'The changing landscape of language teaching and learning that we have witnessed recently has emphasized the need for a greater understanding of nature and significance of out-of-class learning opportunities in second language learning. This handbook provides a valuable account of the nature of LBC; illustrates the diversity of affordances learners make use of; describes the cognitive, affective, linguistic, social and individual dimensions involved; and provides examples of the research methods that can be used in investigating LBC. And in addition the handbook demonstrates how learners' use of out of class learning opportunities are changing our understanding of the nature of second language learning.'

– **Jack C. Richards**, *Honorary Professor, University of Sydney*

'Starting with the recognition that technology has opened a new world for language teachers and learners, this handbook provides an up-to-date and comprehensive look at learning beyond the classroom. Editors Reinders, Lai, and Sundqvist are leading authorities in this domain, and have put together an impressive ensemble of knowledgeable contributors across a broad range of relevant sub-areas. Language teachers, teacher educators, and researchers will find this an invaluable and timely resource.'

– **Phil Hubbard**, *Senior Lecturer Emeritus, Stanford University*

THE ROUTLEDGE HANDBOOK OF LANGUAGE LEARNING AND TEACHING BEYOND THE CLASSROOM

Informal language learning beyond the classroom plays an important and growing role in language learning and teaching. This Handbook brings together the existing body of research and unites the various disciplines that have explored this area, in order to present the current state of knowledge in one accessible resource.

Much of adult learning takes place outside of formal education and for language learning, it is likely that out-of-class experiences play an equally important role. It is therefore surprising that the role of informal language learning has received little attention over the years, with the vast majority of research instead focusing on the classroom. Researchers from a range of backgrounds, however, have started to realise the important contribution of informal language learning, both in its own right, and in its relationship with classroom learning. Studies in the areas of learner autonomy, learning strategies, study abroad, language support, learners' voices, computer-mediated communication, mobile-assisted language learning, digital gaming, and many others, all add to our understanding of the complex and intersecting ways in which learners construct their own language learning experiences, drawing from a wide range of resources, including materials, teachers, self-study, technology, other learners and native speakers.

This Handbook provides a sound and comprehensive basis for researchers and graduate students to build upon in their own research of language learning and teaching beyond the classroom.

Hayo Reinders (www.innovationinteaching.org) is TESOL Professor and Director of Research at Anaheim University, USA, and Professor of Applied Linguistics at KMUTT in Thailand. He is founder of the global Institute for Teacher Leadership and editor of *Innovation in Language Learning & Teaching*.

Chun Lai is an Associate Professor at the Faculty of Education, the University of Hong Kong. Her research interests include self-directed language learning with technology beyond the classroom, technology-enhanced language learning and teacher technology integration.

Pia Sundqvist is Associate Professor of English Language Education at the University of Oslo, Norway. Her main research interests are in the field of applied English linguistics, with a focus on informal language learning, especially Extramural English and gaming, the assessment of L2 oral proficiency and English language teaching.

ROUTLEDGE HANDBOOKS IN APPLIED LINGUISTICS

Routledge Handbooks in Applied Linguistics provide comprehensive overviews of the key topics in applied linguistics. All entries for the handbooks are specially commissioned and written by leading scholars in the field. Clear, accessible and carefully edited *Routledge Handbooks in Applied Linguistics* are the ideal resource for both advanced undergraduates and postgraduate students.

THE ROUTLEDGE HANDBOOK OF THE PSYCHOLOGY OF LANGUAGE LEARNING AND TEACHING
Edited by Tammy Gregersen and Sarah Mercer

THE ROUTLEDGE HANDBOOK OF LANGUAGE TESTING
Second Edition
Edited by Glenn Fulcher and Luke Harding

THE ROUTLEDGE HANDBOOK OF CORPUS LINGUISTICS
Second Edition
Edited by Anne O'Keeffe and Michael J. McCarthy

THE ROUTLEDGE HANDBOOK OF MATERIALS DEVELOPMENT FOR LANGUAGE TEACHING
Edited by Julie Norton and Heather Buchanan

THE ROUTLEDGE HANDBOOK OF CORPORA AND ENGLISH LANGUAGE TEACHING AND LEARNING
Edited by Reka R. Jablonkai and Eniko Csomay

THE ROUTLEDGE HANDBOOK OF LANGUAGE AND THE GLOBAL SOUTH
Edited by Sinfree Makoni, Anna Kaiper-Marquez and Lorato Mokwena

For a full list of titles in this series, please visit www.routledge.com/series/RHAL

THE ROUTLEDGE HANDBOOK OF LANGUAGE LEARNING AND TEACHING BEYOND THE CLASSROOM

Edited by
Hayo Reinders, Chun Lai and Pia Sundqvist

LONDON AND NEW YORK

Cover image: Gettys

First published 2022
by Routledge
4 Park Square, Milton Park, Abingdon, Oxon OX14 4RN

and by Routledge
605 Third Avenue, New York, NY 10158

Routledge is an imprint of the Taylor & Francis Group, an informa business

© 2022 selection and editorial matter, Hayo Reinders, Chun Lai and Pia Sundqvist; individual chapters, the contributors

The right of Hayo Reinders, Chun Lai and Pia Sundqvist to be identified as the authors of the editorial material, and of the authors for their individual chapters, has been asserted in accordance with sections 77 and 78 of the Copyright, Designs and Patents Act 1988.

All rights reserved. No part of this book may be reprinted or reproduced or utilised in any form or by any electronic, mechanical, or other means, now known or hereafter invented, including photocopying and recording, or in any information storage or retrieval system, without permission in writing from the publishers.

Trademark notice: Product or corporate names may be trademarks or registered trademarks, and are used only for identification and explanation without intent to infringe.

British Library Cataloguing-in-Publication Data
A catalogue record for this book is available from the British Library

Library of Congress Cataloging-in-Publication Data
A catalog record has been requested for this book

ISBN: 9780367499389 (hbk)
ISBN: 9780367499396 (pbk)
ISBN: 9781003048169 (ebk)

DOI: 10.4324/9781003048169

Typeset in Bembo
by codeMantra

CONTENTS

List of figures xi
List of tables xii
Notes on contributors xiii

Introduction: Language Learning and Teaching Beyond the Classroom 1
Hayo Reinders, Chun Lai and Pia Sundqvist

PART I
Mapping LLTBC 7

1 The History of Language Learning and Teaching Beyond the Classroom 9
   Jonathon Reinhardt

2 Mapping Language Learning Environments 24
   Phil Benson

3 Interfacing Formal Education and Language Learning Beyond the Classroom 36
   Steven L. Thorne and John Hellermann

4 Participant-driven L2 Learning in the Wild: An Overview and Its Pedagogical Implications 52
   Søren W. Eskildsen

5 Learning Beyond the Classroom and Autonomy 67
   Geoff Sockett

6 CALL in the Wild: A Voyage of Independent Self-directed Learning 81
   Liam Murray, Marta Giralt, Martin A. Mullen and Silvia Benini

7 English Language Learning Beyond the Classroom: Do Learner
   Factors Matter? 98
   Cynthia Lee

8 The Golden Age of Foreign Language Learning: Age and Language
   Learning Beyond the Classroom 112
   Elke Peters

PART II
Supporting LLTBC **127**

9 Digital Game-Based Language Learning in Extramural Settings 129
   Kyle W. Scholz

10 Fostering Learners' Self-regulation and Collaboration Skills and
   Strategies for Mobile Language Learning Beyond the Classroom 142
   Olga Viberg and Agnes Kukulska-Hulme

11 Enhancing Language and Culture Learning Through Social
   Network Technologies 155
   Lina Lee

12 Enhancing Language and Culture Learning in the Case of Study Abroad 168
   Martin Howard

13 Enhancing Language and Culture Learning in Migration Contexts 181
   Silvia Kunitz

14 Learning to Act in the Social World: Building Interactional
   Competence through Everyday Language Use Experiences 195
   Arja Piirainen-Marsh and Niina Lilja

15 Enhancing Language Learning in Private Tutoring 214
   Kevin Wai Ho Yung

16 Enhancing the Quality of Out-of-Class Learning in Flipped Learning 229
   Jun Chen Hsieh, Michael W. Marek and Wen-Chi Vivian Wu

17 Enhancing Language Learning Beyond the Classroom through Advising 244
   Jo Mynard and Satoko Kato

18 Online Learner Communities for Fostering Autonomous Learning
    Beyond the Classroom   258
    Wenli Wu and Qing Ma

19 Self-access Centres for Facilitating Autonomous Language Learning   271
    David Gardner

20 Assessments of and for LBC   286
    Tony Burner

PART III
Researching LLTBC   **297**

21 Ethics, Privacy and Security in Researching LBC   299
    Liss Kerstin Sylvén

22 Evaluation of Instruments for Researching Learners' LBC   312
    Ju Seong Lee

23 Methods and Approaches to Investigating Language Learning in the
    Digital Wilds   327
    Shannon Sauro

24 The Use of Mixed Methods to Study Language Learning Beyond the
    Classroom   340
    Lisbeth M. Brevik and Nils F. Buchholtz

25 Language Learning Diary Studies in Learning Beyond the Classroom
    Contexts   354
    Kathleen M. Bailey

26 Doing LLBC Research With Young Learners   367
    Signe Hannibal Jensen

27 Ethnography in LBC Research   381
    Anastasia Rothoni

28 When Classrooms Aren't an Option: Researching Mobile Language
    Learning through Disruption   395
    Matt Smith, Howard Scott and John Traxler

29 Bringing Beyond into the L2 Classroom: On Video Ethnography and
    the 'Wild' In-class Use of Smartphones   408
    Peter Wikström and Marie Nilsberth

30 Learning Analytics and Educational Data Mining in Learning
   Beyond the Classroom 426
   Michael Thomas

Index *439*

FIGURES

5.1	Contexts, materials and intentions	73
5.2	Interactions between aspects of learner autonomy and learning contexts beyond the classroom	74
14.1	Extract 1: Graphic transcript	202
14.2	Extract 2: Graphic transcript	207
16.1	Characteristics of flipped learning	230
16.2	The four pillars of flipped learning	231
16.3	The seven pillars of flipped learning	232
17.1	The learning trajectory (Kato & Mynard, 2016)	247
26.1	Example of a questionnaire	369
26.2	Example of a language diary (two pages) in Hannibal Jensen (2018)	370
29.1	A student watching YouTube during a break	414
29.2	A student participates in a Kahoot quiz during an L2 English class	415
29.3	Panels 1–4	417
29.4	Panels 5–8	418
29.5	Panels 9–12	419
29.6	Panels 13–17	420
29.7	Panels 18–19	420

TABLES

6.1	Examples from student essays and blog quotations about self-directed learning, self-awareness, self-motivation and agency	86
22.1	Distribution of commonly used research tools in LBC studies from 2010 to 2020	313
24.1	LBC studies using a mixed methods design	347

CONTRIBUTORS

Kathleen M. Bailey is a Professor of Applied Linguistics at the *Middlebury Institute of International Studies at Monterey (MIIS)*. She served as the president of *TESOL* and the *American Association for Applied Linguistics*. In 2009 she became the President of *TIRF*, The international Research Foundation for English Language Education. Dr Bailey has been interested in the diary studies since the late 1970s.

Silvia Benini (PhD, University of Limerick, Ireland) is a researcher in the School of Modern Languages and Applied Linguistics, University of Limerick, Ireland. She is an executive committee member of IRAAL (Irish Association for Applied Linguistics) and member of CALS (Centre for Applied Language Studies). Areas of research interest include CALL, games-based learning, computer-mediated communication and language learning, intercultural communication. Her work has been published in CALICO and ReCALL, among others.

Phil Benson is a Professor in Applied Linguistics and Director of the Multilingualism Research Centre at Macquarie University. He has published extensively on autonomous and informal language learning beyond the classroom. His recent research has focused on the roles of space and language learning environments in second language acquisition.

Lisbeth M. Brevik, PhD, is an award-winning teacher educator and researcher. As a Professor of English didactics at the University of Oslo, Norway, she has developed and taught mixed methods courses, she supervises doctoral and master's students, and is the author of articles, chapters and anthologies. Over the years, she has gained expertise in game-based mixed methods research, in particular the relation between playing online games and reading comprehension.

Nils F. Buchholtz is a Professor of mathematics education at the University of Hamburg (Germany). He studied mathematics and religious education for teaching and got his PhD in mathematics education on teachers' professional knowledge of mathematics in 2014. Buchholtz researches the development of teacher competencies and instructional quality in mathematics both qualitatively and quantitatively, as well as the use of digital tools in doing mathematics in out-of-school learning settings.

Contributors

Tony Burner is a Professor of English Education at the University of South-Eastern Norway. His research interests are assessment, teacher mentoring, diversity, multilingualism, and teacher professional development. He has written the country introductory (Norway) to assessment in secondary education in Bloomsbury Education and Childhood Studies (2019). His most recent publication from concerns a minority language teacher's perspectives on language teaching and citizenship (co-authored with Professor Audrey Osler, published in London Review of Education).

Søren W. Eskildsen is Associate Professor of second language (L2) learning at the Department of Design and Communication, University of Southern Denmark. His primary research interest concerns the usage-based processes and practices in second language learning over time as seen through the lenses of usage-based models of language and conversation analysis. He works with both in- and out-of-class L2 data.

David Gardner teaches English for Academic Purposes and Applied Linguistics at the Centre for Applied English Studies at the University of Hong Kong. His research interests are in self-access learning and the student learning experience in EMI institutions. He is co-author of *Establishing Self-Access* (CUP) and *Managing Self-Access Language Learning* (City University Press), and has written numerous articles and book chapters.

Marta Giralt is a Lecturer in Applied Linguistics and Spanish in the School of Modern Languages and Applied Linguistics, University of Limerick, Ireland. Her research interests are in CALL, Computer-Mediated Communication, Second Language Acquisition and Intercultural Communication. She is involved in various European projects: Erasmus + Dice.Lang (Digital Citizenship Education for Foreign Languages learning) 2019-1-DE01-KA203-005712 and Erasmus + Frames (Fostering resilience through Accredited Mobility for European Sustainable Higher Education innovation) 2020-1-IT02-KA226-HE-095196. For her recent list of publications in various journals and books: https://ulsites.ul.ie/mlal/dr-marta-giralt-0

Signe Hannibal Jensen is an Assistant Professor at the University of Southern Denmark. She holds an MA in English and linguistics and a PhD in second language acquisition. Her research is within the field of second language learning where she is particularly interested in language learning beyond the classroom with focus on young learners (6–11 years of age).

John Hellermann is a Professor in Applied Linguistics at Portland State University, Portland, Oregon (USA). Using methods from conversation analysis, he has investigated the sequential actions and semiotic practices involved in language learning. He also does research on the prosodic organization of language and the linguistic landscapes of urban areas.

Martin Howard is currently Associate Dean in the College of Arts, Celtic Studies and Social Sciences at University College Cork. His research focuses on study abroad and second language acquisition. He is founding co-editor of the journal, *Study Abroad Research in Second Language Acquisition*, and has previously led a European COST Action, Study Abroad Research in European Perspective. He is currently President of the Association for French Language Studies. Recent publications include *Study Abroad and the Second Language Learner* (Bloomsbury) and *Study Abroad, Second Language Acquisition and Interculturality* (Multilingual Matters).

Contributors

Jun (Scott) Chen Hsieh is currently an Assistant Professor of the Department of Foreign Languages and Literature at Asia University in Taiwan. His research has a strong interdisciplinary focus that combines theory and practice in areas of digital technologies, language learning, cognitive psychology, and affective domains, specifically centering on technological innovations for learning (such as robot, virtual reality, artificial intelligence, intercultural telecollaboration, and mobile devices) and affective aspects of learning (such as emotion, grit, demotivation, and willingness to communicate).

Satoko Kato is a Senior Education Coordinator/Lecturer at Research Institute for Learner Autonomy Education (RILAE), Kanda University of International Studies (KUIS) in Japan. She is also a lecturer at the Graduate School of Language Sciences, KUIS, teaching 'learner autonomy' and 'teacher autonomy' in the MA TESOL program. She holds a PhD degree in Education from Hiroshima University, Japan, and a Master's degree in TESOL from Teachers College, Columbia University, NY.

Agnes Kukulska-Hulme is Professor of Learning Technology and Communication in the Institute of Educational Technology at The Open University, UK, where she leads the Future Learning Research and Innovation Programme. Her work encompasses online distance education, mobile learning and language learning. Her publications include over 200 articles, papers, books, and policy and practice reports. She is on the Editorial Boards of *ReCALL,* *RPTEL, International Journal of Mobile and Blended Learning* and *Waikato Journal of Education*.

Silvia Kunitz completed her PhD at the University of Illinois at Urbana-Champaign (USA) in 2013. In her conversation-analytic research she explores how language learning environments are organized and how students and teachers do learning/teaching/testing as socially situated activities in and through embodied talk-in-interaction. In 2018–2021 she worked on a project funded by the Swedish Research Council on language cafés as social arenas where migrants can practice their L2 Swedish.

Chun Lai is an Associate Professor at the Faculty of Education, University of Hong Kong. Her research interests include self-directed language learning with technology beyond the classroom, technology-enhanced language learning and teacher technology integration. She is the author of *Autonomous Language Learning with Technology Beyond the Classroom* (Bloomsbury).

Cynthia Lee is Professor cum Head of Education at the School of Education and Languages, Hong Kong Metropolitan University. Her research interests include second language pragmatics, English language learning and teaching, second language acquisition, English teacher education and computer-assisted writing.

Lina Lee is a Professor of Spanish in the Department of Languages, Literatures and Cultures at the University of New Hampshire where she teaches all levels of Spanish, Spanish linguistics, second language acquisition, and language teaching methods. She has conducted research and published articles on language pedagogy, computer-mediated communication, online intercultural learning and discourse analysis. Her articles have appeared in refereed journals including Foreign Language Annals, Hispania, Language Learning & Technology, Language Awareness, CALICO, CALL, ReCALL, System, and among others.

Contributors

Ju Seong Lee (PhD, University of Illinois at Urbana-Champaign) is Assistant Professor and Associate Head of the Department of English Language Education at the Education University of Hong Kong, specializing in Computer Assisted Language Learning (particularly in Extramural CALL contexts), emotions and motivation in language learning, and English as an International Language. He is the author of *Informal Digital Learning of English: Research to Practice* (Routledge).

Niina Lilja is a Lecturer of Finnish at the University of Tampere. Her areas of expertise include Conversation Analysis, learning in interaction (CA-SLA, Finnish as a second language and learning in the wild.

Qing Ma is an associate professor at the Department of Linguistics and Modern Language Studies, The Education University of Hong Kong. Her main research interests include second language vocabulary acquisition, corpus linguistics, corpus-based language pedagogy, computer-assisted language learning (CALL) and mobile-assisted language learning (MALL).

Michael W. Marek is an emeritus full professor of mass communication at Wayne State College, Wayne, Nebraska, USA, having taught a wide range of media and communication courses. He continues to publish, with research interests focusing on the intersection of instructional technology, language learning and meta-cultural communication; as well as marketing communication and media criticism. Dr. Marek was among the first scholars to publish quantitative research about the worldwide impact of COVID-19 restrictions on teaching and learning.

Martin A. Mullen is a lecturer in the School of Education and Social Sciences at the University of the West of Scotland. His research interests include CALL, MALL and in particular, learner and teacher uses of and attitudes to smartphones. He is currently the Co-chair of the EUROCALL MALL SIG.

Liam Murray is a senior lecturer in French and language technologies and Head of the School of Modern Languages and Applied Linguistics, University of Limerick, Ireland. His research interests range from the exploitation of social media and blog writing for SLA to digital games-based language learning. Recent publications list: *https://ulsites.ul.i/la/od/101*

Jo Mynard is a Professor in the Faculty of Global Liberal Arts, Director of the Self-Access Learning Center and Director of the Research Institute for Learner Autonomy Education at Kanda University of International Studies in Chiba, Japan. She has an MPhil in Applied Linguistics (Trinity College Dublin, Ireland) and an EdD in TEFL (University of Exeter, UK). Her research interests include advising in language learning, the psychology of language learning and learning beyond the classroom.

Marie Nilsberth is associate professor of Educational Work at Karlstad University, specializing in interactional and ethnographic approaches to learning and the digitalization of teaching. She is currently working on research projects concerning connected classrooms as spaces for teaching and learning, with a special focus on literacy practices and classroom discourse in relation to new technologies in education.

Contributors

Elke Peters is an associate professor at the KU Leuven. Her main research interests involve deliberate and incidental FL vocabulary learning inside and outside the classroom and how different types of input can contribute to vocabulary learning (single words and multiword units). She has published her research in *Language Learning*, *Studies in Second Language Acquisition*, *Language Teaching Research* and *TESOL Quarterly*.

Arja Piirainen-Marsh is Professor of English at the Department of Language and Communication Studies, University of Jyväskylä. Her research focuses on social interaction in multilingual and second language interaction. In her recent work, she has investigated the coordination of verbal and bodily resources in classroom interaction, everyday social activities in the wild and technologically mediated work settings.

Hayo Reinders (www.innovationinteaching.org) is TESOL Professor and Director of Research at Anaheim University, USA, and Professor of Applied Linguistics at KMUTT in Thailand. He is founder of the global Institute for Teacher Leadership and editor of Innovation in Language Learning & Teaching. His interests are in out-of-class learning, technology and language teacher leadership.

Jonathon Reinhardt (PhD, Penn State) is Professor of English Applied Linguistics and Second Language Acquisition and Teaching at the University of Arizona, USA. His research interests focus on technology-enhanced second and foreign language pedagogy and learning, especially with emergent technologies like social media and digital gaming, as well as the history of CALL and educational technology.

Anastasia Rothoni holds a PhD in Applied Linguistics from the English Department of the University of Athens. She has taught workshops for undergraduate students and has participated in programs organized for training English teachers. Her research interests lie in the area of literacy practices while she is also interested in ethnography, visual methods, pop culture. Currently, she is working on a project examining the digital literacy practices of Greek neomigrants in Germany and Australia.

Shannon Sauro (PhD, University of Pennsylvania; Docent, Malmö University) is an associate professor in the Department of Education at the University of Maryland, Baltimore County, USA. She has taught at universities in the United States and Sweden. Her areas of research include the intersection of online fan practices and language learning and teaching as well as the role of virtual exchange/telecollaboration in language teacher education.

Kyle W. Scholz holds a PhD in German Applied Linguistics from the University of Waterloo (CAN). He is an Educational Developer in the University of Waterloo's Centre for Teaching Excellence where he supports instructors conduct research on their teaching and student learning. His work focuses on digital game-based language learning, computer assisted language learning and the scholarship of teaching and learning (SoTL).

Howard Scott is a Senior Lecturer in Post-Compulsory Teacher Education and a Researcher at the Education Observatory, University of Wolverhampton, UK.

Geoff Sockett is Professor of language sciences at the Université de Paris, where he currently serves as head of the language sciences department. He obtained his PhD at the Université

Nancy 2 under the direction of Henri Holec. He has published and spoken widely in the topic of online informal language learning and has a particular interest in how young people acquire communicative skills in English through informal online sources.

Matt Smith is a Senior Lecturer in Primary Teacher Education and a Researcher at the Education Observatory, University of Wolverhampton, UK.

Pia Sundqvist is Associate Professor of English Language Education at the University of Oslo, Norway. Her main research interests are in the field of applied English linguistics, with a focus on informal language learning, especially Extramural English and gaming, the assessment of L2 oral proficiency and English language teaching. She is the author of *Extramural English in Teaching and Learning* (with Sylvén, Palgrave Macmillan, 2016) and *Motivational Practice: Insights from the Classroom* (with Henry and Thorsen, Studentlitteratur, 2019).

Liss Kerstin Sylvén is Professor of Language Education at the University of Gothenburg. With a PhD in English linguistics, her research interests include various perspectives of computer-assisted language learning (CALL), content and language integrated learning (CLIL), second language vocabulary acquisition, motivation, individual differences and extramural English. Apart from publishing in a variety of journals, LK has co-authored a book about extramural English (Palgrave MacMillan, 2016), and edited a volume about CLIL (Multilingual Matters, 2019).

Michael Thomas is Professor of Education and Social Justice and Director of the Centre for Educational Research at Liverpool John Moores University. He is the founder of four book series, including Global Policy and Critical Futures in Education, author of three research monographs and editor of over 20 edited volumes. He has worked in Germany, the United Kingdom and Japan and is currently coordinating research projects on UN SDGs in Botswana, Ghana, Nigeria and South Africa.

Steven L. Thorne is Professor of Second Language Acquisition in the Department of World Languages and Literatures at Portland State University (USA), with a secondary appointment in the Department of Applied Linguistics at the University of Groningen (the Netherlands). His professional interests include formative interventions in world languages education contexts, intercultural communication, new media and mobile technologies, Indigenous language revitalization and research that draws upon contextual and sequential traditions of language analysis and usage-based approaches to language development.

John Traxler is Professor of Digital Learning at the Education Observatory, University of Wolverhampton, UK.

Olga Viberg is Associate Professor in Media Technology with specialization in Technology-Enhanced Learning, KTH Royal Institute of Technology, Sweden. Her fields of expertise include technology-enhanced learning, self-regulated learning, learning analytics, mobile-assisted language learning, and learning design. Her current research includes a focus on learning analytics, the design and application of mobile technology in language education, the integration of formal and informal learning environments, and design for learning. Her work has been published in many high-ranked referred journals and conferences.

Contributors

Peter Wikström is associate senior lecturer in English Linguistics at Karlstad University, Sweden, specializing in social media discourse analysis and digital communication. He is currently working on projects concerning informal digital language activities, the reception of public apologies in social media settings, and uses and negotiations of the concepts of "race" and "racism" in Swedish public discourse, as well as teaching in the areas of English and applied linguistics.

Wen-Chi Vivian Wu is a distinguished professor of the Department of Foreign Languages and Literature at Asia University and a consultant of the Department of Medical Research in China Medical University in Taiwan. She has published extensively on CALL and educational technology-related SSCI journals, with research interests focusing on VR, flipped classrooms, PBL, MALL, cross-cultural communication and robotics learning. She has several highly cited SSCI articles on topics, including flipped instruction and learner motivation.

Wenli Wu is currently a lecturer of bilingual communication. She received her PhD in Education from the Institute of Education, University of Warwick, England. Her current research interests include cross-cultural and intercultural communication, English for academic studies and using new technology in teaching and learning.

Kevin Wai Ho Yung is an Assistant Professor at the Department of Curriculum and Instruction, The Education University of Hong Kong. He teaches teacher education courses in pedagogy, curriculum and assessment. His research interests include shadow education, language learning motivation, English for academic purposes and students' learning experiences.

INTRODUCTION

Language Learning and Teaching Beyond the Classroom

Hayo Reinders, Chun Lai and Pia Sundqvist

An estimated 80% of adult learning takes place outside of formal education (Cross, 2007). For additional/foreign/second language (L2) learning, it is likely that out-of-class experiences play an equally important role. The vast amount of time and the diversified experiences essential to language development makes in-class learning insufficient in meeting the language development need. Out-of-class language learning not only constitutes an important context for personally meaningful and authentic language exposure and use, but also plays essential roles in maintaining motivation in learning (Reinders, Dudeney & Lamb, 2022). Language learning beyond the classroom is a common phenomenon among language learners, and is part and parcel in language development (Cole & Vanderplank, 2016; Dressman & Sadler, 2020). It is therefore surprising that the role of informal language learning outside the classroom is not given its due attention in the second language education field, with the vast majority of research instead focusing on classroom methods, materials, and interaction.

In effect, language learning beyond the classroom is not a new phenomenon, and has existed in one form or another since the emergence of 'schooled' second language education. However, its scale has exponentially accelerated with the development of technology, in particular the arrival of the internet in the 90s, as technology makes learning beyond the classroom much more accessible. The increased scale of language learning beyond the classroom raises its importance for language education, and has started to draw researchers' attention. Studies from a range of backgrounds have started to explore the important contribution of informal language learning, both in its own right, and in its relationship with classroom learning and teaching. The rise of research attention aligns with the surge of interest in informal learning in education in general in the early 2000s (Ito et al., 2020; Malcolm, Hodkinson & Colley, 2003), and intertwines with the development in language pedagogy and the use of technology in teaching and learning. Studies in the areas of learner autonomy, learning strategies, study abroad, work-based learning, language support, learners' voices, self-regulated learning, computer-mediated communication (CMC), computer-assisted language learning (CALL), mobile-assisted language learning (MALL), education for migrants, digital gaming, and many others, all add to our understanding of the complex and intersecting ways in which learners construct their own L2 learning experiences, drawing from a wide range of resources, including materials, teachers, self-study, technology, other learners, and native speakers (see, e.g.,

Benson & Reinders, 2011). The existing body of research has generated a rich understanding about informal language learning, which calls for and forms the basis of efforts to solidify and bring together the insights from various disciplines to present the current state of knowledge in one accessible *Handbook*, to provide a sound and comprehensive basis for researchers and graduate students in all languages to build their own research on. This *Handbook of Language Learning and Teaching Beyond the Classroom* provides a comprehensive overview of the existing body of literature related to language learning and teaching beyond the walls of the classroom, presenting current conceptualizations, research findings, and methodological issues on informal L2 learning and teaching in various contexts. While the scope of this *Handbook* is broad, a clear focus on *learning beyond the classroom* (LBC) runs through its three parts and all included chapters.

What do we mean by language learning and teaching beyond the classroom?

As is common in all young fields of research, a plethora of closely related terms tends to emerge, denoting more or less similar concepts. We would like to take this opportunity to position *language learning and teaching beyond the classroom* (LLTBC) in relation to some of these frequently used terms and concepts that have been proposed over the last two decades or so.

Some of these terms highlight the real-life and situated nature of LLTBC. Take one of the most recent concepts, *language learning in the digital wild* (or *wilds*), as an example. Sauro and Zourou (2017) define this as "informal language learning that takes places in digital spaces, communities, and networks that are independent of formal instructional contexts" (Sauro & Zourou, 2017, p. 186). Their definition first appeared in a call for papers for a special issue on 'CALL in the digital wilds' with the journal *Language Learning & Technology*. In the published issue (Sauro & Zourou, 2019) they described learning in the digital wilds as not determined or controlled by educational institutions and as occurring in digital contexts or communities where the main aim is not necessarily L2 teaching or learning. Another feature they highlighted is that learning is driven or initiated by the learner, and not directly mediated by matters such as educational policy and evaluation. We may add that the core term *the wild* was originally coined by Hutchins (1995), to refer to real-life, situated cognition.

Others underscore the informal nature of LLTBC. Examples are Sockett's (2014) *online informal learning of English* (OILE) as well as Lee and Dressman's (2018) *informal digital learning of English* (IDLE). So is Sundqvist's (2009) earlier term *extramural English* (EE), which she coined to refer to "the English [that] learners come in contact with or are involved in outside the walls of the classroom" (p. 1). In stark contrast to OILE and IDLE, extramural English encompasses both digital and non-digital activities and incidental as well as intentional learning, and EE is therefore more clearly unrelated to schooling or educational institutions, which makes that term broader in comparison – and possibly closer in meaning to the recently suggested learning in the (digital) wild(s). The concept of extramural English is explored in more depth in Sundqvist and Sylvén (2016), where they further emphasize the fact that EE always is initiated by the learner. Further, they propose a quadrant model of language learning (and to a certain extent also of teaching). According to their model, L2 learning can be explained with the help of two dimensions: the learner's driving force for learning the target language (which is connected to the level of formality in learning), and the learner's physical location when carrying out (or being exposed to) an activity using the target language (in this case, English). The driving force is illustrated as a horizontal axis (from 100% other-initiated to 100% learner-initiated) and the location as a vertical axis (from the learner sitting at the desk in a classroom in the home country to a place as far away as possible). The symbolic center, then, would correspond to language learning that is partially initiated by the learner and partially by the teacher, and it would take place right at the wall of the classroom in the home country. Learners who step *beyond* that wall and, for example, put their headphones on and start listening to music in English engage in a prototypical extramural activity. Sundqvist (2019) has later proposed the term *extramural L_n* in reference to any L2, because the principles at play in extramural English apply also to other target languages, such as learning Japanese extramurally in Saudi Arabia (Al-Nofaie, 2018).

In addition, a vast number of other terms have also been used in studies from different parts of the world to describe the phenomenon of L2 learning beyond the classroom, such as *after-school, autonomous, extracurricular, independent, informal, naturalistic, non-formal, out-of-class, out-of-school, self-directed, self-instructed,* and *unintentional* language learning. By proposing a general theoretical framework that highlights four distinct dimensions of L2 learning beyond the classroom – *location, formality, pedagogy,* and *locus of control* – Benson (2011) attempts not only to explain the scope of L2 learning that actually takes place beyond classroom walls, but also teaching beyond those walls. While *beyond* teaching may sound like a contradiction in terms, Benson's framework offers guidance. For example, with regard to the first dimension (location), at least in some parts of the world, it is common with tutorial lessons in learners' homes. Benson exemplifies this with reference to Hong Kong, where older students attending the university or secondary school offer tutorial lessons (one-to-one) in the homes of younger students, often as a way of financing their own studies (Benson, 2011). Thus, tutoring is one clear example of teaching beyond the classroom, which can be explained theoretically by considering the location of L2 learning/teaching.

Whether learning/teaching is formal or informal is connected with Benson's (2011) second dimension: formality. In essence, formality refers to "the degree to which learning is independent of organized courses leading to formal qualifications" (p. 10). Whereas LLTBC typically is informal, some learners may perceive that they are also being taught (cf. formal). For instance, in a young learner study from Denmark, one of the participants, Antonio, described how he often searched on the internet to find information related to the digital games he played, letting YouTube teach him (Hannibal Jensen, 2019).

The third dimension (pedagogy) concerns the role of pedagogy as well as types of pedagogy involved in L2 learning beyond the classroom, and especially when learning has an element of instruction to it. Only to give two examples, self-instructed and naturalistic learning (mentioned above) can be explained by this third dimension of LLTBC. These two examples "lie at two ends of a continuum," according to Benson (2011, p. 11), as he explains how L2 learners in self-instructed learning can choose to read certain books or watch certain programs designed for the purpose of learning, while in comparison, in naturalistic learning, regular books or programs can be chosen but without any intent to learn. More precisely, Benson (p. 12) suggests there will be a shift of focus, the moment a learner becomes engaged in the latter activity, from paying attention to the language to focusing on "communication, enjoyment or learning something other than the language itself."

The final dimension is locus of control. He argues that "the underlying conditions for locus of control in language learning are (…) highly variable" (p. 12), but what is clear is that out-of-school settings tend to demand that learners make their own decisions about their own learning. Thus, in language learning beyond the classroom, learners are in control.

With this discussion on closely related terms as a backdrop, we would suggest that LLTBC is the broadest term of them all, and thus the broadest currently used in this field of research. LLTBC distinguishes itself from each of the other terms accounted for, in different ways.

Its closest 'relative' (very similar conceptualization) would be learning through *extramural* L_n engagement, but LLTBC still differs in that the teaching component is much more pronounced in LLTBC.

What are the aims of this handbook?

As this is an emerging research field, and despite the accumulating empirical evidence, the theoretical basis of LLTBC is still quite weak. As the previous section suggests, the field is quite indeterminate with a wide range of terminologies used. What does the theoretical concept of LLTBC entail? What are its different dimensions? How does it relate to associated terms such as autonomy, motivation, and identity? As LLTBC has its theoretical basis in a variety of fields, reaching a clear theoretical demarcation of LLTBC and its constitutive elements might be a daunting task. However, the answers to these questions may provide the initial steps toward achieving conceptual clarity, and will hopefully enable scholars in this field to work from a shared starting point and continue to chart out the field to enrich our understanding.

As LLTBC highlights both language learning and teaching beyond the classroom, we highlight the roles of external parties, other than the learners, in shaping their learning experience, and the interaction of the formal and informal components of language education. Although we have witnessed an increase in research on LLTBC in recent years, the majority of this body of literature has focused on observing and profiling the nature and effects of language learners' self-directed incidental learning beyond the classroom. This handbook aims to accumulate the insights from the field on how learners' experiences beyond the classroom may be shaped by external forces, and hence be better supported. By solidifying these insights, we hope to draw greater attention to the field, in order to facilitate a dialog between researchers in the areas of both formal and informal learning, so as to coordinate the affordances of both in language education.

Researching LLTBC is a difficult task since it is not easy to keep records of learners' behaviors in informal contexts. Thus, many existing studies rely on self-report data, which suffers from a number of methodological challenges. Thus, more innovative approaches are needed in this field to provide more objective, in-depth insights into learners' out-of-class behaviors. This handbook aims to provide a collection of innovative methods and related methodological issues in researching LLTBC so that researchers in this field can have a repertoire of methodological tools to rely on.

What did we ask our contributors to do?

To ensure uniformity in terms of chapter structure, we asked all our contributors to follow a similar outline for their chapter. That is, we instructed them to provide a brief overview of the chapter topic and its importance in an introduction. We then asked for a section on key constructs, which should offer readers an overview of how those constructs have been defined, operationalized, and developed over time. Next we asked our authors to discuss key issues that researchers and practitioners are currently facing related to the specific chapter topic. We also wanted everybody to include a section on the implications of the current state of the field for theory and practice, and to offer some ideas about future directions. In short, where is the field moving to? Each chapter then ends with three reflective questions as well as three annotated Recommended Readings tips. Altogether, we hope the chapter closings will be welcome to those readers who wish to learn more about specific chapter topics.

Introduction

The scope and outline of this volume

This *Handbook* consists of three major sections: Part I – Mapping LLTBC, Part II – Supporting LLTBC, and Part III – Researching LLTBC. This type of division is slightly different from other Handbooks in the series but given the relatively emergent status of the field, we feel that this tripartite division will be the most useful to our readers.

Part I, *Mapping LLTBC*, provides an overview of the broad and emerging field of learning, but also teaching, beyond the classroom. It covers the key concepts, theoretical underpinnings, and historical developments that have contributed to our current understanding of what LLTBC is (and what it is not), its core components, and its manifestations across different learner and environmental characteristics. There are eight chapters in Part I.

Part II, *Supporting LLTBC*, presents an overview of learners' engagement in various informal learning contexts, and reviews the factors that shape these contexts, ranging from teacher instructional practices inside the classroom to learner beliefs and capacities outside the classroom, and to the design of learning experiences and resources across both spheres. This section also discusses how these factors could be facilitated, ranging from explicit preparatory programs (e.g., learner training), to the provision of resources and support that aim to bridge informal and formal education (e.g., self-access and language advising), as well as the design and implementation of resources and environments to be used by learners themselves (e.g., digital games and language exchange). There are 12 chapters in Part II.

Part III, *Researching LLTBC*, includes chapters that target different topics relating to researching LLTBC. This includes overviews and critical evaluations of tools and instruments that have previously been used in LLTBC research, discussions on how to gather and utilize data about both young and adult learners' LLTBC, discussions on learning analytics and data mining, and central methodological issues, such as questions about validity, reliability, and not least ethical issues in LLTBC research. This section also includes empirical papers that address pedagogy and technology in relation to researching LLTBC. There are ten chapters in Part III.

Conclusion

The call for papers and invitations to this Handbook were sent out in January of 2020. Little did we know then about the challenges a pandemic would pose on the work of actually completing this Handbook, not only for us as editors, but of course also for our authors. Finalizing this volume has been a huge joint effort and there are numerous people to whom we owe a debt of gratitude. First of all we would like to thank the authors themselves. We sent invitations to authoritative as well as upcoming scholars in the field, and they all went to great lengths in order to meet our different deadlines and help us with other requests throughout the whole process of completing the volume. We recognize how difficult the process has been and are immensely grateful for all their efforts – and proud of the results. Second, we would like to thank Katie Peace from Routledge whose support and assistance have been much appreciated, from day one when we first proposed the idea of this Handbook. We also appreciate that Routledge was patient when we had to change the time line somewhat because of the unforeseen circumstances. And finally, producing a volume with a total of 30 chapters demands time and we are forever grateful to our families, and particularly to Aylina (Hayo), Jun (Chun), and Martin (Pia).

Acknowledgements

Pia Sundqvist is deeply grateful for funding from the Research Council of Norway [project number 314229].

References

Al-Nofaie, H. (2018). The attitudes and motivation of children towards learning rarely spoken foreign languages: a case study from Saudi Arabia. *International Journal of Bilingual Education and Bilingualism, 21*(4), 451–464. https://doi.org/10.1080/13670050.2016.1184612

Benson, P. (2011). Language learning and teaching beyond the classroom: An introduction to the field. In P. Benson & H. Reinders (Eds.), *Beyond the language classroom* (pp. 7–16). Basingstoke: Palgrave Macmillan.

Benson, P., & Reinders, H. (Eds.). (2011). *Beyond the language classroom.* Basingstoke: Palgrave Macmillan.

Cole, J., & Vanderplank, R. (2016). Comparing autonomous and class-based learners in Brazil: Evidence for the present-day advantages of informal out-of-class learning. *System, 61*, 31–42. https://doi.org/10.1016/j.system.2016.07.007

Cross, (2007). *Informal learning.* Hoboken, NJ: Pfeiffer.

Dressman, M., & Sadler, R. (Eds.). (2020). *The handbook of informal language learning.* John Wiley & Sons.

Hannibal Jensen, S. (2019). Language learning in the wild: A young user perspective. *Language Learning & Technology, 23*(1), 72–86. https://doi.org/10125/44673

Hutchins, E. (1995). *Cognition in the wild.* Cambridge, MA: MIT Press.

Ito, M., Arum, R., Conley, D., Gutiérrez, K., Kirshner, B., Livingstone, S., Michalchik, V., Penuel, W., Peppler, K., Pinkard, N., Rhodes, J., Tekinbaş, K. S., Schor, J., Sefton-Green, J., & Watkins, S. C. (2020). *The connected learning research network: Reflections on a decade of engaged scholarship.* Irvine, CA: Connected Learning Alliance.

Lee, J. S., & Dressman, M. (2018). When IDLE hands make an English workshop: Informal digital learning of English and language proficiency. *TESOL Quarterly, 52*(2), 435–445. https://doi.org/10.1002/tesq.422

Malcolm, J., Hodkinson, P., & Colley, H. (2003). The interrelationships between informal and formal learning. *Journal of Workplace Learning, 15*(7/8), 313–318.

Reinders, H., Dudeney, G., & Lamb, M. (2022). *Using technology to motivate language learners.* Oxford: Oxford University Press.

Sauro, S., & Zourou, K. (2017). Call for Papers for *CALL in the Digital Wilds* Special Issue, *Language Learning & Technology.* http://llt.msu.edu/issues/february2017/call.pdf

Sauro, S., & Zourou, K. (2019). What are the digital wilds? *Language Learning & Technology, 23*(1), 1–7. https://doi.org/10125/44666

Sockett, G. (2014). *The online informal learning of English.* Basingstoke: Palgrave Macmillan.

Sundqvist, P. (2009). *Extramural English matters – out-of-school English and its impact on Swedish ninth graders' oral proficiency and vocabulary.* (Diss.), Karlstad University, Karlstad.

Sundqvist, P. (2019). Commercial-off-the-shelf games in the digital wild and L2 learner vocabulary. *Language Learning & Technology, 23*(1), 87–113. https://doi.org/10125/44674

Sundqvist, P., & Sylvén, L. K. (2016). *Extramural English in teaching and learning: From theory and research to practice.* London: Palgrave Macmillan.

PART I
Mapping LLTBC

1
THE HISTORY OF LANGUAGE LEARNING AND TEACHING BEYOND THE CLASSROOM

Jonathon Reinhardt

Introduction

This chapter explores the history of second, foreign, or additional language (L2) learning and teaching beyond the classroom (LLTBC) by exploring how literacy and communication technologies[1] (LCTs), educational institutions and practices, and L2 learning activity both in and outside of schools have mutually shaped one another in ecologies of use over time. Although LCTs have existed for thousands of years (e.g. writing, manuscripts, ink, etc.), and L2 learning presumably since the mythical age of Babel, the rise of the Internet and digital technologies in the last several decades has led to a veritable explosion of LLTBC practices so noteworthy it has given impetus for a new subfield of scholarly inquiry, and the need for handbooks like this one.

Since a truly comprehensive treatment of the phenomenon would require much more than a single handbook chapter permits, I focus on selected key points to make the argument that LLTBC and LCTs have had a dialectical but complex relationship throughout history. Moreover, although I present the phenomenon from Western European and specifically Anglophone perspectives, since the concept of LLTBC itself is decidedly grounded in that world-view and that history is readily available, in no way do I mean to imply that understandings of language, multilingualism, learning, and schooling situated in non-white, non-Western ontologies are not equally as important to consider. It is hoped that this chapter sparks and informs further inquiry and discussion of these ideas in the fields of CALL (computer-assisted language learning), educational technology, applied linguistics, digital media studies, and language education, with the goal of providing a technology-focused perspective on the growing field of HoLLT (the history of language learning and teaching, McLelland & Smith, 2018), including from historically unheard voices. Because they have been overlooked, they are arguably even more important to consider than the perspective presented here, if a truly comprehensive and informed argument is to be made.

The history of LCTs is itself extensive and could arguably go back as far as the invention of writing (Ong, 1982). The history of language teaching and learning (e.g. Howatt & Widdowson, 2004; McLelland & Smith, 2018) might go back to classical antiquity, and the practice of learning other languages naturalistically even earlier. The current, curious state of affairs is that we now consciously use the phrase 'L2 learning beyond the classroom' to refer to something we feel is happening beyond the control of teachers. Recently the phrase 'digital wilds' (Sauro & Zourou, 2019) is used to refer to something similar, focused on the online, vernacular, user-controlled activities that may involve L2 use and learning incidentally. The word 'wilds' is interesting as it implies that formal education tames, domesticates, or enculturates what is otherwise 'natural', and the history of LLTBC seems to be typified by the periodic unleashing of wild LCT-mediated behavior that must then somehow be tamed, or at least accommodated in classrooms. It makes intuitive sense that formal learning is somehow less natural, and that informal learning is more so, but it is nearly impossible to disentangle the two historically, because literacy itself is not natural and usually must be explicitly learned. An historical perspective that considers the relationship between LLTBC (or learning in the wilds) and LCTs can enlighten our understanding of how this state came to be and provide insight into the future of it.

LCTs mediate and extend our human capacities to inform, interact, and relate by means of language and other symbolic semiotic systems. Analog LCTs like writing and the printing press have been in use for so long and are so widely integrated into human existence they have given rise to phenomena no less monumental than alphabetic literacy itself, even as new digital LCTs continue to engender new forms of literacies and socially semiotic, mediated expression. LCTs have given rise to vernacular media forms like newspapers, film, and digital social media, and some have been adapted for educational uses as textbooks, language labs, teaching methods, and language learning apps. The relationship among these many educational and vernacular technologies, media, literacies, and socio-educational practices is ecologically complex, dynamic, and mutually co-constitutive.

Technologies are products of the practical human need to solve problems and enhance their existence, but solutions and enhancements always lead to new affordances, both negative, which lead to new problems to solve, and positive, which lead to new opportunities for enhancement. However, both the technological deterministic argument that technology impacts societal and cultural development, and the social deterministic notion that society develops separately and influences technology, so that social needs give rise to new technologies, are overly essentialist and teleological. A better metaphor to comprehend how LLTBC, L2 teaching and learning practices, and LCTs have co-evolved throughout human history is the idea of *mutual shaping* (Boczkowski, 1999), the notion that users, institutional structures, and technologies influence one another in non-linear, complex, and ecological fashion over time.

A framework for LLTBC

To frame discussion of the history of LLTBC, this chapter uses Benson's (2011) definition of LLTBC as involving four dimensions: location, formality, pedagogy, and locus of control. First, LLTBC is defined as located *beyond classrooms*. An historical perspective recognizes that what we understand and recognize as classrooms today are themselves an historical phenomenon that developed over time, interrelated with the development and establishment of educational institutions, from Latin schools associated with monasteries in the Early Middle Ages of Europe to online schools today. Indeed, as more learning happens online and learning resources become accessible and pervasive (e.g. with augmented reality), the definition of 'beyond classrooms' continues to evolve.

Second, LLTBC is normally *informal*, meaning it is not done for educational credit or certification purposes, for example, in order to fulfill the requirements of a course or an assignment. An informal practice involving L2 use may have formal qualities like generally recognized levels of skill or expertise, but these are judged by folk measures (e.g. 'working knowledge', 'can get by', 'pretty good', 'fluent', 'can order a beer', etc.). Historically speaking, L2 learning, especially in comparison with something like learning algebra, has always occurred outside of formal schooling frameworks, and multilingualism should be considered the norm rather than the exception. The term 'informal' implies that 'formal' learning is the norm, although it is not when considered historically and globally. It should also be recognized that formality in this sense has served as a means of linguistic imperialism, especially in colonial contexts.

Third, the resources or practices of LLTBC may or may not be intentionally designed as *pedagogical*. Media and texts of all sorts may be didactic to greater or lesser extents (e.g. a newsstory or a museum tour are more didactic than a novel), regardless of intended audience; at the same time, pedagogically mediated materials may be meant for both informal and formal uses, as attested by the proliferation of apps like *Duolingo*, the popularity of educational *YouTube* channels, and the activities of online L2 learner communities. The earliest print resources used for LLTBC like grammars and dictionaries emerged in the Early Modern Era (1500–1800 CE), and were not necessarily meant to be exclusively pedagogical, as instructional genres had not yet distinguished themselves from reference genres. The notions of pedagogical methods and textbook genres coalesced in the industrial era alongside mass education.

Finally, *locus of control* refers to the agency and autonomy of learners, that is, the extent to which decisions about learning are controlled by teachers, administrators, parents, or learners themselves. LLTBC normally requires considerable autonomy on the part of learners insofar as it is engaged in voluntarily, and it is usually directed and managed without authoritative supervision (since it is informal). Centuries ago, when education was not universal and usually only those who wanted or had to engage in L2 learning did, success in LLTBC was measured by meeting needs that might have been a matter of socio-economic survival. A user's sense of agency, competence, and self-efficacy inherent to autonomy were immediately realized and reinforced with pragmatic success. Today, participation in online spaces around affinities like digital gaming (Vasquez-Calvo, 2021) or popular culture fandom (Sauro & Thorne, 2021), while needs may be social or identity-related, may afford LLTBC for the same reasons.

In an overview of the field of LLTBC (2017), Reinders and Benson note that Benson's 2011 framework was meant to be preliminary and might also include dimensions such as trajectory (Chik, 2014), variety (Lai et al., 2015), intentionality, explicitness, and induction, among others. The definitions inherent to the term itself – language, learning, teaching, beyond, and classroom – should also be understood historically. For example, the concept of language has evolved over time in relationship to other societal and cultural developments. Movements to define and standardize the modern European languages of English, French, and German were partially driven by the goal to teach them more efficiently and evolved in reaction and relation to histories and discourses surrounding the education of classical languages, especially Latin. Formal L2 teaching practices developed in conjunction with, and often as intentional application of, developments in fields like phonetics, lexicography, philology, linguistics, and psychology, as well as in response to the concept of 'naturalistic' learning. The pendulum of teaching practice has been swinging between 'application of science' and 'reflection of nature' for quite some time. Today, ongoing and emerging debates over definitions of 'English' vs. 'Englishes', 'variety' vs. 'dialect', 'additional' vs. 'second' vs. 'foreign', and 'native' vs. 'learner' hinge on conceptual paradigms and dichotomies that naturally evolve and shift over time in response to larger scientific and socio-historical developments. Again, non-Western perspectives may be vital to better, more universal understandings of these concepts as they have developed over time.

Medieval and early modern era LLTBC

The historical roots of LLTBC go back to as far as there were classrooms to be beyond, that is, outside of which to learn. Most human civilizations have always had some version of schools – buildings devoted to learning – often originally integrated with places of worship. In Europe starting in the Medieval Period, Latin or grammar schools emerged that were devoted to teaching Latin to new clergy by means of reciting verses, copying manuscripts, and studying grammar. University education as well was conducted in medieval Latin, which would have been an additional language for all students, who would have used vernacular languages at home. Although conversational Latin was sometimes taught, not much was used by students outside of classrooms; Rait (1912) writes that university students were allowed only to converse in Latin, a rule that

> was not merely an educational method; it was deliberately intended to be a check upon conversation. College founders accepted the apostolic maxim that the tongue worketh great evil, and they were convinced that a golden rule of silence was a protection against both ribaldry and quarrels.
>
> *(Rait, 1912, p. 59)*

Latin grew into a diglossic relationship with vernacular Romance (e.g. Italian or French) and Germanic languages (e.g. English or German) among clergy and learned classes, but because it had no true native speakers, it was not particularly feasible to learn it informally outside the classroom.

Clergy aside, only a minority of Europeans had the means to go to grammar school or to university, and only if one were wealthy and privileged enough could one hire a private tutor to learn Latin or classical Greek, or to speak French, the first *lingua franca* of royalty and diplomacy. Any learning of additional languages by the masses was naturalistic and was done primarily by religious refugees seeking shelter (e.g. 17th-century Huguenots in London, see Howatt & Widdowson, 2004), migrants seeking opportunity, traders and businessmen in multilingual guilds, subjugated or enslaved individuals, or children in contact zones or multilingual locales – in other words, there was always a pragmatic and usually economic need to do so. For these learners, all L2 learning was 'beyond the classroom', if classrooms are defined as formal learning spaces for privileged classes.

The impact of the invention of the printing press, the first modern LCT, cannot be overstated. Starting in the 1600s, as printed texts became more widely available in the form of books and affordable pamphlets, general literacy in Europe began to expand; rates in the UK, for example, grew from 16% in 1550 to 53% in 1650 (Mitch, 2005). For a growing middle class, reading knowledge of additional languages became desirable; 80% of the books ever printed in 18th-century Europe, for example, were in English, French, or German, and translations of titles were rare. Throughout the Early Modern Era (1500–1800), bilingual glossaries and dictionaries appeared, some of which included didactic elements like practice dialogs and topically themed word lists; the first Latin-to-vernacular bilingual textbooks are credited to Comenius in the early 1600s. Still, teaching modern languages, especially to speak them, was generally not considered a purpose of formal education; in schools, the purpose of learning grammar, which meant Latin or Greek grammar, was to be able to read what was written, which meant what was written in Latin or Greek.

Industrial era LLTBC

In 1800s Europe, efforts to define and describe modern languages through standardized grammars led to L2 teaching approaches – if one could even use the term 'approach' yet – that exalted grammatical forms and rules through rote memorization. Balch in 1838 wrote that:

> with the mention of grammar, an association of ideas are called up by no means agreeable. The mind involuntarily reverts to the days of childhood, when we were compelled, at the risk of our bodily safety, to commit to memory a set of arbitrary rules, which we could neither understand nor apply in the correct use of language.
>
> *(p. 14)*

Educational reformers in the 1800s sought to inform and standardize teaching through methods that could be efficiently reproduced. Informed by Early Modern dual-translation approaches, methods identifiable today like grammar-translation were mutually shaped by the technological affordances and constraints of learning spaces at the time – books and paper were rare and expensive, but blackboards and slates supported repetition and copying. Since teachers who could speak the L2 fluently were still rare, instruction still necessarily privileged written modalities.

However, outside of classrooms, telegraphs were shrinking temporal distances, and railroads physical distances, which raised popular interest in learning to speak, not just read, other languages. Imperialism and colonialism began accelerating the movement of massive numbers of people around the globe, creating new demands for L2 skills. New private language schools appeared, often centered around a well-known teacher and their method (e.g. Ollendorff or Berlitz), some employing grammar-translation and others new methods that emphasized listening and speaking in 'natural' or 'direct' approaches. Teachers and learners of English in particular had grown frustrated with its highly opaque orthography, which meant learning to speak and listen were quite difficult using grammar-translation methods. The budding new science of phonetics supported the idea that teaching spoken forms before writing might be more effective for learning another language, especially if the intention was to learn to communicate.

In the later 1800s, new audio LCTs in the forms of the wax cylinder and phonograph promised a revolution for L2 learning that would enable individuals not only to read but also hear an L2 without being physically co-present with someone who knew how to speak it accurately. In 1878, as the first Berlitz school was established, Edison himself noted uses for his new invention would include "the preservation of languages by exact reproduction of the manner of pronouncing" and "educational purposes, such as preserving the explanations made by a teacher, so that the pupil can refer to them at any moment, and spelling or other lessons placed upon the phonograph for convenience in committing to memory" (Library of Congress, 2016). By the turn of the 20th century, educational media companies like Linguaphone had become "the first language training company to recognise the potential of combining the traditional written course with the wax cylinder and later with records" (Wikipedia: Lingaphone_(company)). While these resources were relatively expensive and highly structured pedagogically, they were meant to be used informally outside of schools by individuals, not necessarily by groups of students in classrooms.

By the turn of the century, methods had become diverse and some even remarkably progressive by current standards; for example, the Direct Method (e.g. Krause, 1916), which centered on naturalistic dialogs, prohibited the use of the first language, and emphasized form-meaning association. While grammar-translation still dominated many formal classrooms, innovative instructors were already recognizing the value of extra-curricular, affinity-driven, casual, and non-pedagogical uses of the language of study controlled by the learner. In the third issue of the *Modern Language Journal* (1916), American German instructor E.B. Mersereau describes a formal extensive reading activity designed to "create an interest in outside reading", with several guidelines. First, the activity "must not be work to the student" in order to "make the student read so much that he will later read of his own free will" (p. 111). Therefore, as many incentives for casual reading to be as voluntary as possible were necessary, including extra credit for extra books read beyond the minimum. Second, reports could be in English, and third, focus should be on stories and characters, not grammar or literal translation. Finally, the teacher "should try to make the students feel that now they are not in the position of teacher and student, but that they are co-readers of an interesting book", and "to share with the student the lively interest which the student has acquired in the book" (p. 112). It is striking to realize that Mersereau could present his ideas at a conference 100 years later and still be considered progressive.

Modern era LLTBC

By the 1910s, books had become a vernacular technology, accessible for LLTBC as it were, while audio LCTs were considered precious until LCTs like broadcast radio emerged, leading to new forms of LLTBC. In the US, Air of America Educational Radio ran in the 1930s and 1940s. Although none of its programs were focused explicitly on English learning, the many programs in history, literature, geography, and vocational education were appreciated as an informal yet didactic means of learning American English language and culture by the "foreign born – grown-ups often deprived of educational advantages in the old countries who now go to school here" (Pickard, 1932). Pickard noted in his newspaper article the surprising existence of "a growing audience" that had:

> greatly increased since the inauguration of the 'transoceanic lessons,' an outstanding feature of the school's 1931–32 curriculum as nearly 33 1/3 per cent of this nation's citizens is foreign born or of foreign born parentage. The foreign language press in this country has given these programs wide notice and their continuance can undoubtedly attract a vast new audience for the network.
>
> *(p. 11)*

After WWII, with continued internationalization of Western society, quasi-formal activities outside of foreign language (FL) classrooms like foreign exchanges, study abroad, pen pals, and field learning methods grew in popularity, although they were still pedagogical and usually associated with a formal program. Because popular, non-educational media in other languages were not widely accessible outside of bookstores and libraries in larger cities and universities, informal, extramural learning opportunities were not available to most FL learners; resources in second language (immigrant) communities were sometimes available, but they might have been eschewed because their varieties were considered sub-standard. In formal US FL learning contexts, extra-curricular language clubs were growing in popularity, with a suggested purpose "to provide the student with an opportunity to use the language informally with his instructors and fellow students outside of class" (Nealon, 1950, p. 59), to learn to use the language "under practical circumstances" and view it as "a living medium of communication", and to allow direct participation in "activities most commonly pursued by the foreign people" (ibid.). It was advised that students themselves direct FL clubs, and decide on activities based on student interest, with faculty advising only when needed (ibid.). In FL clubs students could read, watch, and share popular media like films and magazines, invite and listen to guest speakers, cook and eat the foods, and learn the customs of the culture of study. With an implication that these activities had no place in the formal classroom of the day, students were the locus of control. In their day such clubs were immensely popular in the US, with nearly every student enrolled in a FL course also a member of its corresponding extra-curricular club.

In the language classrooms of the 20th century, the most progressive formal instruction was informed by psychologists, linguists, and applied linguists, who founded their new discipline in the 1950s with the confidence that every psychological experiment and contrastive analysis would lead to important new pedagogical insights. Until the cognitive turn in the late 1960s, "new key" audiolingual programmed instructional methods reflected behaviorist learning theory (Skinner, 1965) that taught language through highly structured drills and habit formation. Touted as supported by scientific research, these methods were mutually shaped by new, room-filling LCTs or 'language laboratories' replete with audio technological contraptions involving tapes, consoles, speakers, and headphones adapted for learning purposes. A reading of the titles in a 1968 "Selective Bibliography on the Teaching of Foreign Languages, 1920–1966" (Birkmaier & Lange, 1968) shows mostly theories and methods from psychology and linguistics, with no evidence of discussion or consideration of LLTBC; it can be presumed that such ideas were not considered worthy of publication in scholarly journals. In the new field of applied linguistics, even informal learning through acculturation (Schumann, 1978) was explained in cognitive terms. At the same time, social learning experiences outside the classroom, for example by immigrant populations (Durojaiye, 1971), were not overlooked by some scholars, as sociological and anthropological theoretical frameworks were gaining foothold. Eventually theories of language socialization (Ochs & Schieffelin, 1984) and socio-cultural theory (Vygotsky, 1978) would spearhead the social turn (Firth & Wagner, 1997), informing the theoretical frameworks that are ultimately used to interpret LLTBC today.

Starting in the 1970s, communicative language teaching ideals (Canale & Swain, 1980), and by the 1980s new methods (once again) calling themselves "natural" (Krashen, 1985) were (once again) considered revolutionary by positing that learners had to comprehend the content of what they were hearing and saying in order to learn the language mediating that content. Effective learning was possible through authentic tasks (see Gilmore, 2007) and the use of 'realia', that is, authentic, non-literary texts and media not originally meant for pedagogical purposes. Explicit focus on linguistic forms was out, and authenticity of learning experience and meaningful interaction was in. Into the 1990s, scholarly attention to the learner grew rapidly, including learner-centered approaches (Nunan, 1988), self-instruction (Dickinson, 1987), learning strategies (Oxford, 1990), and learner autonomy (Little & Singleton, 1991). L2 pedagogies centered on tasks (Nunan, 1989) and projects (Hutchinson, 1991) offered frameworks that would become more commensurable with the concept of LLTBC.

Outside of classrooms, starting in the 1960s, increasing standards of living, growing international travel and tourism, diversifying broadcast and entertainment media content, and globalizing media and entertainment markets contributed to the emergence of a "global village" (McLuhan, 1964), beginning with economically wealthy countries and slowly expanding to nearly the entire globe today. Audiovisual media content – cinema, music, and television – produced in another country in another language became increasingly accessible to new markets. With market liberalization, consumer goods and items from around the world, including food, fashion, and household goods, became increasingly available to a growing global middle class. By means of these internationalized popular culture consumer and entertainment products, exposure to the cultural discourses and social practices associated with global superlanguages became increasingly possible and probable outside of classrooms. In short, as the millennium was ending, the stage was set for another revolutionary LCT.

Digital era LLTBC

Starting in the 1990s, the Internet began changing the scale at which learners could participate in LLTBC, albeit again, as with material resources and analog technologies, first among socio-economically privileged populations. Users with regular access to the Internet were able to find and participate in affinity groups that shared their interests whose members were not physically co-located, but potentially spread around the planet. Users could connect through personal homepages with discussion boards, webrings, and Internet Relay Chat channels. CALL researchers noted the potential of CMC (computer-mediated communication) as an L2 learning resource to connect learners with each other and with communities of personal interest, both in and outside of classrooms (e.g. Lam, 2000; Warschauer & Kern, 2000).

Outside the classroom, starting around the turn of the millennium, Web 2.0 technologies changed the nature of Internet participation to allow users to contribute content and to connect more easily with one another; consumption and production evolved into 'reprodusage' (Reinhardt & Thorne, 2019). Throughout the 2000s and 2010s, devices to access the Internet and the Web became more affordable and widespread, and broadband allowed faster access from more locations around the globe. Social media emerged in the mid-2000s, allowing individuals to connect and share with one another, and smartphones emerged in the late 2000s allowing individuals anywhere, anytime access to the Web and social media. Some of the digital access gap shrank as global living standards rose.

Smartphone apps grew in popularity, diversity, and number throughout the 2010s, allowing digital LCTs to impact work, play, and everyday life to a much greater extent than they were impacting educational practices in classrooms (Reinhardt, 2022). Digital gaming became a globally networked practice, so that players on one continent could play with others on another simultaneously. Audio streaming and podcasts allowed broadcasts to be listened to on demand, so that the term 'live' had to be specified to refer to broadcasts that were in real time. Thanks to ever-increasing broadband capacity and smartphone camera technology, video production, streaming, and sharing grew massively in the 2010s to the point where 500 hours of content every minute (Iqbal, 2020) is uploaded to *YouTube*, the world's premier video sharing service as of this writing, and sharing images and videos is an ever-increasing practice in social media. In short, by 2020, digital LCTs had been domesticized by large percentages of the populations of most wealthy nations, mediatizing nearly every aspect of everyday life outside of schools. Among teens in the US, for example, time on digital media has displaced time once spent reading and watching TV (Twenge et al., 2019). Books have now become legacy forms of LCTs.

Along with the mediatization of everyday life by digital LCTs has come a cornucopia of resources and practices for LLTBC in a variety of modalities that stretch Benson's (2011) parameters. In the open (non-censored) Internet, authentic, vernacular (i.e. non-educational) resources in other languages became increasingly accessible through the 2010s, to the point where one can now specify the language(s) of use and easily find hundreds of websites, videos, audio recordings, communities, and other digital media resources for expert users of that language; for example, a *Google* search entry (from the US, with interface set to English) of 'como cocinar', 'wie kocht man', or 'comment preparer' generates dozens of automated predictions for searches of recipes in Spanish, German, or French respectively. Because of predictive Web algorithms, users may be incidentally exposed to authentic uses of other languages in their everyday digital lives, especially if they have ever searched for or browsed content in that language, which means incidental exposure to global superlanguages like English has become ubiquitous (Trinder, 2017). Video streaming services like *Netflix*, as they globalize and expand into international markets, offer hundreds of films and television shows in other languages; as of this writing media in 62 languages are offered, with only 55% of nearly 6,000 titles in English (Moore, 2020) and nearly all with subtitled translations and closed captioning in major languages.

Dozens, if not hundreds, of pedagogical apps and online resources are available for informal LLTBC, some associated with traditional schools (e.g. *Deutsch für Dich* by the Goethe Institute) and some with their own semi-formal (internal) achievement, ranking, proficiency, and economy systems (e.g. *DuoLingo*). Like modern day Ollendorffs and Berlitzes, personable language instructors around the globe, some working in teams, maintain *YouTube* channels with millions of viewers devoted to informal language learning. These innovators offer videos that focus on listening, vocabulary, and grammar, as well as on culture and L2 learning strategies, and some offer supplemental activities for subscribers. Some resources like *Lingo-Pie* offer scaffolding services for authentic materials like streamed TV shows in the L2. Other innovators use social media platforms to peddle informal language learning, pushing various pedagogically mediated bits of information and participatory experiences into subscribers' everyday digital lives. With a good Internet connection, LLTBC has never been easier.

Trends in and implications for research and practice

Although research in applied linguistics and language teaching applicable to the study of LLTBC began before the digital turn, as with learner autonomy (Holec, 1981; Little & Singleton, 1991), authenticity (Nunan, 1989), motivation (Oxford & Shearin, 1994), and learning with vernacular media like music (Murphey, 1990) and video (McGovern, 1983), the accessibility, multiplicity, and diversity of online resources for LLTBC have given a new impetus to research in these fields, sparking innovation in theory and practice. Practice-focused research like the pieces in Benson and Reinders' (2011) 'Beyond the Language Classroom' and Nunan and Richards' 'Language Learning Beyond the Classroom' (2015) edited volumes recount formal interventions using vernacular technologies, drawing interconnections between formal and informal practices. These particular volumes have set out to define the nascent field, adapting theories from more established fields and including both analog (e.g. extensive reading and listening logs) and Internet-mediated (e.g. email and social media) practices, bridging the two for the many LLTBC practices that are hybrid or semi-formal in nature.

Sauro and Zourou's (2019) special journal issue on 'CALL in the digital wilds' highlights the descriptive, less interventionist work also emerging as a foundation for the field (see also Chik & Ho, 2017; Han, 2020; and Vasquez-Calvo, 2021 for examples). Theoretical frameworks reflect trends in SLA and CALL more broadly and tend to be social constructivist or ecological in nature, and methodologies tend to be qualitative, ethnographic, and discourse analytic, although they may use some quantitative techniques. The work emphasizes the key role played by social activity and affiliative, identity-related behavior in LLTBC, an element lacking prominence in Benson's (2011) definition. Sauro and Zourou imply that these new

LCT-related practices will lead us (once again) back to a natural, informal state where L2 learning is perhaps more effective and efficient:

> Developments in technology – such as mobile devices that afford connection and social interaction anytime and anywhere, social networking offline and online, horizontal patterns of connectivity that allow users to create natural bonds based on shared interests – all offer possibilities for user-driven, self- and group-initiated practices that redraw models of production, distribution, and reuse of knowledge.
>
> *(p. 1)*

Major implications for formal L2 pedagogy include to integrate interest-driven, identity-engaging tasks and projects that promote learner agency, whether extensive reading online or offline, following *Instagram* influencers, subscribing to podcasts, or playing games in the L2. LLTBC practices should be bridged into formal classrooms, ideally as core activities in the syllabus. Multiliteracies-inspired frameworks that develop critical digital literacies as 'prosumers' or 'reprodusers' of digital media content can focus on computer, information, and media literacies (Reinhardt & Thorne, 2019). Development of digital register and genre awareness, for example the discourse features of a text-based interaction, a social media post, or a *YouTube* instructional video, can contribute to language awareness in general and transfer to academic contexts. Challenges include that digital LLTBC resources are overwhelmingly available only in the global super-languages, especially English, and that bridging LLTBC into formal curricula while maintaining learner autonomy is a considerable balancing act. Letting learners do what they want when they want to do it is difficult to integrate with programmed, sequenced, and objectively assessed instructional practices. Formal instructors must compete with personable *YouTube* instructors who do not call on you or force you to take tests.

LLTBC research and practice can be approached from content, concept, or technology-specific perspectives, for example, content like pop culture (Werner & Tegge, 2021), concepts like informal learning (Dressman & Sadler, 2019) or linguistic landscapes (Niedt & Seals, 2020), or technologies like digital gaming (Peterson, Yamazaki, & Thomas, 2021). With regard to a content focus on culture, both research and practice recognize the globalized and hybrid nature of much modern culture and that many LLTBC practices are not specific to traditional concepts of cultural content; for example, many involve participating in fandoms associated with various global entertainment media and fictional series (e.g. games, novels, films, comics, and television, etc.). Fandoms are massively popular, transcultural, and multilingual and may be leveraged for pedagogical purposes (Sauro & Sundmark, 2019). For users, the language needed to participate in fandoms and most LLTBC practices is incidental to the participation itself, which is "motivated by social and higher cognitive motives" (Hannibal Jensen, 2019, p. 83) and may be personal and interwoven with identity expression and non-academic (i.e. career) development (Han, 2020). Having to use a new language in order to do something meaningful beyond simply using it for its own sake teaches learners how to use it beyond the classroom.

Research and practice on LLTBC should also recognize that many of the theoretical concepts it uses and might consider using have long histories in applied linguistics, although they may need a refresh. Concepts like naturalistic approaches, interest-driven learning, goal-oriented learning, and learner-centeredness have histories much older than applied linguistics itself, and innovative, effective L2 teaching has been happening – sometimes even involving explicit grammar instruction – since far before many key concepts were named, defined, and reified. It can be enlightening to see that something has been tried or considered before under different contextual constraints, but that it was called something else. Indeed, some of the dichotomies used to conceptualize LLTBC now may be artificially imposed and may actually constrain our understanding of the phenomenon; for example, 'formal vs. informal' has led to awkward terms like 'non-formal' to refer to semi-structured pedagogical LLTBC resources. Such resources have actually existed before strictly formal or informal resources and may actually be preferred because of their versatility (Chik & Ho, 2017), but since they do not fit into modern dichotomous nomenclature they are seen as aberrant, rather than normal.

Finally, it's important to recognize that LCTs evolve and change, and by doing so they afford, both positively and negatively, new L2 teaching and learning practices, transforming some traditional practices and rendering others obsolete, or at least putting them out of sight and out of mind until a new technology or development makes them relevant again. Understanding both the constant and mutable aspects of literacy, communication, and technology may help us be critical of new LCTs as they appear and recognize both problems they might solve and new ones they might pose, as well as what aspects of human existence they might both enhance and diminish. Instead of constantly jumping on and off bandwagons and new technological innovations, identifying the more constant qualities of LCTs more broadly both in and beyond classrooms – for example, that they are mediational, relational, and representational – may be a more prudent approach.

Conclusion

In the Western world, LLTBC began first in the Early Modern Era, when the first modern LCT, the printing press, afforded the growth of literacy and made books and printed media more available to the general population. For formal education at the time, the learning of Latin as a written vessel of knowledge had become so deeply entrenched that the learning of modern spoken vernaculars was not considered the charge of formal education. To read in other languages, individuals learned to translate on their own using the first dictionaries and grammars and they learned to speak through what we now might term experiential means in the analog wilds. Over time, as modern languages were standardized, these resources incorporated pedagogical dictates that evolved into methods. These methods first mirrored the grammar and translation-focused techniques of Latin learning, but as industrialization and a shrinking world led to increased demand for L2 speaking proficiency, they began recognizing the value of communicating as much as, or more than, translating texts. The invention of audio technology coincided and perhaps mutually shaped this new focus on more balanced 'natural' approaches. Within a century, however, an over-reliance on audio-centered methods proved that learning to use language solely through mimicry and habit formation was no more effective than solely focusing on grammar and translating texts. As communicative approaches emerged and economic globalization created a global village, LLTBC resources grew increasingly available and L2 teaching attempted to better integrate L2 learning experiences deemed to be 'authentic'. With the development of digital LCTs and the globally networked Internet, a new explosion of multimodal, social media-enhanced, and gameful LLTBC resources are now accessible in the everyday digital lives of half the planet. Formal L2 pedagogical practices, LLTBC, and LCTs continue to mutually shape one another, although in general LLTBC resource creators seem to be more proactive, and formal L2 practitioners reactive, toward new LCTs as they emerge.

Historians of the future may note that for a few hundred years, approx. 1850–2050 CE, considerable amounts of L2 learning took place in physical places called schools, but that it had taken place before, outside of, and after their existence, which reached its peak in the Modern Era. Yet L2 learning is eternal, and no matter where or when it occurs, its relationship with teaching and technologies is dialectical and ecological. The LCTs of writing and manuscripts afforded techniques like memorization and analysis of grammar, suiting the needs of learners of Latin, which didn't need to be spoken. When books appeared and the need to learn to speak other languages emerged, there was little space for innovation to meet the need in formal classrooms. When audio technologies emerged, they were first embraced as the key to natural learning not by storied institutions but by informal language schools. Today, digital LCTs are being embraced by a growing online informal language learning community, many of whom find traditional classrooms mired in the past and unable to provide them the agency and means to learn through practice and pursuit of personal affinities. By conceptualizing and labeling this embrace as LLTBC, scholars of CALL and applied linguistics now recognize that although similar trends have occurred before, new LCTs beckon us to turn a critical lens on concepts like formality, pedagogy, and the classroom.

Reflection questions

1 How do you think additional languages were learned before there were schools and classrooms? Why did people learn them? What motivates people to learn them today, both in and outside of classrooms?
2 What are some problems with dichotomous definitions associated with LLTBC, e.g. informal vs. formal, in vs. outside of the classroom, pedagogical vs. vernacular? What opportunities for learning and innovative teaching are overlooked when we are limited to these parameters? What other parameters are worth consideration?
3 How do you think future technologies, e.g. virtual and augmented reality, might influence informal L2 learning practices and how do you think formal L2 pedagogy will and should respond?

Note

1 A technology is the application, or the product of the application, of systematic knowledge to the practical goals of human life; literacy and communication technologies are those technologies – analog, mechanical, and digital – applied to the goals of the representation, expression, and mediation of language-based knowledge and information.

Recommended readings

Dickinson, L. (1987). *Self-Instruction in Language Learning*. Cambridge: Cambridge University Press.
  Dickinson's work represents a small movement in language teaching to legitimize the study of informal (or rather, non-formal) LLTBC just when learner variables, strategies, and autonomy were gaining interest in applied linguistics. It is useful for its insights into how LLTBC was understood to exist before the Internet, reminding us of the key role of agency.

Howatt, A. & Widdowson, H. (2004). *A History of English Language Teaching*. Oxford: Oxford University Press.
  While there are more comprehensive treatments of the history of language teaching (e.g. McLelland & Smith, 2018; Kelly, 1969), Howatt and Widdowson's book is not only chock full of interesting and enlightening facts and insights, but it is written in an entertaining, refreshing style. It makes clear that far from what we might be taught in methods courses, early L2 instructors were innovative and truly invested in their students' success.

Standage, T. (2013). *Writing on the Wall: Social Media the First 2,000 Years*. New York: Bloomsbury. Standage's history of social media is approachable, fascinating, and enlightening for researchers in CALL and LLTBC, as it illustrates that the human impulse to share, reflect, self-present, and socialize has had a dialectical relationship with various technologies throughout history. While there are more academic treatments of the history of media, it's easy to read and relatable.

References

Balch, W. (1838). *Lectures on Language, as Particularly Connected with English Grammar*. Providence, RI: Cranston.

Benson, P. (2011). Language learning and teaching beyond the classroom: An introduction to the field. In P. Benson & H. Reinders (eds.), *Beyond the Language Classroom* (pp. 7–16). Basingstoke: Palgrave-Macmillan.

Benson, P. & Reinders, H. (2011). *Beyond the Language Classroom*. Basingstoke: Palgrave-Macmillan.

Birkmaier, E. & Lange, D. (1968). A selective bibliography on the teaching of foreign languages, 1920–1966. *Foreign Language Annals, 1*(4), 318–353.

Boczkowski, P. (1999). Mutual shaping of users and technologies in a national virtual community. *Journal of Communication, 49*(2), 86–108.

Canale, M. & Swain, M. (*1980*). Theoretical bases of communicative approaches to second language teaching and testing. *Applied Linguistics, 1*, 1–47.

Chik, A. (2014). Digital gaming and language learning: Autonomy and community. *Language Learning & Technology, 18*(2), 85–100.

Chik, A. & Ho, J. (2017). Learn a language for free: Recreational learning among adults. *System, 69*, 162–171.

Dickinson, L. (1987). *Self-instruction in Language Learning*. Cambridge: Cambridge University Press.

Dressman, M. & Sadler, R. (2019). *The Handbook of Informal Language Learning*. Hoboken: Wiley.

Durojaiye, S. (1971). Social context of immigrant pupils learning English. *Educational Research, 13*(3), 179–184.

Firth, A., & Wagner, J. (1997). On discourse, communication, and (some) fundamental concepts in SLA research. *Modern Language Journal, 81*(3), 285–300.

Gilmore, A. (2007). Authentic materials and authenticity in foreign language learning. *Language Teaching, 40*, 97–118.

Han, Y. (2020). Navigating language learning in the digital wilds: Complexity, autonomy and identity. Unpublished Doctoral Dissertation. Tucson: University of Arizona.

Hannibal Jensen, S. (2019). Language learning in the wild: A young user perspective. *Language Learning & Technology, 23*(1), 72–86.

Holec, H. (1981). *Autonomy in Foreign Language Learning*. Oxford: Pergamon.

Howatt, A. & Widdowson, H. (2004). *A History of English Language Teaching*. Oxford: Oxord University Press.

Hutchinson, T. (1991). *An Introduction to Project Work*. Oxford: Oxford University Press.

Iqbal, M. (2020). Youtube revenue and usage statistics. Downloaded December 30, 2020 from: https://www.businessofapps.com/data/youtube-statistics/

Kelly, L. G. (1969) *Twenty-five Centuries of Language Learning*. Rowley, MA: Newbury House.

Krashen, S. (1985). *The Input Hypothesis: Issues and Implications*. London: Longman.

Krause, C. (1916). *The Direct Method in Modern Languages*. New York: Scribner.

Lai, C., Zhu, W. & Gong, G. (2015). Understanding the quality of out-of-class English learning. *TESOL Quarterly, 49*(2), 278–308.

Lam, W. S. E. (2000). Second language literacy and the design of the self: A case study of a teenager writing on the Internet. *TESOL Quarterly, 34*, 457–483.

Library of Congress (2016). History of the cylinder phonograph. Downloaded December, 30, 2020 from: https://www.loc.gov/collections/edison-company-motion-pictures-and-sound-recordings/articles-and-essays/history-of-edison-sound-recordings/history-of-the-cylinder-phonograph/

Little, D. & Singleton, D. (1991). Authentic texts, pedagogical grammar and language awareness in foreign language learning. In C. James & P. Garrett (eds.), *Language Awareness in the Classroom* (pp. 123–132). London: Longman.

McGovern, J. (1983). *British Council ELT Documents: Video Applications in ELT Teaching*. Oxford: Pergamon.

McLelland, N. & Smith, R. (2018). *The History of Language Learning and Teaching*. Cambridge: Legenda.

McLuhan, M. (1964). *Understanding Media: The Extensions of Man*. New York: McGraw-Hill.

Mersereau, E. B. (1916). How can we create an interest in outside reading in our German classes and how direct it? *Modern Language Journal, 1*(3), 111–112.

Mitch, D. (2005). Education and economic growth in historical perspective. EH.Net Encyclopedia, edited by Robert Whaples. July 26, 2005. Downloaded May 2, 2018 from: http://eh.net/encyclopedia/education-and-economic-growth-in-historical-perspective/

Moore, K. (2020). Does Netflix have too much foreign content? August 5, 2020. Downloaded December 30, 2020 from: https://www.whats-on-netflix.com/news/does-netflix-have-too-much-foreign-content/

Murphey, T. (1990). *Song and Music in Language Learning: An Analysis of Pop Song Lyrics and the Use of Song and Music in Teaching English to Speakers of Other Languages*. Bern: Lang.

Nealon, J. (1950). The foreign language club as an extra-curricular activity. *Modern Language Journal, 34*(1), 58–60.

Niedt, G. & Seals, C. (2020). *Linguistic Landscapes beyond the Language Classroom*. London: Bloomsbury.

Nunan, D. (1988). *The Learner-Centred Curriculum*. Cambridge: Cambridge University Press.

Nunan, D. (1989). *Designing Tasks for the Communicative Classroom*. Cambridge: Cambridge University Press.

Nunan, D. & Richards, J. (2015). *Language Learning Beyond the Classroom*. New York: Routledge.

Ong, W. (1986). Writing is a technology that restructures thought. In G. Baumann (Ed.), *The Written Word: Literacy in Translation* (pp. 23–50). Oxford: Oxford University Press.

Oxford, R. (1990). *Language Learning Strategies: What Every Teacher Should Know*. Boston: Heinle and Heinle.

Oxford, R. & Shearin, J. (1994). Language learning motivation: Expanding the theoretical framework. *Modern Language Journal, 78*(1), 12–28.

Peterson, M., Yamazaki, K. & Thomas, M. (2021). *Digital Games and Language Learning: Theory, Development and Implementation*. London: Bloomsbury.

Pickard, S. (1932). Commercial value of educational programs. *Broadcasting*, p. 11, June 1, 1932. Downloaded December 30, 2020 from: https://worldradiohistory.com/Archive-BC/BC-1932/1932-06-01-BC.pdf

Rait, R. (1912). *Life in the Medieval University*. Cambridge: Cambridge University Press.

Reinders, H. & Benson, P. (2017). Research agenda: Language learning beyond the classroom. *Language Teaching, 50*(4), 561–578.

Reinhardt, J. (2022). Everyday technology-mediatized language learning: New opportunities and challenges. In C. Lütge & M. Stannard (Eds.), *Foreign Language Learning in the Digital Age: Theory and Pedagogy for Developing Literacies* (pp. 67–78). London: Routledge.

Reinhardt, J. & Thorne, S. L. (2019). Digital literacies as emergent multifarious repertoires. In N. Arnold & L. Ducate (Eds.), *Engaging Language Learners through CALL: From Theory and Research to Informed Practice* (pp. 208–239). London: Equinox.

Sauro, S. & Sundmark, B. (2019). Critically examining the use of blog-based fan fiction in the advanced language classroom. *ReCALL, 31*(1), 40–55.

Sauro. S. & Thorne, S. L. (2021). Pedagogically mediating engagement in the wild: Trajectories of fandom-based curricular innovation. In V. Werner & F. Tegge (Eds.), *Pop Culture in Language Education: Theory, Research, Practice* (pp. 226–238). London: Routledge.

Sauro, S. & Zourou, K. (2019). What are the digital wilds? *Language Learning & Technology, 23*(1), 1–7.

Schieffelin, B. & Ochs, E. (1984). Language acquisition and socialization: Three developmental stories and their implications. In R. Shweder, & R. Levine (Eds.), *Culture Theory: Essays on Mind, Self and Emotion* (pp. 276–320). Cambridge: Cambridge University Press.

Schumann, J. (1978). *The Pidginization Process: A Model for Second Language Acquisition*. Rowley: Newbury House.

Skinner, B. F. (1965). *Science and Human Behavior*. New York: Free Press.

Trinder, R. (2017). Informal and deliberate learning with new technologies. *ELT Journal, 71*(4), 401–412.

Twenge, J., Martin, G. & Spitzberg, B. (2019). Trends in U.S. adolescents' media use, 1976–2016: The rise of digital media, the decline of TV, and the (near) demise of print. *Psychology of Popular Media Culture, 8*(4), 329–345.

Vasquez-Calvo, B. (2021). Guerrilla fan translation, language learning, and metalinguistic discussion in a Catalan-speaking community of gamers. *ReCALL 33*(3), 296–313.

Vygotsky, L.S. (1978). *Mind in Society: The Development of Higher Psychological Processes*. Cambridge, MA: Harvard University Press.

Warschauer, M. & Kern, R. (2000). *Network-based Language Teaching: Concepts and Practice*. Cambridge: Cambridge University Press.

Werner, V. & Tegge, F. (2021). *Pop Culture in Language Education: Theory, Research, and Practice*. London: Routledge.

Wikipedia: Lingaphone_(company). Webpage accessed December 30, 2020.

2
MAPPING LANGUAGE LEARNING ENVIRONMENTS

Phil Benson

Introduction

Language learning beyond the classroom (LBC) research takes its cue from classroom language learning research (Allwright & Bailey, 1991; Bailey, 2006; van Lier, 1988), which moved research out of the laboratory and into the classroom settings in which much language learning actually takes place. Initially, classroom language learning research was interested in the influence of classroom settings on language learning. Bailey (2006: 8) argued that 'the classroom is the setting for and *the object of investigation* in language classroom research' (my emphasis). LBC research extends the object of investigation from the classroom to the myriad settings for language learning in the world *beyond* the classroom. Within the LBC research agenda, the classroom and the world beyond the classroom become a single object of investigation (Reinders & Benson, 2017). The problem is to 'map out' worlds of language learning that very often include both the classroom and a variety of out-of-class settings. Using the word 'mapping' in a partly metaphorical, but also partly literal sense, this chapter outlines what I will call a *spatial* approach to LBC research, in which the primary objective is to understand the spatiality of language learning in its many and varied forms.

Key constructs

Theories of space and place

Following the social turn of the 1990s and 2000s (Block, 2003), second language learning research has opened up to all manner of transdisciplinary perspectives, including theories of space, place and environment (e.g., Baynham & Simpson, 2010; Benson, 2021; Canagarajah, 2018; Dong & Blommaert, 2016; Gao & Park, 2015; Higgins, 2015; Murray & Lamb, 2018; van Lier, 2004). Whether one subscribes to the idea of a single sub-divided human language, to that of a multiplicity of separate but interconnected languages, or to a more fluid conception of 'languaging', it is clear that geography has an important part to play in the varied practices of language learning that the global distribution of language and languages entails. In this sense, space has been neglected in second language learning research in the past, much as it has been neglected in the humanities and social sciences more widely (Soja, 2009). However, interest in spatial theory has emerged from a number of factors influencing the global landscape of languages and language learning in the early 21st century (Kramsch, 2014; Thorne, 2013), three of which stand out as being particularly important.

1   Accelerated mobility of people and goods, in the contexts of migration, international education, business and leisure travel, and global trade. This acceleration was especially sharp in the decade up to the commencement of restrictions on air travel in 2020 during the COVID-19 pandemic. The mobilities of people and goods largely explain why people learn languages in the modern world.
2   An exponential growth in the reach of information and communication technologies, global news and entertainment media and, especially, the use of mobile Internet- and GPS-enabled handheld devices. Laptops, tablets and mobile phones are now ubiquitous tools for second language learning and use.
3   A proliferation of spaces for language learning, involving both diversification of classrooms and institutional spaces, and an increase in the number and variety of spaces in which languages are learnt outside classrooms and educational institutions.

The growing importance of LBC is, thus, a factor that is encouraging broader interest in spatial theory in second language learning research. Many of the studies that have drawn on spatial theory use LBC data. It is also important to recognize, however, that the growth of LBC is inseparable from the accelerated mobilities of people, goods and information that furnish language learners with the resources they need for learning.

The key construct that we have to deal with in this chapter is that of space itself, together with the associated constructs of place, setting and environment. Benson (2021) offers a more in-depth account of the arguments that follow, which can only be summarized here. Space is a contested construct and by spatial theory I mean, here, a body of work that has developed mainly, but not exclusively, in the fields of geography and urban studies and is critical of what is seen as taken-for-granted conceptions of space in the humanities and social sciences (e.g., Amin & Thrift, 2002; Harvey, 2006; Lefebvre, 1991; Massey, 2005; Soja, 1989; Tuan, 1977). In order to engage with spatial theory, we need to suspend a number of assumptions that are deeply embedded in everyday thinking and language. These are, notably, the idea that space is empty and infinite, that it is a container for the physical and non-physical world, that it is a background on which events play out, and that geometry structures the contents of empty space. Moreover, this is not simply an everyday conception of space; it is also a scientific conception, based on Newtonian physics. Prigogine and Stenger's (1984) account of complex systems theory in the natural sciences, for example, takes the Newtonian conception of empty space as its counterpoint. At present, however, this conception of space is more prevalent in the social sciences that it is in the natural sciences. Benson (2021) attempts to show how it underpins much of the linguistic theory on which second language learning research is based. The idea that a language is a structured system of relations among forms with an infinite potential for the production of meanings – which is shared by grammars as diverse as those of Chomsky (2006) and Halliday (2003) – is, for example, based on the idea that a language is a self-contained space that provides geometrical structure for its contents.

Although there is no single critical alternative to this idea of space as empty space, the materialist view that I adopt is, perhaps, the most widely acknowledged. On this view, space is a physical entity. There is no dichotomy between empty space and the physical (or non-physical) matter it 'contains'. Rather, space *is* the matter that constitutes it. Similarly, space does not provide geometrical structure for the content that 'fills' it, because space is already 'full' of forms of matter that have their own particular modes of organization. To engage with spatial theory critically, then, we have to stop thinking of things *in* space, and start thinking of things, including language, *as* space. The body of work that I am referring to here has evolved from Marxist, through post-Marxist and postmodern perspectives, and is concerned, in a sense, to recapture the concept of space from Newtonian physics. A parallel humanistic strand of work on 'place' that has been especially influential in the field of environmental psychology, accepts that empty space exists, but treats it as no more than the starting point for the transformation of space into meaningful place through human activity (Tuan, 1977; Low, 2016). Work on ecology tends to view the 'environment' as the physical, inhabited, space in which an organism lives – as a relationship between the organism and space, in which the organism is a component of the spaces or places that it inhabits (Gibson, 1979; Ingold, 2011). However, the differences among the different strands within this body of critical work are less significant than the shared ground of critique of the Newtonian conception of space as empty space. All have something to offer a spatial perspective on LBC.

Language learning environments

Benson (2021) develops an argument linking theories of space to problems of language learning, and LBC in particular. In brief, if language is not an abstract self-contained entity that learners must acquire as a system of forms and relations, language learning must be viewed in terms of physical interactions among mobile 'language-bearing' entities – language learners and other objects (people, things and information) – conceived as physical objects to which the non-physical object, language, is attached. Such interactions always take place in specific spaces that are constituted as spaces for language learning by the language resources that constitute them. Such spaces are described as language learning 'settings', which may be relatively fixed in place as settings for learning (e.g., a classroom or a self-access centre), or constituted on the fly (e.g., a bus-stop at which a language learner strikes up a conversation with an expert speaker of the target language). While language learning settings are always spatially (i.e., geographically) located, the important thing is not the location itself, but the resources (people, things and information) that are gathered at a setting at particular moments in time. A language learning environment is a configuration of settings, viewed either from an areal or individual perspective. From the areal perspective, a language learning environment would consist of all of the settings and potential settings for learning a particular language to be found in, for example, a city. From an individual perspective, a language learning environment would consist of all of the settings that are accessed by a particular person in the course of their learning.

A spatial perspective on the ecology of learning

The term 'environment' links a spatial perspective on LBC to work on the ecology of perception and learning (Barron, 2006, 2010; Bronfenbrenner, 1979; Gibson, 1979; Ingold, 2011). From an ecological perspective, learning is a matter of interaction with environmental resources, or 'affordances' (Gibson, 1979), and adaptation to the environment. The learner does not acquire the object of learning from the environment, but, instead, learns to inhabit an environment where the object of learning is an integral part. Gibson (1979), who is most often cited as the source of the term 'affordances', began his account of the ecology of perception with a critique of the Newtonian conception of empty space. The premise of his approach was that 'we live in a physical world consisting of bodies in space and that what we perceive consists of objects in space' (Gibson, 1979: 12). It is important to the ecological view that environmental affordances are encountered both *in* and *as* space. From an ecological point of view, then, explicitly spatial terms such as 'environment' and 'setting' may be preferred to the less-explicitly spatial term 'context'. It could be said that the aim of a spatial perspective is to ground context in space (Benson, 2021).

Van Lier (2004) is the most cogent account of an ecological perspective on second language learning. Van Lier is clear that language learning is a matter of interaction with environments in which affordances for language learning are present, including the language to be learnt and non-linguistic resources that aid learning. However, his account is less clear on two important points: the spatiality of the environment and the distinction between first and second language learning. First, van Lier tends to use 'environment' and 'context' as synonyms, and the context of language learning is often construed as a context of person-to-person spoken interaction. This reflects a wider overly humanistic tendency in social approaches to second language learning, that tends to push interactions with non-human objects into the background, in spite of their evident importance in multilingual environments (Aronin, Hornsby & Kiliańska-Przybyło, 2018). A spatial perspective would aim to capture the full range of interactions between learners and the human and nonhuman objects that make up the varied spaces of the environment.

Second, van Lier (2004) treats first and second language learning as essentially continuous processes from an environmental point of view (see also Douglas Fir Group, 2016). He tends, therefore, to assume that the necessary language resources are unproblematically present in the environment in each case. However, one of the main differences between first and second language learning concerns the availability of the language to be learnt in the environment. In first language learning, under usual circumstances, the language is ubiquitous in the environment that immediately surrounds the infant, who learns whichever language is 'there'. In second language learning beyond early childhood, however, the language to be learnt is, for various reasons that research needs to explain, a *scarce* resource. From a spatial perspective, one of the tasks of LBC research is to explain how these scarce resources are spatially distributed and the different uses that second language learners make of them.

Key issues and implications for theory and practice

A spatial perspective on LBC offers insight into three key issues in contemporary second language learning. The first concerns the spatial distribution of resources and opportunities for language learning on scales ranging from the global to the local: the question of who gets to learn which languages where. The second, which is especially relevant to present-day LBC, concerns the ways that the mobility of language learners and their uses of global information and communications technologies (ICTs) help them to get around the constraints of the geographical environments in which they live, study and work. The third issue concerns the nature of individual differences and their relationship to uses of space and time. These issues are connected to each other in the relationship between what I have called 'areal' and 'individual' language learning environments. From an areal perspective, a language learning environment is a geographically defined space, an area, characterized by the language learning settings and resources that it makes available and a population of learners who share these settings and resources. The area in question could be a nation state, a region, a city, a district, a school, a workplace and so on. Individual language learning environments are what individuals make of the settings and resources available in an area. They are spatially constrained by the availability of settings and resources, but they are also a factor of individual difference because they are formed within individually different lives and uses of space and time.

The spatial distribution of LBC resources

Viewed globally, there is a high degree of inequity among language learning environments. These inequities are largely a consequence of the global distribution of environmental resources for language learning both in and beyond the classroom. Both conceptually and historically, second language learning begins with contact among persons who speak different languages. One person enters the space of another, or perhaps they meet in a third space, and learning emerges from their interaction. From the perspective of the learner, the other person is an environmental resource. Here we have an elementary form of LBC. In modern times, things are more complex and language contact involves mobilities of many kinds of objects: not only people, but also inanimate physical objects that in some sense carry languages from place to place, such as books, newspapers and magazines, product labels and documentation, audio and video-recordings, and, of particular importance at present, digitally encoded information displayed on the screens of computers and mobile devices. In the context of language learning, these objects can also be roughly divided into those that are packaged as materials intended for language teaching and learning, and those that carry language for other purposes.

These objects constitute the resources that are available within a language learning environment and, when they are brought together in certain ways in certain spaces, they also constitute the settings that make up the environment. From this perspective, a language classroom represents one way of bringing resources – a teacher, students, teaching and learning materials, classroom furniture and materials – together in space as a setting for language learning. LBC settings are constituted in a similar way by bringing together linguistic and non-linguistic resources in more or less formalized, or institutionalized spaces. In this sense, a language learning environment is, typically, a continuous landscape of classroom and LBC settings, in which relationships between the classroom and LBC are of practical interest (Lai, 2015).

To illustrate this point, I will briefly describe the language learning environment in which I first taught English as a second language, at a secondary school in a provincial town in the east of Algeria in the early 1980s. At that time, language education in school was set by national policy: English was taught to all students in the later years of secondary school, and students also learnt either French or Modern Standard Arabic as a second language. In the town in which I taught, the local variety of Arabic was used as a native language and many adults also spoke French. There were local television channels and radio stations, books, newspapers and magazines in Arabic and French, and local products were labelled bilingually in Arabic and French. Significantly, at that time, Algeria was largely closed to international travel and trade country, and in contrast to neighbouring Morocco and Tunisia, there were few overseas travellers or workers and few imported products. It might be said that the town was an impoverished environment for learning English. Classes were only available to secondary school students; teachers were recruited from overseas (there were three of us) or from large cities nearby, and a single textbook was imported from the United Kingdom. LBC resources were few and far between: almost nobody outside the school spoke English and English language media were difficult to obtain. My own use of English was limited to conversations with other teachers, listening to BBC World Service radio, and reading books sent by mail from the British Council library in the capital, Algiers. For other purposes, I used French, and it should be said that although resources were still limited, the town provided a richer environment for learning French and Arabic.

Contrasting this language learning environment with that of Sydney, where I now live and work, it is clear that Sydney is rich in both classroom and LBC resources, not only for learning English, but for a range of additional languages. There is a large private and public sector English language teaching industry and a large population of visiting English language students, who are partly attracted by the many potential informal settings and resources for learning a language that is widely used in the everyday life of a large city. English teachers often express concerns about the extent to which their students engage in LBC, but this is due more to individual factors than the availability of settings and resources (Chappell, Benson & Yates, 2018). As a 'multilingual' city (King & Carson, 2016), Sydney is also rich in settings and resources for learning the languages of its settled migrant communities; formal and informal courses and classes are available in more than 50 different languages, and LBC resources include newspapers, books and media, as well as native-speakers of these languages.

The point of this comparison is simply to suggest that the world is not a level playing field for LBC, or second language learning more generally. LBC depends on the presence of language resources in specific locations, from which various LBC settings emerge. These resources include people, things and information; all of which in some sense carry the language to be learnt and create the conditions for language contact on which second language learning depends. However, the spatial distribution of these resources on a global scale is both uneven and inequitable, especially when it comes to 'desired' international and regional languages (Chowdhury & Phan, 2014; Piller, 2016; Tupas, 2015). The circulation of language resources is mainly influenced by patterns of inequity in global trade and international relations. But it is also influenced by national language policies, which tend to channel desired language resources into formal education and classroom learning, and by regional inequities within nations as resources flow into cities and more developed regions, bypassing rural and remote areas (see, e.g., Hu, 2005, on regional differences in the distribution of imported ELT resources in China).

In recent years, there has been a kind of generalized injunction for language teachers and learners to devote more time and attention to LBC. However, LBC clearly has a head start in parts of the world where valued languages are widely used in everyday life (e.g., English in Australia) and in more economically developed countries where language resources circulate freely in multilingual environments (e.g., in Europe and Japan). LBC research needs to provide a better picture of how LBC and the classroom intersect within global spatial structures of privilege and inequality, and in particular how LBC can work in environments that are poorly furnished with target language resources. As a practical step, teachers can work with students to map out their language learning environments in order to make more realistic recommendations and plans of action for LBC (see, e.g., Ryan, 1997, on a course designed to explore LBC resources in Japan).

Online communication and opportunities for travel

The comparison that I have made between Sydney and a regional town Algeria is not only a comparison of global spaces but also a comparison of two historical times, the 1980s and the 2020s, that are significantly divided by the global economic phenomenon known as 'neoliberalism'. Characterized by the deregulation of international markets, neoliberalism has been seen as having mainly negative sociolinguistic effects, including the commodification of languages and the subordination of second language learning to narrow economic goals (Block, Gray & Holborow, 2012; Duchêne & Heller, 2012; Rojo & Del Percio, 2020). However, it might also be acknowledged that it is responsible for a significant widening of the range and scope of LBC in three ways: (1) the globalization of information and media technologies, (2) an accelerated circulation of people and commodities and (3) increased opportunities for overseas travel. In many parts of the world, where young people, in the 1980s, grew up in relatively impoverished language learning environments, there is now a much wider availability of language resources. This is partly a matter of increased availability of physical resources – people and things – in the places where learners live. More important, however, are the Internet, satellite communication and wireless technologies, which in a sense create a second environmental layer for LBC that interlaces with settings for LBC on the ground. In addition, the falling costs of air travel mean that language learners increasingly spend periods of time studying and using the language they learn overseas. Whether or not the playing field of LBC has been levelled is a moot point, because inequities in access to information and communications technologies and overseas travel remain. Nevertheless, there is no doubt that recent trends in globalization have opened up new windows of LBC to populations of language learners to whom they were previously closed.

At present, the roles of the Internet, media technologies and study abroad in LBC are not well-understood from a spatial point of view. In the past, language learning environments were, by and large, contained within geographically bounded areas, such that they might be mapped using, for example, the street plan of a town. But is no longer possible to think of a language learning environment simply as the place in which a population of learners lives or studies. LBC is becoming increasingly digital, and it is entirely possible to reach high levels of proficiency in a language using only online resources (Cole & Vanderplank, 2016; Sockett, 2014). However, online LBC is especially complex from a spatial perspective. The ubiquitous use of spatial metaphors to talk about online activity, suggests that the Internet is a space of its own kind – and a space of 'sites' and 'platform' that people visit and even inhabit for significant portions of their time (Ciolfi, 2015). However, in the context of language learning, information networks also have a different kind of spatiality, in that the source of the language and its receiver are always located, simultaneously, both somewhere online and somewhere in the physical world. Language resources are conveyed from remote locations and, in this sense, the physical boundaries of language learning environments appear to dissolve into a spatially unconstrained world of LBC. Located in Sydney, Australia, I can, for example, quite easily find online LBC resources to learn Icelandic, and I can probably attain a high degree of proficiency using these resources alone. However, this would not be quite the same as the embodied experience of learning Icelandic at a university in Reykjavik and ordering a hamburger from a food truck on the way back to my residence (Eskildsen & Theodórsdóttir, 2015).

Overseas travel and study abroad open up very different kinds of opportunities for LBC – opportunities of the 'food truck' variety. They also problematize the spatiality of language learning environments through a different kind of doubling, in which different environments are experienced not simultaneously, but sequentially. Study abroad is also a way of transcending the constraints of a geographically defined environment and typically involves a move from an environment with fewer LBC resources to one with more LBC resources, and especially affordances for informal learning with people who use the language in their everyday lives. For learners who have spent years studying a language in classrooms 'at home', study abroad typically involves both more LBC, new relationships between LBC and the classroom, and new conceptions of language learning in the classroom (Kashiwa & Benson, 2018).

Information and communication technologies and overseas travel add layers of complexity to the task of mapping LBC. While mapping out the LBC resources in a geographically defined area can be a useful exercise for researchers, teachers and students, such mappings need to take account of how learners use the spaces of online media, as well as the local spaces in which they use them, which brings into play questions of access and the physical contexts in which devices are used (see, e.g., Kuure, 2011). Incorporating overseas travel suggests, perhaps, that there may be value in mappings of language learning environments that are layered over time and allow comparison the affordances for LBC experienced in different places and at different times.

Individual language learning environments

So far, I have focussed on what I call 'areal' language learning environments, or the affordances for language learning within a particular locality. These are shared environments that both constrain and enable LBC. From the viewpoint of individual learners they are also 'potential' environments, in that they specify the settings and resources that the learners *could* use, rather than those that they *do* use. From a spatial perspective, the main difference between the classroom and LBC, is that the classroom tends towards homogeneity, whereas LBC tends towards diversity. In classroom learning, the learners go to the same place; in LBC, they go to different places. Moreover, the individual diversity engendered by LBC will tend to increase with the range of settings offered by the environment. In an environment with few LBC settings and resources there will certainly be some individual differences, but they will be fewer than they would be in an environment that is rich in settings and resources. As the language learning environment is expanded beyond the immediate locality by opportunities for online engagement and overseas travel, the potential for individual differences increases further. In other words, the spatial complexity of the shared, areal language learning environment becomes a factor of individual difference, as learners trace unique spatial trajectories across increasingly varied maps of settings and resources. This suggests the value of mapping, not only shared language learning environments, but also the individual environments that learners construct in the course of their learning.

Research that we have carried out with international English language students in Sydney confirms this idea of diverse individual environments emerging from unique trajectories of engagement with LBC settings and resources (Benson, Chappell & Yates, 2018; Chappell, Benson & Yates, 2018). This research also confirms the importance of issues of space and place in the individual environments that learners construct for themselves. The factors that explain individual differences among these students are too many to afford a straightforward explanation. They include a range of internal attributes of personality and individual history that influence their creativity and initiative to interpret and make use of the spaces of the city and beyond as spaces for LBC. However, they are also influenced by wider spatio-temporal routines, involving locations of home, school, part-time work, and sites of leisure, time spent at each location, and time spent travelling between them. These routines are shaped by the geographical space of the city and the need to survive financially in a relatively expensive city. In short, these international students have to fit LBC activities into busy spatio-temporal routines and the most successful students are often those who manage to turn everyday situations – interactions at work, journeys from A to B, watching TV with housemates – into informal settings for LBC. In this sense, the English language learning environment of Sydney is not the open field for LBC that it might appear to be. Rather, it is an environment of affordances, some constraining, some enabling, that furnishes the raw spatial material for the construction of individual language learning environments.

Future directions

Interest in issues of space and place is relatively recent in second language learning. The spatial dimensions of second language learning are not well understood, and this is partly because so much research has focussed on a single, assumed space, the language classroom (Murray & Lamb, 2018). There is, no doubt, much of interest to be learnt about the spatiality of classroom learning, but this chapter has suggested that LBC is a more profitable area for research on the spatiality of second language learning. It is suggested that a spatial perspective has much to offer LBC (mainly because the idea of LBC almost immediately prompts the question: *Where* beyond the classroom?), but also that LBC has much to offer the future of research on the spatiality of language learning.

Future research will, I believe, head in three closely related directions:

- Documentation and analysis of LBC settings, from more formalized settings such as self-access learning spaces, to on-the-fly settings of the 'water cooler conversation' variety. What makes one setting different from another? How do they arise? What are the spatial characteristics of such settings, and what affordances for learning do they offer.
- Documentation and analysis of areal language learning environments. What makes one place a 'good place' in which to learn a language and another place not so good? How are the characteristics of these places related to opportunities for online LBC and overseas travel?
- Documentation and analysis of individual language learning environments. How, exactly, do learners go about choosing the LBC settings in which they learn languages? How do they link these settings to each other within the overall framework of a language learning environment? How is the spatiality of LBC related to the spatiality of everyday lives?

Documentation is a keyword in each case, because, in spite of the proliferation of LBC studies in recent years, we have not yet documented the full range of settings for LBC or developed a clear framework for analysing their key features and characteristics. There is, I believe a pressing need for more research that focusses simply on the description of the wild, wonderful and largely undocumented world of LBC.

Online GIS mapping and GPS-enabled applications are among the innovative research tools that can be used to document LBC, either in 'behaviour mapping' (i.e., observation of multiple individuals in one setting) or 'behaviour tracking' (i.e., observation of a single individual in multiple settings) (Ng, 2016). There is also an important role for space in narrative research, a field in which interviews and reports are very often inexplicit in relation to where events took place. Benson et al.'s (2018) study of international students in Sydney, for example, was conceived as a spatially enhanced narrative study, in which narrative interviews were based on records of activity kept in a GPS-enabled mobile phone diary application. Visual methods using, for example, photographs, drawings and sketch maps can also be a useful tool to uncover the spatiality of language learning experiences (Kalaja & Melo-Pfeifer, 2019; Rose, 2016). 'Walking interviews', in which research participants are interviewed on the move, while accompanying a researcher on a route that is relevant to the focus of the research (Ingold & Vergunst, 2008; O'Neill & Roberts, 2020) may also have applications in LBC research, where it has been historically difficult to obtain direct observational data.

Reflection questions

1. Reflecting on your own experiences of language learning, how have they been shaped by space and place? Think, for example, of why and how you chose to learn particular languages and how your learning was constrained and enabled by the settings in which you lived at different times.
2. Reflecting on the current environment in which you work, how conducive is it to LBC? How far are students able to use online resources and opportunities for travel to extend their LBC beyond the classroom?
3. How useful to do think it would be to work with your students to map out their language learning environments? Would you focus on the affordances for LBC in the local area or on students' individual environments? What mapping tools would be most appropriate to your context of work?

Recommended readings

Benson, P. (2021). *Language Learning Environments: Spatial Perspectives on SLA*. Bristol: Multilingual Matters.
   Benson (2021) is the first in-depth discussion of the potential application of theories of space and place to second language learning research. In addition to summarizing relevant areas of theory, it discusses their application to the ontology of language, and the global mobility of languages that is the starting point for much second language learning. The idea of language learning environments introduced in this chapter is discussed in greater depth.

Cresswell, T. (2015). *Place: An Introduction*. (Second edition. First published, 2004). Malden, MA: Blackwell.
   There are a number of introductory overviews on theories of space and place, including Low (2016), which can profitably be read in conjunction with Cresswell (2015). Cresswell's introduction is both shorter and more accessible. It is also a good jumping off point for exploration of specific theories and perspectives. Hubbard, Kitchin and Valentine (2004) includes biographies and short commentaries on the work of 50 'key thinkers'. The editors' introduction also gives a good overview of the history of the field.

Murray, G., & Lamb, T. (eds.) (2018). *Space, Place and Autonomy in Language Learning*. London: Routledge.
   Murray and Lamb (2018) is the first collection of papers to directly address issues of space and place in language learning. Set in the context of research and practice on autonomy, the collection includes papers on a range of LBC settings.

References

Allwright, D., & Bailey, K. M. (1991). *Focus on the language classroom*. Cambridge: Cambridge University Press.
Amin, A., & Thrift, N. (2002). *Cities: Re-imagining the urban*. Oxford: Wiley.
Aronin, L., Hornsby, M., & Kiliańska-Przybyło, G. (2018). *The material culture of multilingualism*. Bern: Springer.
Bailey, K. M. (2006). Looking back down the road: A recent history of language classroom research. *The China Review of Applied Linguistics*, 1, 6–47.
Barron, B. (2006). Interest and self-sustained learning as catalysts of development: A learning ecology perspective. *Human Development*, 49, 193–224.
Barron, B. (2010). Conceptualizing and tracing learning pathways over time and setting. *National Society for the Study of Education*, 109 (1), 113–127.
Baynham, M., & Simpson, J. (2010). Onwards and upwards: Space, placement, and liminality in adult TESOL classes. *TESOL Quarterly*, 44 (3), 420–440.
Benson, P. (2021). *Language learning environments: Spatial perspectives on SLA*. Bristol: Multilingual Matters.

Benson, P., Chappell, P., & Yates, L. (2018). A day in the life: Mapping international students' language learning environments in multilingual Sydney. *Australian Journal of Applied Linguistics*, 1 (1), 20–32.

Block, D. (2003). *The social turn in second language acquisition*. Edinburgh: Edinburgh University Press.

Block, D., Gray, J., & Holborow, M. (2012). *Neoliberalism and applied linguistics*. London: Routledge.

Bronfenbrenner, U. (1979). *The ecology of human development: Experiments by nature and design*. Cambridge, MA: Harvard University Press.

Canagarajah, S. (2018). Translingual practice as spatial repertoires: Expanding the paradigm beyond structuralist orientations. *Applied Linguistics*, 39 (1), 31–54.

Chappell, P., Benson, P., & Yates, L. (2018). ELICOS students' out-of-class language learning experiences: an emerging research agenda. *English Australia Journal*, 33 (2), 43–48.

Chomsky, N. (2006). *Language and mind*. Cambridge: Cambridge University Press.

Chowdury, R., & Phan, L. H. (2014). *Desiring TESOL and international education: Market abuse and exploitation*. Bristol: Multilingual Matters.

Ciolfi, L. (2015). Space and place in digital technology research: A theoretical overview. In S. Price, C. Jewitt & B. Brown (Eds.), *The SAGE handbook of digital technology research* (pp. 159–173). London: SAGE.

Cole, J., & Vanderplank, R. (2016). Comparing autonomous and class-based learners in Brazil: Evidence for the present-day advantages of informal out-of-class learning. *System*, 61, 31–42.

Cresswell, T. (2015). *Place: An introduction* (Second edition. First published, 2004) Malden, MA: Blackwell.

Dong, J., & Blommaert, J. (2016). Global informal learning environments and the making of Chinese middle class. *Linguistics and Education*, 34, 33–46.

Douglas Fir Group (2016). A transdisciplinary framework for SLA in a multilingual world. *The Modern Language Journal*, 100 (Supplement), 19–47.

Duchêne, A., & Heller, M. (Eds.) (2012). *Language in late capitalism: Pride and profit*. London: Routledge.

Eskildsen, S., & Theodórsdóttir, G. (2015). Constructing L2 learning spaces: Ways to achieve learning inside and outside the classroom. *Applied Linguistics*, 38 (2), 143–164.

Gao, S., & Park, J. S. (2015). Space and language learning under the neoliberal economy. *L2 Journal*, 7 (3), 78–96.

Gibson, J. J. (1979). *The ecological approach to visual perception*. Boston: Houghton Mifflin Company.

Halliday, M. A. K. (2003). Introduction: On the 'architecture' of human language. In J. Webster (Ed.), *The collected works of M.A.K. Halliday. Volume 3: On language and linguistics* (pp. 1–30). London: Continuum.

Harvey, D. (2006). *Spaces of global capitalism: A theory of uneven geographical development*. London: Routledge.

Higgins, C. (2015). Intersecting scapes and new millennium identities in language learning. *Language Teaching*, 48 (3), 373–389.

Hu, G. (2005). Contextual influences on instructional practices: A Chinese case for an ecological approach to ELT. *TESOL Quarterly*, 39 (4), 635–660.

Hubbard, P., Kitchin, R., & Valentine, G. (Eds.) (2004). *Key thinkers on space and place*. London: Sage.

Ingold, T. (2011). *The perception of the environment: Essays on livelihood, dwelling and skill* (Reissue. First published 2001). London: Routledge.

Ingold, T., & Vergunst, J. L. (Eds.) (2008). *Ways of walking: Ethnography and practice on foot*. London: Routledge.

Kalaja, P., & Melo-Pfeifer, S. (Eds.) (2019). *Visualising multilingual lives: More than words*. Bristol: Multilingual Matters.

Kashiwa, M., & Benson, P. (2018). A road and a forest: Conceptions of the relationship between in-class and out-of-class learning at home and abroad. *TESOL Quarterly* 52 (4), 725–747.

King, L., & Carson L. (Eds.) (2016). *The multilingual city: Vitality, conflict and change*. Bristol: Multilingual Matters.

Kramsch, C. (2014). Teaching foreign languages in an era of globalization: An introduction. *Modern Language Journal*, 98 (1), 296–311.

Kuure, L. (2011). Places for learning: Technology-mediated language learning practices beyond the classroom. In P. Benson & H. Reinders (Eds.), *Beyond the language classroom* (pp. 35–46). Basingstoke: Palgrave Macmillan.

Lai, C. (2015). Perceiving and traversing in- class and out-of- class learning: accounts from foreign language learners in Hong Kong. *Innovation in Language Learning and Teaching*, 9 (3), 265–284.

Lefebvre, H. (1991). *The production of space* (Translated by D. Nicholson-Smith) Oxford: Blackwell.
Low, S. (2016). *Spatializing culture: The ethnography of space and place*. New York, NY: Routledge.
Massey, D. (2005). *For space*. London: Sage.
Murray, G., & Lamb, T. (Eds.) (2018). *Space, place and autonomy in language learning*. London: Routledge.
Ng, C. F. (2016). Behavioral mapping and tracking. In R. Gifford (Ed.), *Research methods for environmental psychology* (pp. 29–52). Oxford: Wiley Blackwell.
O'Neill, M., & Roberts, B. (2020). *Walking methods: Research on the move*. London: Routledge.
Piller, I. (2016). *Linguistic diversity and social justice: An introduction to applied sociolinguistics*. Oxford: Oxford University Press.
Prigogine, I., & Stengers, I. (1984). *Order out of chaos: Man's new dialogue with nature*. London: Verso.
Reinders, H., & Benson, P. (2017). Language learning beyond the classroom: A research agenda. *Language Teaching*, 50 (4), 561–578.
Rojo, L.M., & Del Percio, L. (Eds.) (2020). *Language and neoliberal governmentality*. London: Routledge.
Rose, G. (2016). *Visual methodologies: An introduction to researching with visual materials* (Fourth edition. First published, 2001). London: SAGE.
Ryan, S. (1997). Preparing learners for independence: Resources beyond the classroom. In P. Benson & P. Voller (Eds.), *Autonomy and independence in language learning* (pp. 215–224). London: Longman.
Sockett, G. (2014). *The online informal learning of English*. Basingstoke: Palgrave Macmillan.
Soja, E. (1989). *Postmodern geographies: The reassertion of space in critical social theory*. London: Verso.
Soja, E. (2009). Taking space personally. In B. Wharf & S. Arias (Eds.), *The spatial turn: Interdisciplinary perspectives* (pp. 11–35). London: Routledge.
Thorne, S. (2013). Language learning, ecological validity, and innovation under conditions of superdiversity. *Bellaterra Journal of Teaching and Learning Language and Literature*, 6 (2), 1–27.
Tuan, Y. (1977). *Space and place. The perspective of experience*. Minneapolis, MN: University of Minnesota Press.
Tupas, A. (Ed.) (2015). *Unequal Englishes: The politics of English today*. Basingstoke: Palgrave Macmillan.
Van Lier, L. (1988). *The classroom and the language learner: Ethnography and second language classroom research*. London: Longman.
Van Lier, L. (2004). *The ecology and semiotics of language learning: A sociocultural perspective*. Boston, MA: Kluwer Academic Publishers.

3
INTERFACING FORMAL EDUCATION AND LANGUAGE LEARNING BEYOND THE CLASSROOM

Steven L. Thorne and John Hellermann

Introduction

It is certainly the case that the majority of research on second language acquisition (SLA) and education more broadly examines processes and outcomes of learning within the tightly bounded confines of classrooms. Yet demonstrably, life and learning are not composed of isolated or strictly isolatable moments and spaces (e.g., Roth et al., 2005; Leander & Lovvorn, 2006; Benson, this volume). This chapter broadens the scope of inquiry to include second language-related (L2) practices that operate in the interstitial spaces and movements back and forth between instructed L2 contexts and experiential realms of engagement. In recent years there has been considerable research and pedagogical experimentation relating to pedagogies that interface L2 education with opportunities for interaction and learning that occur in settings that are primarily or fully outside of institutional classroom contexts, labeled in this book and chapter as 'learning beyond the classroom' (LBC). Formalized educational activity, of course, is a powerful contributor to development, but so too are lived experiences in less or non-explicitly pedagogically structured environments. While it is an obvious point, we begin with the assertion that people can potentially learn and develop in virtually any arena of human activity and that they do so throughout the lifespan (Chaiklin & Lave, 1993). Building on a review of published research, we will suggest that engagement in informal learning environments provides developmentally productive opportunities for learning and that interfacing LBC with instructed learning environments shows evidence of efficacy and great future promise.

This chapter begins with a review of pedagogical approaches and reported learning outcomes that emerge from projects that interface instructed language learning with school-exogenous social formations and environments such as exploration of linguistic landscapes and participation in activities such as fandom and fan fiction, each of which illustrate numerous possibilities for synergistically uniting the analytic rigor of instructed L2 education with the immediacy and vibrancy of language use in non-institutional, informal, and vernacular contexts (Thorne, 2009, 2016; Reinders & Wattana, 2014; Thorne et al., 2015; Sundqvist & Sylvén, 2016; Dubreil & Thorne, 2017; Reinhardt, 2019; Reinhardt & Thorne, 2020). Also described are a set of more recent LBC projects that involve the development and use of locative mobile media, specifically augmented reality (AR) activities, designed to engage world language learners in structured activities outside of the classroom. Locative media, such as smartphones, are ubiquitous across much of the world (Frith, 2015) and have opened up new possibilities for interfacing embodied and virtual experience and for embedding language-intensive tasks in the social world. In conclusion, an evidence-based argument is made for continued exploration of opportunities for learning beyond the classroom and its support and amplification in instructional settings that serve the superordinate goal of increasing the ecological validity and developmental power of language education.

Key constructs

Learning is multifarious and involves many qualities and dynamics, such as increasing the capacity to function autonomously without external aids, gaining the ability to better use available external resources and tools, enhancing one's capacity to communicate and collaborate productively with others, and developing ways to socially present oneself competently and contingently across diverse activity setting. Processes variably described as informal learning (Sawchuk, 2003), apprenticeship (Lave, 1988; Zemel & Koschamann, 2014), language socialization (Ochs, 1993; Duff, 2007), and learning operationalized as becoming a particular kind of person over historical time (e.g., Lave & Wenger, 1991), may include or be enhanced by explicit instruction, but also encompass a wide array of participation in non-instructed culturally organized activity.

LBC is a prominent term in the more general field of research that examines learning occurring outside of classrooms and institution learning settings (Benson & Reinders, 2011; Reinders, 2017). LBC explicitly denotes a spatial reference to the built structures (and rooms) within which formally organized instruction occurs. Because LBC is defined by what it is not (i.e., learning that happens outside of instructed settings such as classrooms), it is potentially inclusive of innumerable settings and activity types. It is also relevant to note additional overlapping terminology that is prevalent in the research and pedagogical studies associated with LBC. Among the more prominent in the arena of language education are the terms informal learning (e.g., Sockett, 2014; Dressman & Sadler, 2020) and extramural learning of languages (Sundqvist & Sylvén, 2016).

Due to the breadth of LBC-related research, and because there are substantial research literatures that already address numerous learning processes occurring partially or predominantly outside of classrooms, for example, study abroad (Kinginger, 2011, for a review) and service and community-based learning (Bruzos, 2017; Clifford & Reisinger, 2018), this chapter is selective in scope and discusses three sets of pedagogical projects that attempt to beneficially interweave experiences occurring outside of classrooms with instructed learning and intact courses. Topical areas addressed include (1) interaction with and pedagogical approaches gleaned from popular culture and fandom communities, (2) pedagogies built around spatial investigation that include the study of linguistic landscapes, the use of natural environments for language learning, and place-based mobile augmented reality activities, and (3) a group of projects self-describing as 'learning in the wild' that have evolved various social infrastructures to support language learning through organic interactions in society. Pedagogical approaches designed specifically to amplify learning that emerges from or includes experiences outside of formal education will also be discussed. These include bridging activities (Thorne & Reinhardt, 2008) and the somewhat conjoined approaches of 'rewilding' language education (Thorne, Hellermann, & Jakonen, 2021) and the aforementioned learning in the wild (Wagner, 2015; Hellermann et al., 2019).

Key issues

Pedagogical projects interfacing LBC with instructed learning

Popular culture and fandom-informed language education

Within formal educational settings, getting students interested in, and further passionate about, the acts of reading and writing is often a challenge for language (and literature) educators. Yet enthusiasm and high levels of engagement related to popular media such as literature and film has a long history that has been dated back to the remixing and derivatives of the works of Chaucer and the fan protests of the killing off of the character Sherlock Holmes, which compelled the author, Sir Arthur Conan Doyle, to resuscitate the fictional detective in later work (Pugh, 2005). In the modern era, visible in venues such as online fan culture and fan fiction sites (e.g., archiveofourown.org, fanfiction.net), a variety of participatory genre writing communities have emerged with linkages to texts as diverse as anime and manga, popular films and books, and online games. Fan participants build from existing figured worlds, tropes, characters, and story lines to create their own works of literature, transforming passive forms of media consumption into creative forms of cultural and community production (Jenkins, 2006). Using the term 'remixing,' Lankshear and Knobel (2007) suggest the following explanation for the immense popularity of fan authoring practices:

> Diverse practices of "remixing"—where a range of original materials are copied, cut, spliced, edited, reworked, and mixed into a new creation—have become highly popular in part because of the quality of product it is possible for "ordinary people" to achieve.
>
> *(2007: 8)*

There are many forms of fan-based textual remixing that range from fan-produced translations of the source material into other languages (translation by individuals and communities; 'fansub' or fan subtitled media) to largely creative and interpretive fan fiction writing that inhabits, often with modifications and twists, the figured literary world that inspires the authors. In producing a fan fiction text, authors may combine or flout genre conventions, use multiple languages and cultural themes, alter or further explore the sexuality or motivation of key characters, or write themselves into the story (author insert) as an original character (referred to as Mary Sue fanfiction) (Leppänen, 2008).

Many studies have documented the often extraordinary effort exhibited by fans to write and assemble complex and lengthy texts, seemingly driven by the high degree of personal interest in the chosen fictional world. As Black (2008) has noted, fanfiction communities often include vibrant reviewing practices in which authors read and respond to one another's writing. Black's (2008) key informant, a Chinese immigrant to the US who wrote in her L2 of English, but also frequently included Chinese and Japanese dialog in her writing, received more than 7,000 written responses to her work over a two-year period. Many other research projects focusing on fan fiction confirm its potential value as a catalyst for meaningful and engaged written (and multimodal) expression (Lam, 2006; Thorne & Black, 2011; Thorne, 2012; Sauro, 2020). Indeed, remixing practices in the service of language learning align very well with Bakhtin's formulation, that "we acquire language through a 'process of assimilation'—more or less creative—of others' words (and not the words of a language)" (1986: 89).

In a series of pedagogical interventions and related studies, Shannon Sauro (with colleagues) has explored the use of fandom practices within formal educational contexts. One example involves incorporating fan community practices into task-based language teaching (TBLT) curricula for use in instructed L2 settings (Sauro, 2014). Target tasks are modified forms of naturally occurring fan practices that include collaborative storytelling, narrating a story with a particular voice or style, creating a (fan-related) thematic wiki, and subtitling video segments of movies and television shows. Each task includes a description of the fandom source, technology needed, linguistic complexity and proficiency levels targeted by each task, and expectations of technical complexity (Behrenwald, 2012; Sauro, 2017).

Recently, Sauro and colleagues culminated a six-year longitudinal and iteratively redesigned pedagogical project embedded in an English teacher education course at a Swedish university that utilized TBLT rooted in fan practices and fan fiction activities. Initially intended to bridge the 'language-literature' divide, the course was initially designed as a required course for future Swedish secondary school teachers of English (Sauro & Sundmark, 2016). Sauro and Thorne (2020) report on the six-year iterative evolution of the course which, based on student feedback and analysis of student learning outcomes, was revised in each of the six years that it was offered. Major revisions included student-suggested changes to the source texts, from initial use of Tolkien's *The Hobbit*, to Conan-Doyle's Sherlock Holmes stories, to Rowling's contemporary Harry Potter series. The course also progressively incorporated fan input (through Sauro's close ties with various fandom communities) on task design, in class writing activities, and identification of examples of fan fiction to analyze and use as models for writing. Across the three primary phases of the curricular iteration (*The Blogging Hobbit, A Study in Sherlock,* and *The Potter Project*), students identified language learning in a variety of linguistic areas, from vocabulary to grammar and punctuation. For example, a student from the 2017 cohort described the following self-assessment of learning:

> This project made me pay attention to grammatical aspects in the Harry Potter books. For example, Rowling doesn't use a lot of transitional words, which we just used a lot in academic writing, but rather she uses colons. I have never used colons before in my writing so that was fun to learn.
>
> *(Sauro & Thorne, 2020, p. 236)*

Other student reported outcomes included a greater capacity to take a particular character's stance in creative writing, the learning of vocabulary and common formulaic expressions, and an overall heightened sense of engagement with the texts and the English language via participation in (to them meaningful) fandom communities (for further exploration of a wide array of popular culture in instructed language learning contexts, see Werner & Tegge, 2020; for a discussion of multilingual youth writing in- and out-of-school, see Yi, 2021).

The spatial turn in LBC: Linguistic landscapes and use of mobile augmented reality

A number of LBC-integrated pedagogical projects have taken 'space' seriously as a dynamic and relational aspect of lived human experience that shapes, and is shaped by, social, cultural, linguistic, and material aspects of urban and natural environments. Termed the 'spatial turn' by human geographers such as Soja (2003; Warf & Arias, 2014), the premise in regard to educational activity is that while time is emphasized in developmental research, spatiality (and by extension, constructs such as context, setting, environment) has been less frequently theorized and explicitly incorporated into analyses and pedagogy (Benson, 2021). The study of linguistic landscapes (LL) in particular, defined as the material manifestation of language in (generally) urban environments, has informed numerous language education projects. In an early study, Cenoz and Gorter (2008) outlined a number of LL affordances for language learning, including authentic and contextualized instances of language use (such as signage) that could enhance pragmatic competence, multimodal literacy, and greater awareness of the social significance, symbolic, and affective dimensions to "discourses in place" (Scollon & Scollon, 2003; see also Malinowski, 2015).

In an innovative project that involved the development of a Spanish language curriculum focused on the diversity, richness, and complexity of urban environments, Charitos and Van Deusen-Scholl (2017) incorporated aspects of place-based learning and analysis of linguistic landscapes that encouraged students to engage with issues of language, identity, and place in Spanish speaking areas of New York City (NYC). In one course, students were introduced to inquiry-based learning (Justice et al., 2007) and asked to design a research proposal on the topic of "Latino/a/Hispanic/Spanish" art in public spaces in NYC. Participants used methods associated with linguistic landscapes studies to explore "how linguistic signs in the built environment interweave with lived experience to construct a sense of spatiality" and to "better understand the linguistic dimension of contemporary globalization" (Charitos & Van Deusen-Scholl, 2017, p. 18–19). Student work included systematic and structured exploration of urban landscapes, written reflections, production of video documentaries, with an overarching emphasis on activities that cultivated "authentic L2 usage inside and outside the classroom space" (p. 26). Inspiring related works include (1) an undergraduate course, designed and taught by David Malinowski, titled Reading the Multilingual City, that had students explore and interpret East Asian languages in the San Francisco Bay Area (Malinowski, 2016), and (2) the development of an L2 specific pedagogical and methodological approach for incorporating LL into language education curricula (Maxim, 2020).

In a unique and inspiring investigation of place, nature, and language built upon the theme of 'land as interlocutor,' Engman and Hermes (2021) documented the land-based pedagogy used in an Indigenous Ojibwe language reclamation project that emphasized engagement with the natural world (e.g., local, rural, and reservation land) as a language-rich opportunity for learning. Using ecological and sociomaterial lenses that blur the human-nonhuman and nature-culture binaries (Latour, 2013) and which align with Indigenous epistemologies, the study asked, "What kind of linguistic, environmental, and relational knowledge is structured through engagements with land as Ojibwe language learning materials?" (Engman & Hermes, 2021, p. 89). The setting for this multimodal empirical analysis of language learning in partnership with the land involves forest walks taken together by an Ojibwe Elder and a young Ojibwe immersion language student. In this case of LBC, the authors illustrate the open-ended processes emerging from engagement with the land that includes naming requests, relational knowing (entanglement; human and nonhuman both understood as agentive), and cooperative action, each of which further the project of decolonizing educational practice and reclaiming Indigenous ways of knowing and using language (Henne-Ochoa et al., 2020).

The use of location aware mobile devices is another way of supporting language learning activities designed to interface learners with contextually relevant social-material settings. Locative media, such as smartphones, are ubiquitous across much of the world and have opened up new possibilities for interfacing embodied and virtual experience with classroom instruction. Applications of locative media, for example, place-based mobile augmented reality (AR), are now regularly used in a variety of educational content areas in order to present opportunities for investigation-based learning, location-situated social and collaborative interaction, and embodied experience of place (Squire, 2009; Holden et al., 2015; Thorne & Hellermann, 2017).

Place-based AR mobile gaming typically involves guiding or drawing players toward specific physical spaces by using GPS locations on a digital map. The AR dimension involves orienting participants' attention to particular places or relevant features of the landscape and then augmenting their experience with semiotic resources, information, tasks, or prompts, with the intention of creating an embodied and experiential in-the-world dynamic for participants.

One of the first projects to use AR technology for language teaching (L2 Spanish) is *Mentira*, a place-based mobile game set in a Spanish-speaking neighborhood in Albuquerque, New Mexico, where learners work together to solve a prohibition-era murder mystery. While playing the game, students complete a jigsaw-puzzle-style activity in which each player receives different clues, prompting collaboration to complete the task. The linguistic focus of the activity was mastery of appropriate forms of Spanish requests and apologies that were central to solving the fictional murder mystery that spatially played out in the real neighborhood of Los Griegos, New Mexico. Analysis of play records (Holden & Sykes, 2011) found that integrating the orientation tutorial into the game narrative resulted in more time on-task. Additionally, students reported being motivated by their place-based experience in a Spanish-speaking neighborhood, which for some participants included interacting with local residents in Spanish. The Mentira game designers, Julie Sykes and Chris Holden, responding to student frustration about each of the multiple endings they had created, decided to encourage the participants to design their own conclusion to the game. This resulted in an entirely student-organized mock trial in which the students played judges, prosecuting and defending lawyers, and witnesses. In this way, the resolution of the murder mystery became open-ended and was entirely determined by the student participants in the project, which yielded much higher levels of satisfaction and increased the participants' sense of agency and decision making.

ChronoOps is a quest-type mobile AR game, created and located in Portland, Oregon (USA), that is currently available in seven languages, including English (Thorne, 2013). Participants play the role of an agent from the future. The game begins by describing that in the year 2070, the planet has suffered massive environmental degradation and they (the player-agents) have been sent back in time in order to learn from the green technology projects that are evident on and around the university campus. *ChronoOps* was designed as a series of open-ended and intentionally underspecified tasks with the pedagogical motivation of having players construct their actions as agents in interaction with the game's goals and content. In research on *ChronoOps* game play while outside of the classroom, Thorne, Hellermann, Jones, and Lester (2015) used ethnomethodological conversation analysis to investigate how groups of L2 English students sharing one smartphone orient to the device and the information it displays, develop practices for wayfinding, and use talk to bring shared attention to features of their physical surroundings. This research emphasized the importance of how the game moves the language experience out of the classroom and how the group dynamic around one device influences students' interactional practices. In related research, Hellermann, Thorne, and Fodor (2017) described the complex interactions associated with the literacy event of reading aloud during mobile AR gameplay, illustrating that collaborative practices for playing the game that involved reading aloud emerged and consolidated over the duration of the activity. Addressing the hypercontextualization and place-based potential of AR, Thorne and Hellermann (2017) analyzed video data of *ChronoOps* gameplay and described how problems in understanding, as well as moving forward to the next action, are often enmeshed with and supported by the immediate physical environment. Their analysis demonstrates the relevance of embodied and distributed approaches to human activity, illustrating that participants utilize gaze, gesture, vocalizations and talk, pointing, and embodied deixis, in an orderly manner, to coordinate virtual-digital (iPhone) and sensory-visual information, to navigate the team's movement to the next location, and to complete the oral narration tasks comprising the game (Hellermann, Thorne, & Haley, 2019). In a study focusing specifically on L2 acquisition, Sydorenko, Hellermann, Thorne, and Howe (2019) employ the widely used construct of language related episodes (LREs) as a unit of analysis (Swain & Lapkin, 1998). This research illustrates that the mobility and contextual embeddedness of AR tasks create opportunities for just-in-time and situationally driven vocabulary learning, with implications for continuing AR game design and pedagogical structuring of hypercontextualized approaches to language learning.

Each of the above studies analyzed interaction and language learning during actual AR game play, but it is relevant to note that instructors prepared participants for game play through familiarization activities and later incorporated the mobile AR experience into the curriculum with in-class debriefings and follow-up activities such as presentations on environmental stewardship, debates on advantages and disadvantages of various green technologies, and individual and collaborative writing projects.

Research on "learning in the wild"

Within the LBC area are a subset of curricular innovations and research programs that are phenomenological in epistemology and influenced by ethnomethodology and conversation analysis. These efforts have been labeled 'language learning in the wild' (LLW) after the work of cognitive anthropologist Edwin Hutchins whose 1995 book (*Cognition in the Wild*) described the situated nature of cognition in the setting of ship navigation. Drawing on Hutchins' (and others') empirical illustrations of the role of situated cultural practices, the LLW researchers designed interventions to more fully exploit the use of the natural 'language input' available in social contexts outside of schools and universities. The program was also influenced by ideas from user-informed design and findings from usage-based linguistics and conversation analysis (Wagner, 1996; Firth & Wagner, 1997; Eskildsen, 2009) to provide minimally structured, learner-led opportunities for engagement in meaningful everyday language practices in the learners' communities.

The number of studies in the area has grown rapidly in the past 10 years and includes such settings as interactions during mealtimes (Greer, 2018, 2019), hotel workers and pharmacists (Nguyen, 2011, 2012, 2019), business transactions (Brouwer & Wagner, 2004), game players (Piirainen-Marsh & Tainio, 2009a, 2009b, 2014; Thorne, 2008), and shop clerks (Kim, 2019). These studies show how the interactions that take place in varied contexts of the everyday lives of participants provide opportunities for meaningful language use and learning.

Building on the interactional research such as the studies mentioned above, Wagner (2004) and others advocated designing more guided opportunities for learners to use the language of the community in the community. Since that time, three projects were developed to encourage language learners' use of the language in the community with explicit structure and support. Rather than designing tasks for learners to accomplish outside of the classroom that are removed from the contingencies of everyday language use, these programs 'harvest' (Wagner, 2015) everyday interactions (usually service encounters) by recording them for use as objects of study and reflection with peers and teachers in the classroom. Materials are designed around these interactions to allow for changes in subsequent interactions. Another innovative aspect is the recruiting of members of the community to contribute to the pedagogical support. In the Nordic countries, proficiency in English is widespread, and so learners of Swedish, Icelandic, or Finnish in those respective countries face the difficulty of having their interlocutors switch to English to complete the interaction when they detect they are communicating with a language learner (Wagner, 2015). In each project, local business owners were contacted as co-participants in the project. They were informed that learners of the local language (Icelandic, Swedish, or Finnish in the three example projects summarized below) would be in the area and would be, potentially, customers in their businesses. They were asked if they could help by doing their best to engage with the learners in the local language thus providing them with opportunities to have meaningful, ecologically valid language use experiences.

In Iceland, Guðrún Theodórsdóttir has been leading a project that has worked with local businesses to instruct clerks at those businesses (a bakery, a hot dog stand, a cafe, a bank) to interact with adult learners of Icelandic who come to their businesses *in* Icelandic, that is, to not switch to English when there are disfluencies in the learner's use of Icelandic (*Icelandic Village:* Theodórsdóttir & Eskildsen, forthcoming; Theodórsdóttir & Friðriksdóttir, 2013). The learners who engaged in the interactions at the local businesses were taking Icelandic language classes at the University of Iceland in Reykjavik and were asked to audio record some of these daily interactions to bring to class to analyze. Some of this data has been used for analysis (Eskildsen & Theodórsdóttir, 2017; Theodórsdóttir, 2011a, 2011b, 2018) in case study research which shows ways that a learner develops particular interactional practices for accomplishing these everyday social actions. These practices include the creating of spaces for language learning outside of the classroom context, co-constructing corrective feedback during service encounters, developing persistence in completing a turn at talk, and displaying a learner identity as a way to facilitate language learning in the wild.

A research group in Sweden worked with the first empirical findings from the Icelandic Village case studies to formalize more explicit pedagogical interventions (Clark et al., 2011). The title of the project (*Språkskap,* that is, 'speech scape') indicates the ecological approach in the design. Learners were treated as emerging community members and Swedish speakers. The Swedish group's intervention took seriously the conceptualization of language as a co-constructed phenomenon and devised strategies for the fluent Swedish speakers in the community to engage with newcomers to Sweden who were learners of Swedish. For example, cards were provided to the learners and their Swedish-speaking interlocutors to log the number of minutes of spoken interaction each engaged in. The cards (labeled 'Swedish Time') included strategies for the Swedish speakers to use when they had interactions with learners of Swedish. In another facet of the project, learners went to a coffee shop near their school where the owner was encouraged to not switch to English in his service encounters with the learners. The learners were encouraged to audio record those interactions and upload them to a language blog as material for other learners to use to prepare for their own interactions in the coffee shop. A more general strategy was the *sit-talk-sit* procedure in which language learners were instructed to sit down before an upcoming Swedish language interaction and prepare particular speech acts to use during the interaction. After accomplishing the service encounter, the learners were instructed to sit down again somewhere outside the shop and to reflect and take notes on the interaction. Language tutors were also brought into the intervention design by using Twitter to foster regular engagement throughout the data with written Swedish.

Also building on the model of the Icelandic Village, researchers in Finland (Tampere and Jyväskylä) worked with instructional designers and classroom teachers to develop a systematic way for learners of Finnish as a second language in Finland to use the language resources in the community (*Co-designing social interactions in everyday life*). As with the other Nordic countries, researchers, teachers, and learners found that for learners of Finnish in Finland, it is very easy to simply switch to speaking English when there are possible communicative difficulties in their Finnish language interactions. The course that was developed to overcome this difficulty, 'The Rally Course' (Lilja et al., 2019), asked learners to create salient reflections of their daily interactions in Finnish using photo journals, maps, and network diagrams of those interactions. Students were also tasked with preparing for future interactions by 'scouting' locations: observing and listening to interactions in particular places to raise awareness of the linguistic and other semiotic resources that were used for the particular interactions that they knew they would need to accomplish (e.g., buying a birthday present for a friend). Students then prepared for the interaction by engaging in the hypothetical interaction in the classroom with peers, recording the rehearsal and analyzing it. Following the practice interaction, the student goes 'into the wild' to accomplish the interaction which is recorded by a peer. That interaction is then brought back to the classroom to be analyzed in the next classroom meeting. Details about the development of interactional competence during these students' interactions can be found in Lilja & Piirainen-Marsh, 2019a, 2019b and Piirainen-Marsh & Lilja, 2019).

The rewilding approach to language education

Similar in some respects to the 'learning in the wild' projects described above (NB: the authors are regular participants in the 'learning in the wild' research network), "rewilding" language education (Thorne, Hellermann, & Jakonen, 2021) involves reverse engineering from studies of learning in the wild (Hutchins, 1995) in order to augment and restore a diversity of real-world activities and interactional affordances into instructional curricula. The term *rewilding,* now a significant conservation movement in Europe (https://rewilding-europe.com/) and beyond, was first introduced by American conservation biologists (Soulé & Noss, 1998) to describe the reintroduction of paleolithic species of fauna and flora to human-affected ecologies that have lost biodiversity through cultivation and urbanization. We apply the rewilding approach to instructed language education to address the challenge of how to dynamically integrate formal learning settings with the vibrancy and diversity of linguistic, experiential, and situational contexts out in the world. The development of the mobile AR activities that are the focus of the analysis were inspired by research on cognition and learning 'in the wild' (Hutchins, 1995), as well as by diverse cases of language use outside of classroom settings (Thorne, 2010; Holden et al., 2015; Sundqvist & Sylvén, 2016; Piirainen-Marsh & Lilja, 2019).

The term 'rewilding' suggests an emphasis on designing supportive conditions for goal-directed interaction in spaces outside of classrooms and then amplifying potential learning processes when back in the classroom context. Empirical cases of language use and learning illustrate that communicative action is multimodal, embodied, and embedded in material environments that catalyze action among heterogeneous arrays of humans and nonhuman actants (Latour, 2005). The use of a mobile phone for the place-based AR game provided a framework for cooperative action among the participants and with their environment. Sequential–temporal analysis showed how human actions such as gaze, pointing, reading aloud, bodily deixis, and audible communication are used in an orderly manner to achieve and maintain intersubjectivity, and importantly, that such human actions, enmeshed with nonhuman contributions, together produce observable morphologies of action (Thorne, 2016; for additional information on rewilding approaches to language education, see Thorne, Hellermann, & Jakonen, 2021 and Hellermann & Thorne, forthcoming).

Bridging activities

The bridging activities framework (Thorne & Reinhardt, 2008; Reinhardt & Thorne, 2011) has the straight-forward goal of bringing learners' interests and everyday communicative practice into the L2 classroom. Aligned with a multiliteracies approach (New London Group, 1996) and initially designed as a structured approach to help students develop digital literacy abilities, the principle of bridging activities is more general and can involve the careful analysis of any student selected, recorded, or created text. The key to bridging activities is learner involvement in selecting the texts for treatment, which helps ensure relevance and motivation. In addition, gaining diagnostic skills by analyzing language use in high-interest areas (recreational, social, professional, academic) enables continued participation in future lifeworld-relevant contexts that may involve new communicative genres and practices. Essentially, the *bridging activities* model involves analyzing student-selected texts within the world language curriculum. Under ideal conditions, this provides vivid, context-situated, and temporally immediate engagement with "living" language use and directly links classroom learning with participant-relevant extramural communicative contexts.

To implement bridging activities, the proposal is to use a three-phase cycle of *observation and collection*, *exploration and analysis*, and *creation and participation* of student selected texts and communicative practices. The first part of each phase, observation, exploration, and creation, is based in situated practice and experiential learning principles, and as such, is grounded in the out-of-class activities and literacy practices that attract learners and involve the L2 contexts or communities of the language they are studying. The analysis and participation phases are analytically oriented and benefit from guided activity and direct instructor intervention in order to methodically assemble a communicative repertoire that aligns with the target L2 context and/or community. An illustrative study using bridging activities with university level elementary Korean learners focused on developing socio-pragmatic awareness around Korean language social media genres of communication. Reinhardt and Ryu (2013) note that the pragmatics associated with Korean honorifics, an obligatory system that indexes features like social distance and status, situational formality, and degree of intimacy is expressed by a nuanced hierarchy of morphosyntactic options. Using bridging activities, students observed expert native use of social media (Facebook in this case), engaged in instructor-guided analysis, collaboratively created Korean language Facebook profiles, engaged in role-play activities to practice new socio-grammatical utterances, and analyzed one another's production. Learning outcomes included heightened socio-pragmatic awareness that was demonstrated by actions such as intentionally flouting expected pragmatic norms and understanding contextual constraints on such behavior.

Implications

Learning an additional language is a difficult and time-intensive process even under ideal conditions, whether in a supportive naturalistic environment or in formally organized instructional settings. Many students in instructional settings find conventional approaches to the teaching of grammar, vocabulary, and the pragmatics of context- and genre-appropriate usage to be largely decontextualized from personally relevant experience and interests. This potentially results in disengagement, and perhaps even boredom, that may preclude the large volume of effortful engagement required to develop advanced language proficiency. In contrast, approaches such as bridging activities, rewilding, learning in the wild, and other techniques that build on LBC experiences and attempt to amplify learning outcomes via classroom-based reflection and peer- and expert guidance, hold great promise for helping students to forge authentic and engaged voices in their second language. There is an obvious need to engage learners in expressive and meaningful uses of the language they are learning; while no single method will serve all students equally well, creating opportunities for students to express agency and choice, to use language in meaningful and relevant contexts outside of classrooms, and to fortify and augment LBC experiences, warrants continued exploration.

Future directions

Many developmentally productive processes occur within the institutional spaces of modern formal education, marked as they are by typically more prescriptivist epistemological norms and pre-defined benchmarks (e.g., exams, high stakes testing) that are primarily oriented toward learning as reproduction of accepted forms of knowledge and skill. Acknowledging the value of the somewhat obvious fact that humans manage social organization through learning new things outside of classrooms, research on LBC has demonstrated the more radical notion that language learning can and frequently does occur outside of conventional expert (teacher)-novice (student) configurations. Further, the pedagogical interventions discussed above, that combine experience beyond the classroom with formal instruction, open new opportunities for synergistically bringing together life experience with the amplification of learning that is possible through reflection, careful analysis of high frequency linguistic and interactional practices, and expert guidance and facilitation by educators.

Reflection questions

1. Think of instances in which you have learned language 'in the wild' or outside of classroom contexts. In what ways might you pedagogically engineer or attune instructed learning activities or curricula to better support LBC?
2. Consider issues of teaching to specific audiences. How might you consider adapting your teaching goals and incorporating LBC opportunities to accommodate different student subject positions and orientations to the target language?

Recommended readings

Sundqvist, P., & Sylvén, L. K. (2016). *Extramural English in teaching and learning*. New York: Palgrave.
  An excellent book-length treatment describing language learning opportunities and outcomes available outside of formal education.
Thorne, S. L., Hellermann, J., & Jakonen, T. (2021). Rewilding language education: Emergent assemblages and entangled actions. *Modern Language Journal*, 105, S1, 106–125.
  This article presents a pedagogical approach called 'rewilding' that seeks to integrate a diversity of real-world activities into instructional curricula, with examples of augmented reality activities for language acquisition.
Wagner, J. (2015). Designing for language learning in the wild: Creating social infrastructures for second language learning. In T. Cadierno & S. Eskildsen (Eds.), *Usage-based perspectives on second language learning* (pp. 75–101). De Gruyter.
  An enlightening discussion of intervention studies that involve supporting language learning 'in the wild' in various social and transactional contexts.

References

Bakhtin, M. (1986). *Speech genres and other late essays.* Austin: University of Texas Press.

Behrenwald, S. J. (2012). Fanfiction practices in ESL writing classrooms. In G. Kessler, A. Oskoz & I. Elola (Eds.), *Technology across writing contexts* (pp. 277–296). San Marcos, TX: Computer Assisted Language Instruction Consortium.

Benson, P. (2021). *Language learning environments: Spatial perspectives on SLA.* Bristol: Multilingual Matters.

Benson, P. (this volume). Mapping language learning environments. In H. Reinders, C. Lai, & P. Sundqvist (Eds.), *Routledge handbook of language learning and teaching beyond the classroom.* New York: Routledge.

Benson, P., & Reinders, H. (Eds.) (2011). *Beyond the language classroom.* London: Palgrave.

Black, R. W. (2008). *Adolescents and online fan fiction.* New York: Peter Lang.

Brouwer, C., & Wagner, J. (2004). Developmental issues in second language conversation. *Journal of Applied Linguistics, 1*(1), 29–47.

Bruzos, A. (2017). *Encuentros con el Español:* A case study of critical service learning in the Latino community. In S. Dubreil & S. L. Thorne (Eds.), *Engaging the world: Social pedagogies and language learning* (pp. 37–63). Boston, MA: Cengage.

Cenoz, J., & Gortler, D. (2008). The linguistic landscape as an additional source of input in second language acquisition. *IRAL: International Review of Applied Linguistics in Language Teaching, 46*(3), 267–87.

Chaiklin, S., &. Lave, J. (Eds.). (1993). *Understanding practice: Perspectives on activity and context.* Cambridge: Cambridge University Press.

Charitos, S., & Van Deusen-Scholl, N. (2017). Engaging the city: Language, space, and identity in urban environments. In S. Dubreil & S. L. Thorne (Eds.), *Engaging the world: Social pedagogies and language learning* (pp. 15–36). Boston, MA: Cengage.

Clark, B., Wagner, J., Lindemalm, K., & Bendt, O. (2011). *Språkskap: Supporting second language learning "in the wild."* https://doi.org/10.13140/RG.2.1.3564.8489

Clifford, J., & Reisinger, D. (2018). *Community-based language learning: A framework for educators.* Washington, DC: Georgetown University Press.

Dressman, M., & Sadler, R. (Eds.) (2020). *The handbook of informal language learning.* Hoboken, NJ: Wiley.

Dubreil, S., & Thorne, S. L. (Eds.) (2017). *Engaging the world: Social pedagogies and language learning.* Boston, MA: Cengage.

Duff, P. (2007). Second language socialization as sociocultural theory: Insights and issues. *Language Teaching, 40*, 309–319.

Engman, M., & Hermes, M. (2021). Land as interlocutor: A study of Ojibwe learner language in interaction on and with naturally occurring 'materials.' *Modern Language Journal, 105*, S1, 86–105.

Eskildsen, S. W. (2009). Constructing another language: Usage-based linguistics in second language acquisition. *Applied Linguistics, 30*, 335–357.

Eskildsen, S. W., & Theodórsdóttir, G. (2017). Constructing L2 learning spaces: Ways to achieve learning inside and outside the classroom. *Applied Linguistics, 38*(2), 143–164.

Firth, A., & Wagner, J. (1997). On discourse, communication, and (some) fundamental concepts in SLA research. *Modern Language Journal, 81*(3), 285–300.

Frith, J. (2015). *Smartphones as locative media.* Cambridge, England: Polity Press.

Greer, T. (2018). Learning to say grace. *Social Interaction: Video-Based Studies of Human Sociality, 1*(1). https://tidsskrift.dk/socialinteraction/article/view/105499

Greer, T. (2019). Initiating and delivering news of the day: Interactional competence as joint-development, *Journal of Pragmatics, 146*, 150–164.

Hellermann, J., Eskildsen, S., Pekarek-Doehler, S., & Piirainen-Marsh, A. (Eds.) (2019). *Language learning 'in the wild': Using conversation analysis to discover the complex ecology of learning-in-action.* New York: Springer.

Hellermann, J., & Thorne, S. L. (in press). Collaborative mobilizations of interbodied communication for cooperative action. *Modern Language Journal.*

Hellermann, J., Thorne, S. L., & Fodor, P. (2017). Mobile reading as social and embodied practice. *Classroom Discourse, 8*(2), 99–121.

Hellermann, J., Thorne, S. L., & Haley, J. (2019). Building socio-environmental infrastructures for learning in the wild. In J. Hellermann, S. Eskildsen, S. Pekarek-Doehler, & A. Piirainen-Marsh (Eds.), *Language learning 'in the wild': Using conversation analysis to discover the complex ecology of learning-in-action* (pp. 193–218). New York: Springer.

Henne–Ochoa, R., Elliot-Groves, E., Meek, B. A., & Rogoff, B. (2020). Pathways forward for Indigenous language reclamation: Engaging Indigenous epistemology and learning by observing and pitching in to family and community endeavors. *Modern Language Journal, 104*, 481–493.

Holden, C., Dikkers, S., Martin, J., & Litts, B. (2015). *Mobile. media learning: Innovation and inspiration*. Pittsburgh, PA: ETC Press.

Holden, C., & Sykes, J. (2011). Leveraging mobile games for place-based language learning. *International Journal of Game-Based Learning, 1*, 1–18.

Hutchins, E. (1995). *Cognition in the wild*. Cambridge: MIT Press.

Jenkins, H. (2006). *Fans, bloggers, and gamers: Exploring participatory culture*. New York, NY: New York University Press.

Justice, C., Rice, J., Warry, W., Inglis, S., Miller, S., & Sammon, S. (2007). Inquiry in higher education: Reflections and directions on course design and teaching methods. *Innovative Higher Education, 31*, 201–214.

Kim, S. (2019). "We limit ten under twenty centu charge okay?": Routinization of an idiosyncratic multi-word expression. In J. Hellermann, S. W. Eskildsen, S. Pekarek Doehler, & A. Piirainen-Marsh (Eds.), *Conversation analytic research on learning-in-action: The complex ecology of second language interaction 'in the wild'* (pp. 25–50). Cham, Switzerland: Springer.

Kinginger, C. (2011). Enhancing language learning in study abroad. *Annual Review of Applied Linguistics, 31*, 58–73.

Lam, W. S. E. (2006). Re-envisioning language, literacy, and the immigrant subject in new mediascapes. *Pedagogies: An International Journal, 1*(3), 171–195.

Lankshear, C., & Knobel, M. (2007). Sampling the "new" in new literacies. In M. Knobel & C. Lankshear (Eds.), *A new literacies sampler* (pp. 1–24). New York: Peter Lang.

Latour, B. (2005). *Reassembling the social: An introduction to actor-network theory*. Oxford, UK: Oxford University Press.

Latour, B. (2013). *An inquiry into modes of existence: An anthropology of the moderns*. Cambridge, MA: Harvard University Press.

Lave, J. (1988). *Cognition in practice: Mind, mathematics, and culture in everyday life*. Cambridge: Cambridge University Press.

Lave, J., & Wenger, E. (1991). *Legitimate peripheral participation*. Cambridge: Cambridge University Press.

Leander, K., & Lovvorn, J. (2006). Literacy networks: Following the circulation of texts, bodies, and objects in the schooling and online gaming of one youth. *Cognition and Instruction, 24*(3): 291–340.

Leppänen, S. (2008). Cybergirls in trouble? Fan fiction as a discursive space for interrogating gender and sexuality. In C. R. Caldas-Coulthard & R. Iedema (Eds.), *Identity trouble: Critical discourse and contested identities* (pp. 156–179). Houndmills, UK: Palgrave Macmillan.

Lilja, N., & Piirainen-Marsh, A. (2019a). Connecting the language classroom and the wild: Re-enactments of language use experiences. *Applied Linguistics, 40*(4), 594–623, https://doi.org/10.1093/applin/amx045

Lilja, N., & Piirainen-Marsh, A. (2019b). Making sense of interactional trouble through mobile-supported sharing activities. In S. Kunitz & R. Salaberry (Eds.), *Teaching and testing L2 interactional competence: Bridging theory and practice* (pp. 260–288). New York: Routledge.

Lilja, N., Piirainen-Marsh, A., Clark, B., & Torretta, N. (2019). The rally course: Learners as co-designers of out-of-classroom language learning tasks. In J. Hellermann, S. W. Eskildsen, S. Pekarek Doehler, & A. Piirainen-Marsh (Eds.), *Conversation analytic research on learning-in-action: The complex ecology of L2 interaction in the wild*. Berlin: Springer.

Malinowski, D. (2015). Opening spaces of learning in the linguistic landscape. *Linguistic Landscape, 1*(1–2), 95–113.

Malinowski, D. (2016). Localizing the transdisciplinary in practice: A teaching account of a prototype undergraduate seminar on linguistic landscape. *L2 Journal, 8*(4), 100–117.

Maxim, H. (2020). A methodological and pedagogical framework for designing L2 student-based linguistic landscape research. In D. Malinowski & S. Tufi (Eds.), *Reterritorializing linguistic landscapes: Questioning boundaries and opening spaces* (pp. 346–363). New York: Bloomsbury.

New London Group (1996). A pedagogy of multiliteracies. *Harvard Educational Review*, 66(1), 60–92.

Nguyen, H. T. (2011). Achieving recipient design longitudinally: Evidence from a phramacy intern in patient consultations. In J. K. Hall, J. Hellermann, & S. Pekarek Doehler (Eds.), *L2 interactional competence and development* (pp. 173–205). Bristol, UK: Multilingual Matters.

Nguyen, H. thi. (2012). *Developing interactional competence: A conversation-analytic study of patient consultations in pharmacy*. New York: Palgrave.

Nguyen, H. thi. (2019). Turn design as longitudinal achievement: Learning on the shop floor. In J. Hellermann, S. W. Eskildsen, S. Pekarek Doehler, & A. Piirainen-Marsh (Eds.), *Conversation analytic research on learning-in-action: The complex ecology of second language interaction 'in the wild'* (pp. 77–104). Cham, Switzerland: Springer.

Ochs, E. (1993). Constructing social identity: A language socialization perspective. *Language and Social Interaction*, 26(3), 287–306.

Piirainen-Marsh, A., & Lilja, N. (2019). How wild can it get? (Re)configuring questions "in the wild". In J. Hellermann, S. W. Eskildsen, S. Pekarek Doehler, & A. Piirainen-Marsh (Eds.) *Conversation analytic research on learning-in-action: The complex ecology of L2 interaction in the wild*. Berlin: Springer. https://www.springer.com/gp/book/9783030221645

Piirainen-Marsh, A., & Tainio, L. (2009a). Other-repetition as a resource for participation in the activity of playing a video game. *Modern Language Journal*, 93(2), 153–169.

Piirainen-Marsh, A., & Tainio, L. (2009b). Collaborative game-play as a site for participation and situated learning of a second language. *Scandinavian Journal of Educational Research*, 53(2), 167–183. https://doi.org/10.1080/00313830902757584

Piirainen-Marsh, A., & Tainio, L. (2014). Asymmetries of knowledge and epistemic change in social gaming interaction. *Modern Language Journal*, 98(4), 1022–1038. https://doi.org/10.1111/modl.12153

Pugh, S. (2005). *The democratic genre: Fan fiction in a literary context*. Brigdend, UK: Seren Press.

Reinders, H. (2017). Research agenda: Language learning beyond the classroom. *Language Teaching*, 50(4), 561–578.

Reinders, H., & Wattana, S. (2014). Can I say something? The effects of digital game play on willingness to communicate. *Language Learning & Technology*, 18(2), 101–123.

Reinhardt, J. (2019). *Gameful second and foreign language teaching and learning*. Basingstoke, England: Palgrave Macmillan.

Reinhardt, J., & Ryu, J. (2013). Using social network-mediated bridging activities to develop socio-pragmatic awareness in elementary Korean. *International Journal of Computer Assisted Language Learning and Teaching*, 3(3), 18–33.

Reinhardt, J., & Thorne, S. L. (2011). Beyond comparisons: Frameworks for developing digital L2 literacies. In Arnold, N., & Ducate, L. (Eds.), *Calling on CALL: From theory and research to new directions in foreign language teaching*, 2nd edition (pp. 257–280). San Marcos, TX: CALICO.

Reinhardt, J., & Thorne, S. L. (2020). Digital games as language-learning environments. In J. Plass, R. Mayer, & B. Homer (Eds.), *Handbook of game-based learning* (pp. 409–435). Cambridge, Mass.: MIT Press.

Roth, W. M., Elmesky, R., Carambo, C., McKnight, Y. M., & Beers, J. (2005). Re/making identities in the praxis of urban schooling: A cultural historical perspective. *Mind, Culture, and Activity*, 11, 48–69.

Sauro, S. (2014). Lessons from the fandom: Task models for technology-enhanced language learning. In M. González-Lloret & L. Ortega (Eds.), *Technology-mediated TBLT: Researching technology and tasks* (pp. 239–262). Amsterdam: John Benjamins.

Sauro, S. (2017). Online fan practices and CALL. *CALICO Journal*, 34 (2), 131–146.

Sauro, S. (2020). Fan fiction and informal language learning. In M. Dressler & R. Sadler (Eds.) *The handbook of informal language learning* (pp. 139–151). Malden: Wiley-Blackwell.

Sauro, S., & Sundmark, B. (2016). Report from Middle Earth: Fanfiction tasks in the EFL classroom. *ELT Journal*, 70(4), 414–423.

Sauro, S., & Thorne, S. L. (2020). Pedagogically mediating engagement in the wild: Trajectories of fandom-based curricular innovation. In V. Werner, & F. Tegge (Eds.), *Pop culture in language education: Theory, research, practice* (pp. 226–237). London: Routledge.

Sawchuk, P. (2003). Informal learning as a speech-exchange system: Implications for knowledge production, power, and social transformation. *Discourse & Society*, 14(3), 291–307.

Scollon, R., & Scollon, S. (2003). *Discourses in place: Language in the material world*. New York: Routledge.

Sockett, G. (2014). *The online informal learning of English*. New York: Palgrave.

Soja, E. (2003). Writing the city spatially. *City, 7*(3), 269–280.

Soulé, M., & Noss, R. (1998). Rewilding and biodiversity: Complementary goals for continental conservation. *Wild Earth, 8*, 19–28.

Squire, K. D. (2009). Mobile media learning: Multiplicities of place. *On the Horizon, 17,* 70–80.

Sundqvist, P., & Sylvén, L. K. (2016). *Extramural English in teaching and learning.* New York: Palgrave.

Swain, M., & Lapkin, S. (1998). Interaction and second language learning: Two adolescent French immersion students working together. *Modern Language Journal, 82,* 320–337.

Sydorenko, T., Hellermann, J., Thorne, S. L., & Howe, V. (2019). Mobile augmented reality and language-related episodes. *TESOL Quarterly, 53*(3), 712–740.

Theodórsdóttir, G. (2011a). Second language interaction for business and learning. In J. K. Hall, J. Hellermann, & S. Pekarek Doehler (Eds.), *L2 interactional competence and development* (pp. 93–116). Bristol, UK: Multilingual Matters.

Theodórsdóttir, G. (2011b). Language learning activities in everyday situations: Insisting on TCU completion in second language talk. In G. Palotti & J. Wagner (Eds.), *L2 learning as a social practice: Conversation-analytic perspectives.* Honolulu: National Foreign Language Resource Center.

Theodórsdóttir, G. (2018). L2 teaching in the wild: A closer look at correction and explanation practices in everyday L2 interaction. *Modern Language Journal, 102,* 30–45.

Theodórsdóttir, G., & Friðriksdóttir, K. (2013). Íslenskuþorpið: Leið til þátttöku í daglegum samskiptum á íslensku [The Icelandic Village: Guided Participation in interaction in Icelandic]. *Milli mála,* 13–42.

Thorne, S. L. (2008). Transcultural communication in open Internet environments and massively multiplayer online games. In S. Magnan (Ed.), *Mediating Discourse Online* (pp. 305–327). Amsterdam: John Benjamins.

Thorne, S. L. (2009). 'Community', semiotic flows, and mediated contribution to activity. *Language Teaching, 42*(1), 81–94.

Thorne, S. L. (2010). The 'intercultural turn' and language learning in the crucible of new media. In F. Helm & S. Guth (Eds.), *Telecollaboration 2.0 for language and intercultural learning* (pp. 139–164). Bern: Peter Lang.

Thorne, S. L. (2012). Gaming writing: Supervernaculars, stylization, and semiotic remediation. In G. Kessler, A. Oskoz, & I. Elola, (Eds.), *Technology across writing contexts and tasks* (pp. 297–316). San Marcos, Texas: CALICO Monograph.

Thorne, S. L. (2013). Language learning, ecological validity, and innovation under conditions of superdiversity. *Bellaterra Journal of Teaching & Learning Language & Literature, 6*(2), 1–27.

Thorne, S. L. (2016). Cultures-of-use and morphologies of communicative action. *Language Learning & Technology, 20*(2), 185–191.

Thorne, S. L., & Black, R. W. (2011). Identity and interaction in Internet-mediated contexts. In C. Higgins (Ed.), *Identity formation in globalizing contexts* (pp. 257–277). New York: Mouton de Gruyter.

Thorne, S. L., & Hellermann, J. (2017). Mobile augmented reality: Hyper contextualization and situated language usage events. *Proceedings of the XVIII International CALL Conference: CALL in Context,* 721–730. ISBN 9789057285509

Thorne, S. L., Hellermann, J., & Jakonen, T. (2021). Rewilding language education: Emergent assemblages and entangled actions. *Modern Language Journal, 105*(S1), 106–125.

Thorne, S. L., Hellermann, J., Jones, A., & Lester D. (2015). Interactional practices and artifact orientation in Mobile Augmented Reality game play. *PsychNology Journal, 13*(2–3), 259–286.

Thorne, S. L., & Reinhardt, J. (2008). "Bridging activities," new media literacies and advanced foreign language proficiency. *CALICO Journal, 25*(3), 558–572.

Thorne, S. L., Sauro, S., & Smith, B. (2015). Technologies, identities, and expressive activity. *Annual Review of Applied Linguistics, 35,* 215–233.

Wagner, J. (1996). Foreign language acquisition through interaction -- A critical review of research on conversational adjustments. *Journal of Pragmatics, 26,* 215–235.

Wagner, J. (2004). The classroom and beyond. *Modern Language Journal, 88,* 612–616.

Wagner, J. (2015). Designing for language learning in the wild: Creating social infrastructures for second language learning. In T. Cadierno & S. Eskildsen (Eds.), *Usage-based perspectives on second language learning* (pp. 75–101). Berlin: De Gruyter.

Warf, B., & Arias, S. (2014). *The spatial turn: Interdisciplinary perspectives.* New York: Routledge.

Werner, V., & Tegge, F. (Eds.). (2020). *Pop culture in language education: Theory, research, practice*. London: Routledge.

Yi, Y. (2021). *Reconceptualizing the writing practices of multilingual youth: Toward a symbiotic approach to in- and out-of-school writing*. New York: Routledge.

Zemel, A., & Koschmann, T. (2014). 'Put your fingers right in here': Learnability and instructed experience. *Discourse Studies*, *16*(2), 163–183.

4
PARTICIPANT-DRIVEN L2 LEARNING IN THE WILD

An Overview and Its Pedagogical Implications

Søren W. Eskildsen

Introduction

This chapter pursues the theme of L2 learning as activities that are socially accomplished through certain displayed behaviors that are recognizable as such by interactional co-participants in situ. In so doing, it builds and expands on a rich body of conversation analytic L2 research (CA-SLA) (e.g., Brouwer & Wagner, 2004; Burch, 2014; Eskildsen, 2019; Eskildsen & Majlesi, 2018; Eskildsen & Theodórsdóttir, 2017; Firth & Wagner, 2007; Hellermann, 2008; Kasper & Burch, 2016; Liddicoat, 1997; Markee & Kasper, 2004; Markee & Kunitz, 2013; Pekarek Doehler, 2010). In particular, I draw on the recent work concerned with building collections of learning behaviors in the wild (Eskildsen 2019; Eskildsen & Theodórsdóttir 2017) to map out systematically the processes and practices involved in the understanding, learning, and teaching activities in which the L2 speakers participate in their everyday lives. This leads to the applied purpose of the chapter, namely, to ground an experiential L2 pedagogy in natural empirical data (Lilja & Piirainen-Marsh, 2019). Specifically, to this end, I present a scaffold-building pedagogy that draws on, exploits, and influences L2 students' social lives through recordings, feedback and challenges and a task-based template that turns curricular assignments into participant-driven activities outside of class, promoting learner autonomy (Little, Dam & Legenhausen, 2017).

L2 learning in and through everyday interaction in the wild is a fundamentally collaborative enterprise in which the L2-speaker is often dependent on the willing participation of locals (Eskildsen, 2019; Greer, 2019; Theodórsdóttir, 2018). Some twenty years after Firth and Wagner (1997) called for a broadening of the SLA database, we are now amassing a body of knowledge about practices and processes of L2 learning in the wild, both in situ and over time (Hellermann et al., 2019). We have mapped out practices for accomplishing repair and doing noticing, learning behaviors, object orientations and the development of L2 interactional competence in the wild. It appears as a principled empirical observation that language learning is a matter of contextualized, biographical discovery of semiotic resources and a matter of discovering, routinizing and diversifying semiotically designed methods to perform social actions that are recognizable to others. In this varied usage-driven process, the key issue for the L2 speaker is to discern, out of all the many bits and pieces of language that filter through to her in her L2 experience, which ones can be used to accomplish what actions. As such, language learning is framed as the learning of a set of semiotic resources for social action.

A few empirical examples will serve as the point of departure to illustrate some basic points and exemplify some phenomena. But before presenting the empirical phenomena, a few words on the data. My data consist of students' self-recorded (audio/video) interactions, amounting to a total of approximately 60 hours of recordings and comprising a variety of uninstructed encounters (e.g., dinner-table talks and service encounters) as well as instructed tasks in which the students discuss non-curricular texts of their own choice. The recordings span up to 16 months allowing for longitudinal investigations.

We meet Lena, Tina (Germans) and Polly (Danish-German) in Extract 1 (transcription conventions at the end of chapter). They are in Polly's kitchen preparing dinner. Tina is peeling the carrots and asks for instructions. However, she runs into trouble with the Danish word for "peel" (line 1).

Extract 1
```
01 T: så, hvor mange gulerødder skal je:g eh s:- skr: (.) skr(  )?=
      so how many carrots shall I p:- pe: pe(  )?
02 P: =skræl[le,
       peel
03 L:       [skrælle
             peel
04 T: skrælle, skrælle? heh[hehheh] hehhehheh .hh
      peel, peel?
05 P:                      [(    )]
06 P: en måske to (.) to, jaer.
      one maybe two (.) two, yeah.
07 T: to? (.) oh okay.
      two? (.) oh okay.
```

Polly hears Tina's speech perturbations and repeated attempts at "skrælle" (peel) as initiating repair, and she provides the term in Danish (line 2). In overlap, Lena repeats the word, either for learning purposes or in support of Polly's candidate (line 3). Tina repeats the word with falling intonation and then once more with rising intonation, followed by laughter. The first repetition of the word indicates noticing and acceptance of the new item. The second repetition of the word is uttered with rising intonation which could be heard as a try-marking of the new item, but it is not oriented to as such by Polly; she orients to it as the completion of the turn at line 1, namely, a request for instructions on how many carrots to peel (line 6). Tina accepts the instruction (line 7).

Of particular interest are lines 1–4. Tina runs into trouble and initiates word search through speech perturbations and attempts at producing a candidate solution to the word search; she initiates repair, and the next speaker, Polly, completes the repair as she provides the sought-for item. Tina then repeats the item and completes her original turn. Elsewhere, I have discussed this as a recurring practice (Eskildsen, 2019) – an example of a type of learning behavior with this recurring sequential format: speaker 1 initiates a word search, speaker 2 provides the word, speaker 1 picks it up and uses it for her immediate communicative purpose. Note that although Polly already knows what Tina is trying to say, she does not respond to the topic-at-hand until Tina has completed her turn at line 4. The speakers co-construct the necessary space for the L2 speaker to notice the new item and hence "do learning" (Eskildsen, 2019; Eskildsen & Theodórsdóttir, 2017).

Word searches, albeit not exclusive to L2 talk (see, e.g., Goodwin & Goodwin, 1986), are opportunities for learning (Brouwer, 2003) and they abound in naturally occurring talk. There are other ways of carrying out word searches – uses of loan words, candidate words with try-marked intonation, explicit word search markers such as *how do you say X?* (Brouwer, 2003; Koshik & Seo, 2012; Kurhila, 2006; Lilja, 2014; Eskildsen, 2018, 2019; Pekarek Doehler & Berger, 2019) – but the learning behavior is visible in the response from the L2 speaker who initiated the word search when she repeats the word and subsequently uses it for what transpires as her planned, communicative purpose; the topical interaction has been put on hold while the word search was resolved. Eskildsen (2018a) demonstrated that (some) word searches have long-term consequences, and, moreover, there is also an increasing amount of evidence from longitudinal usage-based / CA research indicating that encounters with new L2 vocabulary leave traces in people's experience and that learning is a matter of appropriation in multiple encounters over time (Eskildsen & Wagner, 2015b; Y. Kim, 2019). Word searches constitute one kind of encounter, where new L2 items can be highlighted in interaction as "learnables" (Majlesi & Broth, 2012), and are therefore important stepping-stones on the L2 learning path.

The next example, Extract 2, which happens four minutes later, shows a different phenomenon. Having peeled the carrots, Tina is now requesting instructions on how to cut them (line 1). Polly's response at line 2 gets no response as Tina completes her question at line 3. Polly repeats and elaborates her response (line 4), following which Lena initiates repair (line 6). In overlap, Polly self-repairs (line 8). Her repair receives no response; instead Tina repeats the first response with rising intonation (line 9) and Lena explicitly asks for the meaning of the word first used by Polly (line 10). Polly's response is to repeat the repaired version of the response (line 10). The two words used, *terner* and *terninger*, are quite similar in Danish, but they can mean very different things: the latter is plural of "terning" which means "cube", whereas the former is either the plural of "terne" which means "tern" in English (the bird species) or a very infrequent plural form of "tern", another Danish word for something cube-shaped (e.g., bacon cube). Given the likelihood that Polly refers to the shape of a cube throughout, I have interpreted the two words as meaning the same and translated them both into "cubes".

Extract 2
```
01 T: hvordan ska:: gulerødder se ud? så: (.) [ska det være-
      how are the carrots supposed to look? should it be-
02 P:                                          [$terner$
                                                cubes
03 T: stor eller lille stykker->
      big or small pieces->
04 P: terner (.) små terner
      cubes (.) small cubes
05    (0.5)
06 L: [terner?
       cubes?
07 P: [terninger
       cubes
08 T: terner?
      cubes?
09 L: hva betyer terner,
      what does cubes mean?
```

```
10 T: heh heh
11 P: terninger
      cubes
12 L: terninger heh [heh
      cubes
13 T:              [heh heh
14 P: eh würfel,
         cubes
15 L: würfel,
      cubes
16 T: okay ((kitchen noise)) så små: °terninger°,
      okay ((kitchen noise)) so sma:ll °cubes°,
```

Lena repeats Polly's answer followed by laughter in which Tina joins in (lines 12–13). Polly seemingly orients to these actions as displays of non-understanding and, prefaced by a short hesitation token, she translates the word into German (line 14). Lena repeats the German (line 15) and Tina's *okay* indicates her acceptance of the translation as explanation and thus her understanding of the instruction. Her repetition of Polly's responses, as she combines the instruction *små terner* with the corrected word *terninger* (line 16), displays her noticing of not only the new word, but also the repair of "lille" to "små" (lines 3–4). Through this action she displays her orientation to the situation as a learning situation.

The final example, extract 3, showcases another learning behavior as the L2 speakers re-index previously learned items (Eskildsen, 2019). The extract is lengthy, and the focal lines are 15–32. At line 1, Tina is again asking for instructions – this time concerning the number of potatoes. Polly understands and responds even though Tina's question is verbally incomplete (line 2).

Extract 3a
```
01 T: hvor mange kartofler: (.) ska je::[g
      how many potatoes      shall I::
02 P:                                   [ehm: to
                                              two
03 T: t[o
      t[wo
04 L: [to, o:g- kun [to?
      [two a:and- only two?
05 P:          [(   ) store ( [ )
               [       big
06 T:                         [KUN TO?
                              [ONLY TWO?
((kitchen noise))
07 P: der os en masse andre grønsager i
      there are many other vegetables in it
08 L: ja ja det er rigtig.
      yes yes that is right
09    (1.2)
10 T: to stor elle:r
      two big ones o:r
11 P: ja j- jeg tror det blir nok
      yes I- I think that will be enough
((kitchen noise))
```

Tina responds by repeating, and in overlap Lena questions the number of potatoes (lines 3–4). Polly says something largely inaudible in overlap and Tina, also in overlap with Polly, repeats Lena's questioning of the number of potatoes in a raised voice (lines 5–6). Polly's next turn serves a dual purpose: it confirms the number of potatoes and accounts for why they need only two (line 7). Lena acknowledges this explicitly (line 8) and, following a pause, Tina also displays alignment by asking whether the two potatoes should be big (lines 9–10). Polly confirms (line 11).

Next, Tina continues to ask for instructions (Extract 3b). It is not until Lena's contribution at line 15 that we understand what exactly they are talking about: the shape of the potatoes. Lena reuses *terninger* with rising intonation and Polly confirms the word *and* the shape (line 16). That might have been the end of the focus on the word; Tina might have begun cutting the potatoes into cubes. Instead, she repeats *terninger* (line 17), following which they all repeat the word again (Lena even does so twice; lines 18–21).

Extract 3b
```
12 T: eh de ska osse være eh
         they shall also be eh
13 P: jaer.
         yeah.
14 T: som: eh gule[rødder]
         like eh carrots
15 L:            [tern- ] terninger?
                  cu-      cubes?
16 P: ter[ninger.
      cu[bes.
17 T:    [terninger.
         [cubes.
18 L: terninger.
      cubes.
19 P: terninger.
      cubes.
20 T: terninger.
      cubes.
21 L: °terninger°
      °cubes°.
22 T: kay,
      kay,
((Lines omitted))
```

Finally (Extract 3c), Tina makes a comment on all the new words that they are encountering, expressing hope that she will not forget them. Not only does this emphasize their orientation to *doing learning*, but even in this activity there is a potential learning moment as Polly is helping Tina solve a search for the Danish word for "remember" (lines 25–27). Lena expresses agreement with Tina (lines 30–32). The three participants co-construct this sequence, but only the two speakers who are identified as L2 learners in situ display their stance toward the situation as learning-related.

Extract 3c
```
25 T: jeg håber at je:g ik glem: øh
      I hope that I won't for: eh
26 P: glemmer?
```

```
           forget?
27  T:     glemmer
           forget
28  L:     or[dene?
           the words?
29  T:        [alle nye ord
                all new words
30  L:     ja
           yes
31  T:     heh heh
32  L:     det håber jeg heller ikke.
           I don't hope so either.
```

Key issues and constructs

So far, I have focused on lexical items because these visibly attract the attention of L2 users: people demonstrably notice new vocabulary (Greer, 2019). In alignment with usage-based models of language where no principled distinction is made between lexis and grammar, I do not exclude morpho-syntax from my empirical investigations nor do I view such aspects of "grammar" as a priori phenomena detached from "vocabulary" (see discussions in Eskildsen, 2018a, 2019; and Theodórsdóttir, 2018). The crucial issue at stake, however, is that language learning is much more than discovering words and other semiotic items; there is a range of social practices to be learned in a broad range of situations and environments; people learn how to navigate socially in and through the new language. They learn how to perform social actions that call on responses from co-participants. This is the crux of social interaction which, in turn, constitutes the bedrock of L2 learning. The nut to crack for the L2 speaker concerns the understanding of social practices, what actions to be performed when, and how to package them linguistically (Eskildsen, 2018b).

Under the header of "interactional competence" (Hall, Pekarek Doehler & Hellermann, 2011; Pekarek Doehler, 2018), research has investigated L2 speakers' methods to accomplish particular actions and how these methods change and are recalibrated over time. Rooted in ethnomethodological conversation analysis, specifically Harvey Sacks' interest in people's methods to achieve social order in a "basic infrastructure of human sociality" (Hall, 2018: 26), research in L2 interactional competence has documented learning trajectories for L2 speakers' practices for managing turn-taking, classroom task openings and disengagements, story-telling and responding to story-telling, repair, requesting, topic management, sequence organization, and word searches (see overview in Pekarek Doehler & Pochon-Berger, 2015 and subsequent studies (Berger & Pekarek Doehler, 2018; König, 2020; Pekarek Doehler & Berger, 2018, 2019; Pekarek Doehler & Eskildsen, 2022). Moreover, work is accumulating toward principled ways of organizing L2 teaching around interactional competence (Hall, 2018; Huth, 2020; Salaberry & Kunitz, 2019; Waring, 2018).

Research that investigates the intersection between the emergent linguistic repertoire and people's developing interactional competence is scarce and only recently beginning to appear systematically (Pekarek Doehler & Eskildsen, 2022). In the remainder of this section, I will present some data as a glimpse into the process of identifying phenomena at the linguistic-interactional interface. With these data, the longitudinal work remains to be done.

We rejoin Tina, Lena, and Polly in Extract 4, where they are shopping for groceries in preparation for dinner. They are discussing what ingredients to buy and in the first line in the extract, Lena makes a suggestion in this regard (please keep in mind the data are audio-only).

Extract 4
```
01 L: hva m- hva med det her.
      what about this.
02    (1.3)
03 P: nej de: det ser- det se:r [u:Hlækkert ud.]
      no that looks disgHu:sting.
04 L:                           [nå (.) nej m- ] eh heh heh
                                 oh (.) no m-
05    (5.2)
06 P: ja, det ser da oka[y ud.
      Yes, well this looks okay.
07 L:                   [hva betyder disgusting på dansk,
                         what does disgusting mean in Danish,
08 P: ulækkert.
      disgusting.
09 L: ulæk[kert,
      disgusting,
10 T:     [Ulækkert=
           Disgusting=
11 L: =det ser ulækkert ud eh heh heh
      =that looks disgusting
```

Following a pause (line 2), Polly rejects Lena's suggestion and accounts for her rejection by way of an assessment (line 3). In overlap, Lena produces a change of state token and a *no*-token before beginning to laugh (line 4). It appears that she realizes something, probably about the food item, and then agrees with Polly in rejecting her own suggestion. Note that her change of state and rejection-agreement are produced in overlap with Polly's account. Following a more than 5 second pause, Polly appears to have moved to another food item (line 6), but Lena is on a different track: overlapping Polly, she initiates a word search as she asks for the Danish equivalent of "disgusting" (line 7). Polly provides this without hesitation in the next turn (line 8) and both Lena and Tina pick it up publicly (lines 9 and 10). Lena then produces the turn for which she needed the sought-for item. They then continue shopping (not shown).

Lena uses an explicit word search marker to ask for the missing item and although the expression she uses – what does X mean? – is not standardly used for this purpose, it is recognizable enough for the "expert" co-participant to respond, even without the slightest delay. Moreover, the extract, even if brief, illustrates how people reuse linguistic resources – a crucial point in usage-based approaches to L2 learning (Bates & MacWhinney, 1988; Eskildsen, 2017, 2020a, 2020b; Hopper, 1987). Note how Lena and Polly use and repeat the format "det ser ADJ ud" ("it looks ADJ"). Recalling earlier extracts, we can identify further reused expressions: "Hvor mange X skal jeg Y?" (how many X shall I Y?"), other "skal"-("shall")-patterns, and "kun to" ("only two"). We may also indirectly identify other expressions as reuse – "hvad betyder X?" ("what does X mean?") and "hvad med X?" ("what about X?"). While these are not reused in this brief extract, they are both found elsewhere in the data in talk with the same participants. In a previous publication (Eskildsen & Wagner, 2015a), we showed how another L2 speaker of Danish, Katarina, relied heavily on linguistic material that predominantly consisted of reused utterance schemas (Tomasello, 2000) to place an order for food over the phone – e.g., "det / der var X"("it/there was X"); "det skal være X" "it will be X"); "så skal vi have X" ("then we'll have X"). The expressions found in the data, as is the case with Lena's use of "hvad betyder X?" ("what does X mean?"), in Extract

4, may be more or less standard, but they are recognizable to the co-participant; they get the interactional job done. I do not know where the specific linguistic formats in question originated, but the L2 speakers are tapping into their own experience and knowledge to apply them. The L2 speakers in my data were studying Danish and living in Denmark at the time of recording. They were actively participating in Danish in their daily lives. Active participation is the sine qua non of L2 learning in an interactional usage-based perspective; where long-standing theories in SLA debate over issues concerning the necessity and sufficiency of input, I prefer to abandon that metaphor all together to focus instead on social participation. A "second language" is a key to community participation and membership, its learning happens best in and through that, too; i.e., when it is part and parcel of social life in a local community. Input is something we feed to computers so that they may generate an output. The human mind is not a computer and does not work as one. Human language is not output based on input.

Finally, and related to the uses of linguistic expressions, the L2 speakers are continuously learning to interact; i.e., to accomplish social actions in and through language. In the extract, Lena suggests a food item (line 1), displays a change of state and then agrees with the co-participant's rejection of the suggestion (line 4), initiates word search (line 7), displays uptake of the new item (line 9), and finally produces an account, albeit delayed, of her agreeing with Polly's rejection. In the earlier extracts, Tina requested instructions and displayed her stances. To accomplish these actions, the L2 speaker needs to command certain linguistic formats that at least resemble the formats typically and standardly used by L1 speakers to accomplish these actions. This can be done by one-word expressions (e.g., the change of state token ("nå"), ("oh")) and the agreement with the rejection ("nej", ("no")), but usually longer strings of language of a more or less formulaic nature are needed. As mentioned, I do not know how or where in Lena's experience "hva med X?", "hvad betyder X?", and "det ser ADJ ud" have emerged, or how these feed into her emergent L2-grammar-for-interaction (Pekarek Doehler, 2018; Pekarek Doehler & Eskildsen, 2022), but the speakers themselves are demonstrably aware of the importance of such fixed expressions. A final example is given in Extract 5 (adapted with revised line numbering from Eskildsen, 2019), where Lena is talking to a Danish friend, Molly. Lena has been telling Molly about different places in the US that she went to during her au pair sojourn. Just prior to the excerpt Lena has related how much she liked seeing the Grand Canyon. Molly then starts asking Lena a new question (line 1).

Extract 5
```
01 M:   å: hvis [du::
        a:nd if you::
02 L:          [hvad- hvad betyder <at gå:> (.) e::h (0.9) hiking (.) på
03      dansk
               what does to go hiking mean in Danish
04      (0.3)
05 L:   at
        to
06 M:   der ville man- man ville sige det samme (.) man ville enten sige man
        you would- you would say the same (.) you would either say you
07      ska på haik (.) eller man ska ud å vandre.
        go on a hike or you go hiking.
08      (0.5)
09 L:   oka:y?
```

```
10 M: m[m?
11 L:  [så: i grand canyon (.) e:h sku vi på haik?
        so: in grand canyon we went on a hike
12 M: mm?=
13 L: =o:g >det var virkelig dejlig.<
       a:nd it was really lovely
```

Before Molly gets to her question, however, Lena interrupts and asks for the Danish equivalent of "at gå hiking". Interestingly, this is already partly in Danish, as seen in Lena's translation of "to go" into "at gå" which coerces the Danish words into the English phrase "to go hiking". Molly then delivers two alternatives (lines 6–7) and, following another pause and a confirmation check (lines 8–10), Lena accepts Molly's first candidate and in overlap with Molly's confirmation and continuer (line 10), she begins producing a telling that relies on the new item, *så i grand canyon sku vi på haik* (line 11, simplified). This gets another continuer (l. 12) and Lena gives an assessment (l. 13), which Molly aligns with (not shown).

In essence, the data shows the empirical, in situ evidence for the usage-based understanding of learning as the conspiracy of all the memories of all the utterances in a L2 speaker's entire history as language user (Ellis, 2015). People can learn a language, essentially, because it is noticeable; it is derived from real-life encounters as people appropriate the nuts and bolts of language as part of an emergent semiotic repertoire for social action (Eskildsen, 2018b, 2019).

Implications

As mentioned, research investigating the intersection between the linguistic repertoires and interactional competence has only recently begun to appear systematically. These studies have shown how people use specific linguistic items in different interactional contexts over time (e.g., Hauser, 2013; Ishida, 2009; Kim, 2009) and how such instances of use play into the emergent L2-grammar-for-interaction (Eskildsen, 2011, 2018b; Pekarek Doehler, 2018; Pekarek Doehler & Skogmyr Marian, 2022; Theodórsdóttir & Eskildsen, 2022). In a recent volume reporting on CA studies of L2 interaction and learning in the wild (Hellermann et al., 2019), Pekarek Doehler and Berger (2019) documented changes in an au pair's L2 French practices for word searches centering on the phrase comment on dit; Kim (2019) traced an L2 English speaking shopkeeper's routinization of an expression for informing customers about the shop's credit card policy; and Nguyen (2019) showed the emergence and development of English linguistic resources for L2 small-talk in a hotel employee in Vietnam.

I recently summed up research along these lines as being based on the insight that language is a semiotic resource for social action and that learning it is the process of creating one's social, linguistic, and interactional biography through discovery (Eskildsen, 2018). Putting an interactional repertoire to good and proper use is to know what to do how and when and to be able to package it semiotically in a way that can be readily made sense of by others. Experienced language users routinely accomplish social actions in ways, and by use of linguistic resources, that are recognizable to co-participants. Repair is initiated when intersubjectivity is threatened as recognition fails. This is the catch-22 of L2 learning: how do people learn to do something they have never done before in a way that is recognizable to their co-participants?

Whatever language they are learning and whenever they are doing it, people must learn the new language-specific ways of accomplishing social action by participating in interaction with local co-participants. They learn these in a very bottom-up, trial-and-error fashion as they observe, eavesdrop, appropriate, control, and calibrate semiotic resources, picked up from the environment, for accomplishing locally occasioned social actions. In L2 learning, they are crutched by the L1 interactional competence they bring into the task of learning the new language, but little is known about the specifics of this cross-cultural influence (Pekarek Doehler & Pochon-Berger, 2015). Whatever guidance their human biological and biographical experience affords them on the L2 road of discovery, they can learn the linguistic ways of their new community because what people do in interaction, how they put their interactional repertoires to use, is empirically observable, witnessable, and noticeable – and because they can participate in it as legitimate members.

As mentioned, the practices and social actions that have been explored in L2 interactional competence research include taking turns at talk, opening and disengaging from classroom talk, disagreeing, story-telling and responding to such, repairing, requesting, and topic shifting. These are all teachable objects in that they are practices and social actions that can be accomplished through particular observable methods, including semiotic resources. A key to L2 learning, and therefore teaching, is that the correlation between particular semiotic resources and particular social actions is observable and noticeable. The task of the L2 researcher is to work toward a better understanding of this correlation and make her research widely accessible, and the task of the L2 teacher is to make such correlations observable and noticeable.

One way to accomplish such L2 teaching is to make opportunities available for L2 speakers to engage in a wider variety of social situations. Initiatives to support L2 learning in the wild are spreading to accomplish just that (Eskildsen & Wagner, 2015a, 2018). The *Språkskap* project in Sweden, e.g., developed a simple structure for learners to engage in learning through their encounters with service providers (Clark et al., 2011), and likewise *The Icelandic Village* created opportunities for low-level learners of Icelandic to use the new language in everyday service encounters outside the classroom (Wagner, 2015). At the University of Tampere and the University of Iceland, L2 students co-design their excursions into the wild using different material resources that aim at supporting their L2 use and development, record their interactions in the wild and bring them back to the classroom for reflection (Lilja & Piirainen-Marsh, 2019; Lilja et al., 2019). At Portland State University, the use of GPS-enabled mobile games has brought language learning activities into the outside world (Hellermann, Thorne & Hayley, 2019). These efforts move experiential L2 pedagogies to a qualitatively new level.

In my own teaching, I have practiced experiential L2 pedagogies in the form of (1) a scaffold-building pedagogy that draws on, exploits, and influences L2 students' social lives through recordings, feedback and challenges; and (2) a task-based template that turns curricular assignments into participant-driven activities outside of class. The former consists in the L2 students recording themselves and the teacher acting as a counselor providing feedback on the interactional and linguistic accomplishments in the recordings (Brouwer & Nissen, 2003). This can be done on levels ranging from morpho-phonemic to interactional-sequential. To help the students progress, the teacher may also suggest the next challenge to be overcome in the L2; or ask the students to challenge each other. I have often seen my L2 students progress from accomplishing basic service encounters (like ordering a coffee) to more complex service encounters (signing up for a club membership or opening a bank account) to participating freely in everyday social encounters with friends (e.g., shopping for and cooking dinner together, as shown in extracts in this chapter). The challenges posed may profitably reflect this progression.

Many if not most L2 teachers also face curricular and institutional requirements that may not be compatible with the outlined approaches. I would advocate a change in these requirements, but if that is impossible, then initiatives can be taken to accommodate them. A teacher might, e.g., ask the students to hand in oral reading reports on curricular texts based on a questionnaire provided by the teacher. The questionnaire might address the nature and length of the text, the reason for choosing it, the level of difficulty it represents, what reading strategies were employed, how many and which words were new etc. The students then present and discuss their texts on the basis of these questions, record themselves and hand in their recordings, and the feedback and challenge cycle outlined above is then applied. The reading report questionnaire can serve as a template for other task-based assignments, e.g., on the basis of self-chosen texts, that then turn into participant-driven activities outside of class. Although not naturally occurring in the wild, because the teacher is now more in control of the environments, the talk that ensues from reading the texts yields many learning opportunities. Many of my students have handed in video-recordings of their reading reports, and although I have not yet published on these data, I have presented preliminary analyses and findings at conferences, where I have shown embodied learning practices and microgenetic L2 development. Anecdotally, I also know from the students' feedback that they particularly enjoyed talking about the new words they had encountered. The reading report and the subsequent feedback I provided thus seems to be a profitable way of giving the students opportunities to learn new L2 vocabulary.

Future directions

The implication of the previous sections is that everyday mundane interaction is rich in semiotic resources to be harvested by L2 learners. Most of the research from L2 learning in the wild has focused on vocabulary learning, probably due to the highly noticeable nature of lexical items as opposed to say, morphology, and while that is central to L2 learning, it is not the only aspect of it. Moreover, we do not know the details of how such expanded vocabulary knowledge plays into a developing L2 interactional competence, just as we are only beginning to grasp the mutually dependent nature of L2 emergence and L2 interactional competence. A great deal of basic research remains to be done on these issues.

Finally, many of the casually encountered semiotic resources may pass out of the L2 speaker's experience if not encountered again in due course; we saw Tina and Lena expressing this concern in one of the extracts. We need to give them tools to better remember what they encounter. Therefore, we need to pedagogically draw on and intervene with their everyday lifeworlds, and one way to do that is to design tools that support L2 participation and learning in the wild based on experienced everyday situations with learning potential (Clark & Lindemalm, 2011; Wagner, 2015). This can be achieved by applying methods from social and participatory design that allow us to learn with, from, and about the population we work with (for details on Design Thinking, see, e.g., Buchanan, 1992; Plattner et al., 2010). Such work results in tools to enhance the contacts between newcomers and locals, prepare newcomers for the situations in which they engage and enable them to harvest and systematize knowledge and practices from these situations by recording and storing the activities and sharing the recordings (Borg et al., 2018; Lilja et al., 2019; Wagner, 2019). Further work in this vein will aim to design locally adaptable tools to scaffold L2 socialization and learning to the benefit of L2 speakers, e.g., refugees and work migrants, L2 teachers, local communities, and society as a whole.

Reflection questions

1. As an L2 teacher, what activities would you encourage your students to participate in outside of the classroom?
2. In your experience as an L2 learner, what activities and social and linguistic environments have given you the best learning opportunities?
3. If L2 learning is a matter of discovering (noticing and picking up) the relationship between semiotic resources and accomplishing social actions, then what role is there for linguistic awareness in L2 teaching?

Recommended readings

Hellermann, J., Eskildsen, S. W., Pekarek Doehler, S. & Piirainen-Marsh, A. (Eds.) (2019). *Conversation analytic research on L2 interaction in the wild: The complex ecology of learning-in-action.* Cham: Springer. (State-of-the-art volume on conversation analytic L2 learning in the wild).

Huth, T. (2020). *Interaction, language use, and second language teaching.* New York: Routledge. (state-of-the-art volume on interactional, usage-based SLA with implications for L2 teaching).

Salaberry, R. & Kunitz, S. (Eds.) (2019). *Teaching and testing L2 interactional competence: Bridging theory and practice.* New York: Routledge. (State-of-the-art volume on interactional competence in L2 research).

References

Bates, E., & MacWhinney, B. (1988). What is functionalism? *Papers and Reports on Child Language Development 27*, 137–152.

Berger, E., & S. Pekarek Doehler, S. (2018). Tracking change over time in second language talk-in-interaction: A longitudinal case study of storytelling organization. In S. Pekarek Doehler, E. González-Martínez, & J. Wagner (Eds.), *Documenting change across time: Longitudinal studies on the organization of social interaction* (pp. 67–102). Basingstoke: Palgrave Macmillan.

Borg, K. O., Juhl, N. B., Mathiasen, D. D., Petersen, C. H., & Wagner, J. (2018). Dansk i hverdagen – på vej mod en læringsinfrastruktur [Everyday Danish - towards a learning infrastructure]. Sprogforum, *67*, 31–42.

Brouwer, C. E. (2003). Word searches in NNS-NS interaction: Opportunities for language learning? *The Modern Language Journal 87*(4), 534–545.

Brouwer, C. E., & Nissen, A. (2003). At lære dansk som andetsprog i praksis: Et sprogpædagogisk koncept med konversationsanalyse som fagligt grundlag [Learning Danish as a second language: A language pedagogical concept based on conversation analysis]. In B. Asmuss & J. Steensig (Eds.), *Samtalen på arbejde: Konversationsanalyse og kompetenceudvikling* (pp. 52–72). [Talk at work: Conversation analysis and competence development]. Copenhagen: Samfundslitteratur.

Brouwer, C. E., & Wagner, J. (2004). Developmental issues in second language conversation. *Journal of Applied Linguistics 1*, 29–47.

Burch, R.A. (2014). Pursuing information. A conversation analytic perspective on communication strategies. *Language Learning 64*(3), 651–684.

Buchanan, R. (1992). Wicked problems in design thinking. *Design Issues 8*(2), 5–21

Clark, B., & Lindemalm, K. (Eds.). (2011). *Språkskap – Swedish as a Social Language.* Stockholm: Ergonomidesign, Folkeuniversitetet and Interactive Institute.

Clark, B., Wagner, J., Lindemalm, K., & Bendt, O. (2011). Språkskap: Supporting second language learning 'in the wild.' *INCLUDE 11. International conference on inclusive design proceedings.* London: Royal College of Art.

Ellis, N. C. (2015). Cognitive and social aspects of learning from usage. In T. Cadierno & S. W. Eskildsen (Eds.), *Usage-based perspectives on second language learning* (pp. 49–74). Berlin: Mouton de Gruyter.

Eskildsen, S. W. (2011). The L2 inventory in action: Conversation analysis and usage-based linguistics in SLA. In G. Pallotti & J. Wagner (Eds.), *L2 learning as social practice: Conversation-analytic perspectives* (pp. 337–373). Honolulu, HI: University of Hawai'i.

Eskildsen, S. W. (2017). The emergence of creativity in L2 English – a usage-based case-study. In N. Bell (Ed.), *Multiple perspectives on language play* (pp. 281–316). Berlin: Mouton de Gruyter.

Eskildsen, S. W. (2018a). "We're learning a lot of new words": Encountering new L2 vocabulary outside of class. *The Modern Language Journal, 102* (Supplement), 46–63.

Eskildsen, S. W. (2018b). Building a semiotic repertoire for social action: Interactional competence as biographical discovery. *Classroom Discourse, 9*(1), 68–76.

Eskildsen, S. W. (2019). Learning behaviors in the wild: How people achieve L2 learning outside of class. In Hellermann, J., Eskildsen, S. W., Pekarek Doehler, S., & Piirainen-Marsh, A. (Eds.), *Conversation analytic research on learning-in-action: The complex ecology of second language interaction 'in the wild'* (pp. 105–129). Cham: Springer.

Eskildsen, S. W. (2020a). From constructions to social action: The substance of English and its learning from an interactional usage-based perspective. In C. Hall & R. Wicaksono (Eds.), *Ontologies of English. Reconceptualising the language for learning, teaching, and assessment* (pp. 59–79). Cambridge: Cambridge University Press.

Eskildsen, S. W. (2020b). Creativity and routinisation in L2 English – two usage-based case-studies. In W. Lowie, M. Michel, A. Rousse-Malpat, M. Keijzer, & R. Steinkrauss (Eds.), *Usage-based dynamics in second language development*. Bristol, UK: Multilingual Matters.

Eskildsen, S. W., & Majlesi, A. R. (2018). Learnables and teachables in second language talk: Advancing a social reconceptualization of central SLA tenets. Introduction to the Special Issue. *The Modern Language Journal, 102*(Suppl.), 3–10.

Eskildsen, S. W., & Theodórsdóttir, G. (2017). Constructing L2 learning spaces: Ways to achieve learning inside and outside the classroom. *Applied Linguistics, 38,* 148–164.

Eskildsen, S. W., & Wagner, J. (2015a). Sprogbrugsbaseret læring i en tosproget hverdag. Enforskningsoversigt over sprogbrugsbaseret andetsprogstilegnelse og sprogpædagogiske implikationer. [Usage-based learning in everyday bilingual practice. usage-based learning in everyday bilingual practice. A survey of usage-based second language acquisition research with implications for teaching.] *Nydanske Sprogstudier, 48,* 71–104.

Eskildsen, S. W., & Wagner, J. (2015b). Embodied L2 construction learning. *Language Learning, 65*(2), 419–448.

Eskildsen, S. W., & Wagner, J. (2018). "Language learning in the wild" som praksisorienteret sprogundervisning ["Language learning in the wild" as practice-oriented language teaching]. *Sprogforum [Language Forum], 66,* 62–70.

Firth, A., & Wagner, J. (1997). On discourse, communication, and (some) fundamental concepts in SLA research. *The Modern Language Journal, 81*(3), 285–300.

Firth, A., & Wagner, J. (2007). S/FL learning as a social accomplishment: Elaborations on a "reconceptualised" SLA. *The Modern Language Journal 91,* 800–819.

Goodwin, M. H., & Goodwin, C. (1986). Gesture and coparticipation in the activity of searching for a word. *Semiotica, 62,* 51–75.

Greer, T. (2019). Noticing words in the wild. In Hellermann, J., Eskildsen, S. W., Pekarek Doehler, S., & Piirainen-Marsh, A. (Eds.), *Conversation analytic research on learning-in-action: The complex ecology of second language interaction 'in the wild'* (pp. 131–158). Cham: Springer.

Hall, J. K. (2018). *Essentials of SLA for L2 teachers: A transdisciplinary framework*. New York: Routledge.

Hall, J. K., Hellermann, J., & Pekarek Doehler, S. (Eds.). (2011). *L2 interactional competence and development*. Clevedon: Multilingual Matters.

Hauser, E. (2013). Stability and change in one adult's second language English negation. *Language Learning, 63*(3): 463–498.

Hellermann, J. (2008). *Social actions for classroom language learning*. Clevedon, UK: Multilingual Matters.

Hellermann, J., Eskildsen, S. W., Pekarek Doehler, S., & Piirainen-Marsh, A. (Eds.) (2019). *Conversation analytic research on L2 interaction in the wild: The complex ecology of learning-in-action*. Cham: Springer.

Hellermann, J., Thorne, S. L., & Hayley, J. (2019). Building socio-environmental infrastructures for learning. In Hellermann, J., Eskildsen, S. W., Pekarek Doehler, S., & Piirainen-Marsh, A. (Eds.), *Conversation analytic research on learning-in-action: The complex ecology of second language interaction 'in the wild'* (pp. 193–218). Cham: Springer.

Hopper, P. J. (1987). Emergent grammar. In J. Aske, N. Beery, L. Michaelis, & H. Filip (Eds.), *Proceedings of the Thirteenth Annual Meeting of the Berkeley Linguistics Society* (pp. 139–157). Berkeley: Berkeley Linguistics Society.

Huth, T. (2020). *Interaction, language use, and second language teaching.* New York: Routledge.

Ishida, M. (2009). Development of interactional competence: Changes in the use of ne in L2 Japanese during study abroad. In H. T. Nguyen & G. Kasper (Eds.), *Talk-in-interaction: Multilingual perspectives* (pp. 351–386). Honolulu: University of Hawai'i.

Kasper, G., & Burch, A. R. (2016). Focus on form in the wild. In R. A. van Compernolle & J. McGregor (Eds.), *Authenticity, language and interaction in second language contexts* (pp. 198–232). Bristol, UK: Multilingual Matters.

Kim, S. (2019). We limit under twenty century charge okay?: Routinization of an idiosyncratic multi-word expression. In J. Hellermann, S. W. Eskildsen, S. Pekarek Doehler, & A. Piirainen-Marsh (Eds.), *Conversation analytic research on L2 interaction in the wild: the complex ecology of learning-in-action* (pp. 25–49). Cham: Springer.

Kim, Y. (2009). Korean discourse markers in L2 Korean speakers' conversation: An acquisitional perspective. In H. T. Nguyen and G. Kasper (Eds.), *Talk-in-interaction: Multilingual perspectives* (pp. 317–350). Honolulu: University of Hawai'i.

Kim, Y. (2019). What is stoyr- steruh type?": Knowledge asymmetry, intersubjectivity, and learning opportunities in conversation-for-learning. *Applied Linguistics, 40*(2), 307–328.

König, C. (2020). *A conversation analysis approach to French L2 learning: Introducing and closing topics in everyday interactions.* New York: Routledge.

Koshik, I., & Seo, M.-S. (2012). Word (and other) search sequences initiated by language learners. *Text & Talk, 32*(2), 167–189.

Kurhila, S. (2006). *Second language interaction.* Philadelphia/Amsterdam: John Benjamins.

Liddicoat, A. (1997). Interaction, social structure, and second language use. *Modern Language Journal, 81*(3), 313–317.

Lilja, N. (2014). Partial repetitions as other-initiations of repair in second language talk: Re-establishing understanding and doing learning. *Journal of Pragmatics, 71,* 98–116.

Lilja, N., & Piirainen-Marsh, A. (2019). Connecting the language classroom and the wild: Re-enactments of language use experiences. *Applied Linguistics, 40*(4), 594–623.

Lilja, N., Piirainen-Marsh, A., Clark, B., & Torretta, N. (2019). The rally course: Learners as co-designers of out-of-classroom language learning tasks. In J. Hellermann, S. W. Eskildsen, S. Pekarek Doehler, & A. Piirainen-Marsh (Eds), *Conversation analytic research on learning-in-action: The complex ecology of second language interaction 'in the wild'* (pp. 219–248). Cham: Springer

Little, D., Dam, L., & Legenhausen, L. (2017). *Language learner autonomy: Theory, practice and research.* Bristol: Multilingual Matters, September 2017

Majlesi, A. R., & Broth, M. (2012). Emergent learnables in second language classroom interaction. *Learning, Culture and Social Interaction, 1,* 193–207.

Markee, N., & Kasper, G. (2004). Classroom talks: An introduction. *The Modern Language Journal, 88*(4), 491–500.

Markee, N., & Kunitz, S. (2013). Doing planning and task performance in second language acquisition: An ethnomethodological respecification. *Language Learning, 63*(4), 629–664.

Nguyen, H. T. (2019). Turn design as longitudinal achievement: Learning on the shop floor. In J. Hellermann, S. W. Eskildsen, S. Pekarek Doehler, & A. Piirainen-Marsh (Eds.), *Conversation analytic research on L2 interaction in the wild: The complex ecology of learning-in-action* (pp. 77–103). Cham: Springer.

Pekarek Doehler, S. (2010). Conceptual changes and methodological challenges: on language, learning and documenting learning in conversation analytic SLA research. In P. Seedhouse & S. Walsh (Eds.), *Conceptions of 'Learning' in applied linguistics* (pp. 105–127). New York: Palgrave Macmillan.

Pekarek Doehler, S. (2018). Elaborations on L2 interactional competence: The development of L2 grammar-for-interaction. *Classroom Discourse 9*(1), 3–24.

Pekarek Doehler, S., & Berger, E. (2018). L2 interactional competence as increased ability for context-sensitive conduct: A longitudinal study of story-openings. *Applied Linguistics, 39*(4), 555–578.

Pekarek Doehler, S., & Berger, E. (2019). On the reflexive relation between developing l2 interactional competence and evolving social relationships: A longitudinal study of word-searches in the 'Wild'. In J. Hellermann, S. W. Eskildsen, S. Pekarek Doehler, & A. Piirainen-Marsh (Eds.), *Conversation analytic research on L2 interaction in the wild: The complex ecology of learning-in-action* (pp. 51–76). Cham: Springer.

Pekarek Doehler, S. & Eskildsen, S. W. (2022). Emergent L2 Grammars in and for Social Interaction: Introduction to the Special Issue. *Modern Language Journal, 106* (Supplement).

Pekarek Doehler, S., & Pochon-Berger, E. (2015). The development of L2 interactional competence: evidence from turn-taking organization, sequence organization, repair organization and preference organization. In T. Cadierno & S. W. Eskildsen (Eds.), *Usage-based perspectives on second language learning* (pp. 233–268). Berlin: Mouton de Gruyter.

Pekarek Doehler, S., & Skogmyr Marian, K. (2022). Functional diversification and progressive routinization of a multiword expression in and for social interaction: A longitudinal L2 study. *Modern Language Journal, 106* (Supplement 2022).

Plattner, H., Meinel, C., & Leifer, L. (Eds.) (2010). *Design Thinking*. Heidelberg: Springer.

Salaberry, R., & Kunitz, S. (Eds.) (2019). *Teaching and testing L2 interactional competence: Bridging theory and practice*. New York: Routledge.

Theodórsdóttir, G. (2018). L2 teaching in the wild: A closer look at correction and explanation practices in everyday L2 interaction. *Modern Language Journal, 102* (Supplement), 30–45.

Theodórsdóttir, G., & Eskildsen, S. W. (2022). Accumulating semiotic resources for social actions: A case study of L2 Icelandic in the wild. *Modern Language Journal, 106* (Supplement).

Tomasello, M. (2000). First steps toward a usage-based theory of language acquisition. *Cognitive Linguistics, 11*, 61–82.

Wagner, J. (2015). Designing for language learning in the wild: Creating social infrastructures for second language learning. In T. Cadierno & S. W. Eskildsen (Eds.), *Usage-based perspectives on second language learning* (pp. 75–104). Berlin: Mouton de Gruyter.

Wagner, J. (2019). Towards an epistemology of second language learning in the wild. In: J. Hellermann, S. W. Eskildsen, S. Pekarek Doehler, & A. Piirainen-Marsh (Eds.), *Conversation analytic research on L2 interaction in the wild: The complex ecology of learning-in-action* (pp. 251–271). Cham: Springer.

Waring, H. (2018). Teaching L2 interactional competence: Problems and possibilities. *Classroom Discourse, 9*(1), 57–67.

Transcription conventions

01, 02 etc.	line numbering
K:, B:	speaker identification
GLO:	English gloss
Wei[rd w]ord [yeah]	beginning and end of overlap
$word$	sing-song voice
wHord	word-internal aspiration
.hh	in-breath. The number of h's indicates length of in-breath
? / . / , / →	rising / falling-to-low / falling-to-mid / continuing intonation
( )	unintelligible talk
(0.5) / (.)	pause in tenth of seconds / micro-pause (pause shorter than 0.3 seconds
((word))	transcriber's comment

5
LEARNING BEYOND THE CLASSROOM AND AUTONOMY

Geoff Sockett

Introduction

Autonomy in language learning, the ways in which learners take control of their own learning, has been a fruitful field of research in second language acquisition for over 40 years. From Holec's (1981) initial exploration of the field through Reinders and White's (2016) review of 20 years of autonomy and technology to current discussions of space and place (Murray & Lamb, 2018), much has been discovered about the ways in which the theoretical construct of learner autonomy interacts with learning spaces and learning technologies. The focus on learning beyond the classroom offered by this handbook brings these three strands together as learners interact autonomously, often with technology, in their own learning spaces.

Since the aim of this chapter is to discuss learner autonomy in the context of out-of-class learning, it may be helpful to begin by observing some differences between the two concepts. Nunan and Richards (2015) in the preface to their book on language learning beyond the classroom state that "this book offers and important perspective on autonomous learning by focusing on out-of-class learning and the role it can play in facilitating learning" (2015: xi). It is therefore helpful to realise that autonomous learning and out-of-class learning overlap in a number of ways but are not synonymous. Characterising both the places where learning happens and the capacities necessary to learn in those varied contexts allows researchers to focus on two dimensions of the complex system that is language learning in the 21st century. Taking out-of-class learning as a perspective on learner autonomy, as Nunan and Richards (2015) suggested, means that the learner's developing capacity to take control of their own learning may be seen most clearly in out-of-class contexts. Indeed, the extent to which learner autonomy is both a cause and a consequence of out-of-class activities has long been of interest to researchers. Learner autonomy is perhaps the key notion in any discussion of learning beyond the classroom since it questions to what extent and in what conditions language acquisition will actually take place beyond the control of the teacher and therefore to what extent and in what conditions lifelong learning may become a reality going forward.

We will begin this exploration of learner autonomy beyond the classroom by observing how the key concepts necessary to understand these phenomena have evolved through time to bring us to their current definitions and operationalisations. We will then explore the current issues facing researchers and practitioners interested in learner autonomy beyond the classroom. Indeed, as learner practices develop more and more beyond the reach of classroom teachers, there are both opportunities to study and capitalise on new learning phenomena and challenges to the methodologies most widely used to teach and study language learners. These implications for research and teaching will lead naturally enough to a consideration of the future directions to be taken in both theory and practice in order for the field of language teaching and learning to remain relevant in a world where many learner practices have moved behind closed doors. The chapter will conclude with some reflective questions allowing the reader to situate their own approach to this new dimension of learner autonomy with respect to the ideas presented, as well as some suggestions for further reading.

Key constructs in learner autonomy

Many authors, including Benson and Reinders (2011) and Little et al. (2017) have, over the years, offered admirable reviews of the history of the learner autonomy paradigm. In the context of this chapter, any such discussion will necessarily be limited to those aspects which point more specifically to issues surrounding learning beyond the classroom. Important issues such as teacher autonomy and language learning as a facet of general autonomy will therefore fall beyond the scope of this brief review.

As the printing press heralded a democratisation of education around the world, so the evolution of communication technologies has often been mirrored by developments in learning and teaching. In the case of the learner autonomy paradigm, it was as a result of the democratisation of analogue technologies in the 1970s and 1980s, based around audio and video tape, that educators began setting up self-access resource centres for language learning, since audio and video playback equipment began to become available at a fraction of the costs previously encountered. Language pedagogy at this time was moving from an audio-visual method, focussed on structured content, towards a communicative approach focussed on the learner. Since the individual learner, rather than the teacher, was now in a position to select an audio or video cassette of interest and decide when to pause it and what aspects of the language to focus on, these learner-centred considerations became more central to research into learning and teaching. By extension, the issue of how learners could successfully take charge of their learning outside the classroom became an obvious focus, since it was reasoned that learner autonomy was developed through autonomous practices.

What, why, and how?

The aspects of learner autonomy first suggested by Holec (1981), developed by Dickinson (1987) and considered by Benson (2011) to continue to be widely accepted, focus on three questions:

- What are learners doing? What method and materials are being used, for how long and where?
- Why are they doing it? Who made the decision to learn? What motivations are involved?
- How is learning being monitored? By the learner, by others, through certification?

Holec reasoned that the more of these parameters were being decided by the learners, the more they were demonstrating control over their own learning. In many ways, these questions are still relevant for the current wave of research into out-of-class learning, which is the focus of this chapter. A recent review of definitions of autonomy by Murray and Lamb (2018) identifies "goal-orientated action, emotions, community, criticality, empowerment and change" (2018: 2) as dimensions of autonomy which are of particular interest today. It is possible to observe in these terms that goal-orientated action relates to the question "what are learners doing?", that emotions and goals relate to "why are they doing it?" and questions of criticality and community relate to the learner and others monitoring learning activities. Political notions of empowerment and change were also important to Holec who viewed autonomy (literally making one's own laws) as a process of being set free from the control of others.

Discovering what activities learners engage in and what individual differences exist in learner practices has been a fruitful area of research as learners access a range of materials outside the classroom on mobile devices, either for leisure purposes or with the intention to learn. This issue of why, or motivation, is therefore still a key to discovering the difference between leisure-focussed activities such as binge-watching television series and more form-focussed activities such as using non-formal learning apps. The issue of monitoring is a key to identifying questions around the degree of involvement of teachers and other actors in the process. Indeed, learners may be engaging in learning activities outside the classroom on learning platforms such as Blackboard or Moodle under the supervision of teachers in order to gain a formal qualification, they may be using non-formal apps such as Duolingo, which provide automated feedback, with a view to self-improvement, or may simply be enjoying informal online activities including those involving social networking with other target language users who may provide implicit feedback on the learner's language use. In each of these situations, some external feedback on language development is available. In other contexts, such as informal viewing of videos for leisure purposes, the learner may not be aware that learning is taking place and may not have any explicit means of monitoring language acquisition. The implications of these different monitoring systems for autonomous learning outside the classroom may continue to be of interest to researchers today.

Learner autonomy in practice

From my own experience of working as an English teacher in Nancy, France in the 1980s, with Holec, Riley, Zoppis and the other key proponents of the learner autonomy paradigm, it was easy to see the challenges of putting into practice the aspects described above in the concrete setting of higher education. Autonomy, according to Holec's definition: the capacity to take charge of one's own learning, was seen as a natural product of the practice of self-directed learning, or learning in which the objectives, progress and evaluation of learning are determined by the learners themselves. The role of the teacher in this context was to offer advice on the learning process to each learner through a series of interviews. Engineering students trialling the resource-centre model faced altogether more teacher-centred constraints (tests, grades, deadlines) in all of their other subjects. Taking charge of their language learning could therefore easily cease to be a priority in a system where the promotion of learner autonomy was not the norm for the other classes.

Beyond the issue of putting such a model into practice in the real world, two other questions might be considered when looking at the Nancy model of learner autonomy. First, "To what extent does encouraging learners to study independently foster a capacity for autonomous learning?" and second "To what extent might autonomous learning be seized upon by educational administrators as a way of reducing costs in an increasingly difficult financial environment?"

Focussing briefly on the first of these questions, Benson (2011) reminds us that:

> There is no necessary relationship between self-instruction and the development of autonomy (…) under certain conditions, self-instructional modes of learning may even inhibit autonomy (…) learners who engage in technology-based learning do not necessarily become more autonomous as a result of their efforts.
>
> *(2011: 11)*

It is therefore important to consider that, for some learners, studying autonomously may not be a good way of learning to study autonomously and that teachers play a key role in facilitating such learning through instruction focussing on the individual differences (such as learning styles and learning strategies), which might influence the outcomes of autonomous activities. It is therefore important to view learner autonomy as something other than a situation in which the teacher is absent from the learning process.

This leads to second issue which is often raised in discussions of learner autonomy. Given the rapidly developing range of tools available to learners over the past 40 years, the term "autonomously", as well as variations such as "semi-autonomous", quickly came to be used to mean "alone" rather than "using a capacity for self-directed learning". Consequently, investment in new technologies for language learning in the 21st century may be seen by some as an opportunity to limit the costs related to face-to-face teaching such as salaries and other benefits, building costs and transport costs. It is therefore likely that so-called "autonomous learning" may be viewed with suspicion as a strategy of educational administrations to marginalise the role of teachers. Proponents of the Nancy model would of course suggest that it is the nature of the teacher's action which changes rather than the number of hours of contact time, and that resource centres without expert guidance have little chance of offering substantive gains in language skills. This politicisation of an approach to learning initially envisaged as a way of focussing more on the learner is unfortunate if inescapable. Such issues continue to be discussed in the 21st century as increasing moves to put learning contents online (particularly in the context of the 2020 Coronavirus) can be viewed as threatening the status of classroom teachers.

Subsequent developments in learner autonomy

In light of these issues, a second wave of learner autonomy research and practice has sought to situate autonomous learning within the classroom. In the 1990s, researchers such as Dam (2004) developed a view of autonomous learning as interdependent rather than independent, stressing the role of other learners and particularly the teacher in developing a capacity to take control of one's own learning. In this view, the autonomy classroom is seen as a place where learners are communicators, experimenters and intentional learners supported by logbooks and classroom posters. There is also a clear role for the teacher to promote the cycle of planning, implementation and evaluation and "to harness (learners') pre-existing capacity for autonomous behaviour to the business of language teaching" (Little et al., 2017: 17). Little et al. (2017) further remind us that in this view, learner autonomy is a collective as well as individual capacity. The movement from communicative language learning pedagogies in the late 20th century to task-based approaches in the early 21st also favours the development of autonomous action in the classroom as learners solve problems together in small groups rather than focussing on whole-class communication activities led by a teacher. The teacher's role in task-based approaches is essentially one of facilitator and classroom manager, suggesting strategies which learners could use to solve problems together. Therefore, the issue of what autonomous language learning looks like outside the classroom where no teacher is present to promote intentionality, review logbooks and harness learners' capacity for autonomous behaviour is clearly of interest.

In the past ten years, our own research has focussed on online informal learning as a development of the learner autonomy paradigm (Sockett, 2014). It is clear that one of the building blocks of Holec's work, the role of resource centres, supposed that target language materials were beyond the reach of ordinary learners, which is no longer the case in the 21st century where online English functions as a second language omnipresent in the media, accessible to most via the internet and mobile devices. Young people around the world today experience extensive exposure to English in their leisure activities. Many studies have pointed to opportunities for English comprehension through the widespread viewing of original version television series on platforms such as Netflix and vlogs in English on platforms such as YouTube. Language production also takes place for many young people in multiplayer games and on social networking platforms (Sundqvist and Sylven, 2016). These studies have led Reinders and White (2016) ask whether such a view of the informal learning of English using social technologies displaces the learner autonomy paradigm (2016: 149). While such practices in some ways resemble the type of autonomous activity imagined by Holec, and often involve a far greater number of hours of exposure to the language than any formal teaching might typically offer, issues around the role of attention to form in such contexts and to what extent language development is possible with only attention to meaning are key in this type of research.

The view put forward by Sockett and Toffoli (2012), which we described as online informal learning, differs from the learner autonomy paradigm in a number of ways. First it is important to observe that this phenomenon essentially relates to English. We have found relatively limited evidence in the past ten years, at least in Western European contexts, that a large number of learners are acquiring foreign languages other than English informally. Media produced in languages other than English rarely attract large non-native audiences, although there are some exceptions such as the viewing of South American Telenovelas in Romania. There is also some indication that Japanese and Korean are learnt by small numbers of learners using English language subtitles on materials such as Anime and K-pop videos.

Second, the online informal learning paradigm makes very limited reference to the classroom and teachers, except to suggest that informal activities should become a major focus of the formal learning context. While it is of course possible that online informal learners are also enrolled in English classes, it is likely that many or most no longer study English formally. This means that monitoring of learning, the "how" dimension of learner autonomy, is essentially implicit and relies on the learner's metacognitive awareness and implicit feedback from informal interactions.

Third, while it is clear that Holec had in mind an intentional process when conceiving of autonomous learning, much of the learning which falls under the heading of online informal learning is incidental in nature and is merely a by-product of massive exposure to target language resources and interactions encountered in leisure activities which happen to involve the use of English. This means that the "why", or "decision to learn" parameter, which is a significant element of learner autonomy, becomes "decision to participate" and involves a range of learner motivations not limited to a desire to improve one's English.

Therefore, while online informal learning resembles the learner autonomy model, particularly around the issue of what learners are doing, there are significant differences around the questions of why they are doing it and how and by whom they are being evaluated.

Summarising developments in learner autonomy research

When seeking to summarise the development of the learner autonomy paradigm over the past decades, Benson (2011) focusses on four key notions: changing pedagogies, the global development of English, changes in notions surrounding work and changes in conceptions of personal and social identity. These notions are helpful in relating learner autonomy many of the issues raised so far, in particular to task-based learning (pedagogy), to differences between the learning of English and the learning of other languages (globalisation), to lifelong learning (work) and to communities of language users (social and personal identity).

One might therefore argue in summary that learner autonomy paradigm first came to the attention of the research community as technologies allowed individual exposure to, and potentially engagement with, target language contents. Since language use is essentially a social activity, researchers and practitioners then sought to draw this paradigm into a more interactive setting, that of the classroom in the absence of any other feasible context for L2 interaction. A key issue today is whether collaborative online contexts outside the classroom offer similar opportunities for language use in problem-solving activities which offer the potential for significant language development.

Current issues

Having briefly reviewed the learner autonomy paradigm, one might also seek to consider which aspects of the model are the most helpful to practitioners and researchers in an age in which out-of-class learning is becoming the norm. Three concepts which we will review here are distinctions between formal, non-formal and informal learning, the distinction between extramural and extracurricular learning and the distinction between individual and social learning. These dimensions question the relationship of out-of-class learning with learning materials, with classroom learning, and with other learners, mirroring in some ways the pedagogical triangle of learner, teacher and materials.

Formal/non-formal/informal

The interaction between learner autonomy and learning outside the classroom offers an opportunity to consider that for the 21st-century learner of English in particular, work in a classroom with a teacher is only a small part of the learning landscape.

Figure 5.1 illustrates different aspects of English use and learning from the point of view of the learner. It may be helpful to begin by considering that while the learner is in formal education, perhaps from the ages of around 5 to 21, classroom learning (5) and other learning prescribed by the educational structures in question (4) will form part of the learner's interaction with English. Beyond this period or in parallel, the learner may also initiate some activities in order to improve their English. These may include using purpose-made tools such as learning apps (Duolingo, Rosetta Stone) (3) or merely involve taking a more active interest in the language used in the series or YouTube channels they are currently binge-watching (2). The former activities would be best described as non-formal learning, whereas use of resources not designed as educational tools would best be described as informal learning. These categories are by no means uncontroversial. For example, Chik (2019) refers to use of purpose-made tools outside the classroom as informal rather than non-formal. Terminological considerations notwithstanding, Benson (2011) considers that "degree of formality"

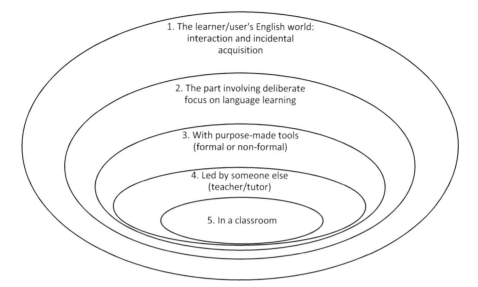

Figure 5.1 Contexts, materials and intentions

is one of the key parameters of out-of-class learning. Figure 5.1 is also a reminder that these activities do not take up equal amounts of time for many learners.

Within the informal learning context (1 and 2), the extent to which learners focus on form when involved in English Language leisure activities has been found to vary (Sockett, 2014) according to a complex range of factors. Learners may, for example, begin watching a series purely for leisure purposes and then re-watch episodes to listen more closely to the dialogue. Choice of subtitles is also an indication of the degree to which binge-watchers are paying attention to the form of dialogues. Language development which takes place when the learner is mostly focussing on the meaning of their favourite series or video is usually referred to as incidental acquisition. The format of Figure 5.1 illustration suggests that a high percentage of the language learner/user's interaction with English falls into the latter category. For example, Lai and Lyu (2019) observe that only 14.7% of the volume of language activities reported on by Hong Kong student learners involved focus on form. In our own research (Sockett, 2014), typical non-specialist language learners in higher education have reported 30–50 hours of class time per year but listening activities which may total several hundred hours per year.

In non-formal learning, the generalisation of the use of smartphones has led to an expansion in a field which previously involved learners purchasing course materials on DVDs or logging onto websites to engage in learning activities. Mobile learning in the non-formal context tends to focus on micro activities such as reviewing vocabulary items for a few minutes while commuting to work or school and makes extensive use of push notifications to encourage learners to persevere in such activities. These pedagogical approaches are not typical of classroom learning which tends to be constructed around longer pedagogical sequences in which language functions are presented, practised and used in production activities or worked on implicitly in problem-solving tasks.

Of course, formal learning activities have long included authentic documents, which are set in a pedagogical context by teachers, and, through the widespread use of learning platforms, can also take place outside the classroom. This means that the context of a learning

	Formal	Non-formal	informal
Choosing activities, approach, duration and location	• Activities and approach prescribed by a teacher. • Moderate duration (homework) • In resource centres, at home or while commuting if platform is mobile-compatible	• Learner selected activities • Apps mostly offer spaced repetition approaches • Short duration (daily micro-learning) • In private or while commuting	• Learner selected activities, • No specific learning approach, • Extensive viewing/gaming time • In private or while commuting
Motivation	• In compulsory education: decision to learn made by others • In higher/further education: decision to learn made by learner/parents	• Self-improvement, • intrinsic or extrinsic motivation	• Leisure, enjoyment • No explicit decision to learn
Monitoring	• Teachers, other learners • Automated feedback from learning platform • Certification from educational structure	• Interaction with other learners • Automated feedback from app • Badges, certificates etc.	• Functional monitoring through interaction with other language users, • Awareness of increasing understanding of media

Figure 5.2 Interactions between aspects of learner autonomy and learning contexts beyond the classroom

activity rather than merely the origin of the documents involved is a key parameter in learning outside the classroom since a learner who has chosen to watch a particular video, for example, will have quite different motivations and monitoring strategies from a learner who has been told to watch the same video as part of a class.

It can therefore be helpful to identify three contexts for out-of-class learning: the formal context where activities are prescribed by teachers, the non-formal context where learners use purpose-built learning tools on their own initiative and the informal context in which naturalistic learning takes place using materials not designed for language learning.

The ways in which these three contexts interact with the three aspects of learner autonomy mentioned earlier are illustrated in Figure 5.2.

Extramural vs Extracurricular

Another pair of terms which has emerged in the recent literature on out-of-class learning is Extramural and Extracurricular. Learning outside the classroom may be envisaged either as beyond the walls of the school, or beyond the scope of a class. Indeed, Holec's original view of learner autonomy was that it involved liberation from the control of others, including teachers. In the 2017 Calico journal issue on learning beyond the classroom, examples are given of learning activities which are mostly teacher-led but which take place outside of class time (extracurricular) and activities which are mostly learner-led (extramural). To use the distinction suggested by Sylven and Sundqvist (2017) "extracurricular and extramural contexts (…) the former type of learning is somehow linked to institutions, but the latter is not" (2017: i). One may think of teacher-led activities outside of class time as homework, but the reality of modern pedagogical practices is more complex than that. Traditional examples of teacher-led extracurricular activities include things like book clubs and language cafés in which the target language is used during the lunch hour or at the end of the school day. It may be more difficult to apply this distinction to online learning activities since the notion of place is more difficult to define. However, the general orientation of extracurricular activities discussed in the Calico special issue is that they resemble activities which a learner may choose to do as a leisure activity, such as engaging in multiplayer gaming (Scholz, 2017; Vosburg, 2017), and they are organised in such a way that the learner has a good deal of choice in the manner in which they engage with the activity. The distinction is somewhat further muddied by examples of extracurricular activities which actually take place in the classroom but have some characteristics of things learners may do at home such as Rodgers and Webb's (2017) learning from television series which involves observing how learners acquire language from materials presented in a classroom setting. It is interesting to observe that Holec's (1981) model of learner autonomy suggests that extracurricular activities would be less "autonomous" in nature than extramural activities, since the decision to initiate extracurricular activities as well as the choice of materials originates with the teacher rather than the learner.

It is therefore helpful when studying autonomous learning to observe whether activities involving learning from videos, music and gaming are initiated by teachers or by learners. It is however sometimes difficult to use the extracurricular/extramural distinction since researchers may wish to investigate extramural activities by asking learners to perform them in a classroom setting. It is likely that the transfer of informal activities to a formal setting will change attentional factors such as focus on form and focus on meaning. The virtual space of the internet also means that formal learning can take place beyond the walls of the classroom, and therefore using the term "extramural" to refer only to informal activities while using "extracurricular" to refer to activities linked to school life may initially lead to some terminological confusion. Since most researchers into second language learning and teaching are themselves language teachers, the extracurricular/extramural distinction can be a helpful way of including more teacher-focussed research in a movement which might otherwise suggest that what goes on in the classroom is somehow less important than what learners do the rest of the time.

Individualisation vs collaboration

As we have seen, a key issue in the learner autonomy paradigm is that of collaboration. We have already considered some collective aspects of the autonomy paradigm and whether or not it isolates the learner from interactions with teachers and other learners. In the three learning contexts outlined above, formal, non-formal and informal, both individualisation and collaboration can be observed to differing degrees.

The formal context. Formal learning beyond the classroom has become a focus of media attention in the 2020–2021 Coronavirus crisis. Language teachers have put into practice a range of pedagogical options including both synchronous and asynchronous elements. Asynchronous approaches typically use learning management systems such as Moodle to allow learners to carry out activities at their own pace, while communication via forums maintains target language interaction and allows learners the opportunity to review and redraft their productions before pressing "send", thus reducing the risk of loss of face from a non-target-like production. Synchronous approaches such as classes held via videoconferencing software such as Zoom seek to recreate classroom conditions and include the option of breaking learners down into pairs or small groups to carry out learning tasks. Ideally a blended approach involving both synchronous and asynchronous activities would permit learners to experience different types of collaboration while allowing for individualisation in terms of times and places.

As an example, our own pedagogical model for distance learning of English for Economics at the University of Paris consisted of listening and reading comprehension activities on Moodle associated with formative assessment exercises, tasks in which groups of learners created videos explaining Economic issues in a film or TV series of their choice and then commented on the productions of other class members, and Zoom classes in which problem-solving tasks prepared individually in the Moodle materials were worked on as a whole class. This model has the advantage freeing up live class time by having learners record their video presentations. Learners also had more time to consider their responses to these productions, which led to extensive asynchronous exchanges in the target language.

The non-formal context. Among current non-formal learning apps, two tendencies can be observed. Content-focussed apps and interaction-focussed apps. Products such as Duolingo or Rosetta Stone continue to focus on content delivery usually through spaced repetition of items recurring in short audio and written texts and use push messaging to motivate learners to continue to log in for a few minutes a day. Interaction-focussed apps such as Speaky and iTalki are essentially social networks designed to put learners in contact with either target language tutors or other learners seeking a language exchange relationship. This context therefore offers the clearest contrast between collaborative and individualised approaches. Learners engaging in non-formal activities may therefore choose whether to emphasise a focus on independent learning or collaboration with others. Products such as Busuu and the recently re-opened Live Mocha offer both learning contents and access to social networks of learning partners.

The informal context. In informal learning, while the vast majority of young people spend a number of hours per week listening to English independently of any teaching structure, many also engage in collaborative activities such as multiplayer gaming or social networking in which English is used as a lingua franca. Research by Las Vergnas (2017) indicates that multiplayer gaming in particular is a favourable context for language acquisition with a majority of participants in Multiplayer Online Battle Arena (MOBA) games such as "League of Legends" reporting significant language gains from very high average engagement times (in excess of 20 hours per week).

As the internet has moved from presenting information to hosting social interaction, the possibilities for autonomous learning outside the classroom through interactions with other target language users have continued to expand. It is likely that with the normalisation of online interaction through the Coronavirus crisis of 2020–2021, this tendency will continue to develop as the idea that a learning space (Murray & Lamb, 2018) can be something other than a classroom to which one travels becomes more widely accepted.

Implications

In the concluding section of this chapter, we will suggest some implications of these current issues for research and practice in the field of learner autonomy outside the classroom.

Implications for practice: How might one go about focussing formal language learning on the practices of fledgling language users today?

The main implication of the preceding arguments for English teachers particularly is that the formal English class is now a key cog in a larger machine, rather than being the machine itself. The existence of formal, non-formal and informal activities in the language eco-system of the learner should by no means be seen as a threat to classroom teaching. Indeed, the learner's wider engagement in learning activities and likely future online learning lifestyle are indications that the English class is a key moment at which skills can be developed to better manage, enjoy and learn from out-of-class activities. So, more than ever, the classroom is a place where learner autonomy can and should be taught, since the 21st century equivalent of the learner's trip to the resource centre to watch a video cassette is no longer the pious hope of the teacher but a daily reality for even the most recalcitrant student.

The classroom offers many opportunities to look critically at non-formal tools, helping learners to see the limits and advantages of micro-learning approaches. It is also a good place in which to assert the value of informal activities as humble as viewing hair and makeup videos which in many ways represent linguistically mediated tasks which many learners are likely to carry out in their everyday lives. While the social or individual nature of autonomous activities is often a matter of individual learner differences, the interactive nature of multiplayer gaming and social networking means that these are often the most valuable out-of-class activities (Sundqvist & Sylven, 2016) and should therefore be explored in the classroom using examples suggested by learners who are perhaps more expert in such fields than the teachers themselves. The extramural/extracurricular distinction discussed above suggests that, while numerically the majority of out-of-class hours will be spent in activities of which the teacher is unaware, there is scope for teachers to be involved in coordinating some activities which sit on the frontier between the classroom and the learners' private worlds.

Implications for research: characterising the impact of learning outside the classroom on teachers and learners

The current focus on various types out-of-class learning has implications for researchers in the field of the teaching and learning of English in particular. Since many researchers are also English teachers, the issue of the stance of the researcher is an important consideration. While it is easy to agree that a change in focus from the teacher and onto the learner is generally a good thing, research needs to continue to value the roles and actions of teachers in a challenging profession in challenging times.

The major issues in the study of what learners do outside the classroom have moved beyond the initial descriptive assessment of whether significant exposure to the target language is taking place and what forms that exposure might take. Indeed, much is known about the balance of receptive and productive activities engaged in by learners in many different parts of the world. As we have suggested above, current issues such as degree of formality, the role of the teacher and the individual or social nature of current autonomous activities, among others, are helpful prisms through which to assess the likely impact of such activities on the learner and their language skills. These aspects and the future directions which will serve as a conclusion to this discussion should provide researchers with a busy agenda for the coming decades.

Future directions

As a tree develops, it branches out in different directions. So it is that the learner autonomy paradigm began in resource centres and is now of interest to researchers in classroom-based learning, out-of-class learning and informal learning to name but three. In the field of informal learning, Godwin-Jones (2019), identifies five future directions which are also a helpful guide to the potential orientations of autonomous and out-of-class learning. These are lifelong independent learning, recreational learning, gaming and social media, non-formal learning, classroom integration, and a focus on emerging devices and technologies. This list is particularly helpful in identifying the dimensions of a field such as learner autonomy. There is a focus on the learner in the first three sub-fields. Learners may indeed be independent of any formal learning structure, as they continue to be exposed to English for many years after school. This learning may predominantly focus on comprehension activities in leisure time such as television series or may also include interactive activities involving other language learner/users. Indeed, current practices surrounding vlogging show that the comments left by the network of fans of a given vlogger can be as much a focus of attention as the videos themselves. Reference to the roles of non-formal and formal learning suggest that the way in which the three different learning contexts interact will continue to be a focus, as learners navigate between the three contexts in their personal learning environments. Finally, focussing on the technologies themselves continues to be a key to understanding how learners interact with materials. It is important to remember that the original learner autonomy paradigm focussed on resource centres which were an expression of the cost and availability of the technology of the day. Since the learner was unlikely to have a video cassette recorder or a language laboratory in their bedroom, creating spaces where such equipment could be made available to large numbers of learners was a logical step. Similarly today, while viewing and gaming were predominantly carried out at home only a few years ago, it is common today to observe commuters viewing series and participating in multiplayer games on their way to and from work. Mobile technologies for activities as varied as dating (Tinder) and fitness (Strava) now use GPS data to indicate the proximity of like-minded people. With the development of interaction focussed non-formal learning apps such as Speaky and iTalki, it is likely that mobile language learning will become more than just trying to do desktop activities on a smaller screen but will actually offer opportunities for hybrid online/face-to-face language activities.

As we begin the third decade of the 21st century, the global COVID-19 pandemic has of course brought about significant changes in the practices of formal education and a renewed emphasis on what it is possible, or more difficult, to do outside the classroom. Synchronous and asynchronous online learning activities have taken on increased importance and are likely to remain a more important part of the learning ecosystem even as the pandemic itself is resolved. While synchronous teleconferencing tools such as Zoom may continue to offer a relatively teacher-centred model of learning beyond the walls of a physical classroom, the expanded use of asynchronous tools will allow researchers to look again at the dimensions of autonomy exercised by learners as they choose when, where and with whom to carry out a range of activities.

As we have seen, the field of learner autonomy began as a result of the development of technologies which facilitated the setting up of audio-visual resource centres for language learners. Similarly, the affordances of 21st-century technologies such as smartphones have led to an array of out-of-class practices offering varying degrees of autonomy for the learner. It might therefore be argued that for English and other languages frequently used in connection with leisure activities, the learner autonomy paradigm is best viewed as a complex system in which language development emerges from an array of social and cognitive factors.

Reflection questions

1 To what extent do current out-of-class activities such as multiplayer gaming and video viewing help learners to develop a capacity to take charge of their learning?
2 To what extent should formal English classes prepare learners to better engage in extramural activities?
3 How would one go about studying online learner/users of English who are not currently in formal education?

Recommended readings

Three major collections on the topic of out-of-class learning were published between 2017 and 2019.

Dressman, M., & Sadler, R. W. (Eds.). (2019). *The handbook of informal language learning*. Hoboken, NJ: John Wiley & Sons.

This volume is helpful because it divides contributions into different sections focussing on theory, practice, type of activity, regions of the world, etc., allowing the reader to select the contributions of particular interest.

Further insights into these questions are also offered by two special issues of journals dealing with Computer Assisted Language Learning (CALL).

Sauro, S., & Zourou, K. (2019). What are the digital wilds? *Language Learning & Technology, 23*(1), 1–7. https://doi.org/10125/44666

The Special issue of *Language Learning and Technology* entitled CALL in the Digital Wilds, edited by Sauro and Zourou (2019) focusses on a range of learner-led practices such as fan-fiction writing, sub-titling, dubbing and participating in fan communities and multiplayer gaming. It also offers some insights into the relationship between informal practices and formal learning outcomes.

These three resources offer a multitude of voices and perspectives on issues around learner autonomy and out-of-class learning. Since each article and chapter is independent, they can be read quickly and allow for focus on specific topics such as gaming.

Sylvén, L. K., & Sundqvist, P. (2017). Computer-assisted language learning (CALL) in extracurricular/extramural contexts. *CALICO Journal, 34*(1), i–iv.

Volume 34.1 of *Calico Journal* edited by Sylven and Sundqvist (2017), entitled Computer-Assisted Language Learning (CALL) in Extracurricular/Extramural Contexts, offers a balanced insight into out-of-class learning from both a teacher-led and a learner-led perspective. Articles on multiplayer gaming by Hannibal Jensen, Vosburg, and Scholze, in particular, offer a variety of approaches to this sub-field which is often under-represented in out-of-class learning publications.

References

Benson, P. (2011). Language learning and teaching beyond the classroom: An introduction to the field. In P. Benson, & H. Reinders (Eds.), *Beyond the language classroom* (pp. 7–16). Basingstoke, UK: Palgrave Macmillan. https://doi.org/10.1057/9780230306790_2

Benson, P., & Reinders, H. (Eds.). (2011). *Beyond the language classroom*. Basingstoke, UK: Palgrave Macmillan.

Chik, A. (2019). Motivation and informal language learning. In Dressman, M., & Sadler, R. W. (Eds.) *The handbook of informal language learning* (pp. 13–26). Hoboken, NJ: John Wiley & Sons, Ltd. https://doi.org/10.1002/9781119472384.ch1

Dam, L. (2004). *From theory to classroom practice* (Reprinted). Dublin: Authentik Language Learning Resources.

Dickinson, L. (1987). *Self-instruction in language learning*. Cambridge: Cambridge University Press.

Dressman, M., & Sadler, R. W. (Eds.). (2019). *The handbook of informal language learning* (1st ed.). Hoboken, New Jersey: Wiley. https://doi.org/10.1002/9781119472384

Godwin-Jones, R. (2019). Future directions in informal language learning. In Dressman, M., & Sadler, R. W. (Eds.) *The handbook of informal language learning* (pp. 457–470). Hoboken, NJ: John Wiley & Sons, Ltd. https://doi.org/10.1002/9781119472384.ch30

Holec, H. (1981). *Autonomy and foreign language learning*. Oxford: Pergamon Press.

Jensen, S. H. (2017. Gaming as an English language learning resource among young children in Denmark. *CALICO Journal*, *34*(1), 1–19. https://doi.org/10.1558/cj.29519

Lai, C., & Lyu, B. (2019). Hong Kong and informal language learning. In *The handbook of informal language learning* (pp. 271–287). Hoboken, NJ: John Wiley & Sons, Ltd. https://doi.org/10.1002/9781119472384.ch18

Las Vergnas, O., (2017). *Le e-learning informel? des apprentissages diffus, noyés dans la participation en ligne*. Paris: Éditions des Archives contemporaines.

Little, D. G., Dam, L., & Legenhausen, L. (2017). *Language learner autonomy: Theory, practice and research*. Bristol, UK: Multilingual Matters.

Murray, G., & Lamb, T. (Eds.). (2018). *Space, place and autonomy in language learning*. New York: Routledge.

Nunan, D., & Richards, J. C. (Eds.). (2015). *Language learning beyond the classroom*. New York: Routledge, Taylor & Francis Group.

Reinders, H., & White, C. (2016). 20 years of autonomy and technology: How far have we come and where to next? *Language Learning & Technology*, *20*(2), 143–154. http://scholarspace.manoa.hawaii.edu/handle/10125/44466

Rodgers, M. P. H., & Webb, S. (2017). The Effects of Captions on EFL Learners' Comprehension of English-Language Television Programs. *CALICO Journal*, *34*(1), 20–38. https://doi.org/10.1558/cj.29522

Sauro, S., & Zourou, K. (2019). What are the digital wilds?,. In Language Learning and Technology: *23*(1), 1–7. http://scholarspace.manoa.hawaii.edu/handle/10125/44666

Scholz, K. (2017). Encouraging free play: Extramural digital game-based language learning as a complex adaptive system. *CALICO Journal*, *34*(1), 39–57. https://doi.org/10.1558/cj.29527

Sockett, G. (2014). *The online informal learning of English*. Basingstoke, UK: Palgrave Macmillan

Sockett, G., & Toffoli, D. (2012). Beyond learner autonomy: A dynamic systems view of the informal learning of English in virtual online communities. *ReCALL*, *24*(2), 138–151. https://doi.org/10.1017/S0958344012000031

Sundqvist, P., & Sylvén, L. K. (2016). *Extramural English in teaching and learning from theory and research to practice*. Palgrave Macmillan UK: Imprint: Palgrave Macmillan.

Sylvén, L. K., & Sundqvist, P. (2017). Computer-Assisted Language Learning (CALL) in extracurricular/extramural contexts. *CALICO Journal*, *34*(1), i–iv. https://doi.org/10.1558/cj.31822

Vosburg, D. (2017). The effects of group dynamics on language learning and use in an MMOG. *CALICO Journal*, *34*(1), 58–74. https://doi.org/10.1558/cj.29524

6
CALL IN THE WILD
A Voyage of Independent Self-directed Learning

Liam Murray, Marta Giralt, Martin A. Mullen and Silvia Benini

Introduction

The recent emergence of Learning Beyond the Classroom (LBC) as a research agenda (Reinders & Benson, 2017) and established field has demanded increased attention from researchers. It may well claim to be part of the widening stream of "Cultural CALL" (Computer-Assisted Language Learning) reaching the "digital wilds" (Gillespie, 2020, p. 140; Thorne, 2015, p. 225). Sauro and Zourou's co-edited special issue of *Language Learning & Technology* offers informative explanations of processes and practices within the digital wilds and notes the lack of: "empirical studies of informal or beyond-the-class digital language learning" (2019, p. 1). Our chapter aims to present, in compact form, such an empirical study and also to attempt Reinders and Benson's 'Research Task 5' which requests:

> a case study of a learner's efforts to learn a language beyond the classroom, focusing on the strategies used to identify, take advantage of, and/or create opportunities to learn and use the language. Examine the factors that affect the learner's success in these efforts.
>
> *(2017, p. 9)*

In addition, we address the same authors' point that: "Relatively little is known about the ways in which teachers encourage, support and prepare students for LBC", by offering an account of our own pedagogical interface consisting of formal, informal and extramural language learning environments, where we have added a strong element of testing LBC in action.

Yet caveats remain. Zourou (2019) has observed that repurposing generic technologies for dedicated CALL use in institutional learning environments can lead to the "taming" of such tools to institutional and curricular needs: "occasionally leading to paradoxical and unreal learner practices", as cited by Sauro and Zourou (2019, p. 1) and Sauro and Sundmark (2019). While accepting the need for pedagogical activities that may bridge informal and formal learning, Zourou (2019, p. 376) astutely points out that: "the landscape around formal and informal learning is *very nuanced* and is composed of far more elements than 'bridges'.

In addition, *students do not necessarily make the connection* between formal and informal L2 practice" (our italics). Zourou goes on to emphasise: "the need to shape a CALL agenda that carefully looks at autonomy, agency, and openness not as by-products of learning but by situating them as core features of the learning experience" (*ibid*). In our chapter, we shall be examining the importance of autonomy, agency and openness in an LBC context, while incorporating Reinhardt's (2018) notions of user-choice and self-directed learning. Thorne (2015), meanwhile, has pushed the agenda further, arguing in favour of the *rewilding* of education, contesting the pedagogical and transformative value of straitjacketed and highly formalised nature of so many learning environments (see also Little & Thorne, 2017). More recently and more cautiously, Thorne, et al. (2021, p. 16), promoting the notion of 'structured unpredictability', advise: "In essence, when creating rewilding opportunities for language learners, the suggestion is to provide pedagogically informed resources and guidance, but not too much".

We have sought to "rewild" such opportunities in the context of teaching and exploring specific *Critical Digital Literacies* (CDL) (Murray et al., 2020) for LBC purposes. It is our contention that if (language) learners are to be unleashed into the wilds of social media, they must be equipped with basic digital literacies for, *inter alia*, self-protection, self-awareness, intercultural awareness, motivation – both intrinsic and extrinsic – and appropriate search string competences and mobile literacy. In addition, we show examples of student meta-learning and scaffolding as our students describe their growing awareness of their own meta-learning in a fully online environment as they use their scaffolding techniques more effectively and more confidently.

We have applied, expanded and trialled Dudeney and Hockly's original digital literacies (2016) within several of our institutional language learning programmes. This has afforded us a valuable opportunity for: "investigating the largely under-explored area of processes and practices that learners develop in out-of-class contexts", as Sauro and Zourou (2019, p. 2) have recently observed. Finally, we cannot ignore the Covid elephant in the digital (class)room or elsewhere. Our case study was completed during a period when universities were compelled into online teaching. This, undoubtedly, will have had some bearing upon our case study as a whole. We cannot claim that what our students and ourselves are currently experiencing represents a 'game changer' nor that the effects (whatever they may be) will be short- or long-term. However, we can agree with Godwin-Jones (2020, p. 10) who, after writing about the effects of the pandemic, contends that: "we can adopt the metaphor of the porous classroom [an expanded model for blended learning] as a vision for inclusive, engaged, and transformative language learning". In working with students to explore CDL for LBC purposes, we have borne in mind that: "Riding the digital wilds successfully involves learner choices and actions, along with the further development of internal attributes of initiative, persistence, and creativity" (Godwin-Jones, 2019, p. 19).

In order to effectively exploit the digital wilds, language learners must be sufficiently prepared. In this chapter, the authors will first describe some of the central constructs relevant to the development of the attributes needed for successful LBC, followed by a section highlighting some of the issues related to the operationalisation of these constructs, with both sections supported by data collected from our own illustrative study. The chapter will continue by offering practical guidance to teachers interested in helping their learners develop the skills necessary to become effective and independent learners beyond the classroom, and will finish by commenting on themes which we see as central to the future of LBC research and practice as they relate to rewilding for critical digital literacy development.

It may be noted here that all data used in our study was elicited from an undergraduate Year 2, 'Language and Technology' module, populated by students of foreign languages (total n=68) over a 12-week semester period, delivered entirely online due to Covid-19 restrictions. The cited quotations here are taken from student essays, blog posts and semi-structured focus group meetings. This produced a searchable corpus of more than 230,000 words. Such a method would provide a greater scope to investigate educational issues (Almalki, 2016). The main goals of the module are to help students develop a set of skills and CDL that may equip them to keep engaging with their language learning and the real world, during the semester and beyond. The augmented CDL may allow learners to navigate in the wilds of the online world and provide them with many of the necessary competencies and abilities to deal with the challenges of the virtual world. Ultimately, they may become optimal learners, independent and autonomous, as well as digital citizens of the world. This benefit of being exposed to successful LBC practices has not yet been fully explored in the literature.

Key constructs

Learning beyond the classroom

A central construct in operationalising LBC is to identify and define what actually constitutes LBC. Early on, Benson (2011) offered a framework for LBC by identifying 4 key characteristics which differentiate LBC from classroom learning: location (out-of-class in contrast to in-class), formality (informal in contrast to formal), pedagogy (non-instructed in contrast to instructed) and level of control (self-directed in contrast to directed by another). Thorne (2010, p. 44) refines this framework by incorporating the theme of informal online learning in contexts which are more social than educational but which nevertheless 'present interesting, and perhaps even compelling, opportunities for intercultural exchange, agentive action, and meaning making'. Sauro and Zourou (2019, p. 1) expand upon these themes with the concept of learning in the Digital Wilds, characterised as 'informal language learning that takes place in digital spaces, communities, and networks that are independent of formal instructional contexts'; these spaces, communities and networks referring to online contexts in which the primary goal is not language learning or teaching and which are not developed or governed by educational institutions. These contexts can include online gaming communities (Godwin-Jones, 2016b), social media (Rosell-Aguilar, 2018) and video streaming sites such as *Netflix* (Alm, 2019) and *YouTube* (Wang & Chen, 2020).

In our own study, our results showed that students perceived that in-class focus on technology enhanced their language learning both inside and outside the classroom, and that the independent technology-mediated work they completed outside the classroom was an extension of what they started discovering in the classroom and transferred beyond the formal class setting. Reinders and Benson (2017) already point out the relationship between LBC and learning in or from the classroom. The intersection between teacher guidance and the self-directed learning (SDL) that happens outside the classroom was achieved by many students, as evidenced by this typical comment that "venturing into the wild environment of online language learning proved to be quite a shock to the system [...] and it can be safely said that telecollaboration and CALL have allowed for a safer venture into the wild". A key point to take from our data was that in order to learn independently and navigate the digital wilds as part of their language learning process, students feel that they need to be digitally competent with their skills but also knowledgeable of themselves as learners, becoming motivated, agentive and critical.

(Critical) digital literacies

Raising learner awareness of the value of these digital resources and how they can be exploited beyond the classroom remains a problem; a problem which the authors of this chapter address by focussing directly on digital literacies. Digital literacies have been heavily and readily discussed in various academic fora and publications for at least the past two decades. With the advent of the internet and social media, this has brought necessary adjustments and refinements to the meanings and definitions of digital literacies. One influential definition from Dudeney et al. (2013, p. 2) described them as: "the individual and social skills needed to effectively interpret, manage, share and create meaning in the growing range of digital communication channels". These skills are grouped into skillsets related to language use, searching and filtering information, building and maintaining networks, and creative expression. Educators have naturally focussed on the learning merits of these literacies, but Buckingham (2010, p. 59) believes it is important not to frame digital literacy merely in terms of how digital media may be used effectively, but to understand that young people 'are not seeing [digital media] primarily as technical tools, but on the contrary as part of their popular culture, and of their everyday lived experience'. In other words, young people are already quite at home in their cultural digital wilds.

During our study it was noted how timely and relevant it was for our students to realise and acknowledge the importance of developing their own digital literacies as language learners and digital citizens:

> I believe **digital literacies and the ability to use technology** efficiently and effectively, has become one of the most important aspects of university life in 2020", "However, **having the resources** there is all well and good, but one must have the **skills to navigate said resources** in order to benefit from them. [Our emphasis in bold].

By 'digital citizens', we may slightly extend Sheppard's (2014) attempted definition of digital literacies, namely: "those capabilities which fit an individual for living, learning and working in a digital society". Indeed, this is what some of our students claimed, with several listing skills that they believe, will stay with them during their whole life:

> This year has proven to me that humans are a highly adaptable species, and **after almost a full year of online college, I feel I have learned skills that will stick with me for life**. I have been **forced to adapt to a more independent style of learning, with the internet being my main source of education**, rather than books. **I have had to use critical skills to assess how suitable certain CALL applications are**.

CDL has been further conceptualised in different ways, with most studies defining it as either technical proficiency or ability to evaluate and critique (Lankshear & Knobel, 2011). However, as digital landscapes become increasingly complex, and as Web 2.0 capabilities allow individuals the opportunity to produce their own online content, issues such as design literacy and curatorship literacy have arisen (Potter, 2012), and there have been calls for new frameworks within which these new literacies can be explored and developed (Avila & Pandya, 2013). Again, the concept itself of digital literacies has been understandably and necessarily cultivated and expanded over time. Pangrazio (2016) stressed the importance of adding an element of design literacy to the existing focus on critical consumption of digital media, while Murray et al. (2020, p. 266) extended the definition by highlighting the importance of 'agentive literacy [which] would give students the capacity to manage effectively their own learning experience', and in particular, to avoid the distractive elements of digital technologies. One strand of the discussion about student digital literacy has focussed on the role that the educator may play in facilitating their students' development of these skills. Godwin-Jones (2016a, p. 6) notes not only the importance of students developing skills that help them to effectively navigate through, interact with, and utilise the different facets of the online world, but also 'the essential role of the teacher in that process'. Similarly, Hauck and Kurek (2017, p. 1) believe that for teachers to be able to assist learners in developing the literacies needed for meaningful and informed online participation, it is 'paramount for teachers to, first, be digitally literate themselves'.

As an example of how students may perceive the development of their CDL, the quotation below is quite illustrative:

> Overall, this module has been the epitome of my life during the last semester as I have learned to hone and **improve my critical thinking skills** and understanding of the **importance of technology in language learning**. It has allowed me to explore avenues I otherwise would not have considered and supplied me with a new found fascination at how computer assisted language learning profoundly affects one's **knowledge of technology as a language learning tool**, but also our **understanding of intercultural communication** and **digital literacies**.
>
> *(Quotation from one of the student essays)*

The quotation highlights the aspects or types of literacy the student declares to be improving and how it is connected with him/herself as a learner and as a digital citizen (see Sheppard, 2014, op. cit.). The next step after this self-realisation (and good example of meta-learning) is the development of agency and taking greater responsibility for their own learning. An agentive literacy appears to be present in the learning process of most of the participants in our study. Such an agency is instigated by self-awareness, self-motivation and ultimately, by becoming a self-directed learner (see Table 6.1 for some examples of student quotations that support this idea).

This process (see also Hellerman & Thorne, 2020, p. 267) brings learners to a more independent and autonomous space and helps them to self-regulate and manage their own learning. The use of technology enables them to achieve this, but not without the development of their CDL. Learner autonomy is linked to digital literacy as previously stated by Fuchs et al. (2012). Due to the current pandemic situation and our enforced online learning contexts, the development of digital literacies is initiated in the virtual class with the guidance of a teacher, but it does (and should) expand beyond the classroom.

> Being **digitally literate is the critical foundation** to becoming a **self-directed learner** in today's society. When considering both the current social climate with regard to COVID-19, and also the increasingly interconnected world of today, the topic of becoming a digitally literate learner becomes both increasingly relevant and essential, especially for self-directed learners. In being digitally literate, a **learner thus has the capacity to elevate their learning experiences far beyond the classroom and form well informed opinions and a well-rounded knowledge of their chosen subject.**

Table 6.1 Examples from student essays and blog quotations about self-directed learning, self-awareness, self-motivation and agency

---

Student A: **Self-directed learning** whether it be for language or something else **is a skill which one has to acquire**. This can be made easier by the range of tools available to aid in a person's learning. From **this semester I have discovered that self-directed learning requires a will and interest** in what you are studying more so than anything else.

Student B: In my opinion, the act of being able to choose my **own learning tools** increased my **intrinsic motivation** and thus my desire to learn.

Student D: I have found that although third level education is not self-directed it still **forces** me to do my own self-directed learning.

At this point, it is relevant to highlight that as learning contexts may consistently change, then so must the literacies. This is the liminal nature of digital literacies, something that Leu (1997, p. 62) saw in the concept of "literacy" as a "deictic" term. As one of our students said:

> Online learning and the increased **use of CALL in our studies was forced for reasons beyond our control**, however, **it could be argued that it is an opportunity in disguise, as we navigate new platforms and develop 21st century skills**. [...] No one can learn languages for us or develop our own competence with technology, thus reiterating that it is a **semi-structured voyage in which we require guidance**.

The new learning context and the obligation to learn online actually provided the students with both the opportunity and the motivation to develop their digital literacies and take greater control of their learning using technology.

Agentive literacy

The role of learner agency is a critical construct that plays a central role in learner engagement with different aspects surrounding their learning process and the transdisciplinarity of this process. In our context, this may be understood as: foreign language discourse competence and CDL. Agency is a key construct that is close to the notion of autonomy – if one is to follow the work of Little (1991, 2007). It would be difficult to give a precise delineation of the similarities, and especially the differences, between agency and autonomy (Van Lier, 2010). Understanding learner agency from the physiological and individual conceptions, we can talk about a property of the individual, usually connected to psychological or cognitive concepts (for example, motivation, self-regulation, learning strategies, affect and intention). Following Martin (2004, p. 135), we may define learner agency as "the capability of individual human beings to make choices and act on these choices in a way that makes a difference in their lives". The centrality of learner agency in facilitating learner engagement is well researched from multiple perspectives and widely acknowledged (Schwartz & Okita, 2009; Reeve & Tseng, 2011; Blin & Jalkanen, 2014, among others). However, there are few studies that focus on its role in (forced) online learning (with notable exceptions from Xiao, 2014; Knight et al., 2017) or in the latent potential for self-directed engagement (see Mercer, 2015) with the use of technology beyond the classroom and how this can enhance the language learning process.

Our challenge resides in promoting and developing an agentive literacy (Murray et al., 2020) via the development of those digital literacies that allow students to engage beyond the classroom in different activities, including technology-mediated activities, to continue learning and practising their target language/s. Facilitating the development of this agentive literacy for learning in the digital wilds represents our main objective with this chapter.

Meta-learning

Another central construct in fostering learners with the agency to learn beyond the classroom is through explicit focus on meta-learning. Flavell's influential 1979 work described three strands to metacognition:

- *metacognitive knowledge*: what learners understand about themselves as cognitive processors, such as which strategies they best employ for different learning tasks;
- *metacognitive regulation*: actions taken to control their learning, such as planning, monitoring and evaluating;
- *metacognitive experiences*: experiences of learning in which the learner recognises the cognitive processing taking place and which may help the learner to revise their existing body of learning behaviours and strategies.

The relationship between these strands is interactive and iterative, with each strand both affecting and being affected by the other strands (Zhang & Zhang, 2019). By helping learners become more aware of what their learning preferences are, in what environments they learn most effectively, and what motivates them as learners, they can take more control of their own learning (Biggs, 1985). It is therefore important not only to equip students with the skills and resources to make informed choices about their own learning, but also to ensure the learners themselves recognise that they have acquired these competencies, in order to give them the confidence needed to effectively employ them (Boström & Lassen, 2006).

The module outlined earlier in the chapter provides direct classroom focus on learning styles and preferences, offers opportunities to experiment with a range of digital resources and then critically reflects on those experiences and heightens student ability to evaluate and exploit CALL materials. The aim of these practices is to allow learners to become more aware of their own learning preferences and strategies, as well as the skills and resources needed to learn more effectively, not just inside but also beyond the language classroom. As was revealed in one student comment, the module was 'a great opportunity for the learner to become more independent and aware of their language learning techniques, as well as to get to know more about themselves in order to achieve goals knowing strengths and limitations'. Combining an emphasis on meta-learning with a focus on CDL mentioned above, helps students become more aware of what works and does not work for them as language learners, and thus, allows them to make more informed decisions about different resources and the roles they can play in the students' learning practices.

In making a clear connection between CDL, meta learning and agency, we may argue that the development of CDL is strictly aligned to the students' ability to exert control over their own cognitive resources, as mentioned earlier when describing meta-learning. Consequently, the meta-learning process facilitates learners in taking self-directed actions aimed at personal growth and development. As strongly indicated by research (Lin-Siegler et al., 2016, p. 297), students who employ agency in their learning are more motivated, experience greater satisfaction in their learning and, consequently, are more likely to achieve academic success or at least, as one of our participants mentioned, to try to improve their abilities:

My own experience with CALL has been extremely redeeming in the sense that as a student of languages who tries to **make an effort improving my abilities** both **inside** and **outside** of college hours, **CALL gives me the opportunity to do as such** using a variety of apps in heavy rotation.

MALL and smartphone literacy

Mobile-Assisted Language Learning (MALL) is another potentially fertile venue for learning beyond the classroom. Smartphone ownership is ubiquitous, and owners are already using the devices heavily for a wide range of activities (Smith, 2015), some of which, such as social media, have obvious language-learning applications. There is no shortage of research into smartphones as language-learning resources, although a frequent criticism of this research is that it tends to focus on formal research projects or in-classroom use of smartphones, and research exploring the extent to which language learners engage in informal or self-directed MALL is still a 'less explored territory in the field of MALL' (Kukulska-Hulme, 2016, p.138). As smartphone capacities continue to develop, and the range of activities which can be conducted on the devices increases (often at the expense of other devices), smartphone literacy will become increasingly important, and more research is needed as to how and to what extent the learning affordances of smartphones are recognised and exploited by their owners.

The data from our own study revealed that the students of the module were active users of language learning apps (LLA) such as *Duolingo, Kahoot!* among others. Although these LLA might not be typically considered the digital wilds, they do indicate the readiness of students for self-directed out-of-class learning on mobile devices, although limitations on this readiness will be described in the Key Issues section. Similarly, on their smartphones, as well as on other devices, students showed a willingness to engage in repurposing non-dedicated resources for language learning purposes. *Netflix* and *Spotify* were regularly mentioned as resources which the learners found beneficial for language learning. Watching content in their target languages on *Netflix*, with or without subtitles in their target language, was a frequently mentioned activity, and there was evidence that the module had helped broaden the learners' perspectives of what could be considered as a language-learning resource:

> I never fully understood or even noticed the power of Netflix and Spotify before studying this module. Both of these apps are ones I use on a daily basis but **never realised the never-ending language learning possibilities** of [them] such as watching movies in other languages with English subtitles or watching them in English or other languages with Spanish or any other subtitles.

Such *Edutainment*-style (Maher, 2011) LBC repurposing of *Netflix, Spotify, YouTube*, and other online platforms shows a willingness among learners to explore and exploit language-learning aspects to their existing entertainment and relaxation activities, including smartphones. Thus, as well as highlighting the merits of dedicated language-learning resources, broadening the focus to include the merits of these non-dedicated resources can be an important part of raising learner awareness of available resources.

Key issues

This section will describe the challenges faced in relation to the key constructs identified in our study. We have already included findings from our own study which revealed how students on the module were able to embrace these key constructs. However, the practical implementation of these constructs was not without its challenges, and those issues are described in this section.

As previously mentioned, fostering digital and technological literacies is central to developing students capable of independent agentive learning. However, from Secondary to Third Level Education, the amount of evidence showing the extent to which teachers have the literacy, or the willingness, to take on a facilitating role in this process of learner development remains quite limited. Indeed, across Europe, "there is no unified approach as to how such technology should be embedded at secondary level" (Marcus-Quinn et al., 2019, p. 774). Concerning the use of mobile devices, for example, Sung et al. (2016, p. 266) report that one of the chief barriers to the implementation of effective mobile learning programmes "is insufficient preparation of the teachers". In Ireland, the *locus* of our study, this is reflected at curricular level, with individual schools having control regarding how much, or how little, emphasis is placed on mobile learning, resulting in significant variation across schools (Marcus-Quinn et al., 2019). Thus, one central issue is the ongoing need for the establishment of a coherent process for educator-facilitated development of learners' digital literacies, or what Hauck (2019) terms a *critical digital pedagogy*, which will help learners not only to develop the skills, but also to acquire the agency necessary to learn effectively beyond the classroom. Increasingly, educators aim not only to straddle both the design and evaluation aspect of digital literacies, but also aim to equip learners with the tools to achieve both strands of literacy beyond the confines of the classroom. However, as highlighted by Hinrichsen and Coombs (2014, p. 1), one key issue is: "the need to define digital literacy sufficiently to implement it institutionally". Hinrichsen and Coombs' own model of critical digital pedagogy proposes:

> In curriculum terms, the development of digital literacy will involve using devices and software but should also be recognised and made explicit in analytical and discursive practices; in syllabus content; in assessment design and grading criteria; and in formal course specification documents
>
> *(2014, p. 13)*

It is this model, in which there is an explicit focus on digital literacies across the curriculum, that we have sought to apply within our own case study. It must be stated that the application of the model outlined by Hinrichsen and Coombs (2014) was not without challenges and many students required some guidance from the teachers. The next quotation below from one of the students illustrates how students believe the teacher must play a significant role in guiding them in developing their digital literacies and in the acquisition of the necessary agency to learn beyond the classroom.

> The teacher has the duty to assist learners to acquire discipline-specific knowledge and develop a set of competencies that support SDL. Consequently, the teacher must depart from their traditional roles and teacher and take up the primary responsibility to facilitate learning through negotiating contracts for goals, providing encouragement, evaluation criteria and strategies to learners.

Many of these challenges, then, concerning independent and autonomous learning have been related elsewhere (see, for example, Lai, 2019). In the past, our students have not made direct references or reflections related to autonomy and independent learning, but talked about them as two concepts related to learning but existing completely separate from their own learning experience and environment. Autonomy was not a concept they readily identified with, possibly because they had not previously been externally forced to become more autonomous, self-directed and independent learners. While the merits of these attributes are extolled each year, it was not until 2020 when the students were externally forced, due to the Covid pandemic, to study completely online do we finally see evidence of them becoming more self-directed, and self-motivated. Earlier manifestations of LBC-type activities had always seemed unattractive and unnecessary for students and placed them outside of their learning comfort zone. Now, one unanticipated positive development from the current pandemic is that we know that students can adapt to LBC practices and experiences.

Other challenges as discussed earlier, concern the wild exploitation of smartphones and social media which are potentially valuable language-learning devices. Yet the extent to which they may be employed for informal, self-directed learning remains difficult and underexplored. As highlighted before (Stockwell & Hubbard, 2013; Murray et al., 2020), frequent and comfortable use of a smartphone for non-study activities cannot be taken as an indication that learners are, firstly, tech-savvy across a range of devices, and secondly, ready and willing to use their smartphones for learning purposes.

While smartphones and social media have become normalised in the everyday lives of our learners outside the classroom, learning via these platforms "has not become normalized or fully integrated into formal language teaching as predicted" (Reinhardt, 2020, p. 235). One potential factor with implications for learning beyond the classroom is the ongoing perceptual hesitance to recognise the learning potential of smartphones and social media. Stockwell (2008, p. 260) quoted a student who 'couldn't get into study mode' on her smartphone, and Trinder (2017) reported a clear preference for traditional study materials even among heavy smartphone users. More recently, Mullen (2021, p. 143) identified a form of 'actual, proper study' among his participants, which also involved traditional materials and study practices, and in which smartphones and social media played only a limited and tangential role, exemplified by a participant comment that: "for like actual like proper study, and schoolwork, I wouldn't use my phone at all really". Changing learner perceptions of what smartphones and social media are 'for', and what role they can play in learning remains a challenge in the fostering of independent learners who can employ these resources beyond the classroom.

Equally, in our case study, one student raised the point that rather than being considered 'digital natives' (Prensky, 2001), it might be more appropriate for her generation to be considered 'mobile natives', citing Gobel and Kano (2014), whose study of Japanese university students found that while the participants were heavy and comfortable users of their mobile phones, their use of and comfort with other digital devices was limited, and a preference for more traditional paper-based learning materials was identified. This sentiment echoes the findings of Mullen's (2021) research on smartphone-based study behaviour, as was mentioned here earlier.

The participants in our study also had a clear perception of what 'actual, proper study' entails, as the following quotation illustrates:

> This is why I think CALL will never be able to fully replace traditional, classroom-based learning. We need that feeling of movement from one building to another, and then being able to go home and not having to worry about anything for a couple of hours. No matter the technology developments we have, nothing will beat the good, old textbook and slightly cold classroom.

The data for our study's corpus showed 633 occurrences of the word 'app', and 380 for the term '*Duolingo*'. *Duolingo*, was repeatedly evaluated as being quite basic, only suitable for those beginning to learn a language, and having little variety in presentation, with one student commenting that:

> I think that those questions were only suitable for the lower level and not for the intermediate level. It would have been more fun if they change the question types for every level so that the learners would not be tired of using the app.

Apart from *Duolingo*, references to other dedicated language learning apps were relatively rare. In a corpus of more than 230,000 words, there were 57 references to *Babbel*, 22 for *Memrise*, 9 for *Busuu*, 7 for *Kahoot* and 7 for *Quizlet*, indicating the limited role these mobile-friendly platforms play in the learning behaviours of the students. The perceptual barrier to learning on smartphones identified in other studies (Trinder, 2017; Rosell-Aguilar, 2018) and was evident among our students also:

> Since so many people these days use their phone as a form of relaxation, mindlessly scrolling through their timelines to numb their brain after a long day of work or college, using your phone for studying all day can really destroy this boundary, meaning our brain won't be able to distinguish whether we're relaxing or working, and we will never be fully able to relax.

With smartphones playing an ever-increasing role in the everyday lives of learners, it is important to ensure that a focus on developing CDL is compatible with smartphone capacities and encompasses, in theory and in practice, the affordances and constraints of smartphones, and an understanding of how they are used and perceived by their owners.

We conclude this section by emphasising that, as outlined, a variety of resources exist, accessible across different devices, all of which can play valuable roles in establishing and curating an informal, self-regulated learning space as part of what Dabbagh and Kitsantas (2012) term the learner's Personal Learning Environment. However, as we wish to highlight in this chapter, learners are not always aware of the potential learning value of such extracurricular and non-dedicated resources. Moreover, simply making learners aware of the existence and learning potential of the digital wilds may not automatically lead to enthusiastic exploitation of these digital spaces. We may lead the proverbial horse to water, but we may also need to ensure that they are thirsty (and curious) enough to try at least a sip.

Practical implications for classroom focus on the skills needed for LBC

The previous sections have highlighted some of the central constructs in LBC and also outlined some of the challenges faced by the authors of this article during their classroom implementation of these constructs. This section will use these challenges to offer practical advice to educators who are keen to introduce the theme of LBC to their own students.

As quoted earlier, there remains a perception that learning takes place with a 'good, old textbook and a slightly cold classroom', and within this perception there are clear expectations of, and boundaries around, how and where learning takes place. The Irish education system (not alone among others) has long been teacher-centred and examination-driven (O'Brien, 2017), and this perception is a result of such a system. In this sense, a discussion of LBC can also mean promoting an attitude towards learning that goes beyond the traditional and rigid perception of learning, characterised by one student as follows: "In second level education I was strictly taught from a textbook and not encouraged to use CALL programmes whatsoever. That mentality was practically ingrained into my brain as I entered university".

An example of this rigidity emerged during this module, when the lecturers, aiming to familiarise students with another form of online learning resource, proposed the introduction of a student-produced podcast to replace the MCQ&A assessment listed on the module outline. This proposal received a primarily negative response from students, resulting in the lecturers offering the students a choice between the two methods of assessment. However, the incident also provided the opportunity for a Critical Incident Analysis (Reinders & Benson, 2017) through exploration of the factors behind the negative reaction to the proposed assessment, particularly in light of comments from students that the main reason for their response was the unexpected change to the syllabus, rather than the podcast itself. Thus, educators aiming to introduce the concept of LBC into their classroom should be prepared to expect a degree of resistance from students who have fixed ideas about what constitutes learning, and what the roles of both teacher and student are in that process.

As well as traditional perceptions of the role of the teacher and student, there may also be fixed ideas regarding what different devices are 'for'. Students are already heavy users of smartphones for a variety of functions, and there may initially be resistance from students to engaging in academic endeavour on the devices. Educators may encounter learner perceptions of laptop computers as devices for study, and smartphones as devices for communication, relaxation, and indeed, for escaping study. Moreover, as our data showed, there can be strongly held attitudes on the times and places that are for study and for leisure. There may be reluctance on the part of such learners to embrace the idea of building a Personal Learning Environment which exposes them to content even when not in study mode. Educators may need to be better equipped with convincing data and arguments than they might imagine.

It must be emphasised that learners may not always display the readiness or willingness to learn independently, and may not always appreciate the importance of acquiring the skills to do so. As our own study showed, it was not until forced into remote learning that our students fully embraced the concept of autonomous, self-directed learning. Thus, teachers must be prepared to understand that for certain students, simply becoming an autonomous learner is not in itself sufficiently motivating for them. Finding a catalyst that will motivate students to embrace the concept of LBC may prove challenging. Current mindsets shared by both teachers and learners must be transformed. Implications from this transformative experience can only be positive.

Future pedagogical and research directions: rewilding for critical digital literacy development

LBC, as we see it, currently lies beyond the pedagogical landscape of many in-service language teachers chiefly because they are so wedded to their professional practices and their various curricula. The recent dramatic changes which were forced upon educators and learners alike by a pandemic may offer the opportunity to explore these traditional perceptions of learning and the practices encompassed within these perceptions. Schools and universities, with staff who may have previously avoided CALL technology, have delivered education almost entirely online for just over a year (at the time of writing), and there are lessons to be learnt regarding the delivery of education, firstly during Covid-19 itself, but also in a post-Covid-19 world, which may never revert completely to its pre-Covid-19 state (Godwin-Jones, 2020).

During the last year the online delivery of education has been far from seamless, with some students lacking either "the resources (laptop, wifi, software) or digital literacy they need to meaningfully engage" (McGillicuddy, 2020, para. 16). Additional research which explores not just the technical delivery of content, but also the broadening of perceptions and the development of the literacies needed to fully engage with it, is crucial. Agentive literacy should become an established CDL and applied research which investigates how to cultivate CDL among in-service and pre-service teachers, is required. Armed with such digital proficiency, teachers may move away from the technophobic neo-Luddite mindset to the more flexible and critical LBC, where they are more confident in rewilding their language education. Again, serious research is required in order to develop such a convincing approach for teachers.

Reiterating what Thorne, Hellermann and Jakonen (*op. cit.*) advised concerning 'structured unpredictability', and "the suggestion is to provide pedagogically informed resources and guidance, but not too much", we need convincing research on the question of balance to be achieved here when helping learners develop the skills to navigate and exploit the digital wilds, yet still leaving the digital wilds to be discovered. How much is 'not too much'?

Our ever-changing world may well involve greater levels of remote learning and study than was the case beforehand. However, we can always learn from the past, from educators such as Rogers: "The only person who is educated is the one who has learned how to adapt and change; the one who has realised that no knowledge is secure; that only the process of seeking knowledge gives a basis for security" (1969, p.104). Just as our work and study environments change, so too do the skills and literacies needed to survive and succeed. It is important that research continues to be conducted to explore whether universities have identified these skills and their curricula have been updated accordingly. This study indicated that the module delivered by the authors of this chapter helped learners become more self-directed and prepared as learners and as digital citizens by developing their CDL and such modules may well need to become more commonplace in universities.

Applied research such as ours on teaching and learning must follow an iterative process with each element sustaining and enhancing the other. Important themes are emerging from these elements and they require greater scrutiny and exploration. We would suggest that additional research be carried out on mobile learning and LBC and the development of an effective "smartphone literacy" for both teachers and learners, where each may exploit their portable device for their own *wild* purposes and interests. Given the ubiquitous presence of mobile technology, then one possible future for LBC may well be mobile. Given the convergence of apps and technology usage onto one mobile device, which also remains a device for social communication, the opportunities for learner distraction are large and continuous. We would therefore call for more research on the question of CDL and learner distraction in the development of meta-learners who are confident and competent in their new LBC comfort zone.

Reflective questions

As mentioned earlier, the data for the 2020 participants, who completed the module and indeed the whole semester entirely online, revealed that concepts such as autonomy and independence were more relevant, more concrete and more immediate than among those who had completed the module in previous years. It would appear that while experiencing typical university life, with face-to-face classes, and with supports such as open computer rooms and libraries, learners were less inclined to take an agentive role in their own learning.

When remote learning was forced upon them, however, they were able to adapt and engage in self-directed learning. Identifying or generating factors which make students continue to place immediate value on the concepts of autonomous and independent learning will be central to successful implementation of a LBC curriculum. What might these factors be?

Another challenge will be to maintain the agentive roles mentioned above in future semesters. Ideally, learners would return to the traditional university environment while retaining the agentive and autonomous attributes developed during remote learning; however, there is a danger that returning to the comforts of the campus and classroom might lead to regression of these attributes and a return to a more passive, teacher-centred form of learning. It is important to identify ways that formal learning can facilitate the maintenance of these positive learner characteristics when their need is perhaps less immediate to the learners themselves. What teacher practices need to change in order to maintain the progress made in LBC, and are teachers tech-savvy enough across a range of platforms to make these changes?

In Ireland, as in many other countries, learners arrive at university from a secondary schooling that is exam-driven and teacher-centred, in which little emphasis is placed on fostering autonomous or independent learners. This leads to fixed perceptions of when, where and how study is done, and what the roles are of teacher and learner alike in that process. These rigid attitudes make the process of fostering LBC among students even more difficult. What changes could be made at earlier education levels to foster broader and more inclusive perceptions of learning, and lay better foundations for LBC later in the students' educational journeys?

Recommended readings

Thorne, S. L, J. Hellermann & T. Jakonen (2021). Rewilding Language Education: Emergent Assemblages and Entangled Actions. *The Modern Language Journal, 105(S1),* 106–125.
  Presenting and situating a pedagogical approach called 'rewilding' strongly within a research agenda, this article reports on three studies of using augmented reality activities for producing material conditions in language acquisition.

Godwin-Jones, R. (2020). Building the porous classroom: An expanded model for blended language learning. *Language Learning & Technology,* 24(3), 1–18. http://hdl.handle.net/10125/44731.
  An apt and timely review of models of instructional delivery for language learning, this article provides a state-of-the-art overview while also extending the blending learning model for language acquisition.

Zourou, K. (2019). A critical review of social networks for language learning beyond the classroom. In M. Dressman & R. Sadler (Eds.), *Handbook of informal language learning* (pp.369–382). Hoboken, NJ: WileyBlackwell.
  This chapter offers a review of research dealing with repurposing social media in language acquisition, mobile-assisted language learning and game-based learning and contextualises them within the themes of agency and openness; and offers scope on future directions for this research.

References

Alm, A. (2019). Piloting Netflix for intra-formal language learning. *CALL and Complexity: Short Papers from EUROCALL,* 13–18. doi: 10.14705/rpnet.2019.38.979

Almalki, S. (2016). Integrating quantitative and qualitative data in mixed methods research--Challenges and benefits. *Journal of Education and Learning,* 5(3), 288–296.

Avila, J., & Pandya, J. Z. (2013). *Critical digital literacies as social praxis.* New York: Peter Lang.

Benson, P. (2011). Language learning and teaching beyond the classroom: An introduction to the field. In P. Benson & H. Reinders (Eds.), *Beyond the language classroom* (pp. 7–16). London, UK: Palgrave Macmillan.

Biggs, J. B. (1985). The role of meta-learning in the study process. *British Journal of Educational Psychology, 55,* 185–212.

Blin, F. & Jalkanen, J. (2014). Designing for language learning: Agency and languaging in hybrid environments. *Apples – Journal of Applied Language Studies, 8,* 147–170.

Boström, L., & Lassen, L.M. (2006). Unraveling learning, learning styles, learning strategies and meta-cognition. *Education + Training, 48*(2/3), 178–189. https://doi.org/10.1108/00400910610651809

Buckingham, D. (2010). Defining digital literacy. In B. Bachmair (Ed.), *Medienbildung in neuen Kulturräumen* (pp. 59–71). Zürich: VS Verlag für Sozialwissenschaften.

Dabbagh, N., & Kitsantas, A. (2012). Personal learning environments, social media, and self-regulated learning: A natural formula for connecting formal and informal learning. *The Internet and Higher Education, 15*(1), 3–8.

Dudeney, G., & Hockly, N. (2016). Literacies, technology and language teaching. In F. Farr & L. Murray (Eds.), *The Routledge handbook of language learning and technology* (pp. 115–121). Abingdon: Routledge.

Dudeney, G., Hockly, N., & Pegrum, M. (2013). *Digital literacies: Research and resources in language teaching.* London: Pearson Education Limited.

Flavell, J.H. (1979). Metacognition and cognitive monitoring: a new area of cognitive–developmental inquiry. *American Psychologist, 34*(10), 906–911.

Fuchs, C., Hauck, M., & Müller-Hartmann, A. (2012). Promoting learner autonomy through multi-literacy skills development in cross-institutional exchanges. *Language Learning & Technology, 16*(3), 82–102. http://llt.msu.edu/issues/october2012/fuchsetal.pdf

Gillespie, J. (2020). CALL research: Where are we now? *ReCALL, 32*(2), 127–144. doi:10.1017/S0958344020000051

Gobel, P., & Kano, M. (2014). Mobile natives: Japanese university students' use of digital technology. In J.-B. Son (Ed.), *Computer-assisted language learning: Learners, teachers and tools* (pp. 21–46). Newcastle upon Tyne, UK: Cambridge Scholars Publishing.

Godwin-Jones, R. (2016a). Looking back and ahead: 20 years of technologies for language learning. *Language Learning & Technology, 20*(2), 5–12.

Godwin-Jones, R. (2016b). Augmented reality and language learning: From annotated vocabulary to place-based mobile games. *Language Learning & Technology, 20*(3), 9–19.

Godwin-Jones, R. (2019). Riding the digital wilds: Learner autonomy and informal language learning. *Language Learning & Technology, 23*(1), 8–25. https://doi.org/10125/44667

Godwin-Jones, R. (2020). Building the porous classroom: An expanded model for blended language learning. *Language Learning & Technology, 24*(3), 1–18. http://hdl.handle.net/10125/44731

Hauck, M. (2019). Virtual exchange for (critical) digital literacy skills development. *European Journal of Language Policy, 11*(2), 187–210.

Hauck, M., & Kurek, M. (2017). Digital literacies in teacher preparation. In S. Thorne & S. May (Eds.), *Language, education and technology* (3rd. ed., pp. 1–13) *Encyclopedia of Language and Education.* Zürich: Springer International Publishing. DOI: https://doi.org/10.1007/978-3-319-02328-1

Hellerman, J., & Thorne, S.L. (2020). Distributed language for learning in the wild. In S. Conrad, A. Hartig & L. Santelmann (Eds.), *Cambridge introduction to applied linguistics* (pp. 264–277). Cambridge: Cambridge University Press.

Hinrichsen, J., & Coombs, A. (2014). The five resources of critical digital literacy: A framework for curriculum integration. *Research in Learning Technology, 21,* 1–16.

Knight, J., Barbera, E., & Appel, C. (2017). A framework for learner agency in online spoken interaction tasks. *ReCALL: The Journal of EUROCALL, 29*(3), 276.

Kukulska-Hulme, A. (2016). Mobile assistance in language learning: A critical appraisal. In A. Palalas & A. Mohamed (Eds.), *The international handbook of mobile-assisted language learning* (pp. 138–160). Beijing: China Central Radio & TV University Press Co., Ltd.

Lai, C. (2019). Learning beliefs and autonomous language learning with technology beyond the classroom. *Language Awareness, 28*(4), 291–309. DOI: 10.1080/09658416.2019.1675679

Lankshear, C., & Knobel, M. (2011). *New literacies.* Berkshire: McGraw-Hill Education.

Leu, D. J., Jr. (1997). Exploring literacy on the Internet: Caity's question: Literacy as deixis on the Internet. *The Reading Teacher, 51*(1), 62–67.

Lin-Siegler, X., Dweck, C. S., & Cohen, G. L. (2016). Instructional interventions that motivate classroom learning. *Journal of Educational Psychology, 108*(3), 295–299.

Little, D. (1991). *Learner autonomy 1: Definitions, issues and problems.* Dublin: Authentik.

Little, D. (2007). Language learner autonomy: Some fundamental considerations revisited. *Innovation in Language Learning and Teaching, 1*(1), 14–29.

Little, D., & Thorne, S. L. (2017). From learner autonomy to rewilding: A discussion. In M. Cappellini, T. Lewis & A. R. Mompean (Eds.), *Learner autonomy and web 2.0* (pp. 12–35). Sheffield, UK: Equinox.

Maher, J. (2011). Towards an appreciation of the place and potential of computer games in education [Unpublished doctoral dissertation]. University of Limerick.

Marcus-Quinn, A., Hourigan, T., & McCoy, S. (2019). The digital learning movement: How should Irish schools respond? *The Economic and Social Review, 50*(4), 767–783.

Martin, J. (2004). Self-regulated learning, social cognitive theory, and agency. *Educational Psychologist, 39*(2), 135–145, DOI: 10.1207/s15326985ep3902_4

McGillicuddy, D. (2020, June 30). Twelve things Covid-19 has taught us about education and schooling. *The Irish Times.* https://www.irishtimes.com/news/education/twelve-things-covid-19-has-taught-us-about-education-and-schooling-1.4285253 [accessed Jan 22 2021].

Mercer, S. (2015). Learner agency and engagement: Believing you can, wanting to and knowing how to. *Humanizing Language Teaching, 17*(4), 1–19.

Mullen, M. (2021). Left to their own devices: An investigation of learner perceptions of smartphones as tools of language learning [Unpublished doctoral dissertation]. University of Limerick.

Murray, L., Giralt, M., & Benini, S. (2020). Extending digital literacies: Proposing an agentive literacy to tackle the problems of distractive technologies in language learning. *ReCALL, 32*(3), 250–271. https://doi.org/10.1017/S0958344020000130

O'Brien, C. (2017, April 17). Is our education system fit for purpose in the 21st-century? *The Irish Times.* https://www.irishtimes.com/news/education/is-our-education-system-fit-for-purpose-in-the-21st-century-1.3051073 [accessed Jan 24 2021].

Pangrazio, L. (2016). Reconceptualising critical digital literacy. *Discourse: Studies in the Cultural Politics of Education, 37*(2), 163–174.

Potter, J. (2012). *Digital media and learner identity.* New York: Palgrave Macmillan.

Prensky, M. (2001). Digital natives, digital immigrants part 2: Do they really think differently? *On the Horizon, 9*(6), 1–6. https://doi.org/10.1108/10748120110424843

Reeve, J., & Tseng, C. (2011). Agency as a fourth aspect of students' engagement during learning activities. *Contemporary Educational Psychology, 36*(4): 257–267.

Reinders, H., & Benson, P. (2017). Language learning beyond the classroom: A research agenda. *Language Teaching, 50*(4), 561–578.

Reinhardt, J. (2018). Social media in the L2 classroom: Everyday agency, awareness, and autonomy. In H. Castañeda Peña (Ed.), *Technology in ELT: Achievements and challenges for ELT development* (pp. 17–34). Bogota: Publicaciones DIE.

Reinhardt, J. (2020). Metaphors for social media-enhanced foreign language teaching and learning. *Foreign Language Annals, 53,* 234–242. https://doi.org/10.1111/flan.12462

Rogers, C. (1969). *Freedom to learn: A view of what education might become.* Columbus, OH: Merrill.

Rosell-Aguilar, F. (2018). Twitter as a formal and informal language learning tool: From potential to evidence. In T. Beaven & M. Fuertes-Guiterrez (Eds.), *Innovative language teaching and learning at university: Integrating informal language into formal language education* (pp. 99–106). Research-publishing.net.

Thorne, S.L. (2010). The "intercultural turn" and language learning in the crucible of new media. In F. Helm & S. Guth (Eds.), *Telecollaboration 2.0 for language and intercultural learning* (pp. 139–164). Bern, Switzerland: Peter Lang.

Sauro, S., & Sundmark, B. (2019). Critically examining the use of blog-based fanfiction in the advanced language classroom. *ReCALL, 31*(1), 40–55.

Sauro, S., & Zourou, K. (2019). What are the digital wilds? *Language Learning & Technology, 23*(1), 1–7. https://doi.org/10125/44666

Schwartz, D., & Okita, S. (2009). The productive agency in learning by teaching. Unpublished manuscript. http://aaalab.stanford.edu/papers/Productive_Agency_in_Learning_by_Teaching.pdf

Sheppard, M. (2014). Developing digital literacies. https://www.jisc.ac.uk/guides/developing-digital-literacies.

Smith, A. (2015, April 1). U.S. Smartphone Use in 2015. Pew Research Center. https://www.pewresearch.org/internet/2015/04/01/us-smartphone-use-in-2015/

Stockwell, G. (2008). Investigating learner preparedness for and usage patterns of mobile learning. *ReCALL, 20*(3), 253–270.

Stockwell, G., & Hubbard, P. (2013). *Some emerging principles for mobile-assisted language learning*. Monterey, CA: The International Research Foundation for English Language Education. Retrieved from http://www.tirfonline.org/english-in-the-workforce/mobile-assisted-language-learning

Sung, Y. T., Chang, K. E., & Liu, T. C. (2016). The effects of integrating mobile devices with teaching and learning on students' learning performance: A meta-analysis and research synthesis. *Computers & Education, 94*, 252–275.

Thorne, S. L. (2015). Rewilding situated and usage-based approaches to second language development and research. Presentation at *Thinking, Doing, Learning: Usage-based Perspectives on Second Language Learning*, Groningen, Netherlands. Here: https://sites.google.com/site/stevenlthorne/

Thorne, S. L., Hellermann, J., & Jakonen, T. (2021). Rewilding language education: Emergent assemblages and entangled actions. *The Modern Language Journal, 105*(S1), 106–125.

Trinder, R. (2017). Informal and deliberate learning with new technologies. *ELT Journal, 71*(4), 401–412.

Van Lier, L. (2010). Foreword: Agency, self and identity in language learning. In B. O'Rourke & L. Carson (Eds.), *Language learner autonomy: Policy, curriculum, classroom: A festschrift in honour of David Little* (Vol. 3). Bern: Peter Lang.

Wang, H.C., & Chen, C.W. (2020). Learning English from YouTubers: English L2 learners' self-regulated language learning on YouTube. *Innovation in Language Learning and Teaching, 14*(4), 333–346.

Xiao, J. (2014). Learner agency in language learning: The story of a distance learner of EFL in China. *Distance Education, 35*(1), 4–17, DOI: 10.1080/01587919.2014.891429.

Zhang, D., & Zhang, L. J. (2019). Metacognition and self- regulated learning (SRL) in second/foreign language. In X. Gao (Ed.), *Second handbook of English language teaching* (pp. 883–897). Zürich: Springer.

Zourou, K. (2019). A critical review of social networks for language learning beyond the classroom. In M. Dressman & R. Sadler (Eds.), *Handbook of informal language learning* (pp. 369–382). Hoboken, NJ: Wiley Blackwell.

7
ENGLISH LANGUAGE LEARNING BEYOND THE CLASSROOM

Do Learner Factors Matter?

Cynthia Lee

In memory of Cynthia Lee, who passed away before the publication of this book
https://mals.hkbu.edu.hk/record/5/detail/140

Introduction

In today's globalized communities, English is a commonly used language – a *lingua franca* for study by and interpersonal communication between speakers and learners from different cultural backgrounds (Björkman, 2011; Konakahara & Tsuchiya, 2020; Sowden, 2012). Many universities, particularly English-medium institutions, have plans to increase the competitiveness of their students who learn and use English as a foreign or additional language (hereafter L2) for personal (e.g., study) and interactive (e.g., intercultural communication) purposes through the provision of English for Academic Purposes (EAP), English for Specific Purposes (ESP) or a variety of English language skills courses within the curriculum (e.g., Schaller-Schwaner, 2015). Furthermore, out-of-class resources and materials provided via self-access centres (Chung, 2013; Gardner & Miller, 2011) or computer technology (Mills & Wake, 2017) are used to support the formal curriculum and empower language learning. Both formal in-class and voluntary out-of-class learning opportunities form a rich English learning and teaching environment for L2 students. However, there is no guarantee that such an external environment will guarantee language learning success. Individual learners' attitudes, beliefs, perceptions and motivation can, to some extent, mitigate the degree of success.

In the literature of English language learning and teaching, the role of learner factors such as learner attitude and self-perceived ability towards language learning in the classroom has been extensively researched (e.g., Honarzad & Rassaei, 2019; Lee, 2018; Lee, Warschauer, & Lee, 2020). As out-of-class activities are often conducted on a voluntary basis, it is assumed that the learners who choose to participate in those activities are always ready to learn and will take an active role in the learning process. The role of learner factors in out-of-class language learning may not be as critical as in the formal curriculum. That said, little is done to prove the truth of this assumption. Thus, this chapter aims to review five key cognitive and psychological elements related to learners, namely attitude, perception, belief, learning desire and motivation, followed by discussion on the key issues regarding the ways in which the five learner factors influence out-of-class language learning, particularly self-directed English language learning (SDLL) and technology use for English language learning purposes in both school and university contexts. Finally, it points out the practical implications and future research directions for investigating and sustaining out-of-class English language learning opportunities.

Key constructs

Language learners' intention to participate in SDLL or use technology for language learning outside the classroom for personal or interactive learning purposes can be influenced by their attitudes, beliefs, motives, learning desires, and perceptions of the usefulness of technology (e.g., Huang, Teo, & Zhou, 2020; Şenbayrak, Ortaçtepe, & Trimble, 2019). Although positive attitudes, beliefs, perceptions, and motives contribute to out-of-class language learning, some learners may withdraw from or revise their goals in the middle of their language learning journey (e.g., Cheng & Lee, 2018). Others may mainly use technology for language learning to enrich personal linguistic knowledge or complete an essay rather than to share or learn from each other (Lee, Yeung, & Cheng, 2019; Lee, forthcoming). Language learners' participation or withdrawal from any activities or programmes may be caused by multiple personal and contextual factors. This section reviews five key cognitive and psychological constructs that affect learners' readiness for and participation in language learning activities, with particular reference to English language learning beyond the classroom.

Attitude

A learner's attitudes, beliefs, and perceptions reveal his or her internal emotional, cognitive, and psychological state, which, in turn, impacts actions and behaviours. According to the Theory of Reasoned Action (Ajzen & Fishbein, 1980) and the Theory of Planned Behavior (Ajzen, 1985, 1991), a person's attitude can predict his or her response or action to an object (Ajzen & Fishbein, 1977), including regulating learning or using technology for foreign language learning. In other words, attitude and action are interrelated. In the domain of English language learning, if an L2 learner has a positive attitude towards English learning activities outside the classroom, it is very likely that he or she will participate more in out-of-class activities. Similarly, if an L2 learner is anxious about learning English beyond the classroom, it is very likely that he or she may do so less.

Many studies on the relationship between attitude and language learning beyond the classroom revolve around SDLL and technology use for language learning. A survey by Şenbayrak, Ortaçtepe and Trimble (2019) of 250 adult Turkish L2 learners in a university in Turkey found that learners' attitudes towards language learning were closely related to their readiness for and frequency of joining their self-access centre's activities. Moreover, learners' regular use of self-access resources resulted in the further development of their positive attitude towards language learning. Nevertheless, some of the infrequent self-access learners might not have taken the initiative to learn through this method as they preferred to follow teachers' instructions.

Perception: perceived usefulness and perceived ease of use

Beside learners' attitudes, their perceptions of usefulness and perceived ease of use of technology could influence the adoption of technology for language learning. Perceived usefulness and perceived ease of use of an object are the crucial elements of the Technology Acceptance Model (TAM) (Davis, 1989) which has been widely used to study technology use for language learning. Studies that investigated learners' attitudes and perceptions found that both factors could affect the adoption of technology for second and foreign language learning beyond the classroom in the Chinese context (Lai, 2013; Lai, Wang & Lei, 2012). The surveys of Huang, Teo and Zhou (2020), Teo and Zhou (2014), Teo, Zhou, Fan and Huang (2019) and Wang and Jeffrey (2017) have also affirmed the findings. Moreover, Cai, Fan, and Du (2017) revealed the differences between male and female learners in terms of their attitudes towards and perceptions of technology use, after analysing numerous articles related to factors influencing the intention to adopt technology. Although the positive attitudes of both genders predicted their acceptance of technology, including learning beyond the classroom, males showed more favourable attitudes, particularly in belief, and greater self-efficacy or familiarity with technology than females. Attitude and perception were also found to vary with cultural backgrounds. Although the above-mentioned studies have revealed the relationship between positive learner attitude, perception and intention to use technology, it does not categorically mean that learners will use technology to achieve their learning purposes in reality. Some studies have already pointed out the discrepancy between intention to use and actual use of technology to achieve personal and interpersonal learning purposes outside the classroom (Lee, Yeung & Cheung, 2019; Lee, forthcoming).

A survey by Lee, Yeung and Cheung (2019) found that while the 193 secondary Chinese learners of English in Hong Kong had positive attitudes and perceptions towards technology use for personal (e.g., looking for information for homework) and interpersonal (e.g., consulting teachers, interacting with peers online) school-related learning purposes beyond the classroom, they actually adopted technology for personal learning purposes rather than for interpersonal learning purposes. They attributed the findings to the school practice that emphasizes individual learning rather than interactive learning with peers or communication with teachers. Following Lee et al.'s work, another survey of 539 tertiary Chinese learners of English in a private Hong Kong university conducted by Lee (2020) yielded similar results. Although the surveyed respondents had positive attitudes and perceived technology to be useful, they might not necessarily actually adopt it for interpersonal learning purposes. Again, they were more inclined to use technology to achieve personal learning (e.g., improving one's linguistic knowledge and English or writing a discipline-related assignment) than interpersonal learning purposes (e.g., interacting with professors and peers online). The study also found that learners' study level (e.g., junior vs senior students), discipline (e.g., education) and school or programme requirements (e.g., medium of instruction and essays) could mediate their attitude and perception, and influence their actual use of technology for English language learning.

Belief

A person's level of self-efficacy in completing a task will affect his or her belief (Bandura, 1982, 1997). If a person has high self-efficacy or confidence, this will impact their motivation, attitude, and learning processes (Riley, 1996). It is also likely that he or she will be able to finish a task successfully (Marsh, Martin, Yeung, & Craven, 2017). Language learners' beliefs towards a task and corresponding learning behaviours can be shown in terms of language learning strategies, which are chosen by learners to regulate their language learning (Griffiths, 2013, p. 15). A positive correlation between learner beliefs, actions and strategies has been shown in various studies on language learning outside the classroom (e.g., Lee, 2016; Navarro & Thornton, 2011). Navarro and Thornton (2011) found that learners' beliefs shaped actions which would, in turn, refine their beliefs, and consequently they would develop language learning skills in self-directed learning. In this way, interaction between belief and action is "cyclical" (p.291). Refinement of beliefs of two Japanese learners of English in the study was related to the language advisors' feedback, learners' continuous practice and successful implementation of their plans. However, interactions among beliefs, actions, and context (i.e., with language advisors and peers) were found to be complex.

Similarly, Lee's investigation (2016) into 23 L2 tutees' beliefs of learning and learning strategies in one-to-one writing consultations, an out-of-class English service, illustrated how their beliefs shaped behaviours in tutor-tutee interactions. Although the L2 tutees' use of the consultation service was attributable to intrinsic motivation – diagnosing writing problems and improving or polishing up their writing skills – their degree of participation and language learning strategies were affected by their beliefs about tutee roles. Some learners, who were categorized as passive, believed that tutees should listen to tutors' advice and wait to be taught, hence tended to speak little during consultations. Some, who were classified as inactive, believed that they would wait for advice but would respond to tutors' questions whenever they were asked. Others who were grouped as active learners believed that they should express their needs, discuss with tutors and ask questions. The instances of questioning tutors, expressing personal need, feelings or uncertainty, checking and confirming advice, and even participating in small talk were in proportion to the three groups of learners' beliefs. As commented on by Lee, the learners, regardless of the group they were in, mainly used the social or socio-cultural-interactive and affective strategies proposed by Oxford (1990, 2011) as well as O'Malley and Chamot (1990).

Learning desire

Drawing on items adapted from Fisher et al. (2001), Fisher and King (2010), Lee et al. (2016), as well as Gardner and MacIntyre (1993), a survey that investigated self-management, self-control, desire for learning, language learning anxiety, application of computer technology for language learning and learning style preference was administered by Lee, Yeung and Ip (2017) to university Chinese learners of English in Hong Kong. They found that desire for learning had a strong association with technology use for SDLL among the university Chinese learners of English. The older university English learners demonstrated a higher level of readiness for and desire to use technology for SDLL than their younger counterparts, while age versus gender interaction was so small that it did not make any significant difference. The researchers argued that the older learners' clear learning goals and desire to learn seemed to contribute to the difference.

Motivation

Another factor that influences language learning and that has been widely discussed in the literature is learner motivation. Gardner's L2 motivation framework (1985), Ryan and Deci's Self-determination Theory (SDT) (2000, 2017) and Dörnyei's L2 motivational self-system (2005, 2009) have given an account of how L2 learners are motivated and types of motivation. Over half a century ago, Gardner and Lambert (1959) began to explain how socio-cultural context motivates L2 learning and differentiates two types of motivation: instrumental and integrative motivation. Instrumental motivation is driven by external reasons such as passing an examination or parents' expectations while integrative motivation refers to learners' desire to be a member of or involved in the target community. In the 1990s, Ryan and Deci's Self-determination Theory (SDT) posited motivation from a cognitive perspective. SDT argues that motivation to learn or perform an act in schools, families and societies rests on individual learners' decisions. It is unique in the sense that it emphasizes "the different types and sources of motivation that impact the quality and dynamics of behavior"

(2017, p. 14). There are two types of motivation which may happen simultaneously, namely intrinsic motivation, which is grown out of one's interest, resulting in autonomous or self-regulated behaviour; and extrinsic motivation, which is caused by external reward or avoidance of punishment, resulting in controlled and other-regulated behaviour (ibid.). In addition to the concept of motivation, Ryan and Deci propose the concept of amotivation which appears in three forms: a person's negative perception of his/her ability to perform the required actions, lack of interest, relevance or value, and defiance or resistance to influence (ibid., p.16). While positive feedback and praise can be given verbally or textually to enhance a person's intrinsic motivation, its impact is subject to interpretation. Different types of tangible rewards for engagement, completion or competition can increase integrative/instrumental motivation, though their effects can be arbitrary (2017, pp. 131–135). Addressing the limitations of socio-cultural and cognitive-oriented language learning motivation theories for the explanation of L2 motivation, Dörnyei (2005, 2009) proposed the L2 Motivational Self System (L2MSS) from the psychological perspective, emphasizing interactions between motivation, self and learning experiences. According to the system, the ways in which learners want themselves to be or desire to be (i.e., the ideal self), or how they think others want them to be (i.e., extrinsic, the ought-to self), such as to be a proficient L2 user, together with experience which has been influenced by parents, peers, teachers, schools and successful experiences (i.e., L2 learning experiences), can impact their learning motivation and performances in learning activities.

The three motivational theories have been adopted to study how L2 learners other than English learners learn the target language(s) or use learning strategies to learn inside and outside the classroom (e.g., Fryer & Roger, 2017; Jang & Lee, 2019; Li, 2014; Lin, Zhang & Zheng, 2017), particularly in self-directed language learning (SDLL) (e.g., Cheng & Lee, 2018; Chung, 2013; Gardner & Yung, 2017), online language learning (e.g., Chen & Jang, 2010; Lin, Zhang & Zheng, 2017) and voluntary study abroad language programmes (e.g., Briggs, 2015; Hernández, 2010). English learners joined out-of-class activities or programmes for both intrinsic and extrinsic reasons. Therefore, the completion or success rate of out-of-class language learning heavily relies on L2 learners' learning motivation. Drawing on Gardner's (1985) integrative and instrumental motivation theory, Hernández (2010) found that integratively motivated American learners of Spanish were more willing to interact with native Spanish speakers than their instrumentally motivated counterparts. In fact, integrative motivation was identified to be a significant predictor of learners' interactions. Adopting Dörnyei's L2MSS as the theoretical framework, Gardner and Yung (2017) found that the 77 surveyed university Science major students, who were required to complete a self-access learning component in a compulsory English for Academic Purposes course, learnt English for study and career rather than for pleasure and interest. When asked about their learning motives, many of them had shifted from their promotion focus (e.g., to improve a weak skill) at the beginning of the term to a prevention focus (e.g., to finish the self-access learning component) near the end of the term. Despite the shift, the statements related to a promotion focus were ranked more highly than those related to a prevention focus that motivated them to finish the component throughout the course. The shift to prevention focus was a practical move in face of limited time for self-access learning in the course.

Aside from the personal or situational factors, many teachers and teacher trainers thought that the use of technology for teaching can enhance learning motivation and develop autonomy. However, technology does not categorically increase learning motivation nor encourage autonomous behaviour (Stockwell & Reinders, 2019). Although many learners are users of technology, they may not use technology for language learning (Lee, Yeung & Cheung,

2019; Lee, 2020). To sustain learners' learning motivation, teacher support is important. On the other hand, teachers should also be prepared to use technology for language teaching, keep on developing the knowledge of mastering different tools through teacher training or interacting with experienced teachers and find out the most appropriate pedagogies for their teaching situations (Stockwell & Reinders, 2019).

Key issues

The previous section shows how the five key constructs influence self-directed language learning and technology use for language learning, particularly out-of-class learning in the tertiary context. While learner factors play a key role in language learning outside the classroom, researchers have pointed out the complexity of this type of learning. This section points out four key issues facing researchers and practitioners in relation to learners' beliefs, attitudes, perceptions, learning desire and motivation for SDLL and technology use for English language learning.

Theoretical issues

Situational factors and learners' cultural values

According to Gan's (2009) investigation, situational factors which include the social environment (i.e., limited teaching resources and English teacher supply versus rich teaching resources and adequate English teacher supply) and institutional context (i.e., large class size versus small class size in two Confucian-inherited regions (i.e., Mainland China and Hong Kong respectively) caused differences in Chinese English learners' beliefs about independent learning, confidence and ability to achieve SDLL. In light of different situational factors, the surveyed 339 Mainland Chinese university L2 students demonstrated stronger beliefs in independent learning, greater confidence and abilities to achieve SDLL, and used more metacognitive and cognitive learning strategies than the 280 Hong Kong Chinese counterparts. The cultural traditions in the two regions, however, did not have much impact. In contrast, with reference to Hofstede's five cultural value dimensions, Lai, Wang, Li, & Hu's survey (2016) reported that the learners who came from countries whose people hold long-term, collectivist and high-power orientations were more likely to use or value technology for self-directed foreign language learning, including English, in the university context. The learners who came from countries characterized by high uncertainty avoidance might not actively engage in technology use for self-directed learning. Their study on the role of culture is consistent with that of Cai, Fan and Du (2017), which also found that a person's attitude and perception could vary with their cultural backgrounds. Cultural backgrounds include unseen cultural beliefs and values, which are "below the water line" (Oxford & Amerstorter, 2018, p. xxvii), and these have been argued as influential, affecting language learning strategies and learners' autonomy (ibid.).

Discrepancy between intention and actual behaviour

While positive attitude and perception boost technology use for language learning, two recent studies (Lee, Yeung & Cheung, 2019; Lee, forthcoming) have shown a discrepancy between intention and actual behaviour. More importantly, they seem to support the claim that attitude towards an object and perceived usefulness of an object can influence learners' intention to act or behave; however, they may not result in actual behaviour due to the influence of discipline and the field of study.

Understanding the reasons of demotivating motivated L2 learners

Finally, it is of crucial importance to understand not only what motivates L2 learners but also what demotivates them. Students' high attrition rate was and has been a problem in many tertiary self-directed English language learning programmes (Cheng & Lee, 2018; Gardner & Yung, 2017; Reinders, 2005, 2007). Cheng and Lee's study (2018) found that the English language learners who persisted in a self-directed language learning scheme were extrinsically motivated, aiming to achieve a good grade. The demotivated learners who dropped out had difficulty in sparing additional time for voluntary language activities given that there was a lack of time and clashes with their discipline-required courses. Lack of time is a common reason for dropout learners, not only in out-of-class and self-directed learning (see Evans & Tragant, 2020). That said, in interviews, the former motivated learners reported improvement after joining the programme while the latter less motivated learners did not.

Practical issues

Self-directed programme design and teacher support

Furthermore, the surveys of Lai (2015) and Lai, Li and Wang (2017) affirmed the impact of teacher support on English learners' use of technology for SDLL in two Hong Kong and United States universities. It was found that various forms of teacher support – encouragement (affection support), guidance and language resources recommendation (capacity support) and technology use in the classroom and assignment (behaviour support) could push L2 learners to use resources with confidence, and have positive perceptions of usefulness towards technology use for SDLL. Age and gender, however, do not have any significant impact on technology use for language learning within or beyond the classroom (Lee, Yeung & Ip, 2016). To boost SDLL, tutors' oral advice and written feedback on university English learners' work and progress (e.g., reflective journals) contributed to the refinement of university learners' beliefs, plans and actions (Navarro & Thornton, 2011). The difficulty level of an SDLL programme or activity, or lack of tutor support will discourage English learners from continuing the out-of-class learning experience or withdrawing from the activities (Cheng & Lee, 2018).

Implications

Theoretical implications

Researchers have suggested various ways to address the five learner factors. To increase L2 learners' motivation on SDLL, researchers have recommended 'creative ideal-self generating activities' (Dörnyei, 2009, p. 34), as well as visual and mental imagery activities (e.g., Chan, 2014; Dörnyei & Chan, 2013; Magid, 2011) to develop an ideal L2 self. Dörnyei and Chan's survey (2013) has confirmed the positive impact of the combined use of visual imagery and auditory style on the development of future self-identities in learning English and Mandarin. The multisensory intervention methods allow learners to visualize or imagine some scenarios in which they perform successfully (see Dörnyei & Kubanyiova, 2014 for more ideas). Magid (2011) and Chan (2014) used scripted and mental imagery activities in workshops and in a compulsory English programme to help university Chinese learners of English form the mental image of their ideal L2 self. Munezane (2015) added goal-setting to visualization. Mackay (2019) conducted 12-hour intervention activities for 47 university Spanish learners of English. The activities consisted of visualization training, visualization activities and practical strategies to develop an action plan. While most learners were able to provide details of their ideal L2 self in their descriptions after training, the extent of the effects did vary with individual learners' ability to form visual and mental images (Chan, 2014).

Furthermore, the issue of discrepancy between learner intention to use technology and actual behaviour is under-researched (Lee, Yeung & Cheung, 2019; Lee, 2020). More research on English language learners with different cultural backgrounds, age groups, levels of study and proficiency levels is deemed necessary.

Practical implications

It is necessary to think of some means to encourage L2 speakers to use technology for self-directed learning and language learning beyond the classroom at the institutional level. These means include providing authentic materials, organizing opportunities for interactions or meetings with target language speakers, and inviting guest speakers to introduce the target language culture in pre-departure activities for voluntary study-abroad programmes launched by institutions (Hernández, 2010). Similarly, explaining the importance of making use of the study-abroad opportunity to increase out-of-class contact, arranging regular voluntary interactive activities with native speakers outside the classroom (Briggs, 2015), making use of the institutional English language resources and projecting one's future self (Bai & Wang, 2020) would also help. Fryer and Roger (2018) investigated arranging host families for study-abroad students. Interacting with host family members and native speakers, the participants increased their self-confidence and changed language learning behaviours after the study abroad experience. The extent of improvement in lexical competence hinged on the length of stay and learner initiation to obtain information (Briggs, 2015).

In addition, integrating out-of-class language learning activities (e.g., English writing support) into the mainstream courses of various departments or offering online language support not only avoids clashes between the activities and students' timetables (Cheng & Lee, 2018) but also stimulates the desire for learning (Lee, Yeung, & Ip, 2017). Institutions could review the difficulty level of activities, for example, self-directed language learning programmes, with a view to increasing the flexibility and students' completion rate (ibid.). In case online language learning is offered to some out-of-class activities, teachers should explain the rationale of online learning, provide choices and flexible learning options, and devise collaborative activities to facilitate peer interactions (Chen & Jang, 2010; Lee, Yeung, & Cheung, 2019). Teachers can select and deliver suitable linguistic or cognitive tasks for their L2 learners via institutional technological platforms (Lee, Yeung, & Ip, 2017) or online training platforms (e.g., Lai, Shum & Tian, 2016). As there are inherent cultural differences and contextual constraints in technology use for SDLL, approaches that consider L2 learners' cultural dispositions (Lai, Wang, Li & Hu, 2016), learning desire and learning environment (Lee, Yeung, & Ip, 2017) deserve greater attention.

Considering that teacher support influences L2 learners' attitudes, beliefs and actions in SDLL and technology use for SDLL (Lai, 2015; Navarro & Thornton, 2011), teachers are advised to act as a role model in using technology to promote language learning in the classroom. Follow-up guidance for L2 learners on recommended resources and how to use them will be beneficial (Lai, 2015). Teachers may have to develop relevant advising skills and technological knowledge to assist L2 learners during their SDLL journey through training or peer interactions (Stockwell & Reinders, 2019), not simply to encourage them (Lai, 2015; Lee, 2015). In this light, pre-service or in-service teacher training and professional development programmes should help teachers become better equipped with both technological and technological pedagogical knowledge and skills to meet the challenges (Mishra & Koehler, 2006).

Future directions

The previous sections have reviewed the theoretical frameworks for and research studies on the investigation of learners' attitudes, beliefs, perceptions, learning desire and motivation for both out-of-class and technology use for English language learning. Each learner factor has been proved to be influential in a learner's intention. However, a learner's positive intention may not result in any action to learn the language outside the classroom. Mediated by a range of socio-cultural and contextual issues, the learner's self-learning trajectory may change in the midst of the journey. A motivated learner may become a demotivated learner. Therefore, teachers' continuous positive feedback and support may increase learners' confidence and self-image, and drive them to integrate into the target community. The language learning trajectory and long-term impact, as well as interactions between different learner factors and learners' home environments, cultural values, pedagogies and programmes (e.g., online materials, exchange programmes, a multisensory intervention method, interactions with peers and native English speakers), ideas for institutional level support to boost individual learners' ideal L2 self, and promote focussed motivation, attitudes, beliefs and perceptions towards language learning beyond the classroom, deserve more in-depth examination in the future.

Although this review has shown evidence that the five learner factors – attitude, perception, belief, desire for learning and motivation – play a key role in their language learning beyond the classroom, contextual and socio-cultural factors could mediate their impact. It is worth noting that a great majority of the studies reviewed in Sections 2 and 3 adopted the quantitative method by means of surveying a group of L2 learners at a specific time and place, and using modelling techniques, while only a few used follow-up qualitative interview data and diary writing. The quantitative analyses, without doubt, have provided insight into the association between different learner factors under investigation and out-of-class English language learning, as well as predictive pathways for curriculum planners, administrators and practitioners. As pointed out by Lee, Yeung and Ip (2017), "causal interpretation of findings needs to be made with caution", particularly when the data and analysis were collected and made based on a relatively small sample size and within a particular cultural group. To complement the limitations, the emic longitudinal method to examine or trace how a learner factor (e.g., motivation) develops or changes, and how a learner refines it over time either in the home or overseas learning environment, is a viable alternative. Longitudinal studies of selected cases would allow researchers to obtain "a thick description of a complex social issue embedded within a cultural context" and provide "an unparalleled understanding of longitudinal processes" (Dörnyei, 2007, p.155). As there is no fixed timeline for starting and closing a longitudinal investigation, researchers also need to be cautious when making interpretations of this kind of data (Thomson & Holland, 2003). That said, longitudinal studies or case studies together with other qualitative methods such as interview or narrative enquiry could shed "in-depth insights into students' motivational trajectory" (Busse and Walter, 2013, p.449). Therefore, Mackay (2019) calls for investigation into the long-term impact of ideal L2 self-activities on language learning over time.

Moreover, many studies have confirmed the influence of learner factors on their intention to use technology. For instance, a positive attitude towards technology for language learning is found to have a positive correlation with the intention to use technology. However, intention is not necessarily equivalent to actual behaviour. Two previously reviewed studies (Lee, 2020; Lee, Yeung & Cheung, 2019) have lent support to the existence of discrepancies between intention and behaviour. As the studies are limited to the Chinese context in three secondary schools and four disciplines in a university, more investigation into the topic in different cultural groups and teaching environments should be made.

In essence, emic investigation into the interactions between each learner factor and other socio-cultural factors or institutional contexts, as well as examination of discrepancies between intention and actual behaviour will further yield research evidence to extend our understanding of the complexity of language learning beyond the classroom, and can support research-informed pedagogy or curriculum design.

Reflection Questions

1. What are the out-of-class English language learning activities in your context? Comment on their strengths and areas for improvement in one of the five learner factors described in this chapter – attitude, perception, belief, learning desire and motivation.
2. To what extent do learner factors play a more/less significant role than teacher factors or the teaching environment in your context? Why?
3. What have you/other teachers done to motivate, promote and sustain learners' participation in out-of-class English language learning activities in your context? To what extent is/are your method(s) effective?

Recommended readings

Inaba, M. (2019). *Second Language Literary Practices and Language Learning Outside the Classroom*. Bristol, UK: Multilingual Matters.
This book examines the relationship between in-class and out-of-class voluntary second language learning tasks (e.g., email with peers) for university L2 learners of Japanese, and investigates how individual factors (e.g., motivation) and social contexts (e.g., literacy practices) affect out-of-class language learning from a socio-cultural perspective. It allows teachers to understand what L2 learners do outside the classroom and adapt in-class language learning tasks to better engage them and promote out-of-class language learning.

Griffiths, C. (2013). *The Strategy Factor in Successful Language Learning*. Bristol: Multilingual Matters.
This book enables readers to better how learner, situational and target variables can influence language learning strategy use. The first three chapters explores the definition of language learning strategy use, the roles of learner variables, situational variables and target variables in relation to strategy use, as well as individual learners' and teachers' views. The final chapter focusses on the pedagogies adopted in various strategy instruction programmes, teachers' perceptions and how instructions can best be conducted. The learner, situational and target variables and need for teacher training are further discussed in this chapter.

Lee, C., Yeung, A., & Cheung, K. W. (2019). Learner perceptions versus computer technology usage: A study of adolescent English learners in Hong Kong secondary schools. *Computers and Education*, 33, 13–26.
This paper found that although computer technology is widely used by adolescent English learners in Hong Kong, this did not necessarily mean that they would apply technology use for school-related learning, particularly collaborative tasks. To address the discrepancy between intention to use and actual use of technology for in-class and out-of-class language learning, the findings called for teachers' attention to developing more collaborative tasks and considering the suitability of their teaching methods.

Lee, C. (2020). Intention to use versus actual adoption of technology by university English language learners: What perceptions and factors matter? *Computer Assisted Language Learning*. Accessible at https://doi.org/10.1080/09588221.2020.1857410.

With reference to Lee, Yeung and Cheung's paper (2019), the study continues to examine the correlation between Hong Kong tertiary English learners' intention to use technology to achieve personal and interpersonal English learning purposes, attitude towards technology, and perceived usefulness of technology through survey questionnaires. It was found that the tertiary English language learners showed a positive attitude and perceptions towards the use of technology for English language learning. However, learners' disciplines and levels of study mediated their attitudes and perceptions, especially in the use of technology for interpersonal learning purposes, resulting in different actual English learning behaviours. In this light, the researcher recommended four ways to practitioners to bridge the gap between learner intention and actual behaviours.

References

Ajzen, I. (1985). From intentions to actions: A theory of planned behavior. In J. Kuhl & J. Beckman (Eds.), *Action-control: From cognition to behavior* (pp. 3–15). Hilladale, NJ: Erlbaum.

Ajzen, I. (1991). The theory of planned behavior. *Organizational Behavior and Human Decision Processes*, *50*(2), 179–211.

Ajzen, I., & Fishbein, M. (1977). Attitude-behavior relations: A theoretical analysis and review of empirical research. *Psychological Bulletin*, *84*(5), 888–918.

Ajzen, I., & Fishbein, M. (1980). *Understanding attitudes and predicting social behavior*. Englewood-Cliffs, NJ: Prentice-Hall.

Bai, L., & Wang, Y. X. (2020). Pre-departure English language preparation of students on 2+2 programs. *System*, *90*, 102219.

Bandura, A. (1982). Self-efficacy mechanism in human agency. *American Psychologist*, *37*(2), 122–147.

Bandura, A. (1997). *Self-efficacy: The Exercise of Control*. New York: W. H. Freeman and Company.

Björkman, B. (2011). Pragmatic strategies in English as an academic lingua franca: Ways of achieving communicative effectiveness? *Journal of Pragmatics*, *43*(4), 950–964.

Briggs, J. G. (2015). Out-of-class language contact and vocabulary gain in a study abroad context. *System*, *53*, 129–140.

Busse, V., & Walter, C. (2013), Foreign language learning motivation in higher education: A longitudinal study of motivational changes and their causes. *The Modern Language Journal*, *97*(2), 435–456.

Cai, Z., Fan, X., & Du, J. (2017). Gender and attitudes toward technology use: A meta-analysis. *Computers and Education*, *105*, 1–13.

Chan, L. (2014). Effects of an imagery intervention on Chinese university students' possible second language selves and learning experiences. In K. Csizér & M. Magid (Eds.), *The impact of self-concept on L2 learning* (pp. 357–376). Bristol, UK: Multilingual Matters.

Chen, K. C., & Jang, S. J. (2010). Motivation in online learning: Testing a model of self-determination theory. *Computers in Human Behavior*, *26*(4), 741–752.

Cheng, A., & Lee, C. (2018). Factors affecting tertiary English learners' persistence in self-directed language learning journey. *System*, *76*, 170–182.

Chung, I. F. (2013). Are Learners becoming more autonomous? The role of selfaccess center in EFL college students' english learning in Taiwan, *Asia-Pacific Educational Research*, *22*(4), 701–708.

Davis, F. D. (1989). Perceived usefulness, perceived ease of use, and user acceptance of information technology. *MIS Quarterly*, *13*(3), 319–340.

Dörnyei, Z. (2005). *The psychology of the language learner: Individual differences in second language acquisition*. Mahwah, NJ: Lawrence Erlbaum.

Dörnyei, Z. (2007). *Research methods in applied linguistics*. Oxford: Oxford University Press.

Dörnyei, Z. (2009). The L2 motivational self-system. In Z. Dörnyei & E. Ushioda (Eds.), *Motivation, language identity and the L2 Self* (pp. 9–42). Bristol, Buffalo, Toronto: Multilingual Matters.

Dörnyei, Z., & Chan, L. (2013). Motivation and vision: An analysis of future L2 self images, sensory styles, and imagery capacity across two target languages. *Language Learning*, *63*(3), 437–462.

Dörnyei, Z., & Kubanyiova, M. (2014). *Motivating learners, motivating teachers: The role of vision in language education*. Cambridge, UK: Cambridge University Press.

Evans, M., & Tragant, E. (2020). Demotivation and dropout in adult EFL learners. *TESL-EJ*, *23*(4), 1–20.

Fisher, M. J., & King, J. (2010). The self-directed learning readiness scale for nursing education revisited: A confirmatory factor analysis. *Nurse Education Today, 30*(1), 44–48.

Fisher, M. J., King, J., & Tague, G. (2001). Development of a self-directed learning readiness scale for nursing education. *Nurse Education Today, 21*(7), 516–525.

Fryer, M., & Roger, P. (2017). Identifying with the L2 self: Study abroad experiences of Japanese English language learners. *The Journal of Asia TEFL, 14*(3), 443–463.

Fryer, M., & Roger, P. (2018). Transformation in the L2 self: Changing motivation in a study-abroad context. *System, 78*, 159–172.

Gan, Z. (2009). Asian learners' re-examined: An empirical study of language learning attitude, strategies and motivation among Mainland Chinese and Hong Kong students. *Journal of Multilingual and Multicultural Development, 30*(1), 41–58.

Gardner, R. C. (1985). *Social psychology and second language learning: The role of attitudes and motivation.* London: Edward Arnold.

Gardner, R. C., & Lambert, W. E. (1959). Motivational variables in second language acquisition. *Canadian Journal of Psychology, 13*(4), 266–272.

Gardner, R. C., & MacIntyre, P. D. (1993). On the measurement of affective variables in second language learning. *Language Learning, 43*(2), 157–194.

Gardner, D., & Miller, L. (2011). Managing self-access language learning: Principles and practice. *System, 39*(1), 78–89.

Gardner, D., & Yung, K. Y. W. (2017). Learner motivation in self-access learning. *Innovation in Language Learning and Teaching, 11*(2), 159–176.

Griffiths, C. (2013). *The strategy factor in successful language learning.* Bristol, Buffalo, Toronto: Multilingual Matters

Hernández, T. A. (2010). The relationship among motivation, interaction, and the development of second language oral proficiency in a study-abroad context. *The Modern Language Journal, 94*(4), 600–617.

Honarzad, R., & Rassaei, E. (2019). The role of learners' autonomy, motivation and self-efficacy in using technology-based out-of-class language learning activities. *The JALT CALL Journal, 15*(3), 23–42.

Huang, F., Teo, T., & Zhou, M. (2020). Chinese students' intentions to use the Internet-based technology for learning. *Educational Technology Research Development, 68*(1), 575–591.

Jang, Y., & Lee, J. (2019). The effects of ideal and ought-to L2 selves on Korean EFL learners' writing strategy use and writing quality. *Reading and Writing, 32*, 1129–1148.

Konakahara, M., & Tsuchiya, K. (2020). *English as a lingua franca in Japan: Towards multilingual practices.* CH: Palgrave MacMillan.

Lai, C. (2013). A framework for developing self-directed technology use for language learning. *Language Learning & Technology, 17*(2), 100–122.

Lai, C. (2015). Modelling teachers' influence on learners' self-directed use of technology for language learning outside the classroom. *Computers & Education, 82*, 74–83.

Lai, C., Li, X., & Wang, Q. (2017). Students' perceptions of teacher impact on their self-directed language learning with technology beyond the classroom. Cases of Hong Kong and U.S. *Educational Technology Research and Development, 65*(4), 1105–1133.

Lai, C., Shum, M., & Tian, Y. (2016). Enhancing learners' self-directed use of technology for language learning: The effectiveness of an online training platform. *Computer Assisted Language Learning, 29*(1), 40–60.

Lai, C., Wang, Q., & Lei, J. (2012). What factors predict undergraduate students' use of technology for learning? A case from Hong Kong. *Computers and Education, 59*(2), 569–579.

Lai, C., Wang, Q., Li, X., & Hu, X. (2016). The influence of individual espoused cultural values on self-directed use of technology for language learning beyond the classroom. *Computers in Human Behavior, 62*, 676–688.

Lee, C. (2015). More than just language advising: Rapport in university English writing consultations and implications for tutor training. *Language and Education, 29*(5), 430–452.

Lee, C. (2016). Second language learners' self-perceived roles and participation in face-to-face English writing consultations. *System, 63*, 51–64.

Lee, C. (2020). Intention to use versus actual adoption of technology by university english language learners: What perceptions and factors matter? *Computer Assisted Language Learning.* Retrieved from https://doi.org/10.1080/09588221.2020.1857410.

Lee, C., Yeung, A.S., & Ip, T. (2016). Use of Computer technology for english language learning: Do learning styles, gender, and age matter? *Computer Assisted Language Learning, 29*(5), 1033–1049.

Lee, C., Yeung, A. S-S., & Ip, T. (2017). University English language learners' readiness to use computer technology for self-directed learning. *System, 67*, 99–110.

Lee, C., Yeung, A., & Ip, T. (2016). Computer technology and language learning: Do language style, gender and age matter? *Computer Assisted Language Learning, 29*(5), 1033–1049.

Lee, C., Yeung, A. S.-S., & Cheung, K. W. (2019). Learner perceptions versus computer technology usage: A study of adolescent english learners in Hong Kong secondary schools. *Computers and Education, 133*, 13–26.

Lee, H., Warschauer, M., & Lee, J. H. (2020). Toward the establishment of a data-driven learning model: Role of learner factors in corpus-based second language vocabulary learning. *The Modern Language Journal, 104*(2), 345–362.

Lee, J. H. (2018). Exploring relationships between second language learners' attitudes towards classroom language and variables that motivate their learning. *Language Awareness, 27*(3), 243–248.

Li, Q. (2014). Differences in the motivation of Chinese learners of English in a foreign and second language context. *System, 42*, 451–461.

Lin, C. H., Zhang, Y., & Zeng, B. (2017). The roles of learning strategies and motivation in online language learning: A structural equation modeling analysis. *Computers & Education, 113*, 75–85.

Mackay, J. (2019). An ideal second language self intervention: Development of possible selves in an English as a foreign language classroom context. *System, 81*, 50–62.

Magid, M. (2011). *A validation and application of the L2 motivational self system among Chinese learners of English*. Unpublished Doctoral Thesis. University of Nottingham.

Marsh, H. W., Martin, A. J., Yeung, A. S., & Craven, R. G. (2017). Competence self-perceptions: A cornerstone of achievement motivation and the positive psychology movement. In A. Elliot, C. Dweck & D. Yeager (Eds.), *Handbook of competence and motivation* (2nd ed.), *Theory and application* (pp. 85–113). New York: Guildford Press.

Mills, M., & Wake, D. (2017). *Empowering learners with mobile open access learning initiatives*. Hershey: IGI Global.

Mishra, P., & Koehler, M. J. (2006). Technological pedagogical content knowledge: A framework for integrating technology in teachers' knowledge. *Teachers College Record, 108*(6), 1017–1054.

Munezane, Y. (2015). Enhancing willingness to communicate: Relative effects of visualization and goal setting. *The Modern Language Journal, 99*(1), 175–191.

Navarro, D., & Thornton, K. (2011). Investigating the relationship between belief and action in self-directed language learning. *System, 39*(3), 290–301.

O'Malley, J. M., & Chamot, A. U. (1990). *Learning strategies in second language acquisition*. Cambridge: Cambridge University Press.

Oxford, R. L. (1990). *Language learning strategies: What every teacher should know*. Boston, MA: Heinle & Heinle Publishers.

Oxford, R. L. (2011). *Teaching and researching language learning strategies*. Harlow, English: Pearson Education Limited.

Oxford, R. L., & Amerstorter, C. M. (Eds.) (2018). *Language learning strategies and individual learner characteristics: Situating strategy use in diverse contexts*. London: Bloomsbury Academic.

Reinders, H. (2005). Non-participation in university language support. *JALT Journal, 27*(2), 205–222.

Reinders, H. (2007). University language advising: Is it useful? *Reflections on English Language Teaching, 5*(1), 79–92.

Riley, P. (1996). "BATs and BALLs": Beliefs about talk and beliefs about language learning. Paper presented at the International Conference: Autonomy 2000: The development of learning independence in language learning, Bangkok. Retrieved from http://web.atilf.fr/IMG/pdf/melanges/09_riley.pdf.

Ryan, R. M., & Deci, E. L. (2000). Self-determination theory and the facilitation of intrinsic motivation, social development, and well-being. *American Psychologist, 55*, 68–78.

Ryan, R. M., & Deci, E. L. (2017). *Self-determination theory: Basic psychological needs in motivation, development and wellness*. New York, London: The Guildford Press.

Schaller-Schwaner, I. (2015). The habitat factor in ELF(A) – English as a lingua franca (in academic settings) – and English for plurilingual academic purposes. *Language Learning in Higher Education, 5*(2), 329–351.

Şenbayrak, M., Ortaçtepe, D., & Trimble, K. (2019). An exploratory study on Turkish EFL learners' readiness for autonomy and attitudes toward self-access centers. *TESOL Journal, 10*(2), 1–16.

Sowden, C. (2012). ELF on a mushroom: The overnight growth in English as a lingua France. *ELT Journal, 66*(1), 89–96.

Stockwell, G., & Reinders, H. (2019). Technology, motivation and autonomy, and teacher psychology in language learning: Exploring the myths and possibilities. *Annual Review of Applied Linguistics, 39*, 40–51.

Teo, T., & Zhou, M. (2014). Explaining the intention to use technology among university students: A structural equation modelling approach. *Journal of Computing in Higher Education, 26*(2), 124–142.

Teo, T., Zhou, M., Fan, A. C. W., & Huang, F. (2019). Factors that influence university students' intention to use Moodle: A study in Macau. *Education Technology Research Development, 67*, 749–766.

Thomson, R., & Holland, J. (2003). Hindsight, foresight and insight: The challenges of longitudinal qualitative research. *International Journal of Social Research Methodology, 6*(3), 233–244.

Wang, P., & Jeffrey, R. (2017). Listening to learners: An investigation into college students' attitudes towards the adoption of e-portfolios in English assessment and learning. *British Journal of Educational Technology, 48*(6), 1451–1463.

8

THE GOLDEN AGE OF FOREIGN LANGUAGE LEARNING

Age and Language Learning Beyond the Classroom

Elke Peters

Introduction

In Flanders, the Dutch-speaking part of Belgium, it is no exception to hear a child utter a few words or sentences in English. Unlike other children in Europe, they only start learning English in secondary school, at the age of 13 or 14. This means that these children must have picked up English when watching (subtitled) English-language TV shows, YouTube clips or when playing computer games. Questions that arise include: do children indeed soak up new languages like sponges from mere exposure to foreign language (FL) input? What are the differences between learning a language in school or outside school? Are both equally effective?

Popular opinion holds that children are at an advantage for learning foreign languages. The positive evidence for this age effect stems from studies investigating language learning in naturalistic learning settings, i.e., immigrants who are "fully immersed in a second language environment" (DeKeyser, 2012, p. 455). These studies have shown that children learning a new language outperform adolescents and adults in the long run (e.g., Bylund, Hylstenstam, & Abrahamsson, 2021; DeKeyser, 2000). 'The earlier, the better' – credo has also found its way to educational policy and formal language instruction. A prime example is the European Commission's educational policy, which has consistently advocated an early start for learning at least two foreign languages in school (European Council, 2019). Consequently, most children in Europe now start learning a FL at an increasingly younger age. Yet, in spite of the positive evidence for age effects in naturalistic learning settings, a different picture emerges in contexts of formal instruction. Early starters do not tend to obtain higher proficiency levels compared to late starters in the long term, as late starters catch up relatively quickly, sometimes even within a few months (e.g., Baumert, Fleckenstein, Leucht, Köller, & Möller, 2020; Jaekel et al., 2017; Pfenninger & Singleton, 2017). Researchers have provided several explanations for the lack of an age effect in classroom research: the transition from primary to secondary education (e.g., Baumert et al., 2020; Pfenninger & Singleton, 2017), late starters' cognitive maturity (DeKeyser, 2012; Muñoz, 2008), literacy skills (Pfenninger & Singleton, 2017), and language learning motivation (Pfenninger & Singleton, 2017). However, one recurrent explanation is the quantity of input, which is more limited in formal instruction than in naturalistic language learning contexts (DeKeyser, 2012; Muñoz, 2008; Pfenninger & Singleton, 2017).

There is a considerable body of research showing the importance of exposure to FL input for language learning regardless of age (e.g., Muñoz, 2008). In schools, input can be increased by means of Content-and-Language-Integrated Learning (CLIL) programs, in which subjects, such as history or geography, are taught in a FL. CLIL learners have been found to benefit substantially from the extra input and interaction in the FL (e.g., Bulté, Surmont, & Martens, 2021; Pfenninger & Singleton, 2017). However, larger amounts of input can also be realized in activities beyond the classroom. Studies on the relationship between learners' out-of-school exposure to FL and their language proficiency (e.g., Dressman & Sadler, 2020; Werner & Tegge, 2020) are clearly on the rise and there is now mounting evidence for the benefits of out-of-school contact with the FL for language learning. The focus in this chapter will be on the role of age in learners' engagement with the FL outside of school.

Key constructs

Ultimate attainment and learning rate

When discussing age and language learning, there are two constructs that are important, even though they will not figure prominently in this chapter: ultimate attainment and learning rate.

Ultimate attainment: Even though the term ultimate attainment is often used synonymously with nativelike proficiency, it is now more commonly used to refer to "the final product of L2 acquisition" (Muñoz, 2008, p. 580). Nevertheless, it should be stressed that "final" by no means implies the end of learning. In educational contexts, on the other hand, ultimate attainment generally refers to the proficiency level reached within obligatory instructional time (Pfenninger & Singleton, 2017).

Learning rate: Learning rate is simply the speed of learning. There is robust evidence that, with equal input, older learners and late starters initially have a steeper learning rate than young learners (Lambelet & Berthele, 2015: Muñoz, 2008). This means that younger learners in naturalistic learning contexts are not faster learners, but better learners because they reach higher ultimate attainment levels than late starters in spite of a slower start (DeKeyser, 2000, 2012). In formal instruction settings, only the initial learning speed advantage has been observed (Muñoz, 2008; Pfenninger & Singleton, 2017). The distinction between ultimate attainment and learning speed illustrates the importance of longitudinal research to study age effects.

Implicit and explicit learning

Age plays a role in how foreign languages tend to be learned, i.e., implicitly or explicitly (DeKeyser, 2003). *Implicit learning* is "learning without awareness of what is being learned" (DeKeyser, 2003, p. 314), while implicit knowledge refers to the unconscious understanding of language forms, which allows learners to use those forms fluently and correctly without being able to verbalize the grammar rules (Ellis & Shintani, 2014). Children, for instance, know how to conjugate verbs, but they do not know how to explain verb conjugation and might not even know that there are grammar rules (DeKeyser, 2018). In this respect, it is important to refer to the critical period hypothesis, which states that the "automatic acquisition from mere exposure to a given language seems to disappear after this age, and foreign languages have to be taught and learned through a conscious and labored effort" (Lenneberg, 1967, p. 167, as cited in DeKeyser, 2018, p. 2) (see Lambelet & Berthele, 2015, for a more detailed discussion). This means that young language learners are at an advantage for implicit language learning, provided they have large amounts of language input, which means that young learners can pick up language from mere exposure. For young learners, quantity and quality of input are determinant factors in their language success. Consequently, in input-poor settings, such as many FL classrooms, children's implicit learning mechanisms cannot be fully exploited (DeKeyser, 2018). Yet, out-of-school contact with the FL offers the potential for learning conditions for implicit learning. It should be noted though that learners' ability to learn a FL implicitly from mere exposure gradually declines with age (DeKeyser, 2018; Ellis & Shintani, 2014).

In *explicit learning*, the focus is on consciously learning specific language aspects, such as grammar rules, while explicit knowledge refers to the conscious knowledge of language forms, i.e., language learners can explain the grammar rules and verbalize their knowledge of facts about language forms (DeKeyser, 2018; Ellis & Shintani, 2014). For instance, adult FL learners might be able to explain verb conjugation, but still struggle to use verb forms correctly and fluently when speaking (DeKeyser, 2018). Older language learners have been found to be at an advantage for explicit learning because of their cognitive maturity and language-analytic ability (DeKeyser, 2018), which explains why they initially have a steeper language learning curve than younger learners, especially in the domain of morphosyntax (Muñoz, 2008). Older learners can engage in explicit learning processes "to bypass the increasingly inefficient implicit mechanisms" (DeKeyser, 2000, p. 518).

Formal and informal language learning

Formal language learning is the language learning that typically takes place in the classroom. Formal language instruction is characterized by (1) a few hours of teaching per week (often no more than two or three hours), (2) FL input that is limited to the textbook and the teacher, (3) a FL that is not the language of communication between peers, and (4) depending on the learning setting (see below,) limited out-of-school contact with the FL (DeKeyser, 2018; Muñoz, 2008). The starting age for foreign languages in formal instructional settings has been lowered in many European countries in the last two decades. Consequently, most European countries now provide early formal language instruction. It is important to note that formal language learning should not be regarded as synonymous with explicit learning, as language learners can also learn a language implicitly in immersion or CLIL settings (DeKeyser, 2012; Pfenninger & Singleton, 2017).

Informal language learning is the language learning that takes place beyond the classroom. Dressman (2020) defines informal language learning, as "any activities taken consciously or unconsciously by a learner outside of formal instruction that lead to an increase in the learner's ability to communicate in a second (or other, non-native) language" (p. 4). His definition is reminiscent of Sundqvist's (2009, p. 6) definition of *extramural English* (for a discussion of other terms, see Sundqvist, accepted):

> In extramural English, no degree of deliberate intention to acquire English is necessary on the part of the learner, even though deliberate intention is by no means excluded from the concept. But what is important is that the learner comes in contact with or is involved in English outside the walls of the English classroom. This contact or involvement may be due to the learner's deliberate (thus conscious) intent to create situations

for learning English, but it may equally well be due to any other reason the learner may have. In fact, the learner might not even have a reason for coming in contact with or becoming involved in extramural English.

The last 25 years have witnessed an unprecedented increase in the opportunities for informal language learning (Dressman, 2020), which is also reflected in the number of studies exploring this phenomenon. It goes without saying that technological advances have played a crucial role in informal language learning and have had a huge impact on the availability and accessibility of FL input, e.g., YouTube clips, streaming platforms (Netflix), digital games. Here it should be noted that informal language learning does not equate to implicit language learning, as language learners might engage in conscious, explicit learning outside of school, e.g., by using language learning apps, like *Duolingo* (DeKeyser, 2012; Dressman, 2020).

Key issues

Language learning setting: second versus foreign language learning. The need for a third category

Language learning has traditionally been approached from two angles, i.e., that of second language and foreign language learning. Second language learning refers to naturalistic learning settings, in which language learners are fully immersed in the new language, being the dominant language of the country. This is typically the context of immigrants, e.g., Syrian refugees starting a new life in Germany. Research has found an age effect on ultimate attainment in naturalistic second language learning contexts. Foreign language learning, on the other hand, refers to language learning in the classroom, in which exposure to the target language is limited to a few hours per week and to the textbook and the teacher. An example would be Flemish or Swedish children learning French in school (e.g., Peters et al., 2019). So far, there is little empirical evidence that an early start for foreign language learning in school results in higher language proficiency (e.g., Pfenninger & Singleton, 2017). One of the main differences between the two settings is the quantity and quality of language input and interaction. However, the traditional distinction between (naturalistic) second language learning and (formal) foreign language learning has become blurred in settings where language learners have extensive contact with the FL through different sources of media (see also Sundqvist & Sylvén, 2016), even though the FL is not an official or dominant language and is usually not spoken outside of the classroom in such contexts. This is typically the case in countries with a subtitling tradition to make FL TV programs accessible, such as Denmark, Sweden, the Netherlands, and Flanders, but this phenomenon is also becoming increasingly common in non-subtitling or dubbing countries (see Schwarz, 2020 for an example of Austria).

In light of this new reality, it is argued that the distinction between second and foreign language learning does no longer adequately reflect the different learning settings of present-day language learners, as it has led to a third hybrid language learning setting: naturalistic foreign language learning. It is a commonplace observation that for English, for instance, being the dominant language in popular culture (Werner, 2018), formal instruction is no longer the only and maybe not even the predominant way of learning the language (Muñoz, 2012), as language learners increasingly pick up English outside of school (e.g., Busby, 2021; Peters, 2018; Schwarz, 2020; Sundqvist, 2019), similar to the way learners in a naturalistic learning setting learn from input and interaction.

Language learning in this hybrid setting shares with naturalistic L2 learning the large amounts of authentic input, even though input is generally limited to popular media. Consequently, language learners have ample opportunities to pick up the FL implicitly, which is especially important if learners have FL contact from a young age onwards, as is the case in many subtitling countries, such as Denmark, Sweden, and the Netherlands. As discussed above, young learners are particularly good at implicit language learning provided they have large amounts of authentic input (DeKeyser, 2000, 2012). In addition to a considerable amount of implicit learning, learners in naturalistic foreign language learning settings also learn the FL explicitly in the classroom. Explicit learning mechanisms play an increasingly important role after childhood, and may be even necessary to bypass the decline in learners' implicit language learning ability (DeKeyser, 2000, 2012).

It is important to acknowledge the characteristics of this hybrid learning setting and its relation with age for theoretical and pedagogical reasons. First, research into language learning in this hybrid setting has great potential for advancing our understanding of FL acquisition by exploring the role of motivation, input, and age. Pedagogically, research into out-of-school language learning can highlight what should be prioritized in the limited classroom time and how teachers can encourage learners to engage with the FL outside of school.

The relationship between out-of-school language contact and language proficiency in different age groups

This section provides an up-to-date account of research into out-of-school language learning. However, it is by no means a comprehensive synthesis, as that would be beyond the scope of this chapter.

Young language learners (aged 12 or younger) with formal English instruction

Most research into young learners' engagement with the FL outside school has been conducted with learners who also received formal instruction, as most countries start with teaching a FL (English) in primary education.

A study with very young children (age 4) was conducted by Unsworth and colleagues (2015) in the Netherlands. Even though the children already had some out-of-school contact with English, it was too limited to predict vocabulary and grammar outcomes. Unsworth et al.'s findings were not corroborated by Hannibal Jensen (2017), who explored Danish learners' (age 8 and 10) extramural English habits and their vocabulary knowledge. Both age groups had received the same amount of formal instruction, but they had a different starting age and consequently were tested at different ages. Hannibal Jensen (2017) found that the young Danish children in her sample engaged with extramural English six hours per week on average. Watching TV, listening to music, and gaming were popular English-language activities in this age group. A striking result is that boys had almost twice as much English-language contact as girls. This is especially the case for gaming (235 minutes versus 47 minutes). There was a positive relationship between gaming with bimodal input (= spoken and written English) and vocabulary knowledge. Interestingly, the late starters (aged 10) performed significantly better than the early starters (aged 8) on the vocabulary test, probably because of their accumulated exposure to English outside school. Motivation plays a key role, as these children learn by doing. Finally, it was pointed out that these children should be regarded as users of English and not just learners of English (Hannibal Jensen, p. 14).

There is slightly more research into learners aged 10–12. Lindgren and Muñoz (2013) investigated young learners' reading and listening comprehension in a large-scale multisite study involving seven countries. Except for the data collection in England, where the target language was French or Spanish, the FL in the other countries was English. Lindgren and Muñoz found that exposure to the FL, and watching FL movies in particular, was positively related to the learners' performance in the tests. Sundqvist and Sylvén (2014) and Sylvén and Sundqvist (2012) explored how vocabulary knowledge, reading and listening comprehension of Swedish EFL learners was affected by their gaming habits. They found that young Swedish learners frequently engage with English outside of school, that is more than seven hours per week of gaming or watching TV/movies, and that frequent gamers (> five hours/week) outperformed the moderate gamers (zero to five hours/week) who, in turn, obtained higher scores than the non-gamers.

Young English language learners (aged 12 or younger) without formal English instruction

There is also research into young learners' informal language learning prior to English instruction (Bollansée et al., 2021; De Wilde et al., 2020; Kuppens, 2010; Lefever, 2010; Puimège & Peters, 2019). Most of these studies have collected data from Flemish children, who have a late starting age for formal English instruction: in grade 7 or 8 (see Lefever, 2010, for an example from Iceland with children aged 7 and 8). Like in many other countries, English is omnipresent in Flanders and Iceland (e.g., music, the internet, subtitled TV shows and movies). Even though these children had not had any English lessons at the time of data collection, they frequently engaged with English outside school, mainly through TV, gaming, songs, social media, which is in line with the out-of-school activities from their peers in Denmark and Sweden who do have weekly English lessons (Puimège & Peters, 2019). Moreover, many children have intensive daily contact with English (De Wilde et al., 2020).

Let me illustrate this with some concrete examples. Almost half of the participants in Puimège and Peters (2019) watch TV with L1 subtitles several times a week, while 15% of the children in De Wilde et al.'s (2020) study indicated watching English-language TV with L1 subtitles for more than two hours per day. One-third of the participants in Puimège and Peters claimed to watch TV without any subtitles several times a week, very often on a computer or a tablet. This finding was corroborated by De Wilde et al., in which 11% of the children watch non-subtitled English-language TV for at least one hour per day. Gaming is an important activity for this age group. One-third of the surveyed children play games several times per week and 15% engage in playing English-language games for more than two hours per day.

Children learn a lot from these activities, even though there is some variance in their English language skills. Most studies have focused on children's vocabulary knowledge in English (Bollansée et al., 2021; Kuppens, 2010; Puimège & Peters, 2019). Puimège and Peters (2019), for instance, found that Flemish children in grade 6 knew on average 3,000 words without ever having had an English lesson. The children's vocabulary knowledge was positively correlated to gaming and audiovisual input. In an earlier study, Kuppens (2010) showed that grade 6 children, especially those who regularly watched subtitled English-language TV shows and movies, could orally translate short sentences from English into Dutch (e.g., *I feel great,* or *What's going on?*) and from Dutch into English (e.g., *Je hebt gelijk* [You're right], or *Het spijt me* [I'm sorry]). More recently, Bollansée et al. (2021) tested whether

Flemish children in grade 5 and 6 could produce the English word when given a picture prompt/word in Dutch. The children did not only know common words, such as *guy* and *animal*, or cognates, such as *compass* and *sardine*, but also low-frequency words, e.g., *mantis* or *contradict*. It is interesting to note that some children specifically referred to computer games as the source for some of the words they knew (e.g., *armor, harvest*) (Bollansée et al., 2021, p. 210). In addition to watching TV without subtitles, gaming was indeed an important predictor of these learners' productive vocabulary knowledge.

Two studies also explored young learners' listening, reading, and speaking skills. Both Lefever (2010) and De Wilde et al. (2020) found that young learners who had not received any formal English instruction are able to understand basic spoken English. In De Wilde et al.'s study, a quarter of the participants (grade 6) obtained an A2-level for listening. These young learners engaged mostly with spoken modes of English via TV and songs outside school. Nevertheless, some learners were also found to understand written English and to have obtained basic literacy skills in the language (Lefever, 2010), even though children rarely read in English. Children's speaking skills tend to vary more than their listening and reading skills, with some children not being able to produce any English, while others can hold an informal conversation (De Wilde et al., 2020; Lefever, 2010). In Lefever's sample, 25% of the participants (aged seven and eight) could fluently interact in English, even though they had not had any English lessons in school yet. The speech samples below illustrate some of Lefever's participants' conversational skills in English.

It is clear that children who have not had any English lessons can pick up English from TV, games, and social media. Further, they engage with English on a regular basis from a young age onwards. This amount of exposure easily surpasses the input in any classroom setting in primary schools, in which learners have only two or three hours of English per week at best. The omnipresence of English and the availability of English-language media create ideal circumstances to learn English implicitly from mere exposure and interaction. As pointed out by DeKeyser (2018), quantity and quality of language input are determinant factors for children's FL learning development.

Adolescent language learners (aged 13 or older) with formal English instruction

The bulk of research into out-of-school language learning has been done with adolescent learners receiving formal English instruction. Most of these studies were carried out in regions with a subtitling tradition (see Schwarz, 2020, for an exception).

Verspoor, de Bot, and van Rein (2011) conducted one of the few longitudinal studies. They compared learners' language proficiency (writing and vocabulary) in two age groups, i.e., 13 and 15-year old Dutch EFL learners with little (to no) English-language media exposure or regular out-of-school contact with English. The group of EFL learners with no exposure to English language media was a small group of pupils from Dutch reformed groups with very little English outside of school for religious reasons. Verspoor et al.'s findings illustrate the importance of out-of-school contact with English-language media for language learning. At the same time, they show that it affects language learning differently over time, and that it may become more effective when learners' proficiency increases.

Sundqvist and colleagues (Sundqvist, 2019; Sundqvist & Wikström, 2015) zoomed in on the role of gaming in Swedish adolescents' (age 15–16) vocabulary knowledge and use. They found that EFL learners who frequently game (>= five hours per week) obtained significantly higher scores on both a receptive and productive vocabulary test than learners who

> Examples taken from Lefever (2010, pp. 11–12)
>
> [1] Researcher: Do you have any more animals?
> Boy 7: No, I had fish … but now he is gone.
> Researcher: What happened?
> Boy 7: My dad sell it, 'cause my cat was trying to eat
> [2] Researcher: Can you tell me the rest of the story? What happens?
> Girl 2: They are laughing at the monkey and now the monkey is taking his hat off and here he is wearing his hat and he is crying and now the monkey gives … they trade with banana and the mother take the hat and gives it to the boy.

gamed less often (zero to five hours per week). Frequent gamers also used more tokens and types as well as more advanced vocabulary in their essay. Finally, they also had the highest rated essays. However, the type of game (single-player, multiplayer, or massively multiplayer online games) did not predict participants' vocabulary score (Sundqvist, 2019).

An important study is that by Schwarz (2020) because she investigated extramural English in a non-subtitling country, Austria, where she collected data from EFL learners in grade 10 in Vienna. The findings from her mixed-methods study largely corroborate the findings from subtitling regions, showing that there is hardly any difference in the types of extramural English activities and in the time spent on extramural English between subtitling and non-subtitling regions. Schwarz also found that there was a positive relationship between extramural English and learners' receptive vocabulary size, but not with their productive vocabulary size. In spite of the few differences, she does point out that the early exposure to English in subtitling countries may result in a different language learning trajectory and higher proficiency level. Interestingly, learners' extramural English explained more variance than their years of English instruction. Yet, when interviewed, participants explicitly indicated that they regard their English lessons as the basis for their out-of-school English-language activities. Schwarz's findings are in line with Pfenninger and Singleton's (2017) study with Swiss learners (age 18), which also showed the benefits of out-of-school contact with English for learners' listening comprehension and vocabulary outcomes. The language experience essays in their study revealed that learners felt they had profited more from out-of-school activities than from their English lessons. An interesting finding is that some of their respondents were more in favor of an early start for French in school than for English because they could learn English outside of school anyway. In Flanders, learners do have an earlier start for French than for English. Yet, Peters et al. (2019) found that learners' English vocabulary was still significantly larger in English than in French as a result of large amounts of out-of-school contact with English. Even though learners start with French in grade 5 and with English in grade 7 or 8, the French language input remains very limited compared to the thousands of hours English-language input through media. This was the case for the three grades tested (grade 8, 10, and first year at university).

A final study that should be mentioned is that by Huang, Chang, Zhi, and Niu (2020), which is one of the few studies conducted outside of Europe. The study investigated the relationship between past and current out-of-school exposure to input and learners' listening performance among 16–17 year old EFL learners in Taiwan. The study showed a positive relationship between out-of-school exposure and listening. Additionally, out-of-school exposure was a more important predictor than input in school.

It is clear that adolescent learners also benefit from large amounts of English-language contact. This holds for learners with early out-of-school exposure to English as well as those who first have English lessons in school and then start engaging with English outside of school. The findings show how language input remains vital for language learning and how its effect may become larger with increased proficiency. However, learners' out-of-school contact with English is in sharp contrast with that of other languages like French (Peters et al., 2019), which illustrates the dominant position of English as the language of pop culture.

Adult language learners (aged 18 or older) with formal English instruction

Recent years have witnessed an increase in research into adult learners' out-of-school language learning. In a series of large-scale studies, Muñoz (2006, 2011, 2014) investigated the relationship between starting age, input, and several language proficiency measures (e.g., vocabulary, speaking, phonetic discrimination) among EFL university students. Starting age for formal instruction was not a predictor of the university students' language proficiency, but informal contact with the FL, such as watching TV and movies, reading, and writing e-mails, was. The stronger impact of input compared to length of instruction has been confirmed in other studies with university students (Busby, 2021; Peters, 2018). Gonzalez-Fernandez and Schmitt's study (2015) is one of the few studies on collocations. In line with the previous studies, they found that collocational knowledge was more strongly correlated with out-of-school English language contact ($r=.56$) than years of English study ($r=.45$). An interesting study on formulaic language is that by Sockett (2014) who investigated the relationship between the audiovisual input to which learners had been exposed and the output they produced in fan fiction. Frequent viewers recycled many multiword units (4-grams) from the TV shows (e.g., *Walking Dead, The Big Bang Theory, House*, ...) to which they had been exposed, such as *what are you doing, he used to tease me*, confirming the beneficial effects of audiovisual input. Most participants watched TV with L1 (French) or English captions.

For young and adolescent learners, gaming and watching TV are the most important sources for learning outside of school, while reading in the FL barely plays a role. Studies with university students show a slightly different picture, viz. that out-of-school reading can also predict language outcomes (Busby, 2021; González-Fernández & Schmitt, 2015; Peters, 2018) because compared to secondary school learners, university students tend to read more often (Peters et al., 2019). It stands to reason that learners need a sufficiently large vocabulary size to read FL books. The fact that young learners engage in fewer FL literacy-based activities can be explained by their lower proficiency that does not yet meet the vocabulary demands for reading FL books.

The aforementioned studies all support the findings from the research with young and adolescent learners showing the importance of out-of-school contact with the FL for language learning. Nevertheless, two studies did not find a relationship between out-of-school FL contact and language learning (Briggs, 2015; Busby & Dahl, 2021). Briggs (2015) focused on a study-abroad context (6–20 weeks in length), i.e., learners' out-of-school contact with English, while studying at a private language institution in the UK. She collected data from adults (18–53 years old). The lack of a positive relationship between out-of-school language contact and vocabulary learning was attributed to the fact that participants may not have had enough out-of-school contact with English. Second, the language to which participants had been exposed may not have been conducive to learning new vocabulary, as it was often limited to activities like "speaking to service personnel" or "reading menus or timetables". Busby and Dahl (2021) examined the association between Norwegian university students' reading speed of academic texts and their extramural English. Unlike in studies with younger EFL learners (Brevik, 2016), Busby and Dahl did not find a positive relationship, probably because the language to which they had been exposed during their extramural English activities (i.e., informal, every-day English) was different from the academic register in the reading texts.

Implications

Age is related to how languages are learned, whereby children are better at implicit learning – provided they have large amounts of FL input – and adolescent and adults at explicit learning. Effective language teaching, thus, takes age-related learning mechanisms into account (DeKeyser, 2018). The research evidence suggests that an early start for formal language instruction has not systematically resulted in higher language proficiency because the FL input in classrooms is often too limited for young learners to successfully engage in implicit learning processes. However, the research into out-of-school language learning shows that in limited input settings of formal instruction regular contact with the FL beyond the school walls may compensate for the limited amount of input in classroom instruction and cater for implicit learning mechanisms that young learners need. Consequently, young learners in these hybrid, naturalistic foreign language settings have plenty of opportunities to pick up English implicitly from mere exposure and interaction. Let me illustrate this with the rankings of the European Survey on Language Competences (2012) and the English Proficiency Index (EF, 2020). What the top performing regions (the Netherlands, Sweden, Denmark, Finland, Flanders) have in common is not an early start for English in school, but large amounts of out-of-school contact with English from a young age onwards. Additionally, most of these regions have linguistically closely related languages to English. We know that learners' L1 can play a facilitative role, as children tend to learn cognates first (Puimège & Peters, 2019). At the same time, the research into informal language learning also demonstrates that FL input is not only important for young language learners, but remains essential for all age groups, even if older learners are faced with a dwindling capacity for implicit language learning. It should be noted that the effect of FL contact increases when learners' proficiency increases (Verspoor et al., 2011).

It is also relevant to look at the relationship between out-of-school language contact and formal instruction. Research comparing the two suggests that there is a prevalence of out-of-school language contact effects over length of instruction/starting age (Busby, 2021; Gonzaléz-Fernandéz & Schmitt, 2015; Huang et al., 2020; Muñoz, 2011, 2014; Peters, 2018; Schwarz, 2020), as informal language learning tends to explain more variance in students' language proficiency than instruction. These findings illustrate the power of input and the large learning gains that can accrue as a result of extensive engagement with FL input. One caveat, however, may be that language learners mainly encounter everyday, conversational language (TV, movies, social media), which is suitable for acquiring basic communication skills, but less appropriate for developing academic language proficiency (Busby & Dahl, 2021).

The pedagogical implications are clear. There is great potential of out-of-school contact with FL media (TV, internet, gaming, reading, social media) for language learning because it is motivating and engaging and provides FL learners with large amounts of authentic high-quality input. As shown in several studies, learners who frequently engage with the FL outside of school identify themselves as FL users, not as FL learners (Sundqvist, 2019). The studies discussed in this chapter show how FL instruction can be better aligned to learners' age by using authentic input (songs, audiovisual input, internet) and encouraging young language learners to engage with the FL outside of school to foster implicit learning mechanisms. Likewise, adolescent and adult learners should also be informed about the value of FL media for language learning. When learners regularly engage with the FL, teachers may want to consider what learners already know from outside of school. This will help them prioritize language content. Similarly, given the differences in language proficiency as a result of out-of-school exposure (e.g., De Wilde et al., 2020), teachers may also wish to differentiate between learners. Finally, because learners mainly encounter spoken English (TV, movies, internet, gaming), specific attention may need to be allocated to academic registers for students pursuing an academic degree, as out-of-school language contact is vital to foster language learning, but not sufficient for the development of academic literacy skills (Busby & Dahl, 2021).

Future directions

The last decade has witnessed an unprecedented number of studies on out-of-school language learning. Research in this domain has a rich tradition of collecting data from different age groups, i.e., young learners in primary schools, adolescents in secondary education, and adults in tertiary education. Yet, little is still known about adult learners who learn a new language later in life. Further, the majority of studies have been conducted in subtitling regions with Germanic languages as L1, like Sweden, Denmark, and Flanders. In order to generalize the benefits of out-of-school language learning, more research is warranted from non-subtitling countries and from regions other than the Nordic countries, Flanders, and the Netherlands (e.g., Huang et al., 2020; Schwarz, 2020; Sockett, 2014). In spite of a few studies addressing French (e.g., Lindgren & Muñoz, 2013; Peters et al., 2019), most data stem from EFL learners. It is clear that future studies, which focus on other languages than English, will need to be undertaken (see Pai & Duff, 2021, for a recent example on Chinese).

The studies conducted in Flanders (Bollansée et al., 2021; De Wilde et al., 2020; Kuppens, 2010; Puimège & Peters, 2019) and Iceland (Lefever, 2010) as well as the study by Pfenninger and Singleton (2017) show that learners start picking up English before learning English in school. What we need is more longitudinal research to map out the extramural English and English learning trajectory of learners who frequently engage with English outside of school and how the introduction of formal English instruction interacts with these activities to determine how out-of-school language learning develops with age (see De Wilde, Eyckmans, & Brysbaert, 2021, for a recent example). The use of mixed-methods research designs with both quantitative (e.g., tests, questionnaires) and qualitative data collection instruments (e.g., diaries, interviews, language learning essays) (see Schwarz, 2020, for an example) seems a fruitful way forward.

Only few studies have explored the differential impact of several activities on different aspects of language proficiency. Out-of-school language activities requiring production may be more beneficial for language learning than activities which are more passive (Bollansée et al., 2021; De Wilde et al., 2020; Puimège & Peters, 2019; Sundqvist, 2019). Additionally, not all activities are equally beneficial for all language proficiency aspects. For instance, gaming and watching non-subtitled TV enhance productive language skills, like learners' vocabulary use in writing or their productive vocabulary knowledge (Sundqvist, 2019), whereas watching L1 subtitled TV does not (Bollansée et al., 2021). However, it remains unclear how the effectiveness of certain activities interacts with age. It stands to reason that watching captioned TV is less effective for young learners than for adults, given the required reading speed (Vanderplank, 2016). Further research is needed to investigate the relationship between out-of-school learning, age, and language proficiency.

The benefits of out-of-school language contact have been established for several language proficiency aspects, such as listening, writing, and most clearly vocabulary. However, much less is known about grammar, speaking, pronunciation, or reading speed (see Busby & Dahl, 2021, for an exception), so these are also areas that merit further research.

Finally, given that learners in second language contexts may need several years to acquire basic and academic language skills and to be on par with L1 speakers, research could explore how exposure to second language media can support learners of different age groups in their language learning trajectory after arrival in a new country (see also Perry & Moses, 2020). Some of the research on audiovisual input for pre-schoolers seems promising in this respect (e.g., Samudra, Wong, & Neuman, 2019).

Reflection Questions

1. What kind of informal language learning activities do your pupils/students engage in?
2. How does the learning setting (second, foreign, naturalistic foreign language setting) affect your teaching practices?
3. How does learners' engagement with extramural English and its effectiveness on language learning change with age?

Recommended readings

Pfenninger, S., & Singleton, D. (2017). Chapter 7. Age and the impact of differential input. In S. Pfenninger, & D. Singleton, *Beyond age effects in instructional L2 learning*. Multilingual Matters.

Dressman, M., & Sadler, R.W. (Eds.) (2020). *The handbook of informal language learning*. Routledge. Part III. Beyond the classroom. In V. Werner & F. Tegge (Eds.) (2021), *Pop culture in language learning*. Routledge.

References

Baumert, J., Fleckenstein, J., Leucht, M., Köller, O., & Möller, J. (2020). The long-term proficiency of early, middle, and late starters learning English as a foreign language at school: A narrative review and empirical study. *Language Learning*, 20(4), 1091–1135.

Bollansée, L., Puimège, E., & Peters, E. (2021). "Watch out! Behind you is the enemy!" An exploratory study into the relationship between extramural English and productive vocabulary knowledge. In V. Werner & F. Tegge (Eds.), *Pop culture in language education* (pp. 199–214). London: Routledge.

Brevik, L.M. (2016). The gaming outliers: Does out-of-school gaming improve boys' reading skills in English as a second language? In E. Elstad (Ed.), *Educational technology and polycontextual bridging* (pp. 39–61). Rotterdam: Sense Publishers.

Briggs, J. G. (2015). Out-of-class language contact and vocabulary gain in a study abroad context. *System*, 53, 129–140.

Bulté, B., Surmont, J., & Martens, L. (2021). The impact of CLIL on the L2 French and L1 Dutch proficiency of Flemish secondary school pupils, *International Journal of Bilingual Education and Bilingualism*. Advance online publication. https://doi.org/10.1080/13670050.2021.2018400

Busby, N. L. (2021). Words from where? Predictors of L2 English vocabulary among Norwegian university students. *ITL - International Journal of Applied Linguistics*, 172(1), 58–84.

Busby, N., & Dahl, A. (2021). Reading rate of academic English texts: Comparing L1 and advanced L2 users in different language environments. *Nordic Journal of English Studies*, 20(1), 36–61.

Bylund, E., Hyltenstam, K., & Abrahamsson, N. (2021). Age of acquisition – not bilingualism – is the primary determinant of less than nativelike L2 ultimate attainment. *Bilingualism: Language and Cognition, 24,* 18–30.

DeKeyser, R. M. (2000). The robustness of critical period effects in second language acquisition. *Studies in Second Language Acquisition, 22*(4), 499–533.

DeKeyser, R. (2003). Implicit and explicit learning. In C. J. Doughty & M. H. Long (Eds.), *The Handbook of second language acquisition* (pp. 313–348). Malden: Blackwell.

DeKeyser, R. (2012). Age effects in second language learning. In S. M. Gass & A. Mackey (Eds.), *The Routledge Handbook of second language acquisition* (pp. 442–460). New York: Routledge.

DeKeyser, R. M. (2018). Age in learning and teaching grammar. In J. I. Liontas (Ed.), *TESOL Encyclopedia of English Language Teaching.* Hoboken: Wiley & Sons.

De Wilde, V., Brysbaert, M., & Eyckmans, J. (2020). Learning English through out-of-school exposure. Which levels of language proficiency are attained and which types of input are important? *Bilingualism: Language and Cognition, 23*(1), 171–185.

De Wilde, V., Brysbaert, M., & Eyckmans, J. (2021). Young learners' L2 English after the onset of instruction: Longitudinal development of L2 proficiency and the role of individual differences. *Bilingualism: Language and Cognition 24*(3), 439–453.

Dressman, M. (2020). Introduction. M. Dressman & R.W. Sadler (Eds.), *The handbook of informal language learning.* Hoboken: Wiley/Blackwell.

EF (Education First) (2020). EF English proficiency index. A ranking of 100 countries and regions by English skills. http://www.ef.com/epi

Ellis, R., & Shintani, N. (2014). *Exploring language pedagogy through second language acquisition research.* New York: Routledge.

European Commission (2012). *First European survey on language competences.* http://ec.europa.eu/languages/library/studies/executive-summary-eslc_en.pdf

European Council (2019). Council Recommendation of 22 May 2019 on a comprehensive approach to the teaching and learning of languages ST/9015/2019/INIT.

González Fernández, B., & Schmitt, N. (2015). How much collocation knowledge do L2 learners have? The effects of frequency and amount of exposure. *ITL-International Journal of Applied Linguistics, 166*(1), 94–126. https://doi.org/doi:10.1075/itl.166.1.03fer

Hannibal Jensen, S. (2017). Gaming as an English language learning resource among young children in Denmark. *CALICO Journal, 34*(1), 1–19.

Huang, B. H., Chang, Y. H. S., Zhi, M., & Niu, L. (2020). The effect of input on bilingual adolescents' long-term language outcomes in a foreign language instruction context. *International Journal of Bilingualism, 24*(1), 8–25.

Jaekel, N., Schurig, M., Florian, M., & Ritter, M. (2017). From early starters to late finishers? A longitudinal study of early foreign language learning in school. *Language Learning, 67*(3), 631–664.

Kuppens, A. H. (2010). Incidental foreign language acquisition from media exposure. *Learning, Media and Technology, 35*(1), 65–85.

Lambelet, A., & Berthele, R. (2015). *Age and foreign language learning in school.* Basingstoke: Palgrave McMillan.

Lefever, S. (2010). English skills of young learners in Iceland "I started talking English when I was 4 years. It just bang...just fall into me." *Ráðstefnurit Netlu – Menntakvika 2010,* December, 1–17.

Lindgren, E., & Muñoz, C. (2013). The influence of exposure, parents, and linguistic distance on young European learners' foreign language comprehension. *International Journal of Multilingualism, 10*(1), 105–129.

Muñoz, C. (Ed.). (2006). *Age and the rate of foreign language learning.* Bristol: Multilingual Matters.

Muñoz, C. (2008). Symmetries and asymmetries of age effects in naturalistic and instructed L2 learning. *Applied Linguistics, 29*(4), 578–596.

Muñoz, C. (2011). Input and long-term effects of starting age in foreign language learning. *IRAL - International Review of Applied Linguistics in Language Teaching, 49*(2), 113–

Muñoz, C. (2012). The significance of intensive exposure as a turning point in learners' histories. In C. Muñoz (Ed.), *Intensive exposure experiences in second language learning* (pp. 141–160). Bristol: Multilingual Matters.

Muñoz, C. (2014). Contrasting effects of starting age and input on the oral performance of foreign language learners. *Applied Linguistics, 35*(4), 1–21.

Pai, R., & Duff, P.1. (2021). Pop culture in teaching Chinese as an additional language. Theory, research, and practice. In V. Werner & F. Tegge (Eds.), *Pop culture in language learning* (pp. 184–197). London: Routledge.

Perry, K. H., & Moses, A. M. (2020). Mobility, media, and multiplicity: Immigrants' informal language learning via media. In M. Dressman, & R.W. Sadler (Eds.), *The handbook of informal language learning* (pp. 215–229). Hoboken: Wiley/Blackwell.

Peters, E. (2018). The effect of out-of-class exposure to English language media on learners' vocabulary knowledge. *ITL - International Journal of Applied Linguistics, 169*(1), 142–168.

Peters, E., Noreillie, A.-S., Heylen, K., Bulté, B., & Desmet, P. (2019). The impact of instruction and out-of-school exposure to foreign language input on learners' vocabulary knowledge in two languages. *Language Learning, 69*(3), 747–782.

Pfenninger, S. E., & Singleton, D. (2017). *Beyond age effects in instructional L2 learning: Revisiting the age factor*. Bristol, England: Multilingual Matters.

Puimège, E., & Peters, E. (2019). Learners' English vocabulary knowledge prior to formal instruction: The role of learner-related and word-related variables. *Language Learning, 69*(4), 943–977.

Samudra, P. G., Wong, K. M., & Neuman, S. B. (2019). Promoting low-income preschoolers' vocabulary learning from educational media: Does repetition support memory for learned word knowledge? *Journal of Cognitive Education and Psychology, 18*(2), 160–173.

Schwarz, M. (2020). Beyond the walls: A mixed methods study of teenagers' extramural English practices and their vocabulary knowledge. Unpublished PhD thesis. University of Vienna.

Sockett, G. (2014). *The online informal learning of English*. Basingstoke: Palgrave Macmillan.

Sundqvist, P. (2009). Extramural English matters: Out-of-school English and its impact on Swedish ninth graders' oral proficiency and vocabulary. (Unpublished doctoral dissertation). Karlstad University Studies, Karlstad, Sweden.

Sundqvist, P. (2019). Commercial-off-the-shelf games in the digital wild and L2 learner vocabulary. *Language Learning & Technology, 23*(1), 87–113.

Sundqvist, P. (2022). Learning across the lifespan: Age, language learning, and technology. In N. Ziegler & M. González-Lloret (Eds.), *The Routledge handbook of SLA and technology* (pp. 343–355). New York: Routledge.

Sundqvist, P., & Sylvén, L. K. (2014). Language-related computer use: Focus on young L2 English learners in Sweden. *ReCALL, 26*(1), 3–20.

Sundqvist, P., & Sylvén, L. K. (2016). *Extramural English in teaching and learning. From theory and research to practice*. London: Palgrave MacMillan.

Sundqvist, P., & Wikström, P. (2015). Out-of-school digital gameplay and in-school L2 English vocabulary outcomes. *System, 51*, 65–76.

Sylvén, L. K., & Sundqvist, P. (2012). Gaming as extramural English L2 learning and L2 proficiency among young learners. *ReCALL, 24*(03), 302–321.

Unsworth, S., Persson, L., Prins, T., & De Bot, K. (2015). An investigation of factors affecting early foreign language learning in the Netherlands. *Applied Linguistics, 36*(5), 527–548.

Vanderplank, R. (2016). *Captioned media in foreign language learning and teaching*. London: Palgrave MacMillan.

Verspoor, M.H., de Bot, K, & van Rein, E. (2011). English as a foreign language. The role of out-of-school language input. In A. De Houwer & A. Wilton (Eds.), *English in Europe today. Sociocultural and educational perspectives* (pp. 147–166). Amsterdam: John Benjamins.

Werner, V. (2018). Linguistics and pop culture: Setting the scene(s). In V. Werner (Ed.), *The language of pop culture* (pp. 3–26). New York: Routledge.

PART III

Supporting LLTBC

9
DIGITAL GAME-BASED LANGUAGE LEARNING IN EXTRAMURAL SETTINGS

Kyle W. Scholz

Introduction

Games are ubiquitous. What may have once been viewed as a niche source of entertainment is now a multibillion-dollar industry (Reuters, 2020). Games that were once rudimentary in design with limited forms of interaction are now complex, player-driven experiences that require problem-solving and communication to immerse the player. These features may look familiar: they are goals second language (L2) instructors may have for their classroom or online language learning environment (de Bot & Larsen-Freeman, 2011).

While interest in digital game-based language learning (DGBLL) has grown increasingly in scholarly discourse (see Cornillie, Thorne & Desmet, 2012; Peterson, 2013; Reinders, 2012; Reinhardt, 2019), its emphasis has been on how instructors can employ these games in traditional, instructor-guided education settings (see Peterson, 2012; Tang & Taguchi, 2020; Zheng et al., 2012 for examples). And yet this is not how games are typically played. Be it alone or with friends, locally or online, games are often enjoyed from the comfort of one's home for entertainment purposes. Particularly with games that are developed with entertainment in mind – often referred to as vernacular games (Sykes & Reinhardt, 2013) – there exists great potential to situate a language learner in an immersive gameplay environment with rich examples of the L2 being studied. As Godwin-Jones (2014) explains, "language learning through gameplay can happen in a wide variety of ways, from a planned learning activity in an instructional environment to an incidental by-product of a gamer's interactions with the game and its associated online activities" (p. 11), but there is decidedly less research being conducted on "incidental" L2 learning (Sundqvist, 2019).

This approach to gameplay – known as extramural DGBLL – does not need to be compromised for L2 learning to occur beyond the classroom. DGBLL can occur with minimal or no intervention from the instructor so long as conditions exist that support active reflection and production of the L2, connecting gameplay to language (Knight et al., 2019). These conditions can take many forms, but in environments removed from the traditional classroom, we often look to spaces that embody communities such as social networking websites (Thorne & Fischer, 2012), discussion boards (Thorne, 2009), and online communities (Godwin-Jones, 2018). These environments form affinity spaces (Gee, 2005) – virtual communities where individuals congregate to discuss their shared interest in a mutual activity.

Engagement in these spaces isn't superfluous to the DGBLL experience but is equally meaningful (Godwin-Jones, 2014).

If we want to encourage students to continue the second language development (SLD) process (Larsen-Freeman, 2015) outside of a formal education context (Godwin-Jones, 2014), we ought to meet them where they are, recognizing that L2 learning and digital gaming share many goals (Sundqvist & Sylvén, 2012, 2014). Does that mean that extramural DGBLL is a magical panacea to combat the apathy students might feel in a traditional classroom? Certainly not, and in many respects, DGBLL loses its luster and excitement if it is forced upon a language learner – the "broccoli" problem, as Reinhardt (2017) explains, where although it may be good for a learner, it may not be as palatable as gameplay designed for entertainment.

For researchers and practitioners of extramural DGBLL, it can be challenging to study how language learners play digital games. We should endeavour to understand the often-uncontrollable nature of DGBLL and the complex gameplay environments that players inhabit.

Key concepts: what is extramural DGBLL?

Scholars have conceptualized the affordances of digital games and their subsequent application to both general learning (Gee, 2008) and specifically L2 learning (Reinhardt, 2019; Sykes, 2017; Sykes & Reinhardt, 2012, 2013) contexts. Of particular interest to extramural DGBLL are the characteristics identified by Sykes and Reinhardt (2013): goals, interaction, feedback, context, and motivation.

- **Goals** are set by players or the digital game itself via a process of goal-orienting. The focus of gameplay – be it solving problems, completing quests, interacting with other players, etc. – is negotiated between game and player, and the resulting language informs the learner's own SLD goals.
- **Interaction** can occur between the player and the game itself, or with others playing the game, the latter of which can spur SLD in unexpected ways dependent upon numerous game-related factors (e.g., frequency of communication, form of communication, vocabulary complexity, etc.).
- **Feedback** is crucial for SLD, and good DGBLL experiences incorporate immediate feedback provision that is meaningful and personalized to the learner (Holden & Sykes, 2013). This feedback may be at times game-oriented, but it serves the critical role of maintaining engagement and sustaining progress.
- **Context**, like authenticity in a L2 task, is embedded in both the game's narrative, as well as the player's approach to the gameplay experience. Good games immerse the player, offering agency and belonging, and so too do effective L2 tasks which situate the learner in an environment that results in meaningful L2 reception and/or production.
- Finally, **motivation** brings many of these other characteristics together to create an experience that players *want* to play, capturing a feeling reminiscent of Csikszentmihalyi's (1990) concept of flow, whereby the games that offer sufficient challenge with requisite skill investment sustain engagement.

Along with these characteristics of DGBLL are theoretical frameworks which conceptualize DGBLL and the roles that educators, learners (as players), and researchers play. These frameworks are independent but can be categorized to establish a starting point due to conceptual similarities. These categorizations can be identified as: *learning-focussed DGBLL*, *entertainment-focussed DGBLL*, and *extramural DGBLL*.

Learning-focussed DGBLL

Learning-focussed DGBLL encompasses games developed primarily for educational purposes, where the focus of the game is to help the player learn something new and therefore positions the player as a learner. To better understand this relationship between game and player, certain metaphors can be employed to represent the forms of interaction that emerge by playing the game.

Digital games can assume either a tutor (*game as instructor*) or tool (*game as facilitator*) role (Levy, 1997). Learning-focussed DGBLL therefore functions as a tutor, as the digital game being played is positioned as an instructor or educator; it aims to provide feedback and teach the player something through an educational lens. This pedagogical approach results in game-based learning (Sykes & Reinhardt, 2012). The games themselves function as the learning experience, without any additional instructor intervention required. Learning-focussed DGBLL studies have focussed on teaching elements of language such as formulaic expressions (Tang & Taguchi, 2020), vocabulary (Neville et al., 2009), or pragmatics through corrective feedback (Cornillie, Clarebout & Desmet, 2012).

Another way to understand the intention of learning-focussed DGBLL is through Arnseth's (2006) distinction between *playing to learn* and *learning to play*. Learning-focussed L2 games expect the player to play the game with the goal to learn – *playing to learn*. Games designed as such ought to be relatively easy to get into, but the challenge (or at times, lack thereof) comes from the education-focussed questions, problems, or tasks in the game (that as a tutor provide the learner with feedback on their success without requiring instructor intervention).

Entertainment-focussed DGBLL

If learning-focussed DGBLL reflects a tutor metaphor, entertainment-focussed DGBLL and its focus on vernacular games functions as a tool (Levy, 1997). Game developers rarely develop these games to focus on both entertainment and education, and therefore, conceptualized as a tool, the game is not designed to be used for SLD purposes. One can argue that many games do in fact "teach" us something (Gee, 2003), but this notion of teaching is different from that which we observe in learning-focussed DGBLL; the feedback players receive, for example, is directed towards game improvement, not L2 proficiency improvement. Nevertheless, vernacular games have been studied to help learn L2 vocabulary (Ranalli, 2008) and practise communication in the L2 (de Haan et al., 2010; Piirainen-Marsh & Tainio, 2009), among other linguistic phenomena. Research has shown too that games played with other players (such as multiplayer games or massive multiplayer online role-playing games) are more beneficial for L2 vocabulary development (Sundqvist, 2019), and these types of games are almost exclusively vernacular in nature.

Entertainment-focussed DGBLL employs a game-enhanced pedagogical approach (Sykes & Reinhardt, 2012), where pedagogy is not embedded in the game itself but is rather mediated by playing games. The types of interaction or tasks that an instructor might encourage a learner to participate in, in conjunction with playing the game, might occur in a classroom, language laboratory, or even in isolation, removed from the gameplay experience. Meaningful SLD is however contingent upon L2 task design or discussion about the game, guided by the instructor (Collentine, 2011).

In turn, this approach to DGBLL follows the *learning to play* analogy (Arnseth, 2006) whereby the mechanics of the game itself may pose challenges, especially for a learner who is unaccustomed to games of a certain genre – or games at all (Rama et al., 2012). Yet these games often teach the player *how* to play the game, and what may be viewed as handholding can in fact be a valuable learning experience in and of itself; the learner may begin implicitly learning the L2 while simultaneously learning to play the game. Once game mastery becomes feasible, a heightened focus can be placed on SLD through the completion of L2 tasks or discussion in the L2 about the gameplay experience.

Learning-focussed and entertainment-focussed DGBLL represent most evidence-based examples of how digital games have been employed for SLD, yet they also remain limited in the scope of analysis that can be done. Regardless of the pedagogy or type of game chosen, these require instructional intervention. Although understandable, what is missing in this dichotomy are digital games that are enjoyed in their intended setting – typically in the comfort of one's own home – and which still support SLD. This form of DGBLL can be conceptualized as extramural DGBLL.

Extramural DGBLL

Understood as an ecological framing of DGBLL (Reinhardt, 2017; Reinhardt & Thorne, 2016), or DGBLL as a complex adaptive system (Scholz, 2017; Scholz & Schulze, 2017), this theoretical framework aspires to understand how interconnected games are with the individuals that play them, their modes of interaction with the game, and the affinity spaces that support further engagement beyond the game itself. Interaction extends beyond player and game to player and other players (local or global), or player and broader gaming community. An ecological/complex adaptive system understanding of extramural DGBLL recognizes that players themselves may be choosing what game to play, so the design of game-specific L2 learning tasks becomes challenging or even questionable (Fischer, 2007).

Rather than ascribing a learning to play or playing to learn distinction to this approach, the players identify their own purpose for playing a game. Those with more familiarity of the game genre may opt to play a game that is second nature and easy to pick up, whereas others may enquire into DGBLL due to an interest in SLD and likely need to learn to play the game first. If we therefore recognize the limitations of prescribing how students ought to interact with a digital game, we can instead embrace the agency and autonomy of authentic gameplay and work in partnership with it, rather than try to control it. Studies that have been conducted on extramural DGBLL have explored the chaotic nature of interaction with the game (Desmarais et al., 1997), the natural emergence of L2 through organic in-game conversations (Thorne, 2008), the impact of compensating linguistic knowledge for gameplay experience (Rama et al., 2012), and the benefits of this form of gameplay for gamers and non-gamers alike (Scholz, 2017; Sundqvist, 2019).

The utility of affinity spaces (Gee, 2005) is requisite to understand how extramural DGBLL void of instructor intervention can still result in meaningful and focussed L2 practice. An affinity space is an online community – a digital game, discussion board, wiki, chat room, etc. – where individuals with a common, shared interest congregate to interact while engaged in a mutual activity (Gee, 2005, 2017; Rama et al., 2012). Affiliation to the space comes from general interest in the activity, and value is placed on experience rather than power (Gee, 2005). As learners interact with other players in the affinity space, they attempt to reproduce language that was produced or observed in the digital game, thereby requiring the ability to understand the meaning of the vocabulary they encountered, or in more advanced scenarios, the ability to formulate linguistic structures that demonstrate knowledge of syntax or pragmatics encountered in-game.

Key issues: key theoretical and practical issues in extramural DGBLL

Extramural DGBLL remains an emergent field of study (Sundqvist, 2019), and as a result, many key issues require further consideration. A robust theoretical understanding of DGBLL has been developing (Cornillie et al., 2012; Peterson, 2013; Reinhardt, 2017, 2019; Sykes, 2017), but extramural forms of DGBLL require further analysis. One can look to the growing body of research on L2 learning in informal contexts (Dressman & Sadler, 2020) to gain an idea of some recommended theoretical or methodological considerations, but DGBLL has its own challenges that compound those faced when attempting to determine how learners develop an L2 in non-classroom contexts (Knight et al., 2019). Practitioners can also look to research on DGBLL-at-large to determine what types of studies have been conducted, which linguistic phenomena are under investigation, and which research methods may have utility, but this too serves as only a starting point and comes with assumptions that may not be relevant to the extramural environment until put into practice.

Extramural DGBLL therefore requires consideration of the following three key issues: *DGBLL proficiency*, *novelty*, and *appropriate methodologies for extramural DGBLL*.

DGBLL proficiency

Educators might expect a certain level of proficiency with digital gaming in order to explain the benefits of DGBLL to students. Learning-focussed DGBLL requires knowledge of what games exist for instructional purposes, whereas entertainment-focussed DGBLL requires knowledge of gaming conventions to design tasks that reflect the L2 phenomena encountered in the vernacular game. Extramural DGBLL may not require such proficiency, but awareness of effective gaming practices and what strengths games have for SLD (Sykes & Reinhardt, 2012) is nevertheless beneficial in guiding conversations about these games or speaking to the affordances of games for L2 learning beyond the classroom. Knowing, for example, which game genres support interaction between players, or which focus more heavily on game narrative, may assist learners as they begin to venture into extramural DGBLL.

Such knowledge cannot, nor should be, assumed. Fortunately, there exists a growing body of literature on the affordances of DGBLL, and even a cursory reading of this field can reinforce the fundamental potential of digital games in extramural settings – the ability to practise the L2 in a digital environment that is removed from the in-person classroom, where the very nature of the games being played requires engagement with technology that goes beyond rote textbook memorization or prescriptive exercises designed to teach a specific concept (Knight et al., 2019; Sundqvist, 2019). But yet even with a core understanding of DGBLL, educators may still feel expected to guide learners, or to locate affinity spaces where learners can discuss the games they have played as a form of SLD. These spaces, removed from the digital game itself but which sustain interaction about the game, are crucial components of the gameplay experience (Thorne & Fischer, 2012); as such, educators may feel faced with a daunting task to identify how best to guide their learners.

Developing DGBLL proficiency is not just a challenge for educators, but for learners as well. Digital gaming arguably does not have the same presence or ubiquity as films, music, or literature among prospective learners, and simultaneously requires an investment that may neither be financially nor be technologically reasonable (Liou, 2012). It is therefore challenging to simply encourage a learner to play any given digital game to help learn an L2. At the very least, educators should be aware that developing proficiency with DGBLL is just as much a task for learners as it is for themselves.

DGBLL novelty

Digital gaming is a fickle pastime. Games quickly lose their lustre as gamers are presented with an almost endless repertoire to choose from. The novelty of digital games can therefore prove problematic for researchers and practitioners alike. Research published within the last ten years is rife with examples of games that are simply not widely played anymore (Urun et al., 2017; Wu et al., 2014), and in some cases, not even playable (Peterson, 2012). The results of the studies are nevertheless insightful and help us to understand the utility of DGBLL, but the practicality is lost – the results are not as easily repeatable if the games cannot be purchased or even made accessible.

This is further complicated by the need to find appropriate affinity spaces to participate in to practise the use of the L2. Should the game be too archaic, or simply of a genre that is less popular, the likelihood that an active affinity space exists is reduced. Since these spaces are created by the players in many cases, or at the very least, sustained by the players, there is little a researcher or educator can do to create an affinity space that serves a similar purpose. In many ways this is directly linked to the issue of DGBLL proficiency: if we can establish a base proficiency with DGBLL, it becomes easier to identify games that do not suffer from issues of novelty, and therefore are more likely to benefit SLD.

Appropriate methodologies for extramural DGBLL

Researching extramural DGBLL requires different methodologies than typical experimental research design. This is due to extramural DGBLL functioning, at its best, in environments that are removed from overt researcher or educator intervention. This comes with potential limitations (Knight et al., 2019), namely, that of rigor: when the approach to DGBLL is defined by its inability to directly monitor the actions of the learner/player, traditional notions of rigor are complicated by the methodology employed (Fischer, 2007). Controlled laboratory conditions are not possible, but nor should they be. Extramural DGBLL should ideally occur at a location and time of the learner's own choosing.

Appropriate methodologies are therefore required to capture gameplay experiences that cannot be directly monitored. Indeed, even with non-extramural DGBLL activities, the importance of employing appropriate methodologies to account for complexity in interaction has been considered (Desmarais et al., 1997; Liou, 2012). Capturing fully and accurately what a game player experiences when playing a game is challenging (Godwin-Jones, 2014), with studies attempting to employ expensive user-tracking technology such as eye-tracking that, while certainly bringing further insight into the DGBLL experience, are not sustainable and still require instructor or researcher intervention (Collentine, 2011). Furthermore, although such methodologies are excellent at capturing rigorous data on what students do when interacting with a game, the rationale behind their choices is less clear (Fischer, 2007).

Methodologies that aim to properly understand extramural DGBLL require an element of trust in the learner, and the researcher's willingness to sift through copious amounts of data that may not directly relate to the identified research question. They can nevertheless provide extensive, authentic, and detailed information (Reinhardt, 2017) that can be analysed to detect phenomena such as frequency of linguistic markers, L2 observation/reception/ production, and others.

Implications: towards a better understanding of extramural DGBLL

Many DGBLL studies remain firmly rooted in the classroom or some form of instructor-controlled environment and have demonstrated their value for SLD (see Hung et al., 2018). We have more nuanced analyses of games and their structures, examining syntax (Zheng, 2012), pragmatics (Sykes, 2017; Sykes & Dubreil, 2019), and other linguistic phenomena. A controlled environment does inherently have limitations, however, as it precludes immersing oneself in a gameplay environment to explore at one's own leisure. Therein lies the value of playing/learning in one's own home or other non-educational setting, and therein also lies the challenge in understanding what aspects of an L2 have been developed through the gameplay experience.

As researchers begin to analyse the many approaches to extramural DGBLL, it is imperative that we allow for and encourage studies that are largely exploratory in nature as opposed to strictly experimental. Experimental research design has many benefits, but it also requires controlled conditions to understand how modified variables produce discernible results. The extramural DGBLL environment ought to be free from as many researcher/educator-controlled parameters as possible to ensure it captures authentic free play. There may nevertheless exist aspects of the gameplay experience that are inauthentic, such as the understanding that indirect observation may be occurring through the recording of chat transcripts, the implicit obligation to interact with other players about the gameplay experience, or simply the participation in a research study in and of itself (Knight et al., 2019).

Of course, research still needs to be conducted, so the entire experience cannot completely omit researcher or practitioner intervention. Rather than impose upon the act of playing the game and monitoring the actions the learner takes, the researcher can be involved after gameplay, understanding how the learner reflects upon or discusses the played experience (Scholz, 2017; Scholz & Schulze, 2017). Regardless of the approach taken, a combination of both comprehensive gameplay data in conjunction with participant response helps to ensure that results are reliable and can provide an accurate indication of the gameplay process' effectiveness.

To understand the multitudinous approaches that a learner can take playing a digital game, and the resulting SLD that may emerge, a theoretical framework that can account for the resulting complexity of this experience is necessary. Researchers have explored complex adaptive systems (Godwin-Jones, 2018, 2019; Larsen-Freeman & Cameron, 2008a, 2008b) and ecological (Reinhardt, 2017; van Lier, 2004) frameworks, and when viewed through a DGBLL lens posit that gameplay does not occur in isolation. In fact, many aspects of gameplay require an understanding of the player, their SLD experiences, their environment, the game, and other players. The interaction among these many interwoven elements results in a complex system where time and change are the primary units of analysis (Larsen-Freeman & Cameron, 2008a), and where we seek to understand all elements of the SLD experience, rather than attempt to reduce an analysis to singular components (Larsen-Freeman, 2002). Schulze and Scholz (2016) identify how characteristics of complex adaptive systems (e.g., nonlinearity, interconnectedness, change, iteration, emergent properties) can be aligned with computer-assisted language learning, exploring their application to various online and DGBLL scenarios (Cornillie et al., 2012; Liou, 2012; Marek & Wu, 2014; Sockett, 2013; Zheng, 2012).

The inherent complexity in a digital game-based complex adaptive system emerges due to interaction between players and the game, resulting in often unpredictable change within the system. Due to the nonlinearity of change that does occur, it is impossible to determine the exact outcome or result of the variation that may be expected (de Bot et al., 2007); rather, we attempt to understand as best as possible the trajectories of change that do occur by analysing the system using retrodictive qualitative modelling (Dörnyei, 2014). If we determine the current point of the system at the time of our analysis, we can attempt to trace it back to its initial conditions and argue, based upon the many variables that comprise the system, which conditions may have led to the emergent change (Dörnyei, 2014, 2017).

This is useful as we learn how players interact with games, such as how increasing player agency via the choices they make may not result in improved L2 production (Collentine, 2011) or that players navigate game environments in complex ways, from linear to chaotic (Desmarais et al., 1997; Fischer, 2007). Particularly in Desmarais et al.'s study, we learn that "a chaotic schema is not always related to problems. It may indicate that the learner is comfortable in a multimedia learning environment that he/she does not want to spend time on activities that do not fit his/her needs and that he/she tries to take full advantage of possibilities of the system" (Desmarais et al., 1997, p. 334). In these cases, beginning with a hypothesis, regardless of how well founded it may be, is challenging due to the immense complexity that exists in gameplay.

For researchers, this requires exploring how language in the system emerges, critically examining the myriad factors which may play a role in the development of L2 proficiency. The goal is to understand the change that occurs via extramural DGBLL by first examining the change (e.g., new vocabulary or grammatical construct developed, modified interaction behaviour, etc.), and then discern through the collected game-reported data which conditions may have caused said change to occur.

To facilitate such an analysis in the extramural environment, we ultimately require some form of computer-based tracking to operationalize what SLD may look like via DGBLL. Computer-based tracking does not need to feel impersonal or void of researcher lens, and instead can be viewed similar to ethnographic research (Fischer, 2007), exploring how learners interact with the complex adaptive system and what SLD emerges as a result. Most commonly this comes in the form of chat transcripts captured by the game as it is being played (Rama et al., 2012; Scholz, 2017), which detail every interaction made and observed by the player and are ideal for thorough analysis.

Naturally, learners too will need support to navigate the complexity of extramural DGBLL. While we may simply defer to their own exploration and judgement to find appropriate games to play (which, provided they are in the L2, many vernacular games *would* adhere to Sykes and Reinhardt's (2013) characteristics of games for L2 learning, and therefore *could* function appropriately), certainly guidance and direction can only help. Some game genres are easier to point learners towards than others – massively multiplayer online role-playing games (MMORPGs) of any variety have been shown to have tangible benefits for extramural DGBLL (Peterson, 2013; Rama et al., 2012; Scholz, 2017; Thorne, 2008). If educators are unsure where to begin, these games provide an affinity space directly embedded in the game due to the social interaction that is fundamental to the game's design.

Future directions: participatory extramural DGBLL

The complex, learner-driven extramural DGBLL environment has significant potential for SLD, yet concerns nevertheless remain. There will always exist limitations with extramural

DGBLL, such as issues relating to access and equity. DGBLL requires additional technology – either a relatively expensive video game console, or a computer with sufficient computing power to run the games that accommodate the most active online communities. Certainly, the act of participating in gameplay itself is valuable for DGBLL, but it raises the question: is it necessary? Can DGBLL still exist without the physical act of playing the game? Does an affinity space still hold value for a member if they do not have active experience playing the game in question?

Research into online communities and Internet-mediated communication has examined at length the role online communities play for SLD (see Gee, 2017; Kessler, 2018; Rama et al., 2012; Sockett & Toffoli, 2012), and there exist many online communities that are game-based, or which solely are designed to discuss a particular digital game or game series. These can be found in social-networking websites such as Reddit (Isbell, 2018; Reinhardt, 2019; Yeh & Swinehart, 2020), or on platforms like Discord (Wulanjani, 2018). The resulting conversations allow for the sharing of stories, experiences, achievements, memes, and more. These communities allow for an interest in digital gaming to be fostered without the financial barriers that can exclude interested learners. To this end, these remain affinity spaces without requiring direct experience playing the game to be able to engage in discussion. And just as we see with extramural DGBLL, the autonomy and agency associated with participating in an online community can result in valuable, meaningful SLD opportunities (Reinhardt, 2019).

We may simultaneously be experiencing a shift away from playing games to observing games *being played*. Livestreaming of games via Twitch.tv, YouTube Gaming, or Facebook Gaming has grown in popularity as individuals resonate more with the personality playing the game than the game itself (Sjöblom & Hamari, 2017). Payne et al. (2017) describe the experience of engaging with others on a streaming service such as Twitch as:

> an informal event where streamers and audiences form organically-based discussions without formal constraints. This means that teachers (streamers) may be experts or novices. Similarly, learners (viewers) may come from a variety of levels of expertise with varying degrees of interest in learning (versus watching for entertainment value). (p. 98)

These streaming services may therefore serve the role of *participatory* extramural DGBLL due to their close alignment with the concept of the affinity space and platform's design being focussed on players of the game and their own tight-knit communities (Payne et al., 2017) without requiring actual gameplay. Although the participatory experience of watching a game being played inevitably varies from the act of playing the game itself, games of various genres, including roleplaying (Piirainen-Marsh & Tainio, 2009) and music (de Haan et al., 2010) games, have been shown to be beneficial for SLD when played in tandem. Individuals often take turns playing the game, where the observer has a heightened ability to reflect on what is occurring and uses the L2 to engage in conversation with the player.

The aforementioned key issues, namely, that of DGBLL proficiency and novelty, may be addressed through this form of participatory extramural DGBLL. Proficiency with games is no longer required, as interested learners can choose to watch a game being played in their chosen L2 without needing to know how to play the game. Issues relating to novelty too are remedied by the stream itself acting as the affinity space; so long as there are a sufficient number of other participants to communicate with in the affinity space, the L2 can be practised.

Do these participatory extramural DGBLL opportunities present similar SLD potential as playing the game? That remains to be seen and requires further research. As the aforementioned observation-based studies argue (de Haan et al., 2010; Piirainen-Marsh & Tainio, 2009), the discussion of the game is fruitful for SLD, and as many other studies have shown, discussion and use of the language encountered in game are crucial to learn the L2.

Conclusion

As we continue to investigate the efficacy of extramural DGBLL, it is imperative that learners, educators, and researchers are guided in navigating what can be seemingly overwhelming terrain. The identified key issues – DGBLL proficiency, novelty, and to some extent, employing appropriate methodologies – can be barriers to entry for any prospective individual interested in further exploring extramural DGBLL. Future research may look towards curating a list of not only vernacular games that have potential for SLD, but in association, the affinity spaces that exist to facilitate interaction around the digital game. In some instances, these may simply be sites of participatory extramural DGBLL.

The strength of extramural DGBLL has always been meeting learners in their own space, creating a learning experience that is entertaining, engaging, and immersive. We nevertheless need to be aware of the challenges that come with encouraging extramural DGBLL, but as research is conducted and technology evolves, we should remain committed to understanding the ubiquitous nature of digital gaming in our lives and its applicability to SLD.

Reflection Questions

1 How might you design a research project that employs DGBLL without direct instructor/researcher observation in your educational context?
2 Which variables influence the complex adaptive systems in your educational and institutional contexts? Are there certain factors that ought to be controlled for?
3 How might participatory extramural DGBLL be studied, and what advantages/disadvantages do you envision in comparison to player-controlled extramural DGBLL?

Recommended Readings

Godwin-Jones, R. (2018). Chasing the butterfly effect: Informal language learning online as a complex system. *Language Learning & Technology, 22*(2), 8–27.
Godwin-Jones draws an explicit connection between complex adaptive systems and informal language learning, focussing on digital environments as complex systems. Three complex adaptive systems characteristics with relevance to informal language learning are highlighted: nonlinear development paths, self-organizational character, and a focus on emergent outcomes. Examples are drawn from online communities, online gaming, and multimedia.

Knight, S. W., Marean, L., & Sykes, J. M. (2019). Gaming and informal language learning. In M. Dressman & R. Sadler (Eds.), *The Handbook of Informal Language Learning* (pp. 101–115). Hoboken, NJ: John Wiley & Sons.
Knight, Marean and Sykes depict the emerging field of informal language learning and digital gaming's contribution to it, including gamified apps such as Duolingo that have game characteristics, without being games themselves. The multifaceted concept of gameplay is unpacked, with its benefits for L2 learning in informal spaces addressed in detail.

Sykes, J., & Reinhardt, J. (2013). *Language at Play: Digital Games in Second and Foreign Language Teaching and Learning.* New York: Pearson.
A definitive source on digital game-based language learning, Sykes and Reinhardt explain the affordances of DGBLL and its applicability to pedagogy in the L2 classroom and beyond. The core characteristics of DGBLL – goals, interaction, feedback, motivation, and context – are identified and explored at length, providing relevance for researchers and educators alike.

References

Arnseth, H. C. (2006). Learning to play or playing to learn – A critical account of the models of communication informing educational research on computer gameplay. *Game Studies*, *6*(1). Retrieved from http://gamestudies.org/0601/articles/arnseth

Collentine, K. (2011). Learner autonomy in a task-based 3D world and production. *Language Learning & Technology*, *15*(3), 50–67.

Cornillie, F., Clarebout, G., & Desmet, P. (2012). Between learning and playing? Exploring learners' perceptions of corrective feedback in an immersive game for English pragmatics. *ReCALL*, *24*(3), 257–278.

Cornillie, F., Thorne, S. L., & Desmet, P. (2012). Editorial: Digital games for language learning: From hype to insight? *ReCALL*, *24*(3), 243–256.

Csikszentmihalyi, M. (1990). *Flow: The Psychology of Optimal Experience*. New York: Harper & Row.

De Bot, K., & Larsen-Freeman, D. (2011). Researching second language development from a dynamic systems theory perspective. In M. H. Verspoor, K. de Bot, & W. Lowie (Eds.), *A Dynamic Approach to Second Language Development* (pp. 5–24). Amsterdam: John Benjamins.

De Bot, K., Lowie, W., & Verspoor, M. H. (2007). A dynamic systems theory approach to second language acquisition. *Bilingualism: Language and Cognition*, *10*(1), 7–21.

De Haan, J., Reed, M., & Kuwada, K. (2010). The effect of interactivity with a music video game on second language vocabulary recall. *Language Learning & Technology*, *14*(2), 74–94.

Desmarais, L., Duquette, L., Renié, D., & Laurier, M. (1997). Evaluating learning and interactions in a multimedia environment. *Language Resources and Evaluation*, *31*(4), 327–349.

Dörnyei, Z. (2014). Researching complex dynamic systems: "Retrodictive qualitative odelling" in the language classroom. *Language Teaching*, *47*(1), 80–91.

Dörnyei, Z. (2017). Conceptualizing learner characteristics in a complex, dynamic world. *Complexity Theory and Language Development: In Celebration of Diane Larsen-Freeman*, 79–96.

Dressman, M., & Sadler, R. W. (Eds.). (2020). *The Handbook of Informal Language Learning*. Hoboken, NJ: John Wiley & Sons.

Fischer, R. (2007). How do we know what students are actually doing? Monitoring students' behavior in CALL. *Computer Assisted Language Learning*, *20*(5), 409–442. https://doi.org/10.1080/09588220701746013

Gee J. P. (2003). *What Video Games Have to Teach Us about Learning and Literacy*. New York: Palgrave Macmillan.

Gee, J. P. (2005). Semiotic social spaces and affinity spaces: From the age of mythology to today's schools. In D. Barton & K. Tusting (Eds.), *Beyond Communities of Practice: Language, Power, and Social Context* (pp. 214–232). Cambridge: Cambridge University Press.

Gee, J. P. (2008). Learning and games. In K. Salen (Ed.), *The Ecology of Games: Connecting Youth, Games, and Learning* (pp. 21–40). Cambridge, MA: MIT Press.

Gee, J. P. (2017). Affinity spaces and 21st century learning. *Educational Technology*, *57*(2) 27–31.

Godwin-Jones, R. (2014). Games in language learning: Opportunities and challenges. *Language Learning & Technology*, *18*(2), 9–19.

Godwin-Jones, R. (2018). Chasing the butterfly effect: Informal language learning online as a complex system. *Language Learning & Technology*, *22*(2), 8–27.

Godwin-Jones, R. (2019). Riding the digital wilds: Learner autonomy and informal language learning. *Language Learning & Technology*, *23*(1), 8–25. https://doi.org/10125/44667

Holden, C., & Sykes, J. M. (2013). Complex L2 pragmatic feedback via place-based mobile games. In N. Taguchi & J. M. Sykes (Eds.), *Technology in Interlanguage Pragmatics Research and Teaching* (pp. 155–183). Amsterdam: John Benjamins. https://doi.org/10.1075/lllt.36. 09hol

Hung, H. T., Yang, J. C., Hwang, G. J., Chu, H. C., & Wang, C. C. (2018). A scoping review of research on digital game-based language learning. *Computers & Education*, *126*, 89–104.

Isbell, D. R. (2018). Online informal language learning: Insights from a Korean learning community. *Language Learning & Technology*, *22*(3), 82–102. https://doi.org/10125/44658

Kessler, G. (2018). Technology and the future of language teaching. *Foreign Language Annals*, *51*(1), 205–218.

Knight, S. W., Marean, L., & Sykes, J. M. (2019). Gaming and informal language learning. In M. Dressman & R. Sadler (Eds.), *The Handbook of Informal Language Learning* (pp. 101–115). Hoboken, NJ: John Wiley & Sons.

Larsen-Freeman, D. (2002). Language acquisition and language use form a chaos/complexity theory perspective. In C. Kramsch (Ed.), *Language Acquisition and Language Socialization: Ecological Perspectives* (pp. 33–46). London: Continuum.

Larsen-Freeman, D. (2015). Saying what we mean: Making the case for second language acquisition to become second language development. *Language Teaching, 48*, 491–505.

Larsen-Freeman, D., & Cameron, L. (2008a). *Complex Systems and Applied Linguistics.* Oxford: Oxford University Press.

Larsen-Freeman, D., & Cameron, L. (2008b). Research methodology on language development from a complex systems perspective. *The Modern Language Journal, 92*(2), 200–213.

Levy, M. (1997). *Computer-Assisted Language Learning: Context and Conceptualization.* New York: Oxford University Press.

Liou, H.-C. (2012). The roles of Second Life in a college computer-assisted language learning (CALL) course in Taiwan, ROC. *Computer Assisted Language Learning, 25*(4), 365–382.

Marek, M. W., & Wu, W.-C. V. (2014). Environmental factors affecting computer assisted language learning success: A complex dynamic systems conceptual model. *Computer Assisted Language Learning, 27*(6), 560–578.

Neville, D. O., Shelton, B. E., & McInnis, B. (2009). Cybertext redux: Using digital game-based learning to teach L2 vocabulary, reading, and culture. *Computer Assisted Language Learning, 22*(5), 409–424.

Payne, K., Keith, M. J., Schuetzler, R. M., & Giboney, J. S. (2017). Examining the learning effects of live streaming video game instruction over Twitch. *Computers in Human Behavior, 77*, 95–109. https://doi.org/10.1016/j.chb.2017.08.029

Peterson, M. (2012). Language learner interaction in a massively multiplayer online role-playing game (MMORPG). In H. Reinders (Ed.), *Computer Games in Language Teaching and Learning* (p. 7092). London: Palgrave Macmillan

Peterson, M. (2013). *Computer Games and Language Learning.* New York: Palgrave Macmillan.

Piirainen–Marsh, A., & Tainio, L. (2009). Collaborative game-play as a site for participation and situated learning of a second language. *Scandanavian Journal of Educational Research, 53*(2), 167–183.

Rama, P. S., Black, R. W., Van Es, E., & Warschauer, M. (2012). Affordances for second language learning in World of Warcraft. *ReCALL, 24*(3), 322–338.

Ranalli, J. (2008). Learning English with The Sims: Exploiting authentic computer simulation games for L2 learning. *Computer Assisted Language Learning, 21*(5), 441–455.

Reinders, H. (Ed.). (2012). *Digital Games in Language Learning and Teaching.* Basingstoke, UK: Palgrave Macmillan.

Reinhardt, J. (2017). Digital gaming in L2 teaching and learning. In C. A. Chapelle & S. Sauro (Eds.), *The Handbook of Technology in Second Language Teaching and Learning* (pp. 202–216). Hoboken, NJ: John Wiley & Sons.

Reinhardt, J. (2019). *Gameful Second and Foreign Language Teaching and Learning.* Basingstoke: Palgrave-Macmillan

Reinhardt, J., & Thorne, S. (2016). Metaphors for digital games and language learning. In F. Farr & L. Murray (Eds.), *The Routledge handbook of language learning and technology* (pp. 415–430). Oxford, UK: Routledge.

Reuters (2020, May 11). *Report: Gaming Revenue to Top $159B in 2020.* https://www.reuters.com/article/esports-business-gaming-revenues-idUSFLM8jkJMl

Scholz, K. (2017). Encouraging free play: Extramural digital game-based language learning as a complex adaptive system. *Calico Journal, 34*(1), 39–57.

Scholz, K., & Schulze, M. (2017). Digital-gaming trajectories and second language development. *Language Learning & Technology, 21*(1), 100–120.

Schulze, M., & Scholz, K. (2016). CALL theory: Complex adaptive systems. In C. Caws & M-J. Hamel's (Eds.), *Language-Learner Computer Interactions: Theory, Methodology and CALL Applications* (pp. 65–87). Amsterdam: John Benjamins.

Sjöblom, M., & Hamari, J. (2017). Why do people watch others play video games? An empirical study on the motivations of Twitch users. *Computers in Human Behavior, 75*, 985–996. 10.1016/j.chb.2016.10.019.

Sockett, G. (2013). Understanding the online informal learning of English as a complex dynamic system: An emic approach. *ReCALL, 25*(1), 48–62.

Sockett, G., & Toffoli, D. (2012). Beyond learner autonomy: A dynamic systems view of the informal learning of English in virtual online communities. *ReCALL*, *24*(2), 138–151.

Sundqvist, P. (2019). Commercial-off-the-shelf games in the digital wild and L2 learner vocabulary. *Language Learning & Technology*, *23*(1), 87–113. https://doi.org/10125/44674

Sundqvist, P., & Sylvén, L. K. (2012b). World of VocCraft: Computer games and Swedish learners' L2 English vocabulary. In *Digital Games in Language Learning and Teaching* (pp. 189–208). Great Britain: Palgrave Macmillan.

Sundqvist, P., & Sylvén, L. K. (2014). Language-related computer use: Focus on young L2 English learners in Sweden. *ReCALL*, *26*(1), 3–20.

Sykes, J. (2017). Technologies for teaching and learning intercultural competence and interlanguage pragmatics In C. A. Chapelle & S. Sauro (Eds.), *The Handbook of Technology in Second Language Teaching and Learning*(pp. 119–133). Hoboken, NJ: John Wiley & Sons.

Sykes, J. M., & Dubreil, S. (2019). Pragmatics learning in digital games and virtual environments. In N. Taguchi's (Ed.) *The Routledge Handbook of Second Language Acquisition and Pragmatics* (pp.387–399). London, UK: Routledge.

Sykes, J., & Reinhardt, J. (2012). Conceptualizing digital game-mediated L2 learning and pedagogy: Game-enhanced and game-based research and practice. In H. Reinders (Ed.), *Digital Games in Language Learning and Teaching* (pp. 32–49). Great Britain: Palgrave Macmillan.

Sykes, J., & Reinhardt, J. (2013). *Language at Play: Digital Games in Second and Foreign Language Teaching and Learning.* New York: Pearson.

Tang, X., & Taguchi, N. (2020). Designing and using a scenario-based digital game to teach Chinese formulaic expressions. *CALICO Journal*, *37*(1), 1–22. https://doi.org/10.1558/cj.38574

Thorne, S. L. (2008). Transcultural communication in open internet environments and massively multiplayer online games. In S. Sieloff Magnan (Ed.), *Mediating Discourse Online* (pp. 305–327). Amsterdam: John Benjamins.

Thorne, S. L. (2009). 'Community', semiotic flows, and mediated contribution to activity. *Language Teaching*, *42*(1), 81–94. doi:10.1017/S0261444808005429

Thorne, S. L., & Fischer, I. (2012). Online gaming as sociable media. *Alsic. Apprentissage des Langues et Systèmes d'Information et de Communication*, *15*(1), 1–25.

Urun, M. F., Aksoy, H., & Comez, R. (2017). Supporting foreign language vocabulary learning through Kinect-based gaming. *International Journal of Game-Based Learning (IJGBL)*, *7*(1), 20–35.

Van Lier, L. (2004). *The Ecology and Semiotics of Language Learning: A Sociocultural Perspective.* Boston, MA: Kluwer Academic.

Wu, M. L., Richards, K., & Saw, G. K. (2014). Examining a massive multiplayer online role-playing game as a digital game-based learning platform. *Computers in the Schools*, *31*(1–2), 65–83.

Wulanjani, A. N. (2018, July). Discord application: Turning a voice chat application for gamers into a virtual listening class. In *English Language and Literature International Conference (ELLiC) Proceedings* (Vol. 2, pp. 115–119).

Yeh, E., & Swinehart, N. (2020). Social media literacy in L2 environments: Navigating anonymous user-generated content. *Computer Assisted Language Learning*, *37*(1), 66–84.

Zheng, D. (2012). Caring in the dynamics of design and languaging: Exploring second language learning in 3D virtual spaces. *Language Sciences*, *34*, 543–558.

Zheng, D., Newgarden, K., & Young, M. F. (2012). Multimodal analysis of language learning in World of Warcraft play: Languaging as values-realizing. *ReCALL*, *24*(3), 339–360.

10
FOSTERING LEARNERS' SELF-REGULATION AND COLLABORATION SKILLS AND STRATEGIES FOR MOBILE LANGUAGE LEARNING BEYOND THE CLASSROOM

Olga Viberg and Agnes Kukulska-Hulme

Introduction

Many second language learners, including older K-12 students, university students and migrant adult learners, are in great need of guidance and support in developing sufficient and appropriate language skills to participate in higher levels of education or to get a job. Language classes alone do not provide sufficient opportunities to progress quickly and in ways that are tailored to the specific needs of people in these groups. Moreover, in view of the recent widespread moves to remote online teaching and learning worldwide (Czerniewicz et al., 2020), effective learner support in settings beyond the physical classroom has become even more critical (Viberg, Wasson, & Kukulska-Hulme, 2020).

Researchers have highlighted that learners in increasingly online learning settings can benefit from the enactment of self-regulated and collaborative learning strategies, skills and knowledge. Self-regulated learning (SRL) can influence positively and predict learners' academic performance (Zimmerman, 1990; Viberg, Khalil, & Baars, 2020) and their ability to acquire a second language efficiently (Oxford, 2016; Botero, Questier, & Zhu, 2019; Viberg & Andersson, 2019; Viberg, Khalil, & Bergman, 2021; Yang, 2020). Collaborative learning activities, assisted by the use of mobile technologies, can "create opportunities for practising language skills and building new knowledge and relationships inside and outside the classroom, as well as in settings where there are no classrooms but there may be other meeting spaces or joint activities" (Kukulska-Hulme & Viberg, 2018, p. 208). Hence, in this chapter we argue that support for language learners should: (1) focus on fostering language learners' *self-regulated learning* and *collaborative learning* strategies and skills that will enable them to take better control over their own learning processes across learning environments and (2) carefully consider the design and situated use of mobile technologies, which have been found to be beneficial for second language learners in developing those strategies and skills (e.g., Shadiev, Liu, & Hwang, 2019; Viberg, Mavroudi, & Ma, 2020; Zhang, Cheng, & Chen,

2020). We also argue that in the mobile-assisted language learning design process, we need to build on recent advances in the fields of learning analytics (see, e.g., Viberg, Wasson, & Kukulska-Hulme, 2020) and artificial intelligence (e.g., Dodigovic, 2020) to be able to offer adaptive language learning paths that address the learners' needs across learning settings.

To examine these issues in more detail, we identified and analysed a sample of published empirical studies concerned with learner self-regulation and collaboration when learning a new language in and beyond the classroom. The sample was bounded by limiting the publication period to peer reviewed papers and chapters in the most recent decade (2010–2020) and searching with keywords related to mobile devices and learning (e.g., smartphones, iPads, mobile assisted language learning, situated language learning, contextual language learning). Related search terms for *self-regulated language learning* included self-directed, self-regulated and autonomous learning, while related search terms for 'collaborative language learning' included cooperative, group and social learning. In these studies, learning was sometimes a combination of in-class and out-of-class (or outdoor) activities, but we excluded papers that were entirely focussed on in-class learning. When making a final selection for our analysis (total of 20 papers), we chose studies where there was a clear concern with the development of skills and strategies and/or consideration of technology or learning designs. In the subsequent analysis of the chosen papers, we paid particular attention to any mechanisms provided by researchers, teachers or system/learning designers to develop or support language learners' self-regulated and collaborative language learning. The results of this analysis contribute to the key constructs and key issues presented in the sections below.

When presenting the key constructs, i.e., self-regulation in language learning and collaborative language learning in relation to mobile contexts, we start with an introduction to the terms, followed by presentation of: (1) central underlying theoretical concepts, (2) the relation of the constructs to mobile learning (m-learning) and mobile-assisted language learning (MALL), (3) how they have been examined in the setting of out-of-class MALL activities, (4) what specifically has been studied and, finally, (5) what support mechanisms have been offered.

Key constructs

Self-regulation in (mobile) language learning

Self-regulated learning (SRL) refers to "the process by which learners personally activate and sustain cognitions, affects and behaviors that are systematically oriented toward the attainment of learning goals" (Zimmerman & Schunk, 2011, p.vii). Strategic SRL is also central and critical to second language acquisition (Oxford, 2011). 'Strategic' points to the way/s in which learners approach learning tasks – offered by the teacher, the intelligent tutor, or the learner if the task is self-initiated – by choosing and enacting a range of relevant strategies and tactics that they believe are "best suited to the situation, and applying those tactics appropriately" (Winne & Perry, 2000, p. 533). Self-regulated language learning involves the use of specific *metastrategies*, *strategies* and *tactics* (Oxford, 2011) that can empower learners to take control of their own learning, and hence to acquire the target language more effectively, for example, in terms of time spent and effort expended on achieving language learning goals.

Language learners can use self-regulated language learning strategies to regulate several interrelated aspects of their learning, including their beliefs, behaviours, their internal mental states and the learning environment (Oxford, 2011). The enactment of these strategies is especially critical for being able to regulate their out-of-class language learning activities, assisted by mobile technologies (Botero et al., 2019). This can be explained by the fact that language learning in out-of-class settings can be undermined by other priorities and obligations in learners' lives. As demonstrated in research findings, learners are not using MALL out-of-class as often as one would expect (e.g., Dashtestani, 2016), and overall "students tend to not self-direct using technology" (Botero et al., 2019, p. 73).

Despite the fact that SRL is beneficial for learner success, it is challenging for learners, because many have difficulty calibrating their own learning processes (Stone, 2000; Viberg, Khalil, & Baars, 2020) and they have poor SRL skills and knowledge when planning, monitoring and reflecting on their learning activities (e.g., Baars & Viberg, in press; Bjork, Dunslosky, & Kornell, 2013). Scholars also stress that learners are not often aware of effective learning strategies and how to employ them (e.g., Dirkx et al., 2019; Cervin-Ellqvist et al., 2021). Nevertheless, SRL strategies and skills can be learnt and taught (Lodge et al., 2018), and to assist learners, teachers and learning designers in this task, we can take advantage of the affordances offered by mobile technology-in-use that can provide relevant individual SRL support at the right place and the right time (e.g., Viberg, Mavroudi, & Ma, 2020).

SRL theoretical lenses are grounded in a number of SRL models (for overview, see Panadero, 2017) that can be used to underpin the design of relevant support mechanisms for self-regulated language learning. One of these models is Zimmerman's SRL model (Zimmerman, 2002). It explains the SRL cyclical process through three phases of self-regulation: the *forethought*, *performance* and *self-reflection* phases. In the *forethought* phase, learners plan their learning activities by, for instance, examining the task (or formulating it if the learning activity is self-initiated), setting their short- and/or long-term goals, and planning how to achieve them. In the *performance phase*, learners carry out the task by monitoring the learning progress and controlling targeted learning activities or actions through the use of selected self-controlling strategies and tactics that keep them engaged so that they complete the task. In the final *self-reflection phase,* learners evaluate their learning performance and reflect on it by considering reasons behind successes and failures. Based on Zimmerman's SRL model, researchers have offered theoretical models of language learner self-regulation. One of them is the *Strategic Self-Regulation* (S2R) model of language learning (Oxford, 2011, 2016). Hitherto, this model has been largely used to monitor and understand various aspects of language learners' self-regulation in their second language acquisition rather than to underpin the design of relevant support mechanisms that would enable the effective use of SRL metastrategies, strategies and tactics (Oxford, 2011) by the learner when acquiring a new language. Peeters et al. (2020) employed the S2R model to reveal second language learners' SRL tactics in an academic writing course. Köksal and Dundar (2018) used it to develop a scale for the use of self-regulated language learning strategies. Others (Saqr, Peeters, & Viberg, 2021) used the S2R model to code language learners' SRL tactics to uncover their dynamics in a computer-supported collaborative learning setting. Based on such understandings, effective ways of supporting language learners in their self-regulated language learning beyond the classroom should be developed and offered.

In a recent review examining the association between m-learning and SRL, Palalas and Wark (2020) reported that the results of the majority of the reviewed studies ($n=38$), including MALL papers, showed that m-learning enhanced learners' SRL and SRL enhanced m-learning, suggesting that mobile technology can be used effectively to foster students' SRL and the other way around, i.e., learners' ability to self-regulate their learning process is advantageous for m-learning and can improve learning outcomes.

In the context of MALL, some scholars have shown that SRL behaviour is the most critical factor in predicting linguistic outcomes (Tseng, Cheng, & Hsiao, 2019). Another study found that language learners' self-regulatory capacity can be facilitated through MALL practices and that self-regulatory capacity plays an important role in determining the magnitude of associations between learning satisfaction and learning intention in MALL settings (Hwang, 2014). Furthermore, researchers have shown that MALL positively affects the enactment of students' SRL behaviours. Kondo et al. (2012) showed that a MALL module encouraged students' self-study in terms of time spent on learning tasks, levels of satisfaction derived from the tasks, and self-measured achievement.

Recent research highlights the importance of *out-of-class contexts* to support learners' engagement with MALL. Botero et al. (2019) examined language learners' engagement with a MALL tool (Duolingo app) and concluded that most students need training and support for their self-directed out-of-class learning. Another study introduced and evaluated a virtual-reality game-based English m-learning application for language learners' SRL (Chen & Hsu, 2020). The results show that the tool influenced students' SRL. They also found that self-efficacy and self-regulation were positively related to each other, i.e., students who had higher confidence believed that they were competent; they were using cognitive strategies, and were increasingly self-regulating using metacognitive strategies. In sum, there is a positive interdependence between SRL and MALL.

Collaborative (mobile) language learning

Collaborative learning is an approach that recognizes the value of social interaction in learning, both from an affective perspective (many people are motivated through learning with others) and from the point of view of learning effectiveness. It is generally derived from Vygotsky's (1978) sociocultural theory of cognitive development, whereby social, cultural and historical forces play a part in an individual's development, and learning is facilitated by social interactions, particularly a learner's interactions with a more knowledgeable person. A key idea is that of the Zone of Proximal Development, which is the gap between what an individual can do on their own and what they can only achieve with some assistance. Crucially, that assistance can come from another learner, not only a teacher. Nowadays, it can also come from a computer-based (increasingly mobile) system playing a similar role. Collaboration can also be seen as a way to promote joint knowledge construction through discussion, reasoning, elaboration and debate.

It has long been acknowledged that collaborative learning is hard to define since it can involve various numbers and configurations of people, the meaning of 'learning' is open to interpretation, and it can be "a truly joint effort" or the learners may divide up the work among themselves (Dillenbourg, 1999). There are also differing perspectives on whether learning together should result in a product/outcome, or if the process of learning is the main focus. Importantly, "the words 'collaborative learning' describe a situation in which particular forms of interaction among people are expected to occur, which would trigger learning mechanisms, but there is no guarantee that the expected interactions will actually occur" (Dillenbourg, 1999, p. 5). Effort therefore needs to be put into planning and supporting interactions among the learners. In cases where collaboration is supposed to take place without support from a teacher, learners can feel helpless; in one study, there was not much discussion among the learners as they felt confused and were "each waiting for someone else to provide a better understanding" of an article they had all read (Chang-Tik & Goh, 2020, p. 7).

In language learning, collaboration offers opportunities for 'collaborative dialogue' (Swain & Watanabe, 2012), for example, one in which learners help each other solve language-related problems such as what to say and how to say it. It can also be an opportunity for learners to engage in more language practice: more speaking, listening, reading, writing, memorizing, rehearsing, especially as a way to extend this activity beyond the classroom. Additionally, peer feedback and corrections enable learners to reflect on their language use and knowledge, which can, in turn, improve the quality of their language production. Collaborative learning also exposes learners to social, emotional, cultural and multilingual dimensions of interaction (Baker, Andriessen, & Järvelä, 2013; Walker, 2018; Kukulska-Hulme & Lee, 2020), often beyond what is available in their classroom.

Research studies reporting technology-supported collaborative activities in language learning tend to report on increased opportunities to communicate, and with more people. It is argued that use of internet-based social media offers opportunities for social networking that may promote language learning (Zourou & Lamy, 2013). MALL extends those opportunities even further through easy and frequent access and thanks to an abundance of applications that enable communication, image, video and audio capture and sharing in multiple settings. In published studies, perceived and documented benefits of mobile collaboration for language learning are centred on: increasing opportunities for communication and negotiation in the target language (Ilic, 2015; Berns et al., 2016) including through peer feedback, commenting, reviewing and rating (Hoven & Palalas, 2013; Hwang et al., 2014; Chai, Wong, & Lind, 2016); listening and speaking practice with reflection on quality (Pellerin, 2014; Hwang et al., 2016); language use during co-creation of artefacts (Hoven & Palalas, 2013; Fomani & Hedayayi, 2016); improving quality and quantity of writing (Hwang et al., 2014); and practising cognitive strategies such as paraphrasing and summarization (Hazaea & Alzubi, 2016).

In the papers reviewed for this chapter, specific collaboration skills and strategies are generally not reported, but there are indications that teachers orchestrate collaboration in various ways. Andujar (2016) describes how a collaborative mobile instant messaging activity to develop ESL writing was carefully structured by the teacher and that there was daily tracking of each student's involvement in the activity. Kirsch (2016) used storytelling to encourage collaboration. In Berns et al. (2016) and in Tai (2012) students had well defined roles in the collaborative tasks. Hoven & Palalas (2013) mention procedures that students had to follow; while Hwang et al. (2014) report that students were instructed on how to give 'meaningful' feedback to their peers. Fomani and Hedayayi (2016) claim that it would be beneficial to train students in artefact creation.

Key issues

Fostering learners' SRL and collaborative learning skills and knowledge for MALL beyond the classroom is a challenging and complex task. There are several interrelated challenges but also some promising results that suggest these approaches are worth pursuing.

First, there is complexity in the 'self-regulated learning' and 'collaborative learning' concepts. Since these concepts consist of many interrelated aspects, dimensions and characteristics, it becomes challenging to select what concrete learning activities and/or aspects of individuals' self-regulated language learning (e.g., goal setting strategies or self-reflection activities) and collaborative language learning processes (e.g., social or cognitive dimension of collaborative learning) should be further developed and adequately supported. This suggests that researchers or practitioners need to identify a problem to be examined and related learning activities to be further developed and supported. In our sample, scholars have frequently studied some chosen aspect/dimension of self-regulation or collaboration in MALL settings, with limited attention to the cyclical and multifaceted nature of these processes. Chen et al. (2018) presented an English vocabulary m-learning app with an SRL mechanism – with a focus on developing learners' goal-setting skills when learning new words – to improve learning performance and motivation. Results indicated that the learners who used the tool with the SRL support exhibited significantly better learning performance and motivation than those who used the app without the SRL support. Others focussed on the affective aspect of SRL and showed that: (1) the use of mobile technologies in second language learning can decrease anxiety for both learners and teachers (Kim, 2018), and (2) a designed Affective Learning SRL app for supporting second language learners with affective learning in their SRL process was seen to increase their awareness of the self-regulated language learning process and their engagement in, and motivation for, self-regulated learning across settings (Viberg, Mavroudi, & Ma, 2020). Also, scholars have focussed on fostering migrant learners' time management skills when acquiring a host language in out-of-class settings and found that using the TimeTracker app to keep track of the time spent on studying a host language enabled learners to devote more time to their second language learning and become more engaged in it through monitoring of their learning activities (via a learning dashboard) and raising awareness of their learning process (Viberg, Khalil, & Bergman, 2019). Andujar's study (2016), which focussed on development of students' accuracy as well as lexical and syntactic complexity in their ESL writing, demonstrated that daily out-of-class collaborative interactions on WhatsApp on their mobile phones improved the students' accuracy.

Second, the definition of m-learning is problematic, and several different definitions of m-learning and MALL are found in the reviewed sample. As stated by Grant (2019), m-learning has become an "'umbrella term for the integration of mobile computing devices within teaching and learning" (p. 361), and the term has been used unsystematically. For this reason, he instead recommends the use of "design characteristics that are essential to mobile learning environments" (p. 368). They are described as follows: Learner is mobile; Device is Mobile; Data services are persistent; Content is mobile; Tutor is accessible; Learner is engaged; and Physical and networked cultures and contexts impact learning or learner (Grant, 2019). These characteristics should be carefully considered when designing relevant support mechanisms aiming to foster language learners' collaborative and SRL strategies and skills in out-of-class MALL settings.

Third, there are difficulties in establishing whether there are language learning gains arising from student collaboration and their ability to self-regulate their own learning processes. In several projects (e.g., Hoven & Palalas, 2013; Berns et al. 2016), learning activities had both individual and collaborative elements that were closely interlinked, so any learning gains cannot be directly attributed to collaboration. Similarly, in Hwang et al. (2014), benefits derived from the situated nature of the activity are intertwined with benefits of peer feedback during collaboration. This finding is supported by earlier research emphasizing that successful collaboration in computer-supported collaborative learning settings requires diverse types of support, including support for promoting individual self-regulatory skills and strategies, peer support, facilitation of self-regulatory competence within the group, and socially shared regulation of learning (Järvelä et al., 2015). This suggests that all these factors may be critical for improved language learning performance in collaborative mobile language learning settings. Also, it has been shown that overall, there is a lack of alignment between the purpose of the tools in supporting self-regulation in online learning settings and the evaluation performed to assess their effectiveness (Pérez-Álvarez, Maldonado-Mahauad, & Pérez-Sanagustín, 2018). In the same review, the scholars found that most of the studies did not evaluate the effect on learners' SRL strategies. This finding relates also to the papers reviewed for this chapter. Similarly, collaboration skills and strategies for MALL are usually not explicitly assessed in the studies we reviewed.

Fourth, there is a challenge in terms of *how* selected aspects of language learners' self-regulation and collaboration should be effectively supported in regard to underlying theoretical lenses of SRL and collaborative learning. In our sample, researchers seldom explicitly present their selected theoretical grounds when designing and examining MALL activities aiming to support language learners' SRL, and this is a limitation since considerable related research is available. For collaborative mobile language learning, relevant theories or frameworks are often mentioned at the start of a paper (e.g., social constructivism) but it is not clear how exactly they were applied in the learning designs. However, there are some exceptions. Kondo et al. (2012), for example, introduced the MALL module based on Zimmerman's model of self-regulation (Schunk & Zimmerman, 1998; Cleary & Zimmerman, 2004). This module was designed to facilitate language students' SRL "in the class, elsewhere in the university, or outside the university" (Kondo et al., 2012, p.174). The same SRL model was used to underpin the design of the Affective Learning SRL mobile app to support Japanese language learners in their self-study of the targeted second language (Viberg, Mavroudi, & Ma, 2020). Botero et al. (2019) applied the lenses of self-directed learning (Garrison, 1997) to study self-directed language learning in a mobile, out-of-class context. To fill the existing gap in the SRL theoretically underpinned MALL designs and tools, researchers have recently offered a conceptual framework, Mobile-Assisted Language Learning for Self-regulated learning (MALLAS; Viberg, Wasson, & Kukulska-Hulme, 2020) aimed at learning designers and grounded in the theoretical lenses of Zimmerman's model (2002) and also the S2R model of language learning (Oxford, 2011, 2016). Hwang et al. (2014) based their research in the value and types of peer feedback within collaborative language learning and used Stanley's (1992) four-step procedure to improve and structure peer feedback.

Moreover, there are several technology-related challenges. These include how we can best design and benefit from existing and emerging technologies (e.g., artificial intelligence (AI), virtual reality, visualization technologies) in combination with mobile technology to adequately address the needs of learners as well as to support them in the development of their SRL and collaborative learning skills when acquiring a new language. Another issue is how to design sustainable adaptive MALL solutions that would support individual learners in their self-study across learning environments. These challenges entail a need to carefully consider learning and technology design (see, e.g., Chen & Hsu, 2020; Viberg, Wasson, & Kukulska-Hulme, 2020), policy-related issues that can contribute to the sustainability of MALL designs over time and space (e.g., the implementation of bring-your-own-device policy, see, e.g., Bartholomew, 2019; Chen & Hsu, 2020), and mobile data-driven language learning solutions that would facilitate the provision of adaptive language learning paths (Viberg, Wasson, & Kukulska-Hulme, 2020). Generally, as emphasized by Pérez-Paredes et al. (2019), the potential of data-driven learning in the MALL context is underexplored.

Finally, there are challenges pertaining to learners' individual characteristics, including their level of motivation for language learning, cultural orientedness, self-regulation capacity and learning orientations (e.g., integrative and instrumental). Regarding learners' self-regulation capacity, Tseng et al. (2019) state that little is known "about the effects of different types of learning orientations and implementation intentions upon the development of self-regulated capacity in L2 m-learning context" (p. 371). Furthermore, they examined the causal relationships between goal orientation, implementation strategies, and SRL behaviour in relation to MALL, and found that SRL behaviour is the most important factor in predicting linguistic outcomes.

Implications

The development of MALL tools aimed at assisting learners in their use of SRL and collaborative language learning strategies in out-of-class settings is a multifaceted task that requires several careful design considerations. Since SRL and collaborative learning strategies and skills can be not only learnt but also taught, such tools can be aimed at learners and teachers, for example, in the form of learner- or teacher-centred learning dashboards that visualize different aspects of the learning process. In the development of such tools, we need to thoroughly consider what indicators of SRL and collaborative learning activities should be visualized (and how) to best address the stakeholders' needs. Knowing which indicators influence stakeholders' understanding of the learning process will lead to a more actionable learner behaviour, and providing extra support on the part of the teacher.

Teacher support and just-in-time feedback is critical, especially at early stages of self-regulation and collaboration. This suggests that in the design process of MALL apps or services, we need to consider *how* such feedback can be provided. It is important to not only consider existing solutions and technologies but also to involve the stakeholders during the design process to best meet learners' needs and preferences.

When developing data-driven MALL approaches, several aspects have to be thought of. First, we need to consider what specific learning activities are targeted and how they will be assessed to be able to track the development of learners' SRL and collaborative strategies and skills. Second, there is a need to carefully think of what learner data to collect and how to collect it, in relation to the development of relevant learning analytics modules that comprise data, analytics and action (for more, see Viberg, Wasson, & Kukulska-Hulme, 2020). Third, since the use of mobile devices allows access to learners' contextual data (e.g., in out-of-class settings), it is of utmost importance to address the issues of learners' privacy and information security. The protection of learner data "is not only a fundamental right among others but the most expressive of the contemporary human condition" (Rodotà, 2009, p. 82). This is not only a legal obligation, but also a moral one. To enact a more responsible use of mobile technologies for language learning, the designers of MALL tools should address key data protection principles associated with lawfulness, fairness, and transparency; purpose limitation; data minimization; accuracy; storage limitation, integrity and confidentiality (European Union, 2017, p. 17).

Designed support for SRL and collaboration in MALL should consider the earlier mentioned essential m-learning characteristics listed by Grant (2019), and how to deal with possible challenges. For example, when learners are mobile, their individual interactions with an application and other learners are likely to vary as to frequency, regularity and intensity. When physical and networked cultures and contexts impact learning, learners may have reduced capacity to pay attention to a task in environments where they are susceptible to distractions, and they may be influenced in their interaction styles by parallel casual conversations with their friends on social media on the same device. Technology designs as well as teaching and learning practices will need to evolve to take account of expected challenges and to capture emerging ones that we may not yet know about. The teacher/tutor should be accessible, but that is not always practical and needs to be carefully managed or supplemented by intelligent tools. Crucially, if teachers have not been trained in SRL and collaborative learning, they need to become familiar with these approaches before they can support their students.

Future directions

Overall, considering that the use of mobile devices is beneficial for fostering learners' self-regulated- and collaborative language strategies and the other way around (i.e., for effective use mobile technologies for second language acquisition in out-of-class contexts, learners are expected to self-regulate their learning process and collaborate effectively with their peers, teachers and the learning environment), and an increasing interest in learning analytics for SRL (Viberg, Khalil, & Baars, 2020) and for understanding and supporting collaborative learning activities (Wise et al., 2021), future pathways to provide adequate MALL support should apply data-driven approaches to learning. Such approaches should be based on sound theoretical lenses and take into account recent advances in the fields of AI and learning analytics to provide more individualized and personalized language learning paths. This will enable learner agency in out-of-class settings. This is important since the teacher is often unavailable in such settings, and access to peers can be likewise limited.

In the development and evaluation of adaptive self-regulated and collaborative learning paths, we also recommend taking a responsible approach to the protection of learners' privacy, ethics and security (see, Viberg, Wasson, & Kukulska-Hulme, 2020). In this regard, there is a need for empirical studies that would target different stakeholders (learners, teachers, school and university leadership, learning designers and developers) and enable more responsible use of student data in out-of-class MALL activities. Another future direction of study is to further validate relevant existing models and frameworks (e.g., Tseng et al., 2019; Viberg, Wasson, & Kukulska-Hulme, 2020) in different cultural and educational contexts. We also need more studies that are explicitly conducted to support L2 learners in out-of-class settings.

Reflection questions

Based on the argumentation and findings presented in this chapter, we offer several questions for the stakeholders' reflection.

For *the teacher*: What SRL and collaboration skills and strategies should your students have, if they are to be effective in the language learning activities or tasks they are expected to undertake, and how might they be developed?

For the *learning designer*: What m-learning design characteristics should be considered in combination with recent advances in the fields of learning analytics and AI to provide adaptive language learning paths?

For *the researcher:* How can you assist learning designers and teachers in the development of relevant support mechanisms, the use of which would provide better conditions for L2 learners' self-regulated and/or collaborative learning in out-of-class settings?

Recommended readings

To deepen the reader's understanding of how learners' self-regulation and collaboration in second language acquisition can be developed through MALL, we suggest the following literature:

Grant, M. (2019). Difficulties in defining mobile learning: Analysis, design characteristics, and implications. *Educational Technology Research and Development, 67*(2), 361–388.
   To better understand existing challenges in defining m-learning, we recommend this paper which reviews definitions of m-learning and argues that they are not helpful in guiding the design of m-learning environments. Instead, it offers a framework of design characteristics for m-learning environments. It also presents implications for future research and instructional design.

Viberg, O., Wasson, B., & Kukulska-Hulme, A. (2020). Mobile-assisted language learning through learning analytics for self-regulated learning (MALLAS): A conceptual framework. *Australasian Journal of Educational Technology, 36*(6), 34–52.

To better grasp how mobile self-regulated language learning can be enacted through learning analytics, we suggest this paper which offers a theoretically grounded conceptual framework and guidelines to its operationalization. The paper includes practice guidelines for teachers in terms of task design and learner support.

Pishtari, F., Rodriguez-Triana, M., Sarmiento-Marques, E., Perez-Sanagustin, M., Ruiz-Calleja, A., Santos, P., Prieto, L., Serrano-Iglesias, S., & Väljataga, T. (2020). Learning design and learning analytics in mobile and ubiquitous learning: A systematic review. *British Journal of Educational Technology, 51* (4), 1078–1100.

To further develop the reader's understanding of learning design and learning analytics in mobile and ubiquitous learning, we recommend this paper which offers an overview and analysis of current research. It proposes addressing mobile and ubiquitous learning beyond higher education settings, reinforcing the link between physical and virtual learning spaces, and more systematically aligning learning design and learning analytics processes.

References

Andujar, A. (2016). Benefits of mobile instant messaging to develop ESL writing. *System* 62, 63–76.

Baars, M., & Viberg, O., Supporting metacognitive and cognitive processes during self-study through mobile learning. In S. Larkin (Ed.), *Metacognition and education: Future trends*. Taylor & Francis Group, in press.

Baker, M., Andriessen, J., & Järvelä, S. (Eds.) (2013). *Affective learning together: Social and emotional dimensions of collaborative learning*. New York: Routledge.

Bartholomew, S. (2019). The impact of mobile devices on self-directed learning and achievement. In: Williams, P., & Barlex, D. (Eds.), *Explorations in technology education research*, 261–275. Singapore: Springer.

Berns, A., Isla-Montes, J.-L., Palomo-Duarte, M., & Dodero, J.-M. (2016). Motivation, students' needs and learning outcomes: A hybrid game-based app for enhanced language learning. *SpringerPlus, 5*(1), 1–23.

Bjork, R. A., Dunlosky, J., & Kornell, N. (2013). Self-regulated learning: Beliefs, techniques, and illusions. *Annual Review of Psychology* [online], *64*, 417–444. https://doi.org/10.1146/annurev-psych-113011-143823

Botero, G., Questier, F., & Zhu, C. (2019). Self-directed language learning in a mobile-assisted out-of-class context: Do students walk the talk? *Computer Assisted Language Learning, 32*(1–2), 71–97. https://doi.org/10.1080/09588221.2018.1485707

Cervin-Ellqvist, M., Larsson, D., Adawi, T., Stöhr, C., & Negretti, R. (2021). Metacognitive illusion or self-regulated learning? Assessing engineering students' learning strategies against the backdrop of recent advances in cognitive science. *Higher Education*, 82, 477–498. http://doi.org/10.1007/s10734-020-00635-x

Chai, C., Wong, L.-H., & Kind, R. (2016). Surveying and modeling students' motivation and learning strategies for mobile assisted seamless Chinese language learning. *Journal of Educational Technology & Society, 19*(3), 170–180. http://www.jstor.org/stable/jeductechsoci.19.3.170

Chang-Tik, C. & Goh, J.N. (2020). Social and cognitive dimensions of collaboration in informal learning spaces: Malaysian social science students' perspectives, *Interactive Learning Environments*, https://doi.org/10.1080/10494820.2020.1799029

Chen, C.-M., Chen, L.-C., Yang, S.-M. (2018). An English vocabulary learning app with self-regulated learning mechanism to improve learning performance and motivation. *Computer-Assisted Language Learning*, http://doi.org/10.1080/09588221.2018.1485708

Chen, Y.-L. & Hsu, C.-C. (2020). Self-regulated mobile game-based English learning in a virtual reality environment. *Computers & Education*. https://doi.org/10.1016/j.compedu.2020.103910

Cleary, T., & Zimmerman, B. (2004). Self-regulation empowerment program: A school-based program to enhance self-regulated and self-motivated cycles of student learning. *Psychology in Schools, 41*, 537–550.

Czerniewicz, L., Agherdien, N., Badenhorst, J. *et al*. (2020). A wake-up call: Equity, inequality and covid-19 emergency remote teaching and learning. *Postdigital Science and Education, 2*, 946–967. https://doi.org/10.1007/s42438-020-00187-4

Dashtestani, R. (2016). Moving bravely towards mobile learning: Iranian students' use of mobile devices for learning English as a foreign language. *Computer Assisted Language Learning, 29*(4), 815–832. https://doi.org/10.1080/09588221.2015.1069360

Dillenbourg, P. (1999) What do you mean by collaborative learning? In P. Dillenbourg (Ed.), *Collaborative-learning: Cognitive and computational approaches.* Oxford: Elsevier, 1–19.

Dirkx, K. J. H., Camp, G., Kester, L., & Kirschner, P. A. (2019). Do secondary school students make use of effective study strategies when they study on their own? *Applied Cognitive Psychology, 33*(5), 952–957. http://doi:10.1002/acp.3584

European Union Agency for Network and Information Security. (2017). Privacy and data protection in mobile applications: A study on the app development ecosystem and the technical implementation of GDPR. https://doi.org/10.2824/114584

Fomani, E., & Hedayayi. M. (2016). A seamless learning design for mobile assisted language learning: An Iranian context. *English Language Teaching, 9*(5), 206–213.

Garrison, D. (1997). Self-directed learning: Toward a comprehensive model. *Adult Education Quarterly, 48*(1), 18–33.

Grant, M. (2019). Difficulties in defining mobile learning: Analysis, design characteristics, and implications. *Educational Technology Research and Development, 67*(2), 361–388. https://doi.org/10.1007/s11423-018-09641-4

Hazaea, A., & Alzubi, A. (2016). The effectiveness of using mobile on EFL learners' reading practices in Narjan University. *English Language Teaching, 9*(5), 8–21.

Hoven, D., & Palalas, A. (2013). The design of effective mobile-enabled tasks for ESP students: A longitudinal study. *CALICO Journal, 30*, 137–165.

Hwang, R. (2014). Exploring the moderating role of self-management of learning in mobile English learning. *Educational Technology & Society, 17*, 255–267.

Hwang, W.-Y., Chen, H., Shadiev, R., Huang, R., & Chen, C.-Y. (2014). Improving English as a foreign language writing in elementary schools using mobile devices in familiar situational contexts. *Computer Assisted Language Learning, 27*(5), 359–378.

Hwang, W.-Y., Shih, T., Ma, Z.-H., Shadiev, R., & Chen, S.-Y. (2016). Evaluating listening and speaking skills in a mobile game-based learning environment with situational contexts. *Computer Assisted Language Learning, 29*(4), 639–657.

Ilic, P. (2015). The effects of mobile collaborative activities in a second language course. *International Journal of Mobile and Blended Learning, 7*(4), 16–37.

Järvelä, S., Kirschner, P.A., Panadero, E., Malmberg, J. Phielix, C., Jaspers, J., Koivuniemi, M., & Järvenoja, H. (2015). Enhancing socially shared regulation in collaborative learning groups: Designing for CSCL regulation tools. *Education Technology Research and Development, 63*, 125–142. https://doi.org/10.1007/s11423-014-9358-1

Kim, Y. (2018). The effects of mobile-assisted language learning (MALL) on Korean college students' English-listening performance and English-listening anxiety. *KOAJ Korea Open Access Journals, 48*, 277-298. https://doi.org/10.17002/sil..48.201807.277

Kirsch, C. (2016). Developing language skills through collaborative storytelling in iTEO. *Literacy Information and Computer Education Journal, 6*(2), 2254–2262.

Köksal, D., & Dundar, S. (2018). Öz-Düzenlemeli Yabancı Dil Öğrenme Strateji Kullanımı Ölçeği'nin Geliştirilmesi (Developing a scale for self-regulated L2 learning strategy use). *Hacettepe Üniversitesi Eğitim Fakültesi Dergisi, 33*(2), 337–352. https://doi.org/10.16986/HUJE.2017033805

Kondo, M., Ishikawa, Y., Smith, C., Sakamoto, K., Shimomura, H., & Wada, N. (2012). Mobile Assisted Language Learning in university EFL courses in Japan: Developing attitudes and skills for self-regulated learning. *ReCALL, 24*(2), 169–187. doi:10.1017/S0958344012000055.

Kukulska-Hulme, A., & Lee, H (2020). Mobile collaboration for language learning and cultural learning. In Mark Dressman & Randall William Sadler (Eds.), *The handbook of informal language learning. Blackwell handbooks in linguistics.* Chichester: Wiley Blackwell, 169–180.

Kukulska-Hulme, A., & Viberg, O. (2018). Mobile collaborative language learning: State of the art. *British Journal of Educational Technology, 49*(2), 207–218. https://doi.org/10.1111/bjet.12580

Lodge, J., Panadero, E., Broadbent, J., & de Barba, P. (2018). Supporting self-regulated learning with learning analytics. In J. Lodge, J. C. Horvath & L. Corrin (Eds.), *Learning analytics in the classroom.* New York: Routledge. https://doi.org/10.4324/9781351113038-4

Oxford, R. (2011). *Teaching and researching language learning strategies.* Pearson Education Limited.

Oxford, R. (2016). *Teaching and researching language learning strategies: Self-regulation in context* (2nd ed). Routledge.

Palalas, A., & Wark, N. (2020). The relationship between mobile learning and self-regulated learning: A systematic review. *Australasian Journal of Educational Technology, 36*(4), 151–172. https://doi.org/10.14742/ajet.5650

Panadero, E. (2017). A review of self-regulated learning: Six models and four directions for research. *Frontiers in Psychology,* https://doi.org/10.3389/fpsyg.2017.00422

Peeters, W., Saqr, M., & Viberg, O. (2020). Applying learning analytics to map students' self-regulated learning tactics in an academic writing course. In So, H.-J., Rodrigo, M., Mason, J., & Mitrovic, A. (Eds.), proceedings of the *International Conference on Computers in Education (ICCE).* Taiwan: Asia-Pacific Society for Computers in Education (APSCE), 245–254. https://apsce.net/icce/icce2020/proceedings/paper_143.pdf

Pellerin, M. (2014). Language tasks using touch screen and mobile technologies: Reconceptualizing task-based CALL for young language learners. *Canadian Journal of Learning and Technology, 40*(1), 1–23.

Pérez-Álvarez, R., Maldonado-Mahauad, J., & Pérez-Sanagustín, M. (2018). Tools to support self-regulated learning in online environments: Literature review. In V. Pammer-Schindler, M. Pérez-Sanagustín, H. Drachsler, R. Elferink, & M. Scheffel (Eds.), *Lifelong technology-enhanced learning. EC-TEL 2018. Lecture notes in computer science, vol. 11082.* Cham: Springer. https://doi.org/10.1007/978-3-319-98572-5_2

Pérez-Paredes, P., Guillamón, C., Van de Vyver, J., Meurice, A., Jiménez, P. A., Conole, G., & Hernandez, P. (2019). Mobile data-driven language learning: Affordances and learners' perception. *System, 84,* 145–159. https://doi.org/10.1016/j.system.2019.06.009

Pishtari, F., Rodriguez-Triana, M., Sarmiento-Marques, E., Perez-Sanagustin, M., Ruiz-Calleja, A., Santos, P., Prieto, L., Serrano-Iglesias, S., & Väljataga, T. (2020). Learning design and learning analytics in mobile and ubiquitous learning: A systematic review. *British Journal of Educational Technology, 51*(4), 1078–1100. https://doi.org/10.1111/bjet.12944

Rodotà, S. (2009). Data protection as a fundamental right. In S. Gutwirth, Y. Poullet, P. De Hert, C. de Terwangne, & S. Nouwt (Eds.), *Reinventing data protection?.* Cham: Springer, 77–82. https://doi.org/10.1007/978-1-4020-9498-9_3

Saqr, M., Viberg, O., & Peeters, W. (2021). Using psychological networks to reveal the interplay between foreign language students' self-regulated learning tactics. In Viberg, O., Mynard, J., Peeters, W., & Saqr, M. (Eds.), *Proceedings of the International Symposium on Harnessing the Potentials of Technology to Support Self-Directed Language Learning in Online Learning Settings,* October 15-16, 2020. http://ceur-ws.org/Vol-2828/article_2.pdf

Schunk, D. H., & Zimmerman, B. (Eds.) (1998). *Self-regulated learning: From teaching to self-reflective practice.* New York: The Guilford Press.

Shadiev, R., Liu, T., & Hwang, W.-Y., (2019). Review of research on mobile-assisted language learning in familiar, authentic environments. *British Journal of Educational Technology, 51*(3), 709–720. https://doi.org/10.1111/bjet.12839

Stanley, J. (1992). Coaching student writers to be effective peer evaluators. *Journal of Second Language Writing, 1,* 217–233.

Stone, N. (2000). Exploring the relationship between calibration and self-regulated learning. *Educational Psychology Review, 12*(4), 437–475. doi: 10.1023/A:1009084430926

Swain, M., & Watanabe, Y. (2012). Languaging: Collaborative dialogue as a source of second language learning. In Carol A. Chapelle (Ed.), *The encyclopedia of applied linguistics.* Wiley & Sons, 1–8. https://onlinelibrary.wiley.com/doi/book/10.1002/9781405198431

Tai, Y. (2012). Contextualizing a MALL: Practice design and evaluation. *Journal of Educational Technology & Society, 15*(2), 220–230.

Tseng, W.-H., Cheng, H.-F., & Hsiao, T.-Y. (2019). Validating a motivational process model for mobile assisted language learning. *English Teaching and Learning, 43,* 369–388.

Viberg, O., & Andersson, A. (2019). The role of self-regulation and structuration in mobile learning. *International Journal of Mobile and Blended Learning, 11*(4), 42–58. https://doi.org/10.4018/IJMBL.2019100104

Viberg, O., Khalil, M., & Baars, M. (2020). Self-regulated learning and learning analytics in online learning environments: A review of empirical research. In C. Rensing & H. Drachsler (Eds.), *Proceedings of the tenth conference on learning analytics and knowledge,* 524–533. https://doi.org/10.1145/3375462.3375483

Viberg, O., Khalil, M., & Bergman, G. (2021). *TimeTracker* App: Facilitating migrants' engagement in their second language learning. In M.E. Auer & T. Tsiatsos (Eds.), *Internet of things, infrastructures and mobile applications. IMCL 2019. Advances in intelligent systems and computing*, Vol. 1192. Cham: Springer. https://doi.org/10.1007/978-3-030-49932-7_91

Viberg, O., Mavroudi, A., & Ma, Y. (2020). Supporting second language learners' development of affective self-regulated learning skills through the use and design of mobile technology. In C. Alario-Hoyos, M. Rodríguez-Triana, M. Scheffel, I. Arnedillo-Sánchez, & S. Dennerlein (Eds.), *Addressing global challenges and quality education: Proceedings of the 15th European conference on technology enhanced learning*. Cham: Springer, 173–186. https://doi.org/10.1007/978-3-030-57717-9_13

Viberg, O., Wasson, B., & Kukulska-Hulme, A. (2020). Mobile-assisted language learning through learning analytics for self-regulated learning (MALLAS): A conceptual framework. *Australasian Journal of Educational Technology, 36*(6), 34–52. https://doi.org/10.14742/ajet.6494

Vygotsky, L. S. (1978). Socio-cultural theory. *Mind in Society, 6*, 52–58.

Walker, U. (2018). Translanguaging: Affordances for collaborative language learning. *New Zealand Studies in Applied Linguistics, 24*(1), 18–39.

Winne, P. & Perry, N. (2000). Measuring self-regulating learning. In M. Boekaerts, P. Pintrich, & M. Zeidner (Eds.), *Handbook of self-regulation*. San Diego: Academic Press, 531–556.

Wise, A., Knight, S., & Buckinghum Shum, S. (2021). Collaborative learning analytics. In Cress, U., Rose, C., Wise, A., Oshima, J. (Eds.) *International Handbook of Computer-Supported Collaborative Learning*. Cham: Springer. https://doi.org/10.1007/978-3-030-65291-3_23

Yang, Z. (2020). A study of self-efficacy and its role in mobile-assisted language learning. *Theory and Practice in Language Studies, 10*(4), 439–444.

Zimmerman, B. (1990). Self-regulated learning and academic achievement: An overview. *Educational Psychologist, 25*(1), 3–17.

Zimmerman, B. (2002). Becoming a self-regulated learner: An overview. *Theory into Practice, 41*(2), 64–70. https://doi.org/10.1207/s15430421tip4102_2

Zimmerman, B., & Schunk, D. (2011). *Handbook of self-regulation of learning and performance*. New York: Routledge.

Zhang, R., Cheng, G., & Chen, X. (2020). Game-based self-regulated language learning: Theoretical analysis and bibliometrics. *PLoS ONE, 15*(12), e0243827. https://doi.org/10.1371/journal.pone.0243827

Zourou, K., & Lamy, M-N. (2013). Introduction. In M.-N. Lamy & K. Zourou (Eds.), *Social networking for language education*. Basingstoke: Palgrave Macmillan, 1–7.

11
ENHANCING LANGUAGE AND CULTURE LEARNING THROUGH SOCIAL NETWORK TECHNOLOGIES

Lina Lee

Introduction

The rise of the proficiency movement has made a paradigm shift in language pedagogy focusing heavily on the development of learners' ability to communicate effectively with speakers of the target language. While in-class instruction prepares students for out-of-class language use in real life, researchers have acknowledged the challenge of limited time spent in the traditional classroom (Nunan & Richards, 2015). The literature suggests that classroom instruction may be necessary but not sufficient. Choi and Nunan (2018), for example, argue that formal instruction is often restricted to structured and predictable discourse that does not allow students to acquire high levels of language competence. Attention has been drawn to language learning and teaching beyond the classroom (LBC) through informal learning that exposure to the target language and culture takes place in real-world contexts (Reinders & Benson, 2017). While there is an array of ways to engage students in out-of-class learning, emerging technologies afford unprecedented opportunities for second or foreign language (L2) learners to expand the use of the target language to enhance language development beyond formal instruction (Dressman & Sadler, 2020). From a pedagogical perspective, technology interventions not only overcome the physical and temporal constraints of conventional classrooms but also empower teachers to create individual and social spaces for L2 learners to engage in authentic experiential learning. According to Benson (2011), technology integration through blended learning or flipped classrooms supports four dimensions of LBC that point to the value of out-of-class (location), informal (formality), less-instructed (pedagogy), and self-directed (locus of control) language learning. Most importantly, the integration of digital technologies into language instruction merges the gap between formal and informal learning, and provides students with immersive learning experiences (Kukulska-Hulme, 2015).

Over the past several decades, L2 researchers and practitioners have developed robust approaches and effective strategies to bring technology to the language classroom and beyond. Unsurprisingly, we have witnessed the growth in computer-assisted language learning (CALL) research aimed at the incorporation of technology-enhanced instruction into L2 learning across a wide variety of contexts (Farr & Murray, 2016; Thomas, Reinders &

Warschauer, 2013). Although CALL embraces large areas covered the breadth of theories, frameworks, approaches, and practices, language learning with social network technologies, including mobile apps is relatively new and has not yet fully implemented in the language classroom. Yet, students routinely use it for informal learning opportunities outside the classroom (Reinhardt, 2020). How can we leverage the potential of social media to facilitate language teaching and enhance student learning? This chapter aims to explore critical issues emerging from a body of research studies to address affordances and constraints of social media use in language learning. To begin, as background, the key concepts of social media and the current scope of L2 learning through social networking are surveyed. Next, the chapter discusses key issues in using social media such as learner motivation and autonomy, and digital literacy and identities. The chapter highlights the importance of adopting task-based instruction as pedagogical framework grounded by second language acquisition (SLA) theories to support technology-mediated language learning. Prominent studies on social media interaction are examined to address task design, language development, and focus on form. The chapter concludes with a discussion of implications for practice, directions for future research, and challenges facing teacher preparation for using multimodal social communication within and beyond the classroom.

Key concepts: Web 2.0, social media, social networking

The concept of social media has gained momentum and has become a 'buzz' word in language learning. While there is no consensus among CALL researchers, different terms are associated with social media and have been used interchangeably such as Web 2.0, social networks and social networking. The literature indicates that these terms share some common key features, including connectivity, content creativity, widened audience, and community building (Boyd & Ellison, 2007). Social media as Web 2.0 applications makes it possible to seamlessly share user-generated content and collaborate with others in real-time or asynchronously (Carr & Hayes, 2015). Moreover, the openness of content exchanging allows for expansive use of social networking that connects people to wider communities (Lamy & Zourou, 2013). To a large extent, virtual communities bring together people with a shared interest and purpose, making interpersonal interaction across geographic distance the central feature of social networking.

Over the years, social media has evolved from early Web 2.0 (wikis, blogs) to social networks (*Instagram, Snapchat*). Each platform has its uniqueness and affordances based on distinct facilities and features. For example, *Facebook* as a naturalistic social media platform allows people to connect with each other to share ideas through informal interaction, whereas *Duolingo* is an online language learning site that brings together learners to practice L2 and interact with native speakers (NSs) through social networking. While some applications highlight individual (blogs) and collective (wikis) ownerships with a target audience, others (social networking sites) underscore identity construction and multimodel communication with a broader community. For example, blogging as a reflective writing tool enables participants to express their opinions through reader comments within a community of practice (Lee, 2017). Despite its popularity and potential for language learning, several key areas dealing with social networks should not be ignored, including ownership, privacy, security, accessibility and compliance with copyright law, and intellectual property rights (Rodriguez, 2011). Thus, it is pivotal to use digital resources wisely and create appropriate virtual learning environments to maximize benefits and diminish drawbacks of social networking.

Key issues of using social networks for language teaching and leaning

According to Kukulska-Hulme (2015), social networking permits students to traverse between in-class and out-of-class spaces that connect the informal (less structured) learning to the formal (highly structured) instruction due to its openness, flexibility, and accessibility. A growing body of research drawing from various theoretical approaches (e.g., psycholinguistic, sociocultural, ecological) has shown positive effects of social media on the development of linguistic, pragmatic, and intercultural competence (Dixon & Thomas, 2015; O'Dowd & Lewis, 2016; Taguchi & Sykes, 2013). For example, Lee (2020) in her recent study grounded in sociocultural theory found that students gained cross-cultural perspectives and interpersonal communication skills through asynchronous video discussions in *Flipgrid*. Unlike in-class practice using simplified rules, social interaction with NSs provided students with an authentic learning context for the development of socio-pragmatic skills, especially speech acts (compliments, apology). Notably, the study demonstrates how out-of-class projects like intercultural exchange can be intentionally designed to incorporate them into the course content to foster cross-cultural communication in informal learning contexts. In spite of the potential of using social media for L2 learning and development, several key aspects have been addressed to facilitate and enhance social interaction and collaboration, as are discussed below.

Motivation and engagement

The interactive and social nature of digital media increase students' motivation to invest their time and energy for personal learning endeavors. As observed by Sykes and Reinhardt (2013), digital games designed for pedagogical purposes have positive effects on learners' willingness to use L2 to improve their language proficiency. For example, language learning commercial sites (*Busuu, Livemocha*) grounded in a mix of social and cognitive approaches to language learning stimulate students' interest in using gamification. Although memorization and pattern drills do not promote language authenticity, the gamified aspect triggers students' enthusiasm for vocabulary and grammar exercises. In a similar vein, Stevenson and Liu (2010) in their survey study found that students were motivated to use the language learning social networking sites (e.g., *Palabea, Babbel*) to interact with NSs via synchronous (chat) and asynchronous (discussion board) computer mediated communication (CMC). As a result, they benefited from cross-cultural communication in socially engaged practices. It is apparent that the opportunity for authentic interaction with other speakers in social network communities plays a fundamental role in motivating language learning outside the classroom. However, students do not necessarily maintain a state of engagement. Zourou and Loiseau (2013) reported on the culture section of *Livemocha* that learners' interaction rate through posting threads was low with only a 10% continuation after a one-month exchange. It is vital for teachers to clearly communicate expectations for online participation to students and help them with community-building activities to increase social engagement.

Digital literacies

It is widely acknowledged that L2 learners need to develop digital literacies to become thoughtful consumers of digital content, effective creators of digital media, and social contributors to virtual communities. Digital literacies have changed from traditional forms of literacy to a communication that is multifaceted and social in nature. According to Reinhardt and Thorne (2019), digital literacies should be considered as 'multifarious repertoires' and skills necessary for successful participation, interaction, and collaboration in social mediated language learning environments; especially outside of instructional contexts. Unlike traditional text-based communication, social interaction via multiple channels (text, image, audio, video) creates a new genre of communication that shapes the way learners make meaning (Kress, 2010). The study by Lee (2019) shows that *VoiceThread* as a multimodal communication platform enables students to bring multiple modes together to create digital stories, and develop audience awareness and multimodal digital literacy as part of the 21st-century skills. Creating digital stories as an extension of in-class instruction empowers L2 learners to share voices and views in an open and interactive learning environment, and build content knowledge and speaking skill. As noted by Lantz-Andersson (2016), social networks offer a casual space of communication using the unplanned and informal style of written and spoken language. Learners use diverse language repertoires to play with the language that extends socially situated vernacular writing and prepares them for the use of L2 in real-world settings.

Multimodal communication caters more easily to different learning styles and modal preferences. Nevertheless, the fact that today's students are digital natives does not guarantee that they can adequately use multimodal communication; especially those who are trained in the traditional learning setting. Thus, it is essential to help students develop new literacies using a variety of representational modes as communication channels to create digital content. Teachers should extend traditional practices to include informal spaces of digital literacies using readily available social media tools and resources (Hafner, 2014). For example, creating stimulation activities using *Facebook* allows students to practice digital literacy and pragmatic skills by playing different famous TV show personalities of various ages and interacting with their peers through postings and comments (Reinhardt & Ryu, 2013). Digital literacy practices are socially bounded with communities of practice in informal learning contexts. Participatory activities such as creating blog and wikis sites or multimodal digital stories should engage students with broader audiences that add authenticity and promote literacy. Activities using leading questions for reflection will help students think critically about benefits and challenges of learning with social networks in out-of-class learning environments.

Digital identities

Given that social networks facilitate real-world connections with authentic audiences and offer many ways to connect, communicate with others, the dynamics of identity has drawn much attention from L2 researchers. Research studies using qualitative methodologies, including interviews and recordings have investigated identity issues in L2 learning (Dooly, 2017) and in open educational practices (Zourou, 2017). Online identity is constructed through the multifaceted engagement in social interaction. Learners construct, change, and maintain their identities and relationships with their interlocutors between formal and informal digital spaces, both online and offline. Individuals identify themselves differently according to conditions and layers of communication in virtual environments. Each type of social network has its own functionalities for identity expression and exploration. For example, students construct their identities as authors, and develop their sense of ownership and awareness of real audience through the creation of wiki pages (King, 2015). *Twitter* as an informal social media platform encourages students to create profile posts to share personal information, make connections, and build group dynamics through peer networking (Lee

& Markey, 2014). Another study by Chen (2013) explored the literacy practices of two multicultural writers in social networking communities. The finding showed that the writers employed different strategies to construct their social, cultural, and professional identities in *Facebook*. The study concludes that *Facebook* can serve as an extension of real life experiences for students to use their linguistic and culture resources to construct and negotiate identities through literacy practices and socialization.

The construction of identity in social networking spaces is a complex phenomenon and can present beneficial and detrimental effects across multiple platforms. For example, digital affordances of *Instagram* allow students to construct self-identities by sharing their own photos, and build a community of people who share interests and cultural identities through the act of liking, tagging, and sharing. Yet, creating a 3D virtual avatar as online 'self' gives students the power to create themselves as someone who does not mirror who they are in the reality. Although learners have the right to express themselves freely, there are also liabilities to doing it. It is important to make students aware of untraditional ways of constructing multiple identities (personal, social, cultural) across multiple social networking platforms to avoid unexpected issues, including conflicts and threats emanating from cyberspace. As Dooly (2017) suggested, language educators should take learners' digital competencies into account and help them 'perform' appropriate identities in out-of-class learning settings. The integration of digital literacies should be part of teaching pedagogies to help students develop critical skills and effective strategies to construct identities, create digital content, and communicate with global audience.

Learner autonomy

Another key aspect emerged from the field of CALL is learner autonomy that takes account of agency (control one's own learning, making choices) in relation to collaboration with others (shared goals, social presence) in formal and informal contexts. Efforts have been made to understand autonomous language learning and its impact on L2 development from a variety of angles (Cappellini, Lewis & Mompean, 2017; Lai, 2017; Reinders & White, 2016). It is commonly recognized that a drive for self-directed learning becomes unequivocally one of the central factors in leading to high performance in technology-mediated language learning. Learner autonomy entails individual and social dimensions of learning that involves independent learning using self-access digital resources and collaborative interaction with others through networked communities. Both underlying individual (personal capacity, knowledge, skills) and social (shared responsibilities, collaboration with others) processes influence how students engage in their own learning.

Studies have shown that teachers play a crucial role in creating learning environments that are conductive to autonomous learning. For example, Lee's study (2016) investigated the affordances for autonomous learning in a fully online learning environment involving the implementation of task-based learning. The results showed that tasks related to real-world language use support social, cognitive, and affective dimensions of autonomous learning by allowing beginning students to learn independently and collaboratively with their peers and instructor. Attitudinal factors, such as beliefs and attitudes toward the use of technology have also been discussed in the literature (Lai, 2019). Students who have greater self-regulated learning dispositions, confidence in their language ability and strong beliefs about the target language use beyond the classroom are more likely to embrace digital technologies to achieve their learning goals and outcomes. However, students may not take advantage of the opportunity for self-regulated learning due to low self-efficacy and poor time management. Thus, teachers have the responsibility to create a conducive learning context that allows students to be fully involved and in charge of their learning.

Implications: supporting students' use of social media beyond the classroom

To effectively integrate social networked technology into L2 instruction, it is essential for teachers to create pedagogically sound learning activities. Task-based instruction (TBI) is arguably one of the most effective approaches to CALL because it promotes authentic use of the target language and supports SLA principles (González-Lloret & Ortega, 2014). Researchers have discussed potential benefits and challenges of TBI for technology-mediated language learning by addressing emerging topics such as task design, language development, focus on form, and more (Chong & Reinders, 2020; Thomas & Reinders, 2012; Ziegler, 2016). Studies have shown promising affordances that derive from implementing authentic tasks for meaningful interaction in technology-mediated learning environments (Lee, 2002; Wang & Vásquez, 2012). For example, Sauro (2014) found that technology-mediated fandom tasks (fans of books, movies) were effective to keep students engaged in learning outside the classroom. Learners created threaded stories and shared them with real audiences through various types of social media platforms. Another example is Lee's (2016) four-skill integrated approach to creating real-world tasks along with various types of CMC tools to expand the use of L2 beyond the classroom setting. From reading and viewing authentic materials (short stories and films) to writing (blogs) and speaking (audio and video recordings) tasks, students used the target language in meaningful contexts to build interpretive, interpersonal, and presentational skills. Significantly, technology-mediated tasks for out-of-class learning shifted the focus of instruction from the teacher to the students to enhance student engagement and promote active learning.

In addition to building language proficiency, developing cultural awareness is an indispensable part of language learning. It broadens students' minds, increases tolerance, and fosters cultural empathy and sensitivity. Accordingly, a three-stage (information exchange, comparing and analyzing, collaborative, and reflective) task sequencing design has been widely adopted to create structured virtual exchanges, and build learners' cultural knowledge and awareness (O'Dowd & Ware, 2009). Giving students the opportunity to reflect on their own perspectives is essential for a profound cultural learning that goes beyond the superficial 'facts only' approach. For example, Lee and Markey (2014) employed culture blogs for students to explore the relationship among the products (tangible and intangible), practices and perspectives of the target culture. Students presented their own cultural views, discussed and reflected upon cross-cultural issues, addressed stereotypes and preconceived judgments through ethnographic interviews with native informants. Consequently, students demonstrated various stages of intercultural competence from understanding cultural differences to demonstrating attitudes of openness and appreciation for the target culture. Nevertheless, teachers may not have pedagogical and digital competences required to make the best use of intercultural exchange (Luo &Yang, 2018). Language proficiency mismatch may challenge instructors to design effective tasks to meet linguistic needs for both groups. Language practitioners should look into successful technology-enhanced task-based models, such as the ones presented in UNICollaboration sponsored by The International Association of Telecollaboration and Virtual Exchange (http://uni-collaboration.eu/) to create engaging CMC tasks.

Focus on form and language accuracy

The literature points to the opportunity for noticing linguistic forms during task performance and its potential impact on L2 development within the context of CMC (Lai & Li, 2011; Ziegler, 2016). Different types of CMC tasks (e.g., jigsaw, problem-solving) have been carefully designed to allow for negotiation of meaning (fluency) and form (accuracy) to help learners build meaning-form connections. Research studies using the psycholinguistic approach have focused on noticing the gap between L1 and L2 from incidental negotiations in response to communication gaps in text chats (e.g., Blake & Zyzik, 2003). The outcomes revealed that learners negotiated meaning due to unknown lexical items. Other studies from sociocultural perspectives have explored how focus on form is noticed and negotiated through peer feedback in a joint collaborative activity. During task performance, learners assisted one another in reconstructing linguistic forms, rather than negotiation of meaning caused by communication breakdowns (e.g., Vinagre & Muñoz, 2011). In addition to noticing in text-based CMC, recent studies have examined focus on form in voice-based communication. For example, Yanguas and Bergin (2018) reported that students produced a high number of lexical language-related episodes and negotiations in the jigsaw tasks via audio mode of communication. Lee (2011) argues that learners tend to make notice of lexical features and ignore syntactical errors because they primarily focus on conveying ideas to reach mutual understanding. As a result, learners make progress in fluency rather than accuracy. One effective way to provide learners with meaningful interaction that goes beyond lexical problems is to include a focus-on-form procedure as a reflective past-task activity in which experts provide linguistic scaffolding to draw learners' attention to syntactic errors.

Although focus on form through corrective feedback has not yet been explored through mobile social networking, there is a concern that the language is being degraded because of the overly casual writing style. It is not uncommon to find grammar, sentence construction and orthographical errors in students' informal writing on their social media apps. As social networks become more prevalent, students are more invested in using text messaging as a central part of social communication. Yet, the blurring line between formal and informal writing viewed as 'text speak' style leads to a decline in their academic writing skills, and diminishes their ability to use correct grammar, vocabulary, and spelling. Pedagogical interventions are necessary to provide students with assistance in drawing their attention to focus on language problems to avoid fossilized errors and improve language accuracy. For example, focused tasks with specific linguistic features in the context of meaning-centered language use will facilitate noticing of lexical, morphological, and syntactic errors. Systematic analysis of errors will provide language practitioners with deep insight into learners' interlanguage process and allow them to design consciousness-raising activities to draw students' attention to focus on form.

Additionally, the instructor should openly discuss the value of focus on form with students, and encourage them to write for both fluency and accuracy in informal digital language learning environments.

Self-regulation outside the classroom

Social media has been increasingly used to foster self-regulated learning beyond the language classroom. Lee (2021) found that the use of technology-enhanced flipped learning model gave students agency over their own learning through self-access learning modules in *Canvas* and ethnographic interviews with NSs via *Zoom*. The findings showed that students demonstrated the capacity of taking charge of their own learning by using their prior knowledge and self-regulated skills to learn course content independently prior to class. Of particular importance, students learned to manage their time wisely and made the best use of digital resources (*YouTube* videos, *Quizlet*). The study concludes that the self-directed nature of flipped instruction presents challenges for students who are not ready for an autonomous approach. In another study, Lai and Zheng (2018) reported a survey study involving more than 200 beginning language students on self-directed use of mobile devices of L2 learning outside the classroom. The study showed that students used mobile devices to support personalized learning by self-selecting authentic resources (e.g., video clips, songs), rather than to connect and interact with the NSs through social networking. The findings revealed that the connectivity of anytime and anywhere mobile learning engaged L2 learners in the individual dimension of learner autonomy. The study suggests that out-of-class mobile learning needs to take into account the design of learning tasks and instructional interventions that will foster self-regulated language learning.

In addition, research studies have demonstrated that social presence and community building through social networks have positive effects on out-of-class autonomous language learning (Chik, 2014; Fornara & Lomicka, 2019). For example, the study by Peeters and Ludwing (2017) showed how the social media site, *Facebook* was used to develop learner autonomy. Students exercised their cognitive, social, and affective strategies to plan, discuss, and carry out writing assignments with their peers. Students established a sense of social presence, held each other accountable, and provided feedback to one another to achieve their shared learning goals. Using an ecological approach, Murray and Fujishima (2013) explored the language affordances in a social learning space called the *L-Café* where Japanese students practiced L2 skills with each other in an informal learning setting. Students valued group autonomy by co-constructing L2 knowledge with other participants and offering emotional support to each other such as compliment and encouragement. However, García Botero, Questier and Zhu (2019) point out that the lack of self-management and self-monitoring affects the degree of learner engagement in less-structured out-of-class settings. In their study, a number of students who used *Duolingo* for informal learning failed to self-manage their own learning due to the lack of time and motivation. To promote learner autonomy beyond the classroom, teachers should provide students with support for self-regulated learning by guiding them in the individual and collaborative process of learning; especially students with limited language proficiency and technological skills.

Future directions

The chapter has discussed and reflected the current trends of social media in the field of language learning focusing on the most prominent issues arising from the existing studies but has certainly not exhausted all the issues. Revolutionary changes in social media have afforded unlimited opportunities for students to engage in learning experiences outside of the classroom to enhance their language development, and build their cultural knowledge and awareness. As such, they have opened a window of possibilities for further research investigations and classroom implementation. Language educators should continue to explore the ways in which social media can be instrumental as a pedagogical tool to support LBC. Such efforts will deepen our understanding of how L2 learning occurs in social network supported environments, and raise learners' awareness of how new technologies can be used effectively for out-of-class learning. Technology does not promote learning on its own. Rather, its effectiveness lies in the way tasks are designed and carried out within the learning objectives supported by theoretical and pedagogical principles. Thus, tasks that meet real-world application and communication needs outside the classroom should be used to engage students in different stages of technology-mediated language learning.

Many more studies are still needed to fully understand the impact of social media on L2 learning and development. Existing research demonstrates that CMC tasks create an authentic learning context for students to interact and collaborate with others in class and beyond the classroom walls. A large number of studies, however, were reported based on qualitative (self-reports, interviews) and anecdotal evidence, providing only perception measures. Thus, multiple methods using both qualitative and quantitative data are needed to generate statistical measures using correctional analyses among different variables to provide a full picture of the role of CMC tasks and its impact on L2 learning (Ziegler, 2016). Due to the lack of a control group performing the same tasks, it is not feasible to document whether students are more productive in terms of the quantity or quality of their language use in out-of-class informal learning as opposed to in-class formal instruction. A future study focusing on the comparison of the results of the control and experimental groups will contribute to a greater understanding of task design and language development through social networking. Additionally, linguistic feedback should move forward with voice feedback that goes beyond written comments.

Adding audio-recorded feedback using digital voice recorders (*SpeakPipe, Vocaroo*) or oral feedback through video conferencing via *Zoom* and *Google Meet* on learners' speaking or writing could provide insights into the comparative effectiveness of written and oral feedback on the development of learners' interlanguage.

Another potential area of investigation is related to multimodel communication through social networking. Traditional forms of communication through social engagements have shifted from one-dimensional to now highly multimodal. Popular social media platforms like *Instagram and WhatsApp* allow for verbal and non-verbal modes of communication. As emphasized by Lomicka and Lord (2016), the future trend of social media communication will move toward more visual communication through sharing photos and images on social media. Since the research in this area is still in its infancy, future studies using multiple lenses (cognitive, social, cultural) of sociocultural perspectives and focusing on multiple semiotic resources should be taken into consideration. These will expand the repertoire of social medial tools that learners can use to engage in meaning making, and construct identity and social bonds. For example, what potential impact does the emergence of multidimensional social networks have on developing L2 language and cultural competencies? Which modes of semiotic resources are most beneficial for students with different learning styles?

It is evident that the technology itself does not determine the degree of learner autonomy. Creating pedagogically promising conditions for fostering out-of-class autonomy will increase our understanding of learners' motivation and engagement to digital-mediated learning environments. As Zourou, Potolia, and Zourou (2017) argued, the majority of existing studies on learner autonomy have focused almost exclusively on learners' perceptions using qualitative data with a few exceptions (e.g., Collentine, 2011; Lee, 2016). Thus, empirical studies using a mixed method approach are needed to find out how the degree of learner autonomy is affected by comparing formal instruction from a pre-designed syllabus to less-structured instruction that takes place outside of class in order to further provide evidence to test whether there is a significant difference in the presence of learner autonomy. Social network technologies have massively boosted content sharing and informal interactions with NSs. It would be worthwhile to investigate whether, over time, learners are self-motivated to engage in CMC tasks and collaborate with others without teacher interventions of monitoring the learning process and progress within the context of out-of-class language learning.

Finally, the fast evolving digital technologies have changed the role of teacher from a traditional knowledge presenter to a facilitator guiding students through the learning process. To ensure that students take full advantage of social media, teachers need to be equipped with pedagogical knowledge and digital literacy to facilitate effective communication, monitor students' involvement and progress, and provide timely feedback. The literature points to a concern over the lack of language teacher preparation in the use of digital technologies both in formal and informal settings (Kessler & Hubbard, 2017). Kessler (2018) argues that teacher preparation for using emerging technologies needs to go beyond short-term professional development and look to ways of engaging teachers in continuous training. Different approaches to the CALL teacher preparation programs have been established to provide pre-service and in-service teachers with opportunities to explore practical ways of using technology and assessment tools to evaluate student performance. Nevertheless, course training should focus on preparing teachers to effectively use social media and mobile technologies to create stimulating learning environments that promote self-directed learning. Future research should explore what strategies teachers use to implement digital-mediated learning activities such as digital games and augmented reality. It should also explore to what extent they are aware of potential benefits offered by social networks for out-of-class language learning and take steps to empower students through digital literacies.

Reflection questions

1. As the landscape of technology is rapidly evolving and is becoming increasingly prevalent in the field of language teaching and learning, what types of technology-mediated tasks and conditions work best for out-of-class learning and development? How can language educators create inclusive digital learning environments for L2 learners from different linguistic, social and cultural backgrounds?
2. Given that self-directed learning plays a central role in language learning and development, to what extent does the integration of social media into informal learning cultivate student interest and ability to learn autonomously? Does teacher intervention affect the way students from different language proficiencies and styles self-regulate their own learning beyond the classroom?
3. What new digital literacies and strategies do language learners need to develop as they navigate digital learning spaces? How does multimodal communication via social networking affect the way they connect and interact with online communities?

Recommended readings

Chapelle, C., & Sauro, S. (Eds.). (2017). *The handbook of technology and second language teaching and learning*. Hoboken, NJ: Wiley-Blackwell.
    The volume covers a wide spectrum of CALL research from a variety of theoretical perspectives and pedagogical applications. The handbook provides a comprehensive exploration of different areas of language learning, teaching and assessment through emerging uses of technology. Discussions highlight critical issues on research and development of technology for language learning.

Stockwell, G., & Reinders, H. (2019). Technology, motivation and autonomy, and teacher psychology in language learning: Exploring the myths and possibilities. *Annual Review of Applied Linguistics, 39*, 40–51.
    The chapter discusses a balanced view of language teaching and learning with technology involving appropriate pedagogies, technological affordances and ongoing training for students and teachers with the goal of developing skills and strategies that leads to higher levels of motivation and autonomy.

Thorne, S., & May, S. (Eds.). (2017). *Language, education, and technology*. Encyclopedia of language and education, 3rd edition. New York: Springer.
    The fully revised third edition offers 34 technology-focused chapters covering a wide range of topics from instructional practice, literacy learning to teacher development in language education. Discussions are drawn from interdisciplinary perspectives with different disciplines and diverse socio-geographic areas in language teaching and learning with technology.

References

Benson, P. (2011). Language learning and teaching beyond the classroom: An introduction to the field. In P. Benson & H. Reinders (Eds.), *Beyond the language classroom* (pp. 7–16). London: Palgrave Macmillan.

Blake, R., & Zyzik, E. C. (2003). Who's helping whom? Learner/heritage-speakers' networked discussions in Spanish. *Applied Linguistics, 24*(4), 519–544.

Boyd, D., & Ellison, N. (2007). Social network sites: Definition, history, and scholarship. *Journal of Computer-Mediated Communication, 13*(1), 210–230.

Cappellini, M., Lewis, T., & Mompean, A. (Eds.) (2017). *Learner autonomy and Web 2.0*. UK: Equinox.

Carr, C. T., & Hayes, R. A. (2015). Social media: Defining, developing, and divining. *Atlantic Journal of Communication, 23*, 46–65.

Chen, H. I. (2013). Identity practices of multilingual writers in social networking spaces. *Language Learning & Technology, 17*(2), 143–170.

Chik, A. (2014). Digital gaming and language learning: Autonomy and community. *Language Learning & Technology, 18*(2), 85–100.

Choi, J., & Nunan, D. (2018). Language learning and activation in and beyond the classroom. *Australian Journal of Applied Linguistics, 1*(2), 49–63.

Chong, S. W., & Reinders, H. (2020). Technology-mediated task-based language teaching: A qualitative research synthesis. *Language Learning & Technology, 24*(3), 70–86.

Collentine, K. (2011). Learner autonomy in a task-based 3D world and production. *Language Learning & Technology, 15*(3), 50–67.

Dixon, E., & Thomas, M. (Eds.) (2015). *Researching language learner interaction online: From social media to MOOCs*. San Marcos, TX: CALICO.

Dooly, M. (2017). Performing identities in social media: Focusing on language learners' identity construction online. *Apprentissage des langues et systèmes d'information et de communication (Alsic), 20*(1). Retrieved from https://journals.openedition.org/alsic/3005

Dressman, M., & Sadler, R. (Eds.) (2020). *The handbook of informal language learning*. Hoboken, NJ: Wiley-Blackwell.

Farr, F., & Murray, L. (Eds.) (2016). *Routledge handbook of language learning and technology*. New York: Routledge.

Fornara, F., & Lomicka, L. (2019). Using visual social media in language learning to investigate the role of social presence. *CALICO Journal, 36*(3), 184–203.

García Botero, G., Questier, F., & Zhu, C. (2019). Self-directed language learning in a mobile-assisted, out-of-class context: Do students walk the talk?. *Computer Assisted Language Learning, 32*(1–2), 71–97.

González–Lloret, M., & Ortega, L. (Eds.) (2014). *Technology-mediated TBLT*. Philadelphia, PA: John Benjamins.

Hafner, C. A. (2014). Embedding digital literacies in English language teaching: Students' digital video projects as multimodal ensembles. *TESOL Quarterly, 48*(4), 655–685.

Kessler, G. (2018). Technology and the future of language teaching. *Foreign language Annals, 51*(1), 205–218.

Kessler, G., & Hubbard, P. (2017). Language teacher education and technology. In C. Chapelle & S. Sauro (Eds.), *The handbook of technology and second language teaching and learning* (pp. 278–292). Hoboken, NJ: Wiley-Blackwell.

King, B. W. (2015). Wikipedia writing as praxis: Computer-mediated socialization of second-language writers. *Language Learning & Technology, 19*(3), 106–123.

Kress, G. (2010). *Multimodality: A social semiotic approach to contemporary communication*. London: Routledge.

Kukulska-Hulme, A. (2015). Language as a bridge connecting formal and informal language learning through mobile devices. In L-H. Wong, M. Milrad & M. Specht (Eds.), *Seamless learning in the age of mobile connectivity* (pp. 281–294). Singapore: Springer.

Lai, C. (2017). *Autonomous language learning with technology beyond the classroom*. London & New York: Bloomsbury Academic.

Lai, C. (2019). Learning beliefs and autonomous language learning with technology beyond the classroom. *Language Awareness, 28*(4), 291–309.

Lai, C., & Li, G. (2011). Technology and task-based language teaching: A critical review. *CALICO Journal, 28*(2), 498–521.

Lai, C., & Zheng, D. (2018). Self-directed use of mobile devices for language learning beyond the classroom. *ReCALL, 30*(3), 299–318.

Lamy, M.-N., & Zourou, K. (2013). *Social networking for language education*. Basingstoke, UK: Palgrave Macmillan.

Lantz-Andersson, A. (2016). Embracing social media for educational linguistic activities. *Nordic Journal of Digital Literacy, 10*(1), 51–77.

Lee, L. (2002). Enhancing learners' communication skills through synchronous electronic interaction and task-based instruction. *Foreign Language Annals, 35*(1), 16–23.

Lee, L. (2011). Focus on form through peer feedback in a Spanish-American telecollaborative exchange. *Language Awareness, 20*(4), 343–357.

Lee, L. (2016). Autonomous learning through task-based instruction in fully online language courses. *Language Learning & Technology, 20*(2), 81–97.

Lee, L. (2017). Learners' perceptions of the effectiveness of blogging for L2 writing in fully online language courses. *International Journal of Computer-Assisted Language Learning and Teaching, 7*(1), 20–34.

Lee, L. (2019). Empowering beginning language learners' voices through digital storytelling: An exploratory study. In F. Nami (Ed.), *Digital storytelling in second and foreign language teaching* (pp. 179–196). New York: Peter Lang Publishing.

Lee, L. (2020). Promoting interpersonal and intercultural communication with Flipgrid: Design, implementation and outcomes. In K. Mariusz & M. Peterson (Eds.), *New technological applications for foreign and second language learning and teaching* (pp. 262–282). IGI Global.

Lee, L. (2021). Exploring self-regulated learning through flipped instruction with digital technologies: An intermediate Spanish course. In C. Fuchs, M. Hauck & M. Dooly (Eds.), *Language education in digital space: Perspectives on autonomy and interaction* (pp. 39–59). Berlin: Springer.

Lee, L., & Markey, A. (2014). A study of learners' perceptions of online intercultural exchange through Web 2.0 technologies. *ReCALL, 26*(3), 1–20.

Lomicka, L., & Lord, G. (2016). Social networking and language learning. In F. Farr & M. Murray (Eds.), *The Routledge handbook of language learning and technology* (pp. 255–268). New York: Routledge.

Luo, H., & Yang, C. (2018). Twenty years of telecollaborative practice: Implications of teaching Chinese as a foreign language. *Computer Assisted Language Learning, 31*(5–6), 546–571.

Murray, G., & Fujishima, N. (2013). Social language learning spaces: Affordances in a community of learners. *Chinese Journal of Applied Linguistics, 36*(1), 141–157.

Nunan, D., & Richards, J. C. (Eds.) (2015). *Language learning beyond the classroom*. New York: Routledge.

O'Dowd, R., & Lewis, T. (2016). *Online intercultural exchange: Policy, pedagogy, practice*. New York: Routledge.

O'Dowd, R., & Ware, P. (2009). Critical issues in telecollaborative task design. *Computer Assisted Language Learning, 22*(2), 173–188.

Peeters, W., & Ludwig, C. (2017). Old concepts in new spaces: A model for developing learner autonomy in social networking spaces. In T. Lewis, A. Rivens Mompean & M. Cappellini (Eds.), *Learner autonomy and Web 2.0* (pp. 117–142). Sheffield: Equinox.

Reinders, H., & Benson, P. (2017). Research agenda: Language learning beyond the classroom. *Language Teaching, 50*(4), 561–578.

Reinders, H., & White, C. (2016). 20 year of autonomy and technology: How far have we come and where to go next? *Language Learning & Technology, 20*(2), 143–154.

Reinhardt, J. (2020). Metaphors for social media-enhanced foreign language teaching and learning. *Foreign Language Annals, 53*(2), 234–242.

Reinhardt, J., & Ryu, J. (2013). Using social network-mediated bridging activities to develop socio-pragmatic awareness in elementary Korean. *International Journal of Computer-Assisted Language Learning and Teaching, 3*(3), 18–33.

Reinhardt, J., & Thorne, S. (2019). Digital literacies as emergent multifarious repertoires. In N. Arnold & L. Ducate (Eds.), *Engaging language learners in CALL: From theory and research to informed practice* (pp. 208–239). London, UK: Equinox.

Rodriguez, J. (2011). Social media use in higher education: Key areas to consider for educators. *The Journal of Online Learning and Teaching, 7*(4), 539–550.

Sauro, S. (2014). Lessons from the fandom: Task models for technology-enhanced language learning. In M. González-Lloret & L. Ortega (Eds.), *Technology- mediated TBLT: Researching technology and tasks* (pp. 239–262). Philadelphia: John Benjamins.

Stevenson, M. P., & Liu, M. (2010). Learning a language with Web 2.0: Exploring the use of social networking features of foreign language learning websites. *CALICO Journal, 27*(1), 233–259.

Sykes, J., & Reinhardt, J. (2013). *Language at play: Digital games in second and foreign language teaching and learning.* New York: Pearson-Prentice Hall.

Taguchi, N., & Sykes, J. (Eds.) (2013). *Technology in interlanguage pragmatics research and teaching.* Philadelphia, PA: John Benjamins.

Thomas, M., & Reinders, H. (Eds.) (2012). *Task-based language learning and teaching with technology.* New York: Continuum.

Thomas, M., Reinders, H., & Warschauer, M. (2013). *Contemporary computer-assisted language learning.* London, UK: Bloomsbury Academic.

Vinagre, M., & Muñoz, B. (2011). Computer-mediated corrective feedback and language accuracy in telecollaborative exchanges. *Language Learning & Technology, 15*(1), 72–103.

Wang, S., & Vásquez, C. (2012). Web 2.0 and second language learning: What does the research tell us? *CALICO Journal, 29*(3), 412–430.

Yanguas, I., & Bergin, T. (2018). Focus on form in task-based L2 oral computer mediated communication. *Language Learning & Technology, 22*(3), 65–81.

Ziegler, N. (2016). Taking technology to task: Technology-mediated TBLT, performance, and production. *Annual Review of Applied Linguistics, 36*, 136–163.

Zourou, K. (2017). Identity and engagement in networked Open Educational Practice. *Apprentissage des langues et systèmes d'information et de communication (Alsic), 20*(1).

Zourou, K., & Loiseau, M. (2013). Bridging design and language interaction and reuse in Livemocha's culture space. In M.-N. Lamy & K. Zourou (Eds.), *Social networking for language education* (pp. 77–99). Basingstoke, UK: Palgrave Macmillan.

Zourou, K., Potolia, A., & Zourou, F. (2017). Informal social networking for language learning: Insights into autonomy stances. In T. Lewis, A. Rivens Mompean & T. Cappellini (Eds.), *Learner autonomy and Web 2.0* (pp. 141–167). San Marcos, TX: CALICO.

12
ENHANCING LANGUAGE AND CULTURE LEARNING IN THE CASE OF STUDY ABROAD

Martin Howard

Introduction

Within the diversity of opportunities for language learning beyond the classroom, study abroad constitutes a more permanent venue in so far as the learner is necessarily located for a period of time, albeit temporary, of varying duration in the target language community. Opportunities extend to all age groups from short-term homestays and residential programmes for children and adults to longer-term school and university exchange programmes. Typically, such study abroad involves 'study' whereby learners follow a programme of instruction, although other opportunities allow for a work placement, a homestay, or simply a sojourn organised by the learner him/herself. In the case of second language (L2) learning, study abroad uptake generally reflects the folk-belief that it offers an ideal combination of instructed input in the foreign language classroom followed by naturalistic exposure through supposed immersion in the target language community (DeKeyser, 1991).

Key constructs

Enquiry into L2 and culture learning in a study abroad context primarily focusses on the nature of learner development during a sojourn abroad as they assume the guise of a pseudo-naturalistic learner, although fundamentally remaining instructed learners (Coleman, 1995). The at-home-instructed learning context is characterised by more restricted opportunities for language contact, often in a drip-feed manner such that the intensity of exposure is more limited compared to the immersion experience abroad. As members of the target language community, study abroad learners thus in principle have more extensive opportunities over longer duration for language use in authentic situations. L2 instruction at home may also include more explicit learning which aims to develop the learner's metalinguistic knowledge in a way that is less true of the more implicit learning that characterises naturalistic learners. Beyond such differences at the level of input exposure and knowledge development, study abroad learners may also come to identify differently as L2 users within the target language community. Study abroad research explores how such change in learning context impacts L2 learning with regard to three fundamental areas of second language acquisition research, namely linguistic development, input and interaction, and individual differences. A further strand is concerned with intercultural competence.

In the case of linguistic development, the traditional investigation into speaking, listening, reading and writing through general language tests and self-evaluation reports has given way to studies of specific components of the learner's linguistic repertoire, such as pronunciation, fluency, lexis, grammar, sociolinguistic and pragmatic competence, and discourse, interactional and literacy skills. Such areas are generally investigated in elicited spoken and written learner data, such as conversations and role-plays, as well as written discourse and judgement tests. Such studies have generally adopted a longitudinal design through pre- and post-test comparisons which capture the scope of development on different language features. While some cross-sectional studies allow comparison with learners who do not venture abroad ('at-home' learners), Rees and Klapper (2008) question the validity of such comparison in so far as the experience of each group is fundamentally different, while learners who venture abroad are motivated to do so in a way that 'at-home' learners may not be.

If study abroad has the potential to impact L2 development, it is based on the premise that learning conditions are different between the foreign language classroom and the target language community. There is thus a need to understand the nature of the learner's engagement with the language input abroad, giving rise to questions of the type of language contact opportunities including both active and passive exposure, quantity and quality of input, and frequency, duration and intensity of contact (see Howard, 2011). Such issues have been investigated using language logs and learner diaries, as well as the Language Contact Profile (LCP [Freed, Dewey, Segalowitz, & Halter, 2004]) which captures the amount of time spent on various activities.

The questions also necessarily pertain to the learner's social networks and integration abroad, such as the range of individuals the learner knows, the depth and closeness of the relationship, and frequency of interaction, among others. As investigated through the Study Abroad Social Interaction Questionnaire (Dewey, Ring, Gardner, & Belnap, 2013), while we often consider the learner to be 'immersed' abroad, such immersion is not automatic or even guaranteed whereby the learner as a new and temporary member of the host community has to develop relationships over a short time span. Coleman's (2013) concentric circles model offers a useful means of conceptualising such social network development: while the learner may initially have contact in the inner circle with fellow compatriots, and then with fellow international sojourners within a middle circle, the challenge to create social networks involving native speakers constitutes a more difficult outer circle. Such interactional opportunities with expert speakers are often restricted to transactional service encounters with opportunities to engage in more creative interactional communication posing a greater challenge (see Devlin, 2014).

If such issues of language contact point to potential differences in the individual learner's experience abroad, a third area of focus provides a broader sweep of the individual differences which arise. Such differences underpin the inter-learner variability seen to be greater in a study abroad context than in the foreign language classroom (Freed, 1995b), whereby the scope of linguistic gains differs across learners. This branch of enquiry investigates socio-biographical and programmatic factors which may condition the scope of development. They include age, gender, motivation, attitudes, aptitude and personality, along with programmatic features such as duration of stay, onset proficiency level and timing of study abroad, learner status abroad (such as a programme of classroom instruction, a work placement, or residence abroad) and residence type (such as a homestay, apartment sharing, or living alone).

The areas identified point to the breadth of issues underpinning language learning abroad. Complementing such a focus, work on culture learning offers mutually informative insights, reflecting that linguistic competence is necessarily entwined with the wide-ranging experiences which the learner engages in. From this point of view, study abroad constitutes a rich area of enquiry for the study of wide-ranging dimensions of the broad concept of 'culture learning' such as in relation to intercultural competence and skills, intercultural awareness and knowledge, intercultural socialisation and intercultural identity. Development of such areas pertains to learner attitudes and experiences of engagement with and reactions to cultural difference between the self and others. Their investigation is complex since intercultural competence is not static or an end product in itself, that someone 'has', but rather fluid and dynamic, mediated during learner discourse construction with the other (see Jackson, 2017).

Intercultural investigation has seen both quantitative and qualitative approaches. In the former case, studies have drawn on questionnaires whereby they attempt to quantify intercultural growth, situating the learner at various stages of development, such as in the case of Hammer's (2012) Intercultural Development Inventory and Bennett's (1993) Development Model of Intercultural Sensitivity which incorporate ethnocentric stages of Denial, Defense, and Minimization and more ethnorelative stages of Acceptance, Adaptation and Integration. Qualitative approaches complement such quantitative analysis in mixed-methods analysis, drawing, for example, on learner interviews, logs and diaries. They capture the relationship between learner experiences, attitudes and feelings over the course of study abroad, offering detail that may not be apparent in quantitative analysis in relation to changes in attitudes such as culture shock, tolerance and open-mindedness.

Key issues

As Pérez-Vidal and Juan-Garau (2011, p. 177) note in relation to the foreign language classroom and study abroad, if "each of the two contexts has differential patterns of input exposure, both quantitatively and qualitatively, their effect on the participants' communicative and motivational development will be different". A key issue therefore concerns the nature of the impact of study abroad on linguistic development. If early research based on general language tests and learner self-evaluations points to greater gains in speaking and listening compared to reading and writing (see, for example, Carroll, 1967, Dyson, 1988, Lapkin, Hart, & Swain, 1995), research from the 1990s onwards highlighted the differential gains made across different components of the learner's linguistic repertoire. Findings support the relative benefits of study abroad in a number of areas, namely, fluency, lexical and sociolinguistic development, and sociopragmatic competence to a certain extent. In the case of fluency, studies note that learners speak faster, attain a higher speech rate, and are more at ease in speaking compared to their at-home counterparts (see Freed, 1995a; Llanes & Muñoz, 2013). In the related area of communication strategies, Lafford's (1995) findings indicate that her study abroad learners develop a greater range of communication strategies such that they are more at ease with dealing with the various difficulties that arise in communicative interaction. Taguchi (2015) offers insight into interactional competence in a study of American learners of Japanese, finding that they became more adept at turn construction during conversation.

In the case of vocabulary, gains extend not only to lexical range but also how that vocabulary is used. Milton and Meara (1994) report that their European learners spending six months in the UK acquired vocabulary "five times faster than for those who took classes at home […] gaining vocabulary at a rate of over 2,500 words per year" (p. 31). Ife, Boix Vives and Meara (2000) observe how their learners of Spanish demonstrate more native-like organisation of the lexicon in terms of collocations.

Sociolinguistic and pragmatic competence respectively relate to the socially appropriate use of variable linguistic forms such as 'ng' vs. 'n' (for example, going vs. goin') variation in English, and the expression of different speech acts such as requests and apologies, pragmatic routines and use of discourse markers. In the case of sociolinguistic competence, studies such as Howard (2012) note the significant impact of study abroad on use of informal variants compared to the overuse relative to native speaker norms of formal variants prior to study abroad. In the case of pragmatic competence, studies have noted gains in production, comprehension and awareness although in some cases, the extent of development is quite minimal. Barron (2003) reports on a longitudinal study of Irish learners in Germany, exploring the expression of refusal, offers and requests. Findings indicate that while they evidenced progress in the direction of native-speaker norms, that progress was very much 'in the direction of' as opposed to reaching such norms. Howard and Shively (2022) note that while progress in production can be made quite quickly such as in the case of service encounter requests, it is in other cases quite slow such as refusals and advice-giving, reflecting an effect for input exposure and saliency. Production skills have been complemented in work on pragmatic comprehension and perception, that is learner awareness of pragmatic norms. In the former case, Howard and Shively (2022) note differences depending on the type of pragmatic routine concerned such as those tied to specific communicative contexts as opposed to those employed in different contexts, although pragmatic awareness is generally seen to develop well.

In contrast to the areas outlined, findings for two components of the learner's linguistic repertoire are more mixed, namely pronunciation and grammar development. In the former area, Díaz-Campos' (2004) study of American learners of Spanish suggests limited gains on pronunciation features known to pose difficulty to L2 learners. In contrast, Mora (2008) reports some development in the production of voiceless oral stops among Spanish learners of English, but notes little progress on learner perception of some phoneme contrasts such as /p/ vs. /b/. Other studies offer complementary findings, exploring perceived foreign accent. Llanes (2016) reports more positive native speaker ratings of learner speech following study abroad even after just a couple of weeks.

The investigation of grammatical development during study abroad has generally seen two approaches. Studies conducted within the framework of complexity, accuracy and fluency (CAF) have noted gains, whereby learner spoken production evidences greater syntactic complexity and morphosyntactic accuracy. For example, in a study of Spanish university learners of English, Pérez-Vidal and Juan-Garau (2011) apply a range of measures which indicate gains, with some exceptions in written complexity. Such an approach contrasts with other studies which have investigated development on specific grammatical features such as verb inflections for the expression of tense, aspect, modality, number and person, as well as nominal and adjectival inflections for gender marking and agreement. In this regard, findings are more mixed, suggesting that the CAF gains evidenced through more global measures may not capture the detail of the more variable levels of development across specific grammatical features. For example, Collentine (2004) finds that his American university learners of Spanish during a semester abroad demonstrate lesser gains, if at all, in comparison to those who remain at home. Some studies, however, note differences depending on the grammatical feature. Marqués-Pascual (2011) reports gains on subject omission and subject-verb inversion, but not for verb agreement in Spanish. Such differential findings raise the question of the role of grammatical feature, but also of other factors impacting linguistic development during study abroad. We consider such issues in the following, firstly in relation to input matters and then individual difference factors.

As Pavlenko (2009) notes, language is not contagious, and we need therefore to better understand the learner's interaction in his/her newfound learning context and the relationship with linguistic gains. Findings are mixed where Freed (1991) and Díaz-Campos (2004), for example, report an effect of different activities such as watching TV and reading, but Juan-Garau, Salazar-Noguera and Prieto-Arranz (2014), Martinsen (2010) and Serrano, Tragant and Llanes (2012) do not. Complementing such work is a focus on learner social networks. On this count, Dewey, Bown and Eggett (2012) find some characteristics especially conducive to linguistic development, namely the range of social networks that the learner develops and intensity of relationships within those networks.

Other work has considered the characteristics of the learner's language contact abroad. Kinginger, Wu, Lee and Tan (2016) offer insight into the role of everyday situations such as family mealtime routines within a homestay context in China. Their work highlights the role of such routines as opportunities for host family engagement and learning. In a further study of Americans in France, Kinginger (2008) presents learner perspectives on such encounters, with some reporting limited engagement on the part of the host who saw the learner in some cases as a paying guest. Wilkinson (2002) notes the repetitive nature of interaction in a homestay context in so far as it replicates the question-response routine of the traditional classroom led by the teacher, leading to limited creative conversation. While the homestay is assumed to offer rich interactional opportunities, Rivers' (1998) comparison of home-stay and non-home-stay learners points to the greater gains made by the latter learners. He interprets such findings as reflecting an effect of co-eval peer interaction in other accommodation types. But beyond residence type, Devlin (2014) notes the learner's difficulty to develop genuine communicative opportunities, observing that more transactional interaction dominates of a formulaic nature in service encounters.

Beyond input matters, issues arise in relation to the role of socio-biographical and programmatic factors in shaping experiences and development abroad. Llanes and Muñoz (2013) investigate age differences among Spanish learners of English, finding greater development on CAF measures among children compared to adults. With regard to gender, Pellegrino Aveni (2005) reports harassment issues among her American female learners in Russia, unlike their male counterparts and which impacted their engagement and linguistic development in the host community. At a socio-psychological level, learner attitudes and motivation have been the focus of investigation. Kinginger (2008) observes how learner attitudes may evolve during a sojourn depending on learner experiences of their host community such that learners react differently, with some learners withdrawing from situations involving host community engagement. Related to the factor of attitudes is motivation. Trenchs-Parera and Juan-Garau (2014) report a positive impact on changes in factors underpinning motivation such as anxiety. Juan-Garau et al. (2014) note increased integrative motivation during study abroad compared to instrumental motivation where the former refers to learner interest in the language for cultural and integrative reasons compared to the more instrumental reasons underpinning the latter. However, such changes did not correlate with the learners' lexico-morphosyntactic development. Learner aptitude is a further factor, relating to cognitive capacity such as in terms of working memory. In this respect, Grey, Cox, Serafini and Sanz (2015) fail to find an effect on morphosyntactic gains in their study of American learners of Spanish. A final factor considered is that of personality where Arvidsson, Eykmans, Rosier and Forsberg Lundell (2018) report a relationship between some dimensions of personality such as cultural empathy and oral skills development, and open-mindedness and cultural empathy and frequency of language usage.

Beyond such factors characterising the learner, programmatic factors are a further area. While we have referred to accommodation type, other factors concern the role of proficiency level and duration of the stay abroad. On the former count, while Freed (1995b) notes that the scope of development is greater for less advanced learners given that they simply have more to gain, other studies note that less proficient learners may not have the requisite linguistic level to cope with the naturalistic input abroad. DeKeyser (2010), for example, exploring grammatical development among American learners of Spanish, notes that they made little progress because their level of proficiency was not sufficiently developed to be able to use the input at a grammatical level. Similarly, in the case of duration of stay abroad, studies differ hugely, ranging from a couple of weeks to a full academic year. While the components of the learner's linguistic repertoire referred to earlier are seen to evidence development even after a short stay abroad of just a couple of weeks, other studies note that development may take longer in some areas. Serrano et al. (2012) observe gains in lexis and fluency after one semester among Spanish learners of English, with grammatical gains only emerging in the second semester.

The wide-ranging factors referred to highlight the complexity of the language learning experience. Such complexity is also seen in the related area of culture learning, where studies similarly point to the considerable individual variability in gains made and the individuality of experiences that shape intercultural development. Jackson (2017), for example, draws on a mixed-methods approach to explore such development in different case studies of Hong Kong university students. Quantitative analysis points to differential levels of development in relation to the stages within the intercultural development models referred to, without necessarily reaching the final stage. Development is also not necessarily linear, with some learners evidencing regression. Qualitative analysis illuminates such findings, showing how diverse factors, especially learner attitudes, shape the potential for such development. While learners may have positive enthusiastic attitudes at the outset and overestimate their sense of intercultural self, the personal challenges of the experience abroad are such that they withdraw from wider engagement to differing degrees as the sojourn progresses. While some learners may embrace the opportunities for intercultural engagement through more passive activities such as cinema-going, as in Alfayez and Hüttner's (2019) study of Saudi learners during a sojourn in the US, other work highlights the challenges of more active socialisation beyond one's group. For example, Durbidge's (2017) work with Japanese adolescent learners of English shows how they maintain a strong affiliation with their home culture and cultural practices. Patron (2007) offers similar findings in the case of French university learners in Australia, for whom national culture held a predominant place even if they did evidence changes in cultural identity in other respects.

Taken together, the threefold approach to the relationship between L2 acquisition and study abroad complemented by work from a culture perspective highlights the complexity of such a relationship with multiple factors at play, ranging from the linguistic to input and social matters to wide-ranging personal and programmatic factors. At a theoretical level, the diverse findings illuminate the complex role of study abroad as a learning context in a theory of second language acquisition. On this count, study abroad research serves to contribute to our understanding of various factors, such as in the case of the role of language contact, the nature of linguistic development during a change in learning context, and the role of individual differences. While there are undoubtedly linguistic gains to be made, there are no guaranteed acquisition miracles that might uphold the folk-belief referred to earlier. In terms of practice, the findings thus provide a more realistic understanding of the complexity of the challenges faced by learners during a sojourn abroad, as they grapple with enhancing their proficiency across the multiple components of their linguistic repertoire, but constrained by difficulties in maximising the input available to them while also being conditioned by the factors that give rise to the individual differences referred to. If the findings point to the complex interaction between language acquisition and learning context underpinned by such a multitude of factors, they also point to the difficulty to generalise the findings across learners. As Coleman (2013) notes, there is no single study abroad experience, but rather the individual's experience as a whole person is unique, shaped by a myriad of factors reflected in the considerable inter-learner variability seen to characterise learner outcomes.

Implications

Given the growing numbers of language learners who embark on a sojourn abroad each year, the global findings across the areas outlined carry important implications for our understanding of language learning among a significant learner cohort. As language practitioners, we need to be cognisant of the reality of that experience, and ensure that the expectations of our learners take account of the challenges they will face abroad. Learners are often victims of overly positive marketing messages that present an idealised picture of the study abroad experience (see Güvendir, Acar-Güvendir, & Dündar, 2021), but as language instructors, we can play an important role in preparing our learners prior to their departure, in mentoring them during the experience, and recognising the specificity of their needs on their return. While they can do very well during study abroad, even in cases of relatively short-term study abroad, our privileged place in shaping their learning trajectory allows us to input to varying levels into their experience abroad. In terms of preparation and mentoring, there is scope to sensitise them to the reality of the experience, providing learning strategies to maximise the benefits to be made, along with coping strategies in facing the challenges that arise (see Moreno Bruna & Goethals, 2020; Oguro & Cottier, 2021). Such preparation and mentoring relate to issues such as language contact opportunities, social integration, learner agency and self-regulation, motivation, and intercultural attitudes and engagement. In the case of intercultural development, Moreno Bruna and Goethals (2020), for example, highlight the importance of critical self-reflection which learners can be sensitised to as a means of making sense of different experiences and encounters, and considering their reactions to differences encountered. While other actors interact in the learner's experience abroad, the learner too plays a key role in shaping that experience, and preparation and mentoring can assist in that process.

A further implication for practice relates to instructional programming in terms of the relationship between the input provided in a classroom context during study abroad and the language situations learners find themselves in. Salaberry, White and Rue Birch (2019) call for greater attention to such a matter whereby the practice opportunities that learners engage in outside the classroom can fruitfully be reflected in the training they receive within the classroom. Instructional issues also relate to the learner's return following study abroad where the findings provide a profile of the potential differential development across components of their linguistic repertoire. That development is not a uniform entity or a case of 'all or nothing', while also underpinned by considerable inter-learner variability, such that our instructional practices need to consider the consolidation of gains made and development in areas more resistant to development during a stay abroad.

A final practical dimension relates to more global programmatic features concerning questions of type of study abroad programme, residence type, duration of stay abroad and timing of study abroad within the learner's programme of study. Such issues are constrained by wider institution factors and learner preferences, but the findings call for reflection on how and when we organise study abroad for our learners, as well as programme design.

While the findings carry wide-ranging practical implications, they also hold theoretical implications for our understanding of the role of learning context. Early second language acquisition research underlined the universality of the psycholinguistic process of acquisition across learners. While the social turn since the early 2000s has highlighted the need to understand contextual factors at play, study abroad research constitutes a rich territory for understanding how such factors shape L2 development and learning experiences. Learning context clearly matters, with developmental changes occurring when the learner switches context from an instructed one to a naturalistic setting. While it might be considered that naturalistic learning simply speeds up development that could otherwise happen in the classroom setting, the naturalistic setting seems especially propitious to development on social language usage such as in the case of spoken language skills, especially fluency, interactional competence, communication strategies, vocabulary usage, sociolinguistic competence and to a certain extent pragmatic competence. Such development suggests a clear role for the language input and the learner's identity as an L2 user in so far as the language contact opportunities characterising the naturalistic setting seem to be conducive to development in these areas in a way that the instructed context is not, or at least to a lesser extent. In contrast, the impact on grammatical development and to some extent pronunciation is less clear-cut, with the possibility that classroom instruction holds greater benefit. It may be the case that as 'instructed' learners, they are not conditioned to utilise the naturalistic input in the implicit manner that 'naturalistic' learners become accustomed to. From a theoretical perspective, the question thus remains as to how study abroad impacts acquisition *processes* especially in relation to grammar, as opposed to simply speeding up acquisition *outcomes* on more social features of language.

Future directions

The findings presented are predominantly based on studies of Western learners in a range of target language countries. The duration of the stay abroad ranges from a couple of weeks to a full academic year. The programme type ranges from the more short-term study abroad increasingly popular in a North American context which has a more 'organised' format where students are often accompanied by home faculty, to the more independent, longer-term transnational Erasmus+ programme in Europe. While the findings available are rich, they thus stem from a diverse range of studies which are often not comparable, giving rise to an equally diverse range of sometimes contradictory findings, making it difficult to draw more substantive conclusions. In this regard, more controlled comparative studies, experimental studies as well as replication studies will be a welcome addition to the field as a means of better understanding programmatic issues surrounding the role of duration of stay abroad, timing of study abroad, type of study abroad programme, and the role of preparation and mentoring within a programme. Questions also remain surrounding the learner's needs post-study abroad and their reintegration in the language classroom. Future studies will be insightful in better understanding the long-term retention of the gains made abroad when the learner is no longer in the host environment.

Beyond such programmatic questions, other questions concern the learner's language contact abroad. The role of English as a global lingua franca (ELF) is especially pertinent whereby many learners necessarily engage in ELF usage, with a need therefore to understand its development as a target language, but also as just one language in the learner's plurilingual repertoire. Indeed, recent studies highlight the plurilingual characteristic of study abroad where various languages are in co-use, such as the target language, the learners' source language, ELF, and others that the learners know (see Moreno Bruna & Goethals, 2020). There is thus increasing need to explore such plurilingual identity during study abroad (see Cots, Mitchell, & Beaven, 2021).

A further issue in language contact is that of instructional programming during study abroad. Experimental work will provide greater insight into how we can better enhance our instructional offerings during study abroad so that learners can maximise the interactional opportunities available to them outside the classroom. There is scope for greater understanding of the relationship between input exposure and linguistic development during study abroad. We know little about how comprehension skills develop with specific regard to issues of input perception, awareness, noticing, parsing and processing of specific features and their relationship to subsequent uptake, use and acquisition of those features. As DeKeyser (2007, p. 208) notes, "research illustrates that transfer of knowledge and skills from a foreign instructed context to a study abroad context is far from obvious". If promotion of study abroad is based on the premise that a change in input conditions is conducive to linguistic development, tracking of such input matters over time will provide crucial insights. A further dimension here relates to the role of technology in learner's access to the target language input. While often frowned upon in so far as it offers a means of maintaining contact with their home culture and language, some studies highlight the role of technology in providing learners with contact to the target language and culture and its members (see Seibert Hanson & Dracos, 2019). Given the link between language and culture, there is thus also potential to explore the interrelationship between the learner's development in both areas.

In sum, the areas outlined as a roadmap for future research reflect fruitful directions for investigation. Study abroad learners are a growing cohort of learners in our institutions, both as sending and host institutions such that it is critical that they not be neglected in development of our language education policy and practices. The findings thus extend to all stakeholders, from language instructors and study abroad organisers, planning and policy makers, to study abroad participants and their families. In considering both existing and future findings, a number of issues underpin how those actors engage with those findings. Firstly, as language instructors and study abroad organisers, we have to reflect on how we can draw upon the rich insights in our own practices. The findings do not necessarily call for change in practice but we can be cognisant of how they may inform language learning among participants who have the privilege to go abroad, but also the many who do not. On the latter count, there may be insights on language learning in a study abroad context that we can transfer to how we engage with and what we offer to learners who do not go abroad. A second issue pertains to planning and policy making where the question of the relationship between research, policy and practice arises. That interface is a long-standing one that remains to be addressed such that the rich insights available should necessarily inform future policy and practice around study abroad matters at micro and macro level. Finally, learners themselves and their parents/guardians constitute central stakeholders where we need to consider how we can engage with them so that they can benefit from the insights available, both in advance of and during study abroad, but also on their return in terms of good learning practices through other means in the short and long term. In sum, as a rich, buoyant sub-field of Applied Linguistics, the findings are ripe for engaging with the wide array of stakeholders whose endeavours are at its core.

Reflection questions

1. Prior to study abroad, how can we best engage with our students in preparing for the learning opportunities and challenges that arise outside the classroom in study abroad?
2. During study abroad, what type of mentoring can the home and host institutions offer to support our students in maximising the learning opportunities available during study abroad?
3. During study abroad, how can we enhance the interface between the students' language and cultural learning in the classroom abroad and their learning experiences as language users in the wider target language community?
4. Following study abroad, how can students be supported in consolidating the linguistic and intercultural gains made abroad as language users on their return home?

Recommended readings

Kinginger, C. *Social and cultural aspects of language learning in study abroad*. Amsterdam/Philadelphia: John Benjamins, 2013.

This edited volume presents a collection of studies which illuminate the complex and diverse intricacies of the learner's experience of social and cultural interaction abroad. Drawing on qualitative approaches, the studies extend to issues of self-regulation, interculturality, lingua franca usage, homestay experiences and negotiation of difference, among others, while a further set of studies focusses on learner identity abroad, with particular attention to pragmatics as a reflection of the expression of learner identity. Taken together, the different studies presented highlight the individual experience that is study abroad for the learner as individual, while also showcasing the need for fuller understanding of the individual as a 'whole' person abroad in relation to the diverse social and cultural issues that serve to shape the individual experience of social and cultural interaction.

Mitchell, R., Tracy-Ventura, N., & McManus, K. *Anglophone students abroad: Identity, social relationships and language learning*. Abingdon/New York: Routledge, 2017.

Stemming from the ambitious LangSnap (Languages and social networks abroad) project at the University of Southampton, this monograph draws on extensive quantitative analysis of British university learners of French and Spanish through a longitudinal prism. On the one hand, it tracks their linguistic development in relation to different measures of complexity, accuracy and fluency (CAF), and on the other hand, offers insights into the relationship between such development and the learners' social integration abroad through social network analysis. The book is groundbreaking in advancing our understanding of social network issues abroad as a key means to providing learners with opportunities for language interaction and development of learner identity as L2 users.

Sanz, C., & Morales-Front, A. *The Routledge handbook of study abroad research and practice*. London: Routledge, 2018.

This handbook presents a comprehensive state-of-the-art collection of chapters addressing wide-ranging dimensions of study abroad, from language learning issues to more global policy, planning and practice matters. The thematic presentation of each chapter allows readers to gain an overview of issues underlying each theme, from approaches to their investigation to the main findings and issues arising, along with comprehensive references for further reading around each theme.

References

Alfayez, H., & Hüttner, C. (2019). Women students from Saudi Arabia in a study abroad programme. *Study Abroad Research in Second Language Acquisition and International Education, 4*, 192–222.

Arvidsson, K., Eyckmans, J., Rosiers, A., & Forsberg Lundell, F. (2018). Self-perceived progress, target language use and personality development during study abroad. *Study Abroad Research in Second Language Acquisition and International Education, 3*, 145–163.

Barron, A. (2003). *Acquisition in interlanguage pragmatics. Learning how to do things with words*. Amsterdam/Philadelphia: John Benjamins.

Bennett, M. (1993). Towards ethnorelativism: A developmental model of intercultural sensitivity. In R. Paige (Ed.), *Education for the intercultural experience* (pp. 21–71). Yarmouth, ME: Intercultural Press.

Carroll, J. (1967). Foreign language proficiency levels attained by language majors near graduation from college. *Foreign Language Annals, 1*, 131–151.

Coleman, J. (1995). The current state of knowledge concerning student residence abroad. In G. Parker & A. Rouxeville (Eds.), *'The Year Abroad': Preparation, monitoring, evaluation* (pp. 17–42). London: AFLS/CILT.

Coleman, J. (2013). Researching whole people and whole lives. In C. Kinginger (Ed.), *Social and cultural aspects of language learning in study abroad* (pp. 17–44). Amsterdam/Philadelphia: John Benjamins.

Collentine, J. (2004). The effects of learning contexts on morphosyntactic and lexical development. *Studies in Second Language Acquisition, 26*, 227–248.

Cots, J. M., Mitchell, R., & Beaven, A. (2021). Structure and agency in the development of plurilingual identities in study abroad. In M. Howard (Ed.), *Study abroad and the second language learner. Expectations, experiences and development* (pp. 165–188). London: Bloomsbury.

DeKeyser, R. (1991). Foreign language development during a semester abroad. In B. Freed (Ed.), *Foreign language acquisition research and the classroom* (pp. 104–119). Lexington, MA: DC Heath.

DeKeyser, R. (2007). Study abroad as foreign language practice. In R. DeKeyser (Ed.), *Practice in a second language: Perspectives from applied linguistics and cognitive psychology* (pp. 208–226). Cambridge: Cambridge University Press.

DeKeyser, R. (2010). Monitoring processes in Spanish as a second language during a study abroad program. *Foreign Language Annals, 43*, 80–92.

Devlin, A. M. (2014). *The impact of study abroad on the acquisition of sociopragmatic variation patterns*. Frankfurt am Main: Peter Lang.

Dewey, D., Bown, J., & Eggett, D. (2012). Japanese language proficiency, social networking, and language use during study abroad: Learners' perspectives. *Canadian Modern Language Journal, 65*, 111–137.

Dewey, D., Ring, S., Gardner, D., & Belnap, R. (2013). Social network formation and development during study abroad. *System, 41*, 269–282.

Díaz-Campos, M. (2004). Context of learning in the acquisition of Spanish second language phonology. *Studies in Second Language Acquisition, 26*, 249–273.

Durbidge, L. (2017). Duty, desire, and Japaneseness. A case study of Japanese high school study abroad. *Study Abroad Research in Second Language Acquisition and International Education, 2*, 205–238.

Dyson, P. (1988). *The year abroad report*. Report for the Central Bureau for Educational Visits and Exchanges, Oxford University Language Teaching Centre.

Freed, B. (1991). Language learning in a study abroad context: The effects of interactive and non-interactive out-of-class contact on grammatical achievement and oral proficiency. In J. Alatis (Ed.), *Linguistics, language teaching and language acquisition: The interdependence of theory, practice and research* (pp. 459–477). Washington DC: Georgetown University Press.

Freed, B. (1995a). What makes us think that students who study abroad become fluent? In B. Freed (Ed.), *Second language acquisition in a study abroad context* (pp. 123–148). Amsterdam/Philadelphia: John Benjamins.

Freed, B. (1995b). Language learning and study abroad. In B. Freed (Ed.), *Second language acquisition in a study abroad context* (pp. 3–32). Amsterdam/Philadelphia: John Benjamins.

Freed, B., Dewey, D., Segalowitz, N., & Halter, R. (2004). The language contact profile. *Studies in Second Language Acquisition, 26*, 349–356.

Grey, S., Cox, J., Serafini, E., & Sanz, C. (2015). The role of individual differences in the study abroad context: Cognitive capacity and language development during short-term intensive language exposure. *Modern Language Journal, 99*, 137–157.

Güvendir, E., Acar-Güvendir, M., & Dündar, S. (2021). Study abroad marketing and L2 self-efficacy beliefs. In M. Howard (Ed.), *Study abroad and the second language learner. Expectations, experiences and development* (pp. 49–68). London: Bloomsbury.

Hammer, M. (2012). The intercultural development inventory: A new frontier in assessment and development of intercultural competence. In M. Vande Berg, R. Paige, & K. Lou (Eds.), *Students learning abroad: What our students are learning, what they're not, and what we can do about it* (pp. 115–136). Sterling, VA: Stylus.

Howard, M. (2011). Input perspectives on the role of learning context in second language acquisition. *International Review of Applied Linguistics, 49*, 71–82.

Howard, M. (2012). The advanced learner's sociolinguistic profile: On issues of individual differences, L2 exposure conditions and type of sociolinguistic variable. *Modern Language Journal, 96*, 20–33.

Howard, M., & Shively, R. (2022). Pragmatic and sociolinguistic development in an intercultural context: the case of study abroad. In I. Kecskes (Ed.), *Cambridge handbook of intercultural pragmatics*. Cambridge: Cambridge University Press.

Ife, A., Vives Boix, G., & Meara, P. (2000). The impact of study abroad on the vocabulary development of different proficiency groups. *Spanish Applied Linguistics, 4*, 55–84.

Jackson, J. (2017). The personal, linguistic, and intercultural development of Chinese sojourners in an English-speaking country. *Study Abroad Research in Second Language Acquisition and International Education, 2*, 80–106.

Juan-Garau, M., Salazar-Noguera, J., & Prieto-Arranz, J. I. (2014). English L2 learners' lexico-grammatical and motivational development at home and abroad. In C. Pérez-Vidal (Ed.), *Language acquisition in study abroad and formal instruction contexts* (pp. 235–258). Amsterdam/Philadelphia: John Benjamins.

Kinginger, C. (2008). *Language learning in study abroad: Case studies of Americans in France*. Modern Language Journal Monograph Series, 1.

Kinginger, C., Wu, Q., Lee, S.-H., & Tan, D. (2016). The short-term homestay as a context for language learning. *Study Abroad Research in Second Language Acquisition and International Education, 1*, 34–60.

Lafford, B. (1995). Getting into, through, and out of a situation: A comparison of communicative strategies used by students studying Spanish abroad and 'at home'. In B. Freed (Ed.), *Second language acquisition in a study abroad context* (pp. 97–121). Amsterdam/Philadelphia: John Benjamins.

Lapkin, S., Hart, D., & Swain, M. (1995). A Canadian interprovincial exchange: Evaluating the linguistic impact of a three-month stay in Québec. In B. Freed (Ed.), *Second language acquisition in a study abroad context* (pp. 67–94). Amsterdam/Philadelphia: John Benjamins.

Llanes, À. (2016). The influence of a short stay abroad experience on perceived foreign accent. *Study Abroad Research in Second Language Acquisition and International Education, 1*, 88–106.

Llanes, À., & Muñoz, C. (2013). Age effects in a study abroad context: Children and adults studying abroad and at home. *Language Learning, 63*, 63–90.

Marqués-Pascual, L. (2011). Study abroad, previous language experience, and Spanish L2 development. *Foreign Language Annals, 44*, 565–582.

Martinsen, R. (2010). Short-term study abroad: Predicting changes in oral skills. *Foreign Language Annals, 43*, 503–530.

Milton, J., & Meara, P. (1994). How periods abroad affect vocabulary growth in a foreign language. *ITL Review of Applied Linguistics, 107–8*, 17–34.

Mora, J. C. (2008). Learning context effects on the acquisition of a second language phonology. In C. Pérez-Vidal, M. Juan-Garau, & A. Bel (Eds.), *A portrait of the young in the new multilingual Spain* (pp. 241–263). Bristol: Multilingual Matters.

Moreno Bruna, A., & Goethals, P. (2020). Intercultural guidance abroad: Impact on social network formation and L2 self-perceived development. *Study Abroad Research in Second Language Acquisition and International Education, 5*, 45–68.

Oguro, S., & Cottier, A. (2021). The complex challenges of delivering a university-wide intercultural mentoring program for study abroad students. In M. Howard (Ed.), *Study abroad and the second language learner. Expectations, experiences and development* (pp. 137–148). London: Bloomsbury.

Patron, M.-C. (2007). *Culture and identity in study abroad contexts*. Frankfurt am Main: Peter Lang.

Pavlenko, A. (2009). Discussant presentation, Language Learning Roundtable, 'Input perspectives on the role of learning context in second language acquisition', Cork, Ireland, September 2009.

Pellegrino Aveni, V. (2005). *Study abroad and second language use: Constructing the self*. Cambridge: Cambridge University Press.

Pérez-Vidal, C., & Juan-Garau, M. (2011). The effect of context and input conditions on oral and written development. *International Review of Applied Linguistics, 49*, 175–185.

Rees, J., & Klapper, J. (2008). Issues in the quantitative longitudinal measurement of second language progress in the study abroad context. In L. Ortega & H. Byrnes (Eds.), *The longitudinal study of advanced L2 capacities* (pp. 89–105). London: Routledge.

Rivers, W. (1998). Is being there enough? The effects of homestay placements on language gain during study abroad. *Foreign Language Annals, 31*, 492–500.

Salaberry, R., White, K., & Rue Birch, A. (2019). Language learning and interactional experiences in a study abroad setting. An introduction to the special issue. *Study Abroad Research in Second Language Acquisition and International Education, 4*, 1–18.

Seibert Hanson, A., & Dracos, M. (2019). The digital dilemma. L1 and L2 technology use, language learning and motivation among US university students studying abroad. *Study Abroad Research in Second Language Acquisition and International Education, 4*, 224–251.

Serrano, R., Tragant, E., & Llanes, À. (2012). A longitudinal analysis of one year abroad. *Canadian Modern Language Review, 68*, 138–163.

Taguchi, N. (2015). *Developing interactional competence in a Japanese study abroad context*. Bristol: Multilingual Matters.

Trenchs-Parera, M., & Juan-Garau, M. (2014). A longitudinal study of learners' motivation and beliefs in at home and study abroad contexts. In C. Pérez-Vidal (Ed.), *Language acquisition in study abroad and formal instruction contexts* (pp. 259–281). Amsterdam/Philadelphia: John Benjamins.

Wilkinson, S. (2002). The omnipresent classroom during summer study abroad: American students in conversation with their French hosts. *Modern Language Journal, 86*, 157–173.

13
ENHANCING LANGUAGE AND CULTURE LEARNING IN MIGRATION CONTEXTS

Silvia Kunitz

Introduction

In recent years, together with a general increase in geographical mobility, there has been a dramatic rise in migration influxes in various countries, which has led to the practical issue of providing material support (i.e., food and shelter) for migrants, while also assisting them in the integration process. Although integration has been variably defined (see below), there is general consensus regarding the role played by language proficiency and cultural knowledge (or cultural fluency: see Kirilova, 2017) as key factors that aid integration. However, what is still an open matter is establishing who is supposed to provide instruction targeting language and culture, and how. Various countries indeed offer state-funded programs that may include language courses, vocational training and citizenship classes. Nonetheless, the efficacy of these programs has often been questioned (see Han, 2009; for more details on this matter, see below). At the same time, the high demand for instructional programs has put a strain on each state's ability to provide access to such programs for all migrants; in response to this issue, members of the civil society have taken various initiatives to provide opportunities for language practice and cultural exchange in more or less informal settings. Finally, and equally importantly, researchers agree on the fact that not all learning occurs in the classroom and that language learners (whether migrants or not) should be offered opportunities for meaningful interaction in the target language with members of the receiving community in their daily life (see Lilja & Piirainen-Marsh, this volume; Wagner, 2015). For all these reasons, exploring the opportunities that the civil society has put in place for language and culture learning is crucial in order to shed light on the integration process and what it entails.

Key constructs

Before engaging in a short overview of key constructs in the literature on language and culture learning in migration contexts, it is important to frame this research strand within the larger field of migration studies. This constantly growing field has become increasingly more internationalized and varied at both the disciplinary and the methodological level (Pisarevskaya, Levy, Scholten, & Jansen, 2020). Essentially quantitative at first, with its initial focus on demography, over the years the field has also seen the growth of qualitative research, mostly conducted with ethnographic methods, though other empirical methods are emerging (e.g., the combination of ethnographic and conversation analytic approaches in a project on language cafés in Sweden: see Jansson, 2021; Kunitz & Jansson, 2021). The rise of qualitative research methods has coincided with the so called "cultural turn" (King, 2012) in migration studies and with an interest for the impact of education and language training on immigrant integration (Pisarevskaya et al., 2020). It is on this qualitative research that this chapter focuses and, more specifically, on studies that have examined experiences of language and culture learning outside of state-funded programs, in order to explore non-governmental initiatives organized by the civil society (including churches and libraries) as well as experiences of language learning on the workplace. Indeed, as has been widely recognized, especially for adult migrants, the majority of the learning experiences occur outside the classroom (e.g., Han, 2009), as they engage in daily activities both on the workplace (on the workplace as a site for language socialization, see, e.g., Strömmer, 2016a) and in other settings.

Navigating key constructs in migration research is no easy task, especially since the field at large seems to be undergoing a phase of reflection and self-criticism, questioning its involvement in the reproduction of a normalization discourse that is the product of the nation-state conceptual apparatus (Dahinden, 2016). Indeed, virtually any term in migration research risks being "politically and normatively loaded" (Dahinden, 2016, p. 2215), from the category of *migrants* (which invokes the idea of a "national container" inhabited by non-migrants; see Dahinden, 2016, p. 2209) to the often monolithic idea of an ethnic/cultural self to the very same concept of *integration*, which has been frequently understood "as a cultural or structural achievement of (ethnically or nationally defined) immigration groups" (Dahinden, 2016, p. 2216). In recent years, some researchers have problematized the normalizing and normative views that these terms index. While it is important to acknowledge the relevance of this internal debate, a detailed account of it is beyond the scope of the present contribution.

In qualitative literature on culture and language learning in migration contexts, the words *immigrants* and *migrants* may be used quite neutrally to refer to "anyone who is on the move" (Jansson, 2021, p. 2) and lives "permanently or temporarily outside of their country of birth" (Johnston, 2018, p. 131), regardless of the reasons for migrating, degree of education, economic status, etc. In other cases, *migrants/immigrants* may be more narrowly defined as underprivileged people, characterized by features of vulnerability and, possibly, undesirability (Jansson, 2021).

As to the place where immigrants live, its denomination is rather sensitive. For example, there are researchers who explicitly refuse to use the term *host* society/community, as it casts on the immigrant the identity of a guest, and ultimately, of an outsider. The preferred term is then *receiving* society/community, which "implies that an immigrant has been received by the society and, therefore, is part" (Johnston, 2018, p. 131) of it.

Another central construct is that of *integration*. In some studies, the concept is left to the reader's intuitive interpretation; in other studies, it is variably defined through different models (e.g., Ager & Strang, 2008; Berry, 1997). Generally speaking, integration is understood in socioeconomic and sociocultural terms and is strictly connected to the migrants' access to community members, schools, and the labor market (on matters of access, see also below). Access to social encounters and to educational and professional opportunities is considered to be mediated by the migrants' proficiency in the language of the receiving community and by their cultural knowledge (e.g., Ager & Strang, 2008; Bonn, 2015; Kirilova, 2017), hence the importance of language and culture learning for migrants' social, educational, and professional integration. Ultimately, the driving force toward integration lies in the social connections that the migrants establish with members of the local community: social bonds help create a sense of belonging (see Jansson, 2021) while also being instrumental to the provision of information that is relevant for the immigrants' life in the receiving society.

The acknowledgement of the importance of developing social relationships in some cases leads to an explicit conceptualization of integration as a dynamic process of *mutual accommodation* of the individuals involved (e.g., Daley, 2009), so that all individuals maintain their cultural identity while "participating as equals in [the] greater society" (Johnston, 2018, p. 132). In this view, in a fully integrated society, immigrants and the majority ethnic group live in harmony, valuing each other's cultures while developing in-group and out-group relations. As Johnston (2018) argues, "these aspects of integration cannot be taught in a classroom, but must be accomplished through face-to-face interaction between members of the respective groups" (p. 132). What is required, then, is a bottom-up approach that allows immigrants and members of the local community to engage in intergroup contact (Pettigrew & Tropp, 2011).

Crucially related to integration is the construct of *participation*, as migrants/novices who actively participate in community-relevant activities are taken to be integrated with the local society. Similar to integration, in the literature the construct of participation either is left undefined or is defined in specific terms. For example, socioculturally oriented studies typically adopt Lave and Wenger's (1991) communities of practice framework, with a focus on the situated learning process through which migrants/novices, under the graduated and contingent assistance of expert community members (Han, 2009), manage to change their degree of participation, initially holding a peripheral role and finally playing a central role in the community activities. Essential are the kind and amount of mediation (i.e., support) that migrants/, novices receive, which is also linked to concrete opportunities of engaging in local activities in visible and meaningful ways (e.g., Han, 2009; Strömmer, 2016b). Research in this area has shown that direct involvement with community members can help establish rapport while also enhancing opportunities to use the language for meaningful communicative purposes and to learn more about the local culture. In other words, increased intercultural contact with community members and direct involvement in the community activities may produce more opportunities to practice the language and may therefore be conducive to language and culture learning.

A clear case is made, for example, by Han's (2009) longitudinal study on the linguistic effects that multiform support provided by members of an evangelical church had in the integration process of a couple of Chinese immigrants in Canada (see the reading tips below). Similarly, Johnston's studies (see Johnston, 2018 in particular, also included in the reading tips) on conversation-based programs organized by municipal libraries show that immigrants participating in these initiatives report: an improvement in their language skills, increased motivation to learn the target language, increased knowledge about the local culture and society, and ultimately a change in preconceived notions about the other participants (Johnston, 2019). On the other hand, the absence of meaningful relationships in a community (e.g., Daley, 2009) and the lack of interaction opportunities on the workplace (e.g., Strömmer, 2016a) may result in isolation and may have a negative impact on the immigrants' linguistic and cultural proficiency.

Whereas studies on participation inspired by Lave and Wenger's (1991) work on situated learning are typically ethnographic and are based on an ethnographic notion of context, a different interpretation of participation, rooted in a local, sequential view of context (for a discussion of the notion of context in conversation analysis vs ethnography, see: Kunitz & Markee, 2016) is at the heart of conversation analytic studies of language and culture learning in interaction (e.g., Kunitz & Jansson, 2021; Kunitz & Majlesi, 2022; Svennevig, 2018). Specifically, these studies focus on how opportunities for participation and learning may emerge in the sequential unfolding of talk-in-interaction between migrants and other members of the local community. Participation then can be conceptualized as active engagement in interaction, rooted in the ability to produce fitting turns-at-talk in pragmatically recognizable ways; in other words, participation is strictly connected to *interactional competence* (Pekarek Doehler, 2019; see also Lilja & Piirainen-Marsh, this volume).

The last construct that requires some attention is *learning*. In the research strand explored here learning is understood as a socially situated activity that occurs in interaction and is not confined to the classroom walls. What is particularly emphasized is the learning *process*, which may occur in different settings, through different life experiences. In this sense, there is a clear connection with the literature on language learning in the wild, which highlights the importance of the complex ecology in which learning-in-action occurs (Hellermann, Eskildsen, Pekarek Doehler, & Piirainen-Marsh, 2019) through everyday experiences of language use (Lilja & Piirainen-Marsh, this volume). Ethnographic studies illustrate accounts of such experiences, while also reporting on the migrants' perceptions of the outcomes of learning. Conversation-analytic studies, on the other hand, focus on the interactional practices through which the migrants and their co-interactants *do* learning/teaching as they engage in a variety of activities, be they specifically aimed at language practice or not. Of interest, then, are the local, immanent pedagogies (Lindwall & Lymer, 2005) through which interactants – either momentarily and incidentally or in more structurally organized ways – orient to learning and teaching.

Current issues

Before illustrating selected issues that practitioners and researchers encounter as they engage in migration contexts, a short description of the issues that migrants face in terms of language and culture learning is in order. As mentioned above, matters of access, support, and participation are crucial for the integration of migrants. Indeed, language and culture learning are typically understood as fundamental to give migrants access to social, educational, and professional opportunities. However, the issue of how migrants actually get access to language and culture learning itself is quite complex.

First of all, migrants typically need to have legal status in the receiving country in order to enroll in state-funded schools and programs. This means that, at the beginning of their stay, they fully rely on informal initiatives for language and culture learning. The existence of such initiatives is therefore crucial to support the migrants during a very delicate phase of their life in the receiving country.

Once they are entitled to attend state-funded schools and programs, the migrants might encounter various problems. For example, young migrants might have difficulties to adjust to the new school environment and consequently might achieve poor academic results (see the overviews in: Makarova & Birman, 2015, 2016). Indeed, there are many factors that might influence the young immigrants' experience in the new school and their academic achievements, such as the quality of the school curriculum, the assimilative pressure it might put on immigrant students, the socio-economic status of both the school and the migrants' family, teachers' attitudes toward migrants and their preparation to work with immigrant students (see Haim, 2019 for a review).

At the same time, state-funded programs for adult migrants do not always seem to cater to migrants' actual needs, neither are they always effective in providing sufficient linguistic and vocational training (see Strömmer, 2017 on the situation in Finland). The weaknesses of these programs, often inspired by old fashioned views of language teaching as based on and targeting the written language, make the linguistic and cultural support that migrants may find in their everyday lives even more crucial (see Lilja & Piirainen-Marsh, this volume).

However, this kind of informal support may not be easy to access either. For example, migrants might not be aware that certain initiatives (like language cafés) have been launched in the receiving community. On the other hand, the support they might receive in their daily and professional life (see Lilja & Piirainen-Marsh) is totally dependent on the specific institution (e.g., a local church or the workplace) and/or on the members of such institution and their attitudes toward migrants. That is, there might be institutionalized practices (see Han, 2009) through which language and culture support is offered to migrants, but this may not always be the case, as all too often migrants are not even afforded participation (and therefore learning) opportunities (Billet, 2001). Furthermore, migrants in vulnerable positions might have jobs that do not require language much (see the case of cleaners in Finland: Strömmer, 2017; though see Lønsmann & Kraft, 2018 on the importance of language use in blue-collar workplaces).

What clearly emerges, then, is the key figure of the *practitioner*. Broadly speaking, in (research on) migration contexts, practitioners are those who are actively involved in the initiatives that aim to foster language and culture learning and, more in general, the integration of migrants in the receiving community. The term *practitioners* then denotes a wide range of people – volunteers, employees of specific organizations (e.g., churches, libraries, etc.), colleagues, mentors, and supervisors – who are long-standing members of the local community regardless of their own ethnic and linguistic background. Some of them happen to be language educators (often retired teachers), but most of them are not education professionals. This makes it all the more interesting for the researcher to study the interactions of practitioners with immigrants, especially in those moments where the participants (i.e., practitioners and immigrants participating in a research study) visibly orient to matters of learning and/or teaching. In these instances, the *local educational order* (Hester & Francis, 2000) achieved by the participants in their interactions might become the object of analysis, together with non-expert, folk ideologies pertaining to what it means to learn/teach a language or a culture.

In line with the theme of the handbook, the research strand briefly illustrated here namely focuses on language and culture learning beyond the classroom. Indeed, the first issue that researchers face is related to the kind of learning that one expects to analyze in non-scholastic environments in migration contexts. That is, one would expect to explore informal learning experiences and the related accounts that immigrants might produce in the form of narratives, interviews, etc. However, it is quite difficult to completely exclude the classroom set-up from the object of study. As it turns out, in fact, many initiatives taken by the civil society actually reproduce the classroom set-up, as has been observed in a project exploring various language cafés organized in a metropolitan area in Sweden (see Jansson & Kunitz, 2020). Though these initiatives typically aim to provide informal venues for social encounters and language practice (see Barraja-Rohan, 2015 on conversations-for-practicing), in some cases they are either set up as full-fledged classrooms or they at least include moments of classroom-like interactions (e.g., information-sharing sessions, reading sessions, etc., in some language cafés in Sweden: see Jansson & Kunitz, 2020; Kunitz & Majlesi, 2022).

The presence or the emergence of classroom-like moments thus poses theoretical and methodological challenges to the researcher, whose object of study might turn out to be quite different from what s/he had originally foreseen. In other words, it might not be possible to establish from the outset whether the immigrants' experiences can be framed through the theoretical and analytical lenses of informal versus formal learning. At the same time, this element of unpredictability is part and parcel of what an empirical investigation entails, especially in qualitative studies that adopt an *emic* (participant-relevant) approach (see Markee, 2013) and that programmatically embrace the multidimensional complexity of the settings they explore in the name of ecological validity.

It should also be noted that, by moving (or attempting to move) beyond the classroom, a variety of settings has to be considered. On the one hand, an immigrant may engage in moments of informal learning in a range of everyday activities occurring in different settings, from the workplace (Strömmer, 2016a, 2016b, 2017; Suni, 2017; Svennevig, 2018) to the church environment (e.g., Han, 2009), which may or may not provide specific support aimed to foster the immigrants' participation in these activities. On the other hand, the initiatives that are more or less explicitly and purposefully organized by the civil society to enhance the immigrants' language and culture learning can also vary greatly. Listed along a continuum from formal to informal activities, we find, among others: full-fledged, community-organized courses (e.g., Chao, 2020 on a church-based citizenship course; Hos, 2016 on a community school for Syrian refugees in Turkey; Minuz & Pugliese, 2012 on language courses organized by volunteer members of local associations); sessions explicitly advertised as homework help; conversation-based programs (such as language cafés and other activities organized by churches, libraries and the Red Cross, for example; see Jansson & Kunitz, 2020; Kunitz & Majlesi, 2022; Johnston, 2018, 2019); tandem programs (such as Buddy Sweden: see https://ec.europa.eu/migrant-integration/); cooking classes and social circus activities (such as those described in Lilja, Eilola, Jokipohja, & Tapaninen, 2021).

Clearly, such variety of activities, goals, and settings might have important implications for researchers, at the methodological level (in terms of adequate data collection tools and kind of data to be collected), at the analytical level (in terms of the focal phenomena that may lend themselves to empirical investigation), and at the theoretical level (in terms of the theoretical points that a researcher might afford to make, especially in research traditions such as conversation analysis, where theory is actually a by-product of empirical analysis; see Markee, 2008).

At a more practical level, researchers working in migration contexts typically face ethical issues that characterize the entire research process, from the recruitment of participants to data collection. Specifically, studying migration contexts means establishing contact with often vulnerable individuals, who have gone through traumatic experiences and/or who many not be legally documented in the receiving society yet. Similar issues are also faced by practitioners who are tasked with creating safe interactional spaces where the migrants can feel free to open up and engage, without incurring in any threat. In sum, developing a sentiment of trust is fundamental for both practitioners, who aim to facilitate the integration of migrants, and researchers, who ultimately need to recruit participants for their studies.

A second practical issue concerns the methods of data collection. As mentioned above, studies on language and culture learning in migration contexts typically involve observations of the immigrants' activities that are collected through more or less extensive periods of fieldwork. Whether studies adopt ethnographic methods (including the collection of fieldnotes, interviews, etc.) or mainly rely on recordings for the analysis of the immigrants' participation in the activities that are the objects of empirical investigation, the researcher needs to be present on the field, taking notes, asking questions, placing cameras, etc. The researcher therefore has to decide whether s/he wants to engage in participant observation

(Hammersley & Atkinson, 2007) or whether s/he would rather take the role of a bystander (on the researchers' participation role, see the special issue edited by Katila, Gan, Goico, & Goodwin, 2021). In any case, it is vital to the research process itself that the researcher gains the trust of whoever is on the field, whether they decide to participate in the study or not.

A third practical (and methodological) issue relates to multilingualism as a key feature of migration contexts. This means that researchers are bound to investigate settings where languages unknown to them are spoken and therefore they need to rely on the help of interpreters and translators. These intermediary figures have an important role in the research process, as their interpreting and translating have direct implications on the data and therefore on the findings of empirical studies.

This issue of potential linguistic barriers is shared by practitioners in their contact with immigrants. Strömmer (2016a), for example, underlines how, in the cleaning sector, providing support for workers with various linguistic backgrounds during orientation, supervision, and teamwork might be challenging for the employer. On the other hand, some conversation-based programs hire multilingual facilitators with the goal of providing extra support and of aiding the immigrants' participation in local activities. As noted by Jansson (in press), these non-professional facilitators do more than translating/interpreting, as they might add information to the ongoing conversation as well as expressing their own stances and taking sides.

The last issue that will be touched upon here concerns both researchers and practitioners. It has to do with establishing the exact object of learning; that is, it proves quite challenging to determine where language learning ends and culture learning begins. Research-wise, some scholars focus on linguistic aspects of support and learning; some focus on cultural aspects; some report on both, while others actually see language and culture as a unified whole, where "cultural skills" include language skills (e.g., Bonn, 2015). Similarly, practitioners in some cases target language forms, while in other cases they seem to focus on the transmission of cultural (and societal) knowledge and see language learning as a by-product. Overall, it might be difficult to tease apart the coextensive constructs of language and culture and the kinds of linguistic and cultural support that may be provided to immigrants.

Implications

As mentioned before, the present chapter concerns qualitative research conducted in migration contexts. This kind of research is typically realized through small case studies which sometimes are longitudinal in nature. That is, in some cases, the researcher has spent months on the field, following the focal participants in the target activities that are the object of study, and is therefore able to monitor the immigrants' progress (or lack thereof) in their interactions with the receiving community. In other cases, despite conducting extensive fieldwork, the researcher is not able to follow the same participants because of the setting itself; for example, in conversation-based programs there may be a core of regular participants, but there can also be substantial turnover, especially in terms of the immigrants who attend these programs.

Whether longitudinal or not, the small scale, qualitative studies conducted in this research strand are very much situated and local in their findings. That is, the participants in these studies cannot necessarily be taken as representative of "immigrants" in general, for example, and no generalizations can be made as to what is to be expected in migration contexts where immigrants and local community members interact in settings that go beyond the institutionalized state-funded courses. While the lack of generalizability is an objection that is commonly raised against any kind of qualitative research, it should be pointed out that: (a) the goal (and the strength) of these studies is precisely that of shedding light on local initiatives with specific participants; and (b) relevant insights can be gained as to "the complex interplay between immigrant settlement and language [and culture] learning, and the kinds of support that may make a difference" (Han, 2009, p. 649). An important implication for the future of this kind of research is thus the need to keep gathering cumulative evidence, to synthesize the findings of such cumulative efforts, and to conduct comparative studies that allow to identify red threads in the experiences of intercultural contact that are the object of investigation.

At the same time, through cumulative and comparative evidence it may be possible to identify features that are common to successful experiences (e.g., indications as to the kind of support that seems to be most effective, etc.) and thus to provide relevant suggestions to practitioners. While research in this area is typically exploratory and inductive, in that it does not set out to test a specific integration model or specific ways to provide linguistic and cultural support to immigrants, its findings can have practical implications, not in terms of prescriptive guidelines, but in terms of examples that can lead practitioners involved in integration initiatives to reflect over the goals of such initiatives and over the tools that might be available to them in order to achieve such goals. As a matter of fact, our own experience[1] with language cafés in Sweden shows that practitioners who participated in our project are interested in our findings. At the same time, since each café was set up in a highly localized context, some practitioners have manifested interest in knowing how similar programs might be organized. In this sense, then, the researcher can create informative, networking occasions for practitioners involved in different settings.

One of the findings that are starting to emerge from studies conducted in different settings (not only in migration contexts) is that language learning – operationalized as the amount and quality of the interaction with local actors – is strictly intertwined with the development of social relationships (see Barraja-Rohan, 2015; Berger & Pekarek Doehler, 2018; Pekarek Doehler & Berger, 2019) and therefore with the growth of affective ties (Johnston, 2019). In other words, there is a social, human aspect connected to the meaningful use of language for communicative purposes within the receiving community and therefore to language learning. Moreover, researchers working with different research traditions seem to converge on the idea that moments of storytelling, where the immigrants and other members of the community share personal experiences, have a crucial role in producing interpersonal relationship work and in strengthening the social bond between the interactants (Kunitz & Jansson, 2021; Wong, 2021). While storytellers "negotiate their social selves" (Barraja-Rohan, 2015, p. 298), story-recipients may (or may not) display active, emotive engagement with the emerging story and through questions, assessments, and empathetic comments help to shape the telling of the story and orient to emerging aspects of the storytellers' identities.

At the level of practice, these findings suggest that creating spaces where the migrants feel safe to share their stories might have positive effects both for language practice and for community-building. For example, the Memory Group initiative (a conversation-based, library-organized program in Norway; see Johnston, 2018) has relied on memory sharing as a way to provide opportunities for language use and to engage immigrants and practitioners in a bonding experience of mutual understanding. At the same time, it has been found that pedagogical participatory approaches such as Learners' Lives as Curriculum and the Language Experience Approach, which rely on the sharing of immigrants' life experiences, seem successful in creating comprehensible and relatable participant-generated content that can be used for explicit language teaching with low literacy adults (Wood, 2011). In other words, the connection between life experiences, interpersonal relationship work, and language (and culture) learning is becoming increasingly more apparent as it emerges in findings on both formal and informal experiences of language support and language practice.

Finally, in light of these findings that highlight the importance of establishing social bonds and sharing life experiences, it has become increasingly more apparent that social approaches to the study of second language acquisition (SLA; see Atkinson, 2011 for an overview) are the best suited to provide an interpretive key of the learning process in migration contexts, where issues of identity come to the fore and seem to be inextricable from accounts of learning experiences. As Han (2009) notes, "self-ascribed and other-assigned learner identities play a critical role in shaping access to resources and participation in learning" (p. 646) the target language and culture. Similarly, the Douglas Fir Group (2016) highlights how "the social-local worlds" (p. 39) of language learners will ultimately shape the SLA field.

Future directions

Though developing a comprehensive account of how immigrants' language and culture learning is supported beyond the classroom is virtually impossible, in the future researchers will hopefully cover an increasingly wider range of settings, with a variety of theoretical and methodological frameworks. Only then it will be possible to provide a synthetic, multidisciplinary account of experiences of more or less informal learning in migration contexts. Despite the practical challenges outlined before and the time-consuming nature of qualitative studies conducted in this line of research, the field needs more longitudinal studies and also more studies that combine different kinds of data, so that self-reported experiences can be analyzed against recordings of what actually happens in the various settings where the immigrants' life experiences take place. Furthermore, by analyzing the details of the interactions between migrants and practitioners, more empirically grounded suggestions can be made to practitioners involved in supporting migrants in their daily lives.

Finally, while there are studies focusing on the support that immigrants receive and studies on the immigrants' own investment (e.g., Strömmer, 2017) in becoming active learners and participants in the receiving community, a few studies are starting to show that integration is really a two-way (or even multi-way; see Daley, 2009) street and that intercultural contact can indeed be a process of reciprocal adaptation and mutual enrichment that brings epistemic changes and affective rewards in the immigrants and in the members of the receiving community as well (e.g., Jansson, 2021; Johnston, 2017). At the same time, even studies that focus on language development (not necessarily in migration contexts) show that interactional competence is a joint accomplishment and is the product of both the learner's and the expert speaker's increased familiarity with each other (e.g., Barraja-Rohan, 2015; Berger & Pekarek Doehler, 2018; Greer, 2019; Pekarek Doehler & Berger, 2019). Altogether, this recognition of the process of reciprocal accommodation, both linguistic and cultural, shows that it is possible to sheer away from the normalization discourse that risks permeating research if the focus is solely on what the immigrants learn. As Dahinden (2016) states, it is time to "de-migranticize" research on migration and integration.

Reflection Questions

Listed below are three reflective questions concerning the research strand illustrated in this chapter.

1. After reading this short overview, what do you think are the greatest challenges in studies of language and culture learning beyond the classroom in migration contexts? If you were to conduct one such study, which caveats would you keep in mind?
2. In the kind of research described here, there are typically three groups of actors: researchers, immigrants, and practitioners. How would you characterize the interplay and potential synergy among these actors and the roles they play?
3. Low language proficiency is often used to explain the immigrants' precarious position in the labor market of the receiving community (see Strömmer, 2017). Put another way, as (Han, 2009) points out, in some cases immigrant settlement policies seem to rely on the belief that language proficiency alone will be somewhat automatically conducive to economic and sociopolitical integration. This author is extremely critical of such assumption, while also maintaining that language learning cannot be "addressed as a purely linguistic matter" (Han, 2009, p. 664), neither in applied linguistics nor in public discourses and policies. Do you agree with Han's point of view? Do you think that applied linguists and ethnographers can (or should) play a role in changing current immigration policies?

Recommended Readings

The readings suggested here are representative examples of empirical studies in the literature presented in this chapter. The rationale motivating the selection lies in the attempt to point the reader toward studies that cover different settings: a church setting in Canada (Han, 2009); a workplace setting in Finland (Strömmer, 2016b, 2017); and conversation-based programs in libraries in the Nordic countries (Johnston, 2018). All three studies were conducted with ethnographic methods.

Han, H. (2009). Institutionalized inclusion: A case study on support for immigrants in English learning. *TESOL Quarterly, 43*(4), 643–668.

The first tip concerns a longitudinal, ethnographic study conducted by Han (2009), who followed a couple of skilled Chinese immigrants as they settled in Canada and analyzed their experiences through the communities of practice framework (Lave & Wenger, 1991), the notion of onstage and offstage performance in the front and back region of an institution (Goffman, 1959), and the notion of identity as social capital (Bourdieu, 1986). Attracted by a free English conversation group organized by Christian retirees, the couple eventually joined two evangelical churches and got baptized. The study details their experiences with the institutionalized mediation practices put in place by one of these churches. Overtime, the couple assumed more central and more visible roles in the church activities (such as singing in the choir, reading the scriptures onstage, and ultimately leading fellowship programs), which led to the development of a positive identity as speakers of English and legitimate (and trustworthy) members of the church. The study advocates for the importance of "allowing newcomers a legitimate speaking position in activities meaningful to them" (Han, 2009, p. 663), while providing adequate mentoring support (see also Billet, 2001). Finally, at the methodological level, the author clearly describes the processes of data collection and data analysis and includes a reflection of her role as an ethnographer.

Strömmer, M. (2016b). Material scaffolding: Supporting the comprehension of migrant cleaners at work. *European Journal of Applied Linguistics, 4*(2), 239–275.

The second tip concerns Strömmer's (2016a, 2016b, 2017) work on the cleaning profession, which is a frequent entry-level occupation for immigrants in Finland. Of particular relevance here is Strömmer's (2016b) study of the learning affordances that the workplace may offer to immigrant cleaners. At the theoretical and methodological level, Strömmer (2016b) combines nexus analysis

(Scollon & Scollon, 2004) with van Lier's (2004) ecological perspective on language learning. Aided by these two approaches, together with methodological tools offered by multimodal conversation analysis (e.g., Goodwin, 2013), the author analyzes the *material scaffolding* that cleaners receive as they engage in work tasks. This kind of material support consists of, for example, embodied demonstrations accompanying verbal descriptions of the task to be accomplished, but also the use of material objects, such as a calendar and a computer, to support the accomplishment of concrete activities, such as changing shifts or filling out electronic forms to apply for leave. Through her analyses, Strömmer (2016b) shows that material mediational means constitute an important form of support for immigrant workers. Strömmer's conclusions are therefore similar to Han's (2009) and are in line with what other researchers have pointed out (see Billet, 2001; Suni, 2017); that is, participation in work activities needs to be adequately supported, be it in structured ways (such as mentoring) or more informally.

Johnston, J. (2018). The use of conversation-based programming in public libraries to support integration in increasingly multiethnic societies. *Journal of Librarianship and Information Science, 50*(2), 130–140.

The third tip concerns an ethnographic study conducted by Johnston (2018), who works within the field of library sciences and explores various conversation-based programs organized by public libraries, such as: the Expat Dinners in Denmark, the Women's Story Circle in Iceland, the Memory Group in Norway, and a language café in Sweden. While rather heterogeneous in their set-ups (e.g., with participants talking in smaller or larger groups and engaging in unstructured or semi-structured conversations), these programs share the goal of providing immigrants with the possibility of practicing the language of the receiving community in an informal environment and expanding their social networks. At the root of these experiences is the organizers' persuasion that "becoming more informed about one another and establishing commonalities may help foster positive intergroup relations" (Johnston, 2018, p. 138). While illustrating a variety of examples of conversation-based programming, this study shows how integration is better understood as a process of mutual accommodation and influence, through which both migrants and local community members acquire greater acquaintance of the other, thereby reducing preconceived notions of one another and eventually re-assessing their own ways of understanding the world (see also Johnston, 2019). The study explicitly relies on Berry's (1997) social-psychological model of integration and on Intergroup Contact Theory (Allport, 1979), which provides the theoretical lens for interpreting the participants' experiences in the programs described by the author.

Note

1 The project on Language cafés as social venues and arenas for language training is financed by the Swedish Research Council (Grant no: 2017e03628). The project leader is Gunilla Jansson, while Silvia Kunitz and Ali Reza Majlesi figure as collaborators in the project.

References

Ager, A., & Strang, A. (2008). Understanding integration: A conceptual framework. *Journal of Refugee Studies, 21*(2), 166–191.

Allport, G.W. (1979). *The nature of prejudice*. Reading: Perseus Books.

Atkinson, D. (2011). *Alternative approaches to second language acquisition*. London, New York: Routledge.

Barraja-Rohan, A.M. (2015). "I told you": Storytelling development of a Japanese learning English as a second language. In T. Cadierno & S. Eskildsen (Eds.), *Usage-based perspectives on second language learning* (pp. 271–304). Berlin, Boston: De Gruyter Mouton.

Berger, E., & Pekarek Doehler, S. (2018). Tracking change over time in storytelling practices: A longitudinal study of second language talk-in-interaction. In S. Pekarek Doehler, J. Wagner, & E. Gonzalez-Martínez (Eds.), *Longitudinal Studies on the organization of social interaction* (pp. 67–102). London: Palgrave Macmillan.

Berry, J.W. (1997). Immigration, acculturation, and adaptation. *Applied Psychology, 46*(1), 5–34.

Billet, S. (2001). Learning through work: Workplace affordances and individual engagement. *Journal of Workplace Learning, 13*(5), 209–214.

Bonn, M. (2015). Migrants' acquisition of cultural skills and selective immigration policies. *Migration Studies, 3*(1), 32–48.

Bourdieu, P. (1986). The forms of capital. In J. G. Richardson (Ed.), *Handbook of theory and research for the sociology of education* (pp. 241–258). Westport: Greenwood Press.

Chao, X. (2020). Language and identity: An inquiry of church-based US citizenship education for refugee-background Bhutanese adults. *Language and Education, 34*(4), 311–327.

Dahinden, J. (2016). A plea for the "de-migranticization" of research on migration and integration. *Ethnic and Racial Studies, 39*(13), 2207–2225.

Daley, C. (2009). Exploring community connections: Community cohesion and refugee integration at a local level. *Community Development Journal, 44*(2), 158–171.

Douglas Fir Group (2016). A transdisciplinary framework for SLA in a multilingual world. *The Modern Language Journal, 100*, 19–47.

Goffman, E. (1959). *The presentation of self in everyday life*. New York, London, Toronto, Sydney, Auckland: Anchor.

Goodwin, C. (2013). The co-operative, transformative organization of human action and knowledge. *Journal of Pragmatics, 46*(1), 8–23.

Greer, T. (2019). Initiating and delivering news of the day: Interactional competence as joint-development. *Journal of Pragmatics, 146*, 150–164.

Haim, O. (2019). "It is hard at school, but I do my best to cope": The educational experience of multilingual immigrant youth in high school. *Intercultural Education, 30*(5), 510–530.

Hammersley, M., & Atkinson, P. (2007). *Ethnography: Principles in practice*. London, New York: Routledge.

Han, H. (2009). Institutionalized inclusion: A case study on support for immigrants in English learning. *TESOL Quarterly, 43*(4), 643–668.

Hellermann, J., Eskildsen, S.W., Pekarek Doehler, S., & Piirainen-Marsh, A. (Eds.) (2019). *Conversation-analytic research on learning-in-action: The complex ecology of second language interaction 'in the wild'*. Cham: Springer.

Hester, S., & Francis, D. (2000). *Local educational order*. Amsterdam: John Benjamins.

Hos, R. (2016). Education in emergencies: Case of a community school for Syrian refugees. *European Journal of Educational Research, 5*(2), 53–60.

Jansson, G. (2021). Negotiating belonging in multilingual work environments: Church professionals' engagement with migrants. *Applied Linguistics Review*, 1–27. https://doi.org/10.1515/applirev-2021-0054

Jansson, G. (in press). Multilingual practices and normative work in the context of a civic integration project in Sweden. *The Translator*.

Jansson, G., & Kunitz, S. (2020). Språkkaféet som arena för språkträning ['Language cafés as arenas for language training']. *Delmi Policy Brief 2020:8*.

Johnston, J. (2018). The use of conversation-based programming in public libraries to support integration in increasingly multiethnic societies. *Journal of Librarianship and Information Science, 50*(2), 130–140.

Johnston, J. (2019). Friendship potential: Conversation-based programming and immigrant integration. *Journal of Librarianship and Information Science, 51*(3), 670–688.

Katila, J., Gan, Y., Goico, S., & Goodwin, M.H. (Eds.). (2021). Researchers' participation roles in video-based fieldwork (special issue). *Social Interaction– Video-Based Studies of Human Sociality, 4*(2). https://doi.org/10.7146/si.v4i2.127184

King, R. (2012). *Theories and typologies of migration: An overview and a primer*. Malmö Institute for Studies of Migration, Diversity and Welfare.

Kirilova, M. (2017). 'Oh it's a DANISH boyfriend you've got': Co-membership and cultural fluency in job interviews with minority background applicants in Denmark. In J. Angouri, M. Marra, & J. Holmes (Eds.), *Negotiating boundaries at work: Talking and transitions* (pp. 29–49). Edinburgh: Edinburgh University Press.

Kunitz, S., & Jansson, G. (2021). Story recipiency in a language café: Integration work at the micro-level of interaction. *Journal of Pragmatics, 173*, 28–47.

Kunitz, S. & Majlesi, A.R. (2022). Multimodal gestalts in reformulating practices at language cafés. *Social Interaction – Video-Based Studies*.

Kunitz, S., & Markee, N. (2016). Understanding the fuzzy borders of context in conversation analysis and ethnography. In S. May (Ed.), *Encyclopedia of language and education*. Vol. 3: *Discourse and education*, 3rd edition (pp. 1–13). Cham: Springer.

Lave, J., & Wenger, E. (1991). *Situated learning: Legitimate peripheral participation*. Cambridge: Cambridge University Press.

Lilja, N., Eilola, L., Jokipohja, A.-K., & Tapaninen, T. (2021). Aikuiset maahanmuuttajat arjen vuorovaikutustilanteissa: Suomen kielen oppimisen mahdollisuudet ja mahdottomuudet ['Adult immigrants in everyday interaction situations: Opportunities and the impossibility of learning the Finnish language']. Vastapaino.

Lilja, N., & Piirainen-Marsh, A. (this volume). Learning to act in the social world: Building interactional competence through everyday language use experiences.

Lindwall, O., & Lymer, G. (2005). Vulgar competence, ethnomethodological indifference and curricular design. In T. Koschmann, D. Suthers, & T-W. Chan (Eds.), *Computer supported collaborative learning 2005: The next 10 years!* Proceedings from the International Conference on Computer Supported Collaborative Learning 2005, Taipei, May 30–June 4, 2005.

Lønsmann, D., & Kraft, K. (2018). Language in blue-collar workplaces. In B. Vine (Ed.), *The Routledge Handbook of Language in the Workplace* (pp. 138–149). London, New York: Routledge.

Makarova, E., & Birman, D. (2015). Cultural transition and academic achievement of students from ethnic minority backgrounds: A content analysis of empirical research on acculturation. *Educational Research, 57*(3), 305–330.

Makarova, E., & Birman, D. (2016). Minority students' psychological adjustment in the school context: An integrative review of qualitative research on acculturation. *Intercultural Education, 27*(1), 1–21.

Markee, N. (2008). Toward a learning behavior tracking methodology for CA-for-SLA. *Applied Linguistics, 29*(3), 404–427.

Markee, N. (2013). Emic and etic in qualitative research. In C. Chapelle (Ed.), *Encyclopedia of Applied Linguistics*. Hoboken: Wiley-Blackwell.

Minuz, F., & Pugliese, R. (2012). Quale didattica per l'italiano L2 nelle classi di volontariato? Risultato di una ricerca-azione su lingua e cultura ['Which didactics for L2-Italian in volunteer classes? Results of an action-research project on language and culture']. In R. Grassi (Ed.), *Nuovi contesti di acquisizione e insegnamento: L'italiano nelle realtà plurilingui* ['New contexts for acquisition and teaching: Italian in plurilingual realities] (pp. 37–60). Perugia: Guerra Edizioni.

Pekarek Doehler, S. (2019). On the nature and the development of L2 interactional competence: State of the art and implications for praxis. In M.R. Salaberry & S. Kunitz (Eds.), *Teaching and testing L2 interactional competence: Bridging theory and practice* (pp. 25–59). London, New York: Routledge.

Pekarek Doehler, S., & Berger, E. (2019). On the reflexive relation between developing L2 interactional competence and evolving social relationships: A longitudinal study of word-searches in the 'wild'. In J. Hellermann, S.W. Eskildsen, S. Pekarek Doehler, & A. Piirainen-Marsh (Eds.), *Conversation-analytic research on learning-in-action: The complex ecology of second language interaction 'in the wild'* (pp. 51–75). Cham: Springer.

Pettigrew, T.F., & Tropp, L.R. (2011). *When groups meet: The dynamics of intergroup contact*. New York, Hove: Psychology Press.

Pisarevskaya, A., Levy, N., Scholten, P., & Jansen, J. (2020). Mapping migration studies: An empirical analysis of the coming of age of a research field. *Migration Studies, 8*(3), 455–481.

Scollon, R., & Scollon, S. W. (2004). *Nexus analysis: Discourse and the emerging internet*. London, New York: Routledge.

Strömmer, M. (2016a). Affordances and constraints: Second language learning in cleaning work. *Multilingua, 35*(6), 697–721.

Strömmer, M. (2016b). Material scaffolding: Supporting the comprehension of migrant cleaners at work. *European Journal of Applied Linguistics, 4*(2), 239–275.

Strömmer, M. (2017). Work-related language learning trajectories of migrant cleaners in Finland. *Apples – Journal of Applied Language Studies, 11*(4), 137–160.

Suni, M. (2017). Working and learning in a new niche: Ecological interpretations of work-related migration. In J. Angouri, M. Marra, & J. Holmes (Eds.), *Negotiating boundaries at work: Talking and transitions* (pp. 197–215). Edinburgh: Edinburgh University Press.

Svennevig, J. (2018). What's it called in Norwegian? Acquiring L2 vocabulary items in the workplace. *Journal of Pragmatics, 126*, 68–77.

van Lier, L. (2004). *Ecology and semiotics of language learning: A sociocultural perspective*. Boston, Dordrecht, New York, London: Kluwer Academic.

Wagner, J. (2015). Designing for language learning in the wild: Creating social infrastructures for second language learning. In T. Cadierno & S. Eskildsen (Eds.), *Usage-based perspectives on second language learning* (pp. 75–101). Berlin, Boston: De Gruyter Mouton.

Wong, J. (2021). Our storied lives: Doing and finding friendship I. In J. Wong, & H.Z. Waring (Eds.), *Storytelling in multilingual interaction: A conversation analysis perspective*. London, New York: Routledge.

Wood, K. (2011). Writing together: Building community through learner stories in adult ESL. *TESOL Journal, 2*(2), 239–248.

14
LEARNING TO ACT IN THE SOCIAL WORLD

Building Interactional Competence through Everyday Language Use Experiences

Arja Piirainen-Marsh and Niina Lilja

Introduction

This chapter discusses how everyday interactions in second language speakers' daily life provide occasions for language learning and how language use experiences can be utilized in developing L2 pedagogy. Following the social turn in Second Language Acquisition (SLA) research in the 1990s, there is now a large body of empirical research that scrutinizes how second language development emerges from the co-constructed practices of social interaction in the learners' lifeworld. Our focus is on research that uses conversation analytic methods to build an empirically based understanding of language learning as situated social activity and achievement. Conversation analysis provides a unique theoretical and methodological framework for understanding the detailed ways in which social action is built and organized, moment-by-moment, by the participants in naturally occurring interaction. The goal of this chapter is twofold. First, it aims to shed light on the new insights that conversation analytic studies of language learning (CA-SLA) have provided into the understanding of second language learning and use as intricately linked to the resources through which social activities are built and organized (Kasper & Wagner, 2014; Wagner, 2015; Hellermann et al., 2019). Second, it discusses how conversation analytic insights can inform and provide a framework for developing second language teaching. To this end, we introduce and discuss examples of research-based practice that aims to support the development of interactional abilities by developing pedagogical procedures, materials and social infrastructures that create opportunities for interactions outside the classroom.

Conversation analytic research has provided new insights into the processes and outcomes of language learning by (1) redefining individualistic notions of cognition and competence as rooted in naturally occurring human social activity, (2) generating empirical analyses of learning-in-action in diverse linguistic, social and cultural settings both inside and outside the language classroom and (3) informing the design of classroom activities and materials to support the development of learners' ability to act in the social world. In what follows, we first discuss how the underlying constructs of cognition and competence have been respecified in conversation analytic research on language learning. After this, we focus on a selection of conversation analytic studies of language learning in the wild and discuss how their results have been used in developing pedagogy for supporting the development of interactional competence. We conclude by addressing some implications for future research and practice.

Key constructs

In this section we discuss how the conversation analytic research has contributed to multidisciplinary SLA and language teaching (The Douglas Fir Group, 2016) by respecifying key concepts used to understand L2 learning.

Cognition

From the outset, the conversation analytic approach to language learning has emphasized the social nature of learning to counter the strong cognitivist orientation in second language acquisition studies (Firth & Wagner, 1997, 2007; Markee & Kasper, 2004; Kasper & Wagner, 2014). Conversation analytic research emphasizes the primacy of interaction as the bedrock of all social and cultural activity, and the natural environment for language use (Garfinkel, 1967; Schegloff, 1991, 2006). From this point of view, cognition is understood as a *socially shared* phenomenon, configured in and adaptive to social practices (Kasper, 2009; Pekarek Doehler, 2010). Language learning is a social endeavour, situated in the sense making practices that participants use in building intersubjectivity. It is the practical, hearable and visible procedures for co-constructing understanding, knowledge and mutual relationships that make language and culture learnable (Garfinkel & Sacks, 1970).

The focus on action, context and naturally occurring interaction is consistent with the view that cognition is *situated* in practical activities in their sociocultural and material environments and *distributed* between human participants and the environment (Hutchins, 1995). Hellermann (2018) argues for a holistic, action-based view that conceptualizes cognition and learning as *enactivism*, that is "the dynamic interplay between mind, body, the environment and action" (p. 43). Aligned with research on distributed cognition and phenomenologically informed views of the self as a "dynamic, unbounded and shared entity" (Hellermann, 2018: 42), this perspective looks at cognition as experienced practice. These views of cognition as situated and socially shared are often referred to as 4E cognition, emphasizing that cognition is (a) *extended*, in other words, uses affordances of artefacts in the environments (such as notebooks, computers), (b) *embedded*, that is situated in material environments, (c) *embodied* – bodily actions and functions influence mental functioning, and (d) *enacted* through agentive activity (Clark & Chalmers, 1998; Atkinson, 2010, 2019; Eskildsen & Markee, 2018; Eilola & Lilja, 2021). The work of Hutchins' (1995) and others on situated cognition informs research on language learning-in-action, which investigates how learning takes place and may be shaped by everyday social activities within specific material ecologies (Wagner, 2015, 2019; Hellermann et al., 2019).

Learning in action

Conversation analytic research is grounded in an action-based view of language and learning (Pekarek Doehler, 2010; Lee, 2010; Lee & Hellermann, 2014): language is seen as a constitutive part of larger ecologies of sociocultural activity and embedded in the activities that people conduct with others in their social world. Research focusses on those aspects of learning that are observable and analysable through detailed attention to the participants' sense-making practices and the procedures through which they manage their participation in social activity. These include the linguistic, vocal and embodied practices of turn-construction and action formation, the moment-by-moment negotiation of turn transitions and accomplishment of sequences of action.

The commitment to trace the participants' displayed understandings of sequentially unfolding turns and actions has led to a reconsideration of what is learnt in interaction and how. The focus of conversation analytic research is on the competencies and capacities that participants deploy – and learn to draw upon – in participating in social tasks. This entails a dialogic, usage-based and practical theory of language in which language and social activity are seen as mutually constitutive and language abilities are seen as intertwined with a wider set of competencies that enable individuals to engage in and manage social tasks (Eskildsen & Wagner, 2015; Wagner, 2015, 2019). These capacities and abilities are captured in the notion of interactional competence.

Interactional competence

The notion of interactional competence has been used in Applied Linguistics and CA-SLA since Claire Kramsch (1986) drew attention to the speaker-centred and restricted view of interaction represented in the "the proficiency movement" in the 1980s (for more detailed discussions tracing the history of the term see Hall & Pekarek Doehler, 2011; Hall, 2018; Salaberry & Kunitz, 2019). More recently, the concept has been respecified in numerous publications documenting how L2 interactional abilities are displayed and developed in diverse activities and settings (Hall, Hellermann & Pekarek Doehler, 2011; Pekarek Doehler & Pochon-Berger, 2015; Skogmyr Marian & Balaman, 2018). At the heart of the notion of interactional competence is the concern with the interacting parties' locally situated practices and their ability to build joint action (Pekarek Doehler, 2019: 34, 38). It is this concern with competence-in-action (Pekarek Doehler, 2010) that distinguishes IC from other related, but more individually oriented concepts such as communicative competence (Hymes, 1972).

From a conversation analytic viewpoint, interactional competence can be defined as the ability to build turns in a context-sensitive way to accomplish recognizable social actions and the ability to respond to the actions of others in situated interaction. This ability rests on the capacity to use and coordinate linguistic resources in the language user's repertoire, and other semiotic resources, such as gaze, gesture and meaningful objects, for joint action in the moment-by-moment unfolding of interaction. This means that interactional competence is dynamic and variable; it involves adaptation and recalibration of interactional resources for specific communicative needs both locally, in making one's utterance recognizable to the recipient, and more generally, when entering into new social engagements and participating in new kinds of communicative tasks (Hellermann et al., 2019; Pekarek Doehler, 2019). Accordingly, the development of interactional competences can be seen as part of larger socialization processes through which second language users gain access to and learn to participate in the practices of a community.

Recent studies have called attention to a need to distinguish between the basic interactional capacities and language-specific resources that can be operationalized as objects of second language learning. Some have also proposed alternative terms such as interactional competencies (Kasper, 2006), interactional practices (Waring, 2018, 2019) and interactional repertoires (Hall, 2018, 2019). Hall (2019), for example, argues for using the term repertoire to talk about objects of language learning, or language knowledge, defined as "conventionalised constellations of semiotic resources for taking action" (p. 86). By contrast, Hellermann (2018) and others (Koschmann, 2012; Kasper & Wagner, 2014; Wagner, 2015, 2019) rely on the ethnomethodological understanding of competence as fundamentally interactional and inseparable from the accountable practices for accomplishing social action and ability to engage in interaction in specific contexts. From this point of view, the development of interactional competence involves developing alternative methods for organizing social interaction such as turn-taking, repair and sequential organization, as well as how these may be adapted according to the local circumstances (Pekarek Doehler, 2019: 29–30).

Empirical studies of interactional competence have covered a wide variety of methods for social action including linguistic practices such as the use of specific lexical features or grammatical constructions in interaction as well as methods for configuring interactional activities such as openings and closings, topic management, repair, disagreement, action sequencing and storytelling in different interactional settings (see Pekarek Doehler & Pochon Berger, 2015 for overview). Overall, the notion of interactional competence or competencies captures the action-based approach to language learning informed by CA by emphasizing the emerging ability to adapt semiotic resources for action in a recipient-designed way and the development of interactional repertoires for context-sensitive social conduct (Eskildsen, 2018; Pekarek Doehler, 2019).

Key issues

In this section, we discuss current issues faced by researchers and practitioners who work towards developing a research-based framework for supporting language learning in the wild.

How do everyday interactions create occasions for learning?

A growing body of empirical research demonstrates the rich learning potential of everyday encounters for language learning. Two strands can be identified in this research. One group of studies focusses on learning as social activity, in other words pays detailed attention to moments where the participants make learning a focal concern in interaction (Koschmann, 2012; Kasper & Wagner, 2014). Another group of studies uses longitudinal data to trace observable changes in L2 speakers' methods for participation in social activity across short or longer time spans (see Pekarek Doehler et al., 2018).

Studies that focus on learning as social activity shed light on learning as a locally occasioned phenomenon that is publicly displayed in the participants' conduct. They demonstrate, for example, how participants momentarily depart from advancing the main line of talk to initiate repair, carry out word searches or focus on the form or meaning of expressions used in prior talk or otherwise observable in the environment (see, e.g. Brouwer, 2003; Kurhila, 2006; Greer, 2013; Lilja, 2014; Kasper & Burch, 2016; Theodórsdóttir, 2011, 2018; Lilja & Piirainen-Marsh, 2019a, 2019b). These studies make visible how language learning activities are embedded in social interaction in a variety of everyday and workplace settings. Kasper and Burch (2016), for example, show how participants in an everyday conversation create a space for learning by shifting the topical focus from everyday matters to language form in order to address a lexical understanding problem and fill a gap in the vocabulary of a L2 speaker of Japanese. Their detailed multimodal analysis demonstrates how this shift to 'focus on form' generates sustained attention to a learning object and involves word definitions, form practice as well as attending to a problem concerning writing the character of a synonym. The study highlights the way that the social organization of the activity enables joint attentional focus on a learning object and augments the L2 speaker's knowledge of linguistic resources, but also makes relevant social relations, in this case 'doing friendship'. Eskildsen and Theodórsdóttir (2017) describe how a Canadian student at Iceland University makes relevant her identity as a second language speaker in everyday service encounters and initiates negotiation for a 'contract' to speak Icelandic with the co-participant.

Studies of learning activity in workplace contexts are still scarce. A few existing studies show that interactional competence is closely intertwined with the work practices of different professions. Kurhila and Lehtimaja (2019a) analyse language use contexts that are typical in nurses' work in hospitals. Their analysis shows that language use in these contexts is situated and tightly connected with nurses' professional expertise (see also Kurhila & Lehti-maja, 2019b). In a study focussing on a migrant worker's interaction in Norwegian as L2 at a construction site, Svennevig (2018) demonstrates how the participants expand a word search sequence beyond identification of the sought for word and thereby orient to the word as a learnable. Learning activity involves repetition and checking the perception of the words and rehearsing pronunciation.

While early studies of such learning behaviours (Markee, 2008) largely focus on repair, recent research draws attention to a range of other features, such as referential practices (Kim, 2012), noticings (Eskildsen, 2019; Greer, 2019) and reindexing previously learned items (Eskildsen, 2018, 2019, see also Jakonen, 2018) as local resources in learning activity. Greer (2019) shows how participants in L2 interaction orient to learning in sequences where they notice and pay explicit attention to new lexical items that occur in the preceding talk or are visible in the physical environment. His multimodal analysis of two distinct cases (a Japanese student interacting with the American host family and a Bolivian man having a haircut in a Japanese hair salon) shows how noticing of a lexical item in interaction can occasion episodes of talk where the participants put the projected trajectory of talk 'on hold' and engage in extended sequences where the noticed items are explained and later re-indexed as recently learned items. The analysis demonstrates how noticings enable the participants to resolve epistemic asymmetries and provide occasions for L2 learners to gain access to new language resources by making use of the expert speakers and assigning them with teacher-like qualities (Greer, 2019: 144).

In sum, studies of mundane interactions in out-of-classroom environments provide empirical insight into the practices that participants deploy to establish spaces for learning, focus joint attention to language forms, solicit assistance from language experts, and engage in sequences where new objects of learning are examined, clarified, explained and co-constructed as learned or understood. Many of the observed practices are similar to those identified in research on classroom interaction and show how everyday interactions can involve pedagogical sequences where the participants orient to roles of novice and expert language user. However, they also suggest how language learning in the wild differs from classroom learning. Pekarek Doehler (2019; see also Berger & Pekarek Doehler, 2018; Pekarek Doehler & Berger, 2018), for example, shows how a L2 speaker of French, who had participated in L2 instruction for 12 years, developed a more varied interactional repertoire of resources in storytelling and was able to deploy these resources in a more context-sensitive way after only two months of homestay in the L2 environment. These and related findings point to the limitations of the classroom as a learning environment and the lack of attention to interactional features in L2 curricula. Recent studies also draw attention to the material environment as a resource for learning activity. Greer (2019) describes how a novice speaker's articulated noticing of an unfamiliar word used about an object in the environment makes public his own hypothesis of the meaning of a lexical item, which leads to an explanation sequence where the participants address different uses of the same word. As he observes, "opportunities to make inferences about incidental language use in relation to description of environmental objects can be limited or at best, artificial" in the classroom (p. 155).

The role of environment and activity-relevant objects for second language use and learning is also illustrated in extract 1 from a cooking class. As the main activities in the class are cooking and baking, the participants' attention is usually not focussed on language. Sometimes, however, language-related noticings are occasioned in the middle of these practical activities. In extract 1 Ali (L2 speaker of Finnish) is guided by Tea (L1 speaker of Finnish) in making cookie dough. While Ali is whisking sugar and butter with a hand-held electric mixer, Tea describes what the dough should be like as a result of the whisking: it should become foam-like (l. 1–2).

Extract 1) Vaahto (foam)

+= TEA's gestures
*= ALI's gestures

```
01 TEA    +siitä pitää saada sem+mosta
          it needs to be made into such like
          +raises right hand to chest level
                              +moves fingers->

02        >ninku< (.)+ vaah*#too, *(.)
          like     (.) foam
                      -->+opens fingers, open palm->
   ali:                   *gazes to teacher,
                          nods *gaze back to bowl->
   fig                    #fig1

03        [vaahto (.) tiedätkö mitä on+
          foam        know-SG2-CLI what is
          foam (.) do you know what is
                                    -->+

04 ALI    [sama #*krema (.) krema (ker-)
          same "krema" (.) "krema" (cre-)
                 *gaze to teacher->
                 #fig 2

05 TEA    =+aaam
           +starts to close and open fingers->

06        (.)

07 ALI    sama kre[ma
          same "krema"
```

```
08 TEA          [foam   #(.) *joo (.)+ joo (.)
                "foam"(.) yes (.) yes
                              -->+
    ali:                      *gaze back to bowl
                #fig3

09              vaahtoo (.) joo (4.0) voit laittaa
                foam    (.) yes (4.0) you can speed it up

10              kovemmalle sitte ku se on semmosta
                when it is like that
```

Concurrently with her verbal turn Tea produces a depictive gesture with her right hand as if squeezing something soft in it (Figure 14.1). She also stresses the first syllable of the word foam (vaahto) (l. 2). Together the gesture and the stress as well as the turn-final position make the word *vaahto* salient in TEA's turn. Simultaneously with ALI's embodied response, Tea continues by directly asking Ali whether he knows what foam means (l. 3). Tea thus orients to the word *foam* as potentially new to Ali. Ali gazes towards Tea and reacts to her instruction by asking whether *vaahto* is the same as *krema*, a word that is not standard Finnish but is recognizable as referring to cream. By seeking confirmation for his understanding of TEA's instruction Ali orients to maintaining mutual understanding of what the dough-in-the-making should become like but also makes a connection between an unfamiliar and familiar vocabulary item. The activity and the objects that enable the whisking thus afford possibilities for language-related talk intertwined with the ongoing larger baking activity. A key question to be addressed in future research is how occasions for similar learning activities arise in different types of social activity and their material ecologies.

CA research highlights how spatial, material and temporal features of practical activities contextualize interaction and create specific kinds of affordances for action. Recent work on objects and mobility in interaction (Haddington et al., 2013; Nevile et al., 2014), for example, show how practices of turn-taking and action formation are sensitive to changes in the physical or spatial environments. So far only a few studies of L2 interaction have considered how the participants' interaction with the environment figures in their interaction and affordances for learning. Hellermann et al. (2019) analyse language learners engaged in playing a place-based augmented reality game in an attempt to explore how their action is "situated in, or catalyzed by, particular aspects of the physical surround and how this might be relevant for language learning" (p. 194). Their focus is on the participants' methods for making unplanned use of resources of the physical context in brainstorming how to accomplish game goals. Their analysis shows how the participants draw on the multiple semiotic fields and a rich array of meaning-making resources in managing the task. For example, written instructions in the game on the mobile device are referred to and understood with respect to salient objects in the physical environment. The participants draw on talk and embodied activity to index features of the environment and make them relevant to their activities. One of the key issues to address in future research concerns the ways in which participants mobilize features of the physical environment in interaction and how this can create affordances for language learning.

A growing number of studies draw on longitudinal data and methods of vertical comparison in Conversation Analysis (Kasper & Wagner, 2014) to investigate the development of interactional competence by documenting observable changes in the methods for participation

Figure 14.1 Extract 1: Graphic transcript

in social activity over time. While the focus has been mostly on instructional settings, increasing attention has been paid to mundane and work settings, including study abroad, homestay contexts and business communication. Longitudinal studies describe changes in the use of L2 linguistic (lexical and syntactic) resources which point to an expanding repertoire of resources and the development of grammar-for-interaction (see, e.g. Ishida, 2009; Hauser, 2013; Pekarek Doehler & Berger, 2019). Another group of studies focus on changes in sequential patterns or overall structural organization of interaction. In a pioneering study Brouwer and Wagner (2004) demonstrated how a second language speaker's practices of opening a business telephone conversation change over the course of three telephone calls in consecutive days. Their analysis shows how the initially disorderly openings are managed in a more coordinated way in later calls, demonstrating the routinization of the social practice of business call openings as well as the evolving social relationship between the participants. In a study focussing on pharmacy consultations, Nguyen (2012, 2018) documents how patterns of action sequencing, topic management and the design of formulations change over time. A few studies shed light on changes in storytelling practices in everyday conversations in a family setting. Barraja-Rohan (2015) reports how a Japanese student's storytelling practices show increasing complexity and evidence of new interactional resources during a 19-week stay in Australia. Kim (2016) shows how a Korean student's recipient conduct manifests widening of resources and more timely and sequentially appropriate deployment of these resources. Two studies focussing on openings (Pekarek Doehler & Berger, 2018) and practices for bringing the story to a climax and close (Berger & Pekarek Doehler, 2018) demonstrate how the storytelling practices of an L2 speaker of French become more attuned to the recipients and more context-sensitive over time. These studies lend support to an understanding of interactional competence as involving diversification of practices for participating in interaction and increased ability for context-sensitive conduct (Pekarek Doehler, 2019).

To summarize, studies of learning activity shed light on social and situated occasions for learning by elucidating how participants in diverse environments outside the classroom make learning a focal concern in interaction. They show how components of social action – including language practices – are made publicly available for learning. In this way, they increase understanding of learning and teaching as "built into the organization of interaction itself" (Goodwin (2018: 102). Although research in this area is accumulating, there are a number of challenges that need to be addressed in future work. One issue that has bearing on both theory and praxis concerns the interrelationship between linguistic resources as part of an individual's interactional repertoire and the holistic understanding of interactional competence as the ability to deploy multiple semiotic resources for action in diverse social activities. This calls for more systematic research on grammar as a set of resources in L2 interaction and the developmental trajectories through which L2 grammar for interaction emerges. Promising steps to this direction have already been taken in studies combining conversation analysis with usage-based linguistics or interactional linguistics (Eskildsen, 2018; Pekarek Doehler, 2018; Pekarek Doehler & Berger, 2019). Another challenge is to broaden the empirical basis of research by investigating affordances of action and learning in a wider array of social activities in the L2 speakers' lifeworld. As learning is embedded in practical activities that are embedded in larger ecologies, studies of L2 interaction need to develop a richer understanding of the practices used in different sociomaterial environments. In addition, longitudinal research is needed to get deeper insight into the factors that impact the development of interactional competence as a social process.

How can research-based insights be applied in designing pedagogical practice?

The study of language learning as embedded in interactions with others has opened up new possibilities for developing L2 instruction by designing materials for teaching interactional competence (Huth, 2006; Huth & Taleghani-Nikazm, 2006; Wong & Waring, 2010; Barraja-Rohan, 2011; Wong, 2011; Betz & Huth, 2014; Kurhila & Kotilainen, 2020). This means focussing on interactionally defined objects of learning such as openings and closings of telephone calls, requests and compliments as well as practices of turn-taking and active listenership. Waring (2018, 2019) adopts the conversation analytic concept of interactional practices as a starting point for developing a model for understanding such practices as pedagogical objects. She argues that practices of turn-taking, sequencing, overall structuring and repair can be taught by designing classroom activities around recordings of naturally occurring interaction and transcripts of these. A more programmatic and systematic effort to develop research-based pedagogical practice was carried out at the Centre for Language and Intercultural Communication (CLIC) at Rice University, where a group of teachers and researchers collaborated to create units of instruction for a curriculum based on interactional competence (Salaberry & Kunitz, 2019). Kunitz and Yeh (2019) describe the steps taken to design instructional materials and discuss the outcomes of a pedagogical intervention aimed at developing the participants' interactional competence in Chinese as a foreign language. The specific focus was on developing practices for active listenership and topic management. They show how a pedagogical cycle consisting of different phases in which students analyse sequences of talk, practise specific learning targets, and reflect on the import of what they have learnt, can be used in raising students' awareness of the practices and skills involved. This work illustrates how a research-based understanding of interactional competence can serve as a useful framework for increasing teachers' and students' awareness of the richness of interaction and for designing materials, teaching strategies and tasks that foster students' participation in interaction. The limitation is that while emphasizing the richness of authentic interaction and details of interactional practices as targets of learning, much of this work focusses on the classroom as the main learning environment.

By contrast, researchers in the language learning in the wild network have argued for more radical changes to teaching of second languages. Wagner (2015) argues for developing a new kind of experiential pedagogy that centres around social encounters that people living in a L2 environment participate in and integrates the learners' experiences of these encounters into pedagogical activities. Two pioneering initiatives to support L2 learning in the wild were carried out in Iceland and Sweden. In Iceland, Gudrun Theodórsdóttir and others created social infrastructures for learning by making agreements with local businesses that enabled novice L2 learners to use Icelandic in actual business encounters in a supportive environment (Wagner, 2015). In Sweden, the Språkskap project brought together researchers, language teachers and interaction designers to develop a framework and material resources to support learners in their interactions outside the classroom. For example, they created materials to guide L2 speakers in mapping their arenas for language use and to support planning interactions to be carried out in the wild and reflecting on them (Clark & Lindemalm, 2011; Clark et al., 2011). In Finland, CA researchers and interaction designers collaborated with language teachers in order to develop tangible materials and experientially based pedagogical practices that would help students extend the spaces for learning, augment their resources for participating in interaction in their social world, and support reflection on their language use experiences. Lilja et al. (2019) provide a detailed description of the structure of the "Rally course", some of the materials used, and the pedagogical process. The materials guided the students to reflect on their needs, goals and opportunities for interaction in the second language, to set challenges and plan their own learning journeys. The students were familiarized with a pedagogic cycle that involved "scouting", that is observing interactions in the wild, preparing for interactions in chosen settings, recording their interactions using their smartphones and reflecting on their language use experiences in 'debriefing activities' (Wagner, 2015) in the classroom. When complementary data sets from classroom discussions and the students' self-recorded interactions were analysed in detail, it was found that the debriefing discussions created opportunities for reflecting and analysing prior language use experiences at several levels. In addition to enabling discussion of objects of learning (ranging from lexical and syntactic to sequential phenomena) identified by the learners themselves, they generated extended discussions focussing on cultural norms and practices (Piirainen-Marsh & Lilja, 2019). In addition, they showed that the smartphone as a personal device enabled language-focussed activity in which students scrutinized moments that they found noteworthy or problematic (Lilja & Piirainen-Marsh, 2019a, 2019b).

Extract 2 (analysed in more detail in Lilja & Piirainen-Marsh, 2019b) illustrates how the smart phone works as a central resource in an extended language-focussed activity which is occasioned by Mark's telling about his service encounter in a café. Prior to the extract Mark has explained that he had difficulties in understanding the clerk's answer to his question asking whether he was expected to pay for a hot chocolate he ordered. This generates a sharing activity, in which the participants watch the video multiple times and collectively work to construct a hearing and understanding of the clerk's answer.

Extract 2) The smartphone as a resource for learning activity

```
34        *Δ #(0.4) (0.6)
  mar   ->*puts the phone on the table so that it is visible to everyone,
            leans towards it->
  joh   ->Δgaze towards phone->
            #pic 1

35 VID    (ok)ei maksaa?
          Okey it costs

36 JOH    Δ^ei [maksa                          ^
              NEG cost-STEM/pay-STEM
            ^points towards the teacher^
          Δgaze towards the teacher->

37 MAR        [*+ei maksa?#
              NEG cost-STEM/pay-STEM
          ->*raises position->
          ->+gaze towards teacher->
                    #pic 2

38 VID    opiskelija?
          student?

39 JOH    see?
```

```
40          +(.)
  mar     ->+gaze towards phone->

41 JOH    Δ^put it a little bit back^#
          ->Δgaze towards the phone ->
                  ^points towards the phone^
                                        #pic3

42          *(.)
  mar     *leans towards phone, handles phone and rewinds the video ->

43 CLA    ei maksaa >maybe<
          NEG cost-INF / pay-INF

44 MAR    we- we'll see when she goes [back, #(.)
                                              #pic 4

45 TEA                                 [ah:

46        se oli ehkä <ei> (.) maksaa:
                       NEG     cost-INF/pay-INF
          it was maybe no  (.) it costs

47          (.)

48 CLA    aah

49 MAR    *now she goes back (.) to ask #
          ->*point towards phone->
                                        #pic5
```

In the beginning of the extract Mark places the phone in the middle of the table for all the participating students to see and starts to play the video (line 34, pic 1) (Figure 14.2). When the clerk's focal answer is hearable, both John and Mark repeat it and Mark directs his gaze towards the teacher as if seeking for her confirmation (lines 36-37, pic 2). Another student, John, asks Mark to replay the answer (line 41, pic 3). While Mark is handling the phone, two other participants, Claire and the teacher, suggest alternative ways of hearing the clerk's turn (lines 43, 46). Mark rewinds the video to moments before the focal response and plays it again, concurrently commenting on what happens on the video while the other participants are watching (pic 4 and 5). After hearing the target turn, the participants again engage with it by repeating the focal answer and clarifying its meaning. This short fragment of the extended activity illustrates how the smart phone as a technological device connects the classroom with the world outside by allowing the participants to retrieve prior language use experiences for retrospective reflection and analysis. The sharing and collective watching of the video enables the participants to co-construct a new understanding of the situation in a way that would not be possible without the recording. As shown in the example, in the classroom the students can also turn to the teacher's expertise in trying to make sense of the turns that cause them trouble in understanding.

Learning to Act in the Social World

Figure 14.2 Extract 2: Graphic transcript

The pedagogical initiatives briefly described above answer the call for developing L2 pedagogy that takes social interaction as its starting point and centres on supporting the L2 speakers' participation and learning from interactions in their life world. Researchers and practitioners face the challenge of designing tools that support L2 users' participation in interactions outside the classroom and creating spaces for 'harvesting' (Wagner, 2015) their experiences.

Implications and future directions

The research discussed above has increased theoretical understanding of interactional competence, provided insights into the in-situ learning activities that are embedded in L2 interactions outside the classroom, and shed light on developmental trajectories by documenting changes in L2 speakers' interactional practices. However, there are still significant gaps in research that need to be addressed to better understand what kinds of infrastructures and pedagogical practices best support the development of interactional competence. There is a need for further development of the programme on language learning in action that pays systematic attention to the following issues: (a) conceptualization of linguistic competencies as part of interactional competence, (b) the tension between conceptualization of IC as locally achieved, co-constructed and situated, and the need to study the emergence of interactional resources in L2 development and (c) the need for a holistic multimodal framework to account for the complexly intertwined resources that participants draw upon to accomplish action. As discussed in previous studies (Nguyen, 2019; Pekarek Doehler, 2019), this also calls for methodological development. It is important to broaden the data base by addressing a wider variety of social activities that L2 speakers participate in their social world. More video-based research is needed to find out about learning opportunities and affordances in workplace interaction, for example. Studies of L2 interaction in the wild also need to refine procedures for systematic analysis and comparison of interactional practices across settings and over time.

An ongoing challenge for researchers and practitioners concerned with supporting the development of IC is the "teachability" of interactional practices. In order to usefully inform pedagogical practice, further efforts are needed to increase awareness of generic organizations of interaction and the detailed practices that these involve among teachers and practitioners. As empirical studies from diverse activities and ecologies accumulate, these can inform our understanding of the ways that interactional competencies are adapted to specific environments and how the participants mobilize linguistic and embodied resources as well as features of the environment in organizing action. Research-based insights are needed to develop infrastructures that widen L2 learners' opportunities for participation in social activity outside the classroom and design materials and support-structures that help them navigate the interactions in their social world.

Reflection questions

1. In your experience, what are the most important aspects of second language use that can be learnt from everyday interactions?
2. What are the advantages of respecifying the object of language learning as interactional competence? What are the advantages of using alternative terms such as interactional interactional repertoires?

3   To what extent is interactional competence teachable? What kind of pedagogy, in your opinion, would best support the development of L2 interactional competence?

Recommended readings

Wagner, Johannes (2015). *Designing for language learning in the wild: Creating social infrastructures for second language learning.*
This article discusses how an action-based view of language can inform the teaching of languages. It argues for redefining language learning as "the range of social possibilities the new language will afford which includes the linguistic competence needed to realize these possibilities" (p 76). The article outlines the basis for experiential pedagogy that centres around the L2 users' encounters in their lifeworld. The role of teaching in this approach is to prepare L2 users for these encounters, furnish them with helpful tools and materials, and provide spaces for reflection and understanding of their experiences.

Salaberry, M. R., & Kunitz, S. (Eds.) (2019). *Teaching and testing L2 interactional competence: Bridging theory and practice.*
This volume presents a selection of research on L2 interactional competence and its pedagogical implications. The book is structured into four sections. After a thorough introduction to the concept of IC, the chapters discuss theoretical and methodological issues (Section 1), research-based insights on teaching (Section 2), research-informed pedagogy (Part III) and testing interactional competence (IV).

Hellermann, J., Eskildsen, S., Pekarek Doehler, S., & Piirainen-Marsh, A. (Eds.) (2019). *Conversation analytic research on learning-in-action. The complex ecology of second language interaction 'in the wild'.* Cham: Springer.
This collection of articles introduces conversation analytic research on language learning outside instructional settings. The articles discuss the complex ecology of second language interactions in a variety of settings ranging from everyday conversation to service encounters and technology-supported place-based games.

References

Atkinson, D. (2010). Extended, embodied cognition and second language acquisition. *Applied Linguistics*, *31*, 599–622.

Atkinson, D. (2019). Beyond the brain: Intercorporeality and co-operative action for SLA studies. *The Modern Language Journal*, *103*(4), 724–738. DOI: 10.1111/modl.125950026-7902/19/724-738

Barraja-Rohan, A.-M. (2011). Using conversation analysis in the second language classroom to teach interactional competence. *Language Teaching Research*, *15*, 479–507.

Barraja-Rohan, A.-M. (2015). "I told you". Storytelling development of a Japanese learning English as a second language. In T. Cadierno & S.W. Eskildsen (Eds.), *Usage-based perspectives on second language learning* (pp. 271–304). Berlin: De Gruyter Mouton.

Betz, E., & Huth, T. (2014). Beyond grammar: Teaching interaction in the German classroom. *Unterrichtspraxis/Teaching German*, *42*(2), 140–163.

Brouwer, C. (2003). Word searches in NNS-NS interaction. Opportunities for language learning? *The Modern Language Journal*, *87*(4), 534–545.

Brouwer, C. E., & Wagner, J. (2004). Developmental issues in second language conversation. *Journal of Applied Linguistics*, *1*, 29–47.

Clark, A., & Chalmers, D. (1998). The extended mind. *Analysis*, *58*(1), 7–19.

Clark, B., & K. Lindemalm (2011). *Språkskap - Swedish as a Social Language*. Ergonomidesign, Folkeuniversitetet & Interactive Institute.

Clark, B., Wagner, J., Lindemalm, K., & Bendt, O. (2011). Språkskap: Supporting second language learning 'in the wild'. *INCLUDE* 11. International conference on inclusive design proceedings. London, Royal College of Art.

The Douglas Fir Group (2016). A transdisciplinary framework for SLA in a multilingual world. *The Modern Language Journal*, *100*(Supplement 2016), 19–47. DOI: 10.1111/modl.123010026-7902/16/19-47

Eilola, L., & Lilja, N. (2021). The smartphone as a personal cognitive artifact supporting participation in interaction. *The Modern Language Journal*, *105*(1), 294–316.

Eskildsen, S. W. (2018). Building a semiotic repertoire for social action: Interactional competence as biographical discovery. *Classroom Discourse, 9*(1), 68–76.

Eskildsen, S. W., & Majlesi, A. R. (2018). Learnables and teachables in second language talk: Advancing a social reconceptualization of central SLA tenets. Introduction to the special issue. *The Modern Language Journal, 102*(Supplement), 3–10.

Eskildsen, S. W., & Markee, N. (2018). L2 talk as social accomplishment. In R. A. Alonso (Ed.), *Learning to speak in an L2* (pp. 69–103). Amsterdam: John Benjamins.

Eskildsen, S., & Wagner, J. (2015). Embodied L2 construction learning. *Language Learning, 65*(2), 419–448.

Eskildsen, S. W., & Wagner, J. (2018a). From trouble in the talk to new resources – The interplay of bodily and linguistic resources in the talk of a speaker of English as a second language. In S. Pekarek Doehler, J. Wagner, & E. González-Martínez (Eds.), *Longitudinal studies on the organization of social interaction* (pp. 143–171). Basingstoke: Palgrave Macmillan.

Firth, Alan, & Wagner, Johannes (1997). On discourse, communication, and (some) fundamental concepts in SLA research. *The Modern Language Journal, 81*(3), 285–300.

Firth, A., & Wagner, J. (2007). Second/foreign language learning as a social accomplishment: Elaborations on a reconceptualized SLA. *Modern Language Journal, 91*(4), 800–819.

Garfinkel, H. (1967). *Studies in ethnomethodology*. Englewood Cliffs: Prentice Hall.

Garfinkel, H., & Sacks, H. (1970). On formal structures of practical action. In J.C. McKinney & E.A. Tiryakin (Eds.), *Theoretical sociology* (pp. 338–366). New York: Appleton-Century-Crofts.

Goodwin, C. (2018). *Co-operative action*. Cambridge: Cambridge University Press.

Greer, T. (2013). Word search sequences in bilingual interaction: Codeswitching and embodied orientation toward shifting participant constellations. *Journal of Pragmatics, 57*, 100–117.

Greer, T. (2019). Noticing words in the wild. In J. Hellermann, S.W. Eskildsen, S., Pekarek Doehler, & A. Piirainen-Marsh (Eds.), *Conversation analytic research on learning-in-action. The complex ecology of second language interaction 'in the wild'* (pp. 131–158), Cham: Springer.

Haddington, P., Mondada, L., & Nevile, M. (Eds.) (2013). *Interaction and mobility. Language and the body in motion*. Berlin: Walter De Gruyter.

Hall, J.K. (2018). From L2 interactional competence to L2 interactional repertoires: Reconceptualising the objects of L2 learning. *Classroom Discourse, 9*, 25–39.

Hall, J.K. (2019). The contributions of conversation analysis and interactional linguistics to a usage-based understanding of language: Expanding the transdisciplinary framework. *The Modern Language Journal, 103*(Supplement 2019), 80–94. DOI: 10.1111/modl.125350026-7902/19/80–94

Hall, J.K., Hellermann, J., & Pekarek Doehler, S. (Eds.) (2011). *L2 interactional competence and development*. Clevedon: Multilingual Matters.

Hauser, E. (2013). Stability and change in one adult's second language English negation. *Language Learning, 63*(3): 463–498.

Hellermann, J. (2018). Languaging as competencing: Considering language learning as enactment. *Classroom Discourse, 9*, 40–56.

Hellermann, J., Eskildsen, S., Pekarek Doehler, S., & Piirainen-Marsh, A. (Eds.) (2019). *Conversation analytic research on learning-in-action. The complex ecology of second language interaction 'in the wild'*. Cham: Springer.

Hellermann, J., Thorne, S., & Haley, J. (2019). Building socio-environmental infrastructures for learning. In J. Hellermann, S.W. Eskildsen, S. Pekarek Doehler, & A. Piirainen-Marsh (Eds.), *Conversation analytic research on learning-in-action. The complex ecology of second language interaction 'in the wild'* (pp. 193–218). Cham: Springer.

Huth, T. (2006). Negotiating structure and culture: L2 learners' realization of L2 compliment-response sequences in talk-in-interaction. *Journal of Pragmatics, 38*, 2025–2050.

Huth, T., & Taleghani-Nikazm, C. (2006). How can insights from conversation analysis be directly applied to teaching L2 pragmatics? *Language Teaching Research, 10*, 53–79.

Hymes, D.H. (1972). On communicative competence. In J.B. Pride & J. Holmes (Eds.), *Sociolinguistics: Selected readings* (pp. 269–293). Harmondsworth: Penguin.

Hutchins, E. (1995). *Cognition in the wild*. Cambridge: MIT Press.

Ishida, M. (2009). Development of interactional competence: Changes in the use of ne in L2 Japanese during study abroad. In H. T. Nguyen and G. Kasper (Eds.), *Talk-in-interaction: Multilingual perspectives* (pp. 351–386). Honolulu: University of Hawai'i.

Jakonen, Teppo (2018). Retrospective orientation to learning activities and achievements as a resource in classroom interaction. *The Modern Language Journal, 102*(4), 758–774.

Kasper, G. (2006). Beyond Repair: Conversation Analysis as an Approach to SLA. *AILA Review 19(1)*, 83–99.

Kasper, G. (2009). Locating cognition in second language interaction and learning: Inside the skull or in public view? *IRAL, 47*, 11–36.

Kasper, G., & Burch, A.R. (2016). Orienting to focus on form in the wild. In R. A. van Compernolle & J. McGregor (Eds.), *Authenticity, language, and interaction in second language contexts* (pp. 198–232). Bristol: Multilingual Matters.

Kasper, G., & Wagner, J. (2011). A conversation-analytic approach to second language acquisition. In D. Atkinson (Ed.), *Alternative approaches to second language acquisition* (pp. 117–142). New York: Routledge.

Kasper, G., & Wagner, J. (2014). Conversation analysis in applied linguistics. *Annual Review of Applied Linguistics, 34*, 171–212.

Kim, Y. (2012). Practices for initial recognitional reference and learning opportunities in conversation. *Journal of Pragmatics, 44*, 709–729.

Kim, Y. (2016). Development of L2 interactional competence: Being a story recipient in L2 English conversation. *Discourse and Cognition, 23*(1), 1–29.

Koschmann, T. (2012). Conversation analysis and learning in interaction. In K. Mortensen & J. Wagner (Eds.), Conversation analysis. In C.A. Chapelle (Ed.), *The encyclopedia of applied linguistics* (pp. 1038–1043). Hoboken, NJ: John Wiley & Sons.

Kramsch, C. (1986). From language proficiency to interactional competence. *The Modern Language Journal, 70*, 366–372.

Kunitz, S., & Yeh, Y. (2019). Instructed L2 interactional competence in the first year. In M.R. Salaberry & S. Kunitz (Eds.), *Teaching and testing L2 interactional competence. Bridging theory and practice* (pp. 228–259). New York/London: Routledge/Taylor & Francis.

Kurhila, S. (2006). *Second language interaction*. Amsterdam/Philadelphia: J. Benjamins.

Kurhila, S., & Kotilainen, L. (2020). Student-initiated language learning sequences in a real-world digital environment. *Linguistics and Education, 56*, 1–11.

Kurhila, S., & Lehtimaja, I. (2019). Ammattikielen tilanteisuus kielenoppimisen haasteena: esimerkkinä hoitoala. In L. Kotilainen, S. Kurhila, & J. Kalliokoski (Eds.), *Kielenoppiminen luokan ulkopuolella* (pp. 143–171). Helsinki: Suomalaisen kirjallisuuden seura.

Kurhila, S., & Lehtimaja, I. (2019). Dealing with numbers: Nurses informing doctors and patients about test results. *Discourse Studies, 21*(2), 180–198. doi.org/10.1177/1461445618802662

Lee, Y. (2010). Learning in the contingency of talk-in-interaction. *Text and Talk, 30*, 403–22. doi: 10.1515/text.2010.020

Lee, Y., & Hellermann, J. (2014). Tracing developmental changes through conversation analysis. Cross-sectional and longitudinal analysis. *TESOL Quarterly, 48*(4), 763–788.

Lilja, Niina (2014). Partial repetitions as other-initiations of repair in second language talk. Re-establishing understanding and doing learning. *Journal of Pragmatics, 71*, 98–116.

Lilja, N., & Piirainen-Marsh, A. (2019a). Connecting the language classroom and the wild: Reenactments of language use experiences. *Applied Linguistics, 40*, 594–623.

Lilja, N., & Piirainen-Marsh, A. (2019b). Making sense of interactional trouble through mobile supported sharing activities. In M. R. Salaberry & S. Kunitz (Eds.), *Teaching and testing L2 interactional competence: Bridging theory and practice* (pp. 260–289). New York/London: Routledge/Taylor & Francis.

Lilja, N., Piirainen-Marsh, A., Clark, B., & Torretta, N. (2019). Learners as co-designers of out-of-classroom language learning tasks. In J. Hellermann, S.W. Eskildsen, S. Pekarek Doehler, & A. Piirainen-Marsh (Eds.), *Conversation analytic research on learning-in-action. The complex ecology of second language interaction 'in the wild'* (pp. 219–248). Cham: Springer.

Markee, N. (2008). Toward a learning behavior tracking methodology for CA-for-SLA. *Applied Linguistics, 29*(3), 404–427.

Markee, N., & Kasper, G. (Eds.) (2004). The special issue: Classroom talks. *The Modern Language Journal, 88*, 491–500.

Neville, M., Haddington, P., Heinemann, T., & Rauniomaa, M. (Eds.) (2014). *Interacting with Objects: Language, materiality, and social activity*. Amsterdam/Philadelphia: Benjamins.

Nguyen, H. T. (2012). *Developing interactional competence: A conversation-analytic study of patient consultations in pharmacy.* Basingstoke, UK: Palgrave-Macmillan.

Nguyen, H. (2018). A longitudinal perspective on turn design: From role-plays to workplace patient consultations. In S. Pekarek Doehler, J. Wagner E., & González-Martínez (Eds.), *Documenting change across time: Longitudinal studies on the organization of social interaction* (pp. 195–224). Basingstoke, UK: Palgrave-MacMillan.

Nguyen, H. T. (2019). Conclusion: Deepening roots and broadening horizons in interactional competence research and praxis. In M. R. Salaberry & S. Kunitz (Eds.), *Teaching and testing L2 interactional competence: Bridging theory and practice* (pp. 397–412). New York/London: Routledge/Taylor & Francis.

Pekarek Doehler, S. (2010). Conceptual changes and methodological challenges: On language and learning from a conversation analytic perspective on SLA. In P. Seedhouse, S. Walsh, & C. Jenks (Eds.), *Conceptualising 'Learning' in applied linguistics* (pp. 105–126). Basingstoke: Palgrave MacMillan.

Pekarek Doehler, S. (2019). On the nature and the development of L2 interactional competence: State of the art and implications for praxis. In R. Salaberry, & S. Kunitz (Eds.), *Teaching and testing L2 interactional competence: Bridging theory and practice* (pp. 25–59). New York/London: Routledge.

Pekarek Doehler, S., & Pochon-Berger, E. (2015). The development of L2 interactional competence: Evidence from turn-taking organization, sequence organization, repair organization and preference organization. In T. Cadierno & S. W. Eskildsen (Eds.), *Usage-based perspectives on second language learning* (pp. 233–268). Berlin: Mouton de Gruyter.

Pekarek Doehler, S., & Pochon-Berger, E. (2018). L2 interactional competence as increased ability for context-sensitive conduct: A longitudinal study of story-openings. *Applied Linguistics, 37*(4), 555–578. https://doi.org/10.1093/applin/amw021.

Pekarek Doehler, S., Wagner, J., & González-Martínez, E. (Eds.) (2018). *Documenting change across time: Longitudinal studies on the organization of social interaction.* Basingstoke, UK: Palgrave-MacMillan.

Piirainen-Marsh, Arja, & Lilja, Niina (2019). How wild can it get? Managing language learning tasks in real life service encounters. In J. Hellermann, S.W. Eskildsen, S. Pekarek Doehler, & A. Piirainen-Marsh (Eds.), *Conversation analytic research on learning-in-action. The complex ecology of second language interaction 'in the Wild'* (pp. 161–192). Cham: Springer.

Salaberry, M. R., & Kunitz, S. (Eds.) (2019). *Teaching and testing L2 interactional competence: Bridging theory and practice.* New York/London: Routledge/Taylor & Francis.

Schegloff, E. (1991). Conversation analysis and socially shared cognition. In L.B. Resnick, J.M. Levine, & S.D. Teasley (Eds.), *Perspectives on Socially Shared Cognition* (pp.150–171). Washington, DC: American Psychological Association.

Schegloff, E. (2006). Interaction: The infrastructure for social institutions, the natural ecological niche for language, and the arena in which culture is enacted. In N. Enfield & S. Levinson (Eds.), *Roots of human sociality* (pp. 70–96). Oxford: Berg.

Skogmyr Marian, K., & Balaman, U. (2018). Second language interactional competence and its development. An overview of conversation analytic research on interactional change over time. *Language & Linguistics Compass, 12*(8), 1–16.

Svennevig, Jan (2018). "What's it called in Norwegian?" Acquiring L2 vocabulary items in the workplace. *Journal of Pragmatics, 126*, 68–77.

Theodórsdóttir, G. (2011). Second language interaction for business and learning. In J. K. Hall, J. Hellermann, & S. Pekarek Doehler (Eds.), *L2 interactional competence and development* (pp. 56–93). Clevedon: Multilingual Matters.

Theodórsdóttir, G. (2018). L2 teaching in the wild: A closer look at correction and explanation practices in everyday L2 interaction. *The Modern Language Journal, 102*(Supplement 2018), 30–45.

Wagner, J. (2015). Designing for language learning in the wild: Creating social infrastructures for second language learning. In T. Cadierno & S. Eskildsen (Eds.), *Usage-based perspectives on second language learning* (pp. 75–101). Berlin: De Gruyter.

Wagner, J. (2018). Multilingual and multimodal interactions. *Applied Linguistics 39*(1), 99–107.

Wagner, J. (2019). Towards an epistemology of second language learning in the wild. In J. Hellermann, S. Eskildsen, S. Pekarek Doehler, & A. Piirainen-Marsh (Eds.), *Conversation analytic research on learning-in-action* (pp. 251–271). Cham: Springer.

Waring, H. Z. (2018). Teaching L2 interactional competence: Problems and possibilities. *Classroom Discourse, 9*(1), 57–67.

Waring, H. Z. (2019). Developing interactional competence with limited linguistic resources. In R. Salaberry, & S. Kunitz (Eds.), *Teaching and testing L2 interactional competence: Bridging theory and practice* (pp. 215–227). New York/London: Routledge.

Wong, J. (2011). Pragmatic competency in telephone conversation openings. In N.R. Houck & D.H. Tatsuki (Eds.), *Pragmatics: Teaching natural conversation* (pp. 119–134). Annapolis Junction: TESOL Classroom Practice Series.

Wong, J., & Waring, H.Z. (2010). *Conversation analysis and second language pedagogy: A gudie for ESL/EFL teachers*. New York: Routledge.

15
ENHANCING LANGUAGE LEARNING IN PRIVATE TUTORING

Kevin Wai Ho Yung

Introduction

Private tutoring is commonly defined as a paid out-of-school activity that students use to supplement their learning of academic subjects after school hours (Bray et al., 2015; Yung & Bray, 2017). Often operating alongside mainstream education, most private tutoring mimics the curriculum of regular schooling. Private tutoring can take various forms. It is offered in a wide range of subjects such as languages, mathematics, sciences, business, and humanities based on students' needs and market demand. Research has shown that many students participate in private tutoring in their national language to prepare for the school and public exams. For instance, in Myanmar, 84% Grade 9 and 93.9% Grade 11 students in a sample of 1,390 students receiving private tutoring had Myanmar language as one of the tutoring subjects (Bray et al., 2020). In a sample of 2,936 Grade 11 students in 127 schools in Russia, approximately 47.9% participated in Russian language private tutoring (Loyalka & Zakharov, 2016, p. 24). In Hong Kong, among a total of 3,329 children aged about nine years, 42.8% received "Chinese alone or Chinese alongside other subject tuition" (Tse, 2014, p. 289). As for English as the first language, learning centres offering courses in reading comprehension, speed reading, and writing are popular in places such as Canada, England and North America (Aurini et al., 2013; Buchmann et al., 2010; Ireson & Rushforth, 2011).

English private tutoring is particularly prevalent in contexts where English is learnt as an additional language. For example, in Hong Kong, a survey of 1,624 students in 16 secondary schools found that 65.2% respondents (58.5% Secondary 3 and 72.4% Secondary 6 students) had received some forms of English private tutoring in the past 12 months (Zhan et al., 2013, p. 500). Of the 177 students in Grade 8 and 10 surveyed in Bangladesh, 84.7% respondents had received English private tutoring (Mahmud & Kenayathulla, 2018). In South Korea, 53.8% of middle school students, 36.6% of high school students, and 42.5% of general high school students received English private tutoring in 2019 (KOSIS, 2020). The popularity of English private tutoring has also been observed in other countries such as China (Zhang, 2013), Germany (Ömeroğulları et al., 2020), and Japan (Allen, 2016).

Private tutoring plays a significant role in students' language learning beyond the classroom. It contributes to the holistic picture of their real language learning experiences and proficiency (Lee, 2010; Yung, 2015) and offers "alternative perspectives on the meaning of, and social and cognitive processes involved in, language learning and teaching" (Benson &

Reinders, 2011, p. 1). Despite increasing attention, research in private tutoring for language learning is still in its infancy. This chapter commences with the definitions of private tutoring and its features in different locales. It then discusses the concepts and constructs that have been operationalised and investigated in the field. Current issues facing various stakeholders and researchers in relation to private tutoring are highlighted. The chapter ends with seeking out further avenues for future research and possibilities for development in theory and practice for language teaching and learning in private tutoring.

Key concepts

Expanding definitions of private tutoring

Private tutoring has been widely known in the literature by its metaphor of *shadow education* because much of it mimics the curriculum of regular schooling – as the content of the curriculum changes in the mainstream, so it changes in the shadow; and as the regular school system expands or contracts, so does the shadow system (Bray, 2009). Alternative vocabularies include private tuition, private tutoring, coaching, extra lessons, and supplementary tutoring, depending on the context of research (see Bray et al., 2015). In the dominant strand of the literature, shadow education is defined by three main dimensions:

- *Privateness*: This dimension limits tutoring to that provided by individuals or organisations in exchange for a fee. It does not include unpaid tutoring offered by families, friends or volunteers, or extra lessons provided by teachers free of charge.
- *Academic subjects*: In many education systems, academic subjects include national languages, English, mathematics, and other subjects that feature in public exams. Domains that are learnt mainly for leisure and/or personal development such as music, art, and sports are excluded from the focus.
- *Supplementation*: Shadow education supplements the provision of schools and is provided outside school hours.

However, as the tutorial industry expands and regular schooling evolves, these characteristics may become less clear-cut. First, the word private may be interpreted as "outside the public space, whether or not in change for a fee" (Zhang & Bray, 2020, p. 324). Even if "private" refers to fee paying, some schools and non-governmental organisations offer fee-free "after-school tutoring" or "supplemental educational services" to help students from low-income families catch up with their studies.

In addition, while English is typically one of the academic subjects in the school curriculum in many educational systems worldwide, some English courses in the market do not directly shadow the mainstream English Language curriculum. One example is tutorial courses for the International English Language Testing System (IELTS). Although mainstream schools generally do not focus on the teaching of English specifically for IELTS, many tutorial companies offer courses for this exam alongside those for the English language exam in the national curriculum because IELTS scores may be used to apply for university admission (Allen, 2016; Bleistein & Lewis, 2015; Jeon & Choe, 2018). This example problematises the third dimension about supplementation, since English courses of this kind may not run in parallel to regular schooling yet are widely offered by tutorial companies.

Moreover, supplementation can be a relative concept from the tutee's perspective. When the tutee values private tutoring over mainstream schooling, the latter becomes supplementary from the tutee's viewpoint. For tutees such as private candidates of public exams who are not enrolled in mainstream schools but attend tutorial courses offered to school candidates after school hours, private tutoring is obviously not a supplement. However, courses offered in private day schools are not considered private tutoring because students attend lessons during regular school hours full-time as in mainstream schools.

Modes of private tutoring for language learning

Over time, the mode of private tutoring has developed and taken various forms. Some tutoring takes place at the tutor's or the tutee's home, some at cram schools or franchised learning centres, and some online. This section illustrates the features of various modes of private tutoring and the different purposes they serve in language learning.

One-on-one tutoring

One-on-one tutoring differs from most types of other tutoring as one tutor works with one learner and is usually unstructured with no planned curriculum. It can take place in assorted settings like home, libraries, classrooms, or coffeeshops. One-on-one tutoring allows the tutor to cater to the specific needs and goals of the language learner, which can be hardly achieved in large group or classroom settings (Barkhuizen, 2017; Bleistein & Lewis, 2015). For instance, the tutor can provide individualised feedback on the learner's writing, engage in conversations with the learner using the target language, and help the learner consolidate or catch up with specific content (e.g., grammar, vocabulary) taught at regular school. Many affluent parents are willing to pay higher tuition fee for one-on-one tutoring because they believe their children can benefit more from the tailor-made, individualised instructions. A shortcoming, however, as Bleistein and Lewis (2015) noted, is that the learner is unable to practise the target language with other people as in authentic social settings, and the tutor may need to make more effort in encouraging communication and practice of the target language.

Small-group tutoring

Similar to one-on-one tutoring, small-group tutoring can also be conducted in various settings. Such small groups may range in numbers depending on the context: two to five students are a suggested group size in South Korea (Kim & Jung, 2019), and two to seven students are generally considered a small group in Hong Kong because more than that would require registration as a 'school' (Yung & Bray, 2017). Compared to one-on-one tutoring, small-group tutoring provides more opportunities for the learners to practise the target language with their peers. This is evidenced in a study conducted by Yung (2015) in which a secondary school student participated in small-group oral English tutoring by a native English-speaking tutor. The lessons allowed the student and his friend to engage in more 'natural' ways of English learning through communicative approaches. When necessary, he could ask the tutor to be more exam-oriented, such as practising group discussions using the questions in past exam papers. In some tutorial institutions operating small-group classes, learners of similar level of the target language are allocated into the same group so that the tutor can prepare tasks and materials suitable for their abilities. For example, as Kim and Jung (2019) observed, advanced learners of English are grouped together and given tasks such as reading the *New York Times* or watching YouTube videos to promote more creative thinking rather than just having a didactic, grammatical oriented lesson typical in lower-ability classes.

Lecture-style tutoring

Lecture-style tutoring usually takes place in classroom settings, sometimes within school premises. Benson and Reinders (2011, pp. 9–10) suggested that:

> Because 'out-of-school' learning only refers to location, the term might also reasonably be applied to attendance at private tutorial schools after the school day is finished. Although the teaching and learning takes place in classrooms, tutorial lessons can be considered as 'out-of-school' activities from the perspective of the main location of the students' learning.

Especially popular in Asian settings are 'cram schools' in which tutors engage students in learning "a large amount of information within a short period of time, such as for a test" (Jeon & Choe, 2018, p. 1). Cram schools can be highly organised and are increasingly school-like with their own set of curricula, time-tabling, and methods of assessment. This has made private tutoring increasingly provided in systems rather than just as a "discrete informal activity" (Bray, 2009, p. 11). Typically, tutors are exam-oriented, focussing on trends and patterns emerging from past exam papers (Chung, 2013; Yung, 2020a). Due to its lecture mode, teaching is inevitably unidirectional and teacher-centred. Compared to the active learning approach adopted in small-group tutoring, lecture-style tutoring demonstrates a greater linkage to grammar-translation rather than communicative language teaching (Yung, 2015).

The number of students in a lecture-style tutorial class can vary drastically. In Hong Kong, for instance, a tutorial lesson can teach over a hundred students at one time with connected classrooms separated by glass walls (Yung & Bray, 2017). Many popular tutors even market themselves as 'stars' or 'celebrities' with expertise in language teaching as well as exam skills (Šťastný, 2017; Yung & Yuan, 2020). Some even video-shoot their live lessons and offer video-recorded classes for students to subscribe to. Because of its cost-effectiveness, video tutoring is prevalent in places where mass schooling is commonplace.

Franchised language learning programmes

As private tutoring is growing in popularity around the world, tutorial companies are seeing an evolution of becoming franchises with increasing standardisations and guidelines. Some franchised tutorial companies are moving beyond supplementation of formal education and have developed their independent curriculum and scaffolded materials (Aurini et al., 2013). For example, the South African franchised company *Active English* offers English as a second language from pre-school to Grade 7 with specialised educational materials such as workbooks and educational games (Fernandez-Martins, 2016).

More internationally, the popular franchise *Kumon* originated from Japan with franchises across the world advertises its unique Kumon Method where tutors give guidance to students through working on step-by-step worksheets that are tailored to students' levels. It offers language programmes as both native and foreign languages. *Oxford Learning* is a Canadian franchised company emphasising developing students' cognitive skills through its unique curriculum, assessment, and coaching. It offers English as the first and second language programmes in reading, writing, vocabulary, and fluency, as well as test preparation. The Australian founded franchised company *Kip McGrath* is notable for its English courses for primary and secondary school students. It offers five key areas in English learning including early reading, reading, spelling, comprehension, and vocabulary and grammar development.

Technology in private tutoring

Amidst the rise of digitalisation, online private tutoring has garnered popularity across the globe. Various online language tutoring companies have become accessible and provided services in homework help, exam preparation, and paper writing (Ventura & Jang, 2010). For instance, English was found to be one of the most highly sought subjects for online tutoring in Russia (Kozar & Sweller, 2014). In China, over 200,000 students subscribe to VIPKid, an online private tutoring service with around 30,000 tutors working from across the world (McClelland, 2018). With its own curriculum, VIPKid finds native English-speaking tutors from Canada and the United States to teach students English online. India is a popular provider of private online English tutoring as it is able to maintain high standard of English while costs are kept low (Ventura & Jang, 2010). Online tutoring can also connect language learners with native speakers of the target language who come from different parts of the world.

In addition, artificial intelligence (AI) has begun to grow in prominence in private tutoring. Based in China, *Tomorrow Advancing Life* advertises itself as a technology-driven, talent centred, and quality focussed leading education and technology enterprise in China. They set up the AI Language Teaching System to help provide more equal education resources to the Yi ethnic minority area. By connecting learning and education with the advances of technology and science, the AI system can effectively evaluate the students' pronunciation and correct students' spoken Yi and Mandarin. It is seen to be able to improve the quality of language learning for the ethnic students in a personalised manner while creating lower costs and promoting educational equality (Wang, 2019).

Key issues

In the field of private tutoring for language learning, various issues are facing researchers and practitioners. The issues involve learners, tutors, and the wider educational and social context.

Uncertain effectiveness on academic performance

Private tutoring has undoubtedly become popular among language learners worldwide, especially as a tool to raise exam scores. However, research has shown inconsistent and contradictory findings regarding its effectiveness on academic performance. Mischo and Haag (2002) compared students who received private tutoring in various subjects including English, Latin and French over a course of nine months in Germany. They found that students who had received private tutoring displayed significant improvements in their school grades on these language subjects compared to those who did not. Hamid et al. (2009) also found some correlation between Bangladeshi secondary school students' participation in private tutoring and their achievement in an English proficiency test. Likewise, Lee (2010) reported on the results of a survey of 43 university freshmen in South Korea and found that those who had experience participating in out-of-school English learning programmes, including private tutoring, had significantly higher English exam scores than those who only relied on regular schooling. Based on 6,403 grade 12 students' performance on the national college entrance exam in China, Zhang (2013) found a significantly positive effect of private tutoring on English test scores but no effect in Chinese, after controlling for other covariates. In Taiwan, Chang (2019) compared the grades of national college entrance exam of students who participated in English private tutoring and those who did not. Although English private tutoring had some positive effect on students' scores, it was found that the time students spent on self-study activities had a more significant positive effect than did private tutoring.

Some studies have shown null or even negative effect of private tutoring on students' language competencies. Luplow and Schneider (2014, as cited in Ömeroğulları et al., 2020) reported no significant differences in the gains of German competencies between tutored and non-tutored primary school students. Zhang and Liu (2016) found no significant effect of private tutoring for Chinese and English on students' scores in the national college entrance exam in China regardless of the size of the tutorial class. Ömeroğulları et al. (2020) conducted secondary analyses using data of two longitudinal studies and found that tutored students received lower test scores in subjects including German and English than their non-tutored counterparts. The study by Tse (2014) also showed a statistically significant difference between the scores of primary school students who received private tutoring in Chinese and those who did not, with the score of the latter group being superior.

Indeed, research attempting to prove the effectiveness of private tutoring in raising students' exam scores and language proficiency is challenging because of the complication with its concurrent regular schooling. Moreover, various conditions are needed to be factored in, such as the content and technique of tutoring, duration of the tutorial lesson, type of language learners, student motivation, and time invested in self-studying. Zhan et al. (2013) observed that studies claiming the effectiveness of private tutoring tend to be "not robust" and criteria evaluating effectiveness should "fit the motivations of the consumers" (p. 2). In this regard, several studies have explored language learners' perceptions of the effectiveness of private tutoring. Although in general students hold a positive attitude towards private tutoring (Hamid et al., 2009), some may criticise it for overly focussing on exam drilling and neglecting the use of the target language for authentic communication (Chung, 2013; Yung, 2015, 2020a).

Diverse motivation of language learners

Research on private tutoring has also focussed on language learners' motivation as well as its related constructs, and findings have been complex. In an earlier study on Indonesian junior high school students' independent learning behaviours, Lamb (2004, p. 239) observed that students attending English private tutoring courses could lead to "sustained autonomous learning behaviour" because motivated learners could turn this out-of-school learning activity into opportunities to supplement their English learning at school. Similarly, Bleistein and Lewis (2015) suggested that one-on-one tutoring could motivate language learners in that the tutor and the learner agree upon a strong ideal L2 self-image as a learning goal and develop individualised learning plans of action. On the other hand, Kim and Kim (2014) found that in South Korea, students' dependence on private tutoring discouraged autonomous language learning because students tended to be guided by their ought-to L2 selves and urged to learn English to the test without self-regulated learning skills. Jung and Seo (2019), however, found a null effect of private tutoring on South Korean middle school students' self-regulated learning in reading and English.

Language learners' motivation in private tutoring in fact depends much on their learning goals and reasons for subscribing to tutorial classes. For instance, Irie and Brewster (2013) reported the preliminary findings of a longitudinal study of three first-year university students in Japan. Two of the participants mentioned their English private tutoring experiences in high school. One of them was intrinsically motivated with an ideal L2 self because she enjoyed "learning grammar, reading passages to solve comprehension questions and understanding listening passages in English" (p. 124) at a cram school. Another learner was motivated extrinsically by an ought-to L2 self because learning English at cram schools helped her to perform better at English level tests, the results of which would determine which university she could pursue.

Many language learners subscribe to private tutoring because of their desire to obtain good results in school and public exams. Chung's (2013, p. 590) study found that Taiwanese senior secondary students attending cram schools were highly instrumentally motivated because of their perceived "utilitarian benefits" of good results for university admission and future career. Similar findings were obtained in Yung's (2019) study on Grade 12 students in Hong Kong. Although some students were initially interested in learning English and engaged in out-of-school language learning activities such as hanging out with native nglish-speaking friends and watching YouTube videos, all participants chose to adopt more exam-oriented tasks such as drilling past exam papers and reciting vocabulary through the subscription of private tutoring when the public exam was approaching. Yung (2019) argued that the learners' future L2 selves consist of dominant ought-to L2 selves and suppressed ideal L2 selves when they learnt English in private tutoring, because of their sacrifice of the language learning activities they enjoyed for the more pragmatic goal of learning English for assessment. Despite this, Yung and Chiu (2020) found that among 2,216 Grade 12 students attending private tutoring courses in a Hong Kong cram school, 80% enjoyed their English learning with their tutors. Language learners were more likely to enjoy private tutoring if they perceived more financial resources in their families, attended schools taught in their first language, internalised their instrumental goals, liked English, were not influenced by advertisements to attend tutoring, attended face-to-face tutoring rather than video tutoring, had a specific tutor, or liked their tutor more than their English teacher at school. Other studies (e.g., Hamid et al., 2009; Yung, 2020a) even show that many students enjoyed and felt motivated to learn English with their tutors more than their schoolteachers.

Complex identities of language tutors

In addition to language learners, researchers in private tutoring have also been interested in tutors, particularly their identities in the language teaching profession. Trent (2016) interviewed six tutors of English in Hong Kong, two of whom also taught Chinese. Employed at different privately owned tutorial centres, the tutors perceived themselves as "shadow teachers" and "subordinate" to teachers in mainstream schools. Since they had to cram the students with teaching content quickly in tutorial lessons, they considered it challenging to develop rapports with their students compared to schoolteachers. Their emphasis on exam techniques attracted stereotypes such as "just exam machines" and "short term goals", and subsequently being positioned as "not really language teachers" (p. 125). Trent argued that there was a professional dichotomy between educators in mainstream schools and private tutors.

A similar phenomenon was observed in Mainland China. Li (2020) investigated the identities of two private English tutors in Nanchang, one employed at a tutorial centre and one self-employed. Through narrative inquiry, she found that the tutors were identified as "service-providers" offering highly time- and labour-intensive teaching to IELTS test-takers and low achieving English language learners. What adds to the complexity of tutors' identities is a participant's feeling of inferiority due to her non-native like English accent. The self-employed tutor was sometimes questioned about his academic qualification, leading to a sense of insecurities in his teacher identity. In a similar vein, Xiong et al. (2020) found that although English language tutors in Guangzhou constructed their identity as "exam experts", they were at the same time perceived as "underdogs" and less competitive than schoolteachers. Tutors were queried on their abilities as there was an assumption that highly qualified graduates would rather teach at a formal school than at a tutorial centre. They were even seen as "salespeople" who must satisfy their clientele and take an active role in showing their passion in improving the students' grades.

Some recent studies have investigated tutors' identities projected in their profiles or advertisements. For example, through multimodal discourse analysis of English language tutors' biographies on tutorial school websites in Hong Kong, Yung and Yuan (2020) found that tutors project identities as "an authoritative exam expert" (e.g., teaching effective exam techniques), "a popular star" (e.g., English exam queen, idol tutor), and "a well-qualified English language teacher" (e.g., King of English grammar). These multiple identities overlap and collectively create an "exam expert-star-teacher" hybrid identity.

On the other hand, Barkhuizen (2017) illustrated a different type of tutors in the New Zealand context. Through analysis of short stories revealed in interviews, he explored the identities of tutors offering one-on-one home English tutoring for immigrants and refugees. He found that, instead of foregrounding "teacher *instructor* identities" as in private tutors offering instructions that shadow the mainstream, the tutors in his study projected "*social inclusion* identities" to help their learners integrate into the social-local community. Their tutoring, either formal or informal, took place beyond the classroom or home to include workplace, the tutor or tutee's social circles, and the wider community. Some tutors became friends with their learners and counselled them in times of need.

Washback on mainstream language education

Apart from its impact on language learners and tutors, private tutoring has also led to both positive and negative washback on mainstream language education. On the positive side, private tutoring can help slow learners to keep up with their peers, which, in turn, reduces disparities in the classroom. Students can also consolidate or even relearn the content taught at school, particularly when the school lessons are conducted in a medium of instruction that is not the students' first language (Yung & Bray, 2017). Private tutoring can also provide gifted students with a special curriculum which may be lacking in regular schools (Kim & Jung, 2019). Nevertheless, when high-achievers receive more tutoring to learn the school content outside school, diversity in the classroom may increase. For students who have already previewed the content in private tutoring, they may lose interest in school (Bray, 2009; Yung & Bray, 2017). In India, Bhorkar and Bray (2018) have noted the shift of private tutoring from "supplementation" to "supplantation" as students skip school lessons for tutoring.

As private tutoring, particularly the lecture-style one, is widely marketed for raising exam scores, students may trust their tutors more than schoolteachers in helping them prepare for public exams. Through an online survey of 477 secondary students in Hong Kong, Yung (2020a) found that cram school tutors were perceived to be more effective than schoolteachers in all identified aspects of effective language teaching, including raising students' learning motivation and confidence, helping them prepare for exams and enhancing their English proficiency. Supposedly, schoolteachers should help learners to develop the necessary competence in the target language for authentic communication rather than teach to the test. This, however, may result in limited focus on exam preparation at school, and hence, schoolteachers may be devalued for they cannot sufficiently cater for the students' exam-oriented needs. Moreover, with most focus on memorising words and phrases for writing and speaking, and learning how to answer questions in reading and listening faster, private tutoring may intensify "banking" education (Yung, 2021). This results in negative washback as the content taught is restricted to tested items rather than the subject matters for authentic communication (Chung, 2013; Yung, 2015). Students tend to adopt ideas and formats similar to model answers and essay exemplars, and avoid creative endeavours for fear of making mistakes and losing marks in exams (Yung, 2020a, 2020b).

In some countries such as Cambodia, Georgia, and Myanmar, much tutoring is provided by schoolteachers to their own students outside regular school hours (Bray et al., 2020; Dawson, 2010; Kobakhidze, 2018). A potential negative washback is that these teachers may put more effort into their after-school tutorial classes than the regular ones, and may even reduce the instructional time and content in their regular classes to promote demand for tutoring from their own students.

Educational and social inequalities

In the wider social context, private tutoring arguably maintains, if not exacerbates, social stratification. Although private tutoring has generally become more affordable, particularly the lecture-style tutoring in large classes, wealthier families are undeniably more able to invest in superior and in greater quantities of private tutoring than less prosperous ones. In the study by Hamid et al. (2009), students from lower-income families reported that being able to receive English private tutoring had an effect on their academic performance. As Bangladesh class sizes can reach up to 50 students per class, private tutoring allows for better quality teaching and more effective learning. The inequality gap widens when such students are unable to invest in private tutoring while their more affluent peers can. This is illustrated in South Korea where the upper 10% income earners reportedly spend eight times the amount lower-income families spend on private education (Dawson, 2010). Students who can afford better and more private tutoring were found to have an advantage in the high-stakes nation-wide college entrance exams.

Nevertheless, an alternative view is that private tutoring indeed benefits students from lower-income families to gain a competitive edge when inequalities already exist in the education system. In a narrative inquiry of a financially deprived secondary student in Hong Kong, Yung (2020b) found that the student invested in English private tutoring to compete against their counterparts from better-off households, who already had more access to resources in terms of books, language learning activities and learning equipment from an early age. Private tutoring offered her more exposure to the target language, which was limited in her social circle but could be rich in wealthier families (e.g., opportunities to study abroad and to communicate in English with foreign domestic helpers at home). She could also make friends with students from prestigious schools who were regarded as her language learning resources in the tutorial class.

Still, some believe that private tutoring acts as a proponent in broadening race and ethnic inequalities. In the United States, for example, private tutoring for SAT preparation may have benefitted East Asian Americans who utilised it. While black students also subscribed to private tutoring, their SAT scores were not drastically enhanced. Buchmann et al. (2010) found that blacks more likely employed private tutors for SAT preparation than whites. They attributed inequalities to mostly social class and not ethnicity as black families were aware of the role of SAT as a gate-keeping tool. Consequently, blacks were active in engaging with test preparation activities. However, Zhou (2008, p. 230) stated that "the concept of ethnicity is inherently interacted with social class" in American society. She furthered that many factors such as community forces, ethnic beliefs, coping strategies interpersonal networks and economic organisations were affecting academic success. Specifically, cram schools were particular to the Asian community. Most establishments offered English private tutoring with an adoption of intensive drilling aiming to improve academic performance. Zhou (2008) believed that this practice popular among the Asian community was a contributing factor to the higher education attainment from American Chinese communities as compared to African Americans and whites and offered the promise of social mobility.

Implications

This chapter has discussed the complex concept of private tutoring for language learning and identified issues regarding its effectiveness on students' academic performance, impact on language learners' motivation, identities of tutors, washback on mainstream education and inequalities in the educational and social contexts. Findings from research in private tutoring offer various implications for the development of theories and practice in language teaching and learning. Theoretically, the blurring boundary between private tutoring and mainstream schooling challenges the concept of shadow education and its ecological positioning in language education. Specifically, the global prevalence of private tutoring has made this out-of-school learning activity increasingly grow "out of the shadows" (Aurini et al., 2013) and become an important part of language learners' experience. The diverse features and modes of private tutoring also interact dynamically with learners who have different motivation and purposes of learning a language (e.g., authentic communication, exam preparation, social integration) as well as other stakeholders in the microsystems such as schoolteachers, tutors, and parents. The macrosystems including the curriculum in mainstream language education, assessment approaches, and the wider sociocultural context (e.g., learning culture, education inequalities, linguistic diversity) also play a crucial role in changing the shape of private tutoring. These considerations offer theoretical implications for the ecosystem of education in which shadow education is embedded.

In addition, the notion of effectiveness of private tutoring for language learning needs to be problematised. As discussed, the diverse reasons for subscribing to private tutoring among different language learners and a wide range of internal (e.g., learner style, motivation, age) and external (e.g., modes of tutoring, tutors' teaching strategies, learning situation at school) factors have led to complications in concluding whether private tutoring is effective; and if so, in what aspects. In this regard, researchers (e.g., Hamid et al., 2009; Yung, 2015) have attempted to explore effectiveness from the learners' perspective. However, another issue is how 'accurate' the students' perceptions are, why they have such perceptions, and how their perceptions may have been influenced by the wider social and educational contexts. An implication, therefore, is to conceptualise effectiveness of private tutoring with caution and consider the various influencing factors within and around the learners. A critical approach may be adopted to problematise students' attitudes and perceptions of private tutoring, as compared to regular schooling, with reference to the wider social, cultural, and educational context.

In practice, the widespread of and students' preference to private tutoring may trigger schoolteachers to reflect on their teaching effectiveness. A question is how to balance enhancing students' language proficiency and preparing them for exams. On the other hand, tutors who have been criticised as overly teaching exam techniques and failing to raise students' language competence may also reconsider their positioning in the education system. In both sectors, schoolteachers and tutors need continuous professional development for the betterment of their teaching to cater for the diversified needs of their learners. In addition, with the rapid development of technology, online tutoring has become increasingly popular. This aspect should also be taken into account in teachers and tutors' professional development such as how to equip their learners with the necessary attitudes and skills to learn languages online.

For language learners, private tutoring can be a double-edged sword for the development of self-regulated learning capacity. While learners can benefit from the extra support from private tutoring in learning the target language outside school, they may become overly reliant on their tutors. Moreover, although they are usually provided with abundant learning materials, those materials can be wasted if learners do not or do not know how to use them effectively. To better benefit from private tutoring, learners need to become more agentic. This means that they need to develop a sense of ownership and control over their learning, so that they can make decisions regarding what tutorial instructions and materials are relevant and beneficial to them. This requires learners' ongoing reflection, clear goals and sustained motivation for learning the target language.

Future directions

Language private tutoring is evolving in a wide range of fields in education, including applied linguistics and language teacher education. The relationships between private tutoring and the various stakeholders and components in the ecology of language education warrant investigation for further conceptual and theoretical development. From the learner perspective research in applied linguistics with a focus on private tutoring such as tutees' motivation has shifted from a cognitive approach (e.g., self-determination theory in Chung, 2013) to a more socio-dynamic perspective (e.g., L2 Motivational Self System in Yung, 2019). Given the social turn in the field of second language acquisition, this line of research is expected to continue considering the complex nature of motivation and identities within language learners. Students' agentic decision-making processes in choosing their tutors, learning content and strategies can be explored to unveil the extent to which and how private tutoring can facilitate self-regulated language learning. Due to the complex interplay between language learner agency and the structure where mainstream and shadow education coexist, further research may analyse learner experience in private tutoring from the complex dynamic systems perspective (Larsen-Freeman, 2019) to capture the emerging and ever-changing agency of learners nested with other stakeholders and the wider sociocultural context. Moreover, given the rise of information technology in the education sector, it is expected that future research on private tutoring will put more emphasis on language learner experiences in the online environment.

In language teacher education, research has primarily focussed on teachers in school settings. Tutors, who are also playing a significant role in students' language learning experience, have been largely neglected. Given the growing attention to shadow education, research in teacher education needs to be extended to tutors. For example, a comparative study between schoolteachers and tutors' identities and teaching strategies may be conducted with reference to their educational background, teaching experience, and self-identification.

Despite increasing attention to shadow education research in comparative education (Zhang & Bray, 2020), studies focussing on language teaching and learning are still scant. At this infant stage, much more research in this area is needed to bridge the gap between shadow education and language learning. Since private tutoring contributes to a significant part in students' out-of-school language learning experience, this line of research needs to become an important agenda in the field of language education and applied linguistics.

Reflection questions

1 Why is private tutoring so popular among language learners worldwide? Does this mean that there are insufficiencies in mainstream language education?
2 Considering the negative washback of private tutoring on regular schooling, should private tutoring be regulated or banned? If so, how?
3 What should schoolteachers do to promote effective language teaching and learning under the influence of private tutoring?

Recommended readings

Bray, M., Kwo, O., & Jokić, B. (Eds.). (2015). *Researching private supplementary tutoring: Methodological lessons from diverse cultures*. Comparative Education Research Centre, The University of Hong Kong, and Springer.
Through methodological lessons from diverse cultures, this edited volume contains chapters that offer valuable insights into the design of quantitative, qualitative, and mixed-methods research in private tutoring from a wide range of settings such as Asia, Caribbean, Europe, and the Middle East.

Yung, K. W. H. (2019). Exploring the L2 selves of senior secondary students in English private tutoring in Hong Kong. *System, 80*, 120–133. https://doi.org/10.1016/j.system.2018.11.003
This article provides an example of researching private tutoring in the field of language education. From the perspective of L2 selves, it investigates the English learning motivation of senior secondary students enrolled in cram school tutorial courses. Although the study was conducted in Hong Kong, the article offers implications to researchers in contexts where high-stakes exams dominate the education system and private tutoring is prevalent.

Zhang, W., & Bray, M. (2020). Comparative research on shadow education: Achievements, challenges, and the agenda ahead. *European Journal of Education, 55*(3), 322–341. https://doi.org/https://doi.org/10.1111/ejed.12413
This paper reviews research on private tutoring across decades, from its initial focus on global mapping in the late 1990s, the interactions between private tutoring and the ecosystems, to the conceptualisation for the futures of education. It offers insights into the development of shadow education across time and cultures.

Acknowledgement

The work described in this paper was partially supported by a grant from the Research Grants Council of the Hong Kong Special Administrative Region, China (Project No. EdUHK 28600919). The author acknowledges the input and assistance from Ms Denise Wu.

References

Allen, D. (2016). Japanese cram schools and entrance exam washback. *The Asian Journal of Applied Linguistics, 3*(1), 54–67. http://www3.caes.hku.hk/ajal/index.php/ajal/article/view/338
Aurini, J., Davies, S., & Dierkes, J. (Eds.) (2013). *Out of the shadows: The global intensification of supplementary education*. Bingley: Emerald.
Barkhuizen, G. (2017). Investigating language tutor social inclusion identities. *101*(S1), 61–75. https://doi.org/https://doi.org/10.1111/modl.12369
Benson, P., & Reinders, H. (Eds.) (2011). *Beyond the language classroom*. London: Palgrave Macmillan.
Bhorkar, S., & Bray, M. (2018). The expansion and roles of private tutoring in India: From supplementation to supplantation. *International Journal of Educational Development, 62*, 148–156. https://doi.org/10.1016/j.ijedudev.2018.03.003

Bleistein, T., & Lewis, M. (2015). *One-on-one language teaching and learning: Theory and Practice*. London: Palgrave Macmillan.

Bray, M. (2009). *Confronting the shadow education system: what government policies for what private tutoring?* Paris: United Nations Educational, Scientific and Cultural Organization; International Institute for Educational Planning.

Bray, M., Kobakhidze, M. N., & Kwo, O. (2020). *Shadow education in Myanmar: Private supplementary tutoring and its policy implications*. Paris: UNESCO and Hong Kong: Comparative Education Research Centre, The University of Hong Kong.

Bray, M., Kwo, O., & Jokić, B. (Eds.) (2015). *Researching private supplementary tutoring: Methodological lessons from diverse cultures*. Hong Kong: Comparative Education Research Centre, The University of Hong Kong, and Switzerland: Springer.

Buchmann, C., Condron, D. J., & Roscigno, V. J. (2010). Shadow education, American style: Test preparation, the SAT and college enrollment. *Social Forces, 89*(2), 435–461. https://doi.org/10.1353/sof.2010.0105

Chang, C.-H. (2019). Effects of private tutoring on English performance: Evidence from senior high students in Taiwan. *International Journal of Educational Development, 68*, 80–87. https://doi.org/10.1016/j.ijedudev.2019.05.003

Chung, I. F. (2013). Crammed to learn English: What are learners' motivation and approach? *The Asia-Pacific Education Researcher, 22*(4), 585–592. https://doi.org/10.1007/s40299-013-0061-5

Dawson, W. (2010). Private tutoring and mass schooling in East Asia: Reflections of inequality in Japan, South Korea, and Cambodia. *Asia Pacific Education Review, 11*(1), 14–24. https://doi.org/10.1007/s12564-009-9058-4

Fernandez-Martins, M. M. (2016). *Evaluation of a franchised supplementary programme in English as a second language in South Africa: A case study North-West University*. Potchefstroom.

Hamid, M. O., Sussex, R., & Khan, A. (2009). Private tutoring in English for secondary school students in Bangladesh. *TESOL Quarterly, 43*(2), 281–308. https://doi.org/10.1002/j.1545-7249.2009.tb00168.x

Ireson, J., & Rushforth, K. (2011). Private tutoring at transition points in the English education system: Its nature, extent and purpose. *Research Papers in Education, 26*(1), 1–19. https://doi.org/10.1080/02671520903191170

Irie, K., & Brewster, D. R. (2013). One curriculum, three stories: Ideal L2 self and L2-self-discrepancy profiles. In M. T. Apple, D. Da Silva, & T. Fellner (Eds.), *Language learning motivation in Japan* (pp. 110–128). Bristol: Multilingual Matters.

Jeon, J., & Choe, Y. (2018). Cram schools and English language education in East Asian contexts. In J. I. Liontas (Ed.), *The TESOL encyclopedia of English language teaching* (pp. 1–14). Chichester: Wiley. https://doi.org/10.1002/9781118784235.eelt0668

Jung, H., & Seo, E. H. (2019). Examining a causal effect of private tutoring in Korea: Does private tutoring damage students' self-regulated learning? *Asia Pacific Education Review, 20*(3), 375–389. https://doi.org/10.1007/s12564-018-9570-5

Kim, T. Y., & Kim, Y. K. (2014). EFL students' L2 motivational self system and self-regulation: Focusing on elementary and junior high school students in Korea. In K. Csizer & M. Magid (Eds.), *The impact of self-concept on language learning* (pp. 87–107). Bristol: Multilingual Matters.

Kim, Y. C., & Jung, J. H. (2019). *Shadow education as worldwide curriculum studies*. London: Palgrave Macmillan.

Kobakhidze, M. N. (2018). *Teachers as tutors: Shadow education dynamics in Georgia*. Hong Kong: Comparative Education Research Centre, The University of Hong Kong, and Dordrecht: Springer.

KOSIS. (2020). *Private education participation rate by school level*. http://kosis.kr/eng/statisicsList/statisticsListIndex.do?menuId=M_01_01&vwcd=MT_ETITLE&parmTabId=M_01_01&statId=1963003&themaId=#SelectStatsBoxDiv

Kozar, O., & Sweller, N. (2014). An exploratory study of demographics, goals and expectations of private online language learners in Russia. *System, 45*, 39–51. https://doi.org/10.1016/j.system.2014.04.005

Lamb, M. (2004). 'It depends on the students themselves': Independent language learning at an Indonesian state school. *Language, Culture and Curriculum, 17*(3), 229–245. https://doi.org/10.1080/07908310408666695

Larsen-Freeman, D. (2019). On language learner agency: A complex dynamic systems theory perspective. *The Modern Language Journal, 103*(S1), 61–79. https://doi.org/10.1111/modl.12536

Lee, B. (2010). The pre-university English-educational background of college freshmen in a foreign language program: A tale of diverse private education and English proficiency. *Asia Pacific Education Review*, 11(1), 69–82. https://doi.org/10.1007/s12564-010-9079-z

Li, W. (2020). Unpacking the complexities of teacher identity: Narratives of two Chinese teachers of English in China. *Language Teaching Research*, 1–19. https://doi.org/10.1177/1362168820910955

Loyalka, P., & Zakharov, A. (2016). Does shadow education help students prepare for college? Evidence from Russia. *International Journal of Educational Development*, 49, 22–30. https://doi.org/10.1016/j.ijedudev.2016.01.008

Mahmud, R., & Kenayathulla, H. B. (2018). Shadow education: Patterns and scale of private supplementary tutoring in English in secondary education at urban Dhaka in Bangladesh. *Compare: A Journal of Comparative and International Education*, 48(5), 702–716. https://doi.org/10.1080/03057925.2017.1340827

McClelland, E. R. (2018). Exploration of positive teacher-student relationships in the online context of VIPKID. *Graduate Education Student Scholarship*, 14. https://mosaic.messiah.edu/gredu_st/14

Mischo, C., & Haag, L. (2002). Expansion and effectiveness of private tutoring. *European Journal of Psychology of Education*, 17(3), 263–273. https://doi.org/10.1007/bf03173536

Ömeroğulları, M., Guill, K., & Köller, O. (2020). Effectiveness of private tutoring during secondary schooling in Germany: Do the duration of private tutoring and tutor qualification affect school achievement? *Learning and Instruction*, 66, 101306. https://doi.org/10.1016/j.learninstruc.2020.101306

Šťastný, V. (2017). Private tutoring lessons supply: Insights from online advertising in the Czech Republic. *Compare: A Journal of Comparative and International Education*, 47(4), 561–579. https://doi.org/10.1080/03057925.2016.1259064

Trent, J. (2016). Constructing professional identities in shadow education: Perspectives of private supplementary educators in Hong Kong [journal article]. *Educational Research for Policy and Practice*, 15(2), 115–130. https://doi.org/10.1007/s10671-015-9182-3

Tse, S. K. (2014). To what extent does Hong Kong primary school students' Chinese reading comprehension benefit from after-school private tuition? [journal article]. *Asia Pacific Education Review*, 15(2), 283–297. https://doi.org/10.1007/s12564-013-9307-4

Ventura, A., & Jang, S. (2010). Private tutoring through the internet: Globalization and offshoring. *Asia Pacific Education Review*, 11(1), 59–68. https://doi.org/10.1007/s12564-009-9065-5

Wang, X. (2019). *TAL 'Using AI language teaching system to innovate language learning of under-resourced students' programme: Progressive evaluation report*. Beijing: Beijing Normal University.

Xiong, T., Li, Q., & Hu, G. (2020). Teaching English in the shadow: Identity construction of private English language tutors in China. *Discourse: Studies in the Cultural Politics of Education*, 1–13. https://doi.org/10.1080/01596306.2020.1805728

Yung, K. W. H. (2015). Learning English in the shadows: Understanding Chinese learners' experiences of private tutoring. *TESOL Quarterly*, 49(4), 707–732. https://doi.org/10.1002/tesq.193

Yung, K. W. H. (2019). Exploring the L2 selves of senior secondary students in English private tutoring in Hong Kong. *System*, 80, 120–133. https://doi.org/10.1016/j.system.2018.11.003

Yung, K. W. H. (2020a). Comparing the effectiveness of cram school tutors and schoolteachers: A critical analysis of students' perceptions. *International Journal of Educational Development*, 72, 102141. https://doi.org/10.1016/j.ijedudev.2019.102141

Yung, K. W. H. (2020b). Investing in English private tutoring to move socially upward: A narrative inquiry of an underprivileged student in Hong Kong. *Journal of Multilingual and Multicultural Development*, 41(10), 872–885. https://doi.org/10.1080/01434632.2019.1660667

Yung, K. W. H. (2021). Shadow education as a form of oppression: Conceptualizing experiences and reflections of secondary students in Hong Kong. *Asia Pacific Journal of Education*, 41(1), 115–129. https://doi.org/10.1080/02188791.2020.1727855

Yung, K. W. H., & Bray, M. (2017). Shadow education: Features, expansion and implications. In T. K. C. Tse & M. Lee (Eds.), *Making sense of education in post-handover Hong Kong: Achievements and challenges* (pp. 95–111). London: Routledge.

Yung, K. W. H., & Chiu, M. M. (2020). Secondary school students' enjoyment of English private tutoring: An L2 motivational self perspective. *Language Teaching Research*, 1–23. https://doi.org/10.1177/1362168820962139

Yung, K. W. H., & Yuan, R. (2020). 'The most popular star-tutor of English': Discursive construction of tutor identities in shadow education. *Discourse: Studies in the Cultural Politics of Education*, 41(1), 153–168. https://doi.org/10.1080/01596306.2018.1488241

Zhan, S., Bray, M., Wang, D., Lykins, C., & Kwo, O. (2013). The effectiveness of private tutoring: Students' perceptions in comparison with mainstream schooling in Hong Kong. *Asia Pacific Education Review, 14*(4), 495–509. https://doi.org/10.1007/s12564-013-9276-7

Zhang, W., & Bray, M. (2020). Comparative research on shadow education: Achievements, challenges, and the agenda ahead. *European Journal of Education, 55*(3), 322–341. https://doi.org/https://doi.org/10.1111/ejed.12413

Zhang, Y. (2013). Does private tutoring improve students' National College Entrance Exam performance?—A case study from Jinan, China. *Economics of Education Review, 32*, 1–28. https://doi.org/10.1016/j.econedurev.2012.09.008

Zhang, Y., & Liu, J. (2016). The effectiveness of private tutoring in China with a focus on class-size. *International Journal of Educational Development, 46*, 35–42. https://doi.org/10.1016/j.ijedudev.2015.11.006

Zhou, M. (2008). The ethnic system of supplementary education: Nonprofit and for-profit institutions in Los Angeles' Chinese immigrant community. In M. Shinn & H. Yoshikawa (Eds.), *Toward positive youth development: Transforming schools and community programs* (pp. 229–254). Oxford: Oxford University Press.

16
ENHANCING THE QUALITY OF OUT-OF-CLASS LEARNING IN FLIPPED LEARNING

Jun Chen Hsieh, Michael W. Marek and Wen-Chi Vivian Wu

Introduction

Empowering students with advanced knowledge and skills has been a priority around the world, yet instructional practices have not always met the changing needs of students in ever-changing educational contexts and instructors often still use teacher-centered, lecture-based methods. Such a conventional pedagogical practice falls short of meeting the individual differences of students with respect to content knowledge comprehension. When teachers spend in-class time lecturing, students are, therefore, left with insufficient time to apply what they have learned, further leading to insufficient guidance from teachers while students are engaged in individual or collaborative learning tasks. Insufficient opportunity for knowledge application also results in unsatisfactory teacher-student interaction, thus making teachers unable to fully understand and solve challenges or problems that students encounter. Furthermore, with unsatisfactory teacher-student interaction, students are not used to interacting with teachers. To be more specific, students might not know how to interact with their teachers, since they are not trained or simply not given the opportunity to do so. Consequently, students become passive learners, afraid of raising questions even if they find something confusing. In conventional instruction, the focus of instruction is lower-order thinking, such as remembering and basic understanding. Such learning does not effectively help students to transfer what they have learned to settings beyond the classroom, thus falling short of empowering students with higher-order skills (i.e., applying, analyzing, evaluating, and creating), which are vital for out-of-class learning and life skills.

In view of the increased emphasis on learner-centered pedagogical practices, higher-order thinking skills, and knowledge/skill transfer beyond the classroom, educators have endeavored to seek innovative instructional methodologies that improve learning and motivate students to become active and lifelong learners. Among those instructional methodologies, flipped learning has received global attention because it reverses the conventional lecture and homework elements. To be more specific, flipped learning is described as a pedagogical practice in which "events that have traditionally taken place inside the classroom now take place outside the classroom and vice versa" (Lage, Platt, & Treglia, 2000, p. 32), inverting the typical cycle of content delivery through face-to-face lectures and knowledge application via homework. Unlike conventional instruction, where students are often expected to receive new knowledge in the classroom through lectures and put that knowledge into practice at

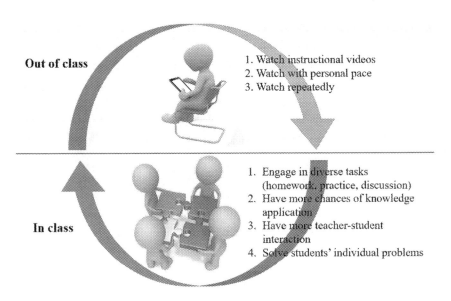

Figure 16.1 Characteristics of flipped learning

home in the form of homework, flipped learning students acquire necessary content knowledge prior to class meetings in out-of-class settings, typically with instructional videos made by the instructor. During classroom meetings, students are then guided by instructors to engage in higher-order thinking, such as meaning clarification and knowledge or skill application (Reidsema, Kavanagh, Hadgraft, & Smith, 2017). Figure 16.1 illustrates the features characteristic of flipped learning.

In other words, class time is freed from lecture and can be optimized for more enriching learning tasks, such as group collaboration and problem solving, which further strengthen the ability of students to deal with tasks in future out-of-class real world contexts. Flipped learning thus shifts lecture-based instruction, which is often teacher-centered, to a student-centered paradigm (Chen Hsieh, Wu, & Marek, 2017), bridging out-of-class and in-class learning with the use of diverse technologies (Hwang, Lai, & Wang, 2015). In fact, such a paradigm shift addresses concerns about the effectiveness of lecture-based teaching practices, which have long been the primary method for teaching. Taken together, the key features that set the flipped learning mode apart from other instructional methods are that students receive initial acquisition of knowledge prior to the physical class meetings (i.e., outside the classroom), allowing class time to be maximized for higher-level guided practice and collaborative tasks. Flipped learning, therefore, is in sharp contrast to non-flipped instruction where a long presentation of a lecture in class is followed by a relatively small amount of guided practice and then individual graded homework. Because instructional videos are created for students to watch during out-of-class time (normally at home), students can watch the videos at their own pace. They might even re-watch the videos until they are satisfied with their understanding. Therefore, in a broader sense, flipped learning embodies personalized learning because it caters to individual preferences and differences. Furthermore, as students schedule their time to study the instructional videos and other pre-classroom learning materials, their self-regulation is fostered, particularly when preparing for the classroom repeatedly for better comprehension.

With the affordances of better cultivating autonomous learning, exploratory ability, and higher-order thinking skills of students (such as synthesizing, analyzing, reasoning, comprehending, application, and evaluation), it is not surprising that more and more flipped learning has been implemented as an alternative to conventional teacher-centered, lecture-based instruction, and as an innovation to facilitate learning beyond the classroom.

Key constructs

Flipped learning is a "pedagogy-first" approach to teaching in which familiar lecture and homework elements are reversed (Bergmann & Sams, 2012). Since the introduction of the flipped classroom by Bergmann and Sams (2012), the flipped learning mode has become a buzzword in education and has gained global attention in recent years. Because the flipped learning practice provides "a dynamic and interactive learning environment where the educator guides students as they apply concepts and engage creatively in the subject matter" (Flipped learning Network, 2014, p. 1), flipped learning thus has been widely adopted across disciplines and subjects, such as the medical field (Ringer, Warkentin, Patel, & Melady, 2019), chemistry (Bokosmaty, Bridgeman, & Muir, 2019), physics (Eldy et al., 2019), nursing (Chung, Lai, & Hwang, 2019), mathematics (Ficano, 2019), and language learning (e.g., Turan & Akdag-Cimen, 2019; Webb & Doman, 2020; Wu, Yang, Chen Hsieh, & Yamamoto, 2020). In addition, its popularity had led to a growing body of literature and systematic reviews aiming to synthesize its effects (e.g., Bond, 2020; Cheng, Hwang, & Lai, 2020; Zou, Luo, Xie, & Hwang, 2020).

The four pillars F-L-I-P™ model by Hamdan, McKnight, McKnight, and Arfstrom (2013), as shown in Figure 16.2, identified four key elements of flipped learning, including *flexible environment, learning culture, intentional content,* and *professional educators. Flexible environment* refers to the emphasis on flexibility in the teaching/learning process, such as using various learning modes to support individual student tasks and collaborative work or remaining flexible in learning expectations and assessments. *Learning culture* means a drastic shift from a teacher-centered, lecture-based pedagogy to a learner-centered and social constructivist approach featuring in-depth discussion and interaction. *Intentional content* highlights the intentionally designed level-appropriate pre-classroom materials, normally in the form of instructional videos, to help students acquire necessary knowledge and to check student comprehension before physical meetings. Finally, instructors in flipped learning are *professional educators* who constantly observe student learning, engagement, and progress before

Figure 16.2 The four pillars of flipped learning

Figure 16.3 The seven pillars of flipped learning

class; adjust subsequent in-class learning tasks based on the level of pre-classroom comprehension; and assess teaching as well as learning effectiveness after class.

Later, Chen, Wang, Kinshuk, and Chen (2014) further expanded flipped learning by adding three elements (as shown in Figure 16.3), namely, (1) progressive networking learning activities; (2) engaging and effective learning activities; and (3) diversified and seamless learning platforms. *Progressive networking learning activities* means enabling students to acquire knowledge, interact, and collaborate via learning communities, both in online pre-classroom tasks and in-class activities. *Engaging and effective learning activities* requires educators to possess strong instructional skills and strategies, as well as awareness of the proper combinations of structure, dialog, and learner autonomy. Finally, *diversified and seamless learning platforms* means that flipped learning features both online learning for pre-classroom tasks (e.g., previewing materials and doing comprehension check exercises) and physical learning contexts in which students improve further via both individual and collaborative activities.

Bishop and Verleger (2013) also found that flipped learning entailed (1) technology-assisted content delivery outside the classroom, typically via video presentations, and (2) interactive group learning tasks inside the classroom. Mok (2014) further stated that in such a pedagogical design, "the teacher 'delivers' lectures before class in the form of prerecorded videos, and spends class time engaging students in learning activities that involve collaboration and interaction" (p. 7). Although flipped learning highlights the reversal of content acquisition, the core of flipped learning goes beyond the mere reordering of teaching and learning activities (Bergmann & Sams, 2012). Students are required to be accountable for the pre-classroom learning and take an active role in in-class learning activities, which are often collaborative and socio-constructive in nature. It is particularly important for students to review the pre-classroom materials and for teachers to check comprehension of the given materials. Because the students come to class prepared, teachers do not have to spend a substantial amount of in-class time lecturing new information. Understanding the preparedness of the students before the physical class meetings, therefore, allows teachers to design advanced learning activities that require students to apply what they have learned. As students are engaged in those learning activities, whether individual or collaborative, they receive feedback from teachers or peer classmates in a timely fashion.

Since the classroom emphasis is more on applying the knowledge gained before class than merely remembering and understating information, students are naturally led to higher-order thinking such as applying, analyzing, and evaluating. It is thus very different from conventional instruction. In conventional instruction, teachers spend a large amount of time lecturing, hoping students to digest the information in class and to apply that information via homework, which is normally challenging because it involves more than memorization.

Without timely assistance from teachers or capable peers, students may feel frustrated and overwhelmed by what they perceive as challenging assignments. Gradually, their motivation to learn can decrease, because they do not feel a sense of confidence or achievement in the learning process (Wu, Yen, & Marek, 2011).

As the world witnesses the growing popularity of flipped learning in education, flipped learning has also been reinventing itself and moving to a new era; referred to as Flipped learning 3.0. According to Flipped Learning Global Initiative (FLGI, 2021):

Flipped learning is not just another teaching tactic. Flipped learning is a meta-instructional strategy because it's a framework that creates *the class time* to enable all other instructional strategies from project-based learning, inquiry learning, game-based learning, mastery learning, makerspaces, and the myriad other active learning strategies. Flipped learning also provides the missing roadmap for the effective application of education technology.

To make sure that students view instructional videos outside the classroom, educators have to take student interests into consideration, focusing on video content that their students will appreciate, in order to keep them engaged. Furthermore, students should be encouraged to create their own video content that is engaging and informative in nature. Educators can take advantage of the tracking mechanism of online platforms to see if students have watched the videos, and to track how many times and for how long. For example, having students respond to question items designed by teachers (or even their classmates) with the use of Kahoot or Quizlet could be an effective way to check student comprehension before class. Online platforms such as Moodle, social networking sites such as Facebook, or even mobile messaging applications such as LINE could also be used for this purpose. With the use of these technologies to help teachers understand students' learning process, in-class learning can be more focused and in-depth.

Taken together, as teachers use carefully chosen modes of delivery, students are given the opportunity to self-monitor their pace through the instructional materials; to interact with the content, the teacher, and their peers in multiple ways; and to demonstrate higher-order thinking skills in both individual and collaborative tasks. Therefore, flipped learning, while building interactivity by connecting pre-class work to group space or making the individual space social, is in itself dynamic and rapidly expanding around the globe with new insights from research, classroom innovation, and education technology, which, in turn, opens new possibilities for researchers, educational practitioners, administrators, technologists, and policymakers.

Current issues facing researchers and practitioners

Although most studies and practitioners have confirmed the benefits and advantages of flipped learning, and conclude that flipped learning can improve student learning outcomes significantly compared to teacher-centered instructional modes, some researchers have remained hesitant about the effectiveness of flipped learning, stating concerns about how to be effective in engaging students in pre-class preparation, enable students to demonstrate what they have learned with the pre-class learning, and foster genuine learning beyond the classroom. For example, O'Flaherty and Phillips (2015), in their scoping review, found "very few studies that actually demonstrated robust evidence to support that the flipped learning approach is more effective than conventional teaching methods" (p. 94). They called for "stronger evidence in evaluating student learning outcomes that particularly improved student learning and development, as critical thinkers, problem solvers and team players; a need to stimulate higher order thinking through the use of creative technologies and applied learning" (p. 94). One potential reason is that the implementation of flipped learning does not necessarily lead to higher student engagement (Chen et al., 2014). Ebbeler (2013) found that about 75% of the students still preferred lecture-based instruction in comparison with the flipped model, possibly because it entails less work. Along a similar vein, Kim, Park, Jang, and Nam (2017) found a low rate of accessing pre-classroom lectures at home.

According to the findings from empirical studies, attention should be drawn to the following issues and challenges faced by both students and instructors when implementing flipped learning instruction. Solutions are also provided to resolve these issues.

Time and effort commitment. As opposed to conventional methods, where student learning begins with classroom instruction, flipped learning starts in "out of class settings", which emphasizes the essential role of learning beyond the classroom walls. A successful flipped learning implementation requires learners to watch videos and understand the contents of learning materials before arriving for classroom meetings. In most cases, this approach requires more time and effort prior to class meetings than a conventional class. More motivated and self-directed learners will realize the benefits of the additional time and effort they need to devote because they feel that flipped learning is worthwhile and rewarding. However, some less motivated students might see the time and effort requirements as invading their leisure time, causing them to prefer a lecture-based approach.

Solutions: Instructors can inform and communicate with students about the advantages and benefits of flipped learning prior to implementation. Students also need to be aware of the detailed assignment schedule as well as individual and group accountability in order to lower student anxiety and any affective filter. Instructors should inform students clearly that flipped learning is not more demanding compared to traditional instruction, and in fact that the amount of time devoted is equal for both instructional approaches. In most countries, teachers will still assign homework for students. It is only the nature of the homework assignments that is different in flipped learning. Students first spend time at home watching less-challenging videos and then they work on more demanding activities in class, either individually or as groups, scaffolded by more capable peers and their instructors. Thus, they can receive more timely support and interventions, whereas when doing traditional homework on their own at home, there is no immediate support and guidance.

Students are unprepared or unready prior to class meetings, which means that students simply do not watch instructional videos or even if they do, it is difficult for instructors to gauge their level of comprehension. Insufficient preparation with pre-classroom materials leads to inadequate pre-class comprehension and will likely impede the implementation of in-class higher-order level activities and tasks. If pre-class video watching and understanding of the intended learned materials is a pre-requisite, instructors cannot overemphasize its important role in flipped learning.

Solutions: Instructors can adopt the "Output-driven/Input-enabled" model, developed by Wen (2008). The core concept of Wen's model emphasizes that the need for producing outcomes drives learners to purse input, and comprehensible input enables learners to produce satisfactory output, thus achieving learning objectives. This model fits perfectly with the pre-requisite element of flipped learning because teachers are responsible for (1) designing authentic output tasks to improve learner proficiency level, (2) providing appropriate, comprehensive input to enhance learner intake, (3) offering appropriate output assistance to improve learner performance, (4) offering targeted feedback and comments rather than general suggestions (Wen, 2013).

Instructors can ask students to write a summary, response, or raise questions immediately after watching the videos. The WSQ technique (watch, summarize, question) proposed by Kirch (2012) can serve as a strategy to enhance the quality of out-of-class learning. This serves two purposes. The first is to urge students to watch the video, then summarize the content, and lastly raise questions of their own based on the learned materials. And the second is to gauge the level of their understanding, so that the instructor can go into more detail in the classroom to clear up confusion and resolve problems with understanding. Instructors can adopt any classroom management platforms or social media approved by their school, such as a learning management system, Line, Facebook, or WhatsApp, to test their understanding of instructional videos. Immediate and timely replies, feedback, or grading from instructors or teaching assistants should be provided. Instructors can praise those students on-the-spot who perform well in these pre-class online tasks/activities. Such encouragement to complete the pre-class learning activities motivates students to become more engaged in subsequent tasks, by which self-confidence in learning is further enhanced. Thus, the pedagogical design of flipped learning, using pre-class introduction of new knowledge, helps students to grow beyond the in-class learning contexts.

Introverted/shy students are often inactive or do not engage actively with in-class activities/tasks. In-class activities in flipped learning are as important as the pre-class video watching, since these activities require students to apply what they have comprehended through watching pre-classroom study. Students who lack confidence in their understanding, or who fear being judged as inadequate by their peers, may be reluctant to speak up or take part.

Solutions: Group dynamics are important when it comes to in-class collaborative activities. Instructors can mix students in terms of student proficiency levels, levels of activeness, personality, and characteristics. Via more capable or active peers helping less capable or active peers, these in-class activities/tasks, which often require higher-order thinking ability and collaborative or communicative competences, can facilitate and reinforce student learning. Engaging in activities requiring not merely memorizing and understanding but engaging in higher-order thinking, such as applying, creating, problem solving, and collaborating, strengthens student readiness for future tasks that go beyond the classroom.

In addition to the students, instructors may also face challenges or problems with flipped learning. Most studies admit that flipped learning is more demanding for both students and instructors. As a result, some instructors might feel intimidated and resist leaving their comfort zone, therefore not being as fully engaged as flipped teaching requires. Such instructors may experience the following challenges.

Instructors with low computer literacy might be reluctant to adopt flipped learning. Some instructors may be unfamiliar with the technology required for flipped instruction. They may be uncomfortable using the portable technology their students favor and they may lack the "know how" for production of instructional videos, or consider it to be too time-consuming to make their own instructional videos.

Solutions: Instructors can locate relevant and appropriate freely available videos via diverse sources if they feel they lack the skill to produce videos or have camera phobia, even though self-produced videos usually yield better learning outcomes.

More broadly, academic programs that prepare future instructors need to incorporate technology literacy into their programs and educational technology design as part of teaching instructional design (Albion et al., 2015). Computer and Information Literacy (CIL), also called Information and Computer Technology (ICT) literacy or simply Digital Literacy, is an essential competency for all students (Vavik & Salomon, 2015; Voogt et al., 2013) and particularly for those preparing to be teachers.

Instructors need to plan various in-class activities ahead of time. Since the in-class time no longer requires lengthy lectures, diverse learning activities/tasks, both individual and collaborative in nature, should be arranged for students to cultivate and demonstrate higher-order thinking skills. These activities must be well-crafted to engage students, stimulate higher-order thinking, and address educational outcome requirements. That is, the challenge centers around how instructors should structure in-class activities to enhance the likelihood that students will engage effectively with the out-of-class learning of flipped learning in order to feel prepared for the classroom time.

Solutions: Instructors need to take an Educational Engineering approach to setting educational outcome requirements and then designing instruction and technology that allows students to achieve those goals (Marek & Wu, 2020), with the designs based on affordances, i.e., the qualities or properties an educational tool or activity offers. By adopting Wen's (2008) "Output-driven/Input-enabled" model, the instructors direct the students' attention to output (i.e., demonstrating what they have learned during in-class activities), which is facilitated by the pursuit of comprehensible input (i.e., the students' ability to comprehend materials acquired in out-of-class settings). Therefore, instructors should design in-class learning activities that enable students to demonstrate their comprehension of, and ability to apply, out-of-class flipped learning.

In-class activities cannot be simply tasks that use the available time. They must be focused on critical thinking, advanced understanding of the subject matter, and advanced proficiency. As a result, instructional designers need criteria and best practices to guide the development, implementation, and evaluation of their in-the-classroom activities. As above, academic programs preparing future teachers need to embrace not just the subject matter expertise, but also the Educational Engineering process of curriculum and technology design.

Those instructors who have not yet been exposed to such pedagogy design should seek, and be offered, professional development. In addition to training offered by their schools, instructors can attend instructional workshops or consult with other instructors who are good at designing the kinds of in-class activities required for flipped teaching.

Stockwell (2017) found that a successful innovative computer assisted language learning instructional design requires three elements: human capital, time, and budget. Likewise, this implementation principle can be applied to flipped learning. Instructors are strongly encouraged to take the three factors into account and learn to manage them appropriately when planning their flipped learning instruction, particularly focusing on how to organize in-class learning tasks to enhance student application of their pre-class, out-of-class flipped learning.

Implications

In any learning endeavor, new knowledge must be introduced and these new ideas must be fit together with what students already know. The ancient "Socratic Method" described in Plato's Theaetetus (Altorf, 2019) is a general term for discussion and critical thinking activities in which the students engage in active exploration of a topic, led by the instructor, resulting in collective judgments based on these interactions. Theorists in the 20th and 21st centuries have studied teaching and learning and developed nuanced theoretical foundations on which sound instructional practice can be based.

Implications for theory

The philosophy about learning in which students evolve or "construct" knowledge through active learning, rather than simple memorization, is known as Constructivism (Bruning, Schraw, Norby, & Ronning, 2011). The more connections that are made between new and existing knowledge, the easier it is for students to recall. These connections are made through higher-order thinking skills in which similarities and differences are compared and contrasted in order to reach conclusions (Ingulsrud et al., 2002; Wu, Yen, & Marek, 2013). When the knowledge is defined as skills or abilities, repetition leads to mastery (Dweck & Leggett, 1998).

John Dewey (1966) stressed the importance of inquiry in the learning process and held that learning is a social, communal process in which students engage with each other to define and explore an idea interactively. Social constructivism (Powell & Kalina, 2009) is at the heart of modern views of learning, invoked in the context of student-centered active learning (Bruning et al., 2011).

Flipped learning aligns well with these foundational theories. Instead of applying new knowledge in isolation at home, students apply their new knowledge in the social setting of the classroom, engaging with others to refine their understanding. Because the teacher has ways of assessing the initial understanding of the students, in-the-classroom activities can be fine-tuned to explore the topic in more detail as needed, and enrich understanding through group activities that apply and strengthen the constructed, interconnected knowledge. The secret to success, of course, is how effective the teacher is in implementing the flipped learning framework.

Implications for practice

The theory of flipped learning, and the associated ideas of Social Constructivism and student-centered active learning, is not challenging to understand. Putting them into operational practice, however, can be daunting, particularly for teachers experienced only with lecture-memorization formats. Even when a teacher is using flipped learning, many factors influence success. The details of the instructional design are vital.

An important focus for the flipped learning instructor is enhancing the quality of out-of-class learning as a preparation for in-class higher-order learning. Higher-quality pre-classroom learning materials prepare the student for classroom better, are more engaging to the student and thus more likely for the student to actually study, and thus better prepare the student for the in-class refinement of learning. The better the student feels the pre-classroom learning experience is, the more likely is it that the student will engage in the learning tasks. It is more desirable that the student engage in pre-classroom learning because it is a good idea (integrative motivation) then because of the consequences if they fail to engage (instrumental motivation), in keeping with Gardner and Lambert's (1972) theory of learning motivation. Better learning materials foster the "it's a good idea" attitude about pre-classroom study.

Videos. Flipped learning usually presents new information to students at home via videos, but young people today are highly sophisticated about online video. A good video will engage them, but if the video is poorly done, students will likely tune it out, even if they are looking at the screen, and the information will not sink in. A poorly done video may be the result of poor technical quality, but it may also be because of things like the teacher not performing well on camera, poor organization of the presentation, or bad audio.

It may also be that the lecture is too long. The optimal length for an online video lecture has been found by some studies to be six minutes and others no more than 15 minutes. Younger students need shorter durations to avoid their attention wandering. Research outside the scope of education reveals that typical online videos lose 33% of their audience after 30 seconds, 45% within a minute, and 60% within two minutes. Even high-level Ted Talks require lengths of no more than 18 minutes (Emporia State, 2018).

This means that teachers need to be active in producing their video lectures, giving strong attention to the overall quality of the production, and carefully focusing the information presented. Students would dread watching an hour-long lecture delivered to a video camera as if it were a conventional classroom, and such a video would be less effective in accomplishing the mission of introducing new knowledge. The best videos are probably those in which the teacher is on the screen, with good audio quality, making direct eye contact with the camera, interspersed with slides and graphics.

In addition, comprehension check mechanisms on video contents, such as questions, summaries, short essays, or reflections for the students, or even having the student raise their own questions, should be included in the pre-class video watching process, since students' out-of-class preparation and engagement before physical class meetings for later meaningful in-class activities is vital in flipped learning. When involving students in watching the videos or previewing the learning materials before class in out-of-class settings, self-regulation is necessary. In addition to than checking students' pre-class comprehension, teachers should also direct their attention to helping students improve self-regulated learning beyond the classroom. Furthermore, because students are allowed to watch the videos or preview the materials repeatedly at will, autonomous learning could be potentially developed. Therefore, the pre-class learning tasks not only help students to become prepared for later in-class activities but, perhaps more importantly, train them to become self-regulated and autonomous lifelong learners.

Classroom Activities. Similar to concerns about instructional video quality, in-class activities in flipped learning are not all equal. They must be crafted carefully to not only engage the students, to transfer the out-of-class learning into physical class meetings, but also to address the essential learning outcomes of the unit or topic. Depending on the subject matter, this might include Socratic exploration of the topic led by the teacher, small group discussion, games, or other relevant activities. Regardless, they must both engage the student and allow reinforcement and application of the information previously provided before class.

Technology Affordances. Teachers and flipped learning instructional designers must make wise decisions about the technology they will use, and how they will use it. It is not the technology, itself, which produces a beneficial learning outcome, but rather the affordances of the overall instructional design, i.e., the benefits or capabilities that the teaching tools and methods offer collectively (van Lier, 2000). Video lectures provide the affordance, if produced well, of an effective way to deliver new information to student before class. The in-class activities that promote higher-order thinking and internalization of knowledge must also be analyzed and engineered in terms of the affordances they provide to allow the students to achieve the desired learning outcome. The overall affordance-based instructional design is not limited to pre-class content delivery and acquisition, or in-class collaboration, but should, furthermore, gear its outcomes to development of self-regulation, autonomous learning, and higher-order thinking skills that are essential for further challenges.

Duration and Novelty Factor. Flipped learning often does not last an entire semester or academic year. At the very least, a few weeks may be needed for orientation and induction training, but the duration of the flipped learning will affect the attainment of the desired outcomes. Very short implementations of flipped learning, such as a "stunt" lasting a week or two, are not really long enough for the intellectual benefits of flipped learning to be felt. This failure is also manifest when research into flipped learning uses very short-term durations. In these cases, the study results may be skewed to the positive, because new ways of learning are more motivating than conventional experiences (Yeh et al., 2021), a phenomenon known as the "Novelty Effect".

The Novelty Effect fades over a period of about eight weeks (Clark & Sugrue, 1991) but an unusual and enjoyable, novel learning experience can boost the motivation of students, at least for the first few weeks. While the Novelty Factor can be problematical for researchers using instructional technology for less than eight weeks (Stockwell & Hubbard, 2014), it, conversely, can provide instructional designers with the affordance of the technology and activities engaging students to a greater extent than conventional instructional methods, at least for the first few weeks, thus helping the students develop positive habits and practices with respect to the flipped learning requirements. As the world becomes increasingly digitalized, familiarizing students with the benefits of the technology-enhanced learning embedded in flipped pedagogical designs helps them to be further empowered with digital literacy—a key lifelong ability to find, evaluate, and compose clear information on various digital platforms.

Planning for Success. The final implication for practice in flipped learning is that unfamiliar technology, or other learning activities that require a significant learning curve, is likely to cause frustration among the students and, as a result, demotivate them (Kao, 2011), thus canceling out the beneficial affordance of the Novelty Effect. Technology the students have used and likely mastered previously is preferred, whether it be school-based technology they have used in other classes, or commercial platforms they use in their personal lives. Classroom activities that are easy to grasp are preferred to those which are complicated to understand.

Scaffolding. Regardless, some induction training will likely be required concerning how the familiar technology will be used in this particular class, or how in-class activities are intended to work. Teachers should make strategic use of Scaffolding (Pelletreau et al., 2018), a teaching method in which instructors initially provide high levels of support as the students learn how the technology or learning activity works. As the students gain more experience and expertise, the instructor withdraws support, step-by-step, to encourage students to become more confident and independent. Scaffolding maximizes the likelihood of student success in the early stages of flipped learning, which increases student confidence, leading, in turn, to increased motivation and, over the long term, more successful learning outcomes (Wu, Chen Hsieh, & Yang, 2017).

Scaffolding is not necessarily limited to assistance provided by teachers. It could also come from the more capable peers. Such peer assistance is also key to the success of flipped learning, whether out-of-class or in-class. If implemented well, engaging students with different proficiency levels in collaborative tasks helps them to develop cognitively and socially through interacting with others—a process that features comprehensible input, i+1, zone of proximal development, and social interaction (Marek & Wu, 2020).

The theoretical foundations and the practical implications of flipped learning are two sides of a coin. Learning designers must make wise use of both the learning tools and the activities promoting higher-order thinking and ability, while preserving the sound theoretical framework of their designs.

Future directions

While most of current research findings and educational practices of flipped learning have shown its advantages over other conventional instruction, more probes into flipped learning are vital before the overall benefits of flipped learning can be validated. Therefore, three main future directions should be taken into consideration in future flipped pedagogical implementations.

First, researchers as well as educational practitioners should move on from the question of whether flipped learning is more effective to when and how flipped learning is most beneficial. As flipped learning continues to gain popularity around the globe, the focus should be directed to the conditions and features that make flipped learning more advantageous than other instructional implementations. Factors such as ways to deliver pre-classroom contents, mechanisms to gauge student pre-classroom comprehension, best classroom grouping of students, and in-class task designs that move students toward the cultivation of higher-order thinking skills should be addressed. Such examination would make the understanding of the affordances and best practices of flipped learning more robust.

Second, the majority of previous research has focused mainly on the students' cognitive domain during flipped learning instruction. Other aspects as behavioral and affective domains (e.g., motivation, anxiety, satisfaction, attitude, etc.) should also be observed so that a more comprehensive picture of flipped learning can be achieved. Nonetheless, cognitive performance is just one aspect of an individual's abilities and does not represent an individual as a whole. Equally important is how students behave and feel during the flipped learning process. The cognitive, behavioral, and affective domains should be included and treated equally, just like the inclusion of cognitive, affective, and psychomotor teaching objectives listed in a lesson plan.

Finally, more attention should be paid to crafting effective in-classroom activities to foster higher-order thinking about the learned knowledge, employing social constructivism. Most flipped learning research has focused on the technology and the pre-classroom introduction of new knowledge. Classroom activities must vary with the discipline being studied, of course, but teachers and instructional designers need criteria and best practices to guide the development, implementation, and evaluation of the in-the-classroom activities which are so important to the beneficial outcomes of the flipped method.

Reflection questions

1 Flipped learning normally requires the use of technology to facilitate pre-classroom material viewing and comprehension check, thus yielding the issue of equal technological access. This concern is particularly important when it comes to learners who are in disadvantaged learning environment where technological resources are limited or simply not available. How might this issue be solved?
2 Flipped learning has been researched primarily in higher education (particularly university-level learners), with relatively few studies among secondary cohorts. In what ways might the flipped learning instructional design be different for younger students?
3 Other than the limitations mentioned in this chapter, have you experienced or observed other challenges while implementing flipped learning instruction?
4 Compare the roles of teachers in flipped learning and conventional lecture-based instruction. Are there similarities or differences? How about the students' roles?

Recommended readings

The Flipped Learning Global Initiative (FLGI) (https://flglobal.org/)
   FLGI is a global coalition of educators, researchers, technologists, and professional development providers who are devoted to effective implementation of flipped learning. This global learning community provides rich resources and tools to support successful flipped learning from K-12 to higher education. Free tutorials for a better understanding of flipped learning as well as paid lessons for advanced certificates are provided to support flipped learning around the globe.

Bergmann, J., & Sams, A. (2012). *Flip your classroom: Reach every student in every class every day*. Oregon: International Society for Technology in Education.
   A practical resource offering a comprehensive view of flipped learning. Topics include what a flipped classroom is, how to implement it, why it works, and the flipped-mastery model. Bergman also has published books about how to apply flipped learning for science, math, English, and social studies instruction.

Talbert, R. (2017). *Flipped learning: A guide for higher education faculty*. Virginia: Stylus Publishing, LLC.
   Talbert makes the point that flipped learning is not about technology, recording your lectures, or physical classrooms, but rather about pedagogy, including motivation, cognitive load, and self-regulated learning.

Walker, Z., Tan, D., Koh, L. (Eds.) (2020). *Flipped classrooms with diverse learners: International perspectives*. Singapore: Springer Nature Singapore Pte Ltd.
   An informative resource that showcases the success of flipped learning across a wide range of learners, examines its strengths and weaknesses, and offers pedagogical guidance on how to implement flipped learning.

References

Albion, P. R., Tondeur, J., Forkosh-Baruch, A., & Peeraer, J. (2015). Teachers' professioal development for ICT integration: Towards a repiprocal relationship between research and practice. *Education and Information Technologies, 20*(4) 655–673. https://doi.org/10.1007/s10639-015-9401-9

Altorf, H. M. (2019). Dialogue and discussion: Reflections on a Socratic method. *Arts and Humanities in Higher Education, 18*(1), 60–75. https://doi.org/10.1177/1474022216670607

Bergmann, J., & Sams, A. (2012). *Flip your classroom: Reach every student in every class every day*. Eugene, OR: International Society for Technology in Education.

Bishop, J. L., & Verleger, M. A. (2013). The flipped classroom: A survey of the research. In *Proceedings of the 120th ASEE Annual Conference & Exposition*. Atlanta, GA: American Society for Engineering Education.

Bokosmaty, R., Bridgeman, A., & Muir, M. (2019). Using a partially flipped learning model to teach first year undergraduate chemistry. *Journal of Chemical Education, 96*(4), 629–639. https://doi.org/10.1021/acs.jchemed.8b00414

Bond, M. (2020). Facilitating student engagement through the flipped learning approach in K-12: A systematic review. *Computers & Education, 151*, Article 103819. https://doi.org/10.1016/j.compedu.2020.103819

Bruning, R. H., Schraw, G. J., Norby, M. M., & Ronning, R. R. (2011). Problem solving and critical thinking. *Cognitive Psychology and instruction* (5th ed., pp., 160–191). Boston: Pearson Education Inc.

Chen Hsieh, J. S., Wu, W.-C. V., & Marek, M. (2017). Using the flipped classroom to enhance EFL learning. *Computer Assisted Language Learning, 30*(1–2), 1–21. https://doi.org/10.1080/09588221.2015.1111910

Chen, Y., Wang, Y., Kinshuk, & Chen, N.-S. (2014). Is FLIP enough? Or should we use the FLIPPED model instead? *Computers & Education, 79*, 16–27. https://doi.org/10.1016/j.compedu.2014.07.004

Cheng, S. C., Hwang, G. J., & Lai, C. L. (2020). Critical research advancements of flipped learning: a review of the top 100 highly cited papers. *Interactive Learning Environments*, 1–17. https://doi.org/10.1080/10494820.2020.1765395

Chung, C.-J., Lai, C.-L., & Hwang, G.-J. (2019). Roles and research trends of flipped classrooms in nursing education: A review of academic publications from 2010 to 2017. *Interactive Learning Environments*. Advance online publication. https://doi.org/10.1080/10494820.2019.1619589

Clark, R. E., & Sugrue, B. M. (1991). Media in teaching. Handbook of research on teaching. New York: Macmillan.

Dewey, J. (1966). *Democracy and education*. New York: Free Press.

Dweck, C. S., & Leggett, E. L. (1988). A social-cognitive approach to motivation and personality. *Psychological Review, 95*(2), 256–273. https://doi.org/10.1037/0033-295X.95.2.256

Ebbeler, J. (2013). Introduction to ancient Rome. The flipped version. *The Chronicle of Higher Education, 59*, 43.

Eldy, E. F., & Chang, J. H. W., Butai, S. N., Basri, N. F., Awang, H., Din, W., Arshad, S. E. (2019). Inverted classroom improves pre-university students understanding on basic topic of physics: The preliminary study. *Journal of Technology and Science Education, 9*(3), 420–427.

Emporia State. (2018). Video Length in Online Courses: What the Research Says. https://emporiastate.blogspot.com/2018/04/video-length-in-online-courses-what.html

Ficano, C. K. C. (2019). Identifying differential benefits from a flipped-group pedagogy in introductory microeconomics. *International Review of Economics Education, 30*, 100–143. https://doi.org/10.1016/j.iree.2018.07.002

Flipped learning Global Initiative. (2021). Flipped learning 3.0. https://flglobal.org/flipped-learning-3-0/

Flipped learning Network. (2014). The four pillars of F-L-I-P™. https://flippedlearning.org/definition-of-flipped-learning/

Gardner, R. C., & Lambert, W. E. (1972). *Attitudes and motivation in second-language learning*. Rowley, MA: Newbury House.

Hamdan, N., McKnight, P., McKnight, K., & Arfstrom, K. M. (2013). A review of flipped learning. Retrieved from http://www.flippedlearning.org/review

Hwang, G. J., Lai, C. L., & Wang, S. Y. (2015). Seamless flipped learning: A Mobile technology-enhanced flipped classroom with effective learning strategies. *Journal of Computers in Education, 2*(4), 449–473. https://doi.org/10.1007/s40692-015-0043-0

Ingulsrud, J. E., Kai, K., Kadowaki, S., Kurobane, S., & Shiobara, M. (2002). The assessment of cross-cultural experience: Measuring awareness through critical text analysis. *International Journal of Intercultural Relations, 26*, 473–491. https://doi.org/10.1016/S0147-1767(02)00030-5

Kao, T-N. R. (2011). Factor analysis of English writing demotivation among central Taiwan university students (Unpublished master's thesis). Providence University, Taichung, Taiwan

Kim, J.-E., Park, H., Jang, M., & Nam, H. (2017). Exploring flipped classroom effects on second language learners' cognitive processing. *Foreign Language Annals, 50*(2), 260–284. https://doi.org/10.1111/flan.12260

Kirch, C. (2012). Flipping with Kirch. Retrieved from http://flippingwithkirch.blogspot.com/p/wsqing.html

Lage, M. J., Platt, G. J., & Treglia, M. (2000). Inverting the classroom: A gateway to creating an inclusive learning environment. *The Journal of Economic Education, 31*(1), 30–43.

Marek, M. W., & Wu, W. V. (2020). Establishing a "Standard Model" for CALL instructional design. *International Journal of Computer-Assisted Language Learning and Teaching (IJCALLT), 10*(3), 79–88. https://doi.org/10.4018/IJCALLT.2020070106

Mok, H. N. (2014). Teaching tip: The flipped classroom. *Journal of Information Systems Education, 25*(1), 7–11.

O'Flaherty, J., & Phillips, C. (2015). The use of flipped classrooms in higher education: A scoping review. *The Internet and Higher Education, 25*, 85–95. https://doi.org/10.1016/j.iheduc.2015.02.002

Pelletreau, K. N., Knight, J. K., Lemons, P. P., McCourt, J. S., Merrill, J. E., Nehm, R. H., & Smith, M. K. (2018). A faculty professional development model that improves student learning, encourages active-learning instructional practices, and works for faculty at multiple institutions. *CBE—Life Sciences Education, 17*(2), es5.

Powell, K., & Kalina, C. (2009). Cognitive and social constructivism: Developing tools for an effective classroom. *Education, 130*(2), 241–250.

Reidsema, C., Kavanagh, L., Hadgraft, R., & Smith, N. (2017). *The flipped classroom. Practice and practices in higher education*. Singapore: Springer Singapore. https://doi.org/10.1007/978-981-10-3413-8

Ringer, T., Warkentin, T., Patel, V., & Melady, D. (2019). Approach to geriatric emergency medicine: A flipped classroom group learning exercise for undergraduate medical trainees. *Journal of Education and Teaching in Emergency Medicine, 4*(2), SG1–23. https://doi.org/10.21980/J8GH03

Stockwell, G. (2017). Moving with the times: Teaching with technology in a changing world. In *The 34th international conference of English teaching and learning*. Kaohsiung, Taiwan.

Stockwell, G., & Hubbard, P. (2014, July). Learner training in mobile language learning. In J. Colpaert, A. Aerts, & M. Oberhofer (Ed's.), *Research challenges in CALL: Proceedings of the Sixteenth International CALL Research Conference* (pp. 320–322). Antwerp: University of Antwerp.

Turan, Z., & Akdag-Cimen, B. (2019). Flipped classroom in English language teaching: A systematic review. *Computer Assisted Language Learning*. Advance online publication. https://doi.org/10.1080/09588221.2019.1584117

Van Lier, L. (2000). 11 From input to affordance: Social-interactive learning from an ecological perspective. *Sociocultural theory and second language learning, 78*(4), 245.

Vavik, L., & Salomon, G. (2015). Twenty first century skills vs. disciplinary studies? In Y. Rosen, S. Ferrara, & M. Mosharaff (Eds.), *Handbook of research on technology tools for real-world skill development* (Vol. 1, pp.1–12). New York, NY: IGI Global.

Voogt, J., Erstad, O., Dede, C., & Mishra, P. (2013). Challenges to learning and schooling in the digital networked world of the 21st century. *Journal of Computer Assisted Learning, 29*(5), 403–413. https://doi.org/10.1111/jcal.12029

Webb, M., & Doman, E. (2020). Impacts of flipped classrooms on learner attitudes towards technology-enhanced language learning. *Computer Assisted Language Learning, 33*(3), 240–274. https://doi.org/10.1080/09588221.2018.1557692

Wen, Q. (2008). On the output-driven hypothesis and reform of English-skill courses for English majors. *Foreign Language World, 2*, 2–9.

Wen, Q. (2013). Application of the output-driven hypothesis in college English teaching; Reflections and suggestions. *Foreign Language World, 6*, 14–22.

Wu, W. C., Chen Hsieh, J., & Yang, J. C. (2017). Creating an online learning community in a flipped classroom to enhance EFL learners' oral proficiency. *Educational Technology & Society, 20*(2), 142–157.

Wu, W. C. V., Yang, J. C., Chen Hsieh, J., & Yamamoto, T. (2020). Free from demotivation in EFL writing: The use of online flipped writing instruction. *Computer Assisted Language Learning, 33*(4), 353–387. https://doi.org/10.1080/09588221.2019.1567556

Wu, W. C. V., Marek, M., & Chen, N. S. (2013). Assessing cultural awareness and linguistic competency of EFL learners in a CMC-based active learning context. *System, 41*(3), 515–528. https://doi.org/10.1016/j.system.2013.05.004

Wu, W-C. V., Yen, L. L., & Marek, M. W. (2011). Using online EFL interaction to increase confidence, motivation, and ability. *Educational Technology & Society, 14*(3), 118–129. https://eric.ed.gov/?id=EJ963205

Yeh, H. C., Tseng, S. S., & Heng, L. (2021). Enhancing EFL students' intracultural learning through virtual reality. *Interactive Learning Environments*, 1–10. https://doi.org/10.1080/10494820.2020.1734625

Zou, D., Luo, S., Xie, H., & Hwang, G. J. (2020). A systematic review of research on flipped language classrooms: Theoretical foundations, learning activities, tools, research topics and findings. *Computer Assisted Language Learning*, 1–27. https://doi.org/10.1080/09588221.2020.1839502

17
ENHANCING LANGUAGE LEARNING BEYOND THE CLASSROOM THROUGH ADVISING

Jo Mynard and Satoko Kato

Introduction

The focal point for this chapter is how best to support language learners as they navigate and negotiate their own learning beyond the classroom (LBC). The traditional classroom environment provides several built-in support systems for learners that are generally absent in LBC approaches, namely: (1) a curriculum which presents the content that needs to be learned, (2) a teacher who normally manages how the curriculum is covered, (3) peers who offer social and linguistic support, (4) a physical space conducive to studying. LBC has the potential to be an effective and motivating approach to language learning, but every learner almost certainly needs to be supported in this process. In this chapter, we are proposing that where possible all decisions about all aspects of learning should come from the learners themselves. In other words, this chapter focuses on how learners can be supported as they develop language learner autonomy, i.e., the process and practice of taking charge of one's own learning (Benson, 2011; Little, 1991; Sockett, this volume) through a process that is known as advising in language learning (ALL).

In the first part of this chapter, we will provide an overview of the key constructs in the field of ALL and explain the vital role that it plays in supporting LBC. ALL has been defined as the practice and process of facilitating one-to-one reflective dialog with language learners with the intention of promoting learner autonomy (Carson & Mynard, 2012; Kato & Mynard, 2016; Mynard, 2020a). As we will see in the following sections of this chapter, ALL takes a learner's goals, interests, context, and other individual differences as a starting point and supports them through individualized, co-constructed, and supportive dialog. This dialog is crucial for sustaining long-term motivation for language learning in the absence of a classroom environment but can of course support classroom-based instruction as well.

After setting the theoretical groundwork, we will examine the key issues in the field and describe ways in which advising occurs in practice and how such powerful dialog can be achieved. Following that we will explore the implications of ALL and look at how educators can be prepared for taking the role of an advisor through training, mentoring, and professional development. Finally, we will turn to the future directions of advising where online formats will take a more central role. In addition, our research methods can be expanded to draw on neuroscience to examine a wider range of evidence to explore—from a neurological perspective—the positive effect that extended engagement with ALL could have on language learners.

Key constructs

ALL is, in simple terms, the process and practice of working with language learners in personally meaningful ways in order to promote language learner autonomy (Carson & Mynard, 2012). For the purposes of this chapter, a practitioner of ALL is known as a learning advisor, but other terms have also been employed such as language counselor (Karlsson, 2012). In essence, a professionally trained learning advisor supports language learners by engaging in careful reflective listening which is done through the skillful use of co-constructed dialog and other tools (Karlsson, 2012; Kato, 2012; Kato & Mynard, 2016; Mozzon-McPherson, 2012). Through the dialog, a learning advisor goes beyond simply giving learning hints or tips, but intentionally promotes deeper-level reflective thinking. This process, in turn, helps the learner to reflect deeply on themselves and their language learning process and progress in order to develop awareness and control over how they study.

Origins

The origin of ALL stems from an early self-access center in Europe in the late 1960s, namely, CRAPEL (Centre de Recherches et d'Applications Pédagogiques en Langues / Centre for Research and Applications in Language Teaching) at the University of Lorraine in Nancy in France (Holec, 2000). Self-access centers were originally designed as places where learners could find materials for continuing to study languages outside of class hours. However, teachers at CRAPEL soon noticed that simply providing materials was insufficient and learners needed support from teachers as well. Our knowledge of ALL has developed substantially since then thanks to a growing number of publications including several collections of edited papers (e.g., Everhard et al., 2011; Ludwig & Mynard, 2012; Mozzon-McPherson & Vismans, 2001; Mynard & Carson, 2012; Rubin, 2007; Thornton & Mynard, 2012; Yamashita & Mynard, 2015). However, ALL is still a relatively new strand of applied linguistics and more research and practice is needed in order to continue to develop the field.

Theoretical perspectives

In terms of the underlying theory, ALL has been explored from different perspectives, but it tends to be situated within a sociocultural view of learning. ALL fits well here as sociocultural theory views language as a tool for facilitating learning while also taking into account the social, historical, psychological and contextual factors that affect learning in addition to the roles of other people in the process (Lantolf & Poehner, 2008; Mynard, 2012). Mediation is a central concept in sociocultural theory which is the development of knowledge through interaction with people and tools (Lantolf & Poehner, 2008). In the case of ALL, interventions in the form of intentional dialogs with learning advisors could be considered an example of such mediation. Learning advisors intentionally use dialog to promote deeper-level thinking so that learners can make connections, challenge previously held assumptions, and increase their understanding of themselves and the learning process (Kato, 2012; Kato & Mynard, 2016; Mynard, 2012).

Researchers have also drawn on literature and practice from several other fields, for example, humanistic counseling, psychology of language learning, and transformation theory. Due to the therapeutic or 'helping' nature of the dialog, the literature and practice of humanistic counseling has influenced the field somewhat (e.g., Karlsson, 2012; Kato & Mynard, 2016; Kelly, 1996; Mozzon-McPherson, 2012), especially where the three fundamental principles of *respect*, *empathy* and *genuineness* are the focus (Mozzon-McPherson, 2012; Rogers, 1951). In addition, with an increased focus on well-being in general and also on proactive learning, the field of coaching has also provided some useful perspectives for the field (e.g., see Kato, 2012; Kato & Sugawara, 2009). More recently, researchers are beginning to draw more heavily on the growing field of the psychology of language learning when framing advising. For example, Shelton-Strong (2020) and Shelton-Strong and Tassinari (2022) examine ALL from a self-determination theory perspective where advising can support one or more of a learner's basic psychological needs which is necessary in order for someone to perform well and thrive as a learner (Ryan & Deci, 2017). Finally, Kato and Mynard (2016) draw on Mezirow's (1991) transformation theory which is when learners are engaged in widening their world view. In order to do this and experience shifts in thinking, learners engage in three kinds of analysis (supported by advisors in ALL): analysis of the content (i.e., what happened and how it happened); analysis of the process (i.e., how one is learning); and analysis of the premise (i.e., how the analysis might challenge one's existing beliefs or assumptions).

One thing that all of these theoretical approaches have in common is that the role of reflection is crucial as part of the process of learning and a key role of ALL is to promote reflection. How this is done might vary as we will see later in the chapter, but we could consider both 'reflective thinking' (Dewey, 1933) and 'reflective practice' (Schön, 1983) as important. Reflective thinking is thinking actively and purposefully from different perspectives in order to solve a problem or puzzle. Reflective practice on the other hand can incorporate conscious thought while working on a task (i.e., reflection-in-action), thinking back on what has already done in order to learn from it (i.e., reflection-on-action), or implementing an intervention based on reflection (i.e., reflection-for-action, Killion & Todnem, 1991; Farrell, 2012).

Kato (2012) proposed the term 'intentional reflective dialogue' (IRD) to describe the process of advising as discourse which intentionally uses dialog and other tools in order to promote deeper-level reflective thinking which facilitates the development of awareness and control over the learning processes. Using the concept of IRD, combined with Mezirow's (1991) transformation theory, Kato and Mynard (2016) developed the concept of 'transformational advising' which is designed to not only promote deeper-level thinking through ALL, but to challenge existing beliefs as part of an ongoing process of learning. In order to help people transform into highly aware learners, an advisor works with a learner at the point they are at on a learning trajectory (Figure 17.1), be it 'getting started' where suggestions might be necessary in order for a largely unaware learner to begin their language learning journey, or working with a highly aware learner in the 'transformation' portion of the trajectory who can be helped to 'self-advise' using tried and tested tools as part of their continuing journey.

Goals of advising

Depending on the context and learners, the goals of advising might vary (Rubin, 2007), but they can broadly be categorized as pedagogical or affective (or both!) (Kato & Mynard, 2016; Rubin, 2007).

Enhancing Learning through Advising

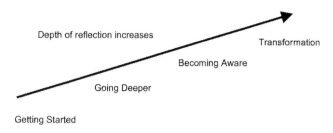

Figure 17.1 The learning trajectory (Kato & Mynard, 2016)

Pedagogical aims

In terms of pedagogical goals, in order to support LBC and learner responsibility, a knowledge of how to learn is important. Advising, combined with a more systematic introduction of skills and knowledge necessary for managing learning is an effective way to promote the kind of knowledge that learners need (Kato & Mynard, 2016). Although this process has been known as learner self-management (Rubin, 2001, 2005), learner training, learner development, or other terms (Sinclair, 2011), Kato and Mynard (2016) use the term 'structured awareness raising' to suggest that ideas should come from the learners themselves. However, support is needed and this includes non-directive suggestions for appropriate strategies and resources when the student needs them. Structured awareness raising could be incorporated into classroom learning so that students will be equipped to create and follow a learning plan that they design for themselves. In order to do this, they should have the opportunity to: (1) explore their motivations, dreams, and interests in order to set learning goals; (2) discover and experiment with different resources and strategies; (3) learn ways for effectively evaluating the learning gain; (4) intentionally reflect on the process. Advising is a very important part of the process of developing a plan, implementing it, and reflecting on and evaluating learning.

Affective aims

A crucial part of the language learning process is understanding oneself and the emotions that influence one's learning. This might include understanding what influences motivation and learning how to manage it; understanding the reasons behind language anxiety and creating an action plan to overcome one's fears of communicating in another language. Through the advising dialog, learners are able to explore affective factors related to learning and to use this knowledge as a resource for autonomous learning beyond the classroom (Tassinari & Ciekanski, 2013; Yamashita, 2015).

Key issues

Even though we have a strong theoretical background on which to situate our practice, in order to implement advising effectively and support learners, there remain some challenges. The key issues are (1) how to translate theoretical perspectives into practice, and (2) how to prepare teachers for such a role.

Advising in practice

Learning advisors accept and respect learners' experiences, goals and feelings without judgment and work with them in personally relevant ways in order to help them to develop understanding of the learning processes. In practice, depending on the context, learning advisors support LBC in various ways (Mozzon-McPherson & Tassinari, 2020). The most common is through face-to-face real-time one-to-one advising sessions. Traditionally, these advising sessions take place in either self-access centers or advising rooms, but recently online advising using teleconferencing or text/video messaging software is also becoming commonplace. Advising can also take place asynchronously through written interaction, for example, through feedback and questions written by learning advisors on learners' self-directed work or learning journals. This process can prompt an ongoing dialog that typically lasts throughout a semester (Mynard & Navarro; Mynard, 2010). Advising is the principal support offered to learners taking independent language learning modules at Kanda University in Japan (Mynard & Stevenson, 2017), at the University of Veracruz (Xalapa) in Mexico (Valdivia et al., 2012), and at the University of Helsinki in Finland (Karlsson et al., 2007). Finally, some institutions support group or peer advising where learners have opportunities to support and empathize with other learners and help each other to find solutions for learning difficulties. This has taken place in classrooms (Horai & Wright, 2016), and also online (Peeters & Mynard, 2019).

Although advising sessions vary based on the needs of the learner, the degree of familiarity, and the style of the advisor, the following is an example of the flow of an advising session. However, as sessions tend to only last between 30 and 50 minutes, it may not be possible to cover all these steps in one session.

1. Ice-breaking talk
2. Discuss background information and issues
3. Help the learner to find the 'real' issue
4. Support the learner in exploring options and making an action plan
5. Support the learner in taking action

In addition to the dialog being intentionally structured within each advising session, the overall process is intentionally structured as well. First, learning advisors intentionally adapt their practice according to where learners are on the learning trajectory; they intentionally apply advising strategies/approaches at appropriate times; and they intentionally focus on building rapport and trust to guide learners into transformative learning processes. This is done naturally by experienced advisors, but new learning can benefit from intentional practice of these processes while they develop their automaticity in advising.

Analyses of advising transcripts shows how the dialog between learners and learning advisors is intentionally structured and sensitive to where a learner is on the learning trajectory. A professionally trained learning advisor effectively uses dialog appropriate to each learner, taking into consideration their awareness level and individual difference factors such as personality, emotions, previous experiences, and the issue being discussed. Advising discourse has been examined and categorized by several researchers (e.g., Kato & Mynard, 2016; Kato & Sugawara, 2009; Kelly, 1996; McCarthy, 2010, 2012; Mozzon-McPherson & Tassinari, 2020; Shelton-Strong & Tassinari, 2022) and these categories include basic advising strategies such as repeating, mirroring, restating, and summarizing, and also more advanced advising strategies such as giving positive feedback, empathizing, complimenting, using metaphor, using powerful questions, intuiting, challenging, and using silence.

Education for advising

Although language teacher education now tends to include content related to language learner autonomy at a theoretical level, advising (and other practical ways of promoting language learner autonomy) does not tend to form part of the curriculum. In addition, if practical applications do form part of a course curriculum, this tends to be related to classroom practice rather than supporting language learners beyond the classroom. Until such time that an LBC component becomes a mainstream and integrated part of a teacher education curriculum, teachers need to overcome this gap in their knowledge by engaging in professional development. However, developing the practical skills necessary for effectively supporting learners through reflective dialog may be a challenge. One of the aims of the (2016) book on advising by Kato and Mynard was to provide examples and practical support to educators engaged in self-directed development of advising strategies. In addition, there are possibilities to earn a professional qualification in advising. The University of Hull in the UK offered a well-respected certificate program in advising, but this unfortunately ceased in 2010 (Mozzon-McPherson & Tassinari, 2020). The National Autonomous University of Mexico has offered an online diploma in advising (in Spanish) since 2004 (http://cad.cele.unam.mx/formasesores/) (Chávez Sánchez & Peña Clavel, 2015), and Kanda University of International Studies in Japan has been offering advisor education in both English and Japanese since 2010, and started to offer advisor education programs (in English) leading to a certificate in advising in 2020 as part of the activities of the Research Institute for Learner Autonomy Education (RILAE, https://kuis.kandagaigo.ac.jp/rilae/education) in collaboration with the university's graduate school.

Implications

The implication of what we have learned from theorizing and examining ALL in practice is that the field is likely to have an increasingly important role to play in language education as the interest in LBC increases. However, it has not yet been widely adopted in language education. Since the 2007 special issue of *System* on language counseling was published, some progress has been made with institutional recognition of the value of ALL, but some of the same challenges outlined by Rubin (2007) still remain, namely, (1) convincing senior administrators of the value of ALL to support LBC, (2) the challenge of training and mentoring learning advisors, and (3) how the effectiveness of advising might be evaluated. This section will focus on the latter two as they will go some way to overcoming the first challenge.

Advisor development and mentoring

As Kato and Mynard (2016) demonstrate, learning advisor education can be mapped on a trajectory not unlike the one described earlier for learners (Figure 17.1).

Through reflection, practice and mentoring, advisors develop a deeper understanding of advising processes and how to work effectively with language learners using IRD. In addition to the dialog being intentionally structured, the process is as well, in terms of the flow of the learning trajectory, the application of advising strategies/approaches, and the processes of building rapport and trust to guide learners into transformative learning processes. Ideally advisor development should be a collaborative process as practicing the strategies and tools used for promoting reflective dialog with colleagues or learners—and reflecting on the process—is necessary to become expert at ALL for supporting the development of learner autonomy. Engaging in reflection by oneself through internal dialog is useful, confidential, and is easier to carry out. However, as learning is limited to one's own experiences and insights, there is a danger of the interpretations being unhelpful, for example: too limiting, too strict, or even overly optimistic. Dialog with others is appealing due to the positive feelings aroused from being listened to by someone who empathizes with you. In addition, the dialog is more powerful as it not only provides new perspectives, but also challenges a mentee or advisee to look beyond their self-imposed boundaries (Brockbank et al., 2002). It is through shared dialog that transformational learning takes place (Brockbank & McGill, 2006).

Having established the need for dialog in mentoring, it is useful to look at an example flow of a mentoring session with an advisor peer.

1. Ice-breaking talk
2. Using a tool to uncover issues and provide background information
3. Setting the focus by using basic advising strategies
4. Broadening perspectives by using advanced advising strategies
5. Clarifying future visions
6. Reflecting on the session together
7. Writing a post-session reflection

This structure and the IRD enables advisors to reflect critically and explore themselves from different perspectives. This process does not occur through casual workplace conversation or through internal dialog alone. In addition, Kato (2012) noticed that the process was effective at building strong rapport between advisors and a mentor. In fact, the mentoring process and being a mentor to others is an integral part of advisor education as taking the role of a mentor is challenging, and normally requires the use of more advanced strategies and approaches than those typically used with language learners. Kato (2022, in press) stresses the importance of mentoring for new advisors to not only support their developing practice, but also ensure their well-being. Kato (2022, in press) maps out a mentoring program for advisors that includes tools that build connections and mutual trust between the mentor and the mentee which have reciprocal benefits.

Evaluating and demonstrating the effectiveness of advising

Anyone who has been involved with ALL firsthand will undoubtedly have experienced the many benefits of the process. Learning advisors witness positive and transformational effects on learners over time, or even within a single session. For example, advisors see learners developing a deeper sense of awareness of themselves and their learning; they see learners demonstrating deeper levels of thinking; and observe how learners create and implement more effective programs of self-directed study over time. In addition, learners achieve their linguistic goals because of their own efforts and experience academic success. Although this firsthand 'evidence' might be sufficient on a personal level, sometimes there is a need to demonstrate these outcomes more systematically to others, such as colleagues or university administrators, especially when applying for funding or other kinds of support. The challenge is demonstrating that these outcomes are as a result of advising specifically and not other experiences that a student may be participating in, such as classroom learning, clubs, hobbies, or part time jobs.

One way of demonstrating the influence of ALL on learning is through collecting and analyzing learner self-reports and reflections. These might take the form of weekly or periodically written journal entries, or responses to guided reflective questions possibly using a tool (Kato & Mynard, 2016). Guided reflection questions might include, for example:

- How is your satisfaction with your learning?
- Do you feel your English has improved? How do you know?
- What were the main reasons for this improvement (if any)?
- What do advising sessions mean to you?
- Looking back at your language learning this semester, were there any powerful moments? Can you explain what happened and why they were powerful?

The analysis of learner reflections can be strengthened with interviews (Noguchi et al., 2018), retrospective interviews or stimulated recall (Castro, 2019; McCarthy, 2012; Mynard, 2010, 2012, 2018), questionnaires (Curry et al., 2017), advisor field notes or reflections (Mynard, 2018), and the examination of learning artifacts (Curry et al., 2017). Taking a longitudinal approach is beneficial for uncovering learner experiences over time and there is a growing number of studies taking this approach (e.g., McLoughlin & Mynard, 2018; Mynard, 2017, 2018a; Noguchi et al., 2018). Through case-study analysis of individual learners, we can see whether ALL has had an influence in specific ways. For example, we can pinpoint actual points in the learning process where shifts occurred. However, more case studies are needed before we are able to see patterns demonstrating general ways in which ALL supports learning.

As university administrators are likely to request quantitative data, the following data might also be useful to collect:

- The number of advising sessions conducted.
- Degrees of learner satisfaction obtained from a Likert-type questionnaire.
- Frequencies of occurrences of evaluative comments from an open-ended questionnaire or series of interview transcripts related to attitudes to advising (e.g., Shelton-Strong, 2020).
- Depth of thinking evident in written reflections as analyzed on a rubric or framework. For example, the levels of reflection chart by Fleck and Fitzpatrick (2010), the learning trajectory by Kato and Mynard (2016), or the community of inquiry framework by Garrison, Anderson, and Archer (2000).

Future directions

We predict that along with an increased focus on outside class learning in teacher training courses and increased research and publications, advising will soon be at the center of how support is provided in practical terms for LBC. However, two specific focus areas that are important for the future of ALL are (1) the development of online practices, and (2) an expanded research agenda.

Online practices for ALL

Until recently, research or even simple descriptions of practices for online ALL have been scarce and most 1-1 advising has taken place in person. However, due to the Covid-19 global pandemic that began in 2020, many advising programs were forced to migrate online, and interest in online ALL suddenly increased. At the time of writing, only a few studies existed related to online advising, but we have seen that it clearly has enormous potential for the future of the field, not just as an emergency provision during a pandemic. For example, it seems that many learners are generally comfortable with attending online advising sessions; Davies et al. (2020) in Japan and Ruiz-Guerrero (2020) in Mexico provided data indicating that advising appointments had increased year-on-year once the service shifted online. Mynard and Shelton-Strong (in preparation) discovered that students reported mainly positive emotions experiences in online advising sessions, and found that in most cases, learners perceived no big difference in the quality of service between online and face-to-face advising. In fact, they identified several benefits of online advising such as convenience, privacy, and comfort. Advisors making the shift to online ALL as reported by Davies et al. (2020) attempted to replicate their practices in the new environment by using tools and strategies and drawing on the technology affordances to facilitate this. One observation was that some of the advisors used more of the L1 than usual when conducting online advising sessions due to technical or acoustic challenges. Results of a study by Guban-Caisido (2020) in the Philippines indicated that a focus on psychosocial and metacognitive issues in online advising sessions was greatly appreciated by learners studying remotely in precarious and stressful times. In general, training was not available to prepare advisors in various contexts for such a big and sudden change in their practice, but informal learning from each other within a community of practice has been reported to be an effective method of developing the necessary new skills (Kelly et al., 2020).

Expanding the diversity of research in ALL

Although research in advising has been increasing in the past ten years, it is still somewhat on the fringes of applied linguistics. As interest in advising and in LBC in general increases, we will also see an increase in the diversity of research in ALL. Researchers to date have investigated several aspects of ALL such as features of the discourse/dialogic features, the role of emotions, and case studies (see Mynard et al., 2018 and Mynard 2020a for summaries). These areas of scholarship are very important as they not only contribute to the field and enhance our knowledge of advising practice, but they also contribute to the continuing professional development of learning advisor both for those conducting the research that examines their practice, but for those new to the field who can see real examples of ALL in practice (Mynard et al., 2018). However, if we are to contribute to the wider field of applied linguistics more substantially, we need to look to other fields to inform our research practices and draw on both psychological and neurological research.

In terms of psychological research, we can look to the developing field of the psychology of language learning, and indeed to mainstream psychology itself. Although applied linguistics developed a parallel literature, there is much overlap when we consider our common interests in, for example, how people learn, why people do what they do, and in ongoing motivation for learning. In recent years, we have become more familiar in theories related to motivation, emotion, and well-being, and acknowledge the central role these psychological factors play in learning. However, more research in ALL from psychological perspectives is needed. This work has begun, for example, drawing on work by Deci and Ryan (1987) and Reeve (2009), we can take a self-determination theory (SDT) perspective when framing and researching our work as learning advisors (Mynard, 2020a; Mynard & Shelton-Strong, 2019; Shelton-Strong, 2020; Shelton-Strong & Mynard, 2020; Shelton-Strong & Tassinari, 2022). SDT is a broad theory of human motivation and wellness that has a robust research tradition. Although SDT has been applied to fields ranging from sports to business, it has not been explored to a large degree in applied linguistics and hardly at all in LBC or advising. SDT has provided evidence from many previous studies and reliable and valid instruments that can be adapted for ALL research.

Neuroscientific research may also have much to contribute to the research agenda to develop our understanding of ALL. It can add a fresh perspective as we can observe and measure changes in the brain, giving a different information that can enhance what we learn from psychological methods (Reeve & Lee, 2018). Drawing on both psychology and neuroscience, for example, we can obtain deeper insights about motivational constructs. Whereas psychological research identifies information related to traits (i.e., an enduring personality feature), neuroscience research can uncover information about states (i.e., situationally or environmentally induced phenomena). Neuroimaging results can be correlated with self-report trait psychological measures for a greater understanding of an educational intervention such as ALL over time (see Mynard, 2020b for a summary of some relevant studies which combine neuroscientific and psychological data in language learning).

Although neuroscience research has not yet been applied to ALL, we can learn from research in the related fields of coaching and counseling. For example, the field of coaching has used brain imaging research to look at the effects of coaching dialogs over time. Using fMRI technology, neuroimages can be examined which show physiological changes in the brain indicating responses such as brain activity showing enhanced future visioning and positive emotions (Cesaro et al., 2010; Jack, Boyatzis, Khawaja, Passarelli, & Leckie, 2013). According to brain imaging research, face-to-face dialog further enhances brain activities in these areas (Boyzatis, 2015). Neuroimaging in addition to psychological and other measures have been used to inform counseling practices (Goncalves & Perrone-McGovern, 2014), for example, by examining approaches and interventions and practices. Clearly, this exciting area has huge potential for the field of ALL. More investment in research is needed in the coming years to continue to inform our practice and to have a more significant influence on accepted practices in applied linguistics in the future.

Reflection questions

1 What do you think are the main differences between *teaching* and *advising*?
2 What do you think are the most important qualities of learning advisors?
3 How would you best support different learners through ALL, for example, (a) a learner with a high degree of awareness about themselves and their learning, and (b) a learner who is largely unaware of how they best learn and has never made decisions about language learning before?

Recommended readings

Mozzon-McPherson, M., & Tassinari, M. G. (2020). From language teachers to language learning advisors: A journey map. *Philologia Hispalensis, 34*(1), 121–139.
 Mozzon-McPherson and Tassinari are two veteran experts in the field of ALL and this recent paper gives an overview of the principles and practices of ALL and how it is an important role that is distinct from language teaching. The article examines how ALL draws on counseling, psychology, and coaching, and how it has become an integrated academic practice. From Mozzon-McPherson and Tassinari's examination of the literature on ALL, they identify four core advisor competences: conceptual knowledge (i.e., how languages are learned and how to use advising strategies to facilitate dialog); socio-cultural competence (i.e., how to build rapport, listen effectively, and empathize with learners); the personal and professional competence (i.e., having self-awareness and

self-management skills); and dialogical competence (i.e., understanding how the environment and use of dialog affect learning). The article also provides a useful taxonomy of 44 advising strategies compiled from the literature.

Rubin, J. (Ed.) (2007). Language counselling. *System, 35*.

This special issue includes five seminal papers on ALL (termed 'counseling' here) and an introduction by Joan Rubin. The special issue was significant in establishing the field and presents experiences of practitioners in the field with a focus on training and support they might need. In the introduction, Rubin gives a brief overview of the origins of ALL, a summary of exemplary training, details of counseling practices, and some challenges faced by those attempting to institutionalize advising. Although we have made headway in terms of expansion of the practice since this special issue was published in 2007, some of the challenges still remain and this collection of papers is essential reading for everyone in the field.

Kato, S., & Mynard, J. (2015). *Reflective dialogue: Advising in language learning.* Routledge, New York.

This book represents our experiences with understanding the practice of advising and of training other colleagues in ALL. Based on thousands of hours of advising practice, this book was designed to be a practical guide for new advisors to the field. It contains 35 sample advising dialogs, 16 basic advising strategies, 8 practical training activities, and 36 tools that can facilitate advising dialog. These are brought together through the concept of transformational advising. The book can be used alone, but ideally it should be used in collaboration with colleagues so that everyone engages in IRD as part of the process.

References

Benson, P. (2011). *Teaching and researching autonomy in language learning* (2nd Ed.). Harlow, UK: Pearson Education.

Boyzatis, R. E. (2015). *Coaching with compassion to inspire sustained learning and development. Module 5.1. Inspiring leadership through emotional intelligence.* Retrieved from: https://www.coursera.org/course/lead-ei

Brockbank, A., & McGill, I. (2006). *Facilitating reflective learning through mentoring and coaching.* London, UK: Kogan Page.

Brockbank, A., McGill, I., & Beech, N. (2002). *Reflective learning in practice.* Aldershot, UK: Gower Publishing.

Carson, L., & Mynard, J. (2012). Introduction. In J. Mynard & L. Carson (Eds.), *Advising in language learning: Dialogue, tools and context* (pp. 3–25). Harlow, UK: Pearson.

Castro, E. (2019). Motivational dynamics in language advising sessions: A case study. *Studies in Self-Access Learning Journal, 10*(1), 5–20. https://doi.org/10.37237/100102

Cesaro, R. L., Boyzatis, R. E., Khawaja, M., Passarelli, A., Barry, K. P., Begany, K., & Kack, A. I. (2010). *Neural correlates of inspirational mentoring.* Paper presented at Society for Neuroscience annual meeting, Chicago, October 19, 2010. Retrieved from http://www.tonyjack.org/sfn2009_inspirationalmentoring.pdf

Chávez Sánchez, M., & Peña Clavel, M. (2015). The development of CELE-UNAM mediateca. *Studies in Self-Access Learning Journal, 6*(2), 219–230. https://doi.org/10.37237/060206

Curry, N., Mynard, J., Noguchi, J., & Watkins, S. (2017). Evaluating a self-directed language learning course in a Japanese university. *International Journal of Self-Directed Learning, 14*(1), 37–57.

Davies, H., Wongsarnpigoon, I., Watkins, S., Vola Ambinintsoa, D., Terao, R., Stevenson, R., Imamura, Y., Edlin, C., & Bennett, P. A. (2020). A self-access center's response to COVID-19: Maintaining stability, connectivity, well-being, and development during a time of great change. *Studies in Self-Access Learning Journal, 11*(3), 135–147. https://doi.org/10.37237/110304

Deci, E. L., & Ryan, R. M. (1987). The support of autonomy and the control of behavior. *Journal of Personality and Social Psychology, 53*(6), 1024–1037. https://doi.org/10.1037/0022-3514.53.6.1024

Dewey, J. (1933). *How we think: A restatement of the relation of reflective thinking to the educative process.* New York, NY: D. C. Heath & Co Publishers.

Everhard, C. J., Mynard, J., with Smith, R. (Eds.) (2011). *Autonomy in language learning: Opening a can of worms.* Hong Kong: Candlin and Mynard.

Farrell, T. S. C. (2012). *Promoting teacher reflection in second language learning.* New York, NY: Routledge

Fleck, R., & Fitzpatrick, G. (2010). *Reflecting on reflection: Framing a design landscape.* OZCHI '10: Proceedings of the 22nd Conference of the Computer-Human Interaction Special Interest Group of Australia on Computer-Human Interaction. November 2010. https://doi.org/10.1145/1952222.1952269

Garrison, D. R., Anderson, T., & Archer, W. (2000). Critical inquiry in a text-based environment: Computer conferencing in higher education model. *The Internet and Higher Education, 2*(2–3), 87–105. https://doi.org/10.1016/s1096-7516(00)00016-6

Goncalves, O. F., & Perrone-McGovern, K. M. (2014). A neuroscience agenda for counseling psychology research. *Journal of Counseling Psychology, 61*, 507–512. https://doi.org/10.1037%2Fcou0000026

Guban-Caisido, D. (2020). Language advising as psychosocial intervention for first time self-access language learners in the time of COVID-19: Lessons from the Philippines. *Studies in Self-Access Learning Journal, 11*(3), 148–163. https://doi.org/10.37237/110305

Holec, H. (2000). Le C.R.A.P.E.L. a travers les ages [CRAPEL through the ages]. *Mélanges, 25*, 5–12. http://www.atilf.fr/IMG/pdf/02_holec.pdf.

Horai, K., & Wright, E. (2016). Raising awareness: Learning advising as an in-class activity. *Studies in Self-Access Learning Journal, 7*(2), 197–208. https://doi.org/10.37237/070208

Jack, A. I., Boyatzis, R., Khawaja, M., Passarelli, A., & Leckie, R. (2013). Visioning in the brain: An fMRI study of inspirational coaching and mentoring. *Social Neuroscience, 8*(4), 369–384. https://doi.org/10.1080/17470919.2013.808259

Karlsson, L. (2012). Sharing stories: Autobiographical narratives in advising. In J. Mynard & L. Carson (Eds.), *Advising in language learning: Dialogue, tools, and context* (pp. 185–204). Harlow, UK: Pearson.

Karlsson, L., Kjisik, F., & Nordlund, J. (2007). Language counselling: A critical and integral component in promoting an autonomous community of learning. *System, 35*(1), 46–65. https://doi.org/10.1016%2Fj.system.2006.10.006

Kato, S. (2012). Professional development for learning advisors: Facilitating the intentional reflective dialogue. *Studies in Self-Access Learning Journal, 3*(1), 74–92. https://doi.org/10.37237%2F030106

Kato, S. (2022, in press). Establishing high-quality relationships through a mentoring programme: Relationships motivation theory. In J. Mynard & S. J. Shelton-Strong (Eds.), *Autonomy support beyond the language learning classroom: A self-determination theory perspective*. Bristol: Multilingual Matters.

Kato, S., & Mynard, J. (2016). *Reflective dialogue: Advising in language learning*. New York: Routledge.

Kato, S., & Sugawara, H. (2009). Action-oriented language learning advising: A new approach to promote independent language learning. *The Journal of Kanda University of International Studies, 21*, 455–476.

Kelly, R. (1996). Language counselling for learner autonomy: The skilled helper in self-access language learning. In R. Pemberton, E. S. L. Li, W. W. F. Or, & H. Pierson (Eds.), *Taking control: Autonomy in language learning* (pp. 93–113). Hong Kong University Press.

Kelly, A., Johnston, N., & Matthews, S. (2020). Online self-access learning support during the COVID-19 pandemic: An Australian university case study. *Studies in Self-Access Learning Journal, 11*(3), 187–198. https://doi.org/10.37237/110307

Killion, J. P., & G. R. Todnem. (1991). A process for personal theory building. *Educational Leadership, 48*(6), 14–16. http://www.ascd.org/ASCD/pdf/journals/ed_lead/el_199103_killion.pdf

Lantolf, J. P., & Poehner, M. E. (2008). Introduction. In J. P. Lantolf & M. E. Poehner (Eds.), *Sociocultural theory and the teaching of second languages* (pp. 1–32). Sheffield: Equinox.

Little, D. (1991). *Learner autonomy 1: Definitions, issues and problems*. Dublin: Authentik.

Ludwig, C., & Mynard, J. (Eds.) (2012). *Autonomy in language learning: Advising in action*. Canterbury: IATEFL.

McCarthy, T. (2010). Breaking down the dialogue: Building a framework of advising discourse. *Studies in Linguistics and Language Teaching, 21*, 39–79.

McCarthy, T. (2012). Advising-in-action: Exploring the inner dialogue of the learning advisor. In J. Mynard & L. Carson (Eds.), *Advising in language learning: Dialogue, tools and context* (pp. 105–126). Harlow: Pearson.

McLoughlin, D., & Mynard, J. (2017). How do self-directed learners keep going? The role of interest in sustained learning. 2017 *PanSIG Journal*, 74–81. https://pansig.org/publications/2017/2017_PanSIG_Journal.pdf

Mezirow, J. (1991). *Transformative dimensions of adult learning*. San Francisco, CA: Jossey-Bass.

Mozzon-McPherson, M. (2012). The skills of counselling in advising: Language as a pedagogical tool. In J. Mynard & L. Carson (Eds.), *Advising in language learning: Dialogue, tools and context* (pp. 43–64). Harlow: Pearson.

Mozzon-McPherson, M., & Tassinari, M. G. (2020). From language teachers to language learning advisors: A journey map. *Philologia Hispalensis, 1*(34), 121–139. http://doi.org/10.12795/PH.2020.v34.i01.07

Mozzon-McPherson, M., & Vismans, R. (2001). *Beyond language teaching: Towards language advising.* London: CELT.

Mynard, J. (2010). Promoting cognitive and metacognitive awareness through self-study modules: An investigation into advisor comments. In W. M. Chan, S. Chi, K. N. Chin, J. Istanto, M. Nagami, J. W. Sew, T. Suthiwan, & I. Walker (Eds.), *Proceedings of the Fourth centre for language studies international conference* (pp. 610–627). Singapore: National University of Singapore.

Mynard, J. (2012). A suggested model for advising in language learning. In J. Mynard & L. Carson (Eds.), *Advising in language learning: Dialogue, tools and context* (pp. 26–41). Harlow: Pearson.

Mynard, J. (2017). The role of advising in developing an awareness of learning processes: Three case studies. *Studies in Linguistics and Language Teaching, 28*, 123–161.

Mynard, J. (2018). "Still sounds quite a lot to me, but try it and see". Reflecting on my non-directive advising stance. *Relay Journal, 1*(1), 98–107. https://doi.org/10.37237/relay/010109

Mynard, J. (2019). Self-access learning and advising: Promoting language learner autonomy beyond the classroom. In H. Reinders, S. Ryan & S. Nakamura (Eds.), *Innovations in language learning and teaching: The case of Japan* (pp.185–220). London: Palgrave Macmillan.

Mynard, J. (2020a). Advising for language learner autonomy: Theory, practice, and future directions. In M. Jiménez Raya & F. Vieira (Eds.), *Autonomy in language education: Present and future avenues* (pp. 46–62). New York: Routledge. https://doi.org/10.4324/9780429261336

Mynard, J. (2020b). Advising, metacognition, and motivation in language learning: A neuroscientific perspective. 64–45. Pp】研究論文）【2020（第26号　言語科学研究　神田外語大学大学院紀要 [*Language Science Research, KUIS Graduate School Bulletin*], *26*, 45–64.

Mynard, J., Kato, S., & Yamamoto, K. (2018). Reflective practice in advising: Introduction to the column. *Relay Journal, 1*(1), 55–64. https://doi.org/10.37237/relay/010105

Mynard, J., & Navarro, D. (2010). Dialogue in self-access learning. In A. Stoke (Ed.), *JALT2009 conference proceedings: The teaching-learning dialogue: An active mirror* (pp. 95–102). http://jalt-publications.org/archive/proceedings/2009/E008.pdf

Mynard, J., & Stevenson, R. (2017). Promoting learner autonomy and self-directed learning: The evolution of a SALC curriculum. *Studies in Self-Access Learning Journal, 8*(2), 169–182. https://doi.org/10.37237/080209

Noguchi, J., Curry, N., Mynard, J., & Watkins, S. (2018). Students' perceptions of the impact of a self-directed learning skills training program on language learning. *Studies in Linguistics and Language Teaching, 29*, 91–117.

Peeters, W., & Mynard, J. (2019). Peer collaboration and learner autonomy in online interaction spaces. *Relay Journal, 2*(2), 450–458. https://doi.org/10.37237/relay/020218

Reeve, J. (2009). Why teachers adopt a controlling motivating style toward students and how they can become more autonomy supportive. *Educational Psychologist, 44*(3), 159–175. https://doi.org/10.1080/00461520903028990

Reeve, J., & Lee, W. (2018). A neuroscientific perspective on basic psychological needs. *Journal of Personality, 87*(1), 102–114. doi: 10.1111/jopy.12390

Rogers, C. (1951). *Client-centred therapy.* Boston: Houghton Mifflin.

Rubin, J. (2001). Language learner self-management. *Journal of Asian Pacific Communication, 11*(1), 25–37. https://doi.org/10.1075%2Fjapc.11.1.05rub

Rubin, J. (2005). The expert language learner: a review of good language learner studies and learner strategies. In: K. Johnson (Ed.), *Expertise in second language learning and Teaching.* London: Palgrave Macmillan.

Rubin, J. (2007). Introduction to a special issue: Language counseling. *System, 35*(1), 1–9. http://doi.org/10.1016/j.system.2006.11.001

Ruiz-Guerrero, A. (2020). Our self-access experience in times of COVID. *Studies in Self-Access Learning Journal, 11*(3), 250–262. https://doi.org/10.37237/110311

Ryan, R. M., & Deci, E. L. (2017). *Self-determination theory: Basic psychological needs in motivation, development, and wellness.* New York: Guilford Press.

Schön, D. (1983). *The reflective practitioner. How professionals think in action.* New York: Basic Books

Shelton-Strong, S. J. (2020). Advising in language learning and the support of learners' basic psychological needs: A self-determination theory perspective. *Language Teaching Research*, 1–23. http://doi.org/10.1177/1362168820912355

Shelton-Strong, S. J., & Tassinari, M. G. (2022). Facilitating an autonomy-supportive learning climate: Advising in language learning and basic psychological needs. In J. Mynard & S. J. Shelton-Strong

(Eds.), *Autonomy support beyond the language learning classroom: A self-determination theory perspective*. Bristol: Multilingual Matters.

Sinclair, B. (2011). Learner training. In C. J. Everhard, J. Mynard, with R. Smith (Eds.), *Autonomy in language learning: Opening can of worms* (pp. 91–98). Hong Kong: Candlin & Mynard.

Tassinari, M. G., & Ciekanski, M. (2013). Accessing the self in self-access learning: Emotions and feelings in language advising. *Studies in Self-Access Learning Journal*, 4(4), 262–280. https://doi.org/10.37237/040404

Thornton, K., & Mynard, J. (Eds.) (2012). Special issue on advising for language learner autonomy. *Studies in Self-Access Learning Journal*, 3(1), 1–132. https://doi.org/10.37237/030101

Valdivia, S., McLoughlin, D., & Mynard, J. (2012). The portfolio: A practical tool for advising language learners in a self-access centre in Mexico. In J. Mynard & L. Carson (Eds.), *Advising in language learning: Dialogue, tools and context* (pp. 105–110). Harlow: Longman.

Yamashita, H. (2015). Affect and the development of learner autonomy through advising. *Studies in Self-Access Learning Journal*, 6(1), 62–85. https://doi.org/10.37237/060105

Yamashita, H., & Mynard, J. (Eds.) (2015). *Special issue, Dialogue and advising in self-access learning, Studies in Self-Access Language Learning*, 6(1), 1–159. https://doi.org/10.37237/060101

18
ONLINE LEARNER COMMUNITIES FOR FOSTERING AUTONOMOUS LEARNING BEYOND THE CLASSROOM

Wenli Wu and Qing Ma

Introduction

With the prevalence of the 5G wireless standard and other forms of mobile technology in the 21st century, autonomous learning beyond the classroom has generated heated discussions. However, it is probable that learners who have access to technology will use it to support their informal learning efforts (Colugh et al., 2009). Many people will agree that 2020 was a year that will be impossible to forget due to COVID-19, which has directly affected millions of lives in terms of health and has reshaped almost every facet of human life (including education). For example, Tam and El-Azar (2020) claim the pandemic has reshaped education because most universities and schools around the world have been forced to adopt online teaching modes to prevent the spread of virus while continuing to deliver their programmes and courses; students have been required to stay at home and interact online with their tutors and peers, either synchronically or asynchronously. In this new era, people are also being urged to update their learning skills and become lifelong learners to keep up with transformations like these (Laal & Salamati, 2012). In other words, learning has become a part of life—a true lifestyle. Thus, learners seek to use whatever techniques, resources, and tools are most suitable for their learning needs and personal preferences beyond the classroom (Colugh et al., 2009). For example, learners can choose to explore the colossal library of the World Wide Web on their own. In contrast, they can also make good use of social networking platforms to learn collaboratively in online learning environments using smartphones or iPads.

According to Ke and Hoadley (2009), the concept of autonomous learning has been successfully integrated into the notion of online learning communities (OLCs), which has become a growing feature in the landscape of educational technology. Whether by accident or intent, learners can enter informal social network sites and engage in language learning, entertainment, and socializing (Lomicka & Lord, 2009). In these settings, they can participate and interact with others as a group and provide/receive feedback. The research of Wu et al. (2017) demonstrated that students become autonomous learners after engaging in OLCs because of "more time engagement in the instruction, lively interaction, and constructive feedback" (p. 151).

In this chapter, we will discuss how OLCs can promote autonomous learning, especially in informal settings after classroom learning takes place. First, some key concepts are reviewed, such as learner autonomy, self-directed learning (SDL), a community of practice, and an OLC. We then discuss the implications of using OLCs for facilitating autonomous learning in informal settings, followed by suggestions for future directions of autonomous learning beyond the classroom. Finally, we provide three reflective questions and three annotated Recommended readings tips for individuals wishing to learn more about this topic.

Key concepts

Autonomous learning

Autonomy was initially addressed in the foreign language (FL) teaching field with the emergence of the communicative approach in the 1970s (Paiva & Braga, 2008). Since then, it has been regarded as an important notion in language learning. Littlewood (1996) proposes that willingness and ability are two important components of autonomous behaviour. In addition, Littlewood (1996) states that an autonomous individual should be a learner, person, and communicator simultaneously. Paiva (2006) claims that autonomy is a socio-cognitive system because it involves an individual's mental states and processes allied with social dimensions. Similarly, Lai (2017) states the multidimensionality of autonomy "is reflected in the duality of meaning, in the nature of autonomy, in the sociality of autonomy and in the teachability of autonomy" (p. 6). Although learner autonomy suffers from not having a clear definition (Thanasoulas 2000), it is agreed that an autonomous learner has the ability to take charge of their learning effectively (Little, 1991). To clarify this term further, Benson (2001) suggests learner autonomy is "a multidimensional capacity" (p. 47). Recently, Huang and Benson (2013) have suggested that autonomous learners should (a) have the desire to take an active role in their learning, (b) have the ability to learn, and (c) have the freedom to learn. The *desire* dimension means autonomous learners are motivated to work towards a goal, take purposeful actions towards that goal, and persist with their attempts. The *ability* dimension refers to autonomous learners possessing the strategies or skills to learn a target language while also being able to plan or organize their learning, take actions to promote the planned actions, and ultimately evaluate their learning process. Finally, the *freedom* dimension refers to the context and chances for adopting an active role in autonomous learning (Huang & Benson, 2013). In this chapter, we subscribe to Huang and Benson's (2013) definition of learner autonomy and their assertion that autonomous learning contains these three dimensions.

Autonomous learning and self-directed learning

According to a definition of learner autonomy by Huang and Benson (2013), in a sense, autonomous learners can also be perceived as self-directed learners. Moreover, self-directed learning (SDL) is a method of coping with constant changes in a new world (Knowles, 1975). If individuals can recognize their self-directing capacities, they enable themselves with the impetus for self-regulatory patterns of research, which then can serve them as the primary agents of their own change (Bandura, 1977). The study of SDL was initiated by Malcom Knowles in the 1970s. He defined SDL as "a process in which individuals take the initiative, with or without the help of others, to diagnose their learning needs, formulate learning goals, identify resources for learning, select and implement learning strategies, and evaluate learning outcomes" (Knowles, 1975, p. 18). Song and Hill (2007) developed a model with the specific aim of understanding SDL in online environments, which was a new perspective for understanding how learning contexts influence SDL in the current era of technology. Further, it emphasizes that the dynamic interactions between the following three components are key to understanding SDL: the learning context, personal attributes, and the learning process.

Learning in the 21st century manifests itself in a variety of contexts, such as face-to-face classroom instruction, web-based courses, computer-based instruction, and a blend of the physical classroom and online environment. As discussed above, autonomous learning overlaps with self-directed learning in many aspects, so they are often used interchangeably by some researchers (e.g., Lai, 2017). For example, the processes of autonomous learning are manifested by certain key features innate to self-directed learning, such as defining tasks, setting goals and planning, implementing strategies, monitoring and reflecting on a task, and self or context. Another similarity lies in that autonomous learners should have the ability to take control of their learning in terms of desire and ability (Huang & Benson, 2013); self-directed learners should also have control over all learning decisions. Finally, both autonomous learning and self-directed learning can take place either in a teacher-guided classroom or beyond it (Guglielmino, 2008).

In contrasting self-directed learning with autonomous learning, the major difference is in the origins of the concepts. Self-directed learning is a concept that originated with adult education in the 1970s (Saks & Leijen, 2014), whereas autonomous learning is a concept that was originally found in the political science and philosophical literature (Lai, 2017). With regard to the popularity of the two concepts, achieving learning autonomy is an important goal for many language courses in the world, and references to learner autonomy can be found in many published textbooks (e.g., Thornton, 2013), while self-directed learning is a step on the path to being a fully autonomous learner (Dickinson, 1987). In other words, self-directed learning is an important feature for becoming an autonomous learner (He et al., 2011).

Autonomous learning and self-regulated learning

Autonomous learning is defined as a learner's ability to take control of their own learning. Accordingly, Palfreyman and Benson (2019) state that a combination of autonomy, learning strategies (e.g., Wenden, 1991), and learner beliefs (e.g., Cotterall, 1995) can help in understanding the cognitive aspects involved in autonomous learning. Self-regulation has been studied extensively in the field of educational psychology and is suggested by Nakata (2014) as a key element that can help autonomous learners to conduct effective strategy training. Moreover, self-regulation can be defined as "self-generated thoughts, feelings and actions that are planned and cyclically adapted to the attainment of personal goals" (Zimmerman, 2000, p. 14). To conceptualize self-regulated learning, Zimmerman (2011) proposed a framework to explain the relationships among SRL processes and paramount learning beliefs and outcomes that contains three phases: forethought, performance, and self-regulation. In this framework, Phase I involves activities such as "goal setting" and "strategic planning", where self-motivated learners prepare for and improve future learning actions. Phase II is the performance stage, where learners use strategies to take control of their own learning and seek help when required. Phase III comprises self-reflection, in which learners self-judge and self-react to their learning efforts, with the intention of maximizing learning outcomes. Zimmerman's framework suggests that the self-regulatory process includes factors other than learner strategies, such as goal setting, strategic planning, and action plans (Tseng et al., 2006). Above all, self-regulation involves learners being active participants in their own learning (Rose et al., 2018).

Autonomous learning and self-regulated learning share some similarities, as both emphasize intrinsic motivation as a key component, and both concepts require the participants' active engagement, goal-oriented behaviour, responsibility, control and metacognition (Deci & Ryan, 2002). However, they should not be confused with each other (Papamitsiou & Economides, 2019). The core of the concept of autonomy is to put the learner at the starting point of the learning task, as they have the freedom to choose (Andrade & Bunker, 2009). In contrast, SRL emphasizes a process that comprises a series of strategies, and the core of this concept is how learners can be effective without relying on the teacher's control or structure (Reeve, 2009; Stefanou et al., 2013).

Autonomous learning and online learning communities

Returning to Huang and Benson's (2013) three dimensions of autonomous learning that we discussed earlier, the freedom dimension means learners have the right to take control of their own learning (Benson, 2009) and that they also have freedom from others' control (Hamilton, 2013). In a similar way, Nunan (1996) states that contextual factors such as the philosophy of a culture or community can influence the degree of autonomy, as individuals could be "autonomous in one area while dependent in another" (Murray, 1999, p. 301).

A community is regarded as important for autonomous learning (Tassinari, 2017) because it provides opportunities and spaces for learners to be active participants (Huang & Benson, 2013). A number of researchers have stated the benefits of learning within a community. For example, Haythornthwait et al. (2000) assert that learners feel less isolated in a learning community in an online context. Further, Dede (1996) claims that membership in a community promotes support from other learners, a speedy exchange of information, collaborative learning among group members, dedication to fulfil the goals of the group, and satisfaction with the efforts and procedures of the group. In agreement with the researchers mentioned previously, Tassinari (2017) states that a community of practice (or a learning community) would be beneficial for autonomous learners to practise within a given context. In a learning community, "newcomers" become more proficient in the areas in which they are practising through collaborative learning with others who also belong to the community (Wenger, 1998). Wenger's view is rooted in a social learning perspective, which asserts that learning takes place when people observe other people in the group (Merriam & Caffarella, 1991). During this learning process, self-regulated individuals serve as the major agents of their own change. Moreover, while learners with higher self-directing capacities could benefit more from a favourable learning environment, it can also foster learners to become more self-directed (Bandura, 1977). Lave and Wenger (1991) propose that "communities of practice" are everywhere and that people are generally engaged in many of them.

In the 21st century, educational technologies provide learners with numerous platforms for selecting information, sharing knowledge and skills, and engaging in collaborative learning. Moreover, advances in digital technologies and internet connections have changed the ways in which people interact with others and develop themselves (Hine, 2000). In other words, there are many new contexts within modern technology where members can engage in common activities and learn from individuals who are more experienced.

An OLC is an environment where continuous learning processes are obtained through receiving, generating, exploring, and shaping information. This is then facilitated in the community through interaction, participation, and communication among learners (Carlen &

Jobring, 2005), which can then be regarded as a special type of community of practice in the context of online learning.

OLCs provide a new domain or context in which SDL can take place, providing more opportunities to foster autonomous learning either within or beyond a classroom setting. In a technology-enhanced OLC, individuals learn to plan, monitor, and evaluate their learning through interaction with peers and more experienced individuals. In practice, OLCs are increasingly being employed for the professional development of teachers, for creating knowledge-sharing settings (such as medical support groups and corporate helpdesks), and for formal education (Chang 2003; Pearson, 1998). Research has indicated that OLCs can take place in various new contexts, such as the online community of Duolingo (Palfreyman & Benson, 2019) and the online communities of Facebook users (Alm, 2015). Other forms may include groups formed around certain media, such as BookTubers (Suarez & Arguello, 2020) or bloggers (Tang & Lam, 2014).

Different types of online learning communities

In a digitally connected world, language learners (especially English language learners) can easily obtain additional learning resources and practice opportunities outside the classroom (Suarez & Arguello, 2020). Moreover, many online social networking platforms provide attractive and interactive learning resources for learners; hence, individuals are motivated to enter and explore them. When members of online social platforms share common features (such as learning goals, interests, identifying characteristics, and values) and deliver or support learning activities, online networking platforms can be considered OLCs (Tang & Lam, 2014). There are various social networking platforms, and we list a few currently well-known platforms below to illustrate why they can be regarded as good venues for accommodating OLCs.

Web forums. Web forums are asynchronous discussion platforms that provide services to people who share a specific interest, such as Fanfiction (Henderson, 2015). They are normally free to join, and participants are allowed to discuss various topics and seek help within the group (Sockett & Toffoli, 2012). A healthy, sustainable web forum normally has at least one administrator to issue memberships and monitor the progress of the forum.

Facebook. The multiple interfaces or roles of Facebook (such as author, commenter, respondent, and approver) provide a supportive environment for language learners. With features such as a wall (which has been renamed a number of times throughout the site's history), information posting, blog-type posts, the ability to like and unlike posts and comments, and the ability to send one-on-one messages, learners have a number of opportunities to collaborate with other individuals on the platform (Liu, 2010; Shih, 2011). For example, Facebook has proved a useful platform for motivating university language students to be active second language learners in New Zealand (Alm, 2015).

YouTube. While audiovisual platforms such as YouTube facilitate informal learning practices, watching YouTube videos normally constitutes one-way communication. However, watching streamed media in its original language provides learners with more opportunities for shared language and values, meaning learners can belong to different communities where they can engage with other members (Sockett & Toffoli, 2012). The BookTuber community introduced by Suarez and Arguello (2020) is another type of OLC, one where members have enhanced their critical thinking skills while also being motivated to make progress.

Others. Other social networking platforms (such as LINE, WeChat, WhatsApp, Instagram, and Twitter) could also be considered OLCs. In these, people communicate and can organize together in various ways through some shared characteristic (such as an interest or learning goal) (Hramiak, 2010), thus creating a sense of belonging to that community.

Key issues

Empirical evidence: OLCs as a promising platform for developing learner autonomy

Some empirical research studies support the idea that OLCs demonstrate the potential to foster autonomous learning (Yang, 2016). For example, in Gao's (2007) study of an online community formed by a group of English learners in mainland China, he described a dynamic community in which the Chinese learners aspired to "satisfy their needs for social exchanges and self-assertion in English" (p. 267), even though their opportunities for using English in real life were limited. The Chinese learners in his study practised language skills in an English club, which can be regarded as a supportive learning community. They gained a sense of belonging, which helped to sustain their continuing efforts of participating in the community. Gao (2007) further reported that strong learners played important roles in maintaining the cohesion of the community and guiding other participants in making friends by using English. The participants in the community felt relaxed and had an opportunity to be themselves, motivating them to voluntarily participate in the community for relatively long periods of time.

Another example is from Ma (2017), which revealed that mobile-assisted online communities can provide more interactions between language learners and other agents (such as teachers, peers, parents, relatives, and friends), who play important roles in facilitating learning, hence enhancing an individual's autonomous learning. Wu et al. (2017) demonstrated the positive effects that an OLC can engender in a flipped classroom in Taiwan. In their study, students were advised to take control of their own learning activities beyond the classroom setting by using LINE (a mobile app). The students were nurtured to gradually become self-directed learners who were responsible for their own learning, which augmented autonomous learning. Further, Suarez and Arguello (2020) reported on creating an out-of-class BookTuber community that motivated university students to make videos and develop their critical thinking skills, which are essential for peer evaluation and career development. Similarly, Ma (2020) reported on an interesting study in which a group of language learners engaged in co-authoring an online book using a wiki as the platform. The peers were motivated to interact and provide useful feedback for each other to improve the quality of the wiki writing.

Underdeveloped role of experts in online learning communities

From Wenger's (1998) perspective, recognized experts are paramount for building a sustainable community of practice because they can help to nurture less experienced members. This view is supported by Lantolf (2013), who states that human agency can only be developed through social interaction in formal or informal teaching or socialization. A number of empirical studies have also demonstrated the importance of having an expert (or teacher) in online communities. For example, we previously mentioned the importance of a group of strong learners (or coordinators) in the informal online English learning community in Gao's (2007) study. Further, the mobile-assisted informal OLC described by Wu et al. (2017) also benefitted from instructor guidance, allowing students to build confidence and take an active role in the LINE-assisted learning community. Correspondingly, a study by Shea et al. (2006) revealed that a strong and active presence of online instructors has a positive association with students developing a stronger sense of a learning community.

Despite sporadic evidence reported by a few studies (e.g., Shea et al., 2006; Wu et al., 2017), there is a lack of empirical studies in language education that have clearly outlined the role of teachers in OLCs beyond the classroom (Lai, 2015). In addition, research shows that many teachers are not aware of the roles that they could play in enhancing students' autonomous learning outside the classroom (Toffoli & Sockett, 2013). As one relevant example, an online writing community did not lead to intended student learning outcomes in a university in Hong Kong due to low participation and interaction rates (Tang et al., 2020). The authors concluded that a lack of face-to-face teacher guidance before the start of the programme and a lack of teacher supervision during the programme were two critical reasons that contributed to the lack of success of the online writing community. Lai (2015) calls for more research attention and effort to understand how teachers can utilize their influence to enhance learners' out-of-class autonomous use of technology to achieve more satisfactory learning outcomes.

Lack of theoretical guidance in developing learner autonomy in OLC

Since the turn of the new millennium, the development of new technologies (especially mobile technologies) has led to more opportunities for out-of-class informal learning in a variety of contexts. Autonomous learning in this technological era needs to be understood from the perspective of looking at the dynamic interactions between learning contexts, personal attributes, and learning processes (Song & Hill, 2007). As previously mentioned, learner autonomy refers to a learner's ability to take control of their own learning (Huang & Benson, 2013), but it is vague as to exactly what "take control" should mean (Thornton, 2013). The flexibility provided by an online context offers more freedom for learners while creating challenges for the planning and monitoring of their learning, the evaluation of the learning, the learners' use of resources and strategies, and learner motivation (Song et al., 2004). Because self-directed learning is counted as a viable alternative to achieve learner autonomy (He et al., 2011), an updated self-directed learning framework might help. Nevertheless, until recently, Song and Hill's (2007) model is still the most current in terms of SDL (Şentürk & Zeybek, 2019) in an online learning environment because of the "learning context" dimension. To date, there is no theoretical framework for guiding the development of learner autonomy within OLCs. Therefore, there is a need to investigate whether and how learner autonomy could be developed with OLCs and to what extent various factors can help boost learning outcomes within a learning community.

Implications for learner autonomy and learning communities

The issue of fostering autonomous learning continues to be a focus for teachers and learners in language learning. Learners of a second language aspire to become autonomous learners so that they can take control of their learning and become successful in their fields. Moreover, teachers would prefer students who have a strong sense of learner autonomy. This would allow more teaching pedagogies to be applied with ease, which would enhance learning. Although teachers and students have different concerns, both are looking for different strategies or skills to foster autonomous learning journeys. It would appear that OLCs, which are a type of technology-enhanced communities of practice, can foster autonomous learning, especially in informal learning settings. OLCs can also be utilized as powerful tools for sustainable and effective learning (Tang & Lam, 2014).

The key characteristics of OLCs that may facilitate learner autonomy beyond the classroom lie in the following three aspects. First, an experienced "recognized expert" who is often a teacher or facilitator, as shown by Gao (2007) and Wu et al. (2017), should be included in the OLC to play an active role and sustain the OLC. Second, having interaction among members is another key feature of successful OLCs; without this interaction, an OLC will eventually fail (Tang et al., 2020). Third, a sense of community can result in positive feelings that lead to engagement, satisfaction, and learning (Liu et al., 2007; Shea et al., 2006). This promotes increased participation and even deeper engagement (Tinto, 1997).

Learners can benefit from successful OLCs that are active and sustainable. Training in self-regulated learning skills, such as setting goals and planning, implementing learning activities, monitoring, and reflecting, can aid learners in gaining more from these communities. It should also be noted that having learners become more self-regulated can facilitate the growth of a healthy and sustainable OLC. This is because "newcomers" can eventually become established members (and leaders) of the group and attract more newcomers to join (Wenger, 1998). The synergies and dynamics created among the OLC are conducive for developing members' learning autonomy.

Finally, contextual factors such as the culture or community can determine the degree of autonomy (Nunan, 1996). As Wood (2017) states, in cultures high in collectivism (such as China), the identities of individuals are deeply connected to their families, clans, and groups. In contrast, people tend to act relatively independently in cultures high in individualism (such as the United States) because there is a higher value placed on individual goals and identity. From the existing literature, it would appear that people from collectivistic cultural backgrounds are more willing to join and participate in online communities. Further, online communities in which the majority of participants value a collectivistic culture are more likely to achieve shared community goals (such as in improving their English proficiency together). This is similar to the finding of Gao (2007), who described that online English learning communities increased their memberships with many people from mainland China. In contrast, Alm (2015) reported that informal language engagement on Facebook by New Zealand university students was not regarded as useful in a formal language learning setting. However, if one considers that people from cultures higher in collectivism (such as China) feel that their identities are deeply connected to groups, it is reasonable that they will be more comfortable with a learning community. Conversely, people from cultures higher in individualism (such as the United States or New Zealand) will act more independently when compared to their counterparts from a collectivistic cultural background. Hence, interaction and engagement in learning communities are less likely to be perceived as comfortable, especially in informal settings.

Future directions

Most human learning takes place in an informal environment (Eraut, 2000, as cited in Rogers, 2008); hence, the development of new technology and the internet has increased the learning contexts in which naturalistic language learning can occur, regardless of geographical boundaries. However, there is a need for further research into how OLCs can foster autonomous learning beyond the classroom and how effective OLCs can be maintained and sustained. Moreover, it takes devotion and skills to create an OLC (Sekulich, 2020). It is easy to dismiss OLCs created informally by learners if no rules and regulations are established or followed; however, they might represent a need that is being unfulfilled. In addition, the maintenance of an active OLC should not be neglected.

In terms of the SDL model created by Song and Hill (2007), an updated model is required to facilitate a more detailed understanding of the *design* and *support* aspects in mobile-assisted online learning. This is particularly relevant as incidental and informal learning has become increasingly more important to learners (Ma, 2017). For example, Chik (2017) reports that profiles, records, and different types of data have been stored in Duolingo forums over an extended period. While the question of how self-directed learners can utilize this type of data from online platforms using their smartphones in an informal context might be a challenge for researchers, an updated model could provide helpful insights.

There is also a need for a more detailed understanding of whether age plays a role in the formation and sustainability of online learner communities. It is reported that young people prefer using online networks and media to develop second language proficiency (Godwin-Jones, 2018). Further, Wu (2011) reported that university students and white-collar staff in the south-west coastal areas of mainland China are more interested in massive open online courses (MOOCs). It is believed that these cohorts are more comfortable financially than people in other regions of China. Other relevant areas that could be addressed in future research could include the online engagement of primary and secondary students (such as whether and how they form any informal online learner communities) and how this new paradigm affects senior citizens.

Finally, although many researchers have emphasized the importance of recognized experts in OLCs (e.g., Sun et al., 2015), few empirical studies have clearly outlined the role of teachers in informal OLCs (Lai, 2015). Key questions for future research in this area could include why teachers should spend time with informal OLCs and what strategies they could adopt to facilitate autonomous learning in informal OLCs.

Conclusion

Although discussions about autonomous learning beyond the classroom have drawn the attention of many people, using OLCs to foster autonomous learning has been inadequately researched. Rooted in social learning theory, an online learner community is an extension of a community of practice, where learners can meet regularly with common learning goals. Importantly, their presence is not restricted by geographical range due to advances in educational technologies, especially mobile technologies. Most learners who join informal OLCs with shared goals do so voluntarily, meaning they are motivated to take purposeful actions to fulfil their goals. Moreover, the online environment provides a context in which learners can take an active role in the pursuit of their learning. Moreover, through collaborating with others and learning from more experienced experts and peers, learners can gain the skills of planning, monitoring, and evaluating their learning processes, which will help them become autonomous learners. Accordingly, we advocate the creation of sustainable OLCs to foster autonomous learning.

Reflection questions

To advance study in this area, we present the following three reflective questions to extend our discussion:

1. How can an informal online learning community be created to foster autonomous learning?
2. How can online learning communities help learners develop their learning agency?
3. How can learners develop SDL skills within online learning, especially in the mobile-assisted online learning context?

Recommended readings

For those wishing to learn more about using online learning communities to foster autonomous learning beyond the classroom, we recommend the following:

Lai, C. (2015). Modeling teachers' influence on learners' self-directed use of technology for language learning outside the classroom. *Computers & Education, 82,* 74–83.
  This article provides a conceptual model of three types of teacher support that could influence how students use self-directed technology beyond the classroom. Further, it is one of the few empirical studies that explores the role teachers could play in online language learning beyond the classroom. We drew on the review of self-directed use of technology to support language learning when writing this chapter. The research findings of this article are inspiring, particularly because a model is proposed that can guide teachers in supporting student language learning beyond the classroom.

Lai, C. (2017). *Autonomous language learning with technology beyond the classroom.* London: Bloomsbury Academic.
  This book provides rich resources and guidance for people who want to know more about fostering autonomous learning beyond the classroom by using technology. The first part of the book introduces key concepts that are related to autonomous learning and provides a theoretical framework to help understand out-of-class autonomous learning in a technology-supported environment. Although this book does not specifically address using online learner communities to foster language learning, it covers many key concepts that we have discussed when writing this chapter, such as "autonomous learning" and "out-of-class learning".

Palfreyman, D. M., & Benson, P. (2019). Autonomy and its role in English language learning: practice and research. In X. Gao (Ed.), *Second handbook of English language teaching* (2nd ed., pp. 661–681). Retrieved from https://doi.org/10.1007/978-3-030-02899-2_38
  This book chapter is an extension of the authors' previous discussions regarding the influence of autonomous learning on applied linguistic and language education. It provides a useful overview of autonomy and the role it plays in language education. In our study, we drew on her definition of autonomous learning and its three dimensions, and the dimensions helped us to link autonomous learning with SDL and technology-enhanced learning. It would be useful reading for anyone seeking further information about autonomous learning.

References

Alm, A. (2015). "Facebook" for informal language learning: Perspectives from tertiary language students. *The EuroCALL Review, 23*(2), 3–18. https://doi.org/10.4995/eurocall.2015.4665
Andrade, M. S., & Bunker, E. L. (2009). A model for self-regulated distance language learning. *Distance Education, 30*(1), 47–61. https://doi.org/10.1080/01587910902845956
Bandura, A. (1977). *Social learning theory.* Prentice Hall: Englewood cliffs.
Benson, P. (2001). *Teaching and researching autonomy in language learning.* London: Longman.
Benson, P. (2009). Making sense of autonomy in language learning. In R. Pemberton, S. Toogood, & A. Barfield (Eds.), *Maintaining control: Autonomy and language learning* (pp. 13–26). Hong Kong: Hong Kong University Press.
Carlén, U., & Jobring, O. (2005). The rationale of online learning communities. *International Journal of Web Based Communities, 1*(3), 272–295.
Chang, C. C. (2003). Towards a distributed web-based learning community. *Innovations in Education and Teaching International, 40*(1), 27–42.
Chik, A. (2017). Learner autonomy and digital practices. In A. Chik, N. Aoki, & R. Smith (Eds.), *Autonomy in language learning and teaching: New research agendas* (pp. 73–92). London: Palgrave.

Colugh, G., Jones, J., McAndrew, P., & Scanlon, E. (2009). Informal learning evidence in online communities of mobile device enthusiasts. In M. Ally (Ed.), *Mobile learning: Transforming the delivery of education and training. Issues in distance education* (pp. 99–112). Athabasca: Athabasca University Press. http://www.aupress.ca/index.php/books/120155

Cotterall, S. (1995). Developing a course strategy for learner autonomy. *ELT Journal, 49*(3), 219–227.

Deci, E. L., & Ryan, R. M. (2002). *Handbook of self-determination research*. New York: University of Rochester Press.

Dede, C. (1996). The evolution of distance education: Emerging technologies and distributed learning. *American Journal of Distance Education, 10*(2), 4–36.

Dickinson, L. (1987). *Self-instruction in language learning*. Cambridge, England: Cambridge University Press.

Gao, X. (2007). A Tale of Blue Rain Café: A study on the online narrative construction about a community of English learners on the Chinese mainland. *System, 35*, 259–270.

Godwin-Jones, R. (2018). Chasing the butterfly effect: Informal language learning online as a complex system. *Language Learning & Technology, 22*(2), 8–27.

Guglielmino, L. M. (2008). Why self-directed learning. *International Journal of Self-Directed Learning, 5*, 1–14.

Hamilton, M. (2013). *Autonomy and foreign language learning in a virtual learning environment*. London: Bloomsbury Academic Publishing.

Haythornthwaite, C., Kazmer, M. M., Robins, J., & Shoemaker, S. (2000). Community development among distance learners: Temporal and technological dimensions. *Journal of Computer-Mediated Communication, 6*(1), 1–24. https://doi.org/10.1111/j.1083-6101.2000.tb00114.x

He, Q., Valcke, M., & Zhu, C. (2011). Promoting a special learning environment for second language learning in a Chinese rural primary school. *Procedia-Social and Behavioral Sciences, 12*, 137–144.

Henderson, S. (2015). *The Hunger Games fanfiction as a community of practice: Forming identities in online communities*. [Master's Thesis/Dissertation, University of British Columbia]. UBC Theses and Dissertations. https://open.library.ubc.ca/collections/ubctheses/24/items/1.0166554

Hine, C. (2000). *Virtual ethnography*. London: Sage.

Hramiak, A. (2010). Online learning community development with teachers as a means of enhancing initial teacher training. *Technology Pedagogy and Education, 19*(1), 47–62.

Huang, J. P., & Benson, P. (2013). Autonomy, agency and identity in foreign and second language education. *CJAL, 36*(1), 7–28.

Ke, F., & Hoadley, C. (2009). Evaluating online learning communities. *Educational Technology Research and Development, 57*(4), 487–510.

Knowles, M. S. (1975). *Self-directed learning: A guide for learners and teachers*. New York: Association Press.

Laal, M., & Salamati, P. (2012). Lifelong learning, why do we need it? *Procedia: Social and Behavioral Sciences, 31*, 399–403. https://doi.org/10.1016/j.sbspro.2011.12.073

Lai, C. (2015). Modeling teachers' influence on learners' self-directed use of technology for language learning outside the classroom. *Computers & Education, 82*, 74–83.

Lai, C. (2017). *Autonomous language learning with technology beyond the classroom*. London: Bloomsbury Academic.

Lantolf, J. P. (2013). Sociocultural theory and the dialectic of L2 learner autonomy/agency. In P. Benson & L. Cooker (Eds.), *The applied linguistic individual: Sociocultural approaches to identity, agency and autonomy* (pp. 17–31). Sheffield, UK: Equinox.

Lave, J., & Wenger, E. (1991). *Situated learning: Legitimate peripheral participation*. Cambridge: Cambridge University Press.

Little, D. (1991). *Learner autonomy 1: Definitions, issues and problems*. Dublin: Authentik Language Learning Resources.

Littlewood, W. (1996). Autonomy: An anatomy and a framework. *System, 24*, 427–435.

Liu, X., Magjuka, R. J., Bonk, C. J., & Lee, S. H. (2007). Does sense of community matter? An examination of participants' perceptions of building learning communities in online courses. *Quarterly Review of Distance Education, 8*(1), 9–24. https://www.learntechlib.org/p/106720/

Liu, Y. (2010). Social media tools as a learning resource. *Journal of Educational Technology Development and Exchange, 3*(1), 101–114.

Lomicka, L., & Lord, G. (2009). Introduction to social networking, collaboration and Web 2.0 tools. In L. Lomicka & G. Lord (Eds.), *The next generations: Social networking and online collaboration in FL learning* (pp. 1–11). San Marcos TX: CALICO Consortium.

Ma, Q. (2017). A multi-case study of university students' language-learning experience mediated by mobile technologies: A socio-cultural perspective. *Computer Assisted Language Learning, 30*(3–4), 183–203. https://doi.org/10.1080/09588221.2017.1301957

Ma, Q. (2020). Examining the role of inter-group peer online feedback on wiki writing in an EAP context. *Computer Assisted Language Learning, 33*(3), 197–216.

Merriam, S. B., & Caffarella, R. S. (1991). *Learning in adulthood*. San Francisco, CA: Jossey-Bass.

Murray, G. L. (1999). Autonomy and language learning in a simulated environment. *System, 27*, 295–308.

Nakata, Y. (2014). Self-regulation: Why is it important for promoting learner autonomy in the school context? *SiSAL Journal, 5*(4), 342–356.

Nunan, D. (1996). Towards autonomous learning: Some theoretical, empirical and practical issues. In R. Pemberton, E. S. L. Li, W. W. F. Or, & H. D. Pierson (Eds.), *Taking control: Autonomy in language learning* (pp. 13–26). Hong Kong: Hong Kong University Press.

Paiva, V. L. (2006). Autonomy and complexity. *Linguagem & Ensino, 9*(1), 77–127.

Paiva, V. L., & Braga, J. D. (2008). The complex nature of autonomy. *DELTA: Documentação de estudos em lingüística teórica e aplicada, 24*(SPE), 441–468.

Palfreyman, D. M., & Benson, P. (2019). Autonomy and its role in English language learning: Practice and research. In X. Gao (Ed.), *Second handbook of English language teaching* (2nd ed., pp. 661–681). https://doi.org/10.1007/978-3-030-02899-2_38

Papamitsiou, Z., & Economides, A. (2019). Exploring autonomous learning capacity from a self-regulated learning perspective using learning analytics. *British Journal of Educational Technology, 50*(6), 3138–3155.

Pearson, J. (1998). Electronic networking in initial teacher education: Is a virtual faculty of education possible? *Computers & Education, 32*(3), 221–238.

Reeve, J. (2009). Why teachers adopt a controlling motivating style toward students and how they can become more autonomy supportive. *Educational Psychologist, 44*(3), 159–175. https://doi.org/10.1080/00461520903028990

Rogers, A. (2008). Informal learning and literacy. In B. Street & N.H. Hornberger (Eds.), *Encyclopedia of language and education* (2nd ed., pp. 1–12). https://doi.org/10.1007/978-0-387-30424-3_41

Rose, H., Briggs, J. G., Boggs, J. A., Sergio, L., & Ivanova-Slavianskaia, N. (2018). A systematic review of language learner strategy research in the face of self-regulation. *System, 72*, 151–163.

Saks, K., & Leijen, Ä. (2014). Distinguishing self-directed and self-regulated learning and measuring them in the e-learning context. *Procedia-Social and Behavioral Sciences, 112*, 190–198. https://doi.org/10.1016/j.sbspro.2014.01.1155

Sekulich, K. M. (2020). Developing an online community of learners. *Delta Kappa Gamma Bulletin, 86*(5), 17–22.

Şentürk, C., & Zeybek, G. (2019). Overview of learning from past to present and self-directed learning. In F.G. Giuseffi (Ed.), *Self-directed learning strategies in adult education context* (1st ed., pp. 138–182). Hershey. PA: IGI Global.

Shea, P., Li, C. S., & Pickett, A. M. (2006). A study of teaching presence and student sense of learning community in fully online and web-enhanced college course. *The Internet and Higher Education, 9*(3), 175–190. https://doi.org/10.1016/j.iheduc.2006.06.005

Shih, R. C. (2011). Can web 2.0 technology assist college students in learning English writing? Integrating Facebook and peer assessment with blended learning. *Australasian Journal of Educational Technology, 27*(5), 829–845.

Sockett, G., & Toffoli, D. (2012). Beyond learner autonomy: A dynamic systems view of the informal learning of English in virtual online communities. *ReCALL, 24*(2), 138–151.

Song, L., & Hill, J. (2007). A conceptual model for understanding self-directed learning in online environments. *Journal of Interactive Online Learning, 6*(1), 27–42. http://www.ncolr.org/jiol/issues/pdf/6.1.3.pdf

Song, L., Singleton, E. S., Hill, J. R., & Koh, H. M. (2004). Improving online learning: Student perceptions of useful and challenging characteristics. *The Internet and Higher Education, 7*(1), 59–70.

Stefanou, C., Stolk, J. D., Prince, M., Chen, J. C., & Lord, S. M. (2013). Self-regulation and autonomy in problem- and project-based learning environments. *Active Learning in Higher Education, 14*(2), 109–122. https://doi.org/10.1177/1469787413481132

Suarez, M. M., & Arguello, M. V. (2020). Becoming a good BookTuber. *RELC Journal, 51*(1), 158–167. https://doi.org/10.1177/0033688220906905

Sun, Y., Franklin, T., & Gao, F. (2015). Learning outside of classroom: Exploring the active part of an informal online English learning community in China. *British Journal of Educational Technology, 48*(1), 57–70. https://doi.org/10.1111/bjet.12340

Tam, G., & El-Azar, D. (2020, March 13). *3 ways the coronavirus pandemic could reshape education.* World Economic Forum. https://www.weforum.org/agenda/2020/03/3-ways-coronavirus-is-reshaping-education-and-what-changes-might-be-here-to-stay/

Tang, E., Cheng, L., & Ng, R. (2020). Online writing community: What can we learn from failure? *RELC Journal,* 1–17. https://doi.org/10.1177/0033688220912038

Tang, E., & Lam, C. (2014). Building an effective online learning community (OLC) in blog-based teaching portfolios. *Internet and Higher Education, 20,* 79–85.

Tassinari, M. G. (2017). Encouraging autonomy through a community of practice: The role of a self-access centre. *Studies in Self-Access Learning Journal, 8*(2), 57–168.

Thanasoulas, D. (2000). What is learner autonomy & How can it be fostered. *The Internet TESL Journal, 6*(11), 37–48. http://iteslj.org/Articles/Thanasoulas-Autonomy.html

Thornton, K. (2013). Supporting self-directed learning: A framework for teachers. *Research and practice in English language teaching in Asia,* 59–77. http://www.leia.org/LEiA/LEiA%20VOLUMES/Download/Research_and_Practice_in_ELT_in_Asia.pdf#page=73

Tinto, V. (1997). Colleges as communities: Taking research on student persistence seriously. *The Review of Higher Education, 21*(2), 167–177.

Toffoli, D., & Sockett, G. (2013). University teachers' perceptions of online informal learning of English (OILE). *Computer Assisted Language Learning.* http://dx.doi.org/10.1080/09588221.2013.776970.

Tseng, W. T., Dornyei, Z., & Schmitt, N. (2006). A new approach to assessing strategic learning: The case of self-regulation in vocabulary acquisition. *Applied Linguistics, 27*(1), 78–102.

Wenden, A. L. (1991). *Learner strategies for learner autonomy.* London: Prentice Hall International.

Wenger, E. (1998). *Communities of practice: Learning, meaning and identity.* Cambridge: Cambridge University Press.

Wood, J. T. (2017). *Communication mosaics: An introduction to the field of communication* (8th ed.). Singapore: Cengage.

Wu, H. (2011). Playing truant, choosing classes or scrounging a free classes?: Reflection on the popularity of open online courses (in Chinese). *Qing Nian Xian Xiang (in Chinese), 9*(85).

Wu, W. V., Chen Hsieh, J., & Yang, J. C. (2017). Creating an online learning community in a flipped classroom to enhance EFL learners' oral proficiency. *Educational Technology & Society, 20*(2), 142–157.

Yang, Y. (2016). Self-directed learning to develop autonomy in an online ESP community. *Interactive Learning Environments, 24*(7), 1–18. https://doi.org/10.1080/10494820.2015.1041402

Zimmerman, B. J. (2000). Attaining self-regulation: A social cognitive perspective. In M. Boekaerts, P.R. Pintrich, & M. Zeidner (Eds.), *Handbook of self-regulation, research, and applications* (pp. 13–39). San Diego, CA: Academic Press.

Zimmerman, B. J. (2011). Motivational sources and outcomes of self-regulated learning and performance. In B. J. Zimmerman & D. H. Schunk (Eds.), *Handbook of self-regulation of learning and performance* (pp. 49–64). New York: Routledge.

19
SELF-ACCESS CENTRES FOR FACILITATING AUTONOMOUS LANGUAGE LEARNING

David Gardner

Introduction

When learners engage in learning beyond the classroom they must of necessity make decisions about their own learning. Taking control in this way will ultimately enable learners to focus on their individual learning needs and learning preferences and thus make learning more meaningful. However, most learners may initially have little experience or confidence in making such pedagogical decisions. This may encourage them to rely on pre-packaged self-instructional materials, thus reducing the level of individual decision-making but also reducing the potential personalisation of learning. However, as Benson (2011a, p. 12) suggests, they may assume the locus of control as they "gain confidence in their ability to learn in more naturalistic, informal ways". One way in which a greater degree of learner autonomy in learning beyond the classroom can be fostered is through the use of self-access centres. The aim of this chapter is look at the role of self-access centres in facilitating autonomous language learning. That is, to assist learners to become autonomous as learners and users of their target language. Before describing and discussing this role it is important to briefly define both the concept of autonomy as it relates to learning, and to clarify what is meant by a self-access centre. Once these terms have been defined, the chapter will review the essential elements of self-access centres which are necessary for the promotion and support of learner autonomy. This is important because without those elements a self-access centre will be an expensive, under-used, white elephant. Next the chapter will look at the opportunities for self-access centres to help learners experience authentic language use, thus giving real-world meaning to their language learning. Then, the chapter will look at the blurring of boundaries between physical and virtual self-access. This is important because while it provides learners with the undoubted advantages of anytime, anywhere learning it also, potentially, produces ethical issues revolving around internet security, especially for those responsible for the provision of educational opportunities for younger learners. Finally, the chapter will discuss the role of a self-access centre in supporting autonomous learning beyond the classroom. This is important because the goal in fostering such learning is to encourage learners to extend themselves beyond what they have learnt in class and individualise their learning.

Key constructs

Autonomy in learning

Autonomy in learning is not a new concept, for example, Krissanapong (1997) recounts stories of the autonomous learning of ancient Thai sages; and Bagheri (2018) and Kashindi (2020) link it to learning in Ancient Greece. However, the concept took on a new importance in language learning in the 1970s and 1980s (see Chapter 1 of Benson, 2011b, for an excellent summary of the history of autonomy in language learning). Alongside a general expansion of education in many parts of the world from this period onwards, new approaches to language learning emerged which revolved around learner-centredness (Nunan, 1988) and communicative language learning (Littlewood, 1981). To accommodate this new focus, researchers also became interested in individualisation in learning (see, for example, British Council, 1978; Brookes & Grundy, 1988; Geddes & Sturtridge, 1982) and in helping learners develop their "ability to take charge of [their] own learning" which is how Holec (1981, p. 3) first defined learner autonomy. Later refinements of this definition by Holec (1985), Little (1991) and Benson (2007), among others, led to a more detailed view of learner autonomy including the "capacity for detachment, critical reflection, decision-making, and independent action" (Little, 1991, p. 4). More broadly, autonomy is considered to encapsulate three distinct aspects which Lai (2017) refers to as "autonomy as language learner, autonomy as language user or communicator, and autonomy as person" (p. 13). The discussion in this chapter relies on Benson's much-cited definition of learner autonomy as "the capacity to take control of one's own learning" (2011b, p. 58). Learner autonomy can be encouraged, supported and fostered in a number of ways, one of which is through the use of self-access centres. It is this connection that is the focus of this chapter.

Self-access centres

Self-access centres, also referred to as independent learning centres or resource centres, began to appear along with the increased interest in learner autonomy in the second half of the 20th century. The early and extensive interest in learner autonomy at the Centre for Research and Applications in Language Teaching (CRAPEL) at the University of Nancy in France quickly led to the development of resources suitable for independent learning and to what might be considered a prototype self-access centre (see, for example, Bouillon, 1971; Cembalo & Holec, 1973; E. Harding & Legras, 1974), which evolved with time. The goal of the CRAPEL self-access centre as it morphed to accommodate developing technologies and new ideas remained firmly focussed on fostering learner autonomy (Riley, 1974). CRAPEL continues to experiment with self-access learning and has inspired developments in many other locations. Various institutions in Europe followed CRAPEL's lead and developed their own self-access centres both in universities (for an early example at the University of Cambridge, see Harding-Esch, 1982; H. Harding & Tealby, 1981; for a more recent discussion, see Tassinari, 2017) and in private language teaching institutions (see, for example, Giblin & Spaldin, 1988; O'Dell, 1992). The British Council also encouraged the development of self-access centres (McCall, 1992; McDowell & Morris, 1989; Moore, 1992) and created them worldwide as part of their language teaching operations. Hong Kong institutions invested heavily in self-access centres from the 1990s onwards, providing early leadership in practical and theoretical aspects of designing, operating and developing self-access centres and self-access learning in general represented by a number of edited collections of papers (see, for example, Gardner & Miller, 1994, 1996; Morrison, 1999; Pemberton et al., 1996; Pemberton et al., 2009) and by research-based papers on specific aspects of self-access learning (for example, Gardner, 1999, 2001; Miller, 1992; Miller et al., 2007).

Other parts of Asia also have a history of developing self-access centres to support learners and to research their use, for example, but not limited to, Thailand (see, for example, Kongchan & Darasawang, 2015; Watson-Todd, 2014), Japan (for example, Mynard & Shelton-Strong, 2020; Mynard & Stevenson, 2017) and elsewhere in Asia (for example, Miller, 1992, 1999). Self-access centres have also been long established in Australia (see Campbell, 1985; Mason, 1985) and New Zealand (for example, Blaker & Burns, 2000; Dofs & Hobbs, 2011), as well as in some parts of South America, of which work in Mexico is particularly well-known (for example, Chávez Sánchez & Peña Clavel, 2015; Domínguez Gaona et al., 2014). For an informative account of the early history of the development of learner autonomy, self-access learning and self-access centres and the inter-connectedness of their development, see Gremmo & Riley (1995).

There is considerable diversity in the design and operation of self-access centres due largely to their development over a considerable period of time, strong influences from surrounding cultural and educational factors, and adaptations for specific target user groups. While their primary, and most important goal is to foster learner autonomy, they may serve additional purposes (for example, providing a convenient location for the completion of homework or for accessing the internet) either because they are considered important functions by the funding body or because they occur incidentally without detracting from the functions of the self-access centre. These centres are most commonly established and managed by educational institutions and are utilised across much of the world and at all educational levels.

Self-access centres provide learners with a range of opportunities for language learning beyond the classroom which are based around physical and virtual resources and activities. Frequently, they also provide learners with support services such as language advising and learner training with the aim of helping learners to discover their learning needs and wants, and to develop their own best learning strategies, thus personalising their learning experience. The contents of self-access centres, and the opportunities and services they provide, vary considerably from one centre to another because they are tailored to a specific set of users and may also be constrained by their operating budgets. While all self-access centres provide a range of freely accessible learning materials and opportunities which learners can independently sample, some also establish links with taught courses to help students of those courses extend their learning and develop a self-access learning habit. The linking of taught programmes with self-access provisions is often referred to as the integration of self-access into the curriculum (for further discussion on integrating self-access into the curriculum, see de Gregorio-Godeo, 2005; Gardner, 2007b; Riley, 1974; Thompson & Atkinson, 2010; Toogood & Pemberton, 2002). Both approaches, that is the entirely independent use of self-access and the integrated approach, are considered to foster learner autonomy.

Having defined self-access centres in terms of the learning opportunities and services they provide, rather than in terms of their facilities, it is important to add that over the years a number of optional extras have become important "add-ons", indeed perhaps even necessary components in some contexts. These add-ons revolve around the development of increasingly useful, sophisticated and affordable technologies. To be clear, the use of technology is not a requirement for pursuing self-access learning although in the modern world, and especially when targeting younger generations of learners, its availability and usage is increasingly expected. Perhaps it has also become a way for funding bodies to indicate their commitment to self-access learning. Cynically, it might also be seen as an attempt to limit the cost of such provisions because the one-off cost of purchasing technology is considerably lower than the ongoing costs of providing additional educators. Technological impacts on self-access centres consist of the provision of equipment that can assist in learning such as media players, recording devices and computers; and in the connectivity provided by networks to connect within an organisation (intranet), between organisations (extranet) and with the entire connected world (internet).

Self-access centres may operate entirely in the physical world, utilising many printed and recorded media resources, as well as face-to-face tutor-led activities (such as workshops) and peer-supported activities (such as peer-tutoring). Such practices were common when centres first became popular beginning in the 1980s and especially when technology was expensive and funding was limited. While some self-access centres may still function in an entirely physical way for valid operational reasons, the majority nowadays make use of the internet to connect their users with each other, with their language advisors, with learning materials and with opportunities to experience authentic language use. The merging of virtual with physical provisions allows the extension of self-access support in terms of access to resources and to people, as well as overcoming barriers related to time and place. Self-access learning has become available at anytime from anywhere for anyone. In recent years, the distinction between a tangible self-access centre and its virtual counterpart has become increasingly blurred. Indeed, many self-access centres have developed their virtual presence to such a degree that their physical presence is dwindling or, on some cases, has disappeared and this will be discussed in more detail below.

From the above it is clear that given the developments over time, the tailoring of self-access centres to their target users and the optional add-ons, it is difficult to describe such centres concisely and definitively because each one may have its own unique configuration. For the purposes of this chapter, and to define them in the broadest terms, self-access centres are considered as physical, virtual or hybrid locations offering a diverse range of learning opportunities and services designed to foster learner autonomy while simultaneously helping learners achieve their learning goals.

Key issues

How a self-access centre supports learner autonomy

Self-access learning brings together a wide range of elements to create a learning environment with which each learner interacts in a unique way (Gardner & Miller, 1999). This emphasis on individualisation is a key concept underpinning self-access learning and the operation of self-access centres. However, it is important to clarify that this does not imply that self-access learners must work individually, or alone. It simply means that each learner should have the freedom to make decisions about their own learning. If after reflecting on their needs, wants, preferred approaches, etc., they find other learners with shared goals, it makes sense for them to work together (if they so desire). Collaborative learning is recognised as a powerful motivator and can provide useful and much-needed language practice, as well as opportunities for peer-assessment.

Careful management of the elements of self-access learning improves the prospect of supporting learners as they develop their learner autonomy by helping them discover their learning styles and preferred learning strategies. The mix of elements and focus within them is often influenced by available resources and institutional philosophy. While some of the elements of self-access learning can and should occur in the classroom context, the broadest and deepest provisions can be made available through a self-access centre.

With proper management a self-access centre supports the development of learner autonomy by providing appropriate and up-to-date resources which appeal to the target users, suit users' needs and are pitched at a range of proficiency levels which allow users a suitable entry level and an opportunity to progress in their learning. These resources should accommodate a range of learning styles to accommodate all types of learners. Guiding documents (often called learning pathways) are frequently provided in self-access centres to give learners tips about how to improve in specific areas of their learning (see, for example, Ivone & Hayati, 2015; Kell & Newton, 1997). They will include references to materials or learning opportunities within the self-access centre, other parts of the host institution or in other nearby facilities, but they may also include reference to learning opportunities accessible via the internet. These learning pathways can also be personalised for individual learners through discussion with a learning advisor (Mozzon-McPherson, 2007) or through technology (for a detailed discussion, see Welch Bacon & Gaither, 2020).

A well-managed self-access centre will make use of people in diverse roles. Unlike a library where users are mostly expected to operate in isolation, self-access centres will provide access to teachers, advisors and peers to encourage learners to consult, collaborate and cooperate in their learning. But the option to operate in isolation should also be available when desired. The various people-related opportunities will be optional so that individual users can make their own decisions about how they want to learn.

The incorporation of teachers into self-access centres adds validity because learners are likely to recognise the expertise of teachers and see their presence as an endorsement. However, teachers with no previous experience of self-access learning may need some support to adapt to the new role. They may have difficulty adapting to being facilitators of learning rather than providers of information and controllers of learning. Whether in the classroom or in a self-access centre, it seems teachers need help re-training to promote learner autonomy (see, for example, Gardner et al., 2013; Reinders & Balcikanli, 2011; Young et al., 2007). It important for the management of self-access centres to ensure that staff have a consistent vision of the goals of the centre. In a study about the effectiveness of a self-access centre it was interesting to discover that the four members of the operational team had different ways of defining the effectiveness of the centre (Gardner, 2001). This disparity had not previously been known to them despite working together for some time. Although there may be challenges coordinating approaches to self-access learning and among teachers in some cases, the use of student assistants to support self-access centres has often proved very reliable (for an interesting account of student assistants' reflection on their role as self-access centre staff, see Tassinari, 2018). Such use is becoming widespread and as well as providing highly motivated, quick-learning (and probably cheap) staff, it is an interesting way of covertly promulgating a view of self-access learning as a normal activity among an institutions' students.

Most importantly, well-managed centres will provide learner training to show users who are new to self-access learning how to take control of their learning, make decisions, evaluate their progress and find their own best learning pathway. Self-access learning can be baffling for learners who have never experienced it and especially so for those who have mostly only known teacher-directed education. The learner training will encourage learners to consider learning approaches they may not have previously encountered and will help them to organise their learning. The organisation of learning is a task often delegated to teachers in classroom learning settings, so may be something learners have previously given little thought to and in which they may have had little or no practice. Planning learning, with its component parts of reflection and decision-making, is considered an important part of developing as an autonomous learner (see, for example, Cooke, 2016; Cotterall & Murray, 2009; Hsieh & Hsieh, 2019; Irie, 2019; Kongchan & Darasawang, 2015; Little, 2015; Morrison, 2005; Trebbi, 2011), although some evidence suggests that while good self-access learners learn to be organised they may have a flexible approach to planning their learning (Candas, 2011), or may replace more recognisable planning of learning with being what Murray (2017) refers to as self-organising learners. There is no single best approach for all learners but the key to successful provision of self-access support is to expose learners to alternatives and ultimately help them recognise what works best for them.

Important elements of the learners' planning process include reflecting on learning needs and wants. That is, those things they must learn and those things they want to learn. Distinguishing between them helps learners set their learning goals, plan their learning and evaluate their progress. The latter is often a challenge for new users of self-access learning because they gain little experience of it when engaged in classroom learning where progress is typically monitored by teachers. Learning to self-evaluate provides learners with a useful skill for life-long learning.

There can be difficulties in persuading learners to engage with self-access learning at the outset. This is largely because it is an unknown entity for them. All learners know what classroom learning is because they have done it as long as they can remember, and because it is a common part of life. Their parents have done it and probably talk to them about it, everyone they know has been in a classroom. Self-access learning, on the other hand, seems alien to those who have not experienced it and have no family members, or friends, or sometimes even teachers, who have experienced it. This lack of common knowledge about self-access learning may cause hesitation among many learners. Such hesitation may be enough to prevent learners from giving self-access learning a fair try. There are accounts of this problem from various parts of the world (so it seems not to be a specifically culture-related problem). A moving, and probably representative, account is provided by Farmer (1994) the manager of a team dedicated to establishing a new self-access centre. They expended considerable efforts establishing a state-of-the art centre to be used as the students desired. When they threw open the doors for the first time they were underwhelmed by the lack of uptake. They quickly researched the problem and discovered many students' attitudes were along the lines of: "I prefer a teacher to teach me the whole programme because he/she knows what I need and the progress in learning" (Farmer, 1994, p. 13). The team introduced learner training programmes to acclimatise students to the notion of self-access learning to help them develop their learner autonomy. Gradually, the students in that institution incorporated self-access learning into their normal learning routines. Twenty years later that institution has a large and thriving self-access centre.

An increasingly popular approach to promoting the use of self-access centres, and one which was introduced to overcome problems like the one highlighted above, is to integrate self-access learning fully into taught courses, promoting it through classroom activities and extending learning by links between the taught course and the self-access centre. This endorsement by teachers of self-access learning as an intrinsic part of a course and of a self-access centre as a useful learning resource, is important for boosting learners' confidence in the approach. This is necessary because, unlike classroom learning, most students have no experience with, and no knowledge of, self-access learning. This lack of familiarity may cause learners to consider self-access learning with some caution and may even consider being asked to self-learn as an avoidance by teachers of their professional duty. Interestingly, there is some evidence to show that the classroom teachers may be wary of self-access learning (Lai, 2011), or interpret it in different ways (Wichayathian & Reinders, 2018) and the degree to which they are comfortable with self-access learning may affect the degree to which they willingly promote it (Young et al., 2007). Also, teachers are more likely to take self-access learning seriously if it is firmly embedded as an integral part of the courses they teach (Lai et al., 2013). Despite the potential hurdles of integrating teaching and self-access learning, it has become relatively common and successful (for some researched examples, see Gardner, 2007a; Gardner & Yung, 2017; Law, 2017; Watson & Agawa, 2016).

Of course, a self-access centre is only one of the possible settings for language learning (as described by Benson, 2017), but if well managed it can greatly facilitate learner autonomy. Conversely, if poorly managed, for example, simply treated as a repository for language teaching materials, it may play only a minimal part in fostering learner autonomy. The management of self-access centres has been widely discussed (Gardner, 2011, 2017; Gardner & Miller, 1999, 2011, 2013a, 2013b, 2014; Hobbs & Dofs, 2017; Kongchan, 2008; Lonergan, 1994; Mooi, 1991; Tassinari, 2018) although there is no recognised training programme available to managers. It seems that most frequently, running a self-access centre is seen by the leaders of host institutions as a simple coordination role which can be assigned to teachers as additional duties with no training, whereas to do the job well requires expertise in management (the correct application of procedures) and leadership (vision and innovation) as well as relevant pedagogical knowledge and experience (Gardner & Miller, 2014).

The potential of self-access centres to expose learners to authentic language use

Self-access centres have always had a strong track record in providing opportunities for studying and practising languages by providing language learning materials (print, audio-visual and computer-based), which are adapted for self-access learning where necessary, study guides, language support and peer activities. Most centres also actively foster learner autonomy by providing learner training and in particular by encouraging reflection, planning and self-assessment. Self-access centres also usually provide access to some authentic language materials such as newspapers, magazines, and audio or video recordings in the target language(s). Notably, the non-interactive nature of such authentic language materials can only provide passive authentic uses. More recently, with the development, affordability and accessibility of technology, it has been possible to promote exposure to the world of authentic language thus providing, potentially, active language use in authentic settings. This includes the relatively controlled environments of email exchanges (Makin, 1994), language exchanges (O'Dowd & Lewis, 2016) and tandem networks (Little, 2015; Stickler & Emke, 2011), all of which have successfully been operated without access to a self-access centre, typically as class projects, but have been, or could be, promoted from within self-access centres. A somewhat less controlled environment for authentic language use could be offered by self-access centres in the form of genuine letters to editors of newspapers or similar contexts, although there seem to be no known examples of such in the literature.

The potential for active authentic language use also extends to uncontrolled environments such as subject-specialist discussion forums, bulletin boards, blogs; and the creation, uploading and unmoderated discussion around YouTube videos, or similar. These are wonderful opportunities for language learners to gain experience in authentic language environments but they present two potential problems. The first problem relates to the language used in the environments. Most problematic is the difficulty learners may have in understanding and in being understood in the discussion. This is reflected in the findings of Lai and Zheng (2018) who found that learners made extensive use of mobile devices to enhance their language learning but used them far less to communicate in authentic language situations. There may also be issues around the levels of formality of the language the learners are exposed to although this seems to present no greater risk than the age-old tradition of exchange visits. Second, there may be ethical issues for institutions which expose their learners to potentially dangerous situations in which there is no way of knowing who the other interlocutors are. Completely unmoderated language activities are the most authentic, and may be most attractive, but they also present the greatest risk for encountering stalkers and scammers.

Not to over-emphasise the risks of authentic language activities, it should be pointed out that they are potentially very motivating because they can be selected by learners based on their own individual interests. This extreme level of individualisation makes such activities difficult for teachers to handle as class activities but, conversely, the challenges of authentic language may make them too challenging for learners to attempt in isolation. A self-access centre would be an ideal location from which to provide help to learners to establish themselves in such authentic language activities.

Implications

The blurring of distinctions between physical and virtual self-access learning

In their initial concept, self-access centres were easy to define as self-contained physical locations (see, for example, McDowell & Morris, 1989; Sheerin, 1989; Sturtridge, 1992). Later, when self-access learning was integrated into taught courses the reach of self-access centres extended but their location remained largely fixed and physical. Even with the introduction of computer-assisted learning into self-access centres little changed in terms of their location. However, as network connectivity blossomed the impact on self-access centres became notable and profound. Intranets make all parts of an institution accessible from all other parts and this carries the implication that the resources of those parts should also be accessible. The internet makes intranets accessible (to valid users) from anywhere. As a result all parts of an institution are available for anywhere. Just as students in universities are becoming used to downloading journal articles and even whole books at any time of the day without physically visiting the library, language learners are increasingly expecting to be able to download their self-access learning materials from anywhere and at any time. Equally, just as students are able to email their teachers, they expect to be able to conduct an online consultation with a self-access language advisor. The degree to which this 24/7 virtual accessibility spreads to all levels of education and permeates institutions may be determined partially by educational culture but, in reality, is probably more determined by financial constraints. It seems likely that such accessibility is the future. Indeed, its introduction was accelerated during the period of the Covid-19 pandemic.

A strong benefit of online accessibility for self-access learning is that it works in both directions, inwards as well as outwards. Learners can access the resources of a self-access centre (for example, learning materials, learner training, advisors) but the self-access centre can also access the learners, providing notifications of upcoming workshops, new materials, and particular learning opportunities. It can also keep in touch with taught courses to provide teachers with notifications of relevant self-access materials and events, and use just-in-time communications for the students of a class to hear about specific learning opportunities as they become relevant to the current part of the course. The self-access centre can also use this online system to personalise its communications with individual learners, tailoring messages to their learning styles, learning goals or upcoming needs in terms of support for course assignments. A self-access centre can also act as a gateway for moderated, or semi-moderated, authentic language opportunities. Thus, reducing or eliminating potential threats arising from students directly accessing forums or other sites.

As self-access becomes more main-stream in courses and as connectivity makes the physical location for providing self-access learning opportunities unimportant, there is a definite blurring of the boundaries of self-access centres. They can no longer be defined so simply. Indeed, there has been some debate over whether their time has come to an end (Mynard, 2012; Reinders, 2012) and some indications that the physical centres are diminishing in floor space (Gardner, 2011) but not necessarily in their provisions.

Whether self-access centres retain a physical presence seems unimportant. As has been the case throughout their history, the centres transform to meet the needs of their users. If face-to-face meet-ups are no longer needed then they should move entirely online. In reality many will probably have a hybrid existence. Of more relevance is that they should continue to foster learner autonomy.

Future directions

From the foregoing discussion it is clear that modern self-access centres, be they physical, virtual or hybrid are able to provide support for classroom learning and for learning beyond the classroom. They are adaptive to learners' needs as they change, are able to provide pedagogical support and promote learner autonomy. While it is difficult to measure autonomy there is some evidence to suggest that self-access centres fulfil this later goal. Hsieh and Hsieh (2019), for example, found a positive correlation between the degree of learner autonomy of university students and their usage of resources in their self-access centre, which led them to recommend that "students be encouraged to learn beyond the classroom through pedagogical activities that link classroom learning to learning-centre resources" (p. 12).

Although they are not the only potential pedagogical tool to support learning beyond the classroom, self-access centres have a considerable history in doing that and should be considered as an important component in the toolbox. A lot has been learnt during the development of self-access centres about balancing learners' freedom to choose and providing structure to support learning. More recently developed learning tools may be less well balanced. For example, Oga-Baldwin (2015) discovered in a study of digital platforms for 21st-century learners that they "offer much of the freedom, but not necessarily the structure and direction, necessary for learning" (p. 31).

Importantly, self-access centres make a contribution on each of the dimensions in the framework for learning beyond the classroom proposed by Benson (2011a).

Location: The learning opportunities provided by self-access centres are always out of the classroom, but can be linked to classroom learning and this may have benefits especially for students new to learning beyond the classroom.

Formality: Self-access centres provide potential for formal settings (for example, workshops) and very informal settings (for example, informal chat sessions, discussion partner matching, chilling). These levels of formality/informality are achievable physically or virtually.

Pedagogy: Self-access centres accommodate the distinction between self-instruction and naturalistic learning. They provide materials specifically designed for learning and which result in intentional learning, such as adapted textbooks and computer-assisted learning materials. They also provide opportunities for naturalistic learning through watching target language videos or TV, or reading newspapers. Potentially, this could also be accommodated through providing access to target language online chats, as discussed above. Some of the peer-learning opportunities like group discussions may also fall into the category of artificially established naturalistic settings in which the learners forget their original language learning intention once they relax into enjoying the conversation.

Locus of control: Learners taking control of their own learning is an important step towards learner autonomy. However, this can be a large and difficult step for learners who are unfamiliar with learner autonomy. A self-access centre can provide a safe and supportive place in which to make the first steps.

In conclusion, despite the concern that self-access centres may be about to disappear it would be wiser to see them as constantly evolving to meet the needs of new generations of learners. In their next incarnation they are likely to morph into fully online or hybrid entities which utilise the wealth of experience behind them to provide a modern take on supporting language learner autonomy. These modern self-access centres will continue to provide important venues for learning beyond the classroom. Fruitful areas of future research would be in looking at how the learning opportunities they provide fit within models of learning beyond the classroom, and the extent to which the new centres continue to foster learner autonomy.

Reflection questions

1 How important is fostering learner autonomy to the development of learning beyond the classroom? What are the benefits and challenges for the learner?
2 How could (or does) a self-access centre contribute to a context with which you are familiar? Consider particularly the locus of control and the physical/virtual/hybrid presence of that centre.

Recommended readings

Gardner, D., & Miller, L. (1999). *Establishing self-access: From theory to practice*. Cambridge: Cambridge University Press.
  This book is rather dated now but is still a good starting point for understanding the theoretical basis of self-access learning and for its discussion of the practical aspects of setting up and maintaining a self-access centre.
Benson, P. (2017). Language learning beyond the classroom: Access all areas. *Studies in Self-Access Learning Journal*, 8(2), 135–146. Retrieved from http://sisaljournal.org/archives/jun17/benson
  This article provides a very accessible discussion of the relationship between self-access centres and learning beyond the classroom.
Mynard, J. (2019). Self-access learning and advising: Promoting language learner autonomy beyond the classroom. In H. Reinders, S. Ryan, & S. Nakamura (Eds.), *Innovation in Language Teaching and Learning: The Case of Japan* (pp. 185–209). Cham: Springer International Publishing
  This book chapter discusses (among other things) the pivotal role in learning beyond the classroom of advising learners as the locus of control moves towards a higher level of learner autonomy.

References

Bagheri, N. (2018). Critical thinking and autonomy in speaking ability: A case study. *International Journal on Studies in English Language and Literature*, 6(5), 73–83.
Benson, P. (2007). Autonomy in language teaching and learning (State of the Art). *Language Teaching*, 40(1), 21–40. https://doi.org/https://doi.org/10.1017/S0261444806003958

Benson, P. (2011a). Language learning and teaching beyond the classroom: An introduction to the field. In P. Benson & H. Reinders (Eds.), *Beyond the language classroom* (pp. 7–16). Basingstoke: Palgrave.

Benson, P. (2011b). *Teaching and researching autonomy* (2nd ed.). Harlow: Pearson Education.

Benson, P. (2017). Language learning beyond the classroom: Access all areas. Studies *in Self-Access Learning Journal*, 8(2), 135–146. http://sisaljournal.org/archives/jun17/benson

Blaker, J., & Burns, T. (2000). *Investigation into independent learning centres in New Zealand, Australia, Hong Kong and England*. Auckland: UNITEC Institute of Technology.

Bouillon, C. (1971). Du Laboratoire de languages a la bibliotheque sonore: L'individualisation de l'apprentissage en langues vivantes. *Mélanges Pédagogiques*, 2, 1–20.

British Council. (1978). *Individualisation in language learning*. London: The British Council.

Brookes, A., & Grundy, P. (Eds.) (1988). *Individualisation and autonomy in Language Learning*. ELT Documents 131. London: Modern English Publications/British Council (Macmillan).

Campbell, R. (1985). Aims and processes of MACE (Migrant Access Centre for English) - the self-access centre at the Institute of Languages, University of NSW. In R. J. Mason (Ed.), *Self-directed learning and self-access in Australia: From practice to theory* (pp. 247–241). Melbourne: Council of Adult Education.

Candas, P. (2011, 2011/07/01). Analyzing student practice in language resource centres of the Louis Pasteur University in Strasbourg: is planning really central to self-directed learning? *Innovation in Language Learning and Teaching*, 5(2), 191–204. https://doi.org/https://doi.org/10.1080/17501229.2011.577534

Cembalo, M., & Holec, H. (1973). Les language aux adultes: Pour une pédagogie de l'autonomie. *Mélanges Pédagogiques*, 4, 77–86.

Chávez Sánchez, M., & Peña Clavel, M. (2015). The development of CELE-UNAM mediateca. *Studies in Self-Access Learning Journal*, 6(2), 219–230.

Cooke, S. D. (2016). Engendering autonomy and motivation through learner reflection tasks. *Studies in Self-Access Learning Journal*, 7(4), 341–354.

Cotterall, S., & Murray, G. (2009). Enhancing metacognitive knowledge: Structure, affordances and self. *System*, 37(1), 34–45. https://doi.org/https://doi.org/10.1016/j.system.2008.08.003

de Gregorio-Godeo, E. (2005). Blended learning as a resource for integrating self-access and traditional face-to-face tuition in EFL tertiary education. In A. Mendez-Vilas, B. Gonzalez-Pereira, J. M. Gonzalez, & J. A. M. Gonzalez (Eds.), *Recent research developments in learning technologies* (pp. 358–362). Badajoz: FORMATEX. http://citeseerx.ist.psu.edu/viewdoc/download?doi=10.1.1.122.8123&rep=rep1&type=pdf

Dofs, K., & Hobbs, M. (2011). *Guidelines for maximising use of Independent Learning CIRIEentres: Support for ESOL learners*. Wellington: Ako Aotearoa. http://akoaotearoa.ac.nz/download/ng/file/group-7/guidelines-for-maximising-student-use-of-independent-learning-centres.pdf

Domínguez Gaona, M. d. R., Romero Monteverde, M., & Crhová, J. (2014). The self-access center as a social landscape: The case of a Mexican self-access center. In R. Watson-Todd (Ed.), *Proceedings of the DRAL2/ILA Conference* (pp. 115–128). Bangkok: King Mongkut University of Technology Thonburi.

Farmer, R. (1994). The limits of learner independence in Hong Kong. In D. Gardner & L. Miller (Eds.), *Directions in self-access language learning* (pp. 13–28). Hong Kong: Hong Kong University Press.

Gardner, D. (1999). The evaluation of self-access centres. In B. Morrison (Ed.), *Experiments and evaluation in self-access language learning* (pp. 111–122). Hong Kong: The Hong Kong Association for Self-Access Learning and Development.

Gardner, D. (2001). Making self-access centres more effective. In D. K. Kember, S. Candlin, & L. Yan (Eds.), *Further case studies of improving teaching and learning from the action learning project* (pp. 161–174). Hong Kong: Action Learning Project.

Gardner, D. (2007a). Integrating self-access learning into an ESP course. In D. Gardner (Ed.), *Learner autonomy 10: Integration and support* (pp. 8–32). Dublin: Authentik.

Gardner, D. (2007b). Introduction. In D. Gardner (Ed.), *Learner autonomy 10: Integration and support* (pp. 1–7). Dublin: Authentik.

Gardner, D. (2011). Looking in and looking out: Managing a self-access centre. In D. Gardner (Ed.), *Fostering autonomy in language learning* (pp. 186–198). Gaziantep: Zirve University. https://doi.org/https://doi.org/10.13140/RG.2.1.2654.8886

Gardner, D. (2017). The evolution and devolution of management and training needs for self-access centre staff. *Studies in Self-Access Learning Journal, 8*(2), 147–156. http://sisaljournal.org/archives/jun17/gardner

Gardner, D., Law, E., & Lai, C. (2013). Training new teachers to promote self-directed learning. In M. Hobbs & K. Dofs (Eds.), *ILAC selections: Autonomy in a networked world* (pp. 68–69). Christchurch: Independent Learning Association. http://www.independentlearning.org/uploads/100836/files/ILA_2012_Proceedings.pdf

Gardner, D., & Miller, L. (Eds.) (1994). *Directions in self-access language learning*. Hong Kong: Hong Kong University Press.

Gardner, D., & Miller, L. (Eds.) (1996). *Tasks for independent language learning*. Alexandria: TESOL International Organisation.

Gardner, D., & Miller, L. (1999). *Establishing self-access: From theory to practice*. Cambridge: Cambridge University Press.

Gardner, D., & Miller, L. (2011). Managing self-access language learning: Principles and practice. *System, 39*(1), 78–89. https://doi.org/https://doi.org/10.1016/j.system.2011.01.010

Gardner, D., & Miller, L. (2013a). The management skills of SALL managers. *Studies in Self-Access Learning Journal, 4*(4), 236–252.

Gardner, D., & Miller, L. (2013b). Self-access managers: An emerging community of practice. *System, 41*(3), 817–828. https://doi.org/https://doi.org/10.1016/j.system.2013.08.003

Gardner, D., & Miller, L. (2014). *Managing self-access language learning*. Hong Kong: City University Press.

Gardner, D., & Yung, K. W. H. (2017). Learner motivation in self-access language learning. *Innovation in Language Learning and Teaching, 11*(2), 159–176. https://doi.org/https://doi.org/10.1080/17501229.2015.1088545

Geddes, M., & Sturtridge, G. (1982). *Individualisation*. London: Modern English Publications.

Giblin, K., & Spaldin, E. (1988). *Setting up a course involving self-directed learning*. Cambridge: Bell Educational Trust.

Gremmo, M. J., & Riley, P. (1995). Autonomy, self-direction and self-access in language teaching and learning: The history of an idea. *System, 23*(2), 151–164.

Harding-Esch, E. M. (1982). The open access sound and video library of the University of Cambridge: Progress report and development. *System, 10*(1), 13–28.

Harding, E., & Legras, M. (1974). La bibliothèque sonore et ses implications pédagogiques. *Mélanges Pédagogiques, 5*.

Harding, H., & Tealby, A. (1981). Counselling for language learning at University of Cambridge: Progress report on an experiment. *Mélanges Pédagogiques, 12*, 96–120.

Hobbs, M., & Dofs, K. (2017). Self-access centre and autonomous learning management: Where are we now and where are we going? *Studies in Self-Access Learning Journal*, 88–101. http://sisaljournal.org/archives/jun17/hobbs_dofs

Holec, H. (1981). *Autonomy and foreign language learning*. Oxford: Pergamon Press.

Holec, H. (1985). Declaration of independence: Autonomy and self-direction in language learning. In R. J. Mason (Ed.), *Self-directed learning and self-access in Australia: From practice to theory* (pp. Jan-19). Melbourne: Council of Adult Education.

Hsieh, H.-C., & Hsieh, H.-L. (2019). Undergraduates' out-of-class learning: Exploring EFL students' autonomous learning behaviors and their usage of resources. *Education Sciences, 9*(3), 159. https://doi.org/https://doi.org/10.3390/educsci9030159

Irie, K. (2019). An insider's view: Launching a university program. In H. Reinders, S. Ryan, & S. Nakamura (Eds.), *Innovation in Language Teaching and Learning: The Case of Japan* (pp. 211–232). Cham: Palgrave Macmillan.

Ivone, F. M., & Hayati, N. (2015). Enhancing independent study program through development of listening learning pathways. *The English Teacher, 44*(3), 96–107.

Kashindi, R. M. (2020). Learner's autonomy: A critical study and research paradigm for ELT curriculum development in Democratic Republic of the Congo higher education. *European Journal of English Language Teaching, 4*. https://doi.org/http://dx.doi.org/10.46827/ejel.v5i4.3209

Kell, J., & Newton, C. (1997, January 1, 1997). Roles of pathways in self-access centres. *ELT Journal, 51*(1), 48–53. https://doi.org/https://doi.org/10.1093/elt/51.1.48

Kongchan, C. (2008). Management of change in a self-access learning centre. *Reflections, 11*(Jan), 8–18.

Kongchan, C., & Darasawang, P. (2015). Roles of self-access centres in the success of language learning. In P. Darasawang & H. Reinders (Eds.), *Innovations in language learning and teaching* (pp. 76–88). Basingstoke: Palgrave Macmillan.

Krissanapong, K. (1997). Autonomy rediscovered. In L. Dickinson (Ed.), *Autonomy 2000: The development of learning independence in language learning* (pp. 93–100). Bangkok: King Mongkut's Institute of Technology Thonburi.

Lai, C. (2011). In-service teacher development for facilitating learner autonomy in curriculum-based self-access language learning. In D. Gardner (Ed.), *Fostering autonomy in language learning* (pp. 148–160). Gaziantep: Zirve University. https://doi.org/https://doi.org/10.13140/RG.2.1.2654.8886

Lai, C. (2017). *Autonomous language learning with technology: Beyond the classroom*. London: Bloomsbury Academic.

Lai, C., Gardner, D., & Law, E. (2013). New to facilitating self-directed learning: The changing perceptions of teachers. *Innovation in Language Learning and Teaching*, 7(3), 281–294 https://doi.org/https://doi.org/10.1080/17501229.2013.836208

Lai, C., & Zheng, D. (2018). Self-directed use of mobile devices for language learning beyond the classroom. *ReCALL*, 30(3), 299–318. https://doi.org/10.1017/S0958344017000258

Law, Y. Y. (2017). *Promoting learner autonomy through a self-access language learning (SALL) component of a taught English course* [Unpublished doctoral thesis, The University of Hong Kong]. Hong Kong. http://hdl.handle.net/10722/261451

Little, D. (1991). *Learner autonomy 1: Definitions, issues and problems*. Dublin: Authentik.

Little, D. (2015). University language centres, self-access learning and learner autonomy. *Recherche et pratiques pédagogiques en langues de spécialité*, 34(1), 13–26. https://doi.org/https://doi.org/10.4000/apliut.5008

Littlewood, W. (1981). *Communicative language teaching: An introduction*. Cambridge: Cambridge University Press.

Lonergan, J. (1994). Self-access language centres: Implications for managers, teachers and learners. In E. Esch (Ed.), *Self-access and the adult language learner* (pp. 119–125). London: Centre for Information on Language Teaching and Research.

Makin, L. (1994). Learner telesupport: Language advising by email. In E. Esch (Ed.), *Self-access and the adult language learner* (pp. 83–96). London: Centre for Information on Language Teaching and Research.

Mason, R. J. (1985). *Self-directed learning and self-access in Australia: From practice to theory*. Melbourne: Council of Adult Education.

McCall, J. (1992). *Self-access: Setting up a centre*. Manchester: British Council.

McDowell, J., & Morris, J. (1989). How to set-up a self-access centre. *EFL Gazette, January*, 4–5.

Miller, L. (1992). *Self-access centres in S.E. Asia*. Hong Kong: City Polytechnic of Hong Kong.

Miller, L. (1999). Self-access language learning in primary and secondary schools: The Malaysian experience and the Hong Kong potential. In B. Morrison (Ed.), *Experiments and evaluation in self-access language learning* (pp. 61–72)). Hong Kong: Hong Kong Association for Self-Access Learning and Development.

Miller, L., Tsang, E. S. C., & Hopkins, M. (2007, July 1, 2007). Establishing a self-access centre in a secondary school. *ELT Journal*, 61(3), 220–227. https://doi.org/https://doi.org/10.1093/elt/ccm029

Mooi, C. T. (1991). Designing and managing a self-access learning system for adult learners. *Guidelines*, 13(1), 74–81. http://search.ebscohost.com/login.aspx?direct=true&db=eric&AN=EJ474501&site=ehost-live

Moore, C. (1992). *Self-access: Appropriate technology*. Manchester: The British Council.

Morrison, B. (Ed.) (1999). *Experiments and evaluation in self-access language learning*. Hong Kong: The Hong Kong Association for Self-Access Learning and Development.

Morrison, B. (2005). Evaluating learning gain in a self-access language learning centre. *Language Teaching Research*, 9(3), 267–293.

Mozzon-McPherson, M. (2007). Supporting independent learning environments: An analysis of structures and roles of language learning advisers. *System*, 35(1), 66–92. 10.1016/j.system.2006.10.008. http://search.ebscohost.com/login.aspx?direct=true&db=aph&AN=24139522&site=ehost-live

Murray, G. (2017). Autonomy in the time of complexity: Lessons from beyond the classroom. *Studies in Self-Access Learning Journal*, 183–193. http://sisaljournal.org/archives/jun17/murray1

Mynard, J. (2012). Does 'self-access' still have life in it?: A response to Reinders (2012). *ELTWorldOnline,* 4. http://blog.nus.edu.sg/eltwo/2012/06/13/does-%E2%80%98self-access%E2%80%99-still-have-life-in-it-a-response-to-reinders-2012/

Mynard, J., & Shelton-Strong, S. J. (2020). Investigating the autonomy-supportive nature of a self-access environment: A self-determination theory approach. In J. Mynard, M. Tamala, & W. Peeters (Eds.), *Supporting learners and educators in developing language learner autonomy.* Hong Kong: Candlin & Mynard.

Mynard, J., & Stevenson, R. (2017). Promoting learner autonomy and self-directed learning: The evolution of a SALC curriculum. *Studies in Self-Access Learning Journal,* 169–182. http://sisaljournal.org/archives/jun17/mynard_stevenson

Nunan, D. (1988). *The learner-centred curriculum: A study in second language teaching.* Cambridge: Cambridge University Press.

O'Dowd, R., & Lewis, T. (Eds.) (2016). *Online intercultural exchange: Policy, pedagogy, practice.* London: Routledge.

O'Dell, F. (1992). Helping teachers to use a self-access centre to its full potential. *ELT Journal, 46*(2), 153–159.

Oga-Baldwin, W. L. Q. (2015). Supporting the needs of twenty-first century learners: A self-determination theory perspective. In C. Koh (Ed.), *Motivation, leadership and curriculum design* (pp. 137–149). New York: Springer.

Pemberton, R., Li, E. S. L., Or, W. W. F., & Pierson, H. D. (Eds.) (1996). *Taking control: Autonomy in language learning.* Hong Kong: Hong Kong University Press.

Pemberton, R., Toogood, S., & Barfield, A. (Eds.) (2009). *Maintaining control: Autonomy and language learning.* Hong Kong: Hong Kong University Press.

Reinders, H. (2012). The end of self-access?: From walled garden to public park. *ELTWorldOnline, 4.* http://blog.nus.edu.sg/eltwo/2012/06/13/the-end-of-self-access-from-walled-garden-to-public-park/

Reinders, H., & Balcikanli, C. (2011). Learning to foster autonomy: The role of teacher education materials. *Studies in Self-Access Learning Journal, 2*(1), 15–25.

Riley, P. (1974). From fact to function: Aspects of the work of the C.R.A.P.E.L. *Mélanges Pédagogiques, 5,* 1–11.

Sheerin, S. (1989). *Self-access.* Oxford: Oxford University Press.

Stickler, U., & Emke, M. (2011). Tandem learning in virtual spaces: Supporting non-formal and informal learning in adults. In P. Benson & H. Reinders (Eds.), *Beyond the language classroom* (pp. 146–160). Palgrave.

Sturtridge, G. (1992). *Self-access: Preparation and training.* Manchester: British Council.

Tassinari, M. G. (2017). Encouraging autonomy through a community of practice: The role of a self-access centre. *Studies in Self-Access Learning Journal, 8*(2), 157–168. http://sisaljournal.org/archives/jun17/tassinari

Tassinari, M. G. (2018). Autonomy and reflection on practice in a self-access language centre: Comparing the manager and the student assistant perspectives. *Studies in Self-Access Learning Journal, 9*(3), 387–412.

Thompson, G., & Atkinson, L. (2010). Integrating self-access into the curriculum: Our experience. *Studies in Self-Access Learning Journal, 1*(1), 47–58. https://sisaljournal.org/archives/jun10/thompson_atkinson/

Toogood, S., & Pemberton, R. (2002). Integrating self-access language learning into the curriculum: A case study. In P. Benson & S. Toogood (Eds.), *Learner autonomy 7: Challenges to research and practice* (pp. 85–109). Dublin: Authentik.

Trebbi, T. (2011). Students planning language learning Case 8. In M. J. Raya & F. Vieira (Eds.), *Understanding and exploring pedagogy for autonomy in language education: A case-based approach.* Dublin: Authentik.

Watson-Todd, R. (Ed.) (2014). *Proceedings of the DRAL2/ILA conference.* Bangkok: King Mongkut University of Technology Thonburi.

Watson, K., & Agawa, G. (2016). Program development for self-access center and core course integration. *SCRIPSIMUS, 25,* 51–73. http://ir.lib.u-ryukyu.ac.jp/bitstream/20.500.12000/36286/1/No25p051.pdf

Welch Bacon, C. E., & Gaither, K. (2020). Personalized learning pathways: Using technology to promote learning beyond the classroom. *New directions for teaching and learning, 2020*(162), 91–102. https://doi.org/10.1002/tl.20394

Wichayathian, N., & Reinders, H. (2018, 2018/04/03). A teacher's perspective on autonomy and self-access: From theory to perception to practice. *Innovation in Language Learning and Teaching, 12*(2), 89–104. https://doi.org/https://doi.org/10.1080/17501229.2015.1103245

Young, J. T., Hafner, C. A., & Fisher, D. W. (2007). Shifting sands: Supporting teachers in facilitating independent learning. In A. Barfield & S. H. Brown (Eds.), *Reconstructing autonomy in language education: Inquiry and innovation* (pp. 196–208). Basingstoke: Palgrave Macmillan.

20
ASSESSMENTS OF AND FOR LBC

Tony Burner

Introduction

This chapter focuses on how assessment, language teaching and language learning are intertwined in ways that not only enhance learning and teaching processes in classrooms, but also extend beyond the classroom. The relations between assessment, motivation, self-efficacy beliefs and self-regulated learning strategies are crucial for the extensions beyond the classroom to take place. Peer assessment, self-assessment and other alternative assessments are assessments that have proven to support learning, collaborative skills and higher order thinking in ways that could be useful for learners' life beyond the classroom. Other topics that will be discussed in this chapter are the power of feedback and washback. Both feedback and washback have societal aspects that can be positive or negative beyond the classroom. Assessment also concerns issues of equity in society, where minority language students and students from lower socio-economic homes often are victims of unintended negative consequences of poor feedback and washback practices. Their home languages are seldom acknowledged or used as a resource in assessments, and they do not have the same support at home as the majority students when language learning is critical to succeed on assessments. Thus, some of these problems of assessment will also be discussed.

Key constructs

Two hundred years ago, the way the classical languages Latin and Greek were taught in schools was used as a model for language learning in general. This model has later been described as the Grammar-Translation Method, where the emphasis was on deductive grammar teaching, learning grammar rules and vocabulary by heart. Tests reflected the language teaching methods of the time. Thus, reproduction of grammar rules and patterns were emphasized in tests. The last 50 years, in tandem with more communicative and contextual approaches to language learning and teaching methods, new ways of assessment have emerged. There have been calls for a shift from a test culture to an assessment culture (Gipps, 2012). Broadfoot and Black (2004) refer to the 1990s and the beginning of the 2000s as the assessment era, "a belief in the power of assessment to provide a rational, efficient and publicly acceptable mechanism of judgement and control" (p. 19). They describe a change where assessments are used to support learning rather than to judge it, based on social-constructivist learning theories (Black & Wiliam, 1998). Others, such as Pryor and Crossouard (2008), conceptualize assessments supporting learning within sociocultural learning theories. The process and the quality of assessment should be emphasized, rather than the product and the quantity (Lantolf & Thorne, 2006), viewing language learning as an ongoing, unfinished and explorative process (Brown, 2000).

Simultaneously, there has been an increased attention on bridging the gap between what students learn at school and what they do outside of school. Learning is not supposed to occur in a vacuum, but support students in their life-long tasks of being a good citizen in democratic societies (Westheimer, 2015). The critique against decontextualized standardized assessments is succinctly posed by Westheimer (2015, p. 27):

> Behind the onslaught of testing and so-called accountability measures lurks the same perverse logic of the man looking for his keys. We know what matters to most teachers, parents, school administrators, board members, and policymakers. But we are far less sure how to find out whether teachers and schools are successful in teaching what matters. Since we have relatively primitive ways of assessing students' abilities to think, create, question, analyze, form healthy relationships, and work in concert with others to improve their communities and the world, we turn instead to where the light is: standardized measures of students' abilities to decode sentences and solve mathematical problems. In other words, *since we can't measure what we care about, we start to care about what we can measure.*

According to Westheimer and Kahne (2004), the good citizen is a personally responsible citizen who acts responsibly in the community, a participatory citizen who is an active member of community organizations and/or improvement efforts, and a social justice-oriented citizen who critically assesses social, political and economic structures. Assessments should have the same purpose: educating children and young adults to become good citizens. Thus, the core argument in this chapter is that assessment *is* learning (Hayward, 2015). Through what has been referred to as "alternative assessments", learners develop skills and knowledge that can be useful for language learning and teaching beyond the classroom (LBC).

Alternative assessments

As a result of the developments mentioned above, the various functions of assessments have become clearer and much debated in recent years. "Alternative assessment" is often used as a term referring to all types of assessments that can support learning when assessing students' *performance*, as opposed to traditional standardized assessments where the objective is to measure students' knowledge in order to rank or rate their performance, for instance, in order to compete for a study program or a specific job. Another term that has been used for alternative assessment is *authentic* assessment. Learners' problem-solving skills and higher-level thinking processes are part of the assessment, in addition to the product of assessment. The point is not that alternative assessment is an alternative to traditional standardized assessments, but that it has an alternative function. Alternative assessments support learning processes in flexible and meaningful ways (Gozuyesil & Tanriseven, 2017) in which learners play a central role (Boud & Falchikov, 2006; Wiliam, 2011); they are *not* used primarily to report ranked data or provide a mark or certificate, but to enhance learners' higher order thinking and skills, which they may benefit from beyond the classroom.

The function of alternative assessments is formative, not summative. The term *formative* in "formative assessment" stems from Scriven's (1967) definition of formative and summative evaluation of study programs. Later, *Assessment for Learning* was coined by the Assessment Reform Group (1989–2010) in the United Kingdom to stress the learning dimension

(Assessment Reform Group, 2002). The UK reform group, consisting of several assessment researchers, put formative assessment on the educational agenda from the mid-1990s (Black & Wiliam, 2003). They define formative assessment as "The process of seeking and interpreting evidence for use by learners and their teachers, to identify where the learners are in their learning, where they need to go and how best to get there" (Assessment Reform Group, 2002). In 1998, in an oft-cited review article, Black and Wiliam (1998) documented formative assessment's learning benefits, which also were researched in foreign language learning contexts (Ross, 2005) and examined critically across subject fields and ages (Gozuyesil & Tanriseven, 2017; Kingston & Nash, 2011). Various assessment tools or methods are used in order to enhance formative assessment practices in schools, for example, self- and peer assessment, reflective logs and portfolio assessment. These assessment tools or methods can be advantageous for LBC since they have a formative purpose. They encourage learner autonomy and involve learners in decision-making where they set goals, reflect upon and evaluate the means they use to achieve their goals (Huang, 2013). However, the quality of formative feedback is essential in order to facilitate the feedback loops necessary for learning and development.

Formative feedback

The significance of formative feedback for assessment to have a positive impact on learners is often highlighted in research (Black & Wiliam, 1998; Hattie & Timperley, 2007). Formative feedback has to be selective and precise, it has to be directed at a process or product, not the person. It has to tell learners how the quality of the process or product is, what the next steps are, and how to get there (Hattie & Timperley, 2007). It has to be understood and acted upon. Moreover, it has to be provided *during* the learning process (Gamlem & Smith, 2013) in order to be useful (Shute, 2008). Only then, feedback can be powerful. Formative feedback offers opportunities for interaction – with oneself (self-assessment) and others (peers, parents and/or other supervisors). No matter what type of alternative assessment learners engage in, the value and effect of formative feedback cannot be overestimated. However, alternative assessments can have varying washback effects.

Potential washback effects of alternative assessments

Washback effect is any effect that assessments have on learning and teaching practices. A washback effect may be positive (beneficial), negative (harmful) or neutral (indifferent). However, assessments have seldom the same washback effects. The effects depend on various factors, such as assessment type, learner motivation, learning support (not the least at home), learners' socio-economic background and their intellectual capacity. Studies show that language skills that are emphasized on assessments, for example, listening skills, may make learners pay particular attention to those skills in out-of-class learning. However, the extent of washback effect can be diverse, including effects on how learners perceive themselves (Zhan & Andrews, 2014). In other studies, high-performing learners prove to have a higher chance of taking advantage of the possibilities provided by portfolio assessment (Burner, 2015) and self-assessment (Panadero et al., 2016).

All in all, alternative assessment methods require that learners seize the opportunities they are given in order to learn, improve and develop skills needed beyond the classroom. Some potential benefits of alternative assessments are stimulation of and reflection upon oral and written interactions with others and their own texts (Black, 2015), and development of intrinsic motivation and transversal skills (Dweck, 2000). In the long term, learners become more autonomous and responsible in general and they become more effective in their learning processes in particular (Brookhart, 2013). Moreover, alternative assessments provide opportunities for learners to critically evaluate their own and others' work. By doing that, and engage formatively in assessments, learners develop the skill that is said to be the only skill with permanent value beyond the classroom: *learning to learn* or *metacognitive strategies* (Black, 2015). In the following, I will describe the most typical examples of alternative assessment tools or methods, i.e. self-assessment, peer assessment and portfolio assessment, and explain their relevance for LBC.

Self- and peer assessment

Self-assessment involves techniques or tools where learners assess the quality of their own learning processes and/or products. Typically, rubrics, logs, reflective journals, scales and checklists are used. However, self-assessment – similar to the other alternative assessments – is not a clearly defined construct. As pointed out by Panadero et al. (2016, p. 810):

> Several factors may importantly alter the nature of making a self-assessment. These include, among others (a) the medium of SSA [student self-assessment], (b) the delay between SSA and the last learning or instructional session, (c) learners' expectations about the type and purposes of assessment for which they will be assessed, and (d) whether learners are provided "no criteria" versus specific criteria.

As a consequence, "… different kinds of SSA are given the same name, while similar kinds of SSA are sometimes given different names" (ibid.). In other words, there are too many factors that influence how studies on self-assessment are conducted, given that its typology is rather heterogeneous. Papanthymou and Darra (2019) reviewed empirical studies from 2008 to 2018, revealing that self-assessment improves academic performance, in addition to enhancing abilities and strategies that are useful for LBC: increasing learning motivation, developing self-regulated learning strategies and increasing self-esteem. The review found that most of the studies concern higher and secondary education, hence calling for more research in primary education. In addition to the above-mentioned advantages, learners can gain increased sense of ownership to their own work through self-assessment (Black & Wiliam, 1998). An increased sense of ownership equips learners with a feeling of responsibility for what they do, which can be advantageous for LBC. Oftentimes, both in research and in classroom practice, self-assessment is accompanied with peer assessment. In fact, peer assessment contributes to self-assessment (Black, 2015).

Peer assessment is any assessment where learners assess their peers' learning processes and/or products. Through peer feedback, learners can develop skills that can be useful for LBC: providing feedback to others (Nigel, 2020), developing their collaboration skills and gaining insight into peers' ideas (Van Gennip et al., 2010). Peer assessment can also improve learners' academic skills (Gielen et al., 2010). It could be argued that peer assessment is a somewhat newer and less researched field than self-assessment (Kollar & Fischer, 2010). A quick search in the database ERIC (Education Resources Information Center – an online library of education research) reveals this fact; searching with the keyword "self-assessment", limited to peer reviewed articles during the years 2000–2021, yields 5,656 hits, whereas the same search for "peer assessment" gives 3,261 hits. Afitska (2014) reviewed studies on self- and peer assessment in the context of formative assessment in lower grades in second and foreign language learning classes. She points out that most of the studies concern adult learners and a few studies from primary levels. Most research on peer assessment has undoubtedly been conducted in higher education settings. Peer assessment is, similar to self-assessment, learner-centered. It requires learners to be active in the process in order for it to be effective (Tillema et al., 2011). Not surprisingly, practice makes perfect also here (Afitska, 2014; Saito, 2008), meaning that even though learners need training and peer assessment needs to be conducted regularly, with time they will need less training since they know more about the processes involved. However, research indicates that the improvement in quality becomes less significant in further sessions (Chen & Tsai, 2009). Nonetheless, the benefits of peer assessment outweigh the difficulties (Kulenovic, 2018). One common critique of peer assessment is, particularly from learners themselves, that the peer feedback lacks the quality that teacher feedback has. However, meta-analyses of peer assessment ratings show a moderately high level of agreement with teacher ratings (Li et al., 2016).

Portfolio assessment

Another well-known and popular alternative assessment method or tool is portfolio assessment. Portfolio assessment is characterized by collecting, reflecting and selecting texts (written, oral or multimodal) (Hamp-Lyons & Condon, 2000, p. 118ff). Collection involves keeping track of one's texts and improving them with the help of formative feedback. Selection involves choosing some of those texts for a summative assessment at the end of a course or school year. The European Language Portfolio (ELP)[1] (Council of Europe, 2001) has played a key role in the European educational context when it comes to developing and promoting the use of portfolio assessment. Portfolio assessment stimulates authenticity, interactivity, reflection, ownership and revision skills (Weigle, 2002). Both self- and peer assessment are normally an integrated part of portfolio assessment (Black et al., 2003). A review of its formative benefits in second and foreign language learning contexts indicates that portfolio assessment can be motivating and can enhance learners' performance, enable process assessment and authentic language use, integrate language teaching, learning and assessment, and foster learner-centeredness, learner autonomy, reflection and responsibility (Burner, 2014) – all of which are skills, attitudes and knowledge useful for LBC. After all, the aim of educational assessment is to build a bridge between learners' in-class learning and development and out-of-class learning and development, and supporting them in becoming good citizens (Westheimer, 2015).

Current issues

There are several issues concerning alternative assessment relating both to theory and practice, among others the lack of a clear construct and evidence, the difficulties of measuring its effect on LBC and ensuring equity or fairness for all learners, and issues pertaining to teachers' and students' perceptions of alternative assessments. These issues will be discussed below.

The construct "alternative assessment" or "formative assessment" can be fuzzy, too broad and definitely not clear-cut. Different definitions are used across research fields (Baird et al., 2017), which makes comparative approaches less fruitful and cumulative research results more challenging. Moreover, as underlined by Bennett (2011) in a critical review, too little attention has been paid to the interpretation of research evidence. There are many studies claiming that alternative/formative assessments lead to or enhance beneficial learner skills, attitudes and knowledge, but few larger longitudinal studies where the effects are controlled and measured exist. The validity of alternative assessments was first based mainly on Black and Wiliam's influential review of its effects (0.4-0.7 effect sizes), but the last two decades lacks good quantitative research of its impacts on learning (cf. Kingston & Nash, 2011). Thus, alternative assessment's effect on learning is thus still disputed (cf. Baird et al., 2017). Not the least, we know too little about its applications outside school; traditionally, effectiveness has been measured with regard to achievement in school contexts.

Assessment's social, cultural and political aspects should not be underestimated. Language use and language learning beyond classroom is not valued in some cases, cf. home language of minority students. This is evident in assessments, such as "national test in reading", which in reality is a test of reading in the country's majority language, not necessarily a test of reading in general. If it had been a test of reading skills in general, the students should have been given the choice to read in the language they know best. This concerns equity or fairness (Gipps & Stobart, 2009), i.e. the quality of opportunities and results being fair for learners, strengthening reliability of alternative assessments. To be fair means differentiating by knowing the learners – both their life at school and beyond the classroom. The distinction between equality and equity or fairness is explained well by Tierney (2013, p. 133): "Equality is maintained with the same tasks and criteria for all learners, while equity involves differentiating according to students' needs". Strengthening reliability of alternative assessments requires the use of assessment criteria (Klenowski, 2002). Using the same standards and criteria for everyone ensures a certain level of reliability, and thus equity or fairness. Another point relating to equity, is the availability of language learning support for LBC. Assessments concern the same syllabus, curriculum, learning speed and available resources at schools for all students. However, even though lots of language learning occurs beyond the classroom, language learning support through formative feedback is not available for all learners beyond the teacher support at school, particularly when it comes to minority language students and students coming from lower socio-economic homes.

Alternative assessments are sometimes perceived as being time-consuming (Al-Nouh et al., 2014) but studies have shown that when teachers who do not have experience with alternative assessments and then, for example, carry out peer assessment, feel they save time and they are surprised by the students' proficiency in providing formative feedback (Burner, 2015). Moreover, skills, knowledge and attitudes that are easy to assess, usually in a short term perspective and limited to a few areas of learning and development – usually mathematics and literacy (Westheimer, 2015) – are prioritized by educational authorities. Thus, it could be argued that alternative assessments stand in contrast to an accountability regime where the assessments at school – that "count" in an easily measurable way – stimulate extrinsic motivation and make alternative assessments seem less important and hence less motivating. This is problematic given that alternative assessments to a greater extent than traditional or standardized assessments stimulate skills, knowledge and attitudes relevant for LBC. Finally, practitioners tend to overestimate their formative assessment practices (Burner, 2016; Pat-El. et al., 2015). In other words, they do a lot they think is formative in their assessment practices, whereas typically the feedback is not formative (enough), the assessment procedures are not clear (enough), or there is a lack of a follow-up system to ensure that learners understand and use the feedback they are provided. Studies also show that students are prone to underestimate the relevance of self- and peer assessment, maintaining that the teacher knows best (Peterson & Irving, 2008). This can hamper the implementation of alternative assessments that could support and enhance LBC. So what possible implications can we draw when it comes to alternative assessments and LBC?

Implications

First, it is important that researchers and practitioners increase their awareness regarding the issues mentioned above. For example, knowing that assessments are equal even though the learners are very different with varying language learning support at home. Second, researchers and practitioners should encourage alternative assessments in schools, highlighting their advantages for LBC. Alternative assessments should be considered as learning in and beyond classroom contexts. They should nurture the advantages of alternative assessments, despite not having exact evidence of accuracy (Panadero et al., 2016). Third, students need to understand that assessment is much more than testing, that things they do during LBC can be meaningful and useful for their lives even though it is not "tested" in a traditional way. As Panadero et al. (2016, p. 817) succinctly put it, we need to "persuade students that there is benefit in reflecting on the quality of work, even if this does not contribute to assessment per se". Fourth, researchers and practitioners need to acknowledge that alternative assessments such as self- and peer assessment need instruction and practice. They need to be conducted regularly and become an integrated part of a holistic learning and teaching system, extending beyond the classroom (Long & Huang, 2015). As pointed out by Panadero et al. (2016, p. 819): "Just as we cannot ask students to perform a novel task with the ease and fluency of an expert, so we should not expect students to conduct SSA [student self-assessment] with ease and accuracy, until they have mastered the relevant skills".

How alternative assessments are introduced and implemented is also context-dependent. In some national contexts, for example, Mainland China, language learning is more exam-driven (Huang, 2013), which makes alternative assessments and consequently LBC a more challenging affair. Connections between assessment and LBC in such contexts, as illustrated by, for example, projects on out-of-class pronunciation learning, have been successful when teachers and learners worked together toward making LBC possible, when learners were given specific tasks to do and strategies to employ, when issues of power relations between teachers and learners were addressed, when learners were given more responsibility and freedom, and when learners had access to appropriate learning materials (Long & Huang, 2015). I believe the challenges and the success criteria from studies like the one mentioned above can shed light on similar challenges in other contexts and help practitioners adopt successful implementation strategies.

Future directions

I believe two areas are in urgent need of attention in the near future. First, studies need to look into and define the components involved in alternative assessments, aiming at approaching a clearer construct than today. It would be useful to be able to unpack the various strategies involved in alternative assessments and relate them more clearly to LBC, such as learner autonomy, transversal skills and metacognitive skills. We know that alternative assessments, when designed and implemented successfully, have positive effects on learning and development that can be useful in out-of-class contexts, but we know less about the extent and the nature of those effects; more research is needed to understand those mechanisms. Second, both researchers and practitioners need to grapple with the tensions between increasing accountability measures and the use of alternative assessments. It is discouraging for all stakeholders – not the least the learners – when so many national and international tests penetrate everyday classroom practices that teachers and parents may lose sight of the formative potentials of assessments of and for LBC. The more assessments in schools focus on what can be measured on standardized tests, the less attention will be paid to what cannot be measured on those tests – which are often the skills and strategies developed through alternative assessments that learners can utilize in LBC.

Reflection questions

1. To what extent can classroom assessments support learning, particularly language learning, beyond the classroom?
2. Are there any assessments in schools that cannot be related to what learners do beyond the classroom? If so, in what ways can they not be related to activities beyond the classroom?
3. Which aspects of alternative assessments do you believe need to be changed in order for them to better support language learning beyond the classroom?

Recommended readings

Brown, G. T. L., & Harris, L. R. (Eds.) (2016). *Handbook of human and social conditions in assessment*. Routledge.
This handbook explores how social and human complexity affect assessment at all levels of learning. Part I deals with teachers' perspectives, Part II with students' perspectives and Part III with classroom conditions. Topics particularly relevant for alternative assessments include self-regulation, self- and peer assessment, students' perceptions of novel forms of assessment, student emotions toward assessment and collaborative learning.

McMillan, J. H. (Ed.) (2013). *SAGE handbook of research on classroom assessment*. SAGE Publications.
This handbook offers a comprehensive source of research on all aspects of K-12 classroom assessment. Section I is about contexts for research on assessment, Section II about technical quality of classroom assessments, Sections III and IV on formative and summative assessment, Section V on methods and Section VI on differentiation in assessment. During my work with this chapter, I found Brookhart's chapter on assessment and motivation theory and Tierney's chapter on fairness useful for assessment of and for LBC.

Nunan, D., & Richards, J. C. (2015). *Language learning beyond the classroom*. Routledge.
I recommend this book to those interested in more practical applications of the theories mentioned in this chapter. The book contains case studies of LBC from various contexts in America, Europe and Asia-Pacific regions. I refer to the chapter by Long and Huang on out-of-class pronunciation learning in Mainland China in the current chapter. Several of the case studies can be related to assessment methods and procedures even though the book is not specifically about assessment.

Note

1 Named LinguaFolio in the United States.

References

Afitska, O. (2014). Use of formative assessment, self- and peer assessment in the classrooms: Some insights from recent language testing and assessment (LTA) research. *i-manager's Journal on English Language Teaching, 4*(1), 29–39. https://doi.org/10.26634/jelt.4.1.2640

Al-Nouh, N. A., Taqi, H. A., & Abdul-Kareem, M. M. (2014). EFL primary school teachers' attitudes, knowledge and skills in alternative assessment. *International Education Studies, 7*(5), 68–84. https://doi.org/10.5539/ies.v7n5p68

Assessment Reform Group. (2002). *Researched-based principles of assessment for learning to guide classroom practice*. http://www.nuffieldfoundation.org/assessment-reform-group

Baird, J-A., Andrich, D., Hopfenbeck, T. N., & Stobart, G. (2017). Assessment and learning: fields apart? *Assessment in Education: Principles, Policy & Practice, 24*(3), 317–350. https://doi.org/10.1080/0969594X.2017.1319337

Bennett, R. E. (2011). Formative assessment: A critical review. *Assessment in Education: Principles, Policy & Practice, 18*(1), 5–25. https://doi.org/10.1080/0969594X.2010.513678

Black, P. (2015). Formative assessment – an optimistic but incomplete vision. *Assessment in Education: Principles, Policy & Practice, 22*(1), 161–177. https://doi.org/10.1080/0969594X.2014.999643

Black, P., Harrison, C., Lee, C., Marshall, B., & Wiliam, D. (2003). *Assessment for learning. Putting it into practice*. Open University Press.

Black, P., & Wiliam, D. (1998). Assessment and classroom learning. *Assessment in Education: Principles, Policy & Practice, 5*, 7–74. https://doi.org/10.1080/0969595980050102

Black, P., & Wiliam, D. (2003). In praise of educational research: Formative assessment. *British Educational Research Journal, 29*(5), 623–637. https://doi.org/10.1080/0141192032000133721

Boud, D. J., & Falchikov, N. (2006). Aligning assessment with long-term learning. *Assessment and Evaluation in Higher Education, 31*(4), 399–413. https://doi.org/10.1080/02602930600679050

Broadfoot, P., & Black, P. (2004). Redefining assessment? The first ten years of assessment in education. *Assessment in Education: Principles, Policy & Practice, 11*(1), 7–26. https://doi.org/10.1080/0969594042000208976

Brookhart, S. M. (2013). Classroom assessment in the context of motivation theory and research. In J. H. McMillan (Ed.), *SAGE handbook of research on classroom assessment* (pp. 35–54). SAGE Publications.

Brown, H. D. (2000). *Principles of language learning and teaching* (4th ed.). Longman.

Burner, T. (2014). The potential benefits of portfolio assessment in second and foreign language writing contexts: A review of the literature. *Studies in Educational Evaluation, 43*(4), 139–149. https://doi.org/10.1016/j.stueduc.2014.03.002

Burner, T. (2015). Processes of change when using portfolios to enhance formative assessment of writing. *Assessment Matters, 9*(2), 53–79. http://dx.doi.org/10.18296/am.0011

Burner, T. (2016). Formative assessment of writing in English as a foreign language. *Scandinavian Journal of Educational Research, 60*(6), 626–648. https://doi.org/10.1080/00313831.2015.1066430

Chen, Y., & Tsai, C. (2009). An educational research course facilitated by online peer assessment. *Innovations in Education and Teaching International, 46*(1), 105–117. https://doi.org/10.1080/14703290802646297

Council of Europe. (2001). *Common European framework of reference for languages: Learning, teaching, assessment*. Cambridge University Press. http://www.coe.int/t/dg4/education/elp/

Dweck, C. S. (2000). *Self-theories: Their role in motivation, personality and development*. Psychology Press.

Gamlem, S. M., & Smith, K. (2013). Student perceptions of classroom feedback. *Assessment in Education: Principles, Policy & Practice, 20*(2), 150–169. https://doi.org/10.1080/0969594X.2012.749212

Gielen, S., Peeters, E., Doucy, F., Onghena, P., & Struyven, K. (2010). Improving the effectiveness of peer feedback for learning. *Learning and Instruction, 20*(4), 304–315. https://doi.org/10.1016/j.learninstruc.2009.08.007

Gipps, C. (2012). *Beyond testing: Towards a theory of educational assessment* (2nd ed.). Falmer Press.

Gipps, C., & Stobart, G. (2009). Fairness in assessment. In C. Wyatt-Smith & J. J. Cumming (Eds.), *Educational assessment in the 21st century: Connecting theory and practice* (pp. 105–118). Springer.

Gozuyesil, E., & Tanriseven, I. (2017). A meta-analysis of the effectiveness of alternative assessment techniques. *Eurasian Journal of Educational Research, 70*, 37–56.

Hamp-Lyons, L., & Condon, W. (2000). *Assessing the portfolio. Principles for practice, theory and research*. Hampton Press, Inc.

Hayward, L. (2015) Assessment is learning: the preposition vanishes. *Assessment in Education: Principles, Policy & Practice, 22*(1), 27–43. https://doi.org/10.1080/0969594X.2014.984656

Hattie, J., & Timperley, H. (2007). The power of feedback. *Review of Educational Research, 77*(1), 81–112. https://doi.org/10.3102%2F003465430298487

Huang, J. (2013). *Autonomy, agency and identity in foreign language learning and teaching*. Peter Lang.

Kingston, N., & Nash, B. (2011). Formative assessment: A meta-analysis and a call for research. *Educational Measurement: Issues and Practice, 30*, 28–37.

Klenowski, V. (2002). *Developing portfolios for learning and assessment. Processes and principles*. Routledge Falmer.

Kollar, I., & Fischer, F. (2010). Peer assessment as collaborative learning: A cognitive perspective. *Learning and Instruction, 20*(4), 344–348. https://doi.org/10.1016/j.learninstruc.2009.08.005

Kulenovic, E. (2018). How can student peer assessment be used to improve the quality of student learning? *Teacher Education Advancement Network Journal, 10*(1), 35–49.

Lantolf, J. P., & Thorne, S. L. (2006). *Sociocultural theory and the genesis of second language development*. Oxford University Press.

Li, H., Xiong, Y., Zang, X., Kornhaber, M. L., Lyu, M. L., Chung, K. S., & Suen, H. K. (2016). Peer assessment in the digital age: A meta-analysis comparing peer and teacher ratings. *Assessment & Evaluation in Higher Education, 41*(2), 245–264. https://doi.org/10.1080/02602938.2014.999746

Long, N., & Huang, J. (2015). Out-of-class pronunciation learning. Are EFL learners ready in China? In D. Nunan & J. C. Richards (Eds.), *Language learning beyond the classroom* (pp. 43–52). Routledge.

Nigel, Q-B. (2020). The effects of peer feedback, within an 'assessment as learning' approach, on the learning and development of student-teachers. *Practitioner Research in Higher Education, 13*(1), 27–36.

Panadero, E., Brown, G. T. L., & Strijbos, J-W. (2016). The future of student self-assessment: A review of known unknowns and potential directions. *Educational Psychology Review, 28*(4), 803–830. https://doi.org/10.1007/s10648-015-9350-2

Papanthymou, A., & Darra, M. (2019). The contribution of learner self-assessment for improvement of learning and teaching process: A review. *Journal of Education and Learning, 8*(1), 48–64. https://doi.org/10.5539/jel.v8n1p48

Pat-El, R. J., Tillema, H., Segers, M., & Vedder, P. (2015). Multilevel predictors of differing perceptions of assessment for learning practices between teachers and students. *Assessment in Education: Principles, Policy & Practice, 22*(2), 282–298. https://doi.org/10.1080/0969594X.2014.975675

Peterson, E. R., & Irving, S. E. (2008). Secondary school students' conceptions of assessment and feedback. *Learning and Instruction, 18*(3), 238–250. https://doi.org/10.1016/j.learninstruc.2007.05.001

Pryor, J., & Crossouard, B. (2008). A socio-cultural theorization of formative assessment. *Oxford Review of Education, 34*(1), 1–20. https://doi.org/10.1080/03054980701476386

Ross, S. J. (2005). The impact of assessment method on foreign language proficiency growth. *Applied Linguistics, 26*(3), 317–342. https://doi.org/10.1093/applin/ami011

Saito, H. (2008). EFL Classroom peer assessment: Training effects on rating and commenting. *Language Testing, 25*(4), 553–581. https://doi.org/10.1177%2F0265532208094276

Scriven, M. S. (1967). The methodology of evaluation. In R. W. Tyler, R. M. Gagne, & M. Scriven (Eds.), *Perspectives of curriculum evaluation* (pp. 39–83). Rand McNally.

Shute, V. (2008). Focus on formative feedback. *Review of Educational Research, 78*(1), 153–189. https://doi.org/10.3102%2F0034654307313795

Tierney, R. D. (2013). Fairness in classroom assessment. In J. H. McMillan (Ed.), *SAGE handbook of research on classroom assessment* (pp. 125–144). SAGE Publications.

Tillema, H., Leenknecht, M., & Segers, M. (2011). Assessing assessment quality: Criteria for quality assurance in design of (peer) assessment for learning – A review of research studies. *Studies in Educational Evaluation, 37*(1), 25–34. https://doi.org/10.1016/j.stueduc.2011.03.004

Van Gennip, N. A. E., Segers, M. S. R., & Tillema, H. H. (2010). Peer assessment as a collaborative learning activity: the role of interpersonal variables and conceptions. *Learning and Instruction, 20*(4), 280–290. https://doi.org/10.1016/j.learninstruc.2009.08.010

Weigle, S. C. (2002). *Assessing writing*. Cambridge University Press.

Westheimer, J. (2015). *What kind of citizen? Educating our children for the common good*. Teachers College Press.

Westheimer, J., & Kahne, J. (2004). What kind of citizen? The politics of educating for democracy. *American Educational Research Journal, 41*(2), 237–269.

Wiliam, D. (2011). What is assessment for learning? *Studies in Educational Evaluation, 37*(1), 3–14. https://doi.org/10.1016/j.stueduc.2011.03.001

Zhan, Y., & Andrews, S. (2014). Washback effects from a high-stakes examination on out-of-class English learning: insights from possible self theories. *Assessment in Education: Principles, Policy & Practice, 21*(1), 71–89. https://doi.org/10.1080/0969594X.2012.757546

PART III
Researching LLTBC

21
ETHICS, PRIVACY AND SECURITY IN RESEARCHING LBC

Liss Kerstin Sylvén

Introduction

Ethics is increasingly found at the center stage of research. From mainly having concerned what information informants have received, and their consent to participate, the ethics section in present-day scholarly publications is usually somewhat more comprehensive (ALLEA – All European Academies, 2017). This chapter goes even further and argues that ethical considerations should permeate all stages of research, from research questions to dissemination of results (see also Hultgren, Erling, & Chowdhury, 2016). The consideration of all possible ethical aspects of investigations involving human informants is vital in order to secure the privacy and well-being of participants as well as the reliability and validity of the research in question (e.g., Moss, Girard, & Haniford, 2006; Shohamy, 2001). This chapter will discuss ethics, privacy and security as they pertain in general to the research of language learning beyond the classroom (LBC) and, as LBC not seldom concerns non-adult individuals, in particular to young informants involved in such research (Larsson, Williams, & Zetterquist, 2019; Silverman, 2017). It will start by a historical overview of the role of ethics followed by a contextualization of ethics in contemporary research. The chapter will then discuss current ethical issues of importance to LBC research, what perspectives need to be considered by researchers, and how they theoretically and practically can be dealt with, before, during and after a study including informants, other collaborators, and dissemination. As a relatively new area of inquiry, LBC research goes beyond the settings of formal education and stretches into the private spheres of the informants, thus giving rise to new ethical considerations. One of the aims of this chapter is to raise an awareness of such issues, and help tackle them.

Key constructs

What is ethics? Etymologically the term ethics comes from the Greek word *ethikos*, which is derived from *ethos*, the meaning of which is *custom* or *character*. Ethics is closely related to moral, insofar as *ethics* is Greek and *moral* Latin, both terms holding basically the same meaning. In some contexts, moral has come to mean the concrete, practical implementation, whereas ethics has been used for abstract, theoretical aspects. In other contexts, however, the two terms are synonymous.

Looking at ethics from an ontological perspective a longstanding philosophical debate on ontology and ethics focuses on the discussion as to whether it can be argued that ethical values indeed have an ontology or not. Aristotle used the Greek term "to kalon", which Schuh (2018, p. 5) argues should be understood as "motivationally admirable actions", and which is often seen as the baseline in the discussion of ontology and ethics. Ethics finds a basis in the field of moral philosophy (Gensler, 2018), and can be encapsulated in the golden rule "treat others as you want to be treated". Taylor (2003, p. 320), in a discussion of the basics of ethics, argues that it is "the affirmation of universal human rights, with their sense that human beings are unconditionally worthy of respect". Ethics, thus, does not lend itself easily to being defined in precise terms. Rather, there are many definitions of the term, all of them pointing in more or less the same direction: ethics is "the philosophical study of good conduct" (Ross, 1930, p. 102); ethics is "the 'right' thing to do" (Hultgren et al., 2016, p. 2). All of the above attempts at defining ethics and morality focus on the responsibility of each individual to hold values that are up to standards expected in a certain context. This is also why discussions around ethical values can be difficult, and entail, as well as merit, vivid and constant thoughts about their implementation in practice.

Ethical perspectives are closely linked to and have a bearing on the validity of any research. Moss et al. (2006), in their text about validity in educational measurement, argue for the importance of the constant presence of interpretations, decisions, and actions, which they refer to as IDAs, in a research process. Validity, just like ethics, does not have one single definition, but many, depending on type of research, context, informants, etc. Messick (1989, p. 5) argues in connection with assessment that "validity is an integrated evaluative judgement of the degree to which empirical evidence and theoretical rationales support the adequacy and appropriateness of inferences and actions based on test scores or other modes of assessment". So, just as validity is dependent on sound IDAs throughout the research process, ethics is an inherent part of the IDAs.

The implementation of ethical values in all phases of research involving learning languages beyond the classroom, then, will be focused on in this chapter, with the aim of making it clear how and why we need to constantly bear these values in mind.

Key issues

Long gone are the times when studies such as those within, e.g., sociolinguistics, or pragmatics from the late 20th century were carried out without even touching upon ethical issues. An example are the groundbreaking studies by William Labov into the sociolects of New York (Labov, 1964, 1966). Labov interviewed and observed individuals with different socioeconomic status and ethnic backgrounds, and was among the first to prove that such individual variables may have a significant impact on pronunciation. However, in none of the publications are issues related to anonymity, informed and voluntary participation, or ethics touched upon.

It should be noted that Labov's studies were administered in a different time, bearing in mind the rules and regulations in force then. In addition, no harm was done to any of the (unaware) participants. Much worse are studies where false information is given to participants, the most famous of which are perhaps the Milgram experiments (Milgram, 1963) where obedience to authority was tested, in some cases leading to traumatic experiences for the participants. Participants were told to deliver shocks of increasingly higher voltage to a person in an adjacent room. The participant could hear this person scream, and eventually, as the voltage increased, go quiet. Unbeknownst to the participant, there was no voltage and the person in the other room was an actor.

Carrying out studies without observing the important elements of anonymity, informed and voluntary consent, and ethics in general is, of course, out of the question today. Gradually, ethics has become part and parcel of any study involving humans.

> "Ethical literacy" is a relatively new term, defined as "more than learning how to achieve a favourable opinion from an ethics committee, it is a matter of research quality and integrity. It means encouraging the development of an attitude to research where ethical issues are foregrounded and one where attention to ethical issues is given throughout the process of conducting research".
>
> (Wiles & Boddy, 2013, pp. 1–2)

In other words, ethical literacy is an understanding of what ethics entails and why it is important in all walks of life in general, and in research in particular. Along with the development of academic institutions and the role of the individual researcher, there has been an increased focus on ethical perspectives involved in research. From having enjoyed the status of an elevated institution in society, creating their own rules and regulations, higher education today takes on a much more society-centered role. In so doing, its activities are more closely scrutinized by outsiders in society. In a similar vein, from having been more or less completely up to the individual researcher to decide what to study and how to do it, as was the case for William Labov for instance, present-day researchers are to a very large degree dependent on external funding. The external funding bodies, governments and others, wish their money to be well spent, and spent on ethically sound projects. As is argued by OECD (2008, p. 1) "[a]t a time when scientific advances are considered to be critical in areas such as economic competitiveness, health, national security, and environmental protection, public officials are strongly motivated – indeed obligated – to ensure the highest levels of integrity in research". In the Helsinki declaration (Declaration of Helsinki, 2013, p. 2192), it is highlighted that "[e]very precaution must be taken to protect the privacy of the research subjects and the confidentiality of their personal information and to minimize the impact of the study on their physical, mental and social integrity". Therefore, rigorous vetting procedures are in place in all application processes, including ethics. Likewise, funding institutions require their ethical guidelines to be adhered to in order to finance research. However, due to the fuzziness connected to the ethical perspective, it has successively become clear that it cannot be left to the individual researcher to decide whether the design of a study is ethically sound or not. Courses in ethics are commonly offered to PhD students in order for anybody embarking on a career involving research to become ethically literate at an early stage of their studies. To lighten the burden and dependency on the individual researcher and his or her moral standpoints, ethical boards and committees are commonplace with the mission to carry out reviews on individual research projects involving human subjects, which we will return to below.

Privacy

At a larger, societal level, the implementation in the European Union (EU) some years ago of the General Data Protection Regulation (https://www.gdprsummary.com/), GDPR, marked an important milestone in the awareness raising of ethical issues in relation to digital spaces among the general public. The underlying purpose of the GDPR is to set out rules for data protection and privacy for all individuals within the EU. Of special interest to us as researchers, is the requirement to pseudonymize or anonymize personal data. The difference between the two is that while a pseudonymized participant can be re-identified by using a code-key, an anonymized individual will forever remain anonymous. The GDPR says that

> [a]nonymization of personal data is the process of encrypting or removing personally identifiable data from data sets so that the person can no longer be identified directly or indirectly. When a person cannot be re-identified the data is no longer considered personal data and the GDPR does not apply for further use.
> *(https://www.gdprsummary.com/anonymization-and-gdpr/)*

It is specified that true anonymization of data is irreversible and makes the identification of a natural person nearly impossible. More specifically for research studies this means, among other things, that not only should individuals not be able to identify; it is also important to keep confidential the schools and specific settings where any study has taken place. Failure to keep such information anonymous may lead to the possible identification of participants, at both group and individual levels. Therefore, any material collected, written, audio and video data, needs to be carefully masked before put into digital storage and/or used as examples in presentations and publications. Such masking involves, for instance, the removal of any geographical and other clues as to where the informant resides.

Technological developments have already enabled voice recognition (see, e.g., techtarget.com). Future progress will probably make it possible also to recognize individuals, even when they speak a second language. This means, that if our data is based on speech samples, in the future it may be possible, and maybe even easy, to decipher what individuals have taken part in a study. This will be particularly true for participants with a less common L1, which may shine through in their L2 pronunciation. This puts a question mark as to what we can promise our informants as regards secrecy and anonymity. Indeed, it is not only speech that can be used for source identification; also written text can be used for the same purpose, namely to figure out who the author is (Erard, 2017). By analyzing certain attributes, such as the use of linking words and adjectives, as well as text and sentence structure, it is possible to identify the person behind the writing. Such technological developments call for very careful handling of any type of data collected.

The GDPR puts ethical perspectives in the spotlight for research studies, and in so doing, creates some dilemmas. The anonymization requirement goes far in the GDPR. If all informants were to be irrevocably anonymized in accordance with the GDPR, then it will be impossible for any participant to "withdraw from further participation", a wording commonly found in many consent forms. Once data have been anonymized, it will be virtually impossible to locate the specific data pertaining to any one individual informant. Therefore, instead of promising total anonymity to participants, it may then be safer to use words like de-identify or pseudonomize, in order to live up to legal requirements.

Another promise sometimes made to informants, is that no one beyond the research team will ever be able to take part of the data collected. This is a promise that, in fact, should not be made, especially given the fact that it is not the researcher him or herself who "owns" the data, but rather the institution of the researcher. In some cases, external revisions or repeated analyses need to be made, and access to data is vital. In other cases, data are seen as official documents, and as such they should be accessible for others than merely those involved in the research. In this case, it may be safer to promise that the data will only be used for academic and research purposes, which is true even if others than those in the specific research team get access to them.

To sum up, there may be several reasons why ethical perspectives have changed from being very peripheral in much research, not least in applied linguistics, to being at the forefront of any present-day study. Suffice it here to conclude that it is clear that much has happened in the relationship between research and ethics during the last couple of decades. From this brief historical overview, let us therefore turn to some current issues in our field.

Ethics in contemporary language research

As touched on above, any research funding institution requires applicants to include a section on ethics in their research applications. A present-day application normally includes a section solely focused on ethical concerns, where not only yes/no questions are asked about, for instance, the inclusion of human data, but also where the applicant is asked to elaborate at some length on the study or project from an ethical perspective. In so doing, the applicant is given the opportunity to show his/her understanding of ethics, and how ethical considerations have been made in the planning stages, and will be made in the implementation of the study. This is also a chance for the individual applicant to carefully consider these aspects already at the preliminary stages of an investigation.

Once an application has received funding, it is often necessary to resubmit it, but this time to an ethical board or committee, not least regarding LBC research, as studies involving language learning and teaching typically entail the inclusion of human beings. The role of such boards is to ensure that ethical core values are adhered to throughout an entire study involving human subjects, and they are found as an inherent part of higher education worldwide. It should, however, be remembered that also ethical boards consist of human beings who hold their own views on ethical issues and how they should be interpreted. Sometimes decisions from ethical boards show evidence of very strict and narrow interpretations of the ethical rules, indicating a standpoint where the rules are at the center, rather than the study and its possible impact and importance. Such cases are unfortunate, as ethical boards are expected to be able to evaluate a study and its context as a whole. Additionally, international collaboration may be hindered as ethical rules and regulations vary between countries. If there is such a risk, it is appropriate to refer to the Helsinki Declaration, which states that a committee "must take into consideration the laws and regulations of the country or countries in which the research is to be performed as well as applicable international norms and standards" (Declaration of Helsinki, 2013, p. 2192).

To sum this section up, practically, the process from application to the actual administration of a study is long and difficult and may sometimes seem insurmountable. It is undoubtedly problematic if and when the red tape caused by these processes leads scholars to decide against initiating new projects. Ideally, we as researchers should instead embrace the opportunity to consider all aspects of our research from ethical points of view, and see the process as a way to ensuring that all aspects are as ethically sound as they possibly can be. And, in relation to international projects, ethical authorities need to be able to adapt to alternative regulations.

Implications

Informants

As LBC research often involves language learners who are not yet adults, the ethical issues at all levels of the research process need to be taken even more seriously than when including adult informants. Individuals who we wish to include in a research study should decide on their own whether they want to take part or not. Age limits vary from country to country; in some countries the age of 15 is a dividing line – if participants are 15 years old or younger, their own consent needs to be accompanied by that of their caretakers. For anybody older than 15, their own consent is in most cases enough. However, even if there are no regulations requiring consent from an adult, it is nevertheless to be advised that for informants up to the age of 18, caretakers be informed about the project in which their child will participate.

It is important that consent is voluntary and informed. Voluntary consent means that the decision to take part in a study is made by each individual (and his/her caretakers) and that no one is forced to participate. That means, for instance, that if a study is classroom based, we as researchers should not view the class as one entity we expect to take part in full. Rather, each and every student in the class needs to come to his/her own decision regarding their possible participation. The consent should also be informed, which means that information about the study, what it entails, its possible effects, dissemination plans, and other relevant details should be offered to participants, ideally both orally and in writing, before they make their decision. If the study is aimed at younger individuals, such information, apart from being formulated in an age-appropriate language, should be directed also toward their caretakers.

Even though this volume is focused on language learning *beyond* the classroom, it should be noted that informants for studies in the LBC-area often are approached in classrooms. The reason for this state of affairs is simply that it is a convenient way of generating large numbers of individuals in an age group of great interest for this type of research. From an ethical perspective, this means that we need to think about a number of ways in which to handle our samples. First of all, should we invite everybody in a class to participate, even though we might only be interested in a smaller sub-sample? From an ethical viewpoint, there are several points to consider here. One is, what happens to the rest of the class if only a select number of students are invited to take part in a study. Is there a risk that they will feel less worthy than those who are selected? Another question is if all students take part in the study, what happens with the data gathered from those individuals in whose contributions we may not be interested for the purposes of a particular study? The question regarding the collection of a surplus of data, by the way, is not only relevant to LBC studies, it is indeed applicable to most data collection. What do we do with data collected, but not used? Is it ethically defendable to leave such data unused? Each individual researcher needs to consider this question, but the basic, most ethically sound conclusion should be that as much of the data collected as possible should also come to some use. Otherwise, the efforts on the part of the informants have been made in vain. This, in turn, may have negative repercussions for, among other things, future collaborations.

An aspect of special importance regarding ethics in connection with language learning and teaching, is the fact that language in many cases is closely linked to ethnicity. That makes LBC research sensitive, in some ways, and higher ethical standards are put on methods and designs. This may be the case, for instance, in connection with research on migrants and endangered languages, where the risk of possible identification of participants may be higher than when more common languages are focused on (see, e.g., Eckert, 2013). While much of the research conducted on LBC normally is harmless to informants, in these specific circumstances the privacy and security of the informants can be decisive to bear in mind.

Ethics in research involving minors

As mentioned above, the Helsinki declaration states that precaution needs to be taken in order to protect informants' privacy and to limit any impact of the research on their lives (Declaration of Helsinki, 2013). When doing research with minors, dilemmas occur. Not seldom, LBC research is more ethnographically oriented, in which case access to the homes of our informants may be offered. In these cases, our ethical senses need to be very alert. First of all, parents, siblings and possible relatives, must be fully informed about the project and must give their voluntary consent to being a part of it, albeit as a background to the informant him/herself. As researchers, we need to be extra particular about our behavior when invited to someone's home for data collection. We need to stay focused on the purpose of the visit, yet flexible enough to adapt to spontaneous events happening while we are there. We should restrict the time we take from the individual, including any family members, yet set aside enough time for the intended data collection to be finalized.

Another aspect relating to young informants is the spaces where LBC take place. A great deal of present-day out-of-school learning takes place digitally on the Internet (e.g., Gee, 2007; Sundqvist & Sylvén, 2016; Reinhardt, 2019). Thus, the informant taking part in a study interacts with (many) others in online spaces, such as digital games and social media. The dilemma of these other individuals involuntarily and unaware actually being part of the research, too, arises. How should such situations be handled? Is it enough that our "primary" informant has given his/her consent, or is it also necessary to obtain the consent of anybody with whom he or she interacts in the process of the language learning situation? If consent is considered necessary from everyone involved, will that have an impact on the authenticity of the activity studied? If so, how does that affect the study as a whole? Here, the concept of IDA (Moss et al., 2006) can be useful, so that informed decisions are made at all stages.

Obtaining consent from minors and their caregivers merits some discussion. As is well known, the attention span for children is limited, and instructions obtained in school may very well be forgotten once inside the door of the home. It is not unusual that consent forms are not returned, not because the child and his/her caregiver are against participation, but because the child has forgotten to show the document, or has lost it in transition. This problem may be augmented in contexts characterized by lower socio-economic status, where caregivers may not be able to or accustomed to checking if there is anything from school that requires their attention. Even more difficult, of course, are contexts where other languages than the majority language are spoken in the homes of the children, making it difficult for caregivers to understand the information provided. Such circumstances require measures to be taken. For instance, information can be given and consent forms distributed at parental meetings, and translations be made available in relevant languages.

In addition, when collaborating with minors, it is important to remember that they, as well as any other informant, may change their minds, and to remind them that it is OK to do so. In certain data collection situations it may therefore be a good idea now and then to remind the child that the procedure only continues as long as he or she wants it to, and that they can take a break at any time.

Collaborators

Doing research is rarely a one-man-job. Many people are involved in one way or another in the process of carrying out a research project. In this section, some ethical aspects to bear in mind as regards collaboration will be discussed.

Be selective when choosing with whom to work. When the first ideas about a study start emerging, there is a need to discuss their feasibility. Such discussions can be held without being too cautious. However, when details are becoming more firm as regards focus, administration, tools, participants, etc., a careful selection of collaborators needs to be made. In this selection, questions such as who do I want to work with, who do I trust, who has the competence, need to be asked. Consider these aspects very carefully, because they are fundamental to the development of any study or project. Needless to say, if an idea is launched by a colleague, he or she has the intellectual property rights ("the rights given to persons over the creations of their minds", wto.org) to it even though it might be in the very early stages of the process of becoming a full-fledged study. Taking someone else's ideas without acknowledging where they originated, or without gaining permission is deeply unethical.

When the selection of collaborators has been made, there should ideally be no changes to the team unless unforeseen circumstances occur. Once a team has been established, whether it consists of 2 or 30 people, each member should know their role, and what is expected of them. Steps should be taken so that the research process is as transparent as possible for all members of the team, and for explanations to be given for parts that for some reason are not disclosed to everyone. A research team is very much built on trust, and if that trust is broken, regaining it requires time and energy.

It is recommended at an early stage to make decisions on data storage and transfer, who should be responsible for the data, the so-called data owner, and who else should have access to data. All of these details are best outlined in a data management plan, DMP. Collaboration agreements should be set up in conjunction with the DMP, in which decisions should be made as to who will take the role as first author on publications that will result from the study. In the case of several publications, a plan should be made as to possible shifts in the role as first author. The Vancouver Protocol (https://research.ntu.edu.sg/rieo/Documents/Foundational%20Documents/Vancouver%20Protocol.pdf) is often referred to in connection with authorship of academic publications, and even though it originally aimed at medical research, it is today used as a standard for many other research areas as, for instance, research on LBC. Among other issues, it states that

> [a]uthorship credit should be based on 1) substantial contributions to conception and design, acquisition of data, or analysis and interpretation of data; 2) drafting the article or revising it critically for important intellectual content; and 3) final approval of the version to be published. Authors should meet conditions 1, 2, and 3.

This is an excellent starting point when discussing the distribution of authorship, as well as inclusion or exclusion of authors, in any publication resulting from a research team.

Should new members join the team, this should have the support of the original group first. Likewise, should an original member of the group leave ahead of the completion of the project, this should be made in an orderly manner: how should his/her contribution be acknowledged when disseminating results? Are there data he/she should have access to, even though not part of the research team anymore?

All of the above aspects of collaboration are not only of ethical importance to have considered. If such decisions have been made early on, the practical implementation and administration of the study or project will be much easier compared with a situation when questions such as these have not been considered at all. For further details on the ethics of collaboration, the APA Ethical Principles are recommended (APA, 2020).

Once a study is defined, it needs to be carried out. As touched on earlier, many of us get access to informants through some educational context, such as kindergarten, school or university. In such cases, we need the help of principals and/or teachers to get into the classrooms or student groups. Such help, especially for the lower grade levels, is decisive, and should be acknowledged in one way or another. Depending on the magnitude of the assistance obtained, various options can be considered. The very least we as researchers can do is to, in one way or another, pay tribute to everybody who has been involved in the project in the acknowledgements of any publication. If the principal/teacher has been more deeply involved, they can also be considered as co-authors to any publication resulting from a study. Being a co-author can open up new horizons for school professionals, and lead to individual and professional development. It is also an effective way of bridging between practice and research, and can have profound effects long-term. However, the balance between anonymity for informants and acknowledging collaborators always needs to be kept in mind.

Dissemination

In the academic context of today, where "publish or perish" to a very large degree is what forms our professional life, disseminating research results in publications and presentations is of utmost importance. In so doing, it is important that all results obtained be discussed, not only those that support a certain hypothesis. Furthermore, opposing arguments should be accounted for and discussed. Data should not have been used for other purposes, and results should not have been published elsewhere before submitting to a journal for a peer review process. These are points commonly put forward by publishing houses and journals, and are what is expected by publishers, reviewers and readers. Unfortunately, they are not always adhered to, due to the pressure to publish, resulting in articles based on the same data with a slightly different perspective taken, or the same article appearing in different languages. In some cases this may be warranted, but if so, the original publication needs to be referred to, otherwise there is a risk for *self-plagiarism*, which is just another form of plagiarism (see below).

Even though many of the ethical perspectives are up to the individual researcher to consider, there are some "hard" limits as to what is allowed or not. Practices beyond those limits are considered as misconduct, and the most regulated examples of misconduct are fabrication and misrepresentation, falsification, and plagiarism (see, e.g., https://ori.hhs.gov/definition-research-misconduct).

Fabrication is when there is no support in empirical evidence for claimed findings, and where data is fabricated to suit a certain outcome. *Misrepresentation* can be said to be a variant of fabrication, where data is not made up but rather where data is represented in a manner that is not entirely true. For instance, omitting so-called outliers in a data set, or simply taking into account such results that are in line with a wished-for outcome or a suggested hypothesis can be ways of misrepresenting the empirical data. It may very well be the case that outliers skew the results to an unreasonable extent. One way of solving that dilemma is to present both sets of data, first the one including the outliers, then the one excluding them, and finally openly discussing the impact the outliers might have had. In that case, it will be up to the reader to determine how to best interpret the findings.

Falsification is similar to misrepresentation as it refers to false data or the false interpretations of results. Data points that are added or removed in order for a specific outcome to be met, or focusing on a certain set of statistical results while leaving out others that may point in another direction, are examples of falsification.

Plagiarism, finally, is when a researcher uses the work of others to make it look as if it was his or her own work. The use of others' (or one's own, see *self-plagiarism* above) work should always be credited to the original source, whether it is an idea, a specific design or results from a study.

Although these three areas, fabrication and misrepresentation, falsification, and plagiarism are the ones most commonly seen as definitely crossing the ethical borders, there are, as always when discussing ethics, dilemmas occurring in the research process. The bottom line, however, in all these cases is that transparency is one way of staying on the right side of the border.

When discussing dissemination, open access needs to be mentioned. Open access, as defined by the Berlin Declaration (https://openaccess.mpg.de/Berlin-Declaration), is the free and open online access to academic publications. Among other things, the Declaration says that "our mission of disseminating knowledge is only half complete if the information is not made widely and readily available to society". In other words, anybody should have access to research data and results without having to pay for them. There is nowadays a host of well-known journals offering open access, for which a fee is paid by the author, his/her institution or the research funder. Indeed, many funding bodies require that results emanating from results obtained in research funded by them are published in an open access format. Ethically, open access should always be the preferred route to publications, as it enables many more access to research findings. However, there is an abundance of so-called predatory journals, whose aim rather is to earn as much money as possible than to distribute scholarly knowledge. Caution is therefore called for when choosing journals for dissemination of results (see, e.g., Eriksson & Helgesson, 2018; Rele, Kennedy, & Blas, 2017).

Theoretical considerations

The fore-fronting of ethical concerns may have various effects on theoretical considerations, depending on the nature of the research. One effect of the need for voluntary participation may be that the building of theory becomes weaker as perhaps not all types of learners are represented in a sample. As an example in LBC research, we can consider a study of young learners' use of computer games to learn English outside of school. If only individuals who already are avid users of such games are those who volunteer to take part in the study, the results and findings will undoubtedly be skewed, and any theoretical assumptions based on such a sample will not be generalizable. In a similar vein, if our informants are representative only of a certain socio-economic group, our results are valid for that group only and cannot be used for generating new theory in a wider sense. Therefore, researchers need to be inventive and ingenious so that our samples are such that the findings are generalizable to a larger population. Case studies, which are quite common within the field of LBC research, need to be carefully contextualized in their social settings as well as within the broader field of research.

Practical considerations

Bearing the theoretical considerations in mind, it becomes clear that there are a great deal of practical considerations in the planning of a study and that sampling is crucial. Steps need to be taken to ensure that a sample is as complete as possible. If, for instance, participants are to be recruited from school classes, visits to those classes on several occasions before the actual study starts and before letters of consent are administered are highly recommended. One purpose of such visits is for the researcher to become a familiar face to the students, and for the researcher to get to know the group of students. Another purpose is to introduce the planned study and to leave ample opportunities for the students to ask questions about it. By allowing time and being very transparent about what the study entails, how data will be collected, and what the data will be used for, chances are that several more individuals will choose to participate than would be the case otherwise. To simply enter a classroom, introduce yourself and your planned research, and then ask students to give their consent to a study which then starts immediately by administering a questionnaire, is often not the best way to initiate a project, and may even be considered unethical. In this case, all the time the researcher possibly can spend in the classroom environment is definitely beneficial, both to the participation ratio and to the quality of the empirical data.

Future directions

In the future, we can expect the ethical perspective to continue having a central role in LBC. However, what needs to be considered are the possible limitations brought by too many and far-reaching restrictions. If we are to be able to continue researching LBC, we need access to informants of all ages. If the ethical standards are set too high, there is an imminent risk of losing not only the important group of minors as our informants, but also others. Researchers will find other ways of doing research, and maybe ending up studying LBC contexts that are easy to research, but not necessarily the ones that are most interesting and informative. If that should become the case, everybody loses. Policy makers, educators at all levels, and not least the language learners themselves. Research needs to take place at the forefront of LBC for it to have any relevance at all. In so doing, ethical considerations need to be made at every step of any study, but the ethical vetting of boards and committees also need to take a holistic grip on the applications they are set to consider. Closer collaboration between decision makers and researchers seems a good way forward in this pursuit.

Reflection questions

This text leads to a number of questions in need of reflection for LBC research. Three of them are as follows:

1. How can I, as a researcher, make sure that my (young) participants understand the purpose of the study and his/her involvement in it?
2. How do I ensure that everybody who in some way has been instrumental in the compilation of data gets acknowledged for his/her contribution without risking the identity of informants?
3. How do I ensure that any dissemination of results indeed provide a true representation of the data?

Recommended readings

A chapter is far too short to be able to do anything more than just touch of some issues in regard to LBC and ethics. For the interested reader, there is an abundance of literature to delve into. The following titles provide easy access to some of the most important perspectives to keep in mind in relation to ethical perspectives on LBC research.

APA Ethical Principles of Psychologists and Code of Conduct https://www.apa.org/ethics/code/?_ga=2.183897638.1628966198.1612112006-291644181.1609771006

The APA Ethical Principles provide guidance on a large number of areas and are a good starting point whenever ethical problems or dilemmas occur. Although the principles are primarily aimed for psychologists, most of them are applicable to researchers in general.

The British Association for Applied Linguistics, Recommendations on Good Practice in Applied Linguistics https://www.baal.org.uk/wp-content/uploads/2016/10/goodpractice_full_2016.pdf

This 19-page document is recommended for any researcher to take part of. It covers researcher's responsibilities and relationships with a number of key stakeholders in the research process, and provides suggestions for further reading in each area.

OECD, 2008 http://www.oecd.org/science/inno/40188303.pdf

This report goes into the area of misconduct in detail, clearly outlining what it is and what it is not, how to deal with it, how to investigate it, and how to respond to misconduct allegations. Highly recommended reading for all researchers.

References

ALLEA - All European Academies. (2017). *The European code of conduct for research integrity*. Berlin: Berlin-Brandenburg Academy of Sciences and Humanities.
APA. (2020). APA ethical principles of psychologists and code of conduct. Retrieved from https://www.apa.org/ethics/code/?_ga=2.183897638.1628966198.1612112006-291644181.1609771006
Declaration of Helsinki. (2013). *Ethical Principles for Medical Research Involving Human Subjects, adopted by the 18th WMA General Assembly, Helsinki, Finland, June 1964, latest revision by the WMA General Assembly, Seoul 2013*. Retrieved from Ferney-Voltaire, France:
Eckert, P. (2013). Ethics in linguistic research. In R. J. Podesva & D. Sharma (Eds.), *Research methods in linguistics* (pp. 11–26). Cambridge: Cambridge University Press.
Erard, M. (2017, November 25). Write yourself invisible. *New Scientist*.
Eriksson, S., & Helgesson, G. (2018). Time to stop talking about 'predatory journals'. *Learned Publishing*(31), 181–183.
Gee, J. P. (2007). *What video games have to teach us about learning and literacy. Revised and updated edition*. New York: Palgrave Macmillan.
Gensler, H. J. (2018). *Ethics. A contemporary introduction* (3rd ed.). New York: Taylor and Francis.
Hultgren, A. K., Erling, E. J., & Chowdhury, Q. H. (2016). Ethics in language and identity research. In S. Preece (Ed.), *Routledge handbooks in applied linguistics*. London: Routledge.
Labov, W. (1964). Phonological correlates of social stratification. *American Anthropologist, 66*(6), 164–176.
Labov, W. (1966). *The social stratification of English in New York City*. Washington, DC: Center for Applied Linguistics.
Larsson, J., Williams, P., & Zetterquist, A. (2019). The challenge of conducting ethical research in preschool. *Early Child Development and Care*. doi:10.1080/03004430.2019.1625897
Messick, S. (1989). Validity. In R. L. Linn (Ed.), *Educational measurement* (7th ed.). New York: Macmillan.
Milgram, S. (1963). Behavioral study of obedience. *Journal of Abnormal and Social Psychology*, (67), 371–378.
Moss, P. A., Girard, B. J., & Haniford, L. C. (2006). Validity in educational assessment. *Review of research in Education, 30*(1), 109–162.

Reinhardt, J. (2019). *Gameful second and foreign language teaching and learning. Theory, research, and practice*. Cham, Switzerland: Palgrave MacMillan.

Rele, S., Kennedy, M., & Blas, N. (2017). Journal evaluation tool. *LMU Librarian Publications & Presentations*, (40), 1–4.

Ross, W. D. (1930). *The right and the good*. Oxford: The Clarendon Press.

Schuh, G. (2018). *The Meaning of To Kalon in Aristotle's Ethics*. Paper presented at the International Society for Neoplatonic Studies, Loyola Marymount.

Shohamy, E. (2001). *The power of tests. A critical perspective on the uses of language tests*. Harlow, Essex: Pearson Education Limites.

Silverman, H. (2017). Children as research participants. In H. Silverman (Ed.), *Research ethics in the Arab region* (pp. 73–81). Cham: Springer.

Sundqvist, P., & Sylvén, L. K. (2016). *Extramural English in Teaching and Learning: From Theory and Research to Practice* London: Palgrave Macmillan.

Taylor, C. (2003). Ethics and ontology. *The Journal of Philosophy, 100*(6), 305–320.

Wiles, R., & Boddy, J. (2013). Research ethics in challenging contexts. *Methodological Innovations Online, 8*(2), 1–5.

22
EVALUATION OF INSTRUMENTS FOR RESEARCHING LEARNERS' LBC

Ju Seong Lee

Introduction

With greater L2 learning opportunities outside the classroom, Language learning and teaching Beyond the Classroom (LBC) has received increasing research attention during the past decade (Benson & Reinders, 2011; Reinders & Benson, 2017). Concurrently, LBC has spawned a number of empirical research studies that use an array of research instruments. Thus, it seems timely to review what research instruments have been used in LBC research and to offer suggestions for future directions.

Key constructs

Broadly, LBC can be divided into two sub-categories: (1) LBC online and offline and (2) LBC online. The first sub-category has been studied by using various approaches, including *Recreational language learning* (Chik & Ho, 2017), *Informal language learning* (Dressman & Sadler, 2020), *Extramural English* (Sundqvist & Sylvén, 2014) and *Extramural L_n* (Sundqvist, 2019). Similarly, the second sub-category has been researched with several methods, such as *CALL in the digital wilds* (Sauro & Zouro, 2019), *Online informal learning of English* (OILE; Sockett, 2013), and *Informal digital learning of English* (IDLE; Lee & Dressman, 2018).

In order to conduct a systematic review of the literature on LBC, the author identified 79 relevant articles by using LBC-related keywords that pertain to articles published from 2010 to 2020 in the Social Science Citation Index (SSCI) and Arts & Humanities Citation Index (A&HCI)-indexed English-language journals. Next, articles irrelevant to L2 learning were excluded from the analysis, which resulted in 35 articles. Lastly, a manual search was conducted based on reference lists of the retrieved articles. These papers appeared in journals from different disciplines (e.g., *International Journal of Bilingual Education and Bilingualism*) and non-SSCI and A&HCI (e.g., *CALICO*), which were nevertheless deemed to be relevant and of high quality. Thus, a total of 76 documents compose the present review. Due to space limitations, research instruments for measuring L2 learning outcomes (e.g., vocabulary and speaking) are excluded from the study. A references list for each research instrument is also provided in the supplemental materials to save space.

Table 22.1 Distribution of commonly used research tools in LBC studies from 2010 to 2020

	2010	2011	2012	2013	2014	2015	2016	2017	2018	2019	2020	Total
Questionnaires	1	3	5	4	3	2	2	6	8	14	9	57
Interviews	0	4	3	2	1	1	3	5	2	11	6	38
Observations	0	1	2	2	2	1	2	5	1	2	2	20
Language logs	0	1	2	2	1	0	1	1	0	1	0	9
Group interviews	0	2	0	1	1	1	0	1	0	1	1	8
Reflective journals	0	0	1	1	0	0	0	2	0	0	1	5
Computer tracking	0	1	1	0	0	0	1	0	0	0	0	3
Stimulated recall	0	1	0	0	1	0	0	0	0	0	0	2
Language learning history	0	1	0	0	1	0	0	0	0	0	0	2
Total	1	14	14	12	10	5	9	20	11	29	19	144

Key issues

In this chapter, research instruments refer to tools that are used to collect and analyze data in research. Among the research instruments presented in Table 22.1, a questionnaire was most prominent in LBC studies ($N = 57$), followed by interviews ($N = 38$), observations ($N = 20$), language logs ($N = 9$), group interviews ($N = 8$), reflective journals ($N = 5$), computer tracking ($N = 3$), stimulated recall ($N = 2$), and language learning history ($N = 2$). On closer inspection, three instruments (i.e., questionnaires, interviews, and observations) have been used frequently and consistently, while the other instruments seem to have been used sparingly in the research of LBC during the past decade. Detailed analyses of each research instrument are presented in subsequent subsections.

Questionnaires

In most of the LBC studies, researchers used a questionnaire to obtain informants' demographic data, such as gender, age, academic year, and length of time learning L2. Apart from that, the questionnaire also has been employed broadly for two purposes: (1) to understand participants' perceptions and behaviors regarding LBC and (2) to understand the relationship between LBC and other variables.

Understanding participants' perceptions and behaviors regarding LBC

Kozar and Sweller (2014) examined how English learners in Russia studied language through private online tutoring. The data were collected from 121 students' application forms, such as students' previous experience in English learning, their English learning goals, and their demographic information. The researchers wrote, "The main advantage of using application forms as a data source...is that employing archival data is able to produce a more representative sample, less affected by response bias commonly found in volunteer-based research" (p. 43). Luef, Ghebru and Ilon (2020) conducted a survey research with 82 Korean

L2 learners, who were learning German and African languages. For a practical reason, the researchers administered the survey twice: first in the classroom (for understanding participants' use of language apps), and then online (for obtaining demographic data). Toffoli and Sockett (2015) conducted a survey study regarding teachers' perceptions of OILE. To this end, 30 university professors of English in France were invited to complete a survey with respect to their awareness and perceptions toward OILE.

Deeper analyses reveal that some researchers initially collected quantitative data, followed by qualitative data. For instance, Mitchell (2012) conducted a preliminary survey with nine ESOL students in the US to understand their participation on Facebook (e.g., the number of interactions on Facebook and the estimated number of times students gained access to Facebook). This data was later triangulated with observations and interview data. In terms of observation, the researcher was added as the participants' Facebook friend and proceeded to monitor their online activity for four weeks. With respect to the interviews, the researcher asked questions such as "current usage, their online friends, their original motivation to join the site, their ability to use the site, and their computer usage" (p. 474). Sylvén and Sundqvist (2012) administered a questionnaire distributed to 86 young Swedish L2 English learners (ages 11–12) in order to measure their Extramural English habits such as "reading books, reading newspapers/magazines, watching TV, watching films, using the Internet, playing digital games, and listening to music" (p. 308). There was an open-ended response option by which participants could type any other Extramural English activities they had practiced. For an in-depth understanding of this behavior, the participants were also asked to keep a diary on how much time they spent on these seven Extramural English activities for one week. Similarly, Sundqvist and Sylvén (2014) administered the same questionnaire with 76 4th graders in Sweden (ages 10–11). The questionnaire data were later triangulated with one-week language diary data. Lai and Zheng (2018) administered an online questionnaire to 256 university L2 learners in Hong Kong with respect to the frequency, nature and tool selection of their self-directed mobile learning in out-of-class settings. Next, 18 participants were invited for a semi-structured interview for an in-depth understanding of the phenomena.

Intriguingly, some other researchers first collected qualitative data, followed by quantitative data. Sockett and Toffoli (2012) had interviews with five EFL university students in France about English-mediated digital activities. Next, a questionnaire was administered to 225 university students to understand the types of informal online learning of English activities that they used. Lai, Hu, and Lyu (2018) conducted an interview regarding resources and experiences of out-of-class L2 learning with 21 university students in Hong Kong, who were learning L2. Based on the findings of the interview, a questionnaire was constructed and administered to 439 L2 university learners who were in Hong Kong ($N = 207$) and the US ($N = 232$).

In some LBC studies that have investigated young L2 learners, parents helped fill out the questionnaire. Terantino (2016) conducted an intervention research study, using seven preschool-aged children (four to five years old) in an American private school. Prior to the research, five free Spanish apps (e.g., Spanish Smash, LinguPinguin, Busuu Kids, Bilingual Child Bubbles, and Bilingual Child) were downloaded to iPads. For a period of six months, the participants' parents were asked to encourage their children to use the apps daily for at least 15 minutes each day. The parents also completed a questionnaire. Lindgren and Muñoz (2013) conducted a large-scale research study with 865 children (10–11 years old) from 38 state schools in Croatia, England, Italy, the Netherlands, Poland, Spain, and Sweden. The participating children brought home a questionnaire that asked the manner of children's out-of-class exposure to L2 (e.g., playing video-computer games, reading, watching films) as well as parents' use of L2 at work, and the parents' educational levels.

Understanding a relationship between LBC and other variables

Lai, Zhu, and Gong (2015) administered a paper-based questionnaire in Mandarin to 82 middle school EFL students in Mainland China. The questionnaire aimed to obtain the frequency, types, and nature of participants' out-of-class English language learning. On open-ended questions, participants could also write the amount of time they spent during the previous six months learning English by using technology outside the classroom. Using a single-item measure of confidence and enjoyment, participants were also asked to indicate their perceived language learning outcomes. Some LBC researchers also employed a single-item question when measuring affective aspects of language learning outcomes, such as self-confidence, enjoyment, and anxiety (Lee, 2019), as well as willingness to communicate in a second language (L2 WTC) online (Lee & Dressman, 2018). More recently, researchers have tried to improve validity and reliability of their findings. For instance, Lee and his colleagues conducted follow-up studies by using a more validated and reliable questionnaire to measure self-confidence (Lee & Drajati, 2019a; Lee & Chen Hsieh, 2019; Lee & Lee, 2020a, 2020b), enjoyment (Lee & Lee, 2020c), and L2 WTC (Lee & Drajati, 2019a; Lee & Chen Hsieh, 2019; Lee & Lee, 2020a, 2020b). In particular, a more rigorous L2 WTC questionnaire, which measures L2 WTC in-class (four items), out-of-class (three items), and extramural digital contexts (four items), was developed through Exploratory (administered to 114 Indonesian university students) and Confirmatory Factor Analysis (with 215 Indonesian university students) by Lee and Drajati (2019c), which was further validated through the use of Rasch analysis ($N = 458$) (Mulyono, Saskia, Arrummaiza, & Suryoputro, 2020).

LBC behavior was investigated in relation to other affective variables, such as self-rated English ability (Jurkovič, 2019), anxiety (Lee, 2019; Lee & Chen Hsieh, 2019), grit (Lee & Chen Hsieh, 2019; Lee & Lee, 2020b), risk-taking (Lee & Lee, 2020b), and motivation (Lee & Chen Hsieh, 2019; Lee & Lee, 2020a, 2020b). Interestingly, Henry, Korp, Sundqvist, and Thorsen (2018) examined L2 motivation from teachers' perspectives, using an open question phrased as "Describe an activity or task that you have carried out with your pupils which in your experience has motivated them" (p. 252). Data were collected from 97 English teachers (Grades 6–9) from 64 secondary schools in Sweden, where students generally become exposed to English in extramural contexts.

Some researchers investigated LBC in relation to:

- speaking skills (e.g., measuring speakers' delivery, language use, and topic development; Lee, 2019a, 2020; Lee & Dressman, 2018; Lyrigkou, 2019; Nielson, 2011);
- writing skills (e.g., measuring complexity, accuracy and fluency of L2 written productions; Eisenchlas, Schalley, & Moyes, 2016; Kusyk, 2017; Mitchell, 2012);
- listening skills (e.g., matching vocabulary words with audio cues; Kondo et al., 2012; Lindgren & Muñoz, 2013; Sylvén & Sundqvist, 2012; Terantino, 2016);
- reading skills (e.g., obtaining reading ability data from the national test; Kondo et al., 2012; Lindgren & Muñoz, 2013; Sylvén & Sundqvist, 2012);
- vocabulary knowledge (e.g., measuring students' receptive and productive vocabulary levels; Jensen, 2017; Lee, 2019a, 2019b, 2020; Lee & Dressman, 2018; Peters, Noreillie, Heylen, Bulté, & Desmet, 2019; Puimège & Peters, 2019; Sundqvist, 2019; Sylvén & Sundqvist, 2012; Terantino, 2016);

- community of inquiry (e.g., finding evidence of teaching social, and cognitive presence; Sun, Franklin, & Gao, 2017);
- perceptions of English as an international language (e.g., measuring perceptions of varieties of English and strategies for multilingual and multicultural communication; Lee & Drajati, 2019b; Lee & Lee, 2019a, 2019b, 2020a, 2020b), and;
- self-directed learning (Lai, Li, & Wang, 2017; Lee, Yeung, & Ip, 2017).

With respect to self-directed learning, Lee et al. (2017) investigated 404 Hong Kong university students, focusing on whether three contracts of self-directed learning—namely, self-management ("I manage my time well"), desire for learning ("I have a need to learn"), and self-control ("I evaluate my own performance")—were associated with the use of technology for language learning. In a comparative study on 418 university students in Hong Kong ($N = 190$) and the US ($N = 228$), Lai et al. (2017) used a cross-culturally validated questionnaire to identify antecedents (e.g., social influence, performance expectancy, teacher support) that may explain self-directed L2 learning with technology outside the classroom.

More recently, and in the same vein, Ghorbani and Golparvar (2020) have conducted survey research with 382 Iranian university students. The researchers explored the relationship between students' socioeconomic status, autonomous out-of-class English learning experiences with technology, and learning outcomes (i.e., English exam scores) using a path analysis test. In a survey-based study with 428 freshmen at a Turkish university, Şad, Özer, Yakar, and Öztürk (2020) looked at LBC behaviors from a different perspective and reported that LBC using smartphones was associated with adverse effects of language learning (e.g., "I am distracted in class because of my smartphone", p. 12).

Interviews

Interviews have been used in LBC studies for clarifying the data as well as for better understanding of a particular phenomenon. Different techniques of the interview have been identified in the analysis.

With respect to clarifying the data, Lee (2019c) adopted an interview technique to check participants' survey responses, such as self-reported TOEIC scores. Sockett and Toffoli (2012) also employed interviews to clarify participants' diary data. In a multiple case-study with four Vietnamese EFL university students, Nguyen and Stracke (2020) also conducted semi-structured interviews on seven occasions to clarify information that had been obtained from observation notes and diary entries.

In some LBC studies, an interview was conducted for gaining an in-depth understanding about a certain phenomenon. For instance, Lee (2019c) conducted individual semi-structured interviews with 77 EFL university students about their IDLE activities. Their responses were subsequently used for analyzing and categorizing the participants' different types of IDLE activities. In a research study using 20 EFL Taiwanese university students, Wang and Chen (2019) conducted semi-structured interviews to "delve into the issues of why these students watched YouTubers' English-teaching videos and how watching these videos had benefited them on different dimensions in great depth" (p. 5). Lai and Gu (2011) purposively selected high-, medium-, and low-tech users for L2 learning based on survey responses. Then, the researchers conducted semi-structured interviews with some of these students ($N = 18$) to "elicit their reasons for, and various factors that affected, their selective use of technologies to regulate their language learning" (p. 322). Similarly, Mitchell (2012) conducted an initial survey with nine ESOL students in the US (two non-Facebook users as well as seven Facebook users). Then, follow-up interviews took place: "Facebook users were asked about their current usage, their online friends, their original motivation to join the site, their ability to use the site, and their computer usage. Non-users were asked about their knowledge of Facebook, their desire to participate on Facebook, and their computer usage" (p. 474).

In a study on digital gameplay, Chik (2011) employed multiple research instruments, one of which was to ask participants (Hong Kong undergraduate video gamers) to interview other gamers about their gaming habits and L2 learning. The interview data were triangulated with other data, such as language learning history, group discussions, and stimulated recall sessions. In Vosburg's (2017) research, 16 German learners in the US ($M = 19.6$ years old) were invited to play *World of Warcraft* on German servers twice a week for eight weeks. They were also asked to keep a journal and participate in an individual interview. According to the researcher, "The journals were designed to give the participants and researcher a chance to further discuss valuable moments of learning during the interviews by reflecting upon the journal notes" (p. 63). Similarly, in Scholz's (2017) study, German learners in a Canadian university were asked to play *World of Warcraft* outside the classroom. The interview was conducted "to determine the students' perception of the gameplay process, as well [as] participants' perceived knowledge of game-specific constructions" (p. 44).

Interestingly, some researchers offered prompts to elicit more responses about certain questions. When conducting semi-structured interviews with 18 participants, for instance, Lai and Zheng (2018) asked each participate to write their out-of-class activities in L2. According to the researchers (p. 303):

> The notes were then used as a stimulus for the interview, and the participants were asked to elaborate on how they engaged in each activity and why they chose the specific digital device(s) for the experience. They were also asked about the reasons for not engaging in some mobile learning experiences discussed in the existing literature.

In some studies, only interview data were used in the analysis. For instance, Lai, Yeung, and Hu (2016) conducted individual semi-structured interviews with 15 university L2 learners and 10 language teachers in Hong Kong. Interview questions included "students' and teachers' attitudes towards students' autonomous use of technology for language learning outside the classroom, and perceptions of how teachers influenced and could support students' autonomous technology use and why" (p. 707). Lee (2019b) conducted semi-structured interviews with 98 EFL students from three Korean universities about their English learning experiences in extramural digital contexts in relation to L2 WTC. Drawing on a ground theory technique, the researcher analyzed, identified and reported emerging themes. In Kashiwa and Benson's (2018) narrative inquiry study with seven Chinese students (ages 23–25) in Australia, the researchers conducted interviews three times, week 1–2, week 5–6, and week 9–10. According to the researchers (p. 731):

> The first interview elicited the students' learning histories and their first impressions of learning English in Australia. The second and third interviews elicited changes in their experiences and activities during the course. This allowed us, first, to compare the participants' conceptions of the relationship between in-class and out-of-class learning in Australia (Interview 3) and, second, to examine the development of their conceptions of learning in Australia over a period of approximately eight weeks (Interviews 1, 2, and 3).

Observations

In LBC research, observations took place both offline and online. With respect to the offline observation, data were collected in the classroom and home settings. For instance, Toetenel (2014) set up a closed network, *Ning*, in the classroom, and the researcher observed whether there had been any change in participants' perceptions and behaviors about the use of *Ning*. The observation data were triangulated with other data, such as diaries and questionnaires. Kashiwa and Benson (2018) conducted a qualitative study with seven Chinese EFL university students (ages 24–25) who attended a study abroad program in Australia. In addition to using a longitudinal interview and a student diary, the researchers observed the participants in the classroom and investigated whether there had been any change (e.g., decisive, gradual, and minimal change) in their learning experience and activities during the research period. In a research study with nine German-English bilingual children (ages five to eight years old) in Australia, Eisenchlas, Schalley, and Moyes (2016) invited parents to observe and take field notes about their children' reactions to three online games (Bubbles, Zoo and Handball) at home. Terantino (2016) conducted an intervention research study regarding how seven young L2 learners (four to five years old) in the US learned and practiced Spanish using five free Spanish apps for a minimum of 15 minutes on a daily basis for six months with "no explicit guidelines for their use" (p. 265). The researcher visited the participants' homes four times to observe firsthand how they use the apps.

With respect to online observations, two types of observation techniques were identified—namely, active observation and passive observation. In the former category, a researcher investigates certain activities through observing and participating in those activities. For instance, Isbell (2018) examined online informal Korean learning in an online community, and observed Reddit r/Korean (e.g., chatlogs from a chatroom) for seven weeks as a participant-observer. In a case study with nine ESOL students in the US, Mitchell (2012) was added as the participants' Facebook friends. Then, for four weeks, the researcher monitored their social media activity. Bytheway (2015) recruited six male ESL students, who played MMORPGs for at least five hours on a weekly basis for more than four years. The researcher observed and video-recorded the participants' gameplay for four hours, which, according to the researcher, "provided data about the gamers' behaviours and actions and allowed the researcher to compare what participants did with what they reported during the interviews" (p. 513).

A passive observation is similar to an unobtrusive observation technique. That is, a researcher collects data without intruding in an investigative context, such as Weblog comments (Hafner & Miller, 2011), digital postings on the Moodle forum (Barrs, 2012), online discussion forums (Chik, 2014), gaming files (e.g., written communication; Scholz, 2017; Vosburg, 2017), GRE AnalyticalWriting Discussion Forum (Sun, Franklin, & Gao, 2017), and fan communities (Vazquez-Calvo, Tian Zhang, Pascual, & Cassany, 2019). Drawing on an innovative digital ethnography, Shafirova and Cassany (2019) conducted both active (e.g., participating in the translating team) and passive observations (e.g., passively monitoring fan output and websites) for a period of six months. The researchers became members of two My Little Pony fandom communities, namely, Russian-language space (https://everypony.ru) and Spanish-language space (https://www.sponisherd.com).

Language Logs

Some researchers used a language log to understand L2 learners' LBC. For instance, Nielson (2011) asked US government employees who learned L2 (e.g., Arabic, Chinese and

Spanish) via self-study materials (e.g., Rosetta Stone and Auralog's TELL ME MORE) to keep a weekly learner log for recording "the time they spent working, technical difficulties, and whether or not they consulted any additional language resources" (p. 115). In Sockett and Toffoli's (2012) eight-week activity-log study, five French university EFL students were asked to record details of OILE, including "the address or description of the resource used, the language skill involved, the time the activity took place, the length of the activity and any comments about the English encountered in the activity" (p. 141). In Chen's (2013) action research, ten Chinese EFL university students were asked to report a daily English learning activity, using a tablet computer. The report included information such as location (e.g., dormitory, library), length (e.g., hours), and purpose of tablet usage (e.g., reading e-books, playing games, listening to music). Sylvén and Sundqvist (2012) asked young English learners in Sweden (ages 11–12) to keep a language diary for one week about the duration of the seven EE activities, namely "reading books, reading newspapers/magazines, watching TV, watching films, using the Internet, playing digital games, and listening to music" (p. 308).

However, when working with younger learners, parents became involved in the data collection process. In Sundqvist and Sylvén's (2014) study, younger Swedish English learners (ages 10–11) were invited to keep a one-week language diary as a homework assignment. At home, guardians or parents were encouraged to regularly remind their children about a language diary. Similarly, in Jensen's (2017) study with young Danish English language learners, a one-week language log was filled out, with parental guidance. In Terantino's (2016) intervention study with preschool-age L2 children (ages four to five), parents also completed an activity log regarding their kids' iPad usage.

More recently, Vazquez-Calvo, Tian Zhang, Pascual, and Cassany (2019) used a more innovative method. That is, three Spanish participants who engaged in video games, anime, and fanfiction activities were asked to provide screencast videos of their informal language activities, which "showcased the full translating process, from the moment that the informants decided to translate a text until it was published" (p. 53).

Group interviews

Group interview or group discussion is a technique by which an interviewer (researcher) simultaneously speaks with multiple interviewees (participants). Hafner and Miller (2011) reported on the implementation of a student-centered digital video project involving 67 university science major students situated in Hong Kong. In addition to questionnaire and weblog comments, the researchers made use of focus group interviews with 21 students about topics such as general perceptions of a digital video project, authenticity and effectiveness, and multiliteracies and technology. Similarly, in Chen's (2013) action research involving 10 freshman English majors in China, the researcher used a semi-structured group interview to delve into their experiences with tablets (e.g., "how the tablets were used to learn English, what advantages and disadvantages the participants thought they had, problems they encountered", p. 23). In Chik's studies (2011, 2014), she collected data from a focus group discussion about participants' gaming habits and L2 learning, along with other data sources that were used (e.g., blog, stimulated recall, interview, and language learning history). Sundqvist (2019) conducted seven interviews with 16 participants (in pairs or groups of three) to understand more about their online gaming. Sundqvist "offered the students a poster (describing typical English-mediated activities in the wild) to look at for inspiration, with the intention of foregrounding the students' views, language use, and 'individual stories'" (p. 93).

Lai et al. (2015) administered a questionnaire with 82 middle school EFL Chinese students about the nature and types of out-of-class language learning. The researchers conducted follow-up focus group interviews with 19 participants "to tap into how the participants selected, perceived, and used different out-of-class activities so as to obtain deeper insights into the nature of their out-of-class learning and to understand the factors that affected the quality of their out-of-class learning experiences" (p. 285). In Lee and Lee's (2020a) research with 112 secondary and 105 university Korean EFL students, the researchers purposefully arranged a focus group discussion with nine participants (six secondary and three university students) "to further elaborate on the quantitative findings" (p. 154), by asking questions such as: "Why do you study English?, Do you think your L2 motivational self-system influences your L2 WTC inside and outside the classroom? If so, how? Is there anything else you would like to add?" (p. 154). After the group discussion, five individual interviews were conducted to gain an in-depth understanding of the findings.

Reflective journals

A total of six studies were found to employ a reflective journal. Casanave (2012) conducted a diary study for her own journey of informally learning Japanese while working as an English instructor at a Japanese university. This autoethnographic type of research was written based on her 758 handwritten pages of journal writing done during 1990 (the date of her first arrival in Japan) to 1998 (a sabbatical). Chik and Ho (2017) took a similar biographical approach to investigate how three adult participants (two of whom were the authors) had learned L2 informally. The researchers analyzed their own diaries, such as blog entries, Facebook posts, and online comments, all of which elaborated on their informal L2 learning experiences.

In Smith and Craig's (2013) action research, the authors provided three learning supports—(1) learner passport ("help[ing] students investigate their learning styles and their study habits, and...help[ing] them identify exactly what role they had to play in advancing their CALL study"; p. 256), (2) the e-language learning portfolio ("a comprehensive electronic document which was to store students' work throughout the [CALL] course"; p. 257), and (3) the e-learner self-reflection diary ("review[ing] and reflect[ing] on their progress and performance in order to inform their future goals and actions"; p. 257). With respect to a self-reflection, students were asked to reflect on their English learning based on guiding questions, such as daily goal, website used, website evaluation, and self-evaluation about their efforts in learning English. According to the researchers, "The Self-Reflection Diary provided an insight into what learners were doing as they systematically planned and reviewed their weekly study, and revealed the kinds of CALL tasks learners were doing, including the websites and software they were exploring" (p. 260). In Kashiwa and Benson's (2018) three-month-long narrative inquiry study about study abroad experiences, participants (seven Chinese prospective MA students) were invited to write a weekly diary entry including texts and photographs in response to an email prompt from the first author. According to the researchers, "These emails elicited complementary introspective data on their current learning experiences and emotional responses to life in Australia" (p. 731). Drawing on a multiple case-study approach, Nguyen and Stracke (2020) examined how four Vietnamese EFL university students (ages 18–22) practiced English inside and outside the classroom. The participants wrote 168 English learning diaries about their autonomous English learning in two contexts.

Computer tracking

Three studies used a computer tracking system to elicit data about the participants' learning progress. Kondo et al. (2012) elicited the total time that participants spent studying TOEIC tasks from the Nintendo DS mobile device. In Nielson's (2011) study, participants (326 US government employees) learned L2 (e.g., Arabic, Chinese and Spanish) by using computer-mediated self-study materials. Although it is not clearly stated, participants' activity data, such as attrition rate, can be obtained from the computer tracking system. In Eisenchlas, Schalley, and Moyes' (2016) study, the young bilingual children engaged in on-line games in German, equipped with the tracking system. The tracking system generated data such as "frequency and length of play, which games children played, and how they performed in terms of success on task and speed" (p. 145).

Stimulated recall

In Chik's (2011, 2014) studies on L2 learning and gaming, she conducted stimulated recall sessions "in which [participants] viewed their recordings and blog entries to discuss what happened in the videos...participants also commented on strategies used by other gamers as recorded in blog entries, and on their interviews with other gamers" (Chik, 2011, p. 33).

Language learning history

According to Oxford (1996), language learning histories or recollective studies allow participants to "describe their own language learning experiences and express their feelings about those experiences" (p. 581). Chik (2011, 2014) employed this technique to learn about participants' out-of-class L2 learning experience.

Implications

Based on these findings, the present study provides several implications for researchers. First, overall data shows that the research tools used in LBC studies have been increased in terms of quantity (amount) and diversity (type). These findings suggest a growing interest and awareness of language researchers and educators in the use of diverse research tools and techniques to understand and facilitate LBC. As such, it is expected that this growing field will continue to expand in the years to come. Second, several research instruments have been used to investigate learners' LBC, which has contributed to advancing the current theoretical understanding of LBC (Reinders & Benson, 2017). For instance, Benson's (2011) four dimensions of LBC model (i.e., formality, location, pedagogy, and locus of control) have been applied and expanded with different perspectives (e.g., a trajectory of LBC learners and a variety of LBC activities; Chik, 2014; Lai et al., 2015; Lee, 2019c).

Nonetheless, more research tools need to be employed to advance the empirical understanding of LBC in relation to other variables. For example, the review findings show the prevalence of certain research tools, namely questionnaires, interviews and observations, over the past decade. In particular, cross-sectional analysis of the questionnaire was frequently used in exploring the link between LBC and other variables (e.g., Lee & Lee, 2020a). Since this can hardly provide evidence for how LBC influences L2 learners' perceptions, behaviors, and learning outcomes, data from other research tools can be combined with the questionnaire findings. Consequently, collecting multiple sources of data and evidence could help us portray a more accurate and comprehensive picture of students' LBC.

Future directions

Although several research instruments are available, diverse and more innovative research tools are needed to expand an understanding of LBC, which can enhance the trustworthiness and richness of the findings. The review findings offer four suggestions for future research.

First, given the rapid development of technology, some information in existing LBC questionnaires can quickly become outdated. Thus, more up-to-date digital resources (e.g., Artificial Intelligence and Natural Language Processing) and correspondent emerging LBC activities (e.g., live-streaming, talking to chatbots, chatting with intelligent personal assistants) can be included in the questionnaire.

Second, since most of the survey results were based on self-reports (e.g., reporting when, where, and how frequently participants consumed and produced L2 outside the classroom), the study is subject to socially desirable responses. To address this issue, several studies have attempted to triangulate survey data with other sources taken from interviews (Lai & Gu, 2011), language logs (Sylvén & Sundqvist, 2012), observations (Toetenel, 2014), group interviews (Hafner & Miller, 2011), and computer tracking (Nielson, 2011). To have a more precise comprehension of the LBC phenomenon, an LBC-track app can be developed and employed. As such, research participants can report their LBC experiences more easily, regularly, and accurately.

Third, and in the same vein, a language log can be recorded using a popular and already-familiar social media app. For instance, participants may regularly report the type and length of LBC activities to the researcher via *WhatsApp*. Since the participants could forget to report, the researcher may send a reminder message to their social media accounts. Thus, the participants can report their LBC activities more accurately and effectively due to the easy accessibility and connectivity with the researchers, which allows the researcher to obtain more reliable and naturally occurring data. Lastly, to collect more naturally occurring instances of LBC, researchers may consider extending the duration of the one-week language diary (e.g., Sundqvist & Sylvén, 2014). To enhance reliability of the data, the one-week language diary can be also collected twice, and the means from "two" one-week language diaries can be used in the analyses (Sundqvist, 2009). Also as demonstrated in Vazquez-Calvo et al. (2019), a researcher may ask participants to provide screencast videos of their LBC activities, which subsequently can be used for stimulated recall. Notably, stimulated recall works best if it takes place immediately after the recording.

Reflection questions

1. What research instruments did you use while investigating LBC? Which ones were especially useful?
2. What is one innovative research instrument you would like to use, and why?
3. What research instruments would you like to develop to advance our understanding of LBC?

Recommended readings

Lai, C. (2017). *Autonomous language learning with technology beyond the classroom*. New York: Bloomsbury Publishing.
   This book provides several LBC-related theoretical frameworks, research agendas, and methodological issues, with a particular focus on autonomy and technology.

Reinders, H., & Benson, P. (2017). Research agenda: Language learning beyond the classroom. *Language Teaching, 50*(4), 561–578. doi:10.1017/S0261444817000192

The authors offer insights into future research areas of LBC including methodological suggestions.

Sundqvist, P., & Sylvén, L. K. (2016). *Extramural English in teaching and learning: From theory and research to practice*. Basingstoke, London: Palgrave Macmillan.

This book provides an overview of LBC-related theory and research and its implications for language practitioners, teacher educators and researchers.

References

Barrs, K. (2012). Fostering computer-mediated L2 interaction beyond the classroom. *Language Learning & Technology, 16*(1), 10–25.

Benson, P., & Reinders, H. (Eds.). (2011). *Beyond the language classroom*. New York, NY: Palgrave Macmillan.

Bytheway, J. (2015). A taxonomy of vocabulary learning strategies used in massively multiplayer online role-playing games. *CALICO Journal, 32*(3), 508–527. doi:10.1558/cj.v32i3.26787

Casanave, C. P. (2012). Diary of a dabbler: Ecological influences on an EFL teacher's efforts to study Japanese informally. *TESOL Quarterly, 46*(4), 642–670. doi:10.1002/tesq.47

Chen, X.-B. (2013). Tablets for informal language learning: Student usage and attitudes. *Language Learning & Technology, 17*(1), 20–36.

Chik, A. (2011). Learner autonomy development through digital gameplay. *Digital Culture & Education, 3*(1), 30–45.

Chik, A. (2014). Digital gaming and language learning: Autonomy and community. *Language Learning & Technology, 18*(2), 85–100.

Chik, A., & Ho, J. (2017). Learn a language for free: Recreational learning among adults. *System, 69*, 162–171. doi:10.1016/j.system.2017.07.017

Dressman, M., & Sadler, R. (Eds.). (2020). *The Handbook of Informal Language Learning* Hoboken, New Jersey: Wiley-Blackwell.

Eisenchlas, S. A., Schalley, A. C., & Moyes, G. (2016). Play to learn: Self-directed home language literacy acquisition through online games. *International Journal of Bilingual Education and Bilingualism, 19*(2), 136–152. doi:10.1080/13670050.2015.1037715

Ghorbani, M. R., & Golparvar, S. E. (2020). Modeling the relationship between socioeconomic status, self-initiated, technology-enhanced language learning, and language outcome. *Computer Assisted Language Learning, 33*(5–6), 607–627. doi:10.1080/09588221.2019.1585374

Hafner, C. A., & Miller, L. (2011). Fostering learner autonomy in English for science: A collaborative digital video project in a technological learning environment. *Language Learning & Technology, 15*(3), 68–86.

Henry, A., Korp, H., Sundqvist, P., & Thorsen, C. (2018). Motivational strategies and the reframing of English: Activity design and challenges for teachers in contexts of extensive extramural encounters. *TESOL Quarterly, 52*(2), 247–273. doi:10.1002/tesq.394

Isbell, D. R. (2018). Online informal language learning: Insights from a Korean learning community. *Language Learning & Technology, 22*(3), 82–102. doi:10125/44658/

Jensen, S. H. (2017). Gaming as an English language learning resource among young children in Denmark. *CALICO Journal, 34*(1), 1–19. doi:10.1558/cj.29519

Jensen, S. H. (2019). Language learning in the wild: A young user perspective. *Language Learning & Technology, 23*(1), 72–86. doi:10125/44673

Jurkovič, V. (2019). Online informal learning of English through smartphones. *System, 80*, 27–37. doi:10.1016/j.system.2018.10.007

Kashiwa, M., & Benson, P. (2018). A road and a forest: Conceptions of in-class and out-of-class learning in the transition to study abroad. *TESOL Quarterly, 52*(4), 725–747. doi:10.1002/tesq.409

Kondo, M., Ishikawa, Y., Smith, C., Sakamoto, K., Shimomura, H., & Wada, N. (2012). Mobile Assisted Language Learning in university EFL courses in Japan: developing attitudes and skills for self-regulated learning. *ReCALL, 24*(2), 169–187. doi:10.1017/S0958344012000055

Kozar, O., & Sweller, N. (2014). An exploratory study of demographics, goals and expectations of private online language learners in Russia. *System, 45*, 39–51. doi:10.1016/j.system.2014.04.005

Kusyk, M. (2017). The development of complexity, accuracy and fluency in L2 written production through informal participation in online activities. *CALICO Journal, 34*(1), 75–96. doi:10.1558/cj.29513

Lai, C., & Gu, M. (2011). Self-regulated out-of-class language learning with technology. *Computer Assisted Language Learning, 24*(4), 317–335. doi:10.1080/09588221.2011.568417

Lai, C., Hu, X., & Lyu, B. (2018). Understanding the nature of learners' out-of-class language learning experience with technology. *Computer Assisted Language Learning, 31*(1–2), 114–143. doi:10.1080/09588221.2017.1391293

Lai, C., Li, X., & Wang, Q. (2017). Students' perceptions of teacher impact on their self-directed language learning with technology beyond the classroom: cases of Hong Kong and U.S. *Educational Technology Research & Development, 65*, 1105–1133. doi:10.1007/s11423-017-9523-4

Lai, C., Yeung, Y., & Hu, J. (2016). University student and teacher perceptions of teacher roles in promoting autonomous language learning with technology outside the classroom. *Computer Assisted Language Learning, 29*(4), 703–723. doi:10.1080/09588221.2015.1016441

Lai, C., Zhu, W., & Gong, G. (2015). Understanding the quality of out-of-class English learning. *TESOL Quarterly, 49*(2), 278–308. doi:10.1002/tesq.171

Lai, C., & Zheng, D. (2018). Self-directed use of mobile devices for language learning beyond the classroom. *ReCALL, 30*(3), 299–318. doi:10.1017/S0958344017000258

Lee, C., Yeung, A. S., & Ip, T. (2017). University English language learners' readiness to use computer technology for self-directed learning. *System, 67*, 99–110. doi:10.1016/j.system.2017.05.001

Lee, J. S. (2019a). Informal digital learning of English and second language vocabulary outcomes: Can quantity conquer quality? *British Journal of Educational Technology, 50*(2), 767–778. doi:10.1111/bjet.12599

Lee, J. S. (2019b). EFL students' views of willingness to communicate in the extramural digital context. *Computer Assisted Language Learning, 32*(7), 692–712. doi:10.1080/09588221.2018.1535509

Lee, J. S. (2019c). Quantity and diversity of informal digital learning of English. *Language Learning & Technology, 23*(1), 114–126. doi:10125/44675

Lee, J. S. (2020a). Informal digital learning of English and strategic competence for cross-cultural communication: Perception of varieties of English as a mediator. *ReCALL, 32*(1), 47–62. doi:10.1017/S0958344019000181

Lee, J. S. (2020b). The role of informal digital learning of English and a high-stakes English test on perceptions of English as an international language. *Australasian Journal of Educational Technology, 36*(2), 155–168. doi:10.14742/ajet.5319

Lee, J. S., & Drajati, N. A. (2019a). Affective variables and informal digital learning of English: Keys to willingness to communicate in a second language. *Australasian Journal of Educational Technology, 35*(5), 168–182. doi:10.14742/ajet.5177

Lee, J. S., & Drajati, N. A. (2019b). English as an international language beyond the ELT classroom. *ELT Journal, 73*(4), 419–427. doi:10.1093/elt/ccz018

Lee, J. S., & Drajati, N. A. (2019c). Willingness to communicate in digital and non-digital EFL contexts: Scale development and psychometric testing. *Computer Assisted Language Learning*, 1–20. doi:10.1080/09588221.2019.1588330

Lee, J. S., & Dressman, M. (2018). When IDLE hands make an English workshop: Informal digital learning of English and language proficiency. *TESOL Quarterly, 52*(2), 435–445. doi:10.1002/tesq.422

Lee, J. S., & Chen Hsieh, J. (2019). Affective variables and willingness to communicate of EFL learners in in-class, out-of-class, and digital contexts. *System, 82*, 63–73. doi:10.1016/j.system.2019.03.002

Lee, J. S., & Lee, K. (2019a). Perceptions of English as an international language by Korean English-major and non-English-major students. *Journal of Multilingual and Multicultural Development, 40*(1), 76–89. doi:10.1080/01434632.2018.1480628

Lee, J. S., & Lee, K. (2019b). Informal digital learning of English and English as an international language: The path less traveled. *British Journal of Educational Technology, 50*(3), 1447–1461. doi:10.1111/bjet.12652

Lee, J. S., & Lee, K. (2020a). Role of L2 motivational self system on willingness to communicate of Korean EFL university and secondary students. *Journal of Psycholinguistic Research, 49*(1), 147–161. doi:10.1007/s10936-019-09675-6

Lee, J. S., & Lee, K. (2020b). Affective factors, virtual intercultural experiences, and L2 willingness to communicate in in-class, out-of-class, and digital settings. *Language Teaching Research, 24*(6), 813–833. doi:10.1177/1362168819831408

Lee, J. S., & Lee, K. (2020c). The role of informal digital learning of English and L2 motivational self system in foreign language enjoyment. *British Journal of Educational Technology.* doi:10.1111/bjet.12955

Lindgren, E., & Muñoz, C. (2013). The influence of exposure, parents, and linguistic distance on young European learners' foreign language comprehension. *International Journal of Multilingualism, 10*(1), 105–129. doi:10.1080/14790718.2012.679275

Luef, E. M., Ghebru, B., & Ilon, L. (2020). Apps for language learning: Their use across different languages in a Korean context. *Interactive Learning Environments, 28*(8), 1036–1047. doi:10.1080/10494820.2018.1558255

Lyrigkou, C. (2019). Not to be overlooked: Agency in informal language contact. *Innovation in Language Learning and Teaching, 13*(3), 237–252. doi:10.1080/17501229.2018.1433182

Mitchell, K. (2012). A social tool: Why and how ESOL students use Facebook. *CALICO Journal, 29*(3), 471–493.

Mulyono, H., Saskia, R., Arrummaiza, V. S., & Suryoputro, G. (2020). Psychometric assessment of an instrument evaluating the effects of affective variables on students' WTC in face-to-face and digital environment. *Cogent Psychology, 7*(1), 1–13. doi:10.1080/23311908.2020.1823617

Nguyen, V., & Stracke, E. (2020). Learning experiences in and outside class by successful Vietnamese tertiary students studying English as a foreign language. *Innovation in Language Learning and Teaching,* 1–13. doi:10.1080/17501229.2020.1801692

Nielson, K. B. (2011). Self-study with language learning software in the workplace: What happens? *Language Learning & Technology, 15*(3), 110–129.

Oxford, R. L. (1996). When emotion meets (meta)cognition in language learning histories. *International Journal of Educational Research, 23*(7), 581–594. doi:10.1016/0883-0355(96)80438-1

Peters, E., Noreillie, A.-S., Heylen, K., Bulté, B., & Desmet, P. (2019). The impact of instruction and out-of-school exposure to foreign language input on learners' vocabulary knowledge in two languages. *Language Learning, 69*(3), 747–782. doi:10.1111/lang.12351

Puimège, E., & Peters, E. (2019). Learners' English vocabulary knowledge prior to formal instruction: The role of learner-related and word-related variables. *Language Learning, 69*(4), 943–977. doi:10.1111/lang.12364

Reinders, H., & Benson, P. (2017). Research agenda: Language learning beyond the classroom. *Language Teaching, 50*(4), 561–578. doi:10.1017/S0261444817000192

Şad, S. N., Özer, N., Yakar, Ü., & Öztürk, F. (2020). Mobile or hostile? Using smartphones in learning English as a foreign language. *Computer Assisted Language Learning,* 1–27. doi:10.1080/09588221.2020.1770292

Sauro, S., & Zourou, K. (2019). What are the digital wilds? *Language Learning & Technology, 23*(1), 1–7. doi:10125/44666

Scholz, K. (2017). Encouraging free play: Extramural digital game-based language learning as a complex adaptive system. *CALICO Journal, 34*(1), 39–57.

Shafirova, L., & Cassany, D. (2019). Bronies learning English in the digital wild. *Language Learning & Technology, 23*(1), 127–144. doi:10125/44676

Shelton-Strong, S. J. (2020). Advising in language learning and the support of learners' basic psychological needs: A self-determination theory perspective. *Language Teaching Research,* 1–23. doi:10.1177/1362168820912355

Smith, K., & Craig, H. (2013). Enhancing the autonomous use of CALL: A new curriculum model in EFL. *CALICO Journal, 30*(2), 252–278.

Sockett, G. (2013). Understanding the online informal learning of English as a complex dynamic system: an emic approach. *ReCALL, 25*(1), 48–62. doi:10.1017/S095834401200033X

Sockett, G., & Toffoli, D. (2012). Beyond learner autonomy: a dynamic systems view of the informal learning of English in virtual online communities. *ReCALL, 24*(2), 138–151. doi:10.1017/S0958344012000031

Sundqvist, P. (2009). *Extramural English matters: Out-of-school English and its impact on Swedish ninth graders' oral proficiency and vocabulary.* (PhD), Karlstad University, Karlstad.

Sundqvist, P. (2019). Commercial-off-the-shelf games in the digital wild and L2 learner vocabulary. *Language Learning & Technology, 23*(1), 87–113. doi:10125/44674

Sundqvist, P., & Sylvén, L. K. (2014). Language-related computer use: Focus on young L2 English learners in Sweden. *ReCALL, 26*, 3–20. doi:10.1017/S0958344013000232,

Sun, Y., Franklin, T., & Gao, F. (2017). Learning outside of classroom: Exploring the active part of an informal online English learning community in China. *British Journal of Educational Technology, 48*(1), 57–70. doi:10.1111/bjet.12340

Sylvén, L. K., & Sundqvist, P. (2012). Gaming as extramural English L2 learning and L2 proficiency among young learners. *ReCALL, 24*(3), 302–321. doi:10.1017/S095834401200016X

Tan, K. E., Ng, M. L. Y., & Saw, K. G. (2010). Online activities and writing practices of urban Malaysian adolescents. *System, 38*, 548–559. doi:10.1016/j.system.2010.09.014

Terantino, J. (2016). Examining the effects of independent MALL on vocabulary recall and listening comprehension: An exploratory case study of preschool children. *CALICO Journal, 33*(2), 260–277.

Toetenel, L. (2014). Social networking: a collaborative open educational resource. *Computer Assisted Language Learning, 27*(2), 149–162. doi:10.1080/09588221.2013.818561

Toffoli, D., & Sockett, G. (2015). University teachers' perceptions of Online Informal Learning of English (OILE). *Computer Assisted Language Learning, 28*(1), 7–21. doi:10.1080/09588221.2013.776970

Vazquez-Calvo, B. (2020). Guerrilla fan translation, language learning, and metalinguistic discussion in a Catalan-speaking community of gamers. *ReCALL*, 1–18. doi:10.1017/S095834402000021X

Vazquez-Calvo, B., Zhang, L. T., Pascual, M., & Cassany, D. (2019). Fan translation of games, anime, and fanfiction. *Language Learning & Technology, 23*(1), 49–71. doi:10125/44672

Vosburg, D. (2017). The effects of group dynamics on language learning and use in an MMOG. *CALICO Journal, 34*(1), 58–74.

Wang, H.-C., & Chen, C. W.-Y. (2019). Learning English from YouTubers: English L2 learners' self-regulated language learning on YouTube. *Innovation in Language Learning and Teaching*, 1–14. doi:10.1080/17501229.2019.1607356

23
METHODS AND APPROACHES TO INVESTIGATING LANGUAGE LEARNING IN THE DIGITAL WILDS

Shannon Sauro

Introduction

The aim of this chapter is to explore methods and approaches for data collection and analysis of language learning beyond the classroom that takes place in the digital wilds, defined as the "digital spaces, communities, and networks that are independent of formal instructional contexts" (Sauro & Zourou, 2019, p. 2), where informal learner-driven language learning occurs. The digital wilds are not a new context for language learning; in fact, it has been more than 20 years since Lam's (2000) case study of Almon, an L2 learner of English, whose experience as a designer of a fan website in the late 1990s fostered new opportunities for English language use that were not available to him in formal classroom contexts. However, the ever-evolving nature of digital media, platforms, and online communities that make up the digital wilds as well as the corresponding opportunities and constraints (practical, legal, and ethical) for conducting research in such spaces and communities necessitate care on the part of those undertaking language-related research.

This chapter, therefore, provides an overview of different research methods carried out on language learning in the digital wilds and unpacks some of the challenges and solutions pioneered in the recent applied linguistics literature. This chapter includes a particular focus on research on language learning on various social media platforms as well as research on language learning in online fan communities, which are "the local and international networks of fans that develop around a particular program, text or other media product" (Sauro, 2014, p. 239) to illustrate some of the particular challenges researchers face when working in the digital wilds. After introducing the considerations facing researchers in these contents, this chapter then suggests different approaches for navigating methodological challenges that may be unique or endemic to the digital wilds and concludes with recommendations for future research directions.

Key constructs

Since the focus of this chapter is on exploring methods for researching learning beyond the classroom in the digital wilds, the key constructs explored will relate to the common methods of research and analysis used in the field so far. This includes case study research, digital ethnography, elicitation measures such as surveys, questionnaires, and interviews, as well as quantitative measures that explore relationships between language use and language learning in the digital wilds and formal measures of language development. This section begins with the most prevalent approach to researching language learning in the digital wilds, case studies.

Case studies of language learning in the digital wilds

Case studies, which represent perhaps the most common approach applied to investigating language learning by fans in the digital wilds, are defined by Casanave (2015) as a type of research "in which the researcher's interest is in an in-depth investigation of the particular rather than the general" (p. 119) and where that which is being investigated "is set in a natural context, is unique (in the sense of the singular) and is bounded" (p. 119). In other words, a case study requires a clear identifiable (bounded) phenomenon situated in an identifiable context and is carried out with the intention of deepening our understanding of an individual, group, process, or phenomenon.

Within the field of applied linguistics, case studies have a rich and established history of elucidating patterns in language development (e.g. Hakuta, 1976) or serving as a basis for the development of hypotheses (see, e.g. Schmidt, 1983, 1984; Schmidt & Frota, 1986 which lay the background to the noticing hypothesis) because their in-depth or longitudinal focus on individuals and focal groups of language learners "have generated very detailed accounts of the processes, outcomes, and factors associated with language learning, use or attrition" (Duff, 2008, p. 35).

In the digital wilds, case studies also have an established history of deepening our understanding of the language learning, literacy practices, and identity development of those engaged in a variety of online practices in different types of online spaces and platforms. Lam's (2000) case study of Almon, mentioned in the introduction to this chapter, stands out as an early example of case study research which emerged from a larger ethnographic study that explored the literacy practices of adolescent immigrant youth in the western part of the United States. This specific case study grew out of in-person interviews in 1996 with students that Lam had observed in an urban secondary school. A year later, when she returned to the school, she learned that one student in particular, Almon, had become heavily involved in designing an online fansite and had markedly improved his English writing ability. Over a six-month period in 1997, Lam collected a wide range of data from Almon in the form of observation, in-depth interviews, and documentation of both his online interactions in the form of text-chats and school-based correspondence and documentation. This in-depth and longitudinal analysis enabled Lam to document the emergence of a new textual online identity that positioned Almon as a productive and knowledgeable user of English, a much broader and more successful identity than that open to him in his formal English as a second language (ESL) classroom context. Through a case study approach on an individual learner, Lam was therefore able to initiate discussion and further investigation into the different practices of other language learners in the digital wilds and what this meant for their language learning and identity both within and beyond formal educational contexts.

Not all case studies of learners in the digital wilds are carried out to connect directly to learning in formal educational contexts, however. Some instead provide close and detailed understanding of the communities and practices found in particular online spaces and what types of learning or language development may be particularly endemic to that specific context. Such case studies therefore support our understanding of the dynamics of particular online affinity spaces or of particular online practices. Black's (2009) multiple case studies of fanfiction writers in the online fan fiction writing communities around the fan fiction archive fanfiction.net provides such an example.

Much like Lam's (2000) case study of Almon, Black's (2009) cases studies emerged from a larger ethnographic study, in this case, a three-year study of the site fanfiction.net (FFN), an archive for fanfiction defined as "fictional writing created by the fans inspired by the objects of their interest" (Duffett, 2013, p. 170), founded in 1998 by then university student and fan Xing Li (Fanlore.org, 2021, January 1). Initially, Black began by carrying out an exploratory study of FFN with the goal of uncovering what aspects of this site could support the literacy and social practices of English language learners who joined it. To do so, she herself became a participant in the FFN community, spending 10–20 hours a week posting her own fan fiction and interacting with other fans. Through her involvement, she came in contact with a number of adolescent fan fiction writers who were English language learners and who later became focal participants in her research. During a three-year period, Black gathered a variety of data from her participants including the fan fiction texts they wrote, reviews of the fan fiction written by other fans, focal fans' profile pages on FFN and their updates, as well as email exchanges and multiple semi-structured interviews carried out via Instant Messenger.

A common research element that emerges from these early case studies of fans and language learning is that these case studies were part of larger ethnographic studies. This leads to the next key related research concepts associated with methods for exploring language learning in the digital wilds: ethnography and its online counterpart, digital ethnography.

Ethnography and participant observation in the digital wilds

Ethnography is a research methodology that has its origins in early 20th-century linguistic and cultural anthropology and sociology and was later adapted by education researchers (Starfield, 2015). It has been defined as research which "involves the direct observation of human behaviour within particular settings and seeks to understand a social reality from the perspectives of those involved" (Mahboob, Paltridge, Phakiti, Wagner, Starfield, Burns, Jones & De Costa, 2016, p. 51). Unpacking this definition further, Nunan (1992) identifies the following six characteristics of ethnographic research: it is (1) contextualized, (2) unobtrusive, (3), longitudinal, (4) collaborative, (5) interpretative, and (6) organic (p. 56). In other words, ethnographic research is carried out over a sustained period of time by a researcher who is immersed in a context that is innate or relevant to the participants (e.g. where they live, study, and interact regularly) but does not manipulate or control it, in collaboration with participants or members of the context. In addition, the analysis of the data elicited is interpretive and there is a recursive relationship between questions and hypotheses and data collection and interpretation. While ethnography has traditionally been applied to in-person contexts and communities, as we see exemplified in Black's (2009) work, ethnographic methods have a rich history of being applied to online contexts and communities. Accordingly, such ethnographic research carried out online has come to be known by one of various related terms including cyber-ethnography, digital ethnography, online ethnography, and virtual ethnography. Throughout the remainder of this chapter, I will use the term digital ethnography (Varis, 2016).

A pair of recent studies of language learning by different groups of fans involved in various amateur translation practices illustrate various ways in which researchers carrying out digital ethnography have immersed themselves in a particular digital context and worked with participants. In both cases, following the stance taken by Hine (2015) who argues that digital ethnography take place within the digital context itself and not over-rely on interviews, researchers for both studies found different ways of embedding themselves in the online communities they chose for their research.

The first of these is a case study of three fans involved in the translation of digital games, anime, and fan fiction from either L2 English or L2 Japanese into Spanish or Catalan (Vazquez-Calvo, Zhang, Pascual & Cassany, 2019). While interviews were used to collect background information on participants and to clarify certain observations, the primary source of data collection were non-participant observations in which researchers observed the fans in their respective fan sites or communities engaged in translation activities. These observations were carried out over a two-month period and averaged one hour every three days. Screenshots taken during the observation provided the researchers with a rich collection of examples of the translation processes as well as of the final products and other fans' feedback and responses to the translations.

A second study which also employed digital ethnography to fan translation practices was carried out on two separate groups of fan translators of the English language animated series *My Little Pony: Friendship is Magic* (Shafirova & Cassany, 2019). Three of the six focal participants were fan translators in the Russian language fan community, and the remaining three were fan translators in the Spanish language fan community. In this study, the researchers augmented a series of semi-structured interviews with a combination of both active and passive participant observation. Specifically, because she was a proficient speaker of Russian, English, and Spanish, the first researcher was perceived of having valuable skills by the fans and invited to take part in translation activities along with them (active participation) and at other times she mainly observed and monitored the fans' activities and their web spaces (passive participation) while also maintaining field notes and taking screenshots. It is important to point out that Shafirova's participation in the translation process, much like Black's (2009) own writing of fanfiction and interaction with other fans during the many hours she spent on FFN, still adheres to Nunan's (1992) quality of unobtrusiveness in that she followed the lead of the participants who invited her to contribute to their process but did not herself lead or manipulate their translation process to elicit certain behaviors or outcomes as one might do in a more interventionist approach to research.

While case studies and digital ethnography represent growing areas of published research on language learning in the digital wilds, which allow for rich longitudinal understanding of the language learning of a small number of participants, the following sections explore research which has been used to elicit or evaluate learning among larger populations in the digital wilds. The first of these are studies that use elicitation tools such as surveys and questionnaires.

Elicitation techniques for language learning in the digital wilds

Elicitation techniques are common in studies of second language acquisition, dating back at least to the 1970s and are defined as methods of obtaining data through means of a stimulus such as a questionnaire, survey or interview (Nunan, 1992). Elicitation techniques are also commonly used in research on language learning in the digital wilds and enable researchers to gather input from a larger number of participants than supported by case studies or digital ethnography. In other cases, elicitation techniques allow for the gathering of data from the digital wilds where participant observation would be disruptive to the context and participants.

The first of these techniques, surveys, relies on the use of questionnaires to gather information about learning and learners that is not directly observable, not generated through production data, and includes such things as "learners' characteristics, beliefs or attitudes" (Wagner, 2015, p. 84). In contrast to the longitudinal nature of case studies and digital ethnographies, surveys are meant to capture a snapshot of a representative population at a single point in time (Nunan, 1992). Because questionnaires can include both closed and open-ended questions, they lend themselves to the collection of data that can be analyzed both quantitatively and qualitatively. For instance, items that can be analyzed quantitatively include closed questions which ask participants to select a relevant category (e.g. whether they are high, mid, or low frequency users of a social networking site), to rank their preference of items (e.g. their preference for different social media platforms to practice a particular language skill), to simply quantify how much or how often they do something (e.g. hours per week spent gaming in the target language), or to indicate their attitude or preference toward something on a scale (e.g. their degree of confidence in their ability to speak the language they are learning).

One researcher who has relied on questionnaires in his work on online language learners and language learning communities is Rosell-Aguilar. In a recent large-scale study of people who use Twitter in their language learning, Rosell-Aguilar (2020) elicited data using a 30-item questionnaire, which consisted of 27 multiple choice questions and three open-ended questions eliciting participant examples and was available in English, French, Italian, and Spanish. He relied on his own extensive Twitter network to disseminate links to the questionnaire in tweets in the four respective languages over a period of seven months. The 370 complete responses he received allowed him to uncover characteristics and particular trends in behavior among this sample of people who use Twitter for the purpose of language learning. For instance, findings revealed a tendency for these learners to focus on communicating meaning in the target language rather than focusing on the use of specific language forms and a corresponding awareness of learning new vocabulary with far fewer recalling the learning of new grammatical features. As can be gleaned, the benefit of this type of survey is the ability to gather a wide swath of data from a much larger number of participants than observation-based research allows for. However, one particular challenge facing researchers who employ survey methods in the digital wilds is also evident in this study as well: it can be a particular conundrum to identify and reach a representative sample in online communities and networks which are not clearly bounded or defined. For instance, as of the fourth quarter of 2020, Twitter had 192 million active users, many of whom tweeted in languages other than English, French, Italian, or Spanish (Twitter Investor Relations, 2021) and therefore were likely not represented by the 370 respondents to Rosell-Aguilar's (2020) questionnaire. This speaks to a particular challenge of survey research, whether online or in person – what sample of the target population it can reasonably access and how representative this sample is. In the case of conducting research on language learning in the digital wilds, where there are not always clearly defined institutional or community boundaries, convenience sampling strategies in which the researcher identifies and reaches out to the nearest reachable individuals (Nunan, 1992) may be an optimal solution. However, not all studies which use questionnaires rely on the same sampling strategies.

For instance, in Zourou, Potolia and Zourou's (2017) investigation of learner autonomy among users of the language learning social networking site Busuu, the researchers screened the public profiles of users from ten countries (five identified as French-speaking and five as English-speaking). Based on further information in user profiles, they then eliminated participants who were determined insufficiently active or overly active to settle on a target population of 1,528 moderately active users to complete a survey in either English or French. Although Zourou et al. (2017) were able to elicit only 47 responses from this initial 1,528, this number did represent a reasonable response rate. As can be seen, an advantage of carrying out a survey on a smaller and more focused social networking site such as Busuu instead of Twitter is that it was feasible for the research team to screen users to locate a complete sample of specific subpopulations. However, one of the drawbacks, as Zourou et al. (2017) note, is that it may result in a low number of total responses, particularly when this population regularly receives a large number of requests to complete questionnaires.

A third study which exemplifies a different approach to the sampling strategies of Rosell-Aguilar (2020) and Zourou et al. (2017) is Lee's (2019) investigation of 71 Korean university students' informal digital learning of English (IDLE). In this study of a purposive sample (Nunan, 1992) of a larger sample of 317 students from three Korean universities, Lee explored whether the amount and type of IDLE these students engaged in shared a relationship with their English learning outcomes, as measured by several formal tests of English. The questionnaire included items which elicited demographic data as well as both closed and open-ended questions. For instance, closed items asked students to rate their confidence, enjoyment and anxiety around using English on a five-point Likert scale. Open ended questions were used to elicit more precise and individualized responses about their IDLE activities such as "On average, how many hours each day did you spend in engaging in IDLE activities outside the classroom in the past 6 months?" (Lee, 2019, p. 117).

Lee's (2019) study also employed another common elicitation technique used in researching language learning in the digital wilds, interviews. Specifically, he carried out semi-structured interviews, typically an interview driven by the researcher but often with a list of topics instead of questions to guide the conversation (Nunan, 1992), with his participants to elicit deeper understanding of the types of IDLE activities they took part in. As we saw earlier in the case studies of Lam (2000) and Black (2009), interviews are a commonly used tool to accompany observational data of smaller groups or communities of participants. However, in cases where observation may not be feasible or ethical, interviews can also serve as the primary source of data elicitation. An example of this can be seen in Hannibal Jensen's (2019) study of 15 Danish primary school aged children on their outside of school English language use. In this study, Hannibal Jensen carried out descriptive ethnographic interviews with both individual and small groups of children who regularly engaged in these English activities together. Specifically, ethnographic interviews are meant to serve two functions: the development of rapport with participants and the elicitation of information (Spradley, 1979). As part of these 60–90 minute interviews, the children engaged in the specific English language activities (e.g. gaming, watching YouTube videos, etc.) that were a regular part of their outside of school lives, thereby taking the researcher on a guided tour of their English language practices that would have otherwise been unobservable to an adult.

The research approaches described so far allow for the documentation and elicitation of language learning and language use in the digital wilds. The final approach I will explore incorporates standardized language assessment measures, such as those one finds in formal educational contexts, to evaluate the language skills and knowledge developed beyond the classroom.

Applying formal language assessment measures to language learning in the digital wilds

A question that is often raised about gaming, fan practices or just interacting in a second language for fun in the digital wilds is what impact this has on the measurable development of specific language skills. Sundqvist's (2019) study of over 1,000 Swedish youth (15–16 year-olds enrolled in year 9 in secondary school) and their online gaming practices addressed this question. In her study, Sundqvist combined both survey approaches and formal language assessment measures including tests of English vocabulary as well as portions of the Swedish national exams for English taken by pupils in year 9. The survey, which asked questions about the amount of time spent gaming in English per week and the type of commercial off-the-shelf (COTS) games these students played enabled Sundqvist to organize students into groups for comparison: non-gamers, low-frequent gamers, moderate gamers, and frequent gamers. By comparing the scores of these groups on the different formal language assessment measures, she was able to identify clear relationships between the type of COTS game played and the amount of time and vocabulary skills and a relationship between the type of COTS game and playing frequency. For instance, one key finding revealed by this study was a clear advantage on assessments of vocabulary knowledge among frequent gamers over all other groups of students. By incorporating formal assessment measures in such a large-scale study, Sundqvist was able to find evidence of a link between a specific type of second language use in the digital wilds (frequent playing of COTS games in L2 English) and productive and receptive vocabulary.

Understandably, such a large-scale study tied to formal educational assessments asks a great deal of researchers who, like Sundqvist, may need to call upon an extensive network of teachers or other researchers to help in data collection, particularly of national tests and national test scores which are often proprietary and protected. However, an advantage can be seen in the high degree of quantitative or quantifiable data collected (e.g. certain scores, number of hours of gameplay) which allows for the use of rapid analysis and of inferential statistics to draw generalizations about a larger population, in this case, Swedish secondary school learners who play COTS games in English in the digital wilds.

In this section, I have discussed several key concepts and implications that emerge from common or emerging approaches to research on language learning in the digital wilds. However, all researchers conducting studies of language learning in the digital wilds will encounter particular challenges endemic to these often ephemeral online spaces and communities. These key issues are the focus of the next section.

Key issues: considerations and recommendations for researching the digital wilds

Carrying out research in online spaces offers researchers many advantages including the opportunity to reach large populations of learners who are geographically dispersed and who might otherwise be inaccessible. However, online research is rife with challenges and potential calamities. In this section, I have grouped these issues together under three substrands (i.e. practical, legal and ethical challenges), and, where possible, share possible solutions to these challenges as have been pioneered by fellow researchers of the digital wilds.

Practical considerations

The first of these challenges, practical issues, often stem from the ephemeral nature of online interactions and online communities which can make longitudinal analysis of language learning or language use a precarious venture. In other words, observational research that relies on analysis of online interactions in particular community spaces or of regular communication with intact online populations can unravel entirely when that community or space suddenly disappears.

Here is an example from my own experience as a member of a vibrant online fan community – in late May 2007, many users of the social media site LiveJournal logged into their accounts to discover that overnight, more than 500 individual and community fan blogs had been deleted. This included role-playing game (RPG) journals, book discussion groups, rape survivor blogs, and an age-restricted Harry Potter fanfiction community which hosted adult-themed Harry Potter fanfiction (Fanlore, 2020, May 11). The reason for this purging was attributed to pressure placed on the company that owned LiveJournal by an online organization threatening to contact vendors who advertised on LiveJournal with evidence that it supported child molestation, incest, child pornography, and pedophilia.

As a result, blogs and communities which had listed topics of interest on their profile pages such as "sexual abuse" and "pedophilia" had been purged regardless of whether these tags were used to describe major themes in fictional texts or lived experiences by survivors. Over time many of the affected blogs and communities were reinstated, but this event, later known as Strikethrough, set the stage for the immediate deletion or locking down of previously publicly available blogs. It also ushered in the long-term exodus of fan communities who sought other platforms where they believed they were less likely to face sudden deletion or censorship in response to financial pressures placed on the company hosting the platform.

What Strikethrough illustrates is the fact that researchers must be mindful that the commercial or ideological interests of social networking sites can lead to the destabilization and even complete dissolution of online communities (and thereby research contexts) where researchers may be carrying out case studies or digital ethnographies. One solution for researchers involved in this type of research is for them to work with participants to archive relevant information, where possible. This leads to the next set of issues prominent in research in the digital wilds – legal considerations which may govern exactly what one can do with online data.

Legal considerations

Legal considerations that researchers investigating the digital wilds must contend with include not only the local laws governing them and the institutions they are affiliated with but also the laws governing the location of the online platform and the participants themselves. To illustrate what this means, what follows is an example of legal considerations applicable to online research of residents of the European Union (EU) and how this has or could impact the research process.

From 2018, the EU has begun enforcing the General Data Protection Regulation (GDPR), a law which concerns data protection and privacy and which is intended to protect EU residents against the leakage of personal information and privacy breaches (Siegert,

Varod, Carmi & Kamocki, 2020). One major concern for researchers under the GDPR is the processing of non-anonymized personal data, defined as "any information relating to an identified or identifiable natural person" (article 4; Regulation (EU) 2016/679). Siegert et al. (2020) provide several examples of research data collection online that hold relevance for researching language learning in the digital wilds and how researchers may comply with the GDPR.

Several examples concern the collection of video recordings in the wild, which contain personal data (e.g. data that could be used to identify a natural person) including their image and voice. In the case of research using case study or digital ethnography, where close involvement with participants makes the research process clear and transparent, researchers will necessarily secure permission to collect data and store participants' personal information in advance. With respect to research, anonymized data or public recorded data with no additional identifying information about the participants do not fall under the GDPR (Siegert et al., 2020), which suggests that researchers could potentially comb the digital wilds for naturally occurring discourse examples. However, voice and facial recognition software make it possible to de-anonymize individuals, thereby requiring researchers to take steps to safeguard the privacy of these individuals (e.g. not including screengrabs of video, not sharing corpora of this data with other researchers in collaboration).

Another challenge with the GDPR concerns its acknowledgment of the need to facilitate different types of research and its corresponding lack of clarification of what constitutes acceptable scientific research. The GDPR's exemptions for research, therefore, are not always applied consistently across the 27 EU member states, and collaborating researchers may find themselves in conflict over how exemptions are applied. In some cases, this can mean researchers who are seeking ethical approval from institutions in different EU member countries may find themselves more limited in approaches they can take to gather, anonymize, or store personal data for use in research. Beyond the limitations imposed by different legal interpretations of data privacy laws, researchers should also be mindful of the ethical considerations of the communities they are researching.

Ethical considerations

For many researchers, ethical practices involve seeking approval for research based on national or institutional standards, securing informed consent from participants, and preserving the confidentiality of participants and participant data. However, when working in the digital wilds, researchers must also be mindful of the values and ethics of the communities they wish to research, although in some cases, the ethics and norms of the online community may be invisible to outsiders (see for instance Minkel, 2015, March 25).

Many fan works, such as fanfiction, are available online through easily accessible archives and websites including the still active FFN explored by Black (2009) or its more recent site fan fiction site Archive of Our Own (AO3) which grew out of the Strikethrough incident on LiveJournal. On the surface, these publicly available collections of stories and comments on stories could potentially serve as a rich source of data for exploring language learning and language use in the digital wilds. However, a less visible understanding of many (but not all) fan communities and fan practices is a desire among many fans that their amateur fanworks remain in the digital wilds to serve as a source of fun and pleasure among other fans and not be brought into more formal spaces for teaching, analysis, critique, or ridicule (see Sauro, 2017). In order to respect the local norms and autonomy of the fan community, it is a good practice to contact the fans themselves to seek their permission to use their work in a research capacity. An example of this can be seen in the acknowledgements section of Cornillie, Buendgens-Kosten, Sauro and Van der Veken (2021), who sought permission from a Harry Potter fanfiction writer to use a summary of one of their stories as well as their replies to fellow fans' comments on their story in a published research article. As a note, reaching out to fans before mining their online discourse for research purposes also recognizes that some fanworks may have been created for specific healing purposes (e.g. processing sexual assault or bereavement through fiction) on the part of the fan creator or fan community.

The future of research in the digital wilds

This chapter provides an overview of common research approaches used to investigate language learning in the digital wilds, the challenges facing researchers as well as innovative and pragmatic solutions to addressing the practical, legal and ethical challenges that arise. Future research can build upon these approaches and also incorporate other emerging practices including, for instance, collaborations between researcher and participant as seen in the work of Dressler and Dressler (2016, 2019), a mother and daughter research team who examined language learning and identity development through the daughter's Facebook postings when she studied abroad as a teenager. Other research may employ corpus-based approaches to analyzing linguistic characteristics of the writing of online fans (Sauro & Sundmark, 2019) or innovative linguistic techniques to capture feedback and interaction moves in online writing communities (Magnifico, Lammers & Curwood, 2020).

Reflection questions

1. What innovative approaches can researchers employ to balance their own ethical obligations with the ethical norms of the online communities in which they research?
2. How can researchers negotiate respecting the autonomy and cultural norms of online communities of practice where language learning occurs while also anticipating inevitable long-term changes in norms and laws regarding privacy and confidentiality that will emerge in response to innovations in technology?
3. What are other methods for eliciting and analyzing language learning, language use and language development in the digital wilds that are optimal for capturing the full range of language learning that takes place in different communities and on different platforms?

Recommended readings

The following Recommended readings have been selected as examples that are methodologically interesting and serve as guiding examples for those who are facing some of the common research challenges that arise when researching language learning beyond the classroom in the digital wilds.

Dressler, R., & Dressler, A. (2016). Linguistic identity positioning in Facebook posts during second language study abroad: One teen's language use, experience, and awareness. *Canadian Journal of Applied Linguistics* (Special Issue: The Culture of Study Abroad), *16*(2), 44–62.

This is a case study of a teenager's use of Facebook during periods of study abroad, to investigate her changes in her L2 German language use and language awareness as well as the successes and challenges that emerged over time. It is noteworthy for representing research beyond the classroom in social media spaces and for detailing steps taken by the researchers, one of which is the teen herself, to comply with both institutional research ethics and with the specific policies of Facebook.com for conducting research. It also serves as an interesting time capsule regarding shifts in social media usage as different platforms emerged or transformed during this time period and served different functions for this young learner/researcher.

Shafirova, L., Cassany, D., & Bach, C. (2020). From "newbie" to professional: Identity building and literacies in an online affinity space. *Learning, Culture and Social Interaction*, 24. https://doi.or/0.101/.lcsi.2019.100370

This article is a longitudinal case study of a 26-year-old fan crafter and member of the My Little Pony: Friendship is Magic fandom from Siberia called Shor. Through analysis of his various social media posts, particularly on the online art community DeviantArt and in interviews, they observed the multimodal development of Shor's English, a language he had not used since middle school, as it grew alongside his skill and expertise in designing and selling polymer figurines based on the show. This study is laudable in how the researchers worked with the participant to negotiate a point of tension between the research ethics of online researchers, intended to protect the confidentiality of participants, and the personal and community ethics of fan creators in the digital wilds, many of whom operate in a culture based upon name recognition as currency for their creative contributions.

Sundqvist, P. (2019). Commercial-off-the-shelf games in the digital wild and L2 learner vocabulary. *Language Learning & Technology*, 23(1), 87–113. https://doi.org/10125/44674

This study stands out as a large-scale predominantly quantitative mixed-methods study, which also incorporated qualitative data and integrated a variety of assessments to identify possible patterns and relationships between informal language learning that resulted from digital gaming and L2 English vocabulary development and use among teenagers in Sweden. In this study, the researcher administered surveys on the type of commercial off-the-shelf games students played and amount of weekly game play as well as two English vocabulary tests, one each targeting productive and receptive knowledge. This was augmented by students' scores on English essays on the Swedish national exam, which were further evaluated for vocabulary use. This study is noteworthy for its well-considered design to answer a question often raised regarding language learning in the digital wilds, especially regarding gaming: what relationship, if any, is there between amount and type of digital gaming (in L2 English) that learners engage in and their English ability in non-gaming contexts?

References

Black, R. W. (2009). Online fan fiction, global identities, and imagination. *Research in the Teaching of English*, 43(4), 397–425

Casanave, C. P. (2015). Case studies. In B. Partridge & A. Phakiti (Eds.), *Research methods in applied linguistics: A practical guide* (pp. 119–136). London: Bloomsbury Publishing.

Cornillie, F., Buendgens-Kosten, J., Sauro, S., & Van der Veken, J. (2021). "There's always an option": Collaborative writing of multilingual interactive fanfiction in a foreign language class. *CALICO Journal*, 38(1), 17–42. https://dx.doi.org/10.1558/cj.41119

Dressler, R., & Dressler, A. (2016). Linguistic identity positioning in Facebook posts during second language study abroad: One teen's language user, experience, and awareness. *The Canadian Journal of Applied Linguistics*, 19(2), 22–43.

Dressler, R., & Dressler, A. (2019). The methodological affordances and challenges of using Facebook to research study abroad. *Study Abroad Research in Second Language Acquisition and International Education*, 4(1), 126–144.

Duff, P. A. (2008). *Case study research in applied linguistics*. New York: Taylor & Francis.

Duffett, M. (2013). *Understanding fandom: An introduction to the study of media fan culture*. New York: Bloomsbury.

Fanlore.org (2020, May 11). Strikethrough and Boldthrough. https://fanlore.org/wiki/Strikethrough_and_Boldthrough

Fanlore.org (2021, January 1). FanFiction.net. https://fanlore.org/wiki/FanFiction.Net

Hakuta, K. (1976). A case study of a Japanese child learning English as a second language. *Language Learning, 26,* 321–351. https://doi.org/10.1111/j.1467-1770.1976.tb00280.x

Hannibal Jensen, S. (2019). Language learning in the wild: A young user perspective. *Language Learning & Technology, 23*(1), 72–86. https://doi.org/10125/44673

Hine, C. (2015). *Ethnography for the Internet: Embedded, embodied, and everyday.* London, UK: Bloomsbury.

Lam, W. S. E. (2000). L2 literacy and the design of the self: A case study of a teenager writing on the internet. *TESOL Quarterly 34*(3), 457–482. https://doi.org/10.2307/3587739

Lee, J. S. (2019). Quantity and diversity of informal digital learning of English. *Language Learning & Technology, 23*(1), 114–126. https://doi.org/10125/44675

Magnifico, A. M., Lammers, J. C., & Curwood, J. S. (2020). Developing methods to trace participation patterns across online writing. *Learning, Culture and Social Interaction, 24.* https://doi.org/10.1016/j.lcsi.2019.02.013

Mahboob, A., Paltridge, B., Phakiti, A., Wagner, E., Starfield, S., Burns, A., Jones, R. H., & De Costa, P. I. (2016). TESOL quarterly research guidelines, *TESOL Quarterly, 50*(1), 42–65.

Minkel, E. (2015, March 25). From the Internet to the Ivy League: Fan fiction in the class-room. Retrieved from https://themillions.com/2015/03/from-the-internet-to-the-ivy-league-fanfiction-in-the-classroom.html

Nunan, D. (1992). *Research methods in language learning.* New York: Cambridge University Press.

Rosell-Aguilar, F. (2020). Twitter as a language learning tool: The learners' perspective. *International Journal of Computer-Assisted Language Learning and Teaching, 10*(4), 1–13.

Sauro, S. (2014). Lessons from the fandom: Task models for technology-enhanced language learning. In M. González-Lloret & L. Ortega (Eds.), *Technology-mediated TBLT: Researching technology and tasks,* (pp. 239–262). Amsterdam/Philadelphia: John Benjamins.

Sauro, S. (2017). Online fan practices and CALL. *CALICO Journal, 34*(2), 131–146. https://doi/org/10.1558/CJ.33077

Sauro, S., & Sundmark, B. (2019). Critically examining the use of blog-based fan fiction in the advanced language classroom. *ReCALL. 31*(1), 40–55, https://doi.org/10.1017/S0958344018000071

Sauro, S., & Zourou, K. (2019). What are the digital wilds? *Language Learning & Technology, 23*(1), 1–7. https://doi.org/10125/44666

Schmidt, R. (1983). Interaction, acculturation and the acquisition of communicative competence. In N. Wolfson & E. Judd, (Eds.), *Sociolinguistics and language acquisition* (pp. 137–174). Rowley, MA: Newbury House.

Schmidt, R. (1984). The strengths and limitations of acquisition. *Language Learning and Communication, 3,* 1–16.

Schmidt, R., & Frota, S. (1986). Developing basic conversational ability in a second language: A case study of an adult learner of Portuguese. In R. Day (Ed.), *Talking to learn* (pp. 237–326). Rowley, MA: Newbury House.

Shafirova, L., & Cassany, D. (2019). Bronies learning English in the digital wild. *Language Learning & Technology, 23*(1), 127–144. https://doi.org/10125/44676

Shafirova, L., Cassany, D., & Bach, C. (2020). From "newbie" to professional: Identity building and literacies in an online affinity space. *Learning, Culture and Social Interaction, 24.* https://doi.or/0.101/.lcsi.2019.100370

Siegert, I., Varod, V. S., Carmi, N., & Kamocki, P. (2020). Personal data protection and academia: GDPR issues and multi-modal data-collections "in the wild". *Online Journal of Applied Knowledge Management, 8*(1), 16–31.

Spradley, J. P. (1979). *The ethnographic interview.* Long Grove, IL: Waveland Press.

Starfield, S. (2015). Ethnographic research. In B. Partridge & A. Phakiti (Eds.), *Research methods in applied linguistics: A practical guide* (pp. 137–152). London: Bloomsbury Publishing.

Sundqvist, P. (2019). Commercial-off-the-shelf games in the digital wild and L2 learner vocabulary. *Language Learning & Technology, 23*(1), 87–113. https://doi.org/10125/44674

Twitter Investor Relations. (9 February 2021). Q4 and fiscal year 2020 letter to shareholders. Available from https://s22.q4cdn.com/826641620/files/doc_financials/2020/q4/FINAL-Q4'20-TWTR-Shareholder-Letter.pdf

Varis, P. (2016). Digital ethnography. In A. Georgakopoulou & T. Spilioti (Eds.), *The Routledge handbook of language and digital communication* (pp. 55–68). London: Routledge.

Vazquez-Calvo, B., Zhang, L. T., Pascual, M., & Cassany, D. (2019). Fan translation of games, anime, and fanfiction. *Language Learning & Technology, 23*(1), 49–71. https://doi.org/10125/44672

Wagner, E. (2015). Survey research. In B. Partridge & A. Phakiti (Eds.), *Research methods in applied linguistics: A practical guide* (pp. 83–99). London: Bloomsbury Publishing.

Zourou, K., Potolia, A., & Zourou, F. (2017). Informal social networking for language learning: Insights into autonomy stances. In M. Cappellini, T. Lewis & A. Rivens Mompean (Eds.), *Learner autonomy and web 2.0* (pp. 141–167). Sheffield: Equinox Publishing Ltd.

24
THE USE OF MIXED METHODS TO STUDY LANGUAGE LEARNING BEYOND THE CLASSROOM

Lisbeth M. Brevik and Nils F. Buchholtz

Introduction

Over the past 50 years, mixed methods has increased in popularity and gained prominence as a research approach within a range of applied disciplines (Alise & Teddlie, 2010; Creamer, 2018), including language research (Brevik, 2022; Riazi, 2017). So-called 'mixing' or integration of qualitative and quantitative methods enables the comparison of information from different perspectives to better understand a phenomenon, such as language learning beyond the classroom (LBC). In this chapter, we discuss how the use of mixed methods designs can enrich our understanding of LBC by allowing for analysis of both qualitative information (e.g. observation, interview, essay) *and* quantitative information (e.g. survey, test results, grades).

Mixed methods is highly relevant for research involving complex phenomena, the study of which typically necessitates examination of both the people *and* the context in which they participate. This is of particular relevance to LBC research, in which people and context are mutually influential via continuous and essential social interaction (Reinders & Benson, 2017). A mixed methods researcher might observe communication and negotiation for meaning in language learning situations beyond the classroom, such as during gameplay, and then survey the participants afterwards for their opinions (e.g. Reinhardt, 2021), or they might interview a gamer concerning his gaming experiences and conduct language tests to measure his language proficiency before and after gaming (e.g. Sylvén, 2021). An increased number of LBC studies have recently begun to utilise mixed methods designs to study, for example, language use in the creation of fan fiction (e.g. Aragon & Davis, 2017), online gaming (e.g. Brevik, 2016, 2019, 2022; Sundqvist, 2019), and social media use (e.g. Trinder, 2017; Velázquez, 2017).

Although the mixing of methods has a long tradition, qualitative and quantitative methods are sometimes combined without being labelled 'mixed methods' (Buchholtz, 2019; Tashakkori et al., 2020). However, we agree with esteemed researchers in the field that mixed methods research, to deserve the label, must integrate analysis of qualitative and quantitative data in order to obtain additional insight:

> Mixed methods involves the collection and "mixing" or integration of both quantitative and qualitative data in a study. It is not enough to only analyse your qualitative and quantitative data. Further analysis consists of integration of the two databases for additional insight into research problems and questions.
>
> *(Creswell & Creswell, 2018, p. xxii)*

The term 'mixed methods' hereby refers to a systematic approach to data collection and analysis that mixes or integrates qualitative and quantitative components, such as data or findings obtained during the course of a study or from a set of closely related studies (Creamer, 2018; Johnson et al., 2007; Tashakkori et al., 2020). The aim of mixed methods research is to deepen and strengthen a study's conclusions by relating different data or results to one another (Buchholtz, 2019). These relations are referred to as 'points of integration' or the 'mixing of methods' (Brevik, 2022).

In this chapter, we discuss how mixed methods contributes interesting—and important—insight and nuance to LBC studies. We do so through the concepts of *multiple perspectives* (Greene, 2007; Johnson, 2017) and *integration* (Brevik, 2022; Creamer, 2018), and we frame these key concepts as 'a mixed methods way of thinking' (Greene, 2007). Next, we present a set of mixed methods research designs and purposes with empirical examples from LBC research. Finally, we address the call for more mixed methods studies in the field of LBC (e.g. Peters, 2022; Reinders & Benson, 2017; Reinhardt, 2021) and discuss the implications of using mixed methods to study language learning beyond the classroom.

Key construct: a mixed methods way of thinking

Aiming to capture *multiple perspectives* in a study, Greene (2007) coined the expression 'a mixed methods way of thinking'. In doing so, she crafted a philosophical mindset that values not only various voices and perspectives but also the differences between them:

> A mixed methods way of thinking aspires to better understand complex social phenomena by intentionally including multiple ways of knowing and valuing and by respectfully valuing differences.
>
> *(Greene, 2007, p. 17)*

This mindset reflects a view of reality as inherently complex. Greene (2007) defined the study of complex social phenomena as one that involves not just one or more individuals, but the individuals *and* their context. When studying humans in context, mixed methods research provides the opportunity to identify both converging and diverging results and to engage with paradox (Johnson, 2017). Challenging monomethod research, it could be argued that a mixed methods way of thinking resonates with the need to explore and deepen our understanding of the complex social phenomena that characterise the field of LBC. For instance, new technologies in informal contexts beyond the classroom (physical and virtual) have considerable implications for language learning (Gee, 2017). The integration of online survey data and digital observation data offers an empirical opportunity to compare reported and actual language use in contexts beyond the classroom (Brevik, 2019). Thus, within the field of LBC, the concept of *multiple perspectives* includes the premise that language learning is a complex social experience that takes place in various physical and virtual contexts (Gee, 2017), among people with different interests and language profiles (Brevik, 2019), and among people of various ages (Peters, 2022).

When both qualitative and quantitative methods are used in a study, it can be challenging to decide how they might best be mixed (the conceptual difference between method combination and integration). In some studies, qualitative and quantitative components are combined without necessarily being framed as a mixed methods design; they are used in separate strands of a study and are not integrated. In such studies, the quantitative strand typically aims to answer a quantitative research question, whereas the qualitative strand aims to answer a qualitative research question (Kelle & Buchholtz, 2015). Perhaps due to recent work that focussed on the relative dominance of qualitative and quantitative methods in mixed methods research (Tashakkori et al., 2020), the mixed methods mindset is increasingly concerned with the notion of integration (Creamer, 2018; Onwuegbuzie et al., 2018; Tashakkori et al., 2020).

Integration refers to the 'explicit conversation between (or interrelating of) the quantitative and qualitative components of a mixed methods study' (Plano Clark, 2019, p. 108). This conversation, which might occur at various stages of a study, can yield findings that are otherwise difficult to achieve (Brevik, 2022; Creamer, 2018). The integration challenge can be expressed quantitatively by two, not necessarily competing, formulas: the $1 + 1 = 3$ partial integration (Fetters & Freshwater, 2015) and the $1 + 1 = 1$ full integration (Onwuegbuzie et al., 2018). The $1 + 1 = 3$ formula suggests that 'qualitative + quantitative = more than the individual components' (Fetters & Freshwater, 2015, p. 115). Conversely, the $1 + 1 = 1$ formula includes crossover analysis that involves either converting qualitative data into a quantitative form (i.e. quantitising) or converting quantitative data into a qualitative form (i.e. qualitising). The points of integration might occur at various stages of a study (Brevik, 2022).

Reinders and Benson (2017) proposed that LBC is emerging as a field that is ripe for new research agendas based on the rapid development of 'online media, communications technologies and opportunities for travel' (p. 561). They argued that, as relatively little is known about the relationship between teachers' beliefs regarding LBC and the influence of such beliefs in their teaching practices, a mixed methods study could address the question of how, for example, teachers' beliefs about student autonomy influence their teaching practices related to encouragement, support, and preparation of students for LBC. In a related vein, Borg and Al-Busaidi (2012) designed a questionnaire to evaluate teachers' beliefs about student autonomy that contained two items on LBC ('autonomy can develop most effectively through learning outside the classroom' and 'out-of-class tasks which require learners to use the internet promote learner autonomy'). That questionnaire could be adapted to include more questions about teachers' beliefs regarding the value and role of LBC in order to quantitatively investigate which beliefs are held by teachers and to what extent. Qualitative observational data, such as video recordings from the classroom, could then provide information about the ways in which teachers with different levels of belief incorporate LBC (see Reinders & Benson, 2017).

Here, the *integration* of quantitative and qualitative findings would provide insight into the relationship between teachers' beliefs and instructional practices and shed light on how to incorporate LBC into classroom instruction in a way that enhances student autonomy. This mixed methods design aligns with the $1 + 1 = 3$ formula (Fetters & Freshwater, 2015); the juxtaposition of qualitative observations and quantitative survey data would provide additional information about teacher beliefs and practices. The inclusion of a crossover analysis (quantitising) could also align this design with the $1 + 1 = 1$ formula (Onwuegbuzie et al., 2018). For instance, the video data could be analysed quantitatively by measuring the total time devoted to LBC discussions or by counting each reference to students' LBC.

Key issue: mixed methods designs

Mixed methods designs refer to studies in which qualitative and quantitative approaches are mixed or integrated (Creswell & Creswell, 2018). Various typologies have been used to describe such designs. In this chapter, we adopt Tashakkori et al.'s (2020) typology of four mixed methods designs: *parallel*, *sequential*, *conversion*, and *hybrid*. Finally, we present five main purposes for performing mixed methods research.

Parallel mixed methods design (one phase)

Parallel designs are also known as concurrent, simultaneous, or convergent designs (Creswell & Creswell, 2018). They comprise one research phase in which quantitative and qualitative strands occur either more or less simultaneously or with some time lapse (Tashakkori et al., 2020). The basic idea is that the *integration* of the two strands (QUAN+QUAL[1]) within the same research phase provides a more holistic picture than does either method separately. Parallel designs are commonly used to validate one dataset with the other. For example, two datasets may be integrated to determine if participants respond similarly to quantitative predetermined scales (e.g. questionnaire) and to open-ended qualitative questions (e.g. interview). These datasets could also capture *different perspectives* if the participants provide information in the open-ended interview that is different from their response to the predetermined questionnaire items. The above example of a study that integrates surveyed opinions of LBC with observation of references to LBC during classroom instruction (Borg & Al-Busaidi, 2012; Reinders & Benson, 2017) could be designed as a parallel mixed methods study. In that case, the two data sources would be collected more or less simultaneously and analysed together, with the results from one method contextualising the other.

To examine practices and preferences related to digital media in informal learning of English beyond the classroom, Trinder (2017) investigated Austrian business students' perceptions of the usefulness of a range of digital resources for the acquisition of language skills and juxtaposed them with opinions on in-class use of technology. She collected quantitative and qualitative data in parallel by means of a questionnaire that included both closed questions with Likert-type ratings and free text responses to open questions. This study found a clear preference for well-established media (e.g. film, online dictionaries, email) in self-regulated contexts beyond the classroom and diverging opinions on the use of technologies in classroom settings. The integrated mixed methods analysis provided multiple perspectives concerning how young adults practise informal language learning beyond the classroom and compared digital tools with more traditional resources.

One of our own studies (Brevik, 2016) in the research project VOGUE (VOcational and General students' Use of English) at the University of Oslo, also used a parallel mixed methods design. The purpose was to identify why a group of adolescents (aged 16–17) read markedly better in English, a second language, than in Norwegian, their first language. The parallel design offered the opportunity to interview five of them—all boys in vocational studies—about their use of English beyond the classroom (qualitative) and to simultaneously collect survey data on their out-of-school use of English (quantitative) and their scores on reading tests in English and Norwegian (quantitative). The data sources captured different perspectives among the boys: open-ended self-reports in the interview, closed-ended self-reports in the survey, and numerical proficiency measures in the test scores. The integrated findings suggested that the boys' use of English beyond the classroom, particularly during online gaming, was decisive for their reading skills.

Sequential mixed methods design (two or more phases)

Sequential mixed methods designs comprise two or more chronological phases in which different types of data (quantitative, qualitative) are mixed (Tashakkori et al., 2020). In sequential designs, the results of one phase influence or initiate the next, offering the opportunity to attend to research in a stepwise fashion and make related decisions during the research process (Brevik, 2022). In sequential designs, *integration* can be accomplished at several points within and across phases. The data within a phase are typically collected in parallel, whereas data across phases are typically collected sequentially.

Sequential designs can be *exploratory* or *explanatory*. The *sequential exploratory design* seeks to generalise findings of a qualitative study. The qualitative data are analysed first and are used to plan the collection and analysis of quantitative data in order to study the phenomenon systematically, commonly with a larger sample (QUAL→QUAN[2]). For instance, a researcher might collect interview data related to participants' opinions on LBC and the conditions for or contexts in which LBC occurs and then analyse the data qualitatively to identify themes. Taking these resulting themes as variables, the researcher can then develop a quantitative survey instrument to assess the overall prevalence of these variables among a large number of participants. The *sequential explanatory design* seeks detailed explanations of quantitative findings; quantitative analysis results are used as the basis for more detailed analysis of qualitative data among fewer participants (QUAN→QUAL). For instance, a researcher might collect and analyse quantitative survey data to identify adolescents' language proficiency and, in order to detect opportunities for LBC, their primary leisure activities. The researcher could then conduct qualitative focus group interviews to more fully explore the results (e.g. how or why adolescents' language proficiency relates to their use of language in certain leisure activities or contexts).

An example of a *sequential exploratory* design is a US study of university students who claim Spanish as a heritage language (Velázquez, 2017). By studying their use of Spanish outside the classroom, Velázquez (2017) examined whether Spanish was relevant in the students' personal networks beyond their families. Methodologically, she first collected interview data to identify language backgrounds before introducing an online survey concerning use of Spanish outside the classroom (QUAL→QUAN). Based on the integrated findings, she found that use of Spanish in music, TV shows, and social media was crucial for social bonding among the students.

Two examples of *sequential explanatory* designs are Sundqvist (2019) in Sweden and Schwarz (2020) in Austria, as the initial quantitative results informed the subsequent qualitative data collection. Both investigated the relationship between engagement with English beyond the classroom and vocabulary knowledge among secondary school students. Sundqvist (2019) specifically examined gaming habits, including types of games and time spent gaming. She first collected quantitative information (survey, vocabulary tests, school leaving certificate) in a large sample, and in the final phase selected a small convenience sample to delve into additional qualitative information on gaming (interview, essay). After integrating the quantitative and qualitative data, she found a positive relationship between English vocabulary and time spent gaming but no relation with types of games. She also found that gamers used advanced vocabulary more often than non-gamers. In the sequential mixed methods study performed by Schwarz (2020), data on the frequency and amount of participants' out-of-school engagement with English were collected by means of a questionnaire, an online language diary, and vocabulary tests. The quantitative data were then used to develop an interview guide; focus group interviews were carried out with six groups of learners to more fully understand their perspectives. Results showed that the majority of participants engaged in English activities on a daily basis in their leisure time and that they evaluated engagement with English beyond the classroom as beneficial to their language and vocabulary acquisition.

In a *sequential explanatory* study by Lee et al. (2019), Korean and Taiwanese students' willingness to communicate in English as a second language in class, out of class, and in digital settings was surveyed using a questionnaire. To identify factors that might have influenced their willingness to communicate in English, the authors conducted follow-up interviews with students who scored above average. Using this sequential design, the researchers were able to identify factors that might have influenced the students' willingness to communicate in English. The initial quantitative results showed that both the Korean and the Taiwanese participants exhibited low willingness to communicate in English inside the classroom, whereas the qualitative data suggested that anxieties related to speaking English might have equally influenced both groups' willingness to communicate. Additionally, while the Korean students scored higher on willingness to communicate outside the classroom, the Taiwanese students scored higher on willingness to communicate in digital settings. Through mixed methods integration, the qualitative data revealed that these discrepancies might have been influenced by the English environment and teaching practice (Lee et al., 2019).

Conversion mixed methods design (one or more phases)

Conversion designs are also known as crossover analysis, designs in which mixing or integration occurs when one type of data is transformed, analysed, and interpreted both qualitatively and quantitatively (Tashakkori et al., 2020). Conversion involves either quantitising or qualitising. *Quantitising* refers to converting qualitative data into a quantitative form that can be statistically analysed, for instance using numeric codes in an observation protocol to analyse a videotaped conversation. *Qualitising* refers to the process of converting quantitative data into a qualitative form, for instance converting numerical data into narratives that can be analysed and understood qualitatively (Onwuegbuzie et al., 2018).

An example of a conversion design might be if a researcher recorded a debate about participants' engagement in LBC activities, such as fan fiction or online gaming, and also conducted individual interviews with the participants. The researcher might analyse the debate data quantitatively by measuring the time allotted to individual speeches or by using an observation protocol and systematically counting specific discourse patterns. Such analysis would be an example of *quantitising*, converting the qualitative data into quantitative form. The interviews could be analysed qualitatively, with the aim of identifying trends in experiences or thematic discourse preferences. Subsequently, the two data sets could be integrated to examine ways that the results converge or diverge.

In another VOGUE study (Brevik, 2022), quantitative data from reading tests and surveys of more than 10,000 adolescents in Norway were converted into qualitative form (*qualitising*) through creation of a poem. The aim of the study was to understand reading proficiency through examination of self-reported language learning beyond the classroom. The tests provided English and Norwegian reading proficiency scores, whereas the survey provided information about self-reported use of the languages beyond the classroom. Analysis of crossover inferences led to the creation of a poem that explores the meaning of the numerical data as a form of qualitative representation (Brevik, 2022, p. 205):

Outliers
mostly vocational boys
at-risk of school dropout
poor readers in the first language
but unexpectedly proficient readers in English
knowing how to make inferences
using strategies to comprehend
revealing how important it is to them
to be good readers of English

In lines 1–6, inferences were drawn from background information and reading scores in the test data. In lines 7–9, inferences were drawn from the self-reports in the survey data. The integration of the two datasets allowed for synthesis and representation of large amounts of quantitative information qualitatively. This also allowed for multiple perspectives to be represented as a poem, thereby enriching our understanding of the value of LBC for these adolescents (Brevik, 2022). This mixed methods conversion design follows the 1 + 1 = 1 full integration formula (Onwuegbuzie et al., 2018), as it includes crossover analysis that involves converting quantitative data into a qualitative form (i.e. qualitising).

Hybrid mixed methods designs (three or more phases)

Hybrid designs combine features of two or more basic designs (parallel, sequential, conversion) into a complex hybrid combination (Tashakkori et al., 2020). Although parallel and sequential designs typically focus on qualitative and quantitative data collection as separate strands of a study, increasing focus on integration has made hybrid designs more common. In these designs, both types of data might be collected in one phase, followed by a new phase that utilises only one type of data: (QUAL+QUAN)→QUAL→(QUAL+QUAN). This example has three phases; a parallel design in the first phase (QUAL+QUAN) is followed by a second phase (QUAL) and a third phase (QUAL+QUAN), thereby mixing parallel and sequential designs. Depending on the research question, many mixed methods studies do not necessarily follow simple designs, and the construction of a complex research design often leads to hybrid designs.

Another of the VOGUE studies is a good illustration of a hybrid design (Brevik, 2019). This study, building on similar prior work (Brevik, 2016), utilised a new context and a larger sample to aggregate LBC findings on the connection between use of English beyond the classroom and language proficiency at school. Brevik (2016) was a parallel design comprising one research phase in which both quantitative and qualitative data were collected. Expanding on this design, the following VOGUE study (Brevik, 2019) comprised three phases: (QUAN+QUAL) →(MIXED) →QUAL. In phase 1, we simultaneously collected test results and survey data (quantitative) and conducted focus groups (qualitative) with 21 adolescents. In phase 2, based on a need to validate the self-reports from the adolescents, we collected language logs with both closed-ended and open-ended questions (mixed) among 18 of them. In phase 3, we interviewed (qualitative) five of the adolescents that seemed to represent different perspectives on the use of English beyond the classroom. Based on this hybrid design (parallel and sequential), the three phases were conducted over seven months. The hybrid design offered the opportunity to enrich our understanding of LBC; based on the adolescents' reported use of English beyond the classroom, three language profiles were identified: the gamer, the internet surfer, and the social media user (Brevik, 2019).

Table 24.1 LBC studies using a mixed methods design

Design	Quantitative data				Qualitative data			Study
Parallel			Survey		Survey			Trinder (2017)
Parallel	Reading test L1	Reading test L2	Survey		Interview			Brevik (2016)
Sequential exploratory			Survey		Interview			Velázquez (2017)
Sequential explanatory			Survey		Interview			Lee et al. (2019)
Sequential explanatory	Vocabulary tests	Test scores	Survey		School leaving certificates	Interview	essay	Sundqvist (2019)
Sequential explanatory	Vocabulary test	Language diary	Survey		Interview			Schwarz (2020)
Conversion	Reading test L1	Reading test L2	Survey		Poetry			Brevik (2022)
Hybrid	Reading test L1	Reading test L2	Survey	Language log	Interview	Focus group	Language log	Brevik (2019)

In Table 24.1, the reviewed studies are summarised in terms of mixed methods design, qualitative data, and quantitative data. Some of the studies in Table 24.1 are also referred to in the following section, which explores multiple purposes for using mixed methods designs.

Multiple purposes for using mixed methods designs

Whereas some mixed methods studies identify one purpose for mixing, many studies list more than one. Greene et al.'s (1989) typology of five purposes for mixing qualitative and quantitative methods is useful for identifying the purpose of mixing. We illustrate each of these five purposes by referencing some of the studies presented above.

1. *Complementarity.* One purpose of a mixed methods study is to include qualitative and quantitative data in order to strengthen one method by including findings from the other. Aiming for complementarity, we seek a more holistic picture by exploring different aspects or perspectives of the same phenomenon (e.g. LBC). Brevik (2016, 2019) and Schwarz (2020) adopted complementarity as a main purpose for their mixing of methods. All three studies included quantitative language tests, which provide information about participants' language proficiency but say very little about why the proficiency in question is developed or how language learning beyond the classroom is perceived by the participants. Integrating qualitative data, such as interviews, complemented the quantitative data and enriched holistic understanding of LBC in these studies.
2. *Initiation.* Another purpose of designing a mixed methods study could be initiation by prior research findings (qualitative or quantitative). The purpose of initiation is then concerned with the examination of surprising or atypical findings from the earlier

studies. Typically, the new study will then aim to examine the phenomenon (e.g. LBC) from a new perspective using new types of data; for instance, conducting interviews to understand previously collected survey responses or conducting language tests to understand previously collected observations. If initiation is the purpose, the researcher should be open to discovery of new perspectives, contradictory findings, paradox, or confirmation of prior results. All three VOGUE studies (Brevik, 2016, 2019, 2022) were initiated by findings from previous research. In these studies, the quantitative test data provided information about adolescents' English reading proficiency, but none about how or why this proficiency was developed. Thus, the main purpose for initiating each of the three studies was to search for explanations for the previous findings by collecting new data (qualitative and quantitative).

3. *Triangulation.* If triangulation is the purpose of a mixed methods study, results are strategically used for validity purposes. An example might be the collection of quantitative and qualitative data about LBC from the same participants in order to examine possible convergence, corroboration, or correspondence of results. In Sundqvist (2019), quantitative data and qualitative data were triangulated to strengthen the answer to the research question. By doing so, her study enriched our understanding of digital gaming for vocabulary development among teenagers in Sweden.

4. *Development.* Another purpose of a mixed methods study is the development of an instrument, for instance a questionnaire, interview guide, or test. Schwarz (2020) aimed for development by integrating qualitative and quantitative data. Quantitative data sources from her study were used to create an interview guide for interviews in the following research phase. Thus, this study had complementarity *and* development as its main purposes.

5. *Expansion.* If expansion is a main purpose of a mixed methods study, it has multiple phases, and findings from one phase inform the next phase. Expansion can be used to extend the breadth or range of enquiry by using different methods for different enquiry components; for instance, self-reported data can be expanded by collecting observation data. This purpose is particularly important in follow-up studies. Brevik (2019) was originally designed with only one phase. However, as the need for validation of the adolescents' LBC arose during the research process, the study was ultimately expanded with two more phases. By building upon and integrating the findings of each phrase, the expansion offered more information about the participants' LBC practices and perspectives than one method alone. The study thus has complementarity *and* expansion as its main purposes.

Implications and future directions

At the core of LBC research are complex phenomena, which resonate with Greene's (2007) notion of a mixed methods way of thinking: research that aims to capture multiple perspectives because it involves humans *and* the context. The notion of multiple perspectives can apply to one or more participants and to one or more contexts. Capturing an individual's perspectives across contexts can be considered an 'intrapersonal' dimension of the research, whereas the comparison of multiple participants' perspectives is considered 'interpersonal'. Mixed methods designs, which are particularly suitable for complex and multi-layered topics, promise to provide additional insight within the assumedly multi-layered and complex field of LBC.

In 2017, Reinders and Benson proposed a research agenda for LBC that emphasised the many opportunities within the field. They addressed the importance of context, the processes involved, the role of the individual learner, and the supportive roles that teachers can play. In order to contribute to such an agenda and move LBC research forward, we argue that mixed methods designs is a particularly fruitful avenue. The integration of qualitative and quantitative approaches reflects a growing interest in designing innovative investigations with multiple—both intrapersonal and interpersonal—perspectives and contexts relevant to LBC studies.

Based on the reviewed studies and in agreement with Reinders and Benson (2017), an essential aspect of LBC research seems to be the study of the roles of spaces in language learning. For instance, the necessity that teachers encourage LBC in the classroom was evident in the studies in which participants did not choose to use the language competence they clearly had (e.g. unwillingness to communicate in English in the classroom compared to online contexts beyond the classroom in Lee et al., 2019) and in those studies where adolescents used their language proficiency inefficiently (e.g. being silent in class despite English competence developed through online gaming, internet surfing, and social media use in Brevik, 2019). In these situations, the integration of qualitative and quantitative approaches to capture multiple perspectives was of utmost importance (Greene, 2007; Johnson, 2017), which supports Reinhardt's (2019) argument that teachers must find ways of making language learning beyond the classroom part of their classroom practices. In light of these findings, it is interesting that participants in some studies reacted negatively to the idea that teachers might include students' LBC experiences because they considered language practices beyond the classroom to be personal (e.g. Brevik, 2016; Trinder, 2017).

Following Reinders and Benson (2017), future LBC research could explore the role of teachers, the complexity of their beliefs regarding LBC, and the potential inclusion of LBC in their teaching. In that case, the research object would be intrapersonal, capturing multiple perspectives by first surveying the teachers about their self-reported beliefs and then adding an observational perspective of their teaching. In such a study, the researcher might integrate the two data sources during data analysis, thereby confirming prior studies that found few connections or contradicting those studies by identifying new links. The added value of the mixed methods design here is the opportunity to integrate the findings and identify whether there seems to be a connection between teachers' beliefs about LBC and their teaching practices. This integration of qualitative and quantitative data might even identify paradox if the teachers express a belief in connecting LBC in the classroom but do not do so in their own teaching.

The role of the individual learner was addressed by Trinder (2017) in her choice to include both open and closed survey questions in order to capture diverging perspectives among her participants. In doing so, she identified diverging views on technology in school contexts and widespread agreement on technology use beyond the classroom. The multi-layeredness in this study captured both intra- and interpersonal perspectives concerning individual views on LBC. Similarly, Lee et al. (2019) captured diverging interpersonal perspectives between two groups of East Asian students of English as a foreign language. They found that Korean students were more willing to communicate in English beyond the classroom than were Taiwanese students. This method of addressing the role of the individual language learner enriches our understanding of LBC as multi-layered and complex. These findings align with Gee's (2017) argument that we must attempt to capture the complexities of language learning across contexts (physical and virtual), in and beyond the classroom, and over time.

The only mixed methods design that was repeatedly used across the reviewed LBC studies was the sequential design. This follows recommendations in mixed methods literature to collect one type of data in the first phase, to analyse that data, and then to follow up with the other type of data to further explore or to explain confusing, contradictory, or unusual responses (Creswell & Creswell, 2018; Tashakkori et al., 2020). In the reviewed studies, we identified sequential *exploratory* designs (e.g. Velázquez, 2017), sequential *explanatory* designs (e.g. Lee et al., 2019; Schwarz, 2020; Sundqvist, 2019), and sequential designs as part of *hybrid* designs (e.g. Brevik, 2019) that were used to study both physical and virtual LBC contexts. The study of virtual contexts beyond the classroom aligns with Sauro and Zourou's (2017) argument on the relevance of studying 'informal language learning that takes place in digital spaces, communities, and networks that are independent of formal instructional contexts' (p. 186).

In this vein, mixed methods designs add value to the complex phenomena that characterise the field of LBC. However, mixed analysis does not always lead to complementary or convergent findings. The results may be incoherent, or the qualitative and quantitative results might diverge or even contradict each other (Kelle & Buchholtz, 2015). However, this identification of dissonance or even paradox in the material might be an important methodological contribution. The challenge is to gain additional value from the integration of approaches with regard to the overarching research question, to 'produce a whole through integration that is greater than the sum of the individual qualitative and quantitative parts' (Fetters & Freshwater, 2015, p. 116). Such an effort is necessary if we want to do justice to the complexity of LBC research.

Mertens (2015) noted that the mixed methods approach is particularly suitable for solving so-called *wicked problems*, which include social inequities and the lack of access to education. She argues that wicked problems 'cannot be resolved by traditional processes of analysing vast amounts of data or more sophisticated statistical analyses' and calls for researchers to 'expand their methods to include qualitative relationship building that gives voice to those who are less powerful in this context' (Mertens, 2015, p. 5). These wicked problems could be placed at the core of LBC research. The ability to communicate in more than one language is key to intercultural understanding and active participation in the current globalised world. Scholars promote linguistic diversity as a matter of social justice; reaffirming the belief that education is one of the most powerful vehicles for language development, they have called for research on comparisons across contexts and languages (De Costa et al., 2017).

The added value of mixed methods designs in LBC research can be justified not only pragmatically but also ontologically by considering the research objects under study. The objects examined in LBC research are typically characterised by a complex structure of multiple intrapersonal and interpersonal perspectives and contexts and the interaction between them, which opens up a corresponding level of complexity in the analysis regarding both the social and psychological layers of the research objects. In addition to these structures, research objects in LBC research can extend over various interacting entities at different levels, including the micro level (individual), the meso level (e.g. group, school class), or the macro level (e.g. country or educational system). The mixing or integration of methods can thus contribute to maximising the scope of research findings by looking at different levels and relating the findings to each other. Consequently, LBC research objects should be integrated in relation to a temporal *and* cultural level of analysis and in relation to educational and social change processes (Brevik, 2022; Buchholtz, 2019). Adoption of a mixed methods way of thinking (Greene, 2007) can raise new questions and encourage the methodological innovations needed to solve increasingly complex problems concerning language learning beyond the classroom, but it also has an inherent pragmatic orientation towards linking the supposedly incompatible.

Reflection questions

1 What are your views on *mixed methods*? Can there be too much focus on research design? Why or why not? Which aspects of mixed methods do you think deserve greater attention, and how might that be accomplished?
2 For a study in the field of LBC, what are the advantages of using quantitative and qualitative approaches, and what is the added value of integrating those approaches in a mixed methods design?
3 Consider the four *MM designs*. Imagine planning an LBC study. How could you draw on these designs to make a visual model of that study?

Recommended readings

For an introduction to research design that covers qualitative, quantitative, and mixed designs: Creswell, J. W., & Creswell, J. D. (2018). *Research design: Qualitative, quantitative & mixed methods approaches*. Thousand Oaks, CA: SAGE.

For a deeper understanding of mixed methods research: Tashakkori, A., Johnson, R. B., & Teddlie, C. (2020). *Foundations of mixed methods research. Integrating quantitative and qualitative approaches in the social and behavioral sciences*. Thousand Oaks, CA: SAGE.

For readers interested in how and when integration can take place in mixed methods research: Creamer, E. G. (2018). *An introduction to fully integrated mixed methods research*. Thousand Oaks, CA: SAGE.

Notes

1 We are taking up the typical notation of mixed methods designs by Morse (2003) here, where QUAL = qualitative, QUAN = quantitative, and + means parallel.
2 Following Morse (2003) the arrow means 'sequential'.

References

Alise, M. A., & Teddlie, C. (2010). A continuation of the paradigm wars? Prevalence rates of methodological approaches across the social/behavioral sciences. *Journal of Mixed Methods Research, 4*(2), 103–126.

Aragon, C., & Davis, K. (2017). *Writers in the secret garden: Fanfiction, youth, and new forms of mentoring*. Cambridge, MA: MIT Press.

Borg, S., & Al-Busaidi, S. (2012). *Learner autonomy: English language teachers' beliefs and practices* (ELT Research Paper 12–07). London: British Council.

Brevik, L. M. (2016). The gaming outliers: Does out-of-school gaming improve boys' reading skills in English as a second language? In E. Elstad (Ed.), *Educational technology and polycontextual bridging* (pp. 39–61). Rotterdam: Sense Publisher.

Brevik, L. M. (2019). Gamers, surfers, social media users: Unpacking the role of interest in English. *Journal of Computer Assisted Learning, 35*, 595–606. https://doi.org/10.1111/jcal.12362

Brevik, L. M. (2022). The emergent multiphase design: Demonstrating an integrated approach in the context of language research in education. In J. H. Hitchcock & A. J. Onwuegbuzie (Eds.), *The Routledge Handbook for Advancing Integration in Mixed Methods Research* (pp. 196–212). Oxford: Routledge.

Buchholtz, N. (2019). Planning and conducting mixed methods studies in mathematics educational research. In G. Kaiser & N. Presmeg (Eds.), *Compendium for early career researchers in mathematics education* (pp. 131–152). Cham: Springer. https://link.springer.com/chapter/10.1007/978-3-030-15636-7_6

Creamer, E. G. (2018). *An introduction to fully integrated mixed methods research*. Thousand Oaks, CA: SAGE.

Creswell, J. W., & Creswell, J. D. (2018). *Research design: Qualitative, quantitative & mixed methods approaches*. Thousand Oaks, CA: SAGE.

De Costa, P. I., Singh, J., Milu, E., Wang, X., Fraiberg, S., & Canagarajah, S. (2017). Pedagogizing translingual practice: Prospects and possibilities. *Research in the Teaching of English, 51*, 464–472.

Fetters M. D., & Freshwater, D. (2015). The 1+1=3 integration challenge. *Journal of Mixed Methods Research, 9*, 115–117. https://doi.org/10.1177/1558689815581222

Gee, J. P. (2017). *Teaching, learning, and literacy in our high-risk high-tech world. A framework for becoming human*. Teachers College Press.

Greene, J. C. (2007). *Mixed methods in social inquiry*. New York: Wiley & Son.

Greene, J. C., Caracelli, V. J., & Graham, W. F. (1989). Toward a conceptual framework for mixed-method evaluation designs. *Educational Evaluation and Policy Analysis, 11*, 255–274. https://doi.org/10.3102/01623737011003255

Johnson, R. B. (2017). Dialectical pluralism: A metaparadigm whose time has come. *Journal of Mixed Methods Research, 11*, 156–173. https://doi.org/10.1177/1558689815607692

Kelle, U., & Buchholtz, N. (2015). The combination of qualitative and quantitative research methods in mathematics education: A "mixed methods" study on the development of the professional knowledge of teachers. In A. Bikner-Ahsbahs, C. Knipping, & N. Presmeg (Eds.), *Approaches to qualitative research in mathematics education. Examples of methodology and methods* (pp. 321–361). Dordrecht: Springer.

Lee, J. S., Lee, K., & Chen Hsieh, J. (2019). Understanding willingness to communicate in L2 between Korean and Taiwanese students. *Language Teaching Research*, online first. https://doi.org/10.1177/1362168819890825

Mertens, D. (2015). Mixed methods and wicked problems. *Journal of Mixed Method Research, 9*(1), 3–6. https://doi.org/10.1177/1558689814562944

Morse, J. M. (2003). Principles of mixed methods and multimethod research design. In A. Tashakkori & C. Teddlie (Eds.), *Handbook of mixed methods in social and behavioural research* (pp. 189–208). Thousand Oaks: Sage.

Onwuegbuzie, A. J., Hitchcock, J., Natesan, P., & Newman, I. (2018). Using fully integrated Bayesian thinking to address the 1+1=1 integration challenge. *International Journal of Multiple Research Approaches, 10*, 1–13.

Plano Clark, V. L. (2019). Meaningful integration within mixed methods studies: Identifying why, what, when, and how. *Contemporary Educational Psychology, 57*, 106–111.

Reinders, H., & Benson, P. (2017). Research agenda: Language learning beyond the classroom. *Language Teaching, 50*(4), 561–578. https://doi.org/10.1017/S0261444817000192

Reinhardt, J. (2019). *Gameful second and foreign language teaching and learning: Theory, research, and practice*. Palgrave MacMillan.

Reinhardt, J. (2021). Not all MMOGs are created equal: A design-informed approach to the study of L2 learning in multiplayer online games. In M. Peterson, K. Yamazaki & M. Thomas (Eds.), *Digital games and language learning: Theory, development and implementation* (pp. 107–131). Bloomsbury Publishing.

Riazi, A. M. (2017). *Mixed methods research in language teaching and learning*. Equinox Publishing.

Sauro, S., & Zourou, K. (2017). Call for papers. *Language Learning & Technology, 21*(1), 186. https://doi.org/10125/44603

Schwarz, M. (2020). *Beyond the walls: A mixed methods study of teenagers' extramural English practices and their vocabulary knowledge* [Doctoral dissertation, University of Vienna]. https://doi.org/10.25365/thesis.63632

Sundqvist, P. (2019). Commercial-off-the-shelf games in the digital wild and L2 learner vocabulary. *Language Learning & Technology, 23*(1), 87–113. https://doi.org/10125/44674

Sylvén, L. K. (2021). Gaming as a gateway to L2 English learning: A case study of a young L1 Swedish boy. In M. Peterson, K. Yamazaki & M. Thomas (Eds.), *Digital games and language learning: Theory, development and implementation* (pp. 288–315). Bloomsbury Publishing.

Tashakkori, A., Johnson, R. B., & Teddlie, C. (2020). *Foundations of mixed methods research. Integrating quantitative and qualitative approaches in the social and behavioral Sciences.* SAGE.

Trinder, R. (2017). Informal and deliberate learning with new technologies. *ELT Journal, 71*(4), 401–12. https://doi.org/10.1093/elt/ccw117

Velázquez, I. (2017). Reported literacy, media consumption and social media use as measures of relevance of Spanish as a heritage language. *International Journal of Bilingualism, 21*(1), 21–33. https://doi.org/10.1177/1367006915596377

25
LANGUAGE LEARNING DIARY STUDIES IN LEARNING BEYOND THE CLASSROOM CONTEXTS

Kathleen M. Bailey

Introduction

Diaries have been used in language learning and teaching research since at least the late 1970s. Diaries (also called *journals*) have been kept by both teachers and language learners, but this chapter will consider only language learning diary studies, focusing on those based on learning done outside of formal coursework. The phrase "learning beyond the classroom" (LBC) encompasses the "types of learning (and the corollary instructional support) that fall outside of or extend teacher-led classroom instruction" (Reinders, 2020, p. 65; see also Reinders & Benson, 2017).

What is a *diary study*? It is "an account of a second language experience as recorded in a first-person journal" (Bailey & Ochsner, 1983, p. 189). Because the diarists' journal entries reflect on their own experiences, readers learn about their subjective perspectives, including their emotions, what they were trying to accomplish, and how successful they felt they may have been. Bailey and Ochsner note that these aspects of second language acquisition "are normally hidden or largely inaccessible to an external observer" (p. 189). It is in revealing these typically hidden factors that the diary studies have been useful in language education and research.

Diary studies have been described as "a research genre defined by the data collection procedures" (Bailey, 1991, p. 60). The source of the data in the language learner diaries comes from the learners themselves, through the processes of observation, introspection, retrospection, and documentation.

Keeping a journal without analyzing the resulting record does not constitute a diary study, though making and rereading the diary entries can be useful to the learner and can be analyzed by other researchers. An example is the report by Rivers (1983) of learning a sixth language on a trip through Latin America. The paper is a fascinating account of an experienced learner and linguist encountering a new language during six weeks of exposure, but the publication provides no analysis. Thus, it is a diary, but not a diary study.

The importance of language learning journals for research can be summarized as being a source of insight into the learners' experiences. Indeed, "diary studies aim to help second language researchers and theorists understand language learning variables from the learner's point of view" (Carson & Longhini, 2002, pp. 402–403).

Key constructs

To the best of my knowledge language learners' diaries were first used as second language acquisition research tools by the Schumanns in the late 1970s (Schumann & Schumann, 1977). Since that time, journals have been kept by language learners in both tutored and untutored contexts.

Language learning diaries (also called "journals" in many publications) have in some instances been analyzed by the learners themselves. This approach was often the case in the early years when the diaries were kept by researchers who were learning languages and studying their own language acquisition (see, e.g., Bailey, 1980, 1983; Schumann, 1980). Matsumoto (1987) referred to this process as *introspective analysis*, but she is careful to note that this term refers to the first-person data analysis – not to the introspection involved in generating the original data.

In other situations, the learners' diary entries were analyzed by researchers who had not themselves been studying a new language (see, e.g., Ellis, 1989; Matsumoto, 1989). Matsumoto (1987) referred to this approach (i.e., someone other than the original diarist analyzing the journal) as *non-introspective analysis*. In considering the studies summarized in this chapter, we should note that language learning experienced of (and the diary data generated by) linguists and trained language teachers may differ substantially from the experiences and records of more typical language learners. We will return to this issue below.

Whether the diary studies involve introspective or non-introspective analyses, journal entries provide interesting insights into the internal, largely private world of the language learners. Issues that are often hidden from teachers and researchers (e.g., language learning anxiety – see Bailey, 1983; Gkonou, 2013; Hilleson, 1996) emerge as the learners track their L2 development (or lack thereof) in regular, frequent written or recorded comments about their experiences.

In keeping a language learning diary, learners report on actions and events, but they also typically reflect on their thoughts, insights, and reactions to those events. Thus, the language learning diary studies rely on both the learners' introspection and retrospection – two key constructs which require some explanation.

Introspection is defined as "a process by means of which we learn about our own currently ongoing, or very recently past, mental states or processes" (Schwitzgebel, 2019, para. 4). Schwitzgebel argues that there are three conditions which determine introspection. First, *the mentality condition* states that "introspection is a process that generates, or is aimed at generating, knowledge, judgments, or beliefs about *mental* events, states, or processes, and not about affairs outside one's mind, at least not directly" (para. 5). Second, it "generates, or is aimed at generating, knowledge, judgments, or beliefs about *one's own mind only* and no one else's" (para. 5). Third, the *temporal proximity condition* holds that introspection is "a process that generates knowledge, beliefs, or judgments about one's *currently ongoing* mental life only; or, alternatively (or perhaps in addition) *immediately past* (or even future) mental life, within a certain narrow temporal window" (para. 5).

Generating a language learning diary entails both introspection and retrospection. The term *introspection* is used in both a general sense and a specific sense. In the former – often the laypersons' use – it means simply reflecting in general (regardless of the time frame) about what we do, think, and/or feel (or have done, thought, and/or felt). But in the latter, more specific sense, it refers to thinking about what a person is doing, thinking and/or feeling at the moment. That is, researchers typically use the term *introspection* in the context of what Schwitzgebel (2019) calls the *temporal proximity condition*.

An early treatment of introspection in language research (Cohen & Hosenfeld, 1981) asserted that *introspection* occurs during the event, *immediate retrospection* right after the event. They note that *delayed retrospection* occurs hours after the event or even later. Bailey (1991) argued that what happens during the events should be called "concurrent introspection," while there might also be "immediate introspection" (p. 64), which then verges into retrospection. Thus, concurrent introspection occurs at a point in time during which the event that is the object of introspection is continuing. Immediate introspection occurs as soon as the event ends but is the beginning point of retrospection (delayed retrospection in Cohen and Hosenfeld's model).

While concurrent introspection for data generation is desirable from the researcher's point of view, it can be problematic for the person doing the introspecting. Fry (1988) noted that introspective data are "gathered from subjects while they carry out the task" (p. 159). In contrast, retrospective data consist of verbalization gathered "after the event" (p. 159). He pointed out that one problem with using introspection as a data generating procedure is that "reporting on how one is doing a task while doing it is a double task" (p. 160). Generating retrospective data circumvents that problem but may lead to a degradation of the data, depending on how long after the focal event the retrospection occurs.

Key issues

In this section I will summarize some of the key issues that have emerged in diary studies conducted in LBC contexts. First, I will discuss those studies where the diarists have been immersed in the target language context. Then I will address a few reports of LBC in non-immersive contexts.

Diary studies of LBC in immersive contexts

One of the earliest diary studies to investigate language learning outside of formal classroom contexts was Schmidt and Frota's (1986) analysis of Schmidt's learning of Portuguese during a five-month sojourn in Brazil. For the first three weeks, he was immersed in Portuguese but was not taking a class. There followed a period of five weeks when he was enrolled in a Portuguese course as well as being immersed in the context. Finally, for the last 14 weeks of his time in Brazil, Schmidt was interacting in Portuguese but was no longer taking a class. This report was the first in which the diary data were analyzed by both the language learner and a colleague who was a linguist (Frota).

The second and third periods of Schmidt's language learning are the most relevant to LBC issues. During the second stage he "started making Brazilian friends with whom he conversed only in Portuguese" (p. 244). In the third stage, that group of friends increased. He believed that his language progress stemmed from talking with those friends: "I think the biggest help has been interacting with lots of people at Trattoria [a club]. There I don't restrict myself to highly negotiated one-on-one conversations, but really strain to understand what everyone is saying" (p. 248).

A study by Carson and Longhini (2002) is similar to the one by Schmidt and Frota in that Carson (an applied linguist and the language learner in this case) went as a Fulbright professor to Argentina. Her co-author, Longhini, was an English teacher in the university. They describe their report as "a case of completely naturalistic language learning: The researcher/diarist was immersed in the target language and received no formal instruction" (pp. 403–404). Also parallel to the Schmidt and Frota study, these authors formed a partnership in which Longhini (like Frota) was the native speaking informant who collaborated on the research project. Carson's journal consisted of 32 single-space pages and focused on her language learning styles and strategies.

Carson taught at an Argentine university for eight weeks. The report states that "during that time she ... successfully developed basic conversational skills" in Spanish (p. 405). Her detailed journal entries document her learning experiences, so that patterns are detectable over time. For instance, several moments of linguistic realization occurred. On August 1 she wrote, "So when Ana said, 'Que Gracioso' it all clicked." On August 5 she said, "All of a sudden something clicked in and I realized she was talking about Snow White...." On August page 25 she wrote, "All of a sudden it clicked – these words are all derived from the same Latin stem" (three quotes from p. 412). These comments led to her awareness of making connections among "various and fragmentary pieces of language input" (p. 413), a process which these authors referred to as the *click phenomenon*.

The bulk of Carson and Longhini's report discussed the diarist's language learning styles and her use of learning strategies. The pattern that emerged was that her "learning styles remained relatively constant throughout her time in the language immersion situation, but her strategies were somewhat more variable over time" (p. 414). Carson encountered several challenges, such as the difficulty of learning vocabulary with only spoken input – a difficulty attributed to her dominant visual learning style. Carson and Longhini acknowledge that as an applied linguist with an interest in language learning styles and strategies, Carson was "a researcher/diarist who may not be a typical language learner" (p. 419).

Carson's diary entries document a kind of dual personality in this situation. She was in Argentina as a visiting professor whose basic identity was as an English speaker. In contrast, she said, "the other person, the one who can't speak Spanish, is an experimental subject and is allowed to say simple things in ungrammatical language without damaging her self-esteem" (p. 424). This comment is closely related to LBC issues: The authors note that "this dual perspective was facilitated by the fact that she was not a classroom language learner, which would have entailed a student identity as well" (p. 424).

Like Carson, Campbell (1996) kept a language learning journal during a two-month trip. She was an experienced language teacher and a doctoral student in applied linguistics when she studied Spanish at a language institute in Mexico. The formal instruction focused on grammar and vocabulary, but with the use of some communication activities. The program included extra-curricular activities, such as singing, games, and skits. Campbell's journal data consisted of "seventy-one separate entries...and five letters, or excerpts of letters" (p. 204) written to friends in California.

What makes Campbell's study fascinating (and particularly relevant to the present report) is that she wrote much more about her out-of-class experiences than about her classroom learning. Based on her prior experience of having developed strong German skills in Germany, she particularly wanted to find a group of Mexican friends she could interact with in Spanish.

The social group she eventually joined consisted of the institute's teachers. Campbell discussed the difficulty of gaining access to them outside of class, partly because they were the teachers (and she was a student), but also because they were all relatives, friends, and co-workers. However, an important development created a dramatic change in Campbell's LBC opportunities. She wrote, "Halfway through my stay in Mexico, I began dating one of the teachers. [T]his dating certainly served as an entrée by placing me in social situation with the group in which I would not otherwise have found myself" (p. 210). Campbell reports that her exposure to conversational Spanish increased when she started dating "Tito."

Campbell notes that "popular opinion holds that a good way to learn a language is to find a boyfriend or girlfriend who is a native speaker of the language" (p. 211). Her diary data document three issues in support of this view. First, she gained access to social events in which she was the only non-Mexican present and the interactions occurred in Spanish. Second, she reports that Tito was patient and she felt confident about asking him for clarification of the Spanish used in those contexts. Third, the social events gave her opportunities to hear "more language from more people speaking in various situations and registers" (p. 211) than would have been possible without that social access.

Campbell summarized the importance of her LBC experiences this way: "By socializing with the teachers as a socially equal member of their circle, I progressed in my acquisition of Spanish by using the language in meaningful and psychologically/emotionally charged situations" (p. 214).

Another diary study based on an adult learning Spanish in an immersion context is by Schulz and Elliott (2000). They analyzed the journal Schulz wrote during a five-month stay as a Fulbright fellow in Colombia when she was 57 years old. The journal consisted of 110 separate entries, and the resulting report focuses on her language learning experiences as an older adult.

Schulz had been determined to be at the ACTFL intermediate-low level in Spanish before going to Colombia. When she arrived there, she started taking a beginning Spanish course which met for 90 minutes a day at the university, but she was moved into an intermediate course after an oral interview. However, in this brief summary, I will comment only on her LBC data. For instance, after about two and a half months she wrote, "I still have problems with TV news, soap operas, and other programs except travelogues or health-related programs where I am already familiar with the content of the broadcast" (p. 112).

Schulz had strategies for dealing with the need to communicate in Spanish beyond the university context, where most of her interactions were in English. After about three and a half months, she wrote, "I still subvocally rehearse what I will say in stores and in other business contacts.... I must appear quite fluent in Spanish when I start out, but break down pretty quickly after my prepared repertoire is exhausted" (pp. 112–113). Schulz was pleased that she had understood much of a play in Spanish, but noted that she "did not always get the humor that caused the audience to laugh" (p. 113).

Schulz (a successful language learner) experienced several emotions: "It is frustrating, challenging, exhilarating, tiring, rewarding, and sometimes discouraging for a relatively articulate adult to have to regress linguistically to an infantile level in terms of topics and style of discussion" (p. 113). The difficulty of understanding natural speech was frequently mentioned in her journal. Fortunately, the data show that she did make progress, "in spite of the many frustrations expressed in her diary" (p. 116).

Casanave (2012) published a diary study based on eight years of journal data she had generated while working as an English professor in Japan. She states that the study documented her "fluctuating desire to invest effort in the self-study of Japanese during a long period" (p. 642). She reports having written every few days or sometimes weeks, and sometimes more often, resulting in an eight-year, handwritten record of 758 pages.

This particular paper reports on what Casanave calls "dabbling" – that is, she was "noticing, attending to, and picking up bits of language" – a process which was "driven by interest and curiosity" (p. 644). She sees dabbling as a viable alternative for busy adults who do not have time to enroll in language lessons. She was also very happy to be free of the kinds of tests, anxiety, and competition that can occur in language classes.

Casanave's learning of Japanese was regularly influenced by ecological factors, such as her health, the weather, environmental noise, and poor sleep, as well as by difficulties in her university department. This candid report accentuates the importance of having fun and the author's desire for conversational practice (as opposed to formal explanations). She actively used a dictionary and worked with a friend as a tutor for a time, but then terminated his tutor role because he was over-explaining grammar points and not providing her with the kinds of interaction she craved.

One of the strongest outcomes of this LBC diary study is Casanave's documentation of the unstable nature of motivation. She describes what she called the *ecology of effort*: "the many influences on my investment of effort to learn something about Japanese" (p. 647). The report provides several examples of both positive and negative influences on her language learning.

All of the studies summarized above are involved introspective analyses of journals kept by language learners who were themselves language teachers and/or linguists. That is, the researcher-authors (or one of the co-authors) who made the journal entries were also the analysts. It is possible (in fact, likely in my opinion) that the experiences and reporting of these professionally qualified language learners may differ from the experiences and journal entries of more typical learners – whether they are school-aged students or adult laypersons.

However, other LBC reports have included diary data recorded by more typical learners and were subsequently analyzed by researchers other than those diarists. These analyses are often well connected to existing research and theory, but sometimes do not share personal factors in as much depth as those studies where the diary data were generated by researchers and/or language teaching professionals.

For instance, Warden, Lapkin, Swain, and Hart (1995) analyzed journals kept by 18 Canadian Anglophone secondary school students who went to Quebec for three months as exchange students. Some of them had been learning French in late immersion contexts (with subject matter courses taught in French starting in the fourth grade), while others had taken traditional French language classes.

The students were asked to focus their diary entries on how they used French in their social lives. These learners' LBC experiences included watching movies and television in French, going to the store, listening to French songs, and talking with their host families. The brief excerpts that are quoted often deal with feeling comfortable with French speakers:

> I love to have one on one conversations. Once I feel comfortable, I can talk for an hour. When I'm uncomfortable, the words just done work. When I'm talking to more than two, people, I'm usually uncomfortable. (p. 541)

Another student commented, "Understanding is getting better as long as they speak directly to me or about me. If it's a big group, I'm totally lost" (p. 541). Some of the students' diary entries document that "the ability to understand swear words, slang, and jokes (and therefore to fit in with one's peers) is a great source of satisfaction" (p. 542).

In another diary study conducted in Canada, Peirce (1994) investigated the opportunities for spoken interaction available to adult female immigrants. She was particularly interested in interactions occurring in the community (e.g., in church) and workplace (in restaurants, in clothing factories). She wanted to study these immigrants' *social identities* – "how a person understands his or her relationship to the social world, how that relationship is socially constructed across time and space, and how the person understands possibilities for the future" (p. 23).

This research project is grounded in a context where the diarists were both taking an ESL class (with Peirce as the teacher) and interacting in English outside those lessons. In addition to making journal entries in English, these five women met with Peirce in her home, initially on a weekly basis for nine weeks and then once a month for three months. At these meetings they would read aloud from their journals. The diary excerpts Peirce shares in this report are lengthy, contextualized, and fascinating. They clearly portray the struggles of non-native speaking immigrant women in Canada.

Diary studies of LBC in non-immersive contexts

There are a few LBC diary studies about learners who were not immersed in the target language context. A good example is a paper by Jones (1994), a British researcher who studied his own strategies for acquiring Hungarian in England, while keeping a diary for 11 months. He studied for about half an hour six times a week, and his diary entries were written in Hungarian. Jones estimates that as a result of these efforts, he was able to move from elementary proficiency to intermediate proficiency.

At first Jones noted that it was quite challenging to write his journal entries in the target language. In the fourth month, however, he wrote, "It's getting easier and easier to write my learner diary in Hungarian. I believe I now know enough vocabulary" (p. 449).

Jones focused largely on acquiring vocabulary and grammar. He reported that he was familiar with the sound system because he had some Hungarian speaking friends. However, he was only in contact with native speakers for about three weeks during the eighth week of the time he kept his diary.

Jones (1994) utilized both pedagogical and non-teaching materials. He described his coursebooks as being dated, stuffy, and dire. He preferred reading comics and popular press items. At 9.5 months into the self-study project, Jones noted, "I've just realized that I've completely stopped using my course books" (p. 446). At ten months, he wrote, "Fantastic feeling: I can read my magazine articles without a dictionary" (p. 446). Near the end of the project, he wrote, "I have decided to read the grammar book ... right to the end. Many things which I read earlier but did not understand ... became clear in a moment!" (p. 447).

In a second report, Jones (1995) discussed his use of two coursebooks and a picture dictionary designed for children in his self-study efforts. He reported that these materials had "a vital input structuring role" (p. 99) during the initial phases of his efforts.

Jones (1995) reports having experienced two thresholds in his study of Hungarian. First, around the eighth month, "enough core lexemes had been acquired for etymology to become a powerful guessing and memorization strategy" (p. 100). Crossing this threshold led to the "ability to cope with simple authentic texts and to the abandonment of studial, textbook-based strategies in favour of autonomous strategies based on comprehensible input" (p. 100). Thereafter he enjoyed reading for pleasure and adopted "a combined approach, integrating authentic input with vocabulary study and output practice" (p. 100).

Another diary study in a non-immersion context was conducted by Leung (2002). She was a bilingual speaker of Cantonese and English who was living in Hawaii when she chose to examine the effect of extensive reading on vocabulary development. About ten years prior to the study, she had taken some Japanese lessons in Hong Kong, in which she had learned basic greetings and how to introduce herself. Leung had also been acquainted with *hiragana* and *katakana* but "she had to relearn hiragana as a beginning learner of Japanese at the time she began this study" (p. 68).

For 20 weeks, Leung investigated her own learning of Japanese through extensive reading. For the first nine weeks she was enrolled in a graduate seminar on teaching reading. During that period, she spent about an hour reading Japanese and then reflecting on what she had learned by writing in her journal on a daily basis. At the end of this phase of the research, she read her journal and took a break from reading Japanese for 2.5 months.

For the next 11 weeks, Leung resumed her reading in Japanese and her journal reflections, writing about herself ("Wendy") in the third person. She also enlisted the support of a colleague who helped her on a weekly basis. She audio-recorded their tutoring sessions, which included "discussions of various reading passages from a first-grade Japanese text, Wendy's questions about Japanese, and her tutor's comments, and oral reading" (p. 69).

Leung said that when she started this project, "she was very excited about her reading project, but then her excitement was quickly replaced by confusion and frustration, mainly because she had a hard time finding the appropriate materials for her study" (p. 73). The issue of learning materials is thus a repeated theme in the LBC diary studies, at least in these two non-immersive contexts (those of Leung and Jones).

Leung's findings showed that her tutor's guidance and the textbooks were helpful, and "reading extensively gave her the opportunity to practice and expand her reading comprehension skills" (p. 73). In addition, her attitude about reading in Japanese became more positive over time. She enjoyed reading children's books in Japanese (e.g., Alice in Wonderland, Sleeping Beauty, and stories about animals).

The diaries by Leung and Jones document the efforts of autonomous learners in non-immersive environments. Because they were the researchers as well as the learners, their diary studies are examples of introspective analyses (Matsumoto, 1987).

Other studies of learners in non-immersive contexts have involved non-introspective analyses (i.e., the researchers analyzed diary data they themselves had not generated). For example, Roswell and Libben (1994) reported on the six-month language learning efforts by 30 adults who were not enrolled in language classes and were not in immersive contexts. The subjects in this study were "English-speaking undergraduate university students who were assigned the task of learning a new language by themselves" (p. 671). These students' diaries yielded "a detailed sequential account of how these independent learners treated their language learning materials and how they addressed the problem of being communicative in isolation" (p. 671).

Based on self-assessment statements at the end of their journals, these learners were categorized as having been successful or unsuccessful in their efforts. The two groups were labeled as high achievers and low achievers, respectively. The researchers analyzed the learners' diary data to see if there were differences in the types of activities the learners in these two groups engaged in as they tried to learn their target language autonomously.

One difference that emerged was that the high achievers tended to create imaginative communicative situations for using their target language. These efforts included talking to "family members, pets, [and] even a teddy bear!" (p. 678) and writing a letter in the target language to someone who did not know that language. Another difference was that the high achieving students created contexts in which they could use the language. One learner imagined talking with her favorite tennis star in his language – an imaginary context she sustained for the entire six-month period. Roswell and Libben concluded that it is the "learners' approach to the meaningful use of the language rather than their approach to the organization of pedagogical tasks that distinguishes between high and low achievement" (p. 681).

Once again, we should note that in the studies by Leung (2002) and Jones (1994, 1995), the diarist-researchers were themselves sophisticated language learners. In the report by Roswell and Libben (1994), however, the diaries were kept by more typical language learners. I am not aware of research that has compared these two types of learners, in either immersive or non-immersive settings. The issue of how typical and atypical leaners may differ, in their language learning experiences and/or their reporting thereof, remains an open question.

Implications

This brief review of some LBC diary studies offers some implications for both theory and practice. Key theoretical issues noted above include identity (Peirce, 1994), motivation (Casanave, 2012), interaction (Campbell, 1996; Schmidt & Frota, 1986), language awareness (Carson & Longhini, 2002), rehearsing speech (Rivers, 1983; Schulz & Elliott, 2000), and the role of reading in language acquisition (Jones, 1994, 1995; Leung, 2002).

A practical issue regarding LBC diary studies is what the learners can gain from the process of keeping a journal. Some authors have commented on the possible benefits of making diary entries for language learners. For instance, in a discussion of autonomy support for language learners, Jiménez Raya (2006) wrote that one goal of keeping a journal

> is to make students' learning more accessible to analysis and scrutiny, so that change become possible. When writing a journal, the learner stands back from the immediacy of the learning experience and reviews it with the freedom of not having to act on it in real time. (p. 131)

Jiménez Raya adds that journal writing aids in metacognitive development and can promote learners' awareness, knowledge generation, and self-confidence.

One likely outcome of keeping a record of language learning is increased retention of target language forms. In Carson and Longhini's (2002) report, for example, Carson reports on her difficulty as a primarily visual learner of retaining vocabulary and syntactic forms without having seen them written – only receiving oral input. Her journal entries include many observations about language forms. I am not aware of diary data from more typical learners using this amount or level of meta-language.

Another possible benefit to learners is enhanced language awareness. This concept has been defined as "the development in learners of an enhanced consciousness of and sensitivity to the forms and function of language" (Carter, 2003, p. 64). For example, Carson and Longhini's (2002) report provides examples of the "click phenomenon" – instances when Carson had sudden realizations about target language forms and functions.

Keeping a language learning journal may also improve confidence and language proficiency – especially if the entries are made in the target language. Peirce (1994) said that the five immigrant women who provided the data for her diary study "made great progress in their writing and appeared to gain confidence in their social interactions with anglophone Canadians" (p. 25). She acknowledges that although she cannot claim that writing their diaries led to these developments, "it is possible that the study made a contribution to this progress" (p. 25).

Peirce also identified three other possible benefits of having learners keep diaries of their LBC experiences when they are also taking language classes. First, teachers can gain insights about how their language lessons are influencing the students' identities and their levels of participation. Second, a language learning diary provides information about "the extent to which a student' social identity is implicated in the kind of learning and interaction that takes place outside the classroom" (p. 28). Finally, language learning diaries can document the gulf that sometimes emerges between classroom instruction and the learners' experiences outside the classroom.

Some reports suggest that keeping a journal of their language learning efforts has allowed the LBC diarists to vent their frustrations and, to some extent, cope with anxiety. For instance, in commenting on not being able to remember a particular Spanish rejoinder, Rivers (1983, p. 169) wrote, "I should have copied it down!" She remarked on her need for "a clear model and a patient one who is willing to repeat and listen over and over again" (p. 173). Without elaborating on the break-down, she wrote, "The emotional problems in all this are clearly important, as witness my breakdown on the first day" (p. 179). Other diary entries included "I still have problems with those wretched verbs and vocabulary" (p. 181) and "I am still struggling with understanding rapid speech between other speakers" (p. 181). When Rivers became frustrated because complications arising (e.g., at a post office) rendered useless her prepared Spanish, she was able to relate to language students: "This is maddening and must be what nervous students undergo when oral exams do not approximate their expectations" (p. 182).

Frustrations were also documented in the diaries of the undergraduate students whose efforts to learn a new language independently were investigated by Roswell and Libben (1994). These comments from three low achievers are particularly salient:

> My communication skills would rate one on a scale of one to ten.
> All I really need to know now is how to swear so that I can scream at myself in another language....I've really disappointed myself.
> The experience was very enlightening. I quickly changed from an eager, excited student to one who was frustrated and angry. (p. 675)

Likewise, frustration emerges in some of the diaries of the Canadian Anglophone students who went to Quebec on the exchange program (Warden et al., 1995):

> Friday was very hard. I felt like I didn't want to get off the bus. I just wanted to go home.
> With all the French I've taken in the last eight years, nothing has prepared me for this.
> At first I was extremely shy about talking because I was worried about sounding really really dumb. (p. 543)

These diary entries show that even students with previous classroom exposure to the target language can be very uncomfortable when faced with the need to actually communicate orally.

Some of the LBC diary studies comment on the use of learning materials (Jones, 1994, 1995; Leung, 2002). Easy access to authentic materials arises in some of the LBC diaries that were written in immersion situations. Authentic (i.e., non-pedagogical) materials have been defined as "oral and written texts that occur naturally in the target language environment and have not been created or edited expressly for language learners" (Larimer & Schleicher, 1999, p. v). For example, near the end of her trip in Latin America, Rivers (1983) wrote that she could read "newspapers, information booklets, police reports, and notices without difficulty" (p. 188).

In LBC diary studies that were not done in immersion contexts, locating authentic materials was more challenging but not impossible. For instance, even though she was in Hawaii, Leung (2002) was able access some authentic Japanese texts in her environment: She reports that she "tried to read Japanese advertisements on campus, directions on the package of children's toys, Japanese instructions on a phone card, Japanese signs everywhere, and items on the menus of a Japanese curry house near a bus stop" (p. 75).

These are just a few of the themes that have emerged in the studies summarized here. There are other reports which could be examined for similar or novel patterns that appear in diaries kept in naturalistic learning contexts. As Leung (2002) noted in her diary study about extensive reading in Japanese, "Self study is not an easy task" (p. 76). Further diary studies conducted in LBC contexts can help the field better understand both the challenges and the reward of language learning beyond the classroom.

Future directions

In the past, language learning diaries have been handwritten or word-processed written, or occasionally audio-recorded. In cases where the journal entries were intended to be the database for a research project, audio-recorded entries had to be transcribed. For example, Campbell (1996) had this to say about transcribing an audio recording:

> Once I tape-recorded a lengthy entry because so much had happened that I didn't have time to write it all down. I was not comfortable with taping and never did it again. The taped entry [was] transcribed and included in the journal. (p. 204)

With the increasing availability of voice-to-text recording, however, it is possible that making diary entries will be less cumbersome. With smart phone recording capabilities, LBC language experiences can be recorded at any time and in any place, although I am unaware of diary studies using this data collection procedure at the time of this writing. This technological development might ease learners' abilities to make journal entries by speaking without having to transcribe the recordings for later analyses.

Another technological development – again, relevant to diaries kept for research purposes – is that there are now software programs that can aid in the analysis of qualitative data, such as journal entries. Even making voice-to-text recordings on a cell phone can save transcription time. Although the analytic process is still demanding, computer-aided data analyses are less laborious than is reviewing massive data sets and coding them by hand.

Finally, it will be interesting to see if any LBC diary studies emerge based on learners' experiences with recently developed language learning apps. There are several programs available now that claim to teach languages effectively, that can be used anytime and anywhere, and that leave the management of learning up to the learner. As of this writing, I am not aware of any diary studies exploring this approach to language acquisition in LBC contexts.

Reflection questions

1 Have you ever kept a diary of your language learning or your teaching? If so, what benefits or challenges did you experience in the process? If not, what benefits or challenges do you think you might encounter?
2 If you were making journal entries about your language learning in non-formal instructional settings (in physical or online classrooms, or with a tutor), what challenges did you experience? How did you overcome them? If you have not learned a language in an LBC context, what challenges would you anticipate? How could you overcome those challenges?

3   Have you had any language learning experiences similar to those of the authors whose work is summarized here? If so, what were those similarities? How did your LBC experiences differ from theirs?

Recommended readings

1   For tips on keeping a journal about language teaching and learning, please see Bailey (2015), Curtis and Bailey (2009), or Nunan and Bailey (2009, pp. 303–304). The article by Curtis and Bailey (2009) also provides a review of the published diary studies that were available at the time.
2   The report by Schmidt and Frota (1986) is one of the earliest published diary studies and, in my view, it is still one of the best. It is a fascinating account of Schmidt's experience acquiring Brazilian Portuguese, in both classroom and LBC contexts.
3   The diary study of Campbell's (1996) experience in Mexico provides a clear contrast of what she learned in her Spanish classes and what affordances her social life with local people provided.

References

Bailey, K. M. (1980). An introspective analysis of an individual's language learning experience. In R. Scarcella & S. Krashen (Eds.), *Research in second language acquisition: Selected papers of the Los Angeles Second Language Research Forum* (pp. 58–65). Newbury House.

Bailey, K. M. (1983). Competitiveness and anxiety in adult second language learning: Looking *at* and *through* the diary studies. In H. W. Seliger & M. H. Long (Eds.), *Classroom oriented research in second language acquisition* (pp. 67–102). Newbury House.

Bailey, K. M. (1991). Diary studies of classroom language learning: The doubting game and the believing game. In E. Sadtono (Ed.), *Language acquisition and the second/foreign language classroom* (pp. 60–102). SEAMEO Regional Language Center.

Bailey, K. M. (2015). Conducting diary studies. In J. D. Brown & C. Coombe (Eds.), *The Cambridge guide to research in language teaching and learning* (pp. 247–252). Cambridge University Press.

Bailey, K. M., & Ochsner, R. (1983). A methodological review of the diary studies: Windmill tilting or social science? In K. M. Bailey, M. H. Long, & S. Peck (Eds.), *Second language acquisition studies* (pp. 188–198). Newbury House.

Campbell, C. C. (1996). Socializing with the teachers and prior language learning experience: A diary study. In K. M. Bailey, & D. Nunan (Eds.), *Voices from the language classroom: Qualitative research on language education* (pp. 201–223). Cambridge University Press.

Carson, J. G., & Longhini, A. (2002). Focusing on learning styles and strategies: A diary study in an immersion setting. *Language Learning, 52*, 401–438.

Carter, R. (2003). Language awareness. *ELT Journal, 57*(1), 654–65.

Casanave, C. P. (2012). Diary of a dabbler: Ecological influences on an EFL teacher's efforts to study Japanese informally. *TESOL Quarterly, 46*(4), 642–670.

Cohen, A. D., & Hosenfeld, C. (1981). Some uses of mentalistic data in second language research. *Language Learning, 31*(2), 285–313.

Curtis, A., & Bailey, K. M. (2009). Diary studies. *OnCUE Journal, 3*(1), 67–85.

Ellis, R. (1989). Classroom learning styles and their effect on second language acquisition: A study of two learners. *System, 17*, 249–262.

Fry, J. (1988). Diary studies in classroom SLA research: Problems and prospects. *JALT Journal, 9*, 158–167.

Gkonou, C. (2013). A diary study on the causes of English language classroom anxiety. *International Journal of English Studies, 13*(1), 51–68.

Hilleson, M. (1996). "I want to talk to them but I don't want them to hear": An introspective study of second language anxiety in an English-medium school. In K. M. Bailey & D. Nunan (Eds.), *Voices from the language classroom: Qualitative research on language education* (pp. 248–275). Cambridge University Press.

Jiménez Raya, M. (2006). Autonomy support through learning journals. In T. Lamb & H. Reinders (Eds.), *Supporting independent learning: Issues and interventions* (pp. 123–140). Peter Lang.

Jones, F. R. (1994). The lone language learner: A diary study. *System, 22*, 441–454.

Jones, F. R. (1995). Learning an alien lexicon: A teach-yourself case study. *Second Language Research*, *11*, 95–111.

Larimer, R., & Schleicher, L. (1999). *New ways in using authentic materials in the classroom*. TESOL.

Leung, C. Y. (2002). Extensive reading and language learning: A diary study of a beginning learner of Japanese. *Reading in a Foreign Language, 14*(1), 66–81.

Matsumoto, K. (1987). Diary studies of second language acquisition: A critical overview. *JALT Journal*, *9*, 17–34.

Matsumoto, K. (1989). An analysis of a Japanese ESL learner's diary: Factors involved in the L2 learning process. *JALT Journal, 11*, 167–192.

Nunan, D. C., & Bailey, K. M. (2009). *Exploring second language classroom research: A comprehensive guide*. Cengage.

Peirce, B. N. (1994). Using diaries in second language research and teaching. *English Quarterly, 26*(3), 22–29.

Reinders, H. (2020). A framework for learning beyond the classroom. In M. Raya & F. Vieira (Eds.), *Autonomy in language education: Theory, research, and practice* (pp. 63–73). Routledge.

Reinders, H., & Benson, P. (2017). Research agenda: Language learning beyond the classroom. *Language Teaching, 50*(4), 561–578.

Rivers, W. M. (1983). *Communicating naturally in a second language: Theory and practice in language teaching*. Cambridge University Press.

Rowsell, L. V., & Libben, G. (1994). The sound of one hand clapping: How to succeed in independent language learning. *Canadian Modern Language Review, 50*, 668–687.

Schmidt, R. W., & Frota, S. N. (1986). Developing basic conversational ability in a second language: A case study of an adult learner of Portuguese. In R. R. Day (Ed.), *Talking to learn: Conversation in second language acquisition* (pp. 237–326). Newbury House.

Schulz, R. A., & Elliott, P. (2000). Learning Spanish as an older adult. *Hispania, 83*, 1, 1207-119.

Schumann, F. (1980). Diary of a language learner: A further analysis. In R. Scarcella & S. Krashen (Eds.), *Research in second language acquisition* (pp. 51–57). Rowley, MA: Newbury House.

Schumann, F. E., & Schumann, J. H. (1977). Diary of a language learner: An introspective study of second language learning. In H. D. Brown, R. H. Crymes, & C. A. Yorio (Eds.), *On TESOL '77: Teaching and learning English as a second language-Trends in research and practice* (pp. 241–249). TESOL.

Schwitzgebel, E. (2019). Introspection. In E. N. Zalta (Ed.), *The Stanford encyclopedia of philosophy*. Retrieved from https://stanford.library.sydney.edu.au/entries/introspection/

Warden, M., Swain, M., Lapkin, S., & Hart, D. (1995). Adolescent language learners on a three-month exchange: Insights from their diaries. *Foreign Language Annals, 28*, 537–550.

26
DOING LLBC RESEARCH WITH YOUNG LEARNERS

Signe Hannibal Jensen

Introduction

Many young children today engage with technology to a hitherto unprecedented degree given the easy access to internet-based entertainment and other types of media for entertainment (De Wilde & Eyckmans, 2017; Sundqvist & Sylvén, 2016). This informal engagement provides rich opportunities for engagement with language other than one's L1, often English given its current status as the global lingua franca, by extension also providing opportunities for informal language learning beyond the classroom.

Most studies on LLBC involve older learners (see, e.g., Lee, 2019; Sundqvist, 2019). The majority of studies on young learners employ quantitative methods typically exploring which types of activities children engage in (e.g., gaming), amount of time spent on activities as well as learning impact (e.g., vocabulary learning) (see, e.g., De Wilde, Bryesbart and Eyckmans, 2019). Such studies are primarily founded in cognitive theories of language learning where mental processes of the individual (i.e., what happens in the mind) are given prominence in the learning process (Peterson, 2016). As such, language 'input' is considered key to language learning because it enables beneficial mental processes to take place such as becoming aware of or noticing language features through repeated exposure (Peterson, 2016). Also, motivation for and using the language productively are considered important factors (pp. 54–55). Findings from quantitative studies confirm that learning takes place beyond the classroom – in particularly, gaming seems to benefit positively to language learning (Hannibal Jensen, 2017; Sundqvist & Sylvén, 2014; Sylvén & Sundqvist, 2012). For other types of activities (such as media use, e.g., watching television and YouTube), results are mixed with younger learners (below age 8) benefitting the least or not at all (Unsworth, Persson, Prins, & De Bot, 2014) and older learners (between 10 and 11) showing greater benefits (De Wilde et al., 2017; Lindgren & Muñoz, 2013).

Few studies are qualitative. These studies focus on uncovering *how* children interact with the language they encounter, for example, by observing (field studies) how they engage with the input (Duran, 2017; Piirainen-Marsh & Tainio, 2009) and by conducting interviews (Hannibal Jensen, 2019; Turgut & Irgin, 2009) related to their engagement. Findings show that children pay attention to some of the input especially because paying attention to, and actively engaging with, the input will enable them to understand and/or progress in their activities, such as making L2 language Google searches for gaining game-specific information (see Hannibal Jensen, 2019). Children also use the L2 productively through, for example, repeating the input they hear and hereby develop their language competence (Piirainen-Marsh &

Tainio, 2009). Findings also show that much learning is afforded through children's socializing in the L2 (Duran, 2017). Such studies are partly grounded in cognitive theories of language learning and partly in more socially oriented theories with focus on how social actors co-create meaning and learning not only in the mind but through the larger social context in which the activities take place such as peer communities (Peterson, 2016).

Key constructs

General concerns in doing research with young children

When doing research with young children, specific attention must be devoted to the operationalization of some central constructs: the role of the child (subject/participant) and the ability of the child (age and maturity) – factors that all have a bearing on ethics, validity and credibility.

Ethical concerns – important in any research project (see Chapter 21 by Sylvén in the present volume) – are key when doing research with children who are not able to protect their own interests (Danby, Ewing & Thorpe, 2011). Moreover, over the past decades research has increasingly moved away from doing research "*on* rather than *with* children" (Greig et al., 2013, p. 112) and as such children are increasingly being viewed as participants rather than subjects in research. Therefore, in addition to getting informed consent from relevant authorities (i.e., research boards, parents, etc.), it is advised to get "informed assent" to participate in the research project from the child him/herself even though it is not legally required (Greig, Taylor & MacKay, 2013, p. 255). This acknowledges the child's status as an autonomous, reflective participant potentially also creating for more engaged participation (Alderson, 2005). Moreover, informing the child of the purpose of the research (Greig et al., 2013) as well as allowing them to ask questions and to withdraw at any time throughout the research process is important ethical considerations. Lastly, ensuring full confidentiality (including ensuring the child that his or her contribution will not be disclosed to, e.g., teachers, peers and parents) is vital (Greig et al., 2013). Importantly, ethical considerations should figure critically in every step of the research process (Alderson, 2005).

Researching with children, the researcher may encounter some age-related challenges, such as limited memory capacity and inattention (Greig et al., 2013), which can have a bearing on, for example, which types of questions or tests children are able to handle and therefore will affect which types of instruments to use and how to use them. Consequently, in the present chapter, a lot of attention is devoted to countering such challenges. Moreover, children are prone to agree with authority figures (Greig et al., 2013). This means that they may provide so-called *socially desired responses* and rather than providing answers based on their own thoughts and feelings may provide the answers that they think the researcher is looking for (Dörnyei, 2010). Specifically, when providing socially desired responses, children below the age of ten tend to do so primarily to please the researcher or other authority figures; whereas, children above the age of ten do so primarily for the benefit of peers (de Leuuw et al., 2004). Such responses naturally pose a challenge to the validity of children's statements and care should be taken to balance such behavior to make sure the facts and opinions voiced are based on personal viewpoints. The above concerns relate to the notion of internal validity (quantitative research) and credibility (qualitative research), that is, the trustworthiness of the study (Johnson & Christensen, 2008) to be discussed in relevant sections below.

Key issues

Mapping and measuring learning: questionnaires and language diaries

As mentioned, most studies on young learners measure out-of-school exposure. Questionnaires (see, e.g., De Wilde et al., 2017; Lindgren & Muñoz, 2013) and language diaries (see, e.g., Hannibal Jensen, 2017; Sylvén & Sundqvist, 2012) are typically used to this end with younger learners. Both instruments elicit retrospective data; that is, participants are asked to recall activities in the past (Bernard et al., 1984). Figures 26.1 and 26.2 illustrate examples of a questionnaire and a language diary:

A key difference between the two instruments lies in the way they elicit data (delayed versus immediate recall) and in the type of information obtained (categorical or specific):

Questionnaires (categorical information through delayed recall)

give *estimates* of time spent on specific L2 mediated categories of interest (e.g., gaming with written input, gaming with spoken input, etc.). In other words, at a random point in time, participants provide general estimates of time spent on specific activity categories over the course of a specific period of time (e.g., weekly or daily). That is, questionnaires rely on delayed recall and on categorical information. Questionnaires typically also incorporate more general questions (e.g., access to L2 through holidays, visits, etc., questions relating to socio-economic status and affective factors (cf. Figure 26.1).

1. Tick the box. How many hours/minutes do you do the activities in the list **per day**:

In ENGLISH	I don't do this.	Less than 30 minutes	30 minutes– 1 hour	1 hour – 1 hour 30 minutes	1 hour 30 minutes – 2 hours	More than 2 hours
Watch TV without subtitles						
Watch TV with English subtitles						
Watch TV with subtitles in the home language						
Listen to English music						
Read English books, magazines, comics						
Gaming in English						
Youtube, use of social media in English						
Speak English						

2. Do you have any contact with people who speak English? Yes / No If yes, where, when, with whom? a. On holiday? Yes / No How often? _____ b. At home? Yes / No How often? _____
c. In other situations? Yes / No How often? _____

Figure 26.1 Example of a questionnaire

Note: Note: De Wilde, V., Brysbaert, M., & Eykmans, J. (2019). Learning English through out-of-school exposure. Which levels of language proficiency are attained, and which types of input are important? *Bilingualism: Language and Cognition* 23(11), 171–185. You find their complete questionnaire in supplementary materials.

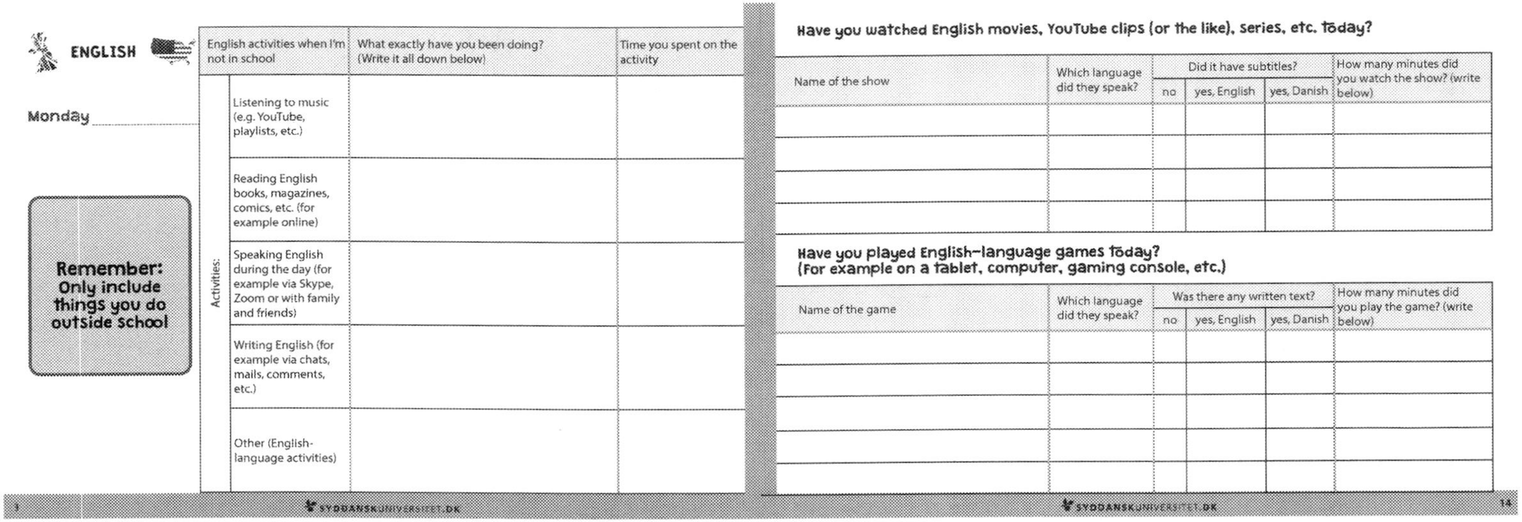

ENGLISH

Monday ____________

Remember: Only include things you do outside school

	English activities when I'm not in school	What exactly have you been doing? (Write it all down below)	Time you spent on the activity
Activities:	Listening to music (e.g. YouTube, playlists, etc.)		
	Reading English books, magazines, comics, etc. (for example online)		
	Speaking English during the day (for example via Skype, Zoom or with family and friends)		
	Writing English (for example via chats, mails, comments, etc.)		
	Other (English-language activities)		

3 SYDDANSKUNIVERSITET.DK

Have you watched English movies, YouTube clips (or the like), series, etc. today?

Name of the show	Which language did they speak?	Did it have subtitles?			How many minutes did you watch the show? (write below)
		no	yes, English	yes, Danish	

Have you played English-language games today?
(For example on a tablet, computer, gaming console, etc.)

Name of the game	Which language did they speak?	Was there any written text?			How many minutes did you play the game? (write below)
		no	yes, English	yes, Danish	

SYDDANSKUNIVERSITET.DK 14

Figure 26.2 Example of a language diary (two pages) in Hannibal Jensen (2018).

Language diaries (specific information through immediate recall)

provide information on *actual* out-of-school L2 engagement (naming specific activities and the actual time spent on these) every day for a specified period of time. Thus, every day before going to bed or perhaps immediately after having engaged in an activity, participants record specific activities (e.g., Minecraft with English text) and time spent on said activities. Language diaries thus rely on immediate recall and on obtaining specific information.

The following sections focus on describing the methodology behind questionnaires and language diaries. Due to their likeness, both instruments are described together through the following sections: content, constructing questions, asking for Language details, recording time, design, choosing an instrument.

Content

A central decision when constructing the instrument relates to deciding on the content in the instrument (i.e., deciding which questions, examples and everyday L2 mediated activities to include) (Dörnyei & Taguchi, 2010). Content can be decided on by looking to existing research studies and/or by conducting focus group interviews (Dörnyei & Taguchi, 2010), that is developing a new instrument or adapting existing instruments to the new context. Turning to existing instruments provides access to validated tools and enables comparisons across studies. However, due to the nature of the digital world with new apps, media and types of entertainment appearing at warp speed, caution to blindly adopt such tools is necessary and, if adopted, must be piloted for the intended population (Dörnyei & Taguchi, 2010). However, it is highly recommended to conduct a focus group interview with participants of the same make-up as the target group to learn which activities are relevant at the given moment. This, in turn, will help ensure the content validity of the instrument (i.e., that the instrument covers all relevant categories) (Gass & Mackey, 2011) which, by extension, will help secure 'face validity' (i.e., that participants find the instrument relevant) (Gass & Mackey, 2011). Finding the instrument relevant is known to greatly help boost participation for children (Stafford, Layborn, Hill, & Walker, 2003).

Constructing questions

General advice on constructing questions in questionnaires such as, keeping wording short and simple (unambiguous) and avoiding negations (Dörnyei & Taguchi, 2010) applies also to children. In addition to this, some advice specifically relates to children.

Young children (especially between seven and ten years of age) can be very literal in their interpretation of questions and thus find 'vague' words difficult to interpret. Thus, for example, it is advisable to avoid the use of "vague quantifiers" when asking for frequency of behavior to instead use clearly defined periods (de Leeuw et al., 2004). Moreover, depersonalized (e.g., "people my age", Heath et al., 2009, p. 139) and indirect questions must be checked for understanding (de Leeuw, p. 414). If scales are used, for example, "How much do you enjoy gaming on a scale from 1–5", it is important to make sure that participants have a conceptual understanding of scales (Greig et al, 2013). And ideally, scales should not exceed more than five options and below the age of ten preferably no more than three options (de Leeuw et al., 2004). For younger participants, using graphics in scales through, for example, smiley faces works well (de Leeuw et al., 2004).

Teachers may prove very helpful in assessing the level of complexity of wordings, category content and conceptual understanding (Puimège & Peters, 2019). Moreover, conducting focus group interviews is valuable for deciding how to formulate the content as interviews offers information on how children talk about activities in which they engage providing relevant terms and expressions.

Asking for target language details

Given that language learning may be tied to the mode in which the target language is used (e.g., spoken or written), such details may be important. In other words, when asking for daily engagement with the L2 through given activities, one may ask in general, for example, "Do you play games in X language?" or in more details "do you play games where X is written/spoken?" (see Figure 26.1). Two important issues must be considered when deciding on the level of detailedness in relation to eliciting information on language. These issues pertain to children's cognitive abilities and thus memory span and attention.

1. Is the target group able to give language-specific information?

    It is important to consider whether children notice, not least, are able to provide information on the language mode. A thorough pilot of the language categories will help decide this. If participants are not able to provide detailed information, the researcher needs to decide whether to call on parents to help or to ask for less details (see Choosing an instrument).

2. Will including language specific details make the questionnaire or language diary excessively long and complex?

    Asking for specific language details inevitably makes the instrument longer. Length should ideally be kept at a minimum (Dörnyei & Taguchi, 2010), not least for children given their shorter attention span which may cause them to quickly loose interest and fall prey to *fatigue effects* (Dörnyei & Taguchi, 2010, p. 9). Asking many language specific details requires of participants to remember how much time they spend on individual activities separately and, as such, demands very detailed recall. Children may give up on answering questions that seem overly complex or they may simply provide a random answer in order to complete the task. Therefore, a careful prioritizing of the content is necessary. Conducting pilot studies and turning to existing studies to see which type of data has been elicited from children of different ages are helpful.

Recording time

As providing information on time is central to the Q and LD methods, it is important to carefully plan the content of the instruments.

The details of the instruments depend in part on the age of the participants and in part on how much the researcher wishes to involve parents/caregivers in the process.

Given that information on time spent on given activities elicited through a questionnaire is based on delayed recall and estimates, and as such may present a complex task, helping the participants fill out the information through premade categories of time spent on given activities is advisable (e.g., 'Please tick the box that matches how much time you spend on X: less than 30 min.., 30 minutes -1 hour, etc. (cf. Figure 26.1). A pilot can help decide on relevant time intervals (i.e., short (1–15 min.) versus long (0–1 hour) intervals). Looking at comparable (in terms of age and cultural background) questionnaires for inspiration is useful. However, a pilot is necessary to decide on the relevance in the new research context (i.e., children in different parts of the world vary in their intensity of engagement in out-of-school habits (see, e.g., Lindgren and Muñoz, 2013, for a diverse European context) and, as such, time intervals are not necessarily readily transferable. It is recommended to ask for weekday versus weekend use separately given that weekend use tends to be more extensive (Schwarz, 2020).

In the language diary, it is advised to have participants fill in time themselves (see Figure 26.1) as a predetermined time grid with different time intervals (Brecht & Robinson, 1993) takes up too much space in the diary and thus make the instrument excessively long (Hannibal Jensen, 2018).

Design

As "half the battle of eliciting data" depends on "an attractive and professional design" (Dörnyei & Taguchi, 2010, p. 13), thought must be put into design. A language diary comes in the form of a printed booklet or in a digital version. A questionnaire typically either comes in the form of a number of printed sheets of paper or in an online format. If the instrument is intended for children to fill out, extra care should be taken to ensure a clear and simple as well as an inviting design (Greig et al., 2013, see also Figure 26.2). If, the researcher has the skills and resources, s/he may consider creating an online format of the tool, for example, for smart phone use which has been found to be a valuable tool for getting data from children (Greig et al., 2013).

Choosing an instrument

Before choosing a tool for the data collection, the researcher must consider participant characteristics and assess the challenges and limitations resulting from such, in turn, also considering the necessary (tolerated) level of parental involvement.

For very young children (approximately below age 9), filling out either instrument requires parental help as the task is too complex (Greig et al., 2013, Hannibal Jensen, 2018) whereas 10- and 11-year olds may be capable of this (De Leuw et.al., 2004; De Wilde, et al., 2017), depending on the complexity of the instrument and subject to piloting. If the child is unable to fill in the desired information on his/her own, the following points should be considered: (1) whether parents and children are able to give a general estimate of time spent over the course of a week or on a daily basis (if yes, both instruments are suitable). Or, (2), whether they are unable to do so – perhaps parents are unaware of their children's habits (found in De Wilde et al., 2017) and, as mentioned, the children are unable to provide an estimate themselves. In this latter case, a language diary is a better option as rather than relying on recall, it relies on recording activities as they occur (or right thereafter). This offers a clear advantage given that events closer in time are easier to remember, not least for children (Bernard, 1984). On the other hand, questionnaires may provide more general estimates of time spent on activities given that they are not, as a language diary, anchored to a specific time frame (i.e., a specific week) and in that sense may be more representative of use. In relation to this, it is imperative to distribute the language diary during what could be considered an average week (not during, e.g., a holiday). Moreover, it is, if possible, advisable to distribute the diary more than once, for example, three times – once every three weeks – and thereby be able to calculate a mean estimated over this longer stretch of time.

When possible, children should ideally fill out the instrument on their own. This provides for an emic approach where the researcher gets as close as possible to the child's own viewpoint (de Leuuw et al., 2004) and, as such, will be doing research 'with' rather than 'on' the child (Greig, et al., 2013, p. 114). As noted, research shows that this is possible above the age of ten. Moreover, whereas children tend to give unreliable responses around topics in which they have little interest, they have good recall (i.e., good memory) when it comes to meaningful events (de Leeuw et al., 2004; Renninger & Wozniak, 1985). Such findings lend further support to an emic approach to LLBC research given the personal and joyful nature of beyond the classroom engagement being initiated solely by the children themselves (Sundqvist and Sylven's, 2016). Moreover, given the implicit topic 'screen time', if called on to help, parents may provide socially desired responses in accordance with socially accepted norms (Dörnyei & Taguchi, 2010). 'Screen time' is a debated issue in society at large, revolving around the argument that too much screen time is bad for children (Ernest, Causey, Newton, Sharkins, Summerlin and Albaiz, 2014). Consequently, when estimating screen time for their children, parents may set the bar lower than the actual time spent. Likewise, if parents elicit time, children may underestimate the time spent on screen-related activities knowing that their parents likely prefer for them to spend only little time on such activities.

Piloting

The importance of piloting cannot be stressed too strongly, not least with children where the suitability of the tool for a specific age group must be assessed (de Leeuw et al., 2004). For the pilot, ideally running over at least two phases, participants need for phase one to (a) fill out the research tool either on their own, or possibly while 'thinking aloud' with the researcher (see de Leeuw et al., 2004, p. 424 for details), for (b) provide feedback on clarity and complexity. In phase 1, parental involvement is advised for feedback on the child's ability to handle the instrument. In phase two, the tool is distributed to a larger pool of pilot participants and an item analysis is carried out (for a detailed description, consult Dörnyei & Taguchi, 2010, pp. 56–57).

Distribution

There are two major issues to consider when distributing the research tool among children: explaining the task and dealing with gatekeepers.

Explaining the task

To make sure the participants understand the task, time is well spent explaining, face-to-face if possible, what is expected. Preferably, the researcher him/herself presents the instrument, not least because children may be reluctant to ask other people (e.g., the teacher) clarifying questions related to the instrument (Strange, Forest, Oakley & the Ripple Study Team, 2003). For the language diary visual aids work well; for example, a large size example diary can be brought to class and filled in with examples of activities based on the children's suggestions (Hannibal Jensen, 2018). This provides for a common understanding of the task, generates talk among the children and, not least, is found to be enjoyable. It is important that the researcher stays neutral when children provide examples of out-of-school activities as they are likely to pick up on the researcher's attitude regarding activities which, in turn, may affect how they fill in the diary (Hannibal Jensen, 2018). Related to the issue of socially desired responses: in order to avoid such, it is key to stress that being a good informant is being an honest informant. For example, in a pilot feedback session, a child said to the author of this chapter: "I watched everything you said!" referring to having put activities in her diary that had been discussed at the handout session – not reflecting actual engagement which turned out to be 0. Thus, it must be stressed to children who do not engage in beyond the classroom activities that this is considered equally interesting. It is important to have all participants feel as valuable and important participants. In this vein, asking participants who do not engage in L2 mediated activities to state which L1 activities they engage in may be considered.

Unless the researcher is certain that the participants can fill out the questionnaire without parental help, it should be filled in at home.

Gatekeepers: ensuring a good return rate

Participants need reminders to fill out the instrument. For the language diary, reminders must be sent during the 'diary week' to boost the return rate: lack of reminders will have the opposite effect (Hannibal Jensen, 2018). If you do not have direct access to your participants and instead must rely on help from gatekeepers, such as parents and teachers, it is very important to gain their support (Dörnyei & Taguchi, 2010). If the participants have their own phones and permission is granted, reminders may be sent directly to them via text messages; a medium that serves well with children for boosting participation (Greig et al., 2013).

Testing, assessing or evaluating the language?

The researcher needs to decide how to record language progress/ability beyond the classroom, that is, whether to employ tests or to evaluate progress in some other way, possibly through observations (Reinders & Bailey, 2020). If you need 'hard figures', a test may be the better option as this allows the opportunity to very concretely measure language ability. However, given the nature of beyond the classroom engagement, which is often not engaged in for learning purposes, measures that consider the whole learner experience, if possible, may be more fitting (see Reinders & Bailey, 2020).

Importantly, if tests are used, care must be taken to ensure that the child is not left feeling inadequate. In my experience, if possible, the test administration room should not be too close to the classroom. This leaves room for a talk on the way to the test about topics with which the participants feel familiar and at ease (e.g., out-of-school activities!) thus easing the atmosphere and creating a space where the child is the knowledgeable other. Additionally, before testing clear instructions must be provided. If the child's attention is drifting during testing, short informal breaks are helpful ensuring that the child feels comfortable and is not simply going through the motions to get the test done with.

Exploring learner engagement: interviews and field observations

Interviews: individual or group?

Many different qualitative approaches can be applied for doing research with young learners. Here, interviews and field observations are described being the most commonly used methods in SLA with young learners.

Conducting interviews is a popular method for doing research with young children for its ability to provide valuable insider (i.e., emic) perspectives from the research participants themselves (Heath, Brooks, Cleaver, & Ireland, 2009). Interviews can be conducted with individuals or groups and can be structured, semi-structured or unstructured in their design and execution. The following section initially describes individual and group interviews. Hereafter, a specific interview type (a so-called *guided tour*) is described which is in particularly well-suited for doing interviews with children.

With children often group interviews are preferred over individual interviews based on the observation that they provide for a more natural conversational context for children given that peer group talks are a common way for children to "create shared meanings and understandings" (Heath et al., 90). In general, group interviews spark more engagement from young children than individual interviews (Greig et al., 2013), and, as such, group interviews are very conducive for generating discussions with participants providing feedback and uptake on each other's statements (Wilkinson, 2004). Moreover, in groups, participants are also more likely to use the 'language' they use for activities beyond the classroom and thereby the researcher gains valuable knowledge on out-of-school peer discourse. In such interviews, care must be taken to ensure that participants pay attention to the questions asked (are not distracted by each other), thus a maximum of five participants is advised (de Leuuw et al., 2004). Moreover, it must be ensured that participants not merely agree with each other when answering questions; recall that children above the age of ten have a tendency to provide peer desirable answers (de Leeuw et al., 2004). Furthermore, apart from asking questions, the researcher needs to make sure that all parties are heard and feel as valuable participants (Greig et al., 2013). Filming the group interview is recommended as telling the recorded voices of young children apart is difficult (Greig et al., 2013). However, make sure that you adhere to all ethical guidelines (consult Sylvén Chapter 21 in the present volume). If the interview is only voice recorded, it is important to have participants state their name or alias at the beginning of the interview for later recognition.

Individual interviews, on the other hand, may elicit more detailed information from the individual child and no attention is needed for keeping a group focused and on track. Depending on personality, some children may be more likely to share their thoughts and experiences when peers are not around. It will be up to the researcher to assess which type of interview works best for the purpose and in relation to the participants. Related to this, it is highly recommended that the researcher visits the research site as often as possible before the interview thereby becoming a familiar face, gaining rapport mitigating as best as possible the asymmetrical relation between the child and the adult researcher (Gibson, 2012) and getting a sense of who the participants are as people (Christensen, 2004).

The guided tour interview

It is advised to use props or doing activities when interviewing young children (Greig et al., 2013). In sociological research a useful method for interviewing children is the so-called *walk and talk* where the child takes the researcher through a *tour*, for example, of his/her neighborhood either while actually walking through this or through watching videos of the neighborhood while talking about relevant issues (Heath et al., 2009). In the case of out-of-school activities, the actual activities children engage in (e.g., games, Social media, etc.) serve as excellent sites (props) to get the conversation going and getting detailed information of beyond the classroom engagement. Such a tour facilitates much talk and makes for a more natural situation than a regular interview. Another benefit is the multimodal nature of the interview making it easier for children to exemplify and describe activities given the contextualized nature of the talk (Greig et al., 2013; Hannibal Jensen, 2018). Moreover, using props (activities) that are related to participants' out-of-school engagement provides an excellent aid for stimulated recall.

In the guided tour-type interview, the research interest will guide the tour. For a completely emic view, for example, the child can engage in out-of-school activities of his/her own choice during the actual interview reflecting what s/he habitually engages in (takes the interviewer on a guided tour) (see Hannibal Jensen, 2019). Ideally, the child brings his/her digital device to the interview so that his/her apps and games are available. If this is not possible, the researcher brings equipment and the child exemplifies activities in whatever form possible (e.g., by showing a YouTube video on a game that s/he plays). Such an interview format may be completely unstructured with no interview guide where instead the researcher develops the interview as the situation unfolds (Mackey & Gass, 2011) and questions take point of departure in on screen activities. Such questions can procure many interesting details rooted in the child's understanding of the activity (i.e., an insider's point of view). Questions may be very general (e.g., "Will you take me through the game and tell me what you have to do?") or very specific (e.g., "What is meant by 'level'?"). The interview may also be semi-structured meaning that an interview guide has been prepared; however, still allowing for the researcher to depart from the guide and ask questions that appear as the interview unfolds (Mackey & Gass, 2011).

There are many advantages to this interview type. For one, it provides the child a guided recall. That is, it is easier for the child to remember and relate what they do when engaging in specific activities when they are engaging rather than abstracting and remembering without any scaffolding (Greig et al., 2013; Heath et al., 2013). Moreover, questions are easier for the child to relate to being concrete rather than abstract. It is also much easier for the child to describe details of engagement when the context of engagement is added (Hannibal Jensen, 2018; Heath et al., 2013).

An additional advantage to this type of interview is that it is fun and given the pleasurable and personal nature of engagement in out-of-school activities, children are likely happy to share their experiences and thoughts on the topic. Being engaged in an activity, furthermore, provides for a more informal atmosphere and one in which the child, rather than the visiting adult, is the expert thus potentially bringing a sense of empowerment.

Due to the unstructured, exploratory nature of the guided-tour interview, it does not necessarily allow for comparison of engagement between participants to this end a structured or semi-structured interview will work better (Greig et al., 2013).

An interview need not necessarily be limited to one format; for example, the interview may start out as a guided tour and be finished as a semi-structured or structured interview or the other way around. Moreover, the researcher may initially use the group interview format to then have information elaborated in individual interviews (Greig et al., 2013). Furthermore, interviews can have a longitudinal design where participants are interviewed several times over a longer period of time (Heath et al., 2009). Focus group interviewees can be selected based on questionnaire data.

When interviewing young children, the general recommendations pertaining to age characteristics addressed in this section, equally relevant in a testing situation, are summed up below (based on Greig et al., p. 115):

- Make sure questions are unambiguous and not leading
- Pay attention to the context of the interview (i.e., make sure the child feels comfortable in the context)
- Use age-appropriate materials to aid memory (e.g., laptops, smartphones, tablets, etc.)

- Make the interview fun
- Focus on attention management.

Importantly, researchers need to practice their interviewing skills before embarking on the real interview as children may prove difficult to interview pertaining to participant characteristics (cf. piloting).

Field observations

Another way to obtain data is through field observations (Greig et al., 2013) (i.e., observing children in their natural surroundings for a natural view of their engagement in out-of-school activities). Data may stand on its own or be a valuable supplement to interview or survey data. The researcher may be present or do video observations (i.e., the participants are filmed). Naturally, such data must be stored in accordance with relevant data protection regulations. If the researcher is present, s/he may take field notes or also film the engagement. If the purpose of the research is to obtain language data, it is advisable to get video data as it is very difficult to get accurate field notes of language data, such as code switching. In relation to the field method, discussions tend to center around the *observer's paradox* (Mackey & Gass, 2011, p. 176); that is, whether participants act differently knowing that they are being observed. However, nowadays, children seem to be accustomed to a great extent to the visual mode so the novelty value of being filmed seems to quickly wear off (Heath et al., 2009).

Another idea is to have children themselves do the field work and film their engagement in different activities (Heath et al., 2009), for example, in the form of a video diary. As noted by Heath et al. (2009), visual methods seem in particularly well-suited for children who seem comfortable with visual media through which they may gain more control of the data collection process. In turn, this provides for an emic view where children share their interests with the researcher. Such data is naturally bound to be messy (i.e., children are unlikely to provide uniform, comparable types of data) but likely to provide very interesting details of children's lives with out-of-school activities which may be elaborated in subsequent interviews (Heath et al, 2009). Naturally, there are a number of ethical issues to consider if employing such types of data (consult, Heath et al., 2009, p. 129 for examples).

Implications: going forward

Existing research on young learners beyond the classroom is sparse and primarily quantitative focusing on measuring extent of and learning from out-of-school habits. More large-scale quantitative research is needed to firmly establish findings across larger and more diverse populations (Sundqvist, 2019). Furthermore, little is known about learning processes over time through out-of-school activities and very little is known of children's engagement with the L2 of the activities. Therefore, more longitudinal and qualitative research is needed. Moreover, as mentioned, employing creative methods and involving children in the research to a greater extent would be helpful. As Heath et al. note: "we need to respect children and young people as experts in their own lives who have a unique and powerful contribution to make to the research" (Greig, et. al, 2013, p. 205). That is, even though children are different than adults, and some precautions are necessary when planning research with children, it would be an error to underestimate the contributions that they themselves are able to make in the research process (see also Reinders & Bailey, 2020).

Reflection questions

1. How can you give your research participants a more active role in the data collection and how may this enrich your research project? You may wish to consult Pinter and Zandian (2014) for some ideas on how to involve children in the research.
2. How will you secure validity in your research project?
3. Which methods in a mixed methods design may help bring about a comprehensive view of beyond classroom L2 engagement?

Recommended readings

For a seminal young learner language diary study, you are recommended to read: Sylvén, L. K., & Sundqvist, P. (2012).

For a valuable guide to constructing age-appropriate questions for children, you are recommended to read De Leeuw, E., et al. (2004).

For an excellent guide to constructing questionnaires, read Dörnyei, Z. & Taguchi, T. (2010). All studies are found in the reference list.

References

Alderson, P. (2005). Designing ethical research with children. In Ann Farrell (Ed.), *Ethical research with children* (pp. 27–37). Berkshire, England: Open University Press.

Bernard, H. R., Killworth, P., Kronenfeld, D., & Sailer, L. (1984). The problem of informant accuracy: The validity of retrospective data. *Annual Review of Anthropology, 13*(1), 495–517. https://doi-org.proxy1-bib.sdu.dk/10.1146/annurev.an.13.100184.002431

Brecht, R. D., & Robinson, J. L. (1993). *Qualitative analysis of second language acquisition in study abroad: The ACTR/NFLC project.* Bloomington, IN: IN National Foreign Language Center.

Christensen, P. H. (2004). Children's participation in ethnographic research: Issues of power and representation. *Children & Society, 18*(2), 165–176. https://doi.org/10.1002/chi.823

Danby, S., Ewing, L., & Thorpe, K. (2011). The novice researcher: Interviewing young children. *Qualitative Inquiry, 17*(1), 74–84. https://doi.org/10.1177/1077800410389754

De Leeuw, E., Borgers, N., & Smits, A. (2004). Pretesting questionnaires for children and adolescents. In S. Presser, J. M. Rothgeb, M. P. Couper, J. T. Lessler, E. Martin, J. Martin & J. Singer (Eds.), *Methods for testing and evaluating survey questionnaires* (pp. 409–429). Hoboken: John Wiley & Sons.

De Wilde, V., Brysbaert, M., & Eyckmans J (2019). Learning English through out-of-school exposure. Which levels of language proficiency are attained and which types of input are important? *Bilingualism: Language and Cognition, 23*(11), 171–185. https://doi.org/ 10.1017/S1366728918001062.

De Wilde, V., & Eyckmans, J. (2017). Game on! Young learners' incidental language learning of English prior to instruction. *Studies in Second Language Learning and Teaching, 7*(4), 673–694. doi: 10.14746/ssllt.2017.7.4.6

Duran, C. S. (2017). "You not die yet": Karenni refugee children's language socialization in a video gaming community. *Linguistics and Education, 42*, 1–9. doi:10.1016/j.linged.2017.09.002

Dörnyei, Z., & Taguchi, T. (2010). *Questionnaires in second language research. Construction, administration, and processing.* New York: Routledge.

Ernest, J. M., Causey, C., Newton, A. B., Sharkins, K., Summerlin, J., & Albaiz, N. (2014) Extending the global dialogue about media, technology, screen time, and young children. *Childhood Education, 90*(3), 182–191, DOI: 10.1080/00094056.2014.910046

Gail, E. (2014). Young learners': Clarifying our terms. *ELTE. Journal, 68*(1), 75–78. https://doi.org/10.1093/elt/cct062

Gibson, J. E. (2012). Interviews and focus groups with children: Methods that match children's developing competencies. *Journal of Family Theory & Review, 4*(2), 148–159. https://doi.org/10.1111/j.1756-2589.2012.00119.x

Greig, A., Taylor, J., & MacKay, T. (2013). *Doing research with children: A practical guide.* London: Sage Publications. https://dx-doi-org.proxy1-bib.sdu.dk/10.4135/9781526402219

Hannibal Jensen, S. (2017). Gaming as an English language learning resource among young children in Denmark. *Calico Journal, 34*(1), 1–19. DOI:10.1558/cj.29519

Hannibal Jensen, S. (2018). Extramural English engagement in a Danish context: A young learner perspective. (Unpublished diss.), University of Southern Denmark, Odense.

Hannibal Jensen, S. (2019). Language learning in the wild: A young user perspective. *Language Learning and Technology, 23*(1), 72–86. https://doi.org/10125/44673

Heath, S., Brooks, R., Cleaver, E., & Ireland, E. (2009) *Researching young people's lives*. London: SAGE Publications Ltd. doi: 10.4135/9781446249420

Johnson, B., & Christensen, L. (2008). *Educational research: Quantitative, qualitative, and mixed approaches*. Thousand Oaks, CA: Sage.

Lee, J. S. (2019). Informal digital learning of English and second language vocabulary outcomes: Can quantity conquer quality? *British Journal of Educational Technology, 50*(2), 767–778. doi:10.1111/bjet.12599

Lindgren, E., & Muñoz, C. (2013). The influence of exposure, parents, and linguistic distance on young European learners' foreign language comprehension. *International Journal of Multilingualism, 10*(1), 105–129. doi:https://doi.org/10.1080/14790718.2012.679275.

Mackey, A., & Gass, S. M. (2011). *Second language research: Methodology and design*. London: Routledge.

Peterson, M. (2016). *Computer games and language learning*. New York: Palgrave Macmillan.

Piirainen-Marsh, A., & Tainio, L. (2009). Other-repetition as a resource for participation in the activity of playing a video game. *The Modern Language Journal, 93*(2), 153–169. doi: https://doi.org/10.1111/j.1540-4781.2009.00853.x.

Pinter, A., & Zandian, S. (2014). 'I don't ever want to leave this room': Benefits of researching 'with' children. *ELT Journal, 68*(1), 64–74.

Puimège, E., & Peters, E. (2019). Learners' English vocabulary knowledge prior to formal instruction: The role of learner-related and word-related variables. *Language Learning, 69*(4), 943–977. https://doi.org/10.1111/lang.12364

Reinders, H., & Bailey, K. M. (2020). Assessing and evaluating language learning beyond the classroom. *The Routledge handbook of second language acquisition and language testing*. New York: Routledge.

Renninger, K. A., & Wozniak, R. H. (1985). Effect of interest on attentional shift, recognition, and recall in young children. *Developmental Psychology, 21*(4), 624–632. https://doi.org/10.1037/0012-1649.21.4.624

Schwarz, M. (2020). *Beyond the walls: A mixed methods study of teenagers' extramural English practices and their vocabulary knowledge*. (Diss.), University of Vienna, Vienna.

Stafford, A., Laybourn, A., Hill, M., & Walker, M. (2003). 'Having a say': Children and young people talk about consultation. *Children & Society, 17*(5), 361–373. https://doi.org/10.1002/CHI.758

Strange, V., Forest, S., Oakley, A., & the Ripple Study Team (2003). Using research questionnaires with young people in schools: The influence of the social context. *International Journal of Social Research Methodology, 6*, 337–346. DOI: 10.1080/1364557021000024749

Sundqvist, P., & Sylvén, L. K. (2014). Language-related computer use: Focus on young L2 English learners in Sweden. *ReCALL, 26*(01), 3–20. doi:https://doi.org/10.1017/S0958344013000232.

Sundqvist, P., & Sylvén, L. K. (2016). *Extramural English in Teaching and Learning*. London: Palgrave Macmillan

Sundqvist, P. (2019). Commercial-off-the-shelf games in the digital wild and L2 learner vocabulary. *Language Learning and Technology, 23*(1), 87–113. https://doi.org/10125/44674

Sylvén, L. K., & Sundqvist, P. (2012). Gaming as extramural English L2 learning and L2 proficiency among young learners. *ReCALL, 24*(03), 302–321. doi:10.1017/SO95834401200016X.

Turgut, Y., & İrgin, P. (2009). Young learners' language learning via computer games. *Procedia-Social and Behavioral Sciences, 1*(1), 760–764. doi:https://doi.org/10.1016/j.sbspro.2009.01.135.

Wilkinson, S. (2004). Focus group research. In D. Silverman (Ed.), *Qualitative research: Theory, method and practice* (pp. 177–199). Thousand Oaks, CA: Sage.

27
ETHNOGRAPHY IN LBC RESEARCH

Anastasia Rothoni

Introduction

As suggested by Lai (2017) and Reinders and Benson (2017), the language-learning landscape beyond the classroom is messy and idiosyncratic. As such, the present chapter aims to illustrate how researchers have attempted to approach such a seemingly messy, and unorganized learning landscape through the use of ethnography. In particular, I focus on ethnography as a particular form of qualitative enquiry because of its long and intimate association with studies of language in education.

In recent years, as the contexts in which languages are used, learnt and taught are constantly changing (Kalaja et al., 2011: 57), there has been a need for alternative approaches to research in the field of language learning, moving beyond approaches which focus almost exclusively on the universal, internal aspects of language learning. In particular, in out-of-school contexts, where literacy and language learning practices tend to occur freely and sometimes without learners noticing them consciously, language learning is better conceived as a process that unfolds in personally meaningful ways and is shaped – in part at least – by an individual's experience of the conditions in which it occurs rather than the assimilation of an autonomous linguistic system resembling that of a native speaker (Divita, 2011: 73). To study language learning, researchers have thus expanded their analytic focus to include social meanings and aspects of language learning that have not traditionally been addressed, foregrounding the role of the individual, whose beliefs, attitudes, emotions and values affect his/her language learning trajectory (see the collection of studies in Kalaja et al., 2008; also Benson & Reinders, 2011). However, these dynamic perspectives of individuals as language learners as well as their learning processes are difficult to trace and cannot be adequately assessed by and accessed through survey (or interview) questions (Livingstone, 2001: 9). Consequently, there is a need for qualitative, ethnographic research projects conducted in non-institutional, out-of-school settings through the use of long-term observations, in-depth interviews and intensive fieldwork in order to establish a better understanding of these processes.

In response to such a need, quite recently, there has been a number of studies that focus on language learning beyond the classroom through a configuration of ethnographic approaches and methodological tools, leading to enhanced understandings of the process of language learning beyond the classroom from a perspective that highlights its social dimensions in all its complexities (see, e.g., Bailly, 2011; Kuure, 2011; Pitkänen-Huhta, & Nikula, 2013; Rothoni, 2019). Briefly introduced here, my own ethnographic project (see Rothoni,

2019) – used as a case study in this chapter – aimed to provide a detailed account of 15 Greek teenagers' out-of-school English literacy and language learning practices and what these practices might reveal about their aspirations, orientations and self-identifications. To achieve this goal, I focussed on the variety of teenagers' everyday engagements with English and their underlying meanings and values situating myself methodologically within the qualitative approach and, specifically, that of ethnography. The study extended over a period of 18 months and employed a combination of ethnographic data collection tools. Theoretically, it subscribed to socio-cultural approaches to language learning (e.g., Norton, 2000; Barron, 2006; Lantolf & Thorne, 2006; Dufva et al., 2011) arguing for the need to look – through an ethnographic lens – at learners' meanings and experiences of languages and how they relate to languages in their daily environment.

Key constructs

Ethnography as a research perspective

Definitions of ethnography abound and vary in the literature depending on the academic tradition in which it is discussed and used (Hammersley & Atkinson, 2007: 1). Heath and Street (2008: 29) define ethnography as "a theory-building enterprise constructed through detailed systematic observing, recording and analysing of human behaviour in specifiable spaces and interactions". In its simplest form, ethnography is "the systematic study of a cultural group or phenomenon based upon extensive field work in one or more selected locales" (Riemer, 2008: 203). Its origins can be traced in the work of early 20th-century researchers (e.g., Malinowski's field work in Trobriand islands) interested in documenting the cultural practices of remote communities in different parts of the world for a number of years. Ethnography has since been employed by scholars in many related fields, including sociolinguistics (e.g., Scollon & Scollon, 1981), literacy studies (e.g., Street, 1984), media studies (e.g., Lemish, 1985) and education (e.g., Willis, 1977). Although these fields share many features with earlier anthropological work, they have broadened the range of sites and issues explored and have combined it with their field-specific theoretical approaches, a fact resulting in pluralistic approaches to ethnography (Creswell, 2007: 69). Still, despite any diversities, a common feature across all approaches and a distinguishing feature from qualitative research, is ethnography's ontological rootedness in the concept of culture (Purcell-Gates, 2004: 92–93) and its epistemological grounding in the study of cultural practices through cultural and social settings (Mason, 2002: 55). This grounding in the notion of cultural practices carries with it ontological, epistemological and methodological entailments for ethnographic studies. The first is that, ethnographic studies must be deeply contextualized, conducted *in situ* over extended periods of time. A further entailment is a focus on the participants' point of view and the meanings they make of practices. Ethnographic accounts, in other words, "are built around and told in the words, views, explanations, and interpretations of the participants in the study" (LeCompte & Schensul, 2010: 16).

The use of ethnography with its interest in broader contexts of cultural practices and social life and its traditional focus on people and their meanings is in strong alignment with the "social turn" in literacy and language acquisition research (Block, 2003). This turn has signalled the shift from traditional, cognitive-based understandings to social views of literacy and language learning which have stressed the importance of the social context in understanding the dynamic nature of literacy and language learning processes (Papen, 2005). Perhaps more importantly, ethnography is particularly effective in offering a "thick description" (Geertz, 1973) and an "emic or insider view" (Riemer, 2008: 205) of the perspectives, emotions, beliefs and values which underlie learners' literacy and language learning practices and processes. Yet, while ethnography has been embraced in the past decades as the preferred research approach in literacy studies (Barton, 2012), it has not hitherto been systematically used as the standard research approach in language learning studies (see, however, Bailly, 2011; Kuure, 2011; Pitkänen-Huhta & Nikula, 2013; Rothoni, 2019), while language learning scholars in different parts of the world are only now starting to pay greater attention to the use of ethnographic or retrospective self-report data to explore learning in non-institutional settings (Benson & Reinders, 2011: 5). This recent interest has been sparked, as will be discussed in detail in the next section, by the shift in the basic assumptions of language learning research among scholars, who no longer view learning in purely cognitive terms, but in terms of participation in communities and contexts of various kinds (ibid.).

Socio-cultural approaches to second/foreign language learning

Within socio-cultural approaches to language learning (e.g., Barron, 2006; Lantolf & Thorne, 2006; Dufva et al., 2011), learning – be it of a first, second or foreign language – is no longer captured as mastering a discrete form of language inside the classroom with the aim to develop an idealized linguistic and communicative competence (cf. Pennycook, 2007). Instead, it is conceptualized as an inherently social process accounting for the various "social, historical and cultural contexts" (Norton & Toohey, 2001: 310) in which individuals engage through language in personally meaningful practices. It is a socially and culturally situated practice where learners are viewed as individuals – that is, as socially and historically situated subjects who navigate and negotiate the experience of language learning in personally meaningful ways (Divita, 2011) – and act as social agents collaborating with other people and using the different tools and resources available to them in their surrounding environment (Kalaja et al., 2011: 47). This emphasis on learners' agency is also evident in the widely used term "out-of-classroom language learning", defined by Phil Benson as "any kind of learning that takes place outside the classroom and involves self-instruction, naturalistic learning or self-directed naturalistic learning" (Benson, 2001: 62). The emphasis here is on the deliberate intention to acquire whatever of the language is needed on the part of the learner. A similar emphasis on intrinsic motivation is also found in Nikula's and Pitkänen-Huhta's (2008) definition of the term "informal learning" as referring to "contacts with the language in everyday settings that arise from the needs and interests of the language users" (ibid.:171). Their definition draws on the socio-cultural view of learning but also sees language users' needs and interests as a driving force behind their contacts with the language.

Informed by such socially based approaches to language and learning, I support the idea that foreign language learning should not be seen only in terms of acquisition of a unitary set of skills but also as a process of effective participation in personally meaningful activities and practices, where learners appropriate semiotic resources – heteroglossic and multimodal – in a situated fashion (Rothoni, 2019: 35–36). Also, in line with research which posits that the overall ecology of literacy and learning is constituted by flows between formal and informal sites and practices (e.g., Barron, 2006), I argue that these activities are no longer solely regulated by, bound by, or confined to educational settings and the associated forms of formal learning as traditionally presented in many foreign language classrooms (Swaffar & Arens, 2005). To the contrary, these activities may take place in various contexts and spaces beyond the formal classroom setting (e.g., home, peer groups, parks, free time or hobbies), may involve family members, peers, friends, interest groups or even strangers and may be facilitated by learners' contacts with different types of media, modes, texts and resources (Rothoni, 2019: 36). Finally, contrary to traditionally held beliefs which question the value of any foreign language learning experience that does not involve grammar and written textbooks arguing that this kind of learning may even "corrupt" the learner's repertoire (Eaton, 2010: 18), I endorse the view that this "passion-based learning" (Lankshear & Knobel, 2010: 20) may enrich and complement learners' formal studies of language.

Key issues

The challenges of conducting a full-scale ethnography of out-of-school language learning

While ethnography is ideally used for studies in specific locations and physically bounded spaces or institutions (e.g., classrooms) in which extensive observation over an extended period of time is possible, there are several shortcomings to it, when it comes to the study of out-of-school literacy and learning practices. By default, such practices that occur in everyday life are not spatially or temporally bounded (cf. Mannion & Ivanič, 2007), permeating a variety of contexts, settings, locations and time periods. As Stickler and Emke (2011: 159) note, "access to the learning process outside the classroom is notoriously difficult". In this sense, full-scale ethnographies of learners' out-of-school learning processes would entail the difficult tasks of "shadowing" them (Hammersley & Atkinson, 2007: 39), as they move in their various social worlds, and engaging in direct participation and close observation of their daily activities in their home lives, school lives, as well as any of their other pastime activities for a prolonged time period. Naturally, such an endeavour would require a significant amount of time and resources as well as a high level of commitment – both from participants and from the researcher – while there could be ethical concerns regarding the relationship established between participants and the researcher and the intrusion of the researcher in participants' lives (see chapter 21 for ethical issues). Besides, full and unrestricted access to participants' day-to-day routines – one that would enable such lengthy naturalistic observations to take place – would be normally difficult to be gained. This is because – contrary to classroom-based ethnographies where access is gained through direct negotiation with the institution – learners' participation in studies conducted in non-institutional settings presupposes an established level of trust and is strongly regulated by their parents or guardians (Emond, 2005: 128).

Taking these constraints into consideration, researchers working in such areas and contexts have instead opted for the use of ethnographic tools and "indirect observational methods" (Pellegrini, 2004: 195) which provide them with the opportunity to be flexible about the nature of their studies (Heath & Street, 2008). This direction is well-suited to the study of out-of-school language learning in that, on the one hand, it offers the opportunity to get around the difficulties imposed by the constraints of fieldwork while, on the other hand, it allows researchers to exploit the benefits of ethnographic understandings. In an example of this, in my study (Rothoni, 2019), I was conscious of the fact that young English language learners are simultaneously situated in a variety of contexts that can contribute to language learning and that the home is only one of the many social and non-institutional settings (e.g., friends' houses, shopping malls, neighbourhood) where they come in contact with English and engage in out-of-school learning activities. Therefore, I employed "indirect observational methods" (Pellegrini, 2004: 195) that would be sensitive to spatial and temporal aspects of data and, at the same time, would not depend on my (the researcher's) continuous physical presence in the field. Overall, such "space-time oriented" (Jorgenson & Sullivan, 2009) methods (i.e., literacy diaries, in-depth interviews, visual data and participants' photos, systematic in-home observations) are extremely useful in home-based ethnographic studies since they can be revealing of participants' daily language learning practices regardless of the space or time of their occurrence.

The use of visual and child-centred methods to complement ethnographic methods

Ethnographic researchers working with young participants and their out-of-school practices argue that the methods used for data collection and the interpretation of research findings bear important ethical implications in that they affect power dynamics within a study (Morrow, 2008). For example, in keeping with the established ethnographic research process, in my study (Rothoni, 2019) I addressed this issue by drawing on a range of child-centred "collaborative or participatory research techniques" (Best, 2007: 14), which would allow me to listen to participants' voices and stories from their own perspectives. Such methods (including photography, role playing, drawing) are not only better suited to young participants but also more empowering, placing them in the position of active participants in the research process rather than powerless and passive objects of study (Veale, 2005). Even though there are still researchers who tend to rely on parents' and teachers' accounts to get a glimpse into their life worlds (Hogan, 2005), there has been a call to give children and adolescents a 'voice' in social research (see, e.g., Lobe et al., 2007). Theoretically, such a view is underpinned by recent sociological research stressing children's agency and by the accompanying shift from conducting research *on* children to conducting research *with* them and *for* them (Livingstone & Lemish, 2001).

In sum, this emphasis on child-centred methodologies has two important implications for ethnographic studies on out-of-school language learning: first, it relates to the conceptualization of participants as social actors (Lobe et al., 2007); second, and as a result of the first, it serves as a guiding framework for the increasing employment of the so-called "collaborative or participatory research techniques" (Best, 2007: 14) (e.g., participant-driven photography, visualization tasks) combined with more traditional ethnographic methods (e.g., informal talks and semi-structured interviews). Perhaps more importantly, such techniques are also in line with the recent interest in visual forms of representation as a means of enhancing understanding of the complexity of young people's literacy and learning practices (e.g., Nikula & Pitkänen-Huhta, 2008; Pitkänen-Huhta & Rothoni, 2018) in that they quite powerfully allow researchers to indirectly access young people's constructions of their own practices (Kendrick & McKay, 2011) by inviting them to become active co-producers of data.

Implications

The need to move beyond quantitative and mixed-method studies documenting the foreign language learning that takes place outside schools

In the European and broader international context there is now a growing body of research focussing on how language learners, on their own initiative, seek opportunities outside the language classroom to enrich and expand their language learning experience (Benson &

Reinders, 2011; Reinders & Benson, 2017), particularly in English as a foreign language. To a large extent, these studies – conducted in different countries across Europe such as Belgium, Denmark, Finland, Germany, Italy, Sweden, Turkey – share similar findings about the learning opportunities provided by young people's English language pastime activities (see, e.g., Grau, 2009; Sundqvist, 2009; Inozu, et al., 2010; Linnakylä, 2010; Olsson, 2011; Menegale, 2013). Despite slight variations in frequency, the most popular, so-called "lighter" (Darasawang & Reinders, 2010), or less conventional, activities that young learners seem to engage in are digital game playing, watching movies or TV shows, listening to music, online chatting with friends, watching YouTube videos, reading books or magazines (Inozu, et al., 2010; Kuppens, 2010; Linnakylä, 2010; Menegale, 2013; Tran, 2017). These activities mostly favour receptive skills and are strongly connected with young people's personal interests and hobbies from outside school. They include the use of global forms of popular culture and new media as well as different types of entertainment material.

What should be noted here, however, is that, while these studies have provided rich evidence concerning learners' learning of English through their engagement in such activities – some of them even combining data on out-of-school activities with specific learning outcomes (e.g., Sundqvist, 2009; Kuppens, 2010) – what they have failed to capture is the social and individual aspects underlying their "passion-based learning" (Lankshear & Knobel, 2010: 20). This is in part at least attributed to the fact that the majority of these studies employ quantitative (e.g., surveys, questionnaires) or mixed method techniques (questionnaires combined with interviews), which cannot adequately focus on and provide a comprehensive view of the individual learner and his/her learning experiences and processes outside school and thus cannot provide access to a variety of key issues such as his/her use of learning strategies, his/her participation in communities or affinity groups, his/her perceptions of the target language and his/her beliefs about the nature of language learning, among others (see, however, Bailly, 2011; Divita, 2011; Kalaja et al., 2011; Pitkänen-Huhta & Nikula, 2013; Rothoni, 2019).

To illustrate with an example related to this limitation of quantitative methods, in my ethnographic study (Rothoni, 2019), although proper English learning was stressed by most teenagers in the opening interviews as a process that mostly occurs in the classroom, at later stages the analysis of ethnographic data revealed important details of their actual learning which took place beyond the classroom: a significant part of young people's learning of English occurred through their socialization in interest-based communities, during their interaction with other people helping them deal with difficulties and "apprenticing" them into new ways of being (Lave & Wenger, 1991). Their learning was thus given a social character and became shared and collaborative occurring spontaneously through immersion in activities in real-life contexts and socialization with experienced others. Indicative examples of such "situated learning" (Lave & Wenger, 1991) or "learning by doing", were some boys' learning of the English terms for the various skateboard tricks they performed from their more experienced friends, a girl's learning experiences occurring through her participation in a meme-sharing online community and young boys' collaborative learning through their game playing with friends or their team of players as they tried to overcome difficulties and get ahead sharing strategies via headphones, microphones or text-based chat (Rothoni, 2019: 246).

Notably, such examples of learning are significant in that they provide useful and detailed insights into the nature of out-of-school language learning as a whole; yet, such insights would have remained uncovered if the analysis had been limited to numerical or quantitative data alone. Thus, although there is now a significant number of studies on young people's language learning practices outside educational contexts which do not rely on quantitative data alone (see, e.g., Sundqvist, 2019 and Schwarz, 2020 for studies employing a combination of quantitative and qualitative methods), examples such as the above stress the need for similar studies to move beyond snapshots of young people's out-of-school language learning as derived merely from tables, figures, checklists, questionnaires and/or single interviews.

The power of ethnography in uncovering the different ideologies and beliefs behind seemingly similar learning practices

Another key point that emerges from the considerations outlined in the previous section is related to the fact that, learners from different contexts and/or countries appear to engage in surprisingly similar types of out-of-school language learning activities (e.g., listening to music, watching TV shows and movies, browsing the Internet, watching online videos). Although appealing, this seemingly straightforward approach to the topic of out-of-school language learning could prove to be misleading, tempting one to assume that young people's everyday learning of a language – English in this case – is uniform and that the various activities carry the same meaning across the different research contexts. The reality, however, is that these seemingly similar learning activities are shaped by different ideologies and beliefs regarding the role and importance of school and out-of-school learning which, in turn, might index more general social structures and values and might be connected to broader discourses in the global and local contexts, which need to be accounted for (Pitkänen-Huhta & Rothoni, 2018: 28–29).

In my study (Rothoni, 2019), for example, despite the wide array of practices with English that occurred in teenagers' everyday lives, a closer look at young people's verbal constructions of their literacy and learning experiences revealed a contrast between formal, school-based literacy and learning, which is systematic and structured, and out-of-school literacy and learning which is meaningful and self-relevant (cf. Menezes, 2008: 212). The former accounts for the metalinguistic terminology used by teenagers when describing their learning experiences (e.g., syntax, grammar, vocabulary, knowledge, attention, concentration, studying, lessons) and the concept of foreign language as a set of grammatical and lexical patterns and rules to be mentally processed and internalized (cf. Dufva et al., 2011). The latter is dynamically described in more social terms as an almost automatic and unconscious process as youngsters use the English language to engage in free-time activities motivated by their individual needs and interests (cf. Nikula & Pitkänen-Huhta, 2008; Pitkänen-Huhta & Nikula, 2013; Sundqvist & Sylvén, 2016).

Perhaps more importantly, though, this juxtaposed discussion of the two also revealed learners' underlying perceptions and the values placed on each world: through the systematic use of concepts arising from educational discourse, the school is described – often in a favourable light – as an important place where legitimately the emphasis is on the formal aspects and norms of the English language (e.g., standard language, grammar, tenses, syntax, vocabulary) and where proper English language learning takes place, while the out-of-school – albeit in a rather less positive light – as a pleasurable and exciting world which, however, is frivolous and less valuable. In other words, my young Greek participants appeared to view themselves as text producers and consumers mainly in classroom settings while, similarly, their perception of English literacy and language learning remained largely framed by the dominant understanding of literacy as a traditional, school-based skill and learning as the mastery of content or subject matter (cf. Kalaja et al., 2008; Nikula & Pitkänen-Huhta,

2008). This, on the one hand, might be seen as illustrative of these learners' traditional and narrow conceptions about what defines English language learning and, on the other, as indicative of the increased emphasis placed on formal English language study in the Greek context (cf. Pitkänen-Huhta & Rothoni, 2018: 24, 28).

Similar findings were also reported by Tran (2017), whose study compared Vietnamese and Finnish learners' perceptions of their out-of-school language learning and their choices of their learning activities. Her Vietnamese participants, heavily driven by achievement in school and coming from an exam-oriented schooling system, stressed the importance of formal learning and its role in the development of their proficiency in English. On the other hand, the Finnish learners were more concerned with their own personal goals in foreign language learning. This proves that the education systems that learners find themselves in might have significant impacts on their underlying beliefs about the learning of English and their choices of learning activities including out-of-school learning activities. Similar conclusions, which highlight the importance of ethnographic investigations in uncovering such issues, were reached by Bailly (2011) in her ethnographic study of young students' language learning outside school in France. While there was continuity between school and home in terms of the learning techniques that students reported to use, the ethnographic data illustrated that students also engaged – albeit rather unconsciously – in "lighter" (Darasawang & Reinders, 2010) everyday activities including popular culture and entertainment material in the target language (e.g., blockbuster films, songs, online games), which they did not consider to be "work", but "fun" and "leisure" and very few seemed to use them as part of a conscious learning strategy.

In sum, the ethnographic data might be seen in these cases to connect to the social discourses, structures and values placed on formal education, functioning, on the one hand, as indexes of the importance granted to the formal learning of English in certain societies (e.g., the Greek and the Vietnamese) when compared to others (e.g., the Finnish) and the idea that school provides a "prestigious" kind of literacy, the basic foundation for learning a foreign language upon which all other learning and literacy practices of everyday life rest. On the other hand, the data can be also considered as representative of the underlying mainstream philosophy in language teaching and language acquisition research that learning a foreign language – in most cases English – is a matter of memorizing formal knowledge (particularly of vocabulary or grammar) (cf. Dufva et al., 2011: 110, 114). This is perhaps understandable, given participants' background as students and the emphasis placed in most local contexts on English language study. The sets of ethnographic data are thus important in that they indirectly – albeit quite powerfully – indicate how language, literacy and learning practices (including values and attitudes) are not neutral but always rooted in broader social discourses and how they arise from historical and cultural values of their immediate societies (Pitkänen-Huhta & Rothoni, 2018: 28).

The need for teachers as ethnographers to raise their own and their learners' awareness of learning practices

In terms of formal classroom practice, the implications of current understandings in the field for educators are equally important. Empirical research has shown that teachers view the classroom as central to their students' learning (Reinders & Benson, 2017: 571) and are surprisingly sceptical of the benefits that non-institutional settings offer their students for second/foreign language learning (Grau, 2009:167), or do not utilize this source of knowledge in lessons in school (Olsson, 2011). Indeed, particularly in the case of learning English, teachers often enough think that the knowledge picked up by learners in their everyday life may "corrupt" their repertoire (Eaton, 2010: 18) or view it as illegitimate to be used in class, while both teachers and learners tend to separate classroom English from the forms of English encountered outside school (see, e.g., Grau, 2009; Menegale, 2013; Tran, 2017; Rothoni, 2019).

One way this can be reversed in practice is through teachers' engagement in contextual, small-scale ethnographic or action research (Reinders & Benson, 2017: 564) aimed at mapping their learners' out-of-school learning and literacy practices (Sundqvist & Sylvén, 2016) through sources, such as document collection (e.g., texts that learners produce themselves), informal interviews or group discussions with learners and observation of youth-dominated spaces in the surrounding community (including skate parks, shopping malls, cinemas). This will help educators to gain a more comprehensive view of their learners' learning practices and experiences in different out-of-school contexts. In addition, equally important is that teachers focus on inviting their learners to self-reflect on the ways they use various learning resources across contexts thus raising their awareness of the affordances and possibilities offered by their ways of learning, their identities and repertoires for meaning-making and individual creative expression in the foreign language (Rothoni, 2019: 263). This suggestion is in line with recent arguments expressed by researchers employing ethnographic data in their studies who stress the importance of "bringing the process of informal learning into the conscious foreground of the learners" (Stickler & Emke, 2011: 158). In other words, the challenge for educators is how to engage with young people's "multiple ways of speaking, being and learning" in the foreign language (Pennycook, 2007: 157) and how to place these at the centre of classroom teaching building thus bridges between the classroom and learners' out-of-school worlds (Thorne & Reinhardt, 2008; Reinders & Benson, 2017: 571).

Future directions

One of the arguments that ran throughout this chapter was that, as socially and culturally situated subjects, learners' learning experiences, practices and trajectories are shaped by their underlying beliefs and perceptions as dynamic and situated processes. It seems that ethnographic approaches are best suited for such investigations as they allow insights into life spheres that are generally not easily accessed by language learning researchers (Kuure, 2011: 46) and create a holistic, retrospective portrait of learners' processes of language learning. Undoubtedly, however, while research in this area is growing and our understanding of out-of-school language learning has increased, there is a need for further, extensive ethnographic projects which will explore in greater depth these social aspects of second/foreign language learning and will give much greater attention to learners' experiences in different out-of-school contexts than they are currently given in the field of second/foreign language education (Benson & Reinders, 2011) by pursuing the forms of qualitative and ethnographic data highlighted in this chapter. Such considerations will complement the field's traditionally cognitive concerns, enabling a deeper understanding of language learning and its non-universal, individualistic dimensions (cf. Divita, 2011: 86).

Furthermore, as young people's out-of-school worlds are now to a great extent interactive, multimodal and digitally mediated (cf. Lankshear & Knobel, 2006), it would be important for future ethnographic studies to further investigate the extent to which learners' out-of-school language learning is affected by the fast-changing technological developments and the widespread dissemination of new media (see, e.g., Lai, 2017). More data collected from young learners' multitasking activities in online everyday environments (including observation logs, ethnographic video-recordings capturing participants' activities and interaction, interviews and various types of computer data) would contribute to such attempts to gain a deeper understanding of learners' complex, yet largely undocumented, language learning processes occurring in such environments (Reinders & Benson, 2017: 565). An indicative example of a study moving in this direction is Kuure's (2011) ethnographic case study of a Finnish learner's out-of-school, technology-mediated, multimodal English language learning practices. An important finding, which needs to be taken further in future studies is that online computer games and activities around such games may provide important affordances for foreign language learning, not as an objective as such, but as a means of nurturing social relationships and participating in collaborative problem-solving and networking among peers.

As a final note, researching out-of-school language learning entails multiple methodological implications: getting access to and observing learning processes outside the classroom is particularly challenging. On the one hand, shifting from viewing the learner as disconnected from the social and physical context to the learner as a person-in-context (Ushioda, 2009) requires an imaginative use of qualitative methods. On the other hand, the dual role of the researcher as insider/outsider necessitates continuous engagement with the learning context. In my study (Rothoni, 2019), for example, I could only record incidents of out-of-school learning through my ongoing involvement and participation. Although I attempted to employ the most promising ethnographic tools in this investigation (participant observation, interviews, diaries, visual methods), further empirical research and more sensitive, innovative and sophisticated research tools (e.g., a combination of photo-based methods and focus groups) are needed (Lai, 2017) to accurately detect and describe learners' out-of-school language learning practices. Future ethnographic projects will hopefully contribute to a better understanding of out-of-school language learning both in terms of theory and practice.

Reflection questions

1 What challenges do you think you would face in uncovering your learners' out-of-school learning practices? Think, for example, of the aspects and features of their learning that would be visible and measurable and those that would continue to remain hidden or implicit.
2 Reflecting on your own teaching experience, how would you guide your learners to reflect more on what they do outside school autonomously, how they learn, what kind of activities they accomplish, and what strategies they use?
3 To what extent and in what way would you adapt curriculum/teaching materials to meet the needs of your learners and make sure that they reflect their out-of-school learning practices? What aspect of their learning would you prioritize/set your focus on and why?

Recommended readings

Divita, D. (2011). Becoming multilingual: An ethnographic approach to SLA beyond the classroom. In P. Benson & H. Reinders (Eds.), *Beyond the language classroom: The theory and practice of informal language learning and teaching* (pp. 72–87). London: Palgrave Macmillan.

Although referring to adult learners, this study is important for its ethnographic perspective on the investigation of out-of-school language learning. In her ethnographic study of two Spanish women who arrived in France as refugees from the Spanish Civil War and learnt French largely "naturalistically", Divita makes the point that, in non-institutional settings, "language acquisition" might be better conceived as a process of becoming multilingual that is shaped by experiences of the sociohistorical conditions in which it occurs. Adopting an approach that pays close attention to language data, Divita seeks evidence for this process in the two women's use of code switching.

Kuure, L. (2011). Places for learning: Technology-mediated language learning practices beyond the classroom. In P. Benson & H. Reinders (Eds.), *Beyond the language classroom: The theory and practice of informal language learning and teaching* (pp. 35–46). London: Palgrave Macmillan.

This is a chapter for those who seek a better understanding of what a home-based ethnographic exploration of a learners' out-of-school language learning entails. In her study, Kuure uses Mediated Discourse Analysis to analyse case study data of a Finnish learner's technology-mediated English language learning. Here the setting is both the home and the virtual gaming environments in which the learner spends much of his spare time. Kuure shows how games and the activities around them provide contexts for English language learning, as a means of developing social relationships through collaborative problem-solving and networking among online peers.

Nikula, T., & Pitkänen-Huhta, A. (2008). Using photographs to access stories of learning English. In P. Kalaja, V. Menezes, & A.M. Barcelos (Eds.), *Narratives of learning and teaching EFL* (pp.171–185). Houndmills, Basingstoke: Palgrave.

Readers of this chapter will find interesting the use of photography as an ethnographic tool in the investigation of young Finns' accounts of learning English. The study is part of a larger project on English in Finnish teenagers' everyday literacy and language learning practices. Making use of methods inspired by ethnographic approaches, the focus is on narratives – triggered by photographs – of informal language learning and the contacts between school-based and everyday learning. The analysis provides evidence of teenagers occupying varying positions among discourses of formal and informal learning, suggesting that conceptualizations of learning depend on learners' experiences both within and outside school.

References

Bailly, S. (2011). Teenagers learning languages out of school: What, why and how do they learn? How can school help them? In P. Benson & H. Reinders (Eds.), *Beyond the language classroom: The theory and practice of informal language learning and teaching* (pp. 119–131). London: Palgrave Macmillan.

Barron, B. (2006). Interest and self-sustained learning as catalysts of development: A learning ecologies perspective. *Human Development, 49*, 193–224.

Barton, D. (2012). Ethnographic approaches to literacy research. In *Encyclopaedia of applied linguistics*. Wiley-Blackwell. https://doi.org/10.1002/9781405198431.wbeal0398

Benson, P. (2001). *Teaching and researching autonomy in language learning*. Harlow: Pearson Education.

Benson, P., & Reinders, H. (2011). Introduction. In P. Benson & H. Reinders (Eds.), *Beyond the language classroom: The theory and practice of informal language learning and teaching* (pp. 1–6). London: Palgrave Macmillan.

Best, A.L. (2007). Introduction. In A.L. Best (Ed.), *Representing youth* (pp. 1–36). New York: New York University Press.

Block, D. (2003). *The social turn in second language acquisition*. Washington, DC: Georgetown University Press.

Creswell, J.W. (2007). *Qualitative inquiry and research design: Choosing among five approaches* (2nd ed.). Thousand Oaks: Sage.

Darasawang, P., & Reinders, H. (2010). Encouraging autonomy with an online language support system, *CALL-EJ Online*, 11. Online journal. http://callej.org/journal/11-2/darasawang_reinders.html, date accessed 19 October 2020.

Divita, D. (2011). Becoming multilingual: An ethnographic approach to SLA beyond the classroom. In P. Benson & H. Reinders (Eds.), *Beyond the language classroom: The theory and practice of informal language learning and teaching* (pp.72–87). London: Palgrave Macmillan.

Dufva, H., Suni, M., Aro, M., & Salo, O.P. (2011). Languages as objects of learning: language learning as a case of multilingualism. *Journal of Applied Language Studies, 5*(1), 109–124.

Eaton, S.E. (2010). Formal, non-formal and informal learning: The case of literacy, essential skills and language learning in Canada. Calgary: Eaton International Consulting. Retrieved January 8, 2012 from: http://www.infed.org/archives/etexts/eaton_literacy_languages_and_types_of_learning.pdf

Emond, R. (2005). Ethnographic research methods with children and young people. In S. Greene & D. Hogan (Eds.), *Researching children's experience: Approaches and methods* (pp.123–139). London: Sage.

Geertz, C. (1973). *The interpretation of cultures*. New York: Basic Books.

Grau, M. (2009). Worlds apart? English in German youth cultures and in educational settings. *World Englishes*, 28(2), 160–174.

Hammersley, M., & Atkinson, P. (2007). *Ethnography: Principles in practice* (3rd ed.). London: Routledge.

Heath, S.B., & Street, B.V., with Mills, M. (2008). *On ethnography: Approaches to language and literacy research*. New York: Teachers College Press.

Hogan, D. (2005). Researching 'the child' in developmental psychology. In S. Greene & D. Hogan (Eds.), *Researching children's experiences* (pp. 22–41). London: Sage.

Inozu, J., Sahinkarakas, S., & Yumru, H. (2010). The nature of language learning experiences beyond the classroom and its learning outcomes. *US-China Foreign Language*, 8, 14–21.

Jorgenson, J., & Sullivan, T. (2009). Accessing children's perspectives through participatory photo interviews. *Forum Qualitative Sozialforschung/Forum: Qualitative Social Research*, 11(1), Art. 8, http://nbn-resolving.de/urn:nbn:de:0114-fqs100189.

Kalaja, P., Menezes, V., & Barcelos, A. M. F. (Eds.). (2008). *Narratives of learning and teaching EFL*. Basingstoke: Palgrave Macmillan.

Kalaja, P., Alanen, R., Palviainen, Å., & Dufva, H. (2011). From milk cartons to English roommates: Context and agency in L2 learning beyond the classroom. In P. Benson & H. Reinders (Eds.), *Beyond the language classroom: The theory and practice of informal language learning and teaching* (pp. 47–58). London: Palgrave Macmillan.

Kendrick, M., & McKay, R. (2011). Drawings as an alternative way of understanding young children's constructions of literacy. In K. Pahl & J. Rowsell (Eds.), *Major works in early childhood literacy* (pp. 261–283). Thousand Oaks: Sage.

Kuppens, A.H. (2010). Incidental foreign language acquisition from media exposure. *Learning, Media and Technology*, 35(1), 65–85.

Kuure, L. (2011). Places for learning: Technology-mediated language learning practices beyond the classroom. In P. Benson & H. Reinders (Eds.), *Beyond the language classroom: The theory and practice of informal language learning and teaching* (pp. 35–46). London: Palgrave Macmillan.

Lai, C. (2017). *Autonomous language learning with technology beyond the classroom*. London: Bloomsbury Publishing.

Lankshear, C., & Knobel, M. (2006). *New literacies: Everyday practices and classroom learning*. McGraw Hill: Open University Press

Lankshear, C., & Knobel, M. (2010). DIY media: A contextual background and some contemporary themes. In M. Knobel & C. Lankshear (Eds.), *DIY media: Creating, sharing and learning with new technologies* (pp.1–24). New York: Peter Lang.

Lantolf, J., & Thorne, S. (2006). *Sociocultural theory and the genesis of second language development*. Oxford: Oxford University Press.

Lave, J., & Wenger, E. (1991). *Situated learning. Legitimate peripheral participation*. Cambridge: University of Cambridge Press.

LeCompte, M. D., & Schensul, J. J. (2010). *Designing and conducting ethnographic research: An introduction*. Lanham, MD: Rowman and Littlefield.

Lemish, D. (1985). Soap opera viewing in college: A naturalistic inquiry. *Journal of Broadcasting & Electronic Media*, 29, 275–293.

Linnakylä, A. (2010). *Learning English informally through authentic literacy practices: A case study of Finnish 8th grade students*. Unpublished Pro Gradu Thesis, University of Jyväskylä, Finland.

Livingstone, D.W. (2001). *Adults' informal learning: Definitions, findings, gaps and future research* (NALL Working Paper, No. 21). Toronto: Ontario Institute and University of Toronto Centre for the Study of Education and Work.

Livingstone, S., & Lemish, D. (2001). Doing comparative research with children and young people. In S. Livingstone & M. Bovill (Eds.), *Children and their changing media environment: A European comparative study* (pp.31–50). Mahwah: Lawrence Erlbaum.

Lobe, B., Livingstone, L., & Haddon, L. (2007). *Researching children's experiences online across countries: Issues and problems in methodology*. London: London School of Economics and Political Science.

Mannion, G., & Ivanič, R. (2007). Mapping literacy practice: Theory, methodology, methods. *International Journal of Qualitative Studies in Education, 20*(1), 15–30.

Mason, J. (2002). *Qualitative researching* (2nd ed.). London: Sage

Menegale, M. (2013). A study on knowledge transfer between in and out-of-school language learning. In M. Menegale (Ed.), *Autonomy in language learning: Getting learners actively involved* (pp. 274–306). Canterbury: IATEFL.

Menezes, V. (2008). Multimedia language learning histories. In P. Kalaja, V. Menezes, & A.M.F. Barcelos (Eds.), *Narratives of learning and teaching EFL* (pp. 199–213). Basingstoke: Palgrave.

Morrow, V. (2008). Ethical dilemmas in research with children and young people about their social environments. *Children's Geographies, 6*(1), 49–61.

Nikula, T., & Pitkänen-Huhta, A. (2008). Using photographs to access stories of learning English. In P. Kalaja, V. Menezes, & A.M. Barcelos (Eds.), *Narratives of learning and teaching EFL* (pp.171–185). Houndmills, Basingstoke: Palgrave.

Norton, B., & Toohey, K. (2001). Changing perspectives on good language learners. *TESOL Quarterly, 35*(2), 307–322.

Olsson, E. (2011). *Everything I read on the Internet is in English': On the impact of extramural English on Swedish 16-year-old pupils' writing proficiency*. Unpublished Licentiate thesis, University of Gothenburg, Sweden.

Papen, U. (2005). *Adult literacy as social practice: More than skills*. Abingdon: Routledge.

Pellegrini, A.D. (2004). *Observing children in their natural worlds: A methodological primer* (2nd ed.). Mahwah: Lawrence Erlbaum.

Pennycook, A. (2007). *Global Englishes and transcultural flows*. London: Routledge.

Pitkänen-Huhta, A., & Nikula, T. (2013). Teenagers making sense of their foreign language practices: Individual accounts indexing social discourses. In P. Benson & L. Cooker (Eds.), *The applied linguistic individual: Sociocultural approaches to autonomy, agency and identity* (pp. 104–118). Sheffield: Equinox.

Pitkänen-Huhta, A., & Rothoni, A. (2018). Visual accounts of Finnish and Greek teenagers' perceptions of their multilingual language and literacy practices. *Applied Linguistics Review, 9*(2–3), 333–364.

Purcell-Gates, V. (2004). Ethnographic research. In N.K. Duke & M. Mallette (Eds.), *Literacy research methodologies* (pp. 92–113). New York: Guilford Publications.

Reinders, H., & Benson, P. (2017). Research agenda: Language learning beyond the classroom. *Language Teaching, 50*(4), 561–578.

Riemer, F. (2008). *Addressing ethnographic inquiry*. In S. Lapan & M. Quarteroli (Eds.), *Research essentials* (pp. 203–221). San Francisco: Jossey Bass Publishers.

Rothoni, A. (2019). *Teenagers' everyday literacy practices in English: Beyond the classroom*. Cham: Palgrave Macmillan.

Scollon, R., & Scollon, S. (1981). *Narrative, literacy and face in interethnic communication*. Norwood: Ablex.

Schwarz, M. (2020). *Beyond the walls: A mixed methods study of teenagers' extramural English practices and their vocabulary knowledge*. Unpublished Doctoral Dissertation, University of Vienna, Austria.

Stickler, U., & Emke, M. (2011). Tandem learning in virtual spaces: Supporting non-formal and informal learning in adults. In P. Benson & H. Reinders (Eds.), *Beyond the language classroom: The theory and practice of informal language learning and teaching* (pp. 146–160). London: Palgrave Macmillan.

Street, B.V. (1984). *Literacy in theory and practice*. Cambridge: Cambridge University Press.

Sundqvist, P. (2009). *Extramural English matters: Out-of-school English and its impact on Swedish ninth graders' oral proficiency and vocabulary*. Unpublished Doctoral Dissertation, Karlstad University, Sweden.

Sundqvist, P. (2019). Commercial-off-the-shelf games in the digital wild and L2 learner vocabulary. *Language Learning & Technology, 23*(1), 87–113.

Sundqvist, P., & Sylvén, L.K. (2016). *Extramural English in teaching and learning*. London: Palgrave Macmillan.

Swaffar, J., & Arens, K. (2005). *Remapping the foreign language curriculum: An approach through multiple literacies*. New York: Modern Language Association of America.

Thorne, S. L., & Reinhardt, J. (2008). "Bridging activities", new media literacies, and advanced foreign language proficiency. *CALICO Journal, 25*(3), 558–572.

Tran, M.P. (2017). *Exploring young learners' informal learning of English language: A comparative study on the perspectives of 11–13-year-old pupils in Finland and Vietnam*. Unpublished Master's thesis, University of Eastern Finland, Finland.

Ushioda, E. (2009). A person-in-context relational view of emergent motivation, self and identity. In Z. Dörnyei & E. Ushioda (Eds.), *Motivation, language identity and the L2 self* (pp. 215–228). Bristol: Multilingual Matters.

Veale, A. (2005). Creative methodologies in participatory research with children. In S. Greene & D. Hogan (Eds.), *Researching children's experiences: Methods and approaches* (pp. 253–272). London: Sage.

Willis, P. (1977). *Learning to labour: How working-class kids get working class jobs*. Farnborough: Saxon House.

28
WHEN CLASSROOMS AREN'T AN OPTION
Researching Mobile Language Learning through Disruption

Matt Smith, Howard Scott and John Traxler

Introduction

This chapter has two aims. Firstly, it seeks to survey the research field of language learning during disruptions and crises, such as occupation, the COVID-19 pandemic and other areas of education-in-emergency situations, when working and researching outside the classroom is the only option. Secondly, it discusses the methodological challenges faced by researchers and offers practical suggestions for helping researchers develop effective tools and techniques that are specifically designed to investigate language-learning in mobile contexts and environments, and to do research with individuals, communities and cultures – social and educational – that can be categorised as different and divergent from established mainstream Global Northern contexts. In order to highlight the latter we will describe, as a case study, a current research project in Palestine, based on Erasmus+ work on language learning in Palestine, which involves as a specific aim "innovating pedagogy through technologies". The geopolitical situation in Palestine has a clear impact on students' motivation to learn foreign languages, and this may be true of other crisis contexts.

For the most part, we are understanding 'research' in this context to be empirical and outcome-oriented research, with specific goals and aims in mind following the analysis of what is collected, rather than 'pure' research for its own sake. Following Traxler and Smith (2020, p. 306), we will argue that the "development of co-designed autonomous and sustainable community digital learning spaces on secure methodological foundations that enhance the understanding of authentic community needs, situations, aspirations, experiences and expectations" relies on researchers adopting and adapting methodological approaches on a 'what-works' basis, particularly during emergent crises, such as the COVID-19 pandemic. We will give a brief oversight of some of the methods derived from diverse disciplines that have been found to be effective when working with marginalised communities, in crisis situations, and with hard-to-reach communities and contexts, as each of these can be understood to have ramifications and implications for studying language learning in these disrupted situations.

We draw on research among, or acknowledge that these techniques can be adapted to work with, communities who are disadvantaged by language, power, access to education, infrastructure, security and capacity. Each of these represents a potential barrier, and we try to offer solutions to these. However, we reiterate a point made in a great deal of the literature we have encountered (for a much fuller list, see Traxler & Smith, 2020; Traxler et al., 2020): working with communities (including the most marginalised) is generally the most powerful methodology for generating an accurate understanding of the situations and contexts under study. Researchers should see themselves as collaborating with communities to ensure local voices are heard in policy decisions and local contextual dynamics are considered in any decision-making processes (see, e.g. Brun & Lund, 2010; von Bayeur, 2018; Park, Freeman & Middleton, 2019; Traxler et al., 2020).

Key constructs

Since its inception, Mobile-Assisted Language Learning (MALL), which grew out of both Computer-Assisted Language Learning (CALL) and the larger mobile learning (mLearn) movement, has focussed on access, communication and portability (see, e.g. Kukulska-Hulme & Shield, 2008; Miangah & Nezarat, 2012). Some of the key methods used have been experimentation, game-based learning, and student-oriented and self-learning tools. For a more comprehensive list, see Viberg & Grönlund, 2012, but – as they state – much of the literature is actually more theoretical than methodological, focussing on one of three broad areas: *technological concepts of learning, techno-centered concepts* and *the learning environment* (p. 6).

Friedrich et al. (2012) have positioned mobile learning as a 'mobile complex' where everyday life-worlds become "learning spaces linked to one's media habits, [which] not only provides an ideal application field for mobile devices for learning but in our view makes the use of mobile devices for learning (in informal contexts) inevitable" (2012, p. 12). The ubiquity of technology in certain parts of the globe has reached a point that it is increasingly accurate to describe humanity as living in a postdigital age where the non-human is seamlessly integrated into human existence (see, e.g. Jandrić & Hayes, 2020). Examples of this include algorithms that decide what we want to see on our smartphones, which we are seldom without, and our unthinking use of, and reliance on, technology in education such as interactive whiteboards, the internet and, increasingly, online classrooms.

Such paradigm shifts in capacity and habits of use lead us to ask whether formal learning environments remain the most suitable contexts for learning facilitated in new ways and using still-evolving technologies, or at least whether mobile learning is itself still a relevant term. Wishart (2015) pre-empted this, invoking Sharples' 2007 assertion that mobile learning was about 'being on the move' with a focus on learning outside supported by devices. Mobile learning has changed from Sharples' original conception: as ever, innovations in technology move faster than reflections on human activities with those technologies can be processed or reified.

We argue here that Pachler, Cook and Bachmair's (2009) definition of mobile learning, which focussed on cultural dimensions, multimodality, informal practices and learning, and aspects such as autonomy and agency are culturally situated and still culturally specific, growing out of a Western European mainstream and history, derived from the ambitions and aspirations of the Western European e-learning research community and a political and economic climate that supported small-scale government-funded curiosity-driven theory-laden pilots that bought into the prevalent rhetoric of trickle-down 'innovation'.

However, mobile devices have great potential to bridge the perceived disconnect between informal learning practices and structures imposed by society and culture, exemplified by the facilitation of individual agency through mobile practices, such as the burgeoning use of digital literacies via mass communication methods in the developing world, or 'Global South', as has been researched extensively by the MALL community. Our work with Palestinian Higher Education Institutions (HEIs) is guided by specific principles which can be understood under the umbrella term 'student-centred learning'. The principles draw in social-constructivist practices where teachers introduce ecologies of digital resources (Cochrane, 2014) to support and initiate self-efficacy in learning (cf. 'heutagogy', or 'leading oneself to knowledge' – Hase and Kenyon, 2000), building on more formal transmission models of teaching and learning. The provision of resources supports the agency of individual identity and social interactions, characterised by enhanced ways of communicating, collaborating and increased autonomy. It both seeks and finds an explicit utilisation of mobile devices appropriated for learning. We return to this Palestinian research later, where it will be apparent that, in partnership with our Palestinian colleagues, we sought to utilise mobile technologies to situate individual identity in social and global contexts through the vehicles of language learning and research into the effectiveness of both the learning and the use of the technology to facilitate it.

Key issues

Education-in-emergencies

The World Bank (2016) stated that nearly 2 billion people live in countries that they classify as "affected by conflict or extreme criminal violence" (online). There are some very useful overviews of the field (see, e.g. Burde et al., 2017; Shah, Paulson & Couch, 2020). Burde et al. note that "this field is changing rapidly and world events have expanded attention to education in these contexts in a way that has never before occurred" (2017, p. 620). They also note that education is not always seen as positive in some of the situations; rather it has a complex relationship with conflict, with the potential for divisiveness instead of cohesion; of disadvantage, inequity or diminishment in access to education – which itself can drive conflict; of a reduction in education altogether; and in gender-based inequity. There is clear evidence that older learners suffer most for a variety of reasons (needing to work when family members are killed or away, being called up to fight, damage to school infrastructure) but that there is greater psychological toll on younger learners, and that distance form school impacts significantly on attendance, particularly for girls. Burde et al. dedicate a substantial portion of their article, which is one of our recommended reads, to demonstrating how education is being used to combat these inequalities and to further peace in these regions. Hopefully it is obvious how research, particularly into language learning, can help achieve similar results and allow local people a voice on a wider stage.

Clearly, conducting rigorous research into language learning in environments and contexts afflicted by violence and emergency is not only difficult and sometimes dangerous, but these problems are compounded when the research is done – or at least led – by investigators who are alien to the context under study. We return to this shortly, when looking at language specifically, but there is a strong argument for the decolonisation of research generally (see, e.g. Desai & Potter, 2006; Simonds & Christopher, 2013; Lambert, 2014; Heleta, 2016). As we noted in Traxler & Smith (2020), lessons from West Africa indicate that responders' unfamiliarity with a local culture can undermine emergency response. As Chelsky & Kelly

(2020, online) note, this is because "when people's lives are threatened, they want to hear from those closest to them – those who speak their language".

Research ethics must also be considered. Kruger, Ndebele, & Horn (2014) wrote very articulately about the decolonisation of ethics (i.e. not allowing them to be governed by the dominant Western worldview but to take account of local understanding), and Binns (2006) and Bozalek (2011) are both powerful voices on research project governance. We see both of these as crucial foundations for decolonised research. Brun and Lund (2010) explored including all stakeholders through language.

Returning to the MALL concept of learning environments, we note that to these difficulties must be added the notion that researchers working in areas defined by emergency or conflict must also work within geopolitical realities and contexts that are – charitably – characterised by motion, as alliances, allegiances and needs shift and realign in unprecedented ways. We do not here offer solutions, but recommend that researchers – especially those on the ground – are mindful of these realities.

Digital access

Even leaving aside the so-called digital divide (see, e.g. Ortega, 2017), digital access is a complex issue, involving a tangled skein of necessary problems and problematic necessities including cost, access, infrastructure and culture. We in the global North take access for granted and are outraged when denied it anywhere or for any length of time. Across much of the world, however, access to the web is much more difficult – people need to be able to afford the hardware and the software and even with it they still need the infrastructure to send and receive. Learning beyond the classroom happens, but not everyone has access to mobile devices – or they are the exclusive preserve of (almost always) male heads of households (see, e.g. Mukharya, 2020), so we must move beyond MALL methods alone.

The International Telecommunication Union (2018) have demonstrated that the percentage of internet users had grown from around 15% of the world's population in 2005 to over 50% by December 2018. This seems an enormous success story. In Africa, the balancing act website (balancingact-africa.com) provides more useful statistics but we posit here that it can be easier – and more rigorous – not to try to summarise these but to point out the limitations under which people gain access (e.g. on gender or patriarchal lines), the granularity of coverage (in Africa and elsewhere this may be only along highways and railways, and in resorts and cities), the problem of access to mains electricity and the tendency to talk about South Africa and Kenya as representative which we maintain they are absolutely not – not of the rest of the continent, nor the wider Global South.

So access is never free, and not always uninhibited either. This is even more so in the case of Palestine where Israel controls the spectrum and monitors the traffic.

Learning through crises, disruption and emergency

Rasmussen & Ihlen (2017) note several key points in their comprehensive review of crisis responses. Firstly, they share the definition of crisis as described by Boin et al. (2005, pp. 2–3): "situations where widely shared values are under immediate threat, leading both to demands for prompt action and to uncertainties regarding the full extent and consequences of the event and possible remedies" (in Rasmussen & Ihlen, 2017, p. 2).

They further state that researchers in the fields of risk and crisis management are increasingly conceptualising and describing risk and crisis as "transboundary" (e.g. Falkheimer,

2013; Boin, Rhinard & Ekengren, 2014; Olsson, 2015), meaning that the origins and effects of crises traverse functional, national, and cultural boundaries – as can clearly be seen during the COVID-19 pandemic – and the distinct political and jurisdictional mandates embedded within these bounds, demanding collaboration across nations and fields (e.g. Olsson, 2015), which we here take further to include the need for cooperation among researchers too, collaborating and drawing on one another for their mutual benefit and that of the communities under study – in our case either language communities or language learners. Moving learning beyond the classroom has clear implications for communication, collaboration and cooperation, both for good and for ill: for example, normalising the use of videoconferencing and the maintenance of close relationships between learners and teachers, and for both groups with the research community, but forcing learning to be at the mercy of infrastructure and access. It is also worth noting that merely outside a traditional learning environment does not necessarily mean 'mobile' – for example, communication could be via radio, or learning delivered by television (Bozkurt et al., 2020).

Decolonisation of language

When studying language learning, we must also be aware of the language we use, especially when we are coming from a global North position that Merritt and Bardzell (2011), for example, challenge researchers to "face assumptions, cultural communication, and the potential repercussions in cross-cultural design" (p. 1675), as the creation of "responsible, successful designs and (becoming aware) of inadvertent Western language culture embedded in (research) design" (p. 1675) requires a decolonisation of the language used. Chelsky and Kelly (2020, online) clearly state the "need to be culturally and linguistically appropriate".

This has been an issue for decades – see, for example, Ndemo (2014), who noted that it has become easier for Africans to express themselves in foreign languages as new words, particularly such as those for technological innovations, have not been reflected in local languages. Bennett (2013) goes even further, using the term "epistemicide" to delineate the insidious impact of alien epistemologies, usually Northern ones inherent in language, technology and learning, on indigenous cultures (and cf. the "information imperialism" of Mulder, 2008). Pasch (2015) also warns that the danger of imposing a colonial perspective is particularly acute when looking at language.

Implications: the implications of the current state of the field for (a) theory and (b) practice

Methods for research in crisis situations are discussed in greater detail in the first of our recommended further reading texts, but we give here a quick overview of current methods that you may wish to consider using. Lupton (2020) gives an excellent analysis of current fieldwork methods that are being used during the COVID-19 pandemic, including the use of wearable cameras (cf. Pink, 2015; Fors, Berg & Pink, 2016), online discussion platforms (Chen & Neo, 2019), digital mapping (Martin and & Schuurman, 2020) and live streaming apps, among others. We posit that these ideas are worth experimenting with to support language learning research beyond the classroom. Mukharya (2020, online) is in line with the 'what works' model we described earlier. She describes having to downsize her fieldwork team and relying on methods that she confesses are less effective at connecting with her subjects. While not ideal, she does however note that the use of big data, feedback surveys and simple opinion polls will continue to enable "governments and corporate bodies to… gain key data insights from those at the bottom of the pyramid". Provided language learners can participate in feedback, either virtually or in person, researchers can gain these important perspectives.

Further methods we would think are worthy of consideration when working with language learners include 'simple' tools that can be used across language barriers and literacy barriers such as card-sorts (Rugg & McGeorge, 2005) and Q-methodology (Hunter, 2014; Brown & Rhoades, 2019). These tools help surface understanding or values that might explain survey or questionnaire responses. The various techniques that make up Soft Systems Methods (see, e.g. Bell & Morse, 2013; Walker, Steinfort & Maqsood, 2014) also have considerable potential for adaptation to language learning research, especially among the young or low-literate. Belay, McCrickard and Besufekad (2016) give a useful report from disparate field researchers on working with low-literate participants.

We turn now to a specific example of how we have acted and operated within this field, through a discussion of how we have enacted some of this theory in practice in a large Erasmus+ funded project in Palestine. We have stated elsewhere that, in research and beyond, "the goal for educators will be to include the voices of the learners – and preferably in their own languages, with their own cultural reference points and – in time – their own ecologies and tools" (Traxler et al., 2020, pp. 38–39). Research into learning and teaching beyond the classroom must take place within those over-arching concerns, as we attempted to enact in Palestine.

Palestine's education systems have challenges both familiar and unique. In conversation with our colleagues from the four participating Higher Education Institutions, we recognise that institutional hegemony with little trust and autonomy for tutors and poor funding leaves a dependency on archaic resources; more alarmingly practice is routinely disrupted due to the military occupation under which they exist. Educational practice in HE, even in language learning, is largely situated within the conservative and traditional hierarchic nature of Palestinian society. Our part in the Erasmus+ project sought to improve teachers' capacity for technology-enhanced learning via skills and knowledge, while an over-arching aim was for developing students' English language through eLearning as the "initiative that (can) bridge educational and socio-political gaps" (TEFL-ePAL project, online).

We mentioned earlier that this research sought to understand and then support a philosophical shift desired by tutors, who were looking to augment the didactic approach as the commonest experience of language teaching in Higher Education with more active, social-constructivist student-centred practices, where teachers introduce ecologies of digital resources (Cochrane, 2014) to support and initiate heutagogic self-efficacy in learning, characterised by individual agency, social interaction and increased student autonomy through greater communication and collaboration. Through our work we aspire to promote the use of technologies to facilitate self-determination, yet what has typically arisen illuminates the ways in which learning with technologies have potentially failed to meet the theoretical hypes and hopes that accompanied devised mobile frameworks (e.g. Laurillard, 2007; Sharples, 2007). Rather, technology appears to have reverted to a tool aligned to traditional and conservative educational paradigms. Indeed, if one is looking at the present shape of mobile learning, it has been appropriated by formal education, consumed through a suite of commercial applications and very much gone indoors and returned to the classroom. Cochrane and Antonczak cautioned against this as the retrofit of "traditional pedagogical strategies and pre-existing course activities onto mobile devices and social media" (2014, p. 1). Such approaches have become common and potentially undermine the situating of learning into broader cultural contexts: the convergence of

> Technologies cited:
> Social media; WhatsApp; Edmodo; Facebook; Messenger; Zoom; use of smartphone to create video; Kahoot; virtual learning environments (VLEs)/platforms; the suite of Google apps; BigBlueButton; Padlet

physical and virtual spaces into a 'third space' (Kearney, Schuck and Burden, 2010), which has promising capacity to be the basis for community life and creative action as a nexus of learning between the formal and informal. For mobile learning depends upon a reflexive awareness to contexts which "can be seen as the process of interacting with, and relating to the inner, personal world and the outside, social world" (Pachler, Cook and Bachmair, 2010, p. 7), where "learners can react and respond to their environment and their changing experiences" (Traxler and Wishart, 2011, p. 7).

Methods of mobile learning, operationalised in the Palestinian contexts are outlined below and show certain distinctions across demographics. We note that younger teachers have a readiness and confidence with innovation that enables learning to be assimilated more easily into the everyday Arab culture outside of the institution – in the home, the community and the wider social context. Younger teachers are creative and imaginative with approaches and understand the value of social learning to invigorate and enhance learning activities that they would themselves have experienced in schools and HEIs. Other practitioners are intuitive of the affordances that technologies enable, but appear constrained to facilitate the learning by institution or curriculum.

In forum discussions with Palestinian practitioners, we reviewed the technological practices teachers had introduced into their work. These are outlined below. It must be noted that the project as well as the practices of our teacher partners was disrupted by COVID-19. This would certainly have forced the hand of the educators in Palestine to change the ways they practise as face-to-face physical environments were curtailed and practice pivoted to online. We highlight that the disruption caused by the pandemic in a nation that faces near-constant upheaval in socio-political and geo-political terms may add to the sense of burden and distress of its students and teachers, as well as a precarious view of education generally. It should be noted, for instance, that Palestinians' right to travel, live and work abroad is greatly diminished and we might imagine this has an impact on students' motivation to learn foreign languages, which is the context of teaching and learning explored here. In other instances, stable internet connections or electricity supply are vulnerable, meaning online practice is far from straightforward.

The above list reflects individual responses from the teachers in the forum, rather than collective use. What is immediately apparent is the familiarity of a standard repertoire of homogenous apps and platforms that we also use in education in the UK. These technologies are mainly communication tools for conferencing and messaging that enhance student-teacher and student-student discourse, exchange of knowledge and resources, though within the list we also identify Kahoot, as an assessment tool. Kahoot is one of a plethora of applications and websites that now afford teachers and students the opportunities to build upon what they know and have 'acquired' through some formal learning input with participatory opportunities for 'doing', usually through quizzes and games.

On first impression, it appears to be a list that builds participation, but which still mainly stems from the teacher's direction (as may be initially expected). *WhatsApp*, however, is often

> Pedagogies mentioned:
>   Flipped; project-based; gamification; active learning; inquiry-based learning
>   Learning activities:
>   Interviews; data collection; student presentations; report-writing; keeping up to date with knowledge of tech itself; 'think, pair, share' (dialogic practice within lessons or sessions)

used by students exclusively to form their own community discourses and may typically exclude the teacher presence. As such, it can be regarded as a 'third space', though it is anchored to learning defined on the curriculum and through the teacher's reading and relaying of it.

We also asked respondents in the forum about the new forms of teaching and learning they were enacting in practice, which resulted in the following responses:

Of those, the opportunities for 'outside-the-classroom-learning' are common features. We can see that these are immediately 'student-centred'. They also reflect the pedagogical workshops we held with our partners, where these formats were divulged and explored for the partners' contexts.

What we can see from more detailed responses is a consideration by teachers of planning for participation, despite the impact of COVID-19 which may have impelled some teachers to revert to standard lectures or one-to-many transmission of content knowledge:

> ...I started thinking of creative methods to replicate the typical F2F environment. For example, I designed a breakout activity using Google Meet and had my students complete an in-class activity in groups of 5.

It is interesting to see in this response that the teacher seeks to recreate what they formally do, which reveals a participatory approach to teaching and learning from the outset. There also appears to be both an institutional and individual inclination to be in creative control of resources and teaching and learning, rather than utilise widely available Open Educational Resources (OER).

This data, limited though it is, points to the earlier notion that mobile learning has indeed come to encompass a range of now relatively accustomed tools that are perfectly suited to both in-class Blended use and Apps that provide access from the home to formal settings. The nexus – or Third Space between the formal and informal – remains to be seen and raises further questions, namely: what competencies arise for students from integrating social technologies and pedagogies into the teaching and learning culture? How do these transfer to informal contexts?

We have argued that there is a disjunction between 'mobile learning' within formal education and what happens in 'real life' (cf. Traxler, 2018). This 'mobile learning' paradigm of the 2000s may nevertheless be a good match to Palestinian circumstances and conceptions of education and learning despite its contemporary critics. Furthermore, we would also argue that Palestinian (for which one could substitute Levantine or Middle Eastern and Near Asian [MENA]) societies are documented as very different in terms of risk-taking, hierarchy, individualism, long-termism etc. that makes them authoritarian and conservative so maybe models of 'mobile learning' that reinforce the pedagogic status quo and the status of teachers are no surprise.

A further discussion involves the difference located here between 'self-organised' cooperative learning, which is played out in informal WhatsApp groups, where the teacher presence is sidelined, and the kind of demanding approaches that are required for metacognitive or even heutagogical learning. The former is a useful prop for formal learning endeavours, while the latter requires highly sophisticated actions from students that are not necessarily borne out through social technologies or innate to the practices therein. Given that one aim of heutagogical learning (Blaschke, 2012) is developing a competency for 'learning to learn', it would seem a stretch to claim that social technologies present the nuance needed for metacognitive approaches to learning required during disruptive crises such as COVID-19. However, it is paramount to induce the confidence in students to pursue their own learning through appropriating those social technologies in formal contexts. Much of the formal findings of this project are yet to be published, but some preliminary results can be found in Qaddumi, Bartram & Qashmar (2020).

Future directions: where is the field moving to?

While mobile learning was originally conceived as a 'mobile complex' (Pachler, Cook and Bachmair, 2010) – loosely situated and on the move between the fields of community, culture and existing media – and as informal, as stemming from individual agency, it has arguably become something more static. 'Mobile' has been institutionalised, formalised, commercialised and – arguably – neutralised from its potential to subvert formal ways of doing, being and knowing and taken indoors to the classroom, to support instructional and transmission models of teaching and learning. It could be argued that, on the one hand, the traditional 'mobile' learning research community, including that part working on mobile-assisted language learning, are still largely constrained by the ambitions, theories, findings, methods and settings set out at the turn of the century, and on the other hand, the fact that personal mobiles are ubiquitous, pervasive and universal – nearly – is facilitating people and communities empowered to create and share their own learning, not necessarily 'good' learning but massive nevertheless (Traxler, 2018). This latter includes all manner of mobile language learning opportunities from apps, podcasts, social media groups, online video and downloads. So, in answering, where is the field moving to? The answer is an increasing discrepancy between the traditional 'mobile' learning research community supporting learning within and from the institutions of formal learning and emerging research on, but not for, societies transformed by ever increasing mobility and connectivity (as documented in the research journal *Mobilities*) and the learning that is happening within them. This argument does however assume language is separate and different from technology and from the societies being transformed, however imperceptibly, by those technologies. This is however naïve and we see the nature, survival, ownership, distribution and balance of languages, dialects, idioms and vocabulary and their social context being transformed by mobile technologies and the global and national digital corporations whose interests they serve (Traxler, 2017).

These contrasting depictions of the nature of languages and their learning, and of the contrasting learning environments inside and outside the institutions of formal learning, have dramatically different implications for research methods and research tools. The mainstream mobile learning research community, including language learning within this paradigm, continues to draw on its heritage and traditions based within, for example, cognitive psychology, computer technology, and within positivist science and the edtech industry, while the emerging but massively under-researched topic of the dynamics of learning, language, digital technology and societal change has not yet acquired an agreed and trust portfolio of research tools and research methods. This is unfinished business. In fact it is almost un-started business.

Reflection questions

1. How will you conduct LBC research in areas defined by disruption, be that conflict, emergency or crisis, manmade or natural? How will you keep yourselves, your research teams and your participants as safe as possible – how will you mitigate risk?
2. Is there a distinction between slow onset crises (climate change, pandemics, economic degradation) and sudden ones (floods, earthquakes, war)? Or localised and globalised? What do the responses need to be from LBC researchers? What is our place in this? Part of the response, or mere observers?
3. In the light of our concluding discussion, how do you feel learning beyond the classroom is reflective of the needs of students in emergency and/or crisis situations, as it can be seen to be rather less mobile than originally intended and visualised? The classroom has been rendered largely superfluous in the current disruption. As an alternative space, in what ways can 'mobile' circumvent the reproductions of inequality that classrooms manifest by creating new environments and ways of being and doing?

Recommended readings

Traxler, J., & Smith, M. (2020) Data for development: Shifting research methodologies for Covid-19. *Journal of Learning for Development*, 7(3), 306–325.
  This immediate and current text has formed the basis for some of the discussions in this chapter and describes in much greater detail and with a wider literature base our understanding of the needed move from 'traditional' research methodologies (what we call in the book "the usual suspects") to a broader range of methodological approaches using a simple 'what-works' attitude in situations of disruption, emergency and crisis, such as that created by the COVID-19 pandemic. While this text is necessarily broader than language learning only, many of the research strategies discussed, including those using mobile technologies, work well with communities at the margins, many of whom see language learning as a crucial way out, as with the Palestinian project we describe in the later section of this chapter.

Burde, D., Kapit, A., Wahl, R. L., Guven, O., & Skarpeteig, M. I. (2017). Education in emergencies: A review of theory and research. *Review of Educational Research*, 87(3), 619–658.
  We drew on this in our section on Education-in-emergencies. It gives a useful overview of the field, and describes in much greater detail than we could here many of the issues that educationalists and students face, from famine to war, and gives clear insights into how education can be, and is being, used to combat these issues. It further details how research can be effected in such situations. As in our first selection, it will be for language researchers to sift through to work out what might work for them in the field.

Traxler, J., Smith, M., Scott, H., & Hayes, S. (2020). *Learning through the crisis: Helping decision-makers around the world use digital technology to combat the educational challenges produced by the current COVID-19 pandemic.* Retrieved from https://docs.edtechhub.org/lib/CD9IAPFX
  This wide-reaching review was funded by the EdTech Hub, which at the time was part of the UK's Department for International Development. In it, we drew on research from across the globe with two key aims: we sought out digital ideas that were aimed at maintaining the continuity of education systems around the world that had been affected by the COVID-19 pandemic, and second that had the potential to stop existing or prospective disadvantages being further intensified or exacerbated by COVID-19 or the responses to it. We have drawn on many of the ideas we discovered in writing this chapter.

References

Belay, E. G., McCrickard, D. S., & Besufekad, S. A. (2016, November). Designing mobile interaction for low-literacy (D-MILL). In *Proceedings of the first African conference on human computer interaction* (pp. 251–255).

Bell, S., & Morse, S. (2013). How people use rich pictures to help them think and act. *Systemic Practice and Action Research, 26*(4), 331–348.

Bennett, K. (2013). English as a lingua franca in academia: Combating epistemicide through translator training. *The interpreter and translator trainer, 7*(2), 169–193. https://doi.org/10.1080/13556509.2013.10798850

Binns, T. (2006). Doing fieldwork in developing countries: Planning and logistics. In V. Desai., & R. B. Potter. (Eds.), *Doing development research*. Newbury Park, CA: Sage Publications.

Blaschke, L. M. (2012). Heutagogy and lifelong learning: A review of heutagogical practice and self-determined learning. *The International Review of Research in Open and Distance Learning, 13*(1), 56–71

Boin, A., Hart, P., Stern, E., & Sundelius, B. (2005). *The politics of crisis management: Public leadership under pressure*. Beverly Hills, CA: Sage.

Boin, A., Rhinard, M., & Ekengren, M. (2014). Managing transboundary crises: The emergence of European Union capacity. *Journal of Contingencies and Crisis Management, 22*(3), 131–142.

Bozalek, V. (2011). Acknowledging privilege through encounters with difference: Participatory Learning and Action techniques for decolonising methodologies in Southern contexts. *International Journal of Social Research Methodology, 14*(6), 469–484.

Bozkurt, A., Jung, I., Xiao, J., Vladimirschi, V., Schuwer, R., Egorov, G., Lambert, S. R., Al-Freih, M., Pete, J., Olcott, Jr., D. Rodes, V., Aranciaga, I., Bali, M., Alvarez, Jr., A. V., Roberts, J., Pazurek, A., Raffaghelli, J. E., Panagiotou, N., de Coëtlogon, P., Shahadu, S., Brown, M., Asino, T. I. Tumwesige, J., Ramírez Reyes, T., Barrios Ipenza, E., Ossiannilsson, E., Bond, M., Belhamel, K., Irvine, V., Sharma, R. C., Adam, T., Janssen, B., Sklyarova, T., Olcott, N. Ambrosino, A., Lazou, C., Mocquet, B., Mano, M., & Paskevicius, M. (2020). A global outlook to the interruption of education due to COVID-19 pandemic: Navigating in a time of uncertainty and crisis. *Asian Journal of Distance Education, 15*(1), 1–126. https://doi.org/10.5281/zenodo.3878572

Brown, Z., & Rhoades, G. (2019). Q methodology. In Z. Brown & H. Perkins (Eds.), *Using innovative methods in early years research: Beyond the conventional*. London: Routledge.

Brun, C., & Lund, R. (2010). Real-time research: Decolonising research practices–or just another spectacle of researcher–practitioner collaboration? *Development in Practice, 20*(7), 812–826.

Burde, D., Kapit, A., Wahl, R. L., Guven, O., & Skarpeteig, M. I. (2017). Education in emergencies: A review of theory and research. *Review of Educational Research, 87*(3), 619–658.

Chelsky, J., & Kelly, L. (2020). *Bowling in the dark: Monitoring and evaluation during COVID-19 (Coronavirus)*. https://ieg.worldbankgroup.org/blog/mande-covid19

Chen, J., & Neo, P. (2019). Texting the waters: An assessment of focus groups conducted via the WhatsApp smartphone messaging application. *Methodological Innovations, 12*(3). https://journals.sagepub.com/doi/full/10.1177/2059799119884276

Cochrane, T. D. (2014). Critical success factors for transforming pedagogy with mobile Web 2.0. *British Journal of Educational Technology, 45*(1), 65–82.

Cochrane, T., & Antonczak, L. (2014). Implementing a mobile social media framework for designing creative pedagogies, *Social Sciences, 3*(3), 359377.

Desai, V., & Potter, R. (Eds.) (2006). *Doing development research*. Newbury Park, CA: Sage Publications.

Falkheimer, J. (2013). Transboundary and cultural crisis communication. In A. Thießen (Ed.), *Handbuch Krisenmanagement*. Wiesbaden: Springer Fachmedien Wiesbaden.

Fors, V., Berg, M., & Pink, S. (2016). Capturing the ordinary. Imagining the user in designing and using automatic photographic lifelogging technologies. In S. Selke (Ed.), *Lifelogging: Theoretical approaches and case studies about self-tracking*. New York: Springer VS.

Friedrich, K., Ranieri, M., Pachler, N., & de Theux, P. (2012). *The "My Mobile" Handbook. Guidelines and scenarios for mobile learning in adult education*. Brussels: Media Animation.

Hase, S., & Kenyon, C. (2000). From andragogy to heutagogy. *ultiBASE In-Site*.

Heleta, S. (2016). Decolonisation of higher education: Dismantling epistemic violence and Eurocentrism in South Africa. *Transformation in Higher Education, 1*(1), a9.

Hunter, W. C. (2014). Performing culture at indigenous culture parks in Taiwan: Using Q method to identify the performers' subjectivities. *Tourism Management, 42*, 294–304.

International Telecommunications Union (2018). *ITU statistics show more than half the world is now using the internet.* https://news.itu.int/itu-statistics-leaving-no-one-offline/

Jandrić, P., & Hayes, S. (2020). Postdigital we-learn. *Studies in Philosophy and Education, 39*, 285–297. https://doi.org/10.1007/s11217-020-09711-2

Kearney, M., Schuck, S., & Burden, K. (2010). Locating mobile learning in the third space. In *Proceedings of mlearn2010: 10th world conference on mobile and contextual learning* (pp. 108–115). Valetta: University of Malta.

Kruger, M., Ndebele, P., & Horn, L. (2014). *Research ethics in Africa: A resource for research ethics committees.* Stellenbosch, SA: SUN MeDIA.

Kukulska-Hulme, A. and Shield, L. (2008). An overview of mobile assisted language learning: From content delivery to supported collaboration and interaction. *ReCALL, 20*(3), 271–289. http://oro.open.ac.uk/11617/6/11617.pdf

Lambert, L. (2014). Spaces between us: Queer settler colonialism and indigenous decolonization. *Tribal College, 25*(4), 48.

Laurillard, D. (2007). Pedagogical forms of mobile learning: framing research questions in In: Pachler, N. (Ed.), *Mobile learning: towards a research agenda.* https://discovery.ucl.ac.uk/id/eprint/10000627/1/Mobile_C6_Laurillard.pdf

Lupton, D. (Ed.). (2020). Doing fieldwork in a pandemic (crowd-sourced document). https://docs.google.com/document/d/1clGjGABB2h2qbduTgfqribHmog9B6P0NvMgVuiHZCl8/edit?ts=5e88ae0a#

Martin, M. E., & Schuurman, N. (2020). Social media big data acquisition and analysis for qualitative giscience: Challenges and opportunities. *Annals of the American Association of Geographers, 110*(5), 1335–1352. https://doi.org/10.1080/24694452.2019.1696664

Merritt, S., & Bardzell, S. (2011). Postcolonial language and culture theory for HCI4D. In *CHI'11 Extended Abstracts on Human Factors in Computing Systems*, pp. 1675–1680.

Miangah, T. M., & Nezarat, A. (2012). Mobile-assisted language learning. *International Journal of Distributed and Parallel Systems, 3*(1), 309. https://citeseerx.ist.psu.edu/viewdoc/download?doi=10.1.1.1066.5613&rep=rep1&type=pdf

Mukharya, P. (2020). *Data collection, research and evaluation services across India during COVID-19.* https://blogs.lse.ac.uk/southasia/2020/05/06/data-collection-research-and-evaluation-services-across-india-during-covid-19/

Mulder, J. (2008). *Knowledge dissemination in Sub-Saharan Africa: What role for open educational resources (OER).* Amsterdam: University of Amsterdam, 14.

Ndemo, B. (2014). Is modernity destroying African education? *The eLearning Africa Report*, 8–9.

Olsson, E.-K. (2015). Transboundary crisis networks: The challenge of coordination in the face of global threats. *Risk Management, 17*(2), 91–108.

Ortega, L. (2017). New CALL-SLA research interfaces for the 21st century: Towards equitable multilingualism. *CALICO Journal, 34*(3), 285–316. https://doi.org/ 10.1558/cj.33855

Pachler, N., Bachmair, B., & Cook, J. (2009). *Mobile learning: Structures, agency, practices.* Springer Science & Business Media.

Park, S. Freeman, J., & Middleton, C. (2019). Intersections between connectivity and digital inclusion in rural communities. *Communication Research and Practice, 5*(2), 139–155. https://doi.org/10.1080/22041451.2019.1601493

Pasch, T. J. (2015). Towards the enhancement of Arctic digital industries:'Translating'cultural content to new media platforms. *Jostrans, the Journal of Specialized Translations, 24*,187–213. https://www.researchgate.net/publication/291696761

Pink, S. (2015). Going forward through the world: Thinking about first-person perspective digital ethnography between theoretical scholarship and applied practice. *Integrative Psychological and Behavioral Science, 49*(2), 239–252.

Qaddumi, H., Bartram, B., & Qashmar, A.L. (2020). Evaluating the impact of ICT on teaching and learning: A study of Palestinian students' and teachers' perceptions. *Education and Information Technologies.* https://doi.org/10.1007/s10639-020-10339-5

Rasmussen, J., & Ihlen, Ø. (2017). Risk, crisis, and social media: A systematic review of seven years' research. *Nordicom Review, 38*(2), 1–17. https://doi.org/10.1515/nor-2017-0393

Rugg, G., & McGeorge, P. (2005). The sorting techniques: A tutorial paper on card sorts, picture sorts and item sorts. *Expert Systems, 22*(3), 94–107.

Shah, R., Paulson, J., & Couch, D. (2020). The rise of resilience in education in emergencies. *Journal of Intervention and Statebuilding, 14*(3), 303–326.

Sharples, M., Taylor, J., & Vavoula, G. (2007). A theory of learning for the mobile age. In R. Andrews & C. Haythornthwaite (Eds.), *The SAGE handbook of e-learning research* (pp. 221–224). London: Sage.

Simonds, V. W., & Christopher, S. (2013). Adapting Western research methods to indigenous ways of knowing. *American Journal of Public Health, 103*(12), 2185–2192.

Smith, M., & Gurton, P. (2020). Flipping the classroom in teacher education. In Z. Walker D. Tan, & N. Koh (Eds.), *Flipped classrooms with diverse learners*. Springer Texts in Education. Singapore: Springer. https://doi.org/10.1007/978-981-15-4171-1_13

Traxler, J. (2017). Learning with Mobiles in developing countries –technology, language and literacy. *International Journal of Mobile & Blended Learning, 9*(2), 1–15.

Traxler, J. (2018). Learning with mobiles in the digital age. *Pedagogika, Special Monothematic Issue: Education Futures for the Digital Age: Theory and Practice, 68*(3), 293–310.

Traxler, J., & Smith, M. (2020). Data for development: shifting research methodologies for Covid-19. *Journal of Learning for Development, 7*(3), 306–325.

Traxler, J., & Wishart, J. (Eds.) (2011). *Making mobile learning work: Case studies of practice*. Bristol: ESCalate.

Traxler, J., Smith, M., Scott, H., & Hayes, S. (2020). Learning through the crisis: Helping decision-makers around the world use digital technology to combat the educational challenges produced by the current COVID-19 pandemic. Retrieved from https://docs.edtechhub.org/lib/CD9IAPFX

Viberg, O., & Grönlund, Å. (2012). Mobile assisted language learning: A literature review. In *11th world conference on mobile and contextual learning*. https://www.diva-portal.org/smash/get/diva2:549644/REFERENCES01

von Bayeur, S. L. (2018). "Thinking Outside the Camp": Education solutions for Syrian refugees in Jordan. *Ethnographic Praxis in Industry Conference Proceedings*, ISSN 1559–8918, https://doi.org/10.1111/1559-8918.2017.01163

Walker, D., Steinfort, P., & Maqsood, T. (2014). Stakeholder voices through rich pictures. *International Journal of Managing Projects in Business, 7*(3), 342–361.

Walker, Z., Tan, D., & Koh, N. (Eds) (2020). *Flipped classrooms with diverse learners*. Springer Texts in Education. Singapore: Springer. https://doi.org/10.1007/978-981-15-4171-1_13

Wishart, J. (2015, October). Assimilate or accommodate? The need to rethink current use of the term 'mobile learning'. In *International conference on mobile and contextual learning* (pp. 229–238). Cham: Springer.

World Bank. (2016). *Fragility, conflict, and violence. Overview*. Retrieved from www.worldbank.org/en/topic/fragilityconflictviolence/overview

29
BRINGING BEYOND INTO THE L2 CLASSROOM

On Video Ethnography and the 'Wild' In-class Use of Smartphones

Peter Wikström and Marie Nilsberth

Introduction

Just as everyday social life increasingly plays out in, around, and surrounded by digital and online technologies, so too does language learning. Mobile and always-online devices – most obviously, the smartphone – are an increasingly ubiquitous presence in the backpacks and lockers, if not pockets and hands, of students. Therefore, digitally mediated language learning beyond the classroom, for instance, in the guise of extensive exposure to and spontaneous opportunities to make use of an L2, can also find its way into the classroom. This chapter concerns the topic of young people's incidental or informal language learning opportunities as they engage in smartphone-mediated, self-initiated activity. It does so through the lens of the conceptual notion of the *digital wilds* (Sauro & Zourou, 2019), and in terms of the potential such activity may have for *rewilding* (Little & Thorne, 2017; Thorne, 2015) L2 language education. Most importantly, we focus on how to approach researching this topic in an empirically grounded way through the use of video ethnographic methods.

In what follows, we briefly introduce the key concepts of *digital wilds* and *rewilding*, map a context of the increased presence of personal mobile devices in the lives of school-aged learners, and discuss the video ethnographic approach to studying learning in the classroom and beyond. After this, we focus on an empirical example from an L2 classroom to illustrate how a particular implementation of video ethnographic methodology makes it possible to study the rewilding potential of the smartphone. Finally, we discuss what we take to be the broader implications of applying video ethnographic methods to this topic area, making some suggestions for future directions.

Key concepts: the digital wilds and rewilding

Beyond e-learning and related perspectives, increasingly scholarly attention is being paid to the informal or incidental learning potential of digital technologies, including research on social media, mobile devices, and digital games. A particularly promising avenue for research into the role of digital artifacts in language learning beyond the classroom comes in the form of the notion of the *digital wilds*. In the introduction to a special issue on computer-assisted language learning in the digital wilds, Sauro and Zourou (2019, p. 1) outline a research agenda focusing on the possibilities afforded by digital artifacts, as well as to the increasingly natural and fluid digitally assisted human interaction, which we consider crucial in enabling spontaneous, user-driven, bottom-up practices that support learning.

Importantly, this notion of digital wilds highlights contexts beyond the classroom, where the use of digital technologies is driven by non-institutional agendas, such as personal interest or peer-group engagement, and integrated into activities that are intrinsically motivated and personally meaningful to the actors (e.g., Richards, 2015). As the present handbook shows, a wide range of issues are addressed by researchers focused on learning beyond the classroom. One central issue is that of learner autonomy (Lai, 2017; Reinders & White, 2016), and of how informal learning happens through – and how formal learning might potentially draw on – authentic engagement in existing communities of practice or affinity spaces (Gee, 2004), popular culture, fandom spaces, and the like (Chik, 2015; Sauro et al., 2020).

The literature on learning in the digital wilds specifically raises the question of how the power of such learning could be harnessed in formal learning contexts without losing the very thing that makes it powerful – its wildness. Notably, Zourou (2019, p. 374) has critically examined how technologies are at risk of being "amed" to fit the institutional agenda of the classroom, leading to "unreal learner practices" (Sauro & Zourou, 2019, p. 1). Here the notion of "rewilding" comes in, as Thorne (2015, see also Little & Thorne, 2017) employs this notion to call for a kind of structured unpredictability in resistance to the tendency of educational institutions to tame unpredictable elements and enmesh opportunities for learner agency and transformation in the predictable routines of the "traditional" classroom. As Sauro and Zourou (2019, p. 2) note, "the word wild emphasizes the dynamic, unpredictable, erratic character of technologies, especially those not designed for learning purposes, and wants against a pedagogical use in a way that overcontrols this wilderness." The complex and dynamic quality of naturalistic learning in a digital and connected landscape is both a challenge and an opportunity – not least for L2 teachers and learners, but also for researchers in this field.

The notion of the digital wilds is a fresh contribution to the plethora of terms and frameworks employed in research on L2 learning that does not center formal instructed classroom learning as the norm. The notion of rewilding even more so calls for further development. In this chapter, we wish to contribute to the development of a scholarly approach to a digital rewilding of L2 learning by focusing on the pressing consequences of the omnipresence of always-online digital devices such as smartphones: the personally and socially meaningful digitally mediated activities that learners are engaging in beyond the classroom often also follow them into the classroom.

Key issues

In this section, we highlight the two central key issues raised by this chapter for researching L2 learning beyond the classroom, namely the increased presence of personal mobile devices in classroom spaces and the methodological issue of approaching this topic through video ethnography.

Personal mobile devices in the classroom

It is of course nothing new that students engage in "off-task" social activities in the classroom, even during class. However, connected personal mobile devices such as the smartphone open yet another, and a different kind of, window to the world outside the classroom. In Ott's (2017, p. 221) words, "the use of the mobile phone in school opens a boundary space between school work and leisure activities." Via mobile devices, students in the classroom can stay connected in real time to family, friends, communities, and platforms – in short, to their extramural lives. This could pose challenges for the extant educational order, but also opens up opportunities for rethinking that order (Godwin-Jones, 2018, 2020), and expand the restricted range of affordances for learning available inside the classroom (Richards, 2015). In short, connected personal digital devices in classrooms offer a rewilding potential, which should be of interest for researchers in the field to capture and analyze.

The context with which we are most familiar ourselves is that of Sweden, a highly digitalized society. Swedish teenagers and young adults are especially connected, with personal smartphone ownership being almost ubiquitous (Statens Medieråd, 2019, p. 21). Below, we focus especially on this context, all the while recognizing that the development of digitalization is unequal across the globe, despite an overall trend toward increasing online connectedness, and increasing global rates of personal smart device ownership (e.g., O'Dea, 2020; Silver, 2019).

In Sweden, as in many places, digitalization policies have led to massive investments in digital technologies like personal laptops or tablets to be used by students for schoolwork (Player-Koro & Tallvid, 2015). Simultaneously, classrooms have been connected from within via the students' own smartphones, frequently used for both on- and off-task purposes during lessons (Olin-Scheller et al., 2020; Sahlström, Tanner & Olin-Scheller, 2019). Students today are more or less constantly connected through different devices, providing resources for a broad range of interactional purposes and challenging the formal boundaries of the classroom. This development has provided young people with new possibilities to connect to or create self-controlled extramural social spaces also during their time in school, which has been shown to change the participation frameworks of classrooms toward personalization and differentiation (Sahlström et al., 2019). In addition, research in the field of digital discourse and sociolinguistics has pointed out how the online/offline distinction itself has increasingly become blurred, as individuals move seamlessly between face-to-face interaction and digital spaces in their everyday social lives (Bolander & Locher, 2020).

Whereas personal computers for students have been seen as important for school development, smartphones have been seen primarily as a disturbance (Ott, 2017). In public political debate in many countries there have been calls for banning phones in classrooms as they have mainly been regarded as disruptive. However, research shows a divided picture. While some have focused on correlations between phone bans and decreasing student results (e.g., Kessel et al., 2019), others point out advantages from an e-learning perspective (Kuznekoff & Titsworth, 2013). Students' use of phones is often coordinated with official classroom interaction during "in-between spaces" in teaching (Olin-Scheller et al., 2020). Further, it is possible for students to participate in screen-mediated interactions without diminishing the interactional space of the teacher (Sahlström et al., 2019). Further, personal phones offer students agency and opportunities to take their own initiatives during school-work (Asplund, Olin-Scheller, & Tanner, 2018). However, from the perspective of formal teaching and learning, these initiatives are often performed "under the teacher's radar" (ibid.).

The picture that emerges from previous research on students' use of mobile devices is scattered and gives no easy answers. Depending on perspective, smartphones and other devices could be seen either as a distraction and a challenge to teaching or as a powerful resource for learner autonomy and exploration. There is clearly a need for more knowledge about language and learning in the connected classroom, and in line with Barton and Lee (2013), we think that the most interesting starting point for further examination is to start in the lives of the participants and the social practices they engage with, in order to rethink from a non-normative stance what the digitally mediated language practices mean to them. This leads us to an ethnographic point of departure, where we turn to video- and screen capture methods, which we consider to be a methodological key issue for research in this area.

Video ethnography in classrooms

A video ethnographic approach allows the researcher to build an empirical account of young people's self-initiated learning activities involving digitally mediated resources. Importantly, it allows this from an emic perspective, that is, with a grounding in the endogenous practices, perspectives, and understandings of the participants. To distinguish video-use in ethnographic studies from, for example, analysis of professionally produced videos or video-analysis based on quantitative coding, Knoblauch and Schnettler (2012) suggests "videography" (p. 349) as a useful notion to describe video analytic work based on audiovisual recordings from the field taking the ethnographic dimension into account methodologically. This includes both a systematic account of actors' and researchers' subjectivity as well as the relevance of context knowledge. The methods we suggest in this chapter are very much in line with this, as we draw on ethnomethodological understandings to systematically analyze video recordings of students' social interaction in language learning activities.

The ethnographic approach means taking an emic perspective and engage in concrete research activities 'from within' to explore a broader culture (Knoblauch & Schnettler, 2012). Here, we specifically focus on how this also involves using video recordings that enable the researcher to return to the data through repeated watching of events and how analysis of how these are constituted in social interaction (Luff & Heath, 2012). As a result of a rapid technological development, video has become ubiquitous in social research on human behavior and interaction (for a brief history of video in social research, see Erickson, 2011). For classroom ethnographic research, easy lightweight video-cameras, wireless microphones and small head-mounted action cameras has made it easier to document the complex multi-party interaction of classrooms from different angles and with different magnification (see Blikstad-Balas, 2017; Maltese et al., 2016; Rusk et al., 2017). As social interaction in classrooms today also to a large extent is screen-mediated, there has also been a development of video methods to study interaction via digital platforms (Melander-Bowden & Svahn, 2020). Additionally, the projects described in this chapter are examples of methodological development, where we have used methods to record students' screen-mediated interaction and activities to study how this is coordinated with face-to-face interaction in the physical classroom.

However, there are several challenges that have to be considered when doing video studies in classrooms, such as challenges related to selection, analysis, technology, and ethics (Derry et al., 2010). Mondada (2006) proposes a "praxeological approach… focusing on the way in which videos are locally produced by social scientists" (p.1). The different choices that the researcher makes in relation to how cameras are set up, camera angles, movements and anticipation of courses of action and how participants interact with the camera are some of the crucial aspects that have to be taken into consideration. Different choices of camera-angles limit what kinds of analysis will be possible to carry out, where, for example, roving cameras that try to follow courses of events often make systematic analysis difficult (Luff and Heath, 2012). Blikstad-Balas (2017) points out challenges related to contextualization, and the balance of going close enough with the camera to capture details in actions and texts without losing sight of the surrounding framing of the action. Rusk et al. (2017) specifically problematizes different approaches to studying learning in interaction from an emic perspective, and discerns three main approaches that in different ways will project the subsequent analysis. A *setting-centered approach*, primarily focusing on aspects of classroom interaction, will generate results on the affordances for learning and the social organization and how classroom interaction is structured. A *participant-centered* approach can provide evidence of longitudinality of learning and the development from one participants' perspective, while *content-centered* studies capture interactional practices linked to a specific learning content or practice.

To make our methodological suggestions more concrete, this chapter draws on experiences from two parallel projects in Sweden and Finland studying upper secondary students' use of smartphones in classrooms.[1] Wi-Fi technology was used to mirror the screens of focus students' smartphones (one or two focus students per recording), casting the screen onto a researcher's laptop where it was recorded. These screen-recordings were then compiled with simultaneous classroom video recordings from different angles, including at least one camera actively operated by one researcher, whose task was to monitor whatever artifacts the focus students oriented to in their interaction. The design of the video-data in our project reflects an ambition to grasp all three of the approaches discussed above – *setting-centered*, *participant-centered*, and *content-centered*. This makes for an intense research activity that may require the presence of more than one researcher to continuously handle the instruments with reflexivity in relation to the overarching purpose of following the students' use of digital resources in classroom interaction. In total, the field work of the Swedish project that we mainly draw on in this chapter resulted in 70 hours of recordings, from eight classrooms involving 25 different focus students. Recordings cover several different school subjects, but for the purpose of this chapter we focus on examples from L2 English classrooms.

Doing video ethnographic research like this involves methods that come very close to the research participants' personal sphere, both in the physical and the digital space, and there is an obvious risk that this is experienced as intrusive (ref. to Chapter 21 on research ethics). Another ethical consideration concerns how participants as well as the researchers are able to overview the full ethical consequences of using data from the internet. Researchers within the AoIR (Association of Internet Researchers) point out some tensions in this kind of research (Markham & Buchanan, 2012), ultimately recommending a case-based and process-focused approach to address and resolve the ethical issues that arise in each stage of the process. In the project described here, ethical considerations have been an integrated part of the research process in a continuous dialog about the recordings, what they focus on and for what purposes they could be used. The methods were carefully introduced to the students, who were also instructed in how to disable the mirroring whenever they wished to. Thus, processes of informed consent can be seen as a continuous process in mutual dialog.

Describing the process of selecting short pieces of data from a large dataset, Blikstad-Balas (2017) discusses the risk of "magnification of events" (2017, p. 516) referring to a paradox that while a strength of video analysis is the opportunity to do repeated, detailed analysis of a certain episode there is a risk that its representativity in relation to the dataset as a whole is lost. This calls for a need for systematic accounts of how selected examples in qualitative analysis relates to patterns in data as a whole, she argues. A first coding generating an overview of the data can help the researcher to identify general patterns but also to find the unusual or deviant cases that are just as important in qualitative analysis. A first coding then provides a basis for selection of cases for further qualitative analysis. In the following section, we continue by illustrating these principles through a more in-depth discussion of observations from our own project, describing the steps of our analysis of the digitally mediated rewilding practices in our dataset.

Implications

In this section, we demonstrate potential research implications of a video ethnographic approach to the topic area of personal connected mobile device. We do this by exemplifying a range of what we call "rewilding potential" evident from our own work with a video ethnographic classroom dataset and a closer look at a specific empirical example from an L2 classroom.

A range of rewilding potential on display in a video ethnographic dataset

For the specific purpose of this chapter, we returned to our data overview in order to investigate how students in language classrooms participated in activities with what we considered to have a rewilding potential in the sense that they oriented to learning activities with a high degree of learner agency and unpredictable elements in contrast to the routines of the traditional classroom (Little & Thorne, 2017). Activities including different mobile devices were specifically focused on in the analysis. In this initial analysis we found several examples of more or less 'wild' learning activities as they varied in terms of how they were initiated and by whom (i.e., student-initiated vs. teacher-initiated) and to what extent the content were related to or conducted in adherence to formal or instructed teaching and tasks in the classroom. We could thus describe a range in terms of Benson's (2011) factors of location, formality, pedagogy, and locus of control, where, in our case, the location is always the classroom, but the other factors are variable. Hence, the different examples of activities with a rewilding potential could not be given one unified definition, but could more be understood as forming a broad range of activities that manifest 'wildness' to different degrees. For reasons of space, we will not go into depth with all different examples but more give an overview of some specific nodes of interest in relation to rewilding in the classroom that we understand as forming a kind of range of rewilding practices.

Personal interest-driven, student-initiated

At one end of the range, we discovered how many students in the language classrooms used smartphones and laptops to engage in personal interests without an obvious connection to any assigned task, like, for example, reading blogs about fashion or yoga, watching YouTube-clips of artists or films, reading about wild-life animals, or looking for aesthetic inspiration for creating own works of art. These activities were often recurring throughout lessons or across multiple lessons, as a specific student with an interest in, for example, fashion blogs would return to such content whenever an opportunity presented itself. Students used the micro-pauses in schoolwork that occur in the 'in-between spaces' of teaching

Figure 29.1 A student watching YouTube during a break

(Olin-Scheller et al., 2020), for example, while waiting for further instructions or help from the teacher. Figure 29.1, for example, shows one of the focus students using a break during a group assignment to watch a YouTube video of a Japanese figure skater on her laptop. During several in-between spaces, this student would make image searches for Japanese figure skaters and for Japanese winter landscapes, and read online Manga comics on her smartphone, cultivating an interest in Japanese culture through both English-language and Japanese-language online sources. She could also sometimes be observed using some of these materials to create fan artifacts of her own. Her activities during these in-between spaces in her school desk clearly involve a self-initiated and agentic learning dimension on a topic beyond the official classroom context.

Integrated into teaching/learning activity, student-initiated or teacher-initiated

There were also instances where students used their smartphones in self-initiated searches during school-work, which often consisted of googling, Wikipedia-searches, translations, and similar information seeking, using web services that are mainly not constructed for formal educational purposes. This was sometimes done for off-task purposes, but more often to solve instructed tasks (albeit on the students' initiative). In other examples, the students used their phones to search for web pages, articles, images, or the like, to show their peers or the teacher, using real-time searches for web content as a resource for accomplishing exemplification, demonstration, or trouble resolution. These instances were generally occasioned by some teacher-initiated learning activity, but also open for the students to add on dimensions of their personal interests, often connected to a popular culture domain. In these examples, the students' personal interests could connect the formal tasks to their personal experiences which were sometimes also shared with peers in joint discussion. An example of this is presented at length in Section 6.

Gamification of teaching, mostly teacher-initiated

At the other end of this range, we placed examples where the teacher-initiated activities that seemed more informal and influenced by 'wild' practices, often with an ethos of gamification (e.g., Dichev & Dhicheva, 2017), such as the use of quizzes in the form of real-time online quizzes, and showings of popular cultural audiovisual content (films, music, etc.). The introduction of these elements into the classroom by the teachers as part of instructed practice has been discussed in the literature as running the risk of 'taming' the wild interests of learners (Little & Thorne, 2017; Zourou, 2019). Nevertheless, we also observed the gamification of the classroom quiz in the form of Kahoot (a popular application for the purpose in Swedish classrooms) to create a higher level of energy and interest from the students, not least in relation to the competitive element. Figure 29.2 shows a moment from a sequence where a student participates in a teacher-initiated Kahoot quiz during an English class, having just lost a streak of correct answers. The student was previously observably unengaged in the ongoing structured learning activities, but was very engaged by the quiz and the possibility of doing well in the 'competition' against his peers. At this end of the range, however, it might be argued that the rewilding potential is quite limited, as these practices are very much integrated into formal teaching practices and leave little room for learner autonomy or spontaneity.

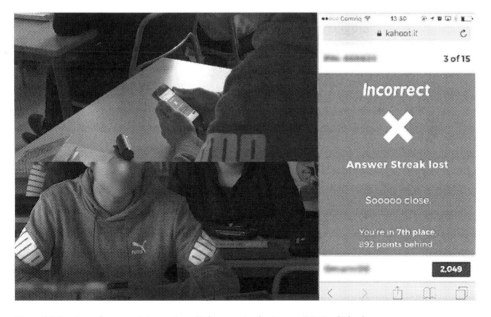

Figure 29.2   A student participates in a Kahoot quiz during an L2 English class

An empirical example from an L2 classroom

In this section, we present an example of how an interactional sequence of analytical interest may be approached. Departing from the ethnomethodologically grounded approach of Conversation Analysis (EMCA), we understand social interaction as organized through verbal as well as non-verbal resources into participation frameworks (Goodwin, 2007). We especially focus on epistemic aspects of the interaction and how these are displayed and negotiated into a cohesive learning trajectory (Tanner & Sahlström, 2018). This example was selected to represent a fairly mundane and typical, based on our review of an extensive ethnographic material. The sequence best exemplifies the second category of rewilding mentioned in the previous section, namely one integrated into the playing out of a planned and structured learning activity. The learning activity was designed and initiated by the teacher, but the students initiate a rewilding of the activity when they discover a shared interest in a work of popular culture.

To begin with, a few things may be noted about our presentation. We present the sequence, spanning approximately two minutes, using a comic-style visual transcript of embodied and screen-mediated activity. This transcript permits us to create a sense of the flow of an extended sequence of interaction. In terms of temporality, it allows us to gloss over less analytically relevant moments and cover more relevant moments in greater detail. Thus, a single panel may be used to summarize 30 seconds of activity (e.g., Panel 3) or one or two seconds (as in Panel 6). Needless to say, temporality can be dealt with both more flexibly and more stringently, on larger or smaller timescales (see Laurier, 2014). The analysis we present is also based on a complete EMCA-style transcript of the sequence. This detailed transcription allowed us to select what to include in the panels in order to represent the flow of the entire interaction and highlight specific analytically salient moments. We would ordinarily prefer to present the full detailed transcript in conjunction with the comic panels. For purposes of length, however, we include only a short example of the detailed transcript below. In Panels 1–4, the students are speaking English, and in Panels 5–20, they are speaking Swedish. These latter panels show our translation into English of their conversation, with some parts elided. The translation into English is idiomatic rather than literal, however for a fully EMCA approach to the same material a more technical translation may have been preferable, and, of course, the original Swedish transcription would be included.

The sequence comes from a 70-minute long English class. The class begins with around 20 minutes of silent reading from novels that the students have been allowed to choose themselves. At video timestamp 19:14, the teacher instructs the students, in English, to finish up their reading. The instructions continue at 19:48 with the teacher telling the students to "tell your friends about what you've just read, in English of course." The students visible on camera are Lotta (left) and Agnes (right). The students spend around 25 seconds negotiating who should go first. Agnes goes first, and presents her book for around 30 seconds. Throughout, both Lotta and Agnes mostly sit back with crossed arms, and Agnes appears tired. At time 21:10 (Panel 1), Agnes trails off in her account of her reading. Lotta takes this as her cue to begin her account at 21:11 (Panel 1) (Figure 29.3).

Lotta is reading the 2009 novel *The Maze Runner*, the first installation of a very popular young adult speculative fiction franchise. In Panel 2 (time 21:13), Lotta holds the book up toward Agnes and transitions into describing the plot of an early part of the novel. Lotta names some of the main characters and the situation that they are currently in (Panel 3; 21:13–21:47). Agnes' gaze is on Lotta, and at one point she yawns. In Panel 4 (21:48), Lotta mentions an experiment. These panels make visible how the two students establish a shared

Bringing Beyond into the L2 Classroom

Figure 29.3 Panels 1–4

epistemic stance (Goodwin, 2007) toward the text (i.e., the story about the maze runner) using their bodily stance, the semiotic structure of the book cover and talk where the word *experiment* is emphasized. In order to illustrate how we have selected from the interaction to construct the visual transcript, Transcript 29.1 presents the detailed CA transcription of the interaction throughout Panels 3–4. The lines in bold (11–12, 15, and 18–19) correspond to what is represented in the comic panels.

Transcript 29.1. Detailed transcript of talk throughout Panels 3–4.
```
P3 11  Lotta:   he and Newt have just come to world and (0.7) he just saw
   12           the grie↑vers that are (0.6) big (0.5) animals in the maze
   13  Agnes:   mm
   14  Lotta:   and he: try- and he is trying to explain to Thomas why (0.6)
P3 15  Agnes:              ((yawn in overlap with Lotta's talk))
   16  Lotta:   they are in the maze
   17  Agnes:   mm
P4 18  Lotta:   and that is because they are going to try to find a way out
   19           because they are in an experiment
   20           (0.4)
   21  Lotta:   ((clicking sound))
```

Following the mention of the experiment, there is a brief pause, after which Agnes switches language to Swedish and asks for clarification (Panel 5; 21:49; our translations into English forthwith), which could be understood as a request for a repair (Schegloff, 1992) (Figure 29.4).

Figure 29.4 Panels 5–8

A change of pace in the interaction is evident here, as Lotta and Agnes lean in toward one another (Panel 5; 21:50), and Agnes' gaze shift back and forth between Lotta and the book lying on the desk (Panels 5–7; 21:50–22:04). It becomes evident in Panel 7 that Agnes was not just initiating repair, but rather something about the idea of the experiment really caught her interest. At this instance, an asymmetry in relation to their epistemic status is demonstrated, where Lotta clearly is positioned as the knowing party and Agnes as unknowing as she asks for more information about the book. Both students here orient to issues of knowing, an action that Tanner and Sahlström (2018) have described as epistemic topicalizations. Agnes leans in over the book and pokes at it with her right hand, as she makes the assessment "that's exciting" and asks what the book is about. Lotta seems taken aback by the question (Panel 8, 22:05–22:08), jerking her head backwards and asking incredulously if Agnes has not in fact "seen" *The Maze Runner*. In this continued epistemic topicalization referring to what Agnes knows, she clarifies that she means the movie (the adaptation of the novel, released in 2014). Lotta's reiterated question indexes her expectation that Agnes should be familiar at least with the movie, which she further emphasizes through an assessment in Panel 9. They still orient to a shared focus on the text as the learning content, but here broaden the construction of this context to encompass the text both as book and as film (Figure 29.5).

Lotta moves her hands to her smartphone (Panel 9; 22:10). Agnes smiles and raises her eyebrows as her gaze follows Lotta's hands. What follows is a sequence of Lotta picking up the phone and performing a web search (Panels 11–12; 22:14–22:23). During the search, she does not share the screen with Agnes, which is a pattern that has been observed also in previous studies in the project (Sahlström et al., 2019b). Agnes waits and looks around the

Figure 29.5 Panels 9–12

classroom while Lotta clears a previous search, mistypes, and retypes the search phrase "maze runner." As the page with top search results loads, Lotta angles the phone toward Agnes and says "here" (Panel 13; 22:23), which works as an invitation to now share the visual focus of the screen (Figure 29.6).

The screen shows the top Google search result, which is an overview of the 2014 film with information from Wikipedia. Among other things, the overview shows an image of the main cast of the film, and Lotta identifies the actor in the center, who plays the main character, as "the guy in Teen Wolf" (Panel 14; 22:25–22:28) projecting him as potentially recognizable by Agnes and as such a continued epistemic topicalization that works to negotiate issues of knowing. Agnes confirms that she has not seen the film, and perhaps does not recognize the actor either, this time orienting to the presumption of shared familiarity through the formulation "haven't had a chance." The way she puts it works as a kind of apology for not knowing, which illustrates how issues of knowledge often include moral aspects of what one should or is supposed to know in a certain context (Stivers et al., 2011). In Panels 15–16 (22:31–22:34), having established the (lack of) shared knowledge, Lotta recommends the movie to Agnes by means of an assessment of the movie itself and a *sotto voce* assessment of the actor. While doing this, she exits the browser application and directs her gaze to Agnes. Agnes makes a suggestive "ooh" sound (approximately oh↑u:↓o::) and smiles, a minimal confirmation displaying a changed epistemic stance. Lotta smiles back and makes a face (pulling her head backward and raising her eyebrows), saying "just kidding" (Figure 29.7).

419

Figure 29.6 Panels 13–17

Figure 29.7 Panels 18–19

Closing the sequence, Lotta redirects the trajectory of the talk to answering Agnes' questions about the story from almost a minute ago. Lotta gives a fuller account of the story (Panels 18–19), approximately 30 seconds in length, and Agnes' gaze shifts between the book and Lotta. The teacher is visible in Panel 19, walking by the students' desk and leaving them a task sheet for the next part of the lesson. Shortly thereafter (Panel 20), Lotta provides a closing of the sequence by referring back to the experiment (cf. Panels 4–6), as Agnes' embodied conduct displays a noticeably higher degree of interest than during the beginning of the sequence.

While we cannot offer a full analysis in this chapter, we do wish to provide a sketch of such an analysis, to demonstrate the potential research implications of the methodology we are presenting. In this example of an L2 classroom situation, clearly a designed learning activity is initially taking place. The students have been instructed by their teacher to read from their individually selected book, and then, after a timed period of reading, to discuss their reading with one another in the target language, L2 English. The design of the learning activity seems already to be based on a recognition of the importance of making activities interesting and relevant to the individual learners and their lifeworlds. Indeed, the curriculum for English at all levels in the Swedish school system calls for this. However, our analysis demonstrates that as the students are conducting the assigned task, they do so briefly – barely 30 seconds of talk each – and with little actual interaction and low engagement evident in their embodied conduct. The learning activity was thus unsuccessful in so far as the immanent object of the instructed task was for the students to engage in extended L2 conversation. However, during these minutes we instead see a learning trajectory initiated where Agnes' epistemic stance is changed from demonstrating a routine acceptance of the formal task to actively asking for more information about the text, that now is not only about the book but directed to a wider popular-culture phenomenon. Agnes begins to develop a genuine interest in the *Maze Runner* story, and Lotta catches on to this opportunity of introducing a peer to a popular culture franchise that she is herself committed to, the students' embodied orientation to the interaction transforms. The connected smartphone is an actor in how this moment plays out, as it becomes a tool and a resource for Lotta to on-the-fly demonstrate her interest, to search for and establish shared knowledge and interest with Agnes, and to argue – with evident success – that Agnes should be interested too. In this, as in many other situations, the smart device quickly and effectively opens a window to the students' extramural engagements, and affords a multimodal alignment of the students' wild interests and their institutional interests as second-language learners of English. While a smartphone might not be necessary for something like this to play out, the smartphone was central in this event playing out *as it did*, functioning as a compelling mediator in this learning trajectory making an extramural interest more richly and readily present in the classroom than it otherwise would have been, and as a ready-at-hand resource for Lotta and Agnes to become agents in rewilding and personalizing a previously rather tame and institutionalized classroom interaction on English literature. Thus, this learning situation provided for the possibility of authentic engagement with a source material relevant to the learners' shared cultural interests and frame of reference to emerge.

In the presentation of this example, we have of course only scratched the surface of what is available for detailed microanalysis, but hopefully we have illustrated some possibilities for researching L2 learning using this approach. More analytical attention could be paid to a number of aspects of the sequence which are all variously relevant to the intersected topics of language learning, rewilding, and the role of mobile devices – for instance, the precise mechanics of language shifting or of the joint orientation to the mobile device, or a more detailed analysis of the epistemic dimension of the sequence. A video ethnographic dataset such as the one we are demonstrating here thus features a wealth of analytically salient sequences of learners interacting with and through digital devices. Each sequence has its own local contingencies, but all come with various implications to be derived to further scholarly and educational policy debate on the learning potentials of rewilding formal L2 learning, and using digital connectivity to open up the L2 classroom.

Discussion and future directions

Our aim in this chapter has been to argue for the relevance of video ethnographic methods for studying digitally mediated practices with a special focus on the identification and detailed analysis of how such practices afford a potential rewilding of L2 learning, and for bringing the digital wilds into the L2 classroom. Video ethnography comprising camera recording of learners' embodied conduct combined with screen-recordings of screen-mediated practices can make visible a wide range of practices that afford such rewilding potential in various ways and to various extents. Focusing specifically on a classroom context, using video ethnography with a focus on capturing when and how learners make use of digital devices, is becomes possible to study both in aggregate and with moment-by-moment precision how personal connected devices render the walls of the classroom porous (cf. Godwin-Jones, 2020), and bring the learners' extramural lives, relationships, and interests into the classroom, potentially rewilding it.

After a very brief survey of some of the ways in which we have ourselves observed the potential rewilding of the classroom space afforded by connected mobile devices, we focused especially on one empirical example of two learners in a classroom situation abandoning an assigned L2 English speaking task in favor of engaging in a more authentically motivated discussion in their L1 Swedish concerning an English language popular cultural franchise. In this example, the learner's smartphone played a mediating role in the interactants' process of establishing shared knowledge and cultural frame of reference, and adding a multimodal demonstration element to the interaction which the learners could jointly orient around. Though the learners were in some sense abandoning the instructed task for an interaction that is at face value of much lesser relevance to the L2 learning agenda set by the teacher, we instead see the initial formation of a more authentic relationship with what may arguably be a much more valuable learning resource than a few minutes of classroom interaction in English. Of course, without follow-up investigation, we do not know whether this student did in fact end up watching the movie, reading the book, or becoming a fan of the franchise. However, we do see that this moment is the kind of unpredictable spark that can set off a complex trajectory of substantial learning (cf. Godwin-Jones, 2018). Follow-up interviews or observations were not conducted in this case, but could be very useful in research in this area.

There is a still growing recognition of the importance of understanding how learning happens outside of the classroom. At the same time, we need to trouble the tradition of imagining the classroom and the home as a binary (Wohlwend, 2015). This goes doubly in a time that important affinity spaces are available to learners through digital mediation across physical and institutional settings (Gee, 2004; Sauro et al., 2020). Little and Thorne (2017) stress the contingency of authentic learning, and importance of creating opportunities for "stochastic events" to occur (p. 21). In a similar vein, Godwin-Jones (2018) proposes a learning framework inspired by complexity theory. Video ethnography is well-suited to empirically capturing the complexities and contingencies of how wild learning transpires and how institutional or formal learning may be, or are already in the process of being, rewilded through the presence of connected digital technologies. This much, we have ourselves observed unfolding in a large number of ways in our own video ethnographic materials, in learners' off-task activities, as well as in their approaches to structured learning activities. Connected personal mobile devices open up new ways for learners to carry on their productive engagement with the digital wilds, bringing the beyond into the classroom. In this chapter, we have argued for the importance and relevance of researching these processes through video ethnography, for a grounded and participant-oriented knowledge base on the rewilding potential of the connected L2 classroom.

Reflection questions

1. Digitalization is a global, yet unequally distributed, development. This chapter focuses mainly on a Western, and specifically Swedish, context. To what extent are connected mobile devices available to learners, and what digital practices might be observed, in L2 classrooms in different parts of the world?
2. This chapter focuses on observing potentials for rewilding learning on a micro-level of social interaction, and with a learner-centric perspective. What are the implications of observations on this level for the policy levels enacted by teachers, school officials, and politicians?
3. How could the video ethnographic approach outlined in this chapter be adapted to study L2 learning practices in other institutional or extramural spaces?

Recommended readings

Little, D., & Thorne, S. (2017). From learner autonomy to rewilding: A discussion. In M. Cappellini, T. Lewis, & A. Rivens Mompean (Eds.), *Learner autonomy and Web 2.0*. (pp. 12–35). London, UK: Equinox.

This article presents an interview with applied linguists David Little and Steven Thorne, conducted by Tim Lewis, in which the interlocutors discuss challenges and opportunities for learner autonomy, and research on learner autonomy, in the context of new digital communication technologies. In the discussion, Thorne develops the idea of 'rewilding' language education as one of providing opportunities for structured unpredictability.

Rusk, F., Pörn, M., Sahlström, F., & Slotte-Lüttge, A. (2015) Perspectives on using video recordings in conversation analytical studies on learning in interaction. *International Journal of Research & Method in Education*, 38(1,) 39–55, DOI:10.1080/1743727X.2014.903918

In this article, Rusk and colleagues present an overview of video-based EMCA approaches to studying learning in interaction. The authors outline three main thematic focus areas for such studies, and give recommendations for how the desired area of focus should impact the construction of data for such a project.

Olin-Scheller, C., Tanner, M., Asplund, S., Kontio, J., & Wikström, P. (2020). Social excursions during the in-between spaces of lessons. Students' smartphone use in the upper secondary school classroom. *Scandinavian Journal of Educational Research* (published online). DOI: 10.1080/00313831.2020.1739132

In this article, Olin-Scheller and colleagues investigate when and why students use their smartphones during lessons. Based on their findings, the authors argue that student-initiated use of smartphones most often occurs in so called in-between spaces during lessons, and could be seen as social excursions that are smoothfully integrated in the social order of the classroom.

Note

1. Connected Classrooms (Swedish Research Council reg. no. 2015-01044) and Textmöten (The Swedish Cultural Foundation in Finland, 2014–2017). The Swedish study replicated field methods that were originally developed by Finnish researchers Fritjof Sahlström, Antti Pakkari, and Verneri Valasmo (cf. Sahlström et al., 2019).

References

Asplund, S., Olin-Scheller, C., & Tanner, M, (2018). Under the teacher's radar: Literacy practices in task-related smartphone use in the connected classroom. *L1 Educational Studies in Language and Literature*, 18. doi: 10.17239/L1ESLL-2018.18.01.03

Barton, D., & Lee, C. (2013). *Language online. Investigating digital texts and practices*. London: Routledge.

Blikstad-Balas, M. (2017) Key challenges of using video when investigating social practices in education: contextualization, magnification, and representation. *International Journal of Research & Method in Education*, 40(5), 511–523, DOI: 10.1080/1743727X.2016.1181162

Bolander, B., & Locher, M., (2020). Beyond the online offline distinction: Entry points to digital discourse. *Discourse, Context & Media, 35*, 1–8.

Chik, A. (2015). Popular culture, digital worlds and second language learners. In J. Rowsell & K. Pahl (Eds.), *The Routledge handbook of literacy studies* (pp. 339–353). London: Routledge.

Derry, S. J., Pea, R., Barron, B., Engle, R., Erickson, F., Goldman, R., Hall, R., Koschmann, T., Lemke, J.L., Sherin, M.G., & Sherin, B.L. (2010). Conducting video research in the learning sciences: Guidance on selection, analysis, technology, and ethics. *Journal of the Learning Sciences, 19*(1), 3–53.

Dichev, C., & Dicheva, D. (2017). Gamifying education: what is known, what is believed and what remains uncertain: A critical review. *International Journal of Education Technology in Higher Education, 14*(9). https://doi.org/10.1186/s41239-017-0042-5

Erickson, F. (2011) Uses of video in social research: A brief history. *International Journal of Social Research Methodology, 14*(3), 179–189, DOI: 10.1080/13645579.2011.563615

Gee, J. P. (2004). *Situated language and learning: A critique of traditional schooling.* London: Routledge.

Godwin-Jones, R. (2018). Chasing the butterfly effect: Informal language learning online as a complex system. *Language Learning and Technology, 22*(2), 8–27. https://doi.org/10.125/44643

Godwin-Jones, R. (2020). Building the porous classroom: An expanded model for blended language learning. *Language Learning & Technology, 24*(3), 1–18.

Goodwin, C. (2007). Participation, stance and affect in the organization of activities. *Discourse and Society, 18*, 53–73.

Kessel, D., Lif Hardardottir, H., & Tyrefors, B. (2019). The impact of banning mobile phones in Swedish secondary schools (Working Paper Series 1288). Research Institute of Industrial Economics.

Knoblauch, H., & Schnettler, B. (2012). Videography: analysing video data as a 'focused' ethnographic and hermeneutical exercise. *Qualitative Research, 12*(3) 334–356, DOI: 10.1177/1468794111436147

Kuznekoff, J. H., & Titsworth, S. (2013). The impact of mobile phone usage on student learning. *Communication Education, 62*(3), 233–252.

Lai, C. (2017). *Autonomous language learning with technology beyond the classroom.* London: Bloomsbury. https://doi.org/10.1177/1748895811401979

Laurier, E. (2014). The graphic transcript: Poaching comic book grammar for inscribing the visual, spatial and temporal aspects of action. *Geography Compass, 8*(4), 235–248. https://doi.org/10.1111/gec3.12123

Little, D., & Thorne, S. L. (2017). From learner autonomy to rewilding: A discussion. In M. Cappellini, T. Lewis, & A. R. Mompean (Eds.), *Learner autonomy and web 2.0* (pp. 12–35). Sheffield: Equinox.

Luff, P., & Heath, C. (2012). Some 'technical challenges' of video analysis: social actions, objects, material realities and the problems of perspective. *Qualitative Research, 12*(3), 255–279.

Maltese, A., Danish, J., Bouldin, R., Harsh, J., & Bryan, B. (2016) What are students doing during lecture? Evidence from new technologies to capture student activity. *International Journal of Research & Method in Education, 39*(2), 208–226, DOI: 10.1080/1743727X.2015.1041492

Markham, A., & Buchanan, E. (2012). Ethical decision-making and internet research: Recommendations from the AoIR ethics working committee (version 2.0). https://aoir.org/reports/ethics2.pdf.

Melander-Bowden, H., & Svahn, J. (2020). Collaborative work on an online platform in video-mediated homework support. Social interaction. *Video-based Studies of Human Sociality, 3* (3), DOI: 10.7146/si.v3i3.122600

Mondada, L. (2006). Video recording as the reflexive preservation and configuration of phenomenal features for analysis. In H. Knoblauch, J. Raab, H.-G. Soeffner, B. Schnettler (Eds.), *Video analysis.* Bern: Lang.

O'Dea, S. (2020). Number of smartphone users worldwide 2016–2021. https://www.statista.com/statistics/330695/number-of-smartphone-users-worldwide/

Olin-Scheller, C., Tanner, M., Asplund, S., Kontio, J., & Wikström, P. (2020). Social excursions during the in-between spaces of lessons. Students' smartphone use in the upper secondary school classroom. *Scandinavian Journal of Educational Research* (published online). DOI: 10.1080/00313831.2020.1739132

Ott, T. (2017). *Mobile phones in school.* Gothenburg: University of Gothenburg.

Player-Koro, C., & Tallvid, M. (2015). One laptop on each desk: teaching methods in technology rich classrooms. *Seminar.net: Media, Technology and Lifelong Learning, 11*(3).

Reinders, H., & White, C. (2016). 20 years of autonomy and technology: How far have we come and where to next?. *Language Learning & Technology, 20*(2), 143–154.

Richards, J. C. (2015). The changing face of language learning: Learning beyond the classroom. *RELC Journal, 46*(1), 5–22. https://doi.org/10.1177/0033688214561621

Rusk, F., Pörn, M., Sahlström, F., & Slotte-Lüttge, A. (2015). Perspectives on using video recordings in conversation analytical studies on learning in interaction. *International Journal of Research & Method in Education, 38*(1), 39–55. DOI:10.1080/1743727X.2014.903918

Sahlström, F., Tanner, M., & Olin-Scheller, C. (red.). (2019a). Smartphones in classrooms: Reading, writing and talking in rapidly changing educational spaces. *Learning, Culture and Social Interaction, 21*, 1–5. DOI: 10.1016/j.lcsi.2019.100319

Sahlström, F., Tanner, M., & Valasmo, V. (2019b). Connected youth, connected classrooms. Smartphone use and student and teacher participation during plenary teaching. *Learning, Culture and Social Interaction, 21*, 311–331. https://doi.org/10.1016/j.lcsi.2019.03.008

Sauro, S., & Zourou, K. (2019). What are the digital wilds? *Language Learning and Technology, 23*(1), 1–7. DOI: 10..125/44666

Sauro, S., Buendgens-Kosten, J., & Cornillie, F. (2020). Storytelling for the foreign language classroom. *Foreign Language Annals, 53*(2), 329–337. DOI: 10.1111/flan.12467

Schegloff, E. (1992). Repair after next turn. The last structurally provided defense of intersubjectivity in conversation. *American Journal of Sociology, 97*(5), 1295–1345.

Silver, L. (2019). Smartphone ownership is growing rapidly around the world, but not always equally. *PEW Research Center.* https://www.pewresearch.org/global/2019/02/05/smartphone-ownership-is-growing-rapidly-around-the-world-but-not-always-equally/

Statens Medieråd. (2019). Ungar och medier 2019. https://statensmedierad.se/download/18.126747f-416d00e1ba946903a/1568041620554/Ungar%20och%20medier%202019%20tillganglighetsanpassad.pdf

Stivers, T., Mondada, L., & Steensig, J. (Eds.). (2011). *The morality of knowledge in conversation.* Cambridge: Cambridge University Press.

Tanner, M., & Sahlström, F. (2018). Same and different: Epistemic topicalizations as resources for cohesion and change in classroom learning trajectories. *Discourse Processes, 55*(8), 704–725, DOI: 10.1080/0163853X.2017.1319168

Thorne, S. L. (2015). *Rewilding situated and usage-based approaches to second language development and research.* Presentation at Thinking, Doing, Learning: Usage-based Perspectives on Second Language Learning, Groningen, Netherlands.

Wohlwend, K. (2015). Making, remaking, and reimagining the everyday: Play, creativity, and popular media. In J. Rowsell & K. Pahl (Eds.), *The Routledge handbook of literacy studies*, 548–560. London: Routledge.

Zourou, K. (2019). A critical review of social networks for language learning beyond the classroom. In M. Dressman & R. W. Sadler (Eds.), *The handbook of informal language learning*, 369–382. New Jersey: Wiley Blackwell. DOI: 10.1002/9781119472384.ch24

30
LEARNING ANALYTICS AND EDUCATIONAL DATA MINING IN LEARNING BEYOND THE CLASSROOM

Michael Thomas

Introduction

Over the last three decades the number of students engaged in higher education around the world has increased dramatically and led to debates about how to maintain the quality of the student experience in a mass global marketplace (Block & Gray, 2016; Block, Gray & Holborow, 2012). It is no coincidence that the growth in student numbers has developed in tandem with a rising interest in the role of digital technologies to administer, support, teach and assess learning at scale and with the promise of ever greater efficiency, predictability and effectiveness (Godwin-Jones, 2017). Pre-dating the emergence of remote online learning that has rapidly transformed how universities operate during the COVID-19 pandemic, digital education has been making inroads since the emergence of Learning Management Systems (LMS) in the early years of the new millennium (Means, Bakia & Murphy, 2014). Digital education is now a field incorporating areas from neural networks to artificial intelligence (AI) in which 'big data' and 'data-driven learning' (DDL) are becoming central components (Cope, & Kalantzis, 2016; Meunier, 2019). Collecting data about learner interactions in these platforms has produced large datasets which appeal to administrators who seek to identify and understand patterns of student engagement. Data driven learning is also being sold to practitioners and researchers from a variety of disciplines, as it offers the potential to quantify and evaluate learner performance in increasingly testing-oriented systems (Boulton, 2017; Flowerdew, 2015).

Imported from the world of business and marketing, learning analytics and data mining techniques have emerged as a result of neoliberal educational reforms in which the student experience, student progression and retention have become strategically important (Giroux, 2014). In the corporate context, analytics and data mining are used to understand and predict trends related to products, consumers and markets, and their use in the increasingly corporatised educational context mirrors substantive changes in the function and purpose of education across all sectors, as it has moved from being a 'public good' to an international commodity associated with discourses of 'innovation' and 'enterprise' (Campbell, Debloi & Oblinger, 2007). While learning analytics often deals with teacher interventions, educational data mining focusses more on automated systems and remains a relatively underexplored area in need of more empirical research (Attewell, Monaghan & Kwong, 2015; Warschauer, Yim, Lee & Zheng, 2019).

Computer-Assisted Language Learning (CALL), an interdisciplinary sub-field of Second Language Acquisition (SLA), has often been at the forefront of digital innovations and has started to engage with learning analytics with greater regularity over the last five years (Thomas & Gelan, 2018), building on previous research in corpus linguistics (Chambers, 2019), ICALL (Intelligent Computer-Assisted Language Learning) and adaptive CALL, which sought to personalise learning materials based on learners' interests, performance or interactions with conversational agents (Fryer, Coniam, Carpenter & Lăpuşneanu, 2020; Ruiz, Rebuschat & Meurers, 2019). While CALL has grown as an international field, larger scale meta-analyses continue to suggest that technology usage in language learning is inconclusive in terms of enhanced language learning performance (Plonsky & Ziegler, 2016).

Regardless of the hype associated 'big data' in debates about how best to deploy digital technologies to enhance learning, it has also led to several areas of concern, such as surveillance, data privacy, the development of 'fake' computer generated audio and video, the effect on learner motivation and ethics, and it is important to recognise that analytics may also have negative implications for language teachers and learners which need to be discussed to maintain transparency and equity (JISC, 2015; Reinders, 2018; Slade & Prinsloo, 2013). While face to face education has been the primary concern of analytics in language learning as in other disciplines, more interest is being shown in the area of self-regulated learning (SRL) as a way to support learners by developing their metacognitive awareness outside formal language learning contexts (Azevedo & Gasevic, 2019; Azevedo, Mudrick, Taub & Bradbury, 2019). Indeed, with many lifelong and casual language learners now studying in their spare time rather than attending face-to-face language classrooms due to work and other commitments, learners in mobile contexts may need more support to learn effectively, as they "possess poor SRL skills and practices, including the ability to calibrate their own learning processes" (Viberg, Wasson & Kukulska-Hulme, 2020, p. 34; see also Viberg & Kukulska-Hulme this volume). Without supplementary input learners may be unable to manage their time effectively, develop appropriate learning strategies, decide which resources are most valuable for their particular objectives, understand gaps in their knowledge or identify which language skills to work on (Baars et al., 2018; Huang & Yu, 2019). The use of analytics in self-regulated mobile language learning contexts 'beyond the classroom' may then present challenges to learners in that it can require extra time to understand the data, in addition to undertaking their own learning, and may be best suited to learners with higher levels of proficiency rather than beginners (Dawson, Gasevic & Mirriahi, 2015; Lee et al., 2019). While the use of learning analytics as a student-centred approach has emerged as one way of repositioning the field so that it is perceived as enhancing teaching and learning, it may not suit every learner in every context all of the time, and may be seen as an attempt by 'big EdTech', an increasingly powerful economic and political lobby, to mask the controversies and promote uncritical approaches to digital technology adoption that promote "over-monitoring and micro-managing" (Reinders, 2018, p. 84).

Key constructs

Learning Management Systems and other forms of online learning platforms such as massive open online courses (MOOCs) act as electronic interfaces between language learners and teachers, enabling the collection of vast amounts of click through data, as users interact with and navigate these platforms and their accompanying tasks and resources. Added to this, collecting similar data from students' interactions with other devices such as smart phones, tablets, e-books and library resources, have become commonplace. Given the diverse range of skills required to design, extract and analyse these large amounts of data, learning analytics includes researchers from a variety of disciplines such as computer science, psychology, statistics and machine learning, often combined in the term 'data scientist'.

Following Long and Siemens (2011, p. 34), the Society for Learning Analytics defines learning analytics as "the measurement, collection, analysis and reporting of data about learners and their contexts, for purposes of understanding and optimising learning and the environments in which it occurs" (SoLAR, n.d.). The Horizon Project (2016, p. 38) takes this definition further, aligning it with 'learner profiling', while also aiming to 'empower learning' and describing it is "an educational application of web analytics aimed at … gathering and analysing details of individual student interactions in online learning activities. The goal is to build better pedagogies, empower active learning, target at-risk student populations, and assess factors affecting completion and student success".

Related to this, educational data mining is defined as the process of turning these large datasets into meaningful and useful information to inform action (Bienkowski, Feng & Means, 2012). For Romero and Ventura (2020, p. 601) data mining is "the development of methods to explore data originating in an educational context", while Warshauer, Yim, Lee and Zheng (2019, p. 93) describe it more precisely as the "process of discovering hidden patterns" via the "interdisciplinary practice involving methods at the intersection of machine learning, pattern recognition, and statistics".

Although seemingly obvious, the related term 'big data' is used to describe information that is "huge in volume, high in velocity, diverse in variety, exhaustive in scope" (Tsai et al., 2020., p. 555). Here 'big' implies 'comprehensive' and 'totalising', as if to imply that large amounts of data can lead to greater objectivity in decision-making, while ignoring the fact that data is implicitly selective, may not include data from marginalised voices (disabled or marginalised students, for example), and fails to acknowledge uncertainty, ambiguity, serendipity, contradictions or contextual differences such as socio-economic factors (Anwaruddin, 2019; D'Ignazio & Klein, 2020). Unlike data that is selected to represent populations in empirical studies, 'big data' in this context seems to imply that size eliminates bias. Indeed, the visualised data is often purely focussed on performance that decontextualises the learner and there is a tendency in viewing self-regulated language learning supported by big data to eradicate the need for any kind of teacher support. This techno-determinism is potentially dangerous in the language learning context, however, in that the data may be used to simplify complex processes based on the frequency of access rather than the quality of decision-making and the contingent, creative and coincidental process of learning. Large datasets may tell us something about *what* is happening or quantify performance based on language tests but struggle to say anything about the *quality* of the communicative interaction, explain ambiguities or *why* something happened in a particular context and at that particular time.

Even before the large-scale turn towards remote online learning precipitated by COVID-19, learning analytics and educational data mining were nevertheless developing a growing profile (Youngs, Moss-Horwitz & Synder, 2015). From the pedagogical perspective, analytics aims to provide evidence to help understand students' learning behaviour that might justify pedagogical interventions, especially if students are not making progress as expected towards pre-identified learning outcomes (Calderon & Sood, 2018; Kuromiya, Majumdar & Ogata, 2020). Thus, the data can be used to operate like an early warning system to aid teachers, particularly when dealing with large numbers of face to face, online or students connected via mobile devices (Dychoff, Zielke, Bültmann, Chatti & Schroeder,

2012). While analytics can also contribute to an understanding of learner engagement, participation, or task completion, particularly aimed at targeting learners who are not on track, a key assumption is that they can also be used reliably to predict future actions. In the context of language learning, behavioural data may also help researchers to understand the pathways learners choose and the individual choices and processes they undertake to achieve gains in performance and proficiency (Corrin, Scheffel & Gašević, 2020). In summary, Van Hermelen and Workman (2012) usefully identify several main areas where analytics can be used: enhancing retention by addressing 'at risk' learners; identifying recommended resources for learners; suggesting where improvements can be made and measuring the results of these suggested performance indicators; personalising learning; identifying teachers' performance; aiding student recruitment processes; and sending email alerts and notifications to teachers.

Several different types of analytics exist. Synchronous analytics relies on data being collected and visualised in real-time, for example, as students work on a particular task, to measure their level of engagement (Hsiao, Lan & Kao & Li, 2017; Youngs, Prakash & Nugent, 2018). The synchronous collection of real-time data can occur in face to face or online education, as long as students are connected with an internet-enabled device. Asynchronous analytics in contrast collects data from students outside of their face-to-face class. Large datasets using the synchronous approach aim to enable predictions about how learners will react and respond in real-time during the instruction, while asynchronous data may be used to produce predictions that teacher and learners can reflect on post-lesson (Zhu, 2016).

According to Siemens and Baker (2012) the main difference between educational data mining and learning analytics is that the former involves automated processes that seek to adapt pedagogical processes, whereas learning analytics aim to provide evidence to improve students' and teachers' engagement with learning. Just as neoliberal values have influenced the transfer of analytics from business and corporate contexts to education, placing renewed emphasis on individual agency, self-directed or self-regulated and autonomous learning have been strongly allied with lifelong learning. Self-directed learning can be defined in terms of the process which enables language learners to assume control of their approach to learning which involves several interconnected aspects such as ownership, self-management, and the ability to extend their learning, each of which, in envisaging learners as rational and capable of seamlessly understanding their own learning process, aims to allow them to control the direction of their own learning pathways (Tan et al., 2011; Zimmerman, 1989, 1990). Assuming control and ownership of the direction of their own learning by establishing their own objectives can also aid motivation and engagement (Rienties, Lewis, McFarlane, Nguyen & Toetenel, 2018). Associated with this learners will acquire skills in monitoring their own progress and becoming more effective at time-management. Students' metacognition is central to a reflective approach to strategies that promote self-directed learning (Pilling-Cormick & Garrison, 2007), alongside goal-directed behaviour, establishing a learning plan, and evaluating its achievement at regular intervals (Kovanovic, Joksimovic, Mirriahi, Blaine, Gasevic, Siemens & Dawson, 2018; Loyens, Magda & Rickens, 2008).

Some studies identify differences between self-directed and self-regulated learners, in that in the former the decision-making of the learners is paramount, whereas in the latter it is the aspects of the environment and context in which the learning takes place that is important (Loyens, Magda & Rickens, 2008). Self-directed learning has often been explored in non-institutional or non-formal learning contexts such as adult education. The introduction of digital tools and applications has focussed on aiding language learners in these processes described above, particularly planning, exploring and evaluating their learning, and it is clear how analytics has emerged as a way of aiding processes related to task completion, and the appropriate use of resources, providing summative feedback on performance, and aiding learners in providing an overview of their own metacognitive behaviour (Bartolomé, Bergamin, Persico, Steffens & Underwood, 2011).

Learning analytics data can help with language learners' monitoring and reflective processes in relation to feedback. Whereas traditionally feedback is provided by teachers, analytics can provide language learners with instant feedback on their performance through the use of dashboards (Pilling-Cormick & Garrison, 2007). This is a rather disruptive notion however in that most data is used by teachers to adapt their instructional approach (Knight et al., 2013), and students may not be willing to invest time to sample, explore and seek to understand their own performance data through the use of personalised dashboards (Roberts-Mahoney, Means & Garrison, 2016). First generation Learning Analytics Dashboards (LADs) typically included performance data in terms of individual test scores, as well as the time students had spent on individual and/or aggregated tasks, enabling them to measure their progress in the context of their learning goals (Verbert, Govaerts, Duval, Santos, Assche, Parra & Klerkx, 2013). Later LADs have included attempts to visualise cognitive and behavioural process data in more dynamic formats. While data on LADs may be individual, it may also visualise student performance relative to the average in a particular class, peer or year group, and this has led to concerns about the implications of a more competitive or 'gamified approach' to data visualisation (Aguilar, Karabenick, Teasley & Baek, 2021).

Self-regulated learning plays an increasingly important role in language learning as the process often combines face to face instruction in formal instructional contexts and/or supplementary study of an individual nature beyond the classroom via a blended approach (Youngs, Moss-Horwitz and Synder, 2015). Zimmerman's (1990) model of SRL is still relevant in this respect, as it describes the importance of cognitive, affective and sociocultural factors in terms of how a learner constructs and applies knowledge (cognitive), harnesses their emotions and attitudes (affective) and learns to communicate in different contexts and identities (sociocultural) that is particularly valuable in a blended self-regulated context (Viberg, Wasson & Kukulska-Hulme, 2020).

Key issues

As we have seen above, and as with many digital technologies that were first developed for primarily corporate reasons and later adapted by educators, learning analytics and data mining present several areas of potential as well as numerous areas of concerns for the theory and practice of language learning and teaching. The speed with which analytics is being deployed from a managerial and/or administrative or perspective may be at the cost to transparency for teachers and learners. New technology innovations are not neutral; they shape teacher-student relationships, and their implications have to be carefully examined from the bottom-up rather than uncritically imposed from the top-down.

The issue of who owns student data, for example, is a central one and some recent research has argued that designers need to embrace open formats (Yousuf & Conlan, 2020). In opposition to proprietary business models (Yousuf & Conlan, 2020), this approach promotes the idea that data can be stored in the cloud, owned by the learners themselves rather than the provider by a particular app, and learners will be able to upload and contribute their own data from their particular context (Rosell-Aguilar, 2018). Consequently, this approach has potential to turn students from passive to active agents and have a knock-on effect on their motivation, as they are not merely subject to the authoritative algorithm but co-designers or co-researchers in their own learning in which data is viewed as always partial and never complete (Bull, 2020). This approach challenges the type of closed, proprietary use of user log data that is often found in popular games, suggesting instead the possibility of developing greater interoperability between applications and learning systems. Indeed, one recurrent challenge facing many generations of technology-enhanced learning and computer-assisted language learning applications and tools has been their lack of sustainability and context awareness.

Another area of potential in the context of self-regulated learning is the extent to which it can build on previous research in adaptive learning (Kerr, 2015) which aims to use data to respond in personalised ways to the pathways learners take through learning materials (Lodge, Panadero, Broadbent & de Barba, 2018). One important area of research in this respect is clarifying the difference as Kerr (2015) argues between several key terms which are sometimes, as in other areas of e-learning, prone to be used interchangeably with less care. Personalisation in autonomous language learning refers to how learning objectives, input materials, methods and the speed of delivery may change according to the particular learner. Individualisation varies in the sense that while learners' goals may be the same, individual students can develop different approaches and pathways through the input materials, and work at their own pace. Finally, differentiation is also based on having similar learning goals, however, the instructional approach has been adapted to the preferences of individual students (Kerr, 2015, p. 88). While 'big data' can help with each of these processes, a key issue is how a more nuanced and granular understanding of learner pathways can be determined, one that is less focussed on micro-managing the process and more attuned to how change and unexpected encounters can also develop language learning (Reinders, 2018).

In terms of self-regulated language learning, the use of student dashboards is one such area (Verbert, Duval, Klerkx, Govaerts and Santos, 2013). Research suggests that they are more widely used by teachers than by students. While much of the focus has been on the use of student log data, the use of quantitative data alone raises several questions about its ability to given autonomous learners anything more that superficial insights into their motivation or provide information about why the process tasks in the way they do (Fischer, 2007; Link & Li, 2015). Dashboards may struggle to provide the granular insights into the social interaction that is typically a part of language learning in instructed contexts as communication is not predictable, linear or consistently uniform (Coffrin, Corrin, de Barba and Kennedy, 2014). Indeed, Link and Li's (2015) framework for the use of analytics and SLA theory such as interactionism and complexity theory, applies to instructed contexts but omits consideration the example data points that apply in self-regulated and autonomous learning. Psycholinguistic approaches using interactionism can draw on several data points such as visualisation of social networks and interaction in social forums, as well as eye tracking (Carolan, 2014; Chun, 2013; Miller, Lindgren & Sullivan, 2008). Language in social context using complexity theory can be examined via error analysis reports and keystroke logging. Language acquisition in self-directed contexts based on viewing language as a skill acquired as a result of continuous practice may rely on performance data arising from exercises and assessments, the time spent on the e-system, the use of particular documents and learning tools, and learner corpus data (Lee, Warschauer & Lee, 2018; Leijten & Van Waes, 2013; Link & Li, 2015).

A related key issue suggests that just as teachers have required training in order to use analytics in instructed language learning contexts, students will also need training to improve their metacognitive awareness beyond the classroom (Ali, Asadi, Gasevic, Jovanovic & Hatala, 2013). Indeed, Link and Li's (2015, pp. 379–80) questions remain under-researched: Do the analytics demonstrate a correspondence between target language activities and tasks beyond the classroom? What evidence do the analytics provide that suggests learners see the connection between classroom activities and outside tasks?

As has been indicated above, analytics is a contested area and like all technology usage it is not neutral. Given the neoliberal origins of analytics in the corporate context, the main critiques relate to the commercial aspects of analytics alongside the ethical and data protection issues (see Sylvén, this volume). As much as it is related to personalisation, analytics can also depersonalise feedback (Buckingham Shum & Ferguson, 2011) and potentially make students rather passive receivers of information that purports to provide an authoritative institutional perspective, promoting ideas of student agency and then leaving little room for creativity (Kruse & Pongsajapan, 2012). Duval (2012), Clow (2012), Kruse and Pongsajapan (2012) argue in response for student-centred analytics which aids metacognition by providing meaningful data that can be visualised to enhance reflection (Coffrin, Corrin, de Barba & Kennedy, 2014). Arising from this key questions can be formulated in the area of self-directed learning using analytics: What types of data is meaningful for self-directed learners? How can data be most effectively visualised to aid self-directed learning?

Implications

As with other areas of digital technologies in education more broadly and language learning in particular, there is an increasing interest in the potential of learning analytics and educational data mining techniques from managers and administrators to teachers and learners. Self-directed and self-regulated language learning is a growth area with new applications appearing at a regular pace to meet the demand for learners using mobile devices to learn outside instructed classrooms. Learners are used to dashboards providing data on their performance via smart watches, phones, fitness and other health and wellbeing related devices (Verbert, Duval, Klerkx, Govaerts & Santos, 2013). Rather than assuming that learners will intuitively be able to read and use the data presented to them in beneficial ways, research suggests that they will need mentoring, guidance and practice to use them effectively. Rather like in the field of corpus linguistics, analytics has often tended to provide some evidence for conclusions that language teachers intuitive already know (Gelan et al., 2018; Vyatkina, 2020a, 2020b). Sometimes in order to justify the use of analytics, rather obvious conclusions have been presented as if they were ground-breaking to sustain the commercial hype, and there is a strong tendency towards the use of a one-sided casual and deterministic approach which lacks nuance (Gandomi & Haider, 2015). Data mining techniques may be more promising, however, as they seek to identify patterns in the data often within larger datasets, and the visualisation of these more focussed studies can uncover meaningful network interactions among smaller groups of learners (Volk, Kellner & Wohlhart, 2015).

Most studies have been of analytics to monitor language learning activities in instructed second language contexts, while in learning beyond the classroom, several apps have emerged that can help teachers track learner interaction such as Socrative, and familiar aspects of gamification may be used to engage the learners. Nevertheless, analytics underlines the importance of a rather deterministic, rationalistic and mechanistic approach to learning which leaves little room for interpreting the complexity of learners or the learning process (Reinders, 2018). It also suggests that learners in self-regulated contexts can fully comprehend and act upon the visualised data presented simply by processing it (Tsai et al., 2020). In seeking to empower learners' agency, which is a tendency of neoliberal educational discourse, the result may in fact be, as Tsai suggests, to remove it: "The emphasis on action informed predictive models has ... a tendency to prioritise effects and indicators (signals) over causes, thus leading to narrow remedial strategies in which students and teachers are channelled along predefined trajectories of educational performance that, paradoxically, leave little room for agency" (Tsai et al., 2020, p. 557). While such an approach may appeal to STEM subjects, language learning involves complex processes in which learning is iterative, complex, multidimensional, dynamic, contingent and organic rather than linear and rational (Prinsloo & Slade, 2017).

Added to this, as analytics involves the collection of personal data, there are concerns about issues of privacy, confidentiality, and ethics (see also Sylvén, this volume), and in the autonomous self-regulated context, of potentially adverse effects in relation to student motivation given the constant focus on measuring performance related outcomes.

Future directions

Data about language learning can provide potentially valuable insights into the digital language learning behaviour of students, and as in the field of corpus linguistics, provide some evidence for assumptions that were previously thought to be true but lacked an empirical base (Biber & Reppen, 2015). The ethical and data security challenges that the use of data presents are real, however, and future research needs to be more nuanced to critique the highly deterministic aspects evident in the emerging field of data science. Historically, in the first generation of learning analytics in education, the use of data were initially motivated by administrative priorities related to decreasing drop-out rates and aiding teacher interventions. Developments in AI, the 'Internet of Things' and predictive analytics suggest that more sophisticated attempts to profile learners based on past history may become increasingly influential. The growth in the recreational use of smart phones, tablets and mobile apps to learn languages 'on the go' promises to continue to be increasingly popular, especially through the use of gamification (e.g., leader boards, competition, badges) enabling learners to compete against themselves or perhaps via social networks with other learners around the world both with and/or 'beyond the classroom', and teachers need to develop the skills to deal with these new sources of data. Engaging language learners in the design of dashboards based on open and co-designed data may help to provide information that is more valuable, but in the highly corporate led field of mobile app production, a risk is that the data may shape the learning process without much opportunity to shape the data (Smith & Seward, 2020). More longitudinal studies involving qualitative research and co-design may empower learners and teachers to advocate for greater transparency (Reinders & Lan, 2021). Above all, the debate about the value of learning analytics and techniques such as educational data mining also have a valuable role to play in providing a vantage point to explore some of our most taken-for-granted and normalised assumptions about the role of learning and the place of teachers, learners, digital technologies and increasingly, artificial intelligence, within them. Teachers and learners shape data; thereafter data must not be allowed uncritically to shape them.

Reflection questions

1 What pressures do the use of analytics add to student learning in self-regulated learning contexts?
2 What data can learners also contribute to provide a more nuanced understanding of their own performance?

3. What are the risks and opportunities for teachers and learners if analytics becomes increasingly normalised in language learning beyond the classroom?

Recommended readings

Warschauer, M., Yim, S., Lee, H., & Zheng, B. (2019). Recent contributions of data mining to language learning research. *Annual Review of Applied Linguistics, 39*, 93–112.

This paper explores data mining in research on second language learning, examining in particular examples from three areas of data mining (clustering techniques, text-mining and social network analysis). Addressing the gaps in current research, the paper is valuable in that the examples show how data can be used in corpus-based vocabulary learning, collaborative written and computer-mediated discussion and it provides an up-to-date discussion of the implications for the field.

Pérez-Paredes, P., Ordoñana Guillamón, C., Van de Vyver, J., Meurice, A., Aguado Jiménez, P., Conole, G., & Sánchez Hernández, P. (2019). Mobile data-driven language learning: Affordances and learners' perception, *System, 84*, 145–159.

This paper examines data-driven learning (DDL) as a learner-focussed approach, which encourages language learners' discovery of linguistic patterns through the detailed exploration of samples of language use. The study is valuable in that it examines the use of a mobile language learning app with several groups of European learners and findings indicated that DDL can be useful for providing instant and personalised feedback, although there is a need for specialised learner training if the potential of DDL and mobile-assisted language learning (MALL) are to be harnessed effectively.

Viberg, O., Wasson, B., & Kukulska-Hulme, A. (2020). Mobile-assisted language learning through learning analytics for self-regulated learning (MALLAS): A conceptual framework. *Australasian Journal of Educational Technology, 36*(6), 34–52.

Mobile learning is increasingly being used for self-regulated language learning but there are numerous challenges relating to how prepared and aware learners are of the resources available to them. This paper is the first to identify a conceptual framework for using mobile assisted language learning and self-regulated learning and is valuable for curriculum and learning designers in that it aims to move beyond the rather limiting view of analytics based on log data to recognise its multimodal aspects.

References

Aguilar, S.J., Karabenick, S.A., Teasley, S.D., & Baek, C. (2021). Associations between learning analytics dashboard exposure and motivation and self-regulated learning. *Computers & Education, 162*, 1–11.

Ali, L., Asadi, M., Gasevic, D., Jovanovic, J., & Hatala, M. (2013). Factors influencing beliefs for adoption of a learning analytics tool: An empirical study. *Computers & Education, 62*, 130–148.

Anwaruddin, S. M. (2019). Teaching language, promoting social justice: A dialogic approach to using social media. *CALICO Journal, 36*(1), 1–18.

Attewell, P., Monaghan, D. B., & Kwong, D. (2015). *Data mining for the social sciences: An introduction.* Oakland, CA: University of California Press.

Azevedo, R., & Gašević, D. (2019). Analyzing multimodal multichannel data about self-regulated learning with advanced learning technologies: Issues and challenges. *Computers in Human Behavior, 96*, 207–210.

Azevedo, R., Mudrick, N., Taub, M., & Bradbury, A. (2019). Self-regulation in computer-assisted learning systems. In J. Dunlosky & K. Rawson (Eds.), *The Cambridge handbook of cognition and education* (pp. 587–618). Cambridge University Press.

Baars, M., Leopold, C., & Paas, F. (2018). Self-explaining steps in problem-solving tasks to improve self-regulation in secondary education. *Journal of Educational Psychology, 110*, 578–595.

Bartolomé, A., Bergamin, P., Persico, D., Steffens, K., & Underwood, J. (Eds.) (2011). *Self-regulated learning in technology enhanced learning environments: Problems and promises.* Berlin: Shaker Verlag.

Biber, D., & Reppen, R. (Eds.) (2015). *The Cambridge handbook of English corpus linguistics.* Cambridge, UK: Cambridge University Press.

Bienkowski, M., Feng, M., & Means, B. (2012). *Enhancing teaching and learning through educational data mining and learning analytics: An issue brief.* U.S. Department of Education, Office of Educational Technology.

Block, D., & Gray, J. (2016). 'Just go away and do it and you get marks': The degradation of language teaching in neoliberal times. *Journal of Multilingual and Multicultural Development, 37*(5), 481–494.

Block, D., Gray, J., & Holborow, M. (2012). *Neoliberalism and applied linguistics.* London: Routledge.

Boulton, A. (2017). Data-driven learning and language pedagogy. In S. Thorne & S. May (Eds.), *Language, education and technology: Encyclopedia of language and education 3* (pp.181–192). Berlin: Springer.

Buckingham Shum & Ferguson, R. (2011). *Social learning analytics.* Milton Keynes: The Open University, UK.

Bull, S. (2020). There are open learner models about! *IEEE Transactions on Learning Technologies, 13*(2), 425–448.

Calderon, O., & Sood, C. (2018). Evaluating learning outcomes of an asynchronous online discussion assignment: A post-priori content analysis. *Interactive Learning Environments, 28*(2), 1–15.

Campbell, J. P., Deblois, P. B., & Oblinger, D. G. (2007). Academic analytics: A new tool for a new era. *EDUCAUSE Review, 42*(4), 41–57.

Carolan, B. (2014). *Social network analysis and education.* Thousand Oaks, CA: SAGE.

Chambers, A. (2019). Towards the corpus revolution? Bridging the research–practice gap. *Language Teaching, 52*(4), 460–475.

Chun, D. M. (2013). Contributions of tracking user behavior to SLA research. *CALICO Journal, 30,* 256–262.

Clow, D. (2012). The learning analytics cycle: Closing the loop effectively. *Proceedings of the 2nd international conference on learning analytics and knowledge - LAK '12,* p. 134.

Coffrin, C., Corrin, L., de Barba, P., & Kennedy, G. (2014). Visualising patterns of student engagement and performance in MOOCs. In *Proceedings of the fourth international conference on learning analytics and knowledge – LAK 14* (pp. 83–92). New York: ACM Press.

Cope, B., & Kalantzis, M. (2016). Big data comes to school: Implications for learning, assessment, and research. *AERA Open, 2*(2). https://doi.org/10.1177/2332858416641907

Corrin, L., Scheffel, M., & Gašević, D. (2020). Learning analytics: Pathways to impact. *Australasian Journal of Educational Technology, 36*(6), 1–6.

Dawson, S., Gasevic, D., & Mirriahi, N. (2015). Challenging assumptions in learning analytics. *Journal of Learning Analytics, 2*(3), 1–3

D'Ignazio, C., & Klein, L. F. (2020). *Data feminism.* Cambridge, MA: MIT Press.

Duval, E. (2012). Attention please! Learning analytics for visualization and recommendation. *Proceedings of the 1st international conference on learning analytics and knowledge,* LAK 2011, Banff, AB, Canada, February 27–March 01.

Dychoff, A. L., Zielke, D., Bültmann, M., Chatti, M. A., & Schroeder, U. (2012). Design and implementation of a learning analytics toolkit for teachers. *Educational Technology & Society, 15*(3), 58–76.

Fischer, R. (2007). How do we know what students are actually doing? Monitoring students' behavior in CALL. *Computer Assisted Language Learning, 20*(5), 409–442.

Flowerdew, L. (2015). Data-driven learning and language learning theories: Whither the twain shall meet. In A. Leńko-Szymańska & A. Boulton (Eds.), *Multiple affordances of language corpora for data-driven learning* (pp. 15–36). Amsterdam: John Benjamins.

Fryer, L. K., Coniam, D., Carpenter, R., & Lăpușneanu, D. (2020). Bots for language learning now: Current and future directions. *Language Learning & Technology, 24*(2), 8–22.

Gandomi, A., & Haider, M. (2015). Beyond the hype: Big data concepts, methods, and analytics. *International Journal of Information Management, 35*(2), 137–144.

Giroux, H. (2014). *Neoliberalism's war on higher education.* Chicago: Haymarket.

Godwin-Jones, R. (2017). Scaling up and zooming in: Big data and personalization in language learning. *Language Learning & Technology, 21*(1), 4–15.

Horizon Project (2016). *2016 Higher education.* New York: New Media Consortium.

Hsiao, I. Y. T., Lan, Y.-J., & Kao, C.-L., & Li, P. (2017). Visualization analytics for second language vocabulary learning in virtual worlds. *Educational Technology & Society, 20*(2), 161–175.

Huang, R.-T., & Yu, C.-Y. (2019). Exploring the impact of self-management of learning and personal learning initiative on mobile language learning: A moderated mediation model. *Australasian Journal of Educational Technology, 35*(3), 118–131

JISC (2015). Code of practice for learning analytics. https://www.jisc.ac.uk/guides/code-of-practice-for-learning-analytics

Kerr, P. (2015). Adaptive learning. *ELT Journal*, 70(1), 88–93.

Knight et al. (2013). Epistemology, pedagogy, assessment and learning analytics. *LAK '13: Proceedings of the third international conference on learning analytics and knowledge, epistemology, pedagogy, assessment and learning analytics*, 75–84.

Kovanovic, V., Joksimovic, S., Mirriahi, N., Blaine, E., Gasevic, D., & Siemens, G., & Dawson, S. (2018). Understand students' self-reflections through learning analytics. In S. Buckingham Shum, R. Ferguson, A. Merceron, & X. Ochoa (Eds.), *Proceedings of the 8th international conference on learning analytics and knowledge management* (pp. 389–398). Association for Computing Machinery.

Kruse, A., & Pongsajapan, R. (2012). Student-centered learning analytics. https://cndls.georgetown.edu/m/documents/thoughtpaper-krusepongsajapan.pdf

Kuromiya, H., Majumdar, R., & Ogata, H. (2020). Fostering evidence-based education with learning analytics: Capturing teaching-learning cases from log data. *Educational Technology & Society*, 23(4), 14–29.

Lee, H., Warschauer, M., & Lee, J. H. (2018). The effects of corpus use on second language vocabulary learning: A multilevel meta-analysis. *Applied Linguistics*, 40, 721–753.

Lee, H., Warschauer, M., & Lee, J. H. (2019). Advancing CALL research via data mining techniques: Unearthing hidden groups of learners in a corpus-based L2 vocabulary learning experiment. *ReCALL*, 31(2), 135–149.

Leijten, M., & Van Waes, L. (2013). Keystroke logging in writing research: Using Inputlog to analyze and visualize writing processes. *Written Communication*, 30(3), 358–392.

Link, S., & Li, Z. (2015). Understanding online interaction through learning analytics: Defining a theory-based research agenda. In Dixon, E. & Thomas, M. (Eds.), *Researching language learner interactions online: From social media to MOOCs* (pp. 369–385). San Marcos, TX: Texas State University.

Lodge, J., Panadero, E., Broadbent, J., & de Barba, P. (2018). Supporting self-regulated learning with learning analytics. In J. Lodge, J. C. Horvath & L. Corrin (Eds.), *Learning analytics in the classroom* (1st ed., pp. 45–55). London: Routledge

Long, P., & Siemens, G. (2011). Penetrating the fog: Analytics in learning and education. *EDUCAUSE Review*, 46(5), 31–37.

Loyens, S.M.M., Magda, J., & Rikers, R.M.J.P. (2008). Self-directed learning in problem-based learning and its relationships with self-regulated learning. *Educational Psychology Review*, 20, 411–427.

Means, B., Bakia, M., & Murphy, R. (2014). *Learning online: What research tells us about whether, when and how*. New York: Routledge.

Meunier, F. (2019). Data-driven learning: From classroom scaffolding to sustainable practices. *EL.LE*, 8(2), 423–434.

Miller, K. S., Lindgren, E., & Sullivan, K. P. (2008). The psycholinguistic dimension in second language writing: Opportunities for research and pedagogy using computer keystroke logging. *TESOL Quarterly*, 42(3), 433–454.

Pérez-Paredes, P., Ordoñana Guillamón, C., Van de Vyver, J., Meurice, A., Aguado Jiménez, P., Conole, G., & Sánchez Hernández, P. (2019). Mobile data-driven language learning: Affordances and learners' perception. *System*, 84, 145–159.

Pilling-Cormick, J., & Garrison, D. R., 2007. Self-directed and self-regulated learning: Conceptual links. *Canadian Journal of University Continuing Education*, 33(2), 13–33.

Plonsky, L., & Ziegler, N. (2016). The CALL-SLA interface: Insights from a second-order synthesis. *Language Learning & Technology*, 20, 17–37.

Prinsloo, P., & Slade, S. (2017). Big data, higher education and learning analytics: Beyond justice, towards an ethics of care. In B. Daniel (Ed.), *Big data and learning analytics in higher education* (pp. 109–124). Heidelberg: Springer.

Reinders, H. (2018). Learning analytics for language learning and teaching. *JALT CALL Journal*, 14(1), 77–86.

Reinders, H., & Lan, Y. J. (2021). Big data in language education and research. *Language Learning & Technology*, 25(1), 1–3.

Rienties, B., Lewis, T., McFarlane, R., Nguyen, Q., & Toetenel, L. (2018). Analytics in online and offline learning environments: The role of learning design to understand student online engagement. *Computer Assisted Language Learning*, 31(3), 273–293.

Roberts-Mahoney, H., Means, A. J., & Garrison, M. J. (2016). Netflixing human capital development: Personalized learning technology and the corporatization of K-12 education. *Journal of Education Policy*, *31*(4), 405–420.

Romero, C., & Ventura, S. (2020). Educational data mining and learning analytics: An updated survey. *Wiley Interdisciplinary Reviews: Data Mining and Knowledge Discovery*, *10*(3), 1–21.

Rosell-Aguilar, F. (2018). Autonomous language learning through a mobile application: A user evaluation of the Busuu app. *Computer Assisted Language Learning*, *31*(8), 854–881.

Ruiz, S., Rebuschat, P., & Meurers, D. (2019). The effects of working memory and declarative memory on instructed second language vocabulary learning: Insights from intelligent CALL. *Language Teaching Research*. https://doi.org/10.1177/1362168819872859

Siemens, G., & Baker, RSJD (2012). Learning analytics and educational data mining: Towards communication and collaboration. In *AK '12: Proceedings of the 2nd international conference on learning analytics and knowledge*, April 2012 (pp. 252–254).

Slade, S., & Prinsloo, P. (2013). Learning analytics: Ethical issues and dilemmas. *American Behavioral Scientist*, *57*(10), 1509–1528.

Smith, M. & Seward, R. (2020). Updating open development: Open practices in inclusive development. In M. Smith & R. Seward (Eds.), *Making open development inclusive* (pp. 1–22). Cambridge, MA: MIT Press.

SoLAR. (n.d.). What is learning analytics. https://www.solaresearch.org/about/what-is-learning-analytics/

Tan, S. C., Divaharan, S., Tan, L., & Cheah, H. M. (2011). *Self-directed learning with ICT: Theory, Practice and Assessment*. Singapore: Ministry of Education.

Thomas, M., & Gelan, A. (2018). Special edition on language learning and learning analytics. *Computer Assisted Language Learning*, *31*(3), 181–184.

Tsai, Y. S., Perrotta, C., & Gašević, D. (2020). Empowering learners with personalised learning approaches? Agency, equity and transparency in the context of learning analytics. *Assessment & Evaluation in Higher Education*, *45*(4), 554–567.

van Harmelen, M., & Workman, D. (2012). *Analytics for learning and teaching*. London: CETIS Analytics Series.

Verbert, K., Duval, E., Klerkx, J., Govaerts, S., & José, L.S. (2013). Learning analytics dashboard applications. *American Behavioral Scientist*, *57*(10), 1500–1509.

Verbert, K., Govaerts, S., Duval, E., Santos, J.L., Assche, F.V., Parra, G., & Klerkx, J. (2013). Learning dashboards: An overview and future research opportunities. *Personal and Ubiquitous Computing*, *18*, 1499–1514.

Viberg, O., Wasson, B., & Kukulska-Hulme, A. (2020). Mobile-assisted language learning through learning analytics for self-regulated learning (MALLAS): A conceptual framework. *Australasian Journal of Educational Technology*, *36*(6), 34–52.

Volk, H., Kellner, K., & Wohlhart, D. (2015). Learning analytics in English language teaching. *Journal of Universal Computer Science*, *21*(1), 156–174.

Vyatkina, N. (2020a). Corpora as open educational resources for language teaching. *Foreign Language Annals*, *53*(2), 359–370.

Vyatkina, N. (2020b). Corpus-informed pedagogy in a language course: Design, implementation, and evaluation. In M. Kruk & M. Peterson (Eds.), *New technological applications for foreign and second language learning and teaching* (pp. 306–335). Hershey, PA: IGI Global.

Warschauer, M., Yim, S., Lee, H., & Zheng, B. (2019). Recent contributions of data mining to language learning research. *Annual Review of Applied Linguistics*, *39*, 93–112

Youngs, B., Moss-Horwitz, S., & Snyder, E. (2015). Educational data mining for elementary French on-line: A descriptive study. In E. Dixon & M. Thomas (Eds.), *Researching language learner interactions online: From social media to MOOCs* (pp. 362–368). San Marcos, TX: CALICO.

Youngs, B. L., Prakash, A., & Nugent, R. (2018). Statistically-driven visualizations of student interactions with a French online course video. *Computer Assisted Language Learning*, *31*(3), 206–225.

Yousuf, B., & Conlan, O. (2020, July). Assessing the impact of controllable open learner models on student engagement. In *2020 IEEE 20th International Conference on Advanced Learning Technologies (ICALT)* (pp. 47–49). IEEE. https://ieeexplore.ieee.org/document/9156066

Zheng, B., & Warschauer, M. (2015). Participation, interaction, and academic achievement in an online discussion environment. *Computers & Education*, *84*, 78–89.

Zhu, E. (2016). Interaction and cognitive engagement: An analysis of four asynchronous online discussions. *Instructional Science, 34*(6), 451–480. https://doi.org/10.1007/s11251-006-0004-0

Zimmerman, B.J. (1989). A social cognitive view of self-regulated academic learning. *Journal of Educational Psychology, 81*, 329–339.

Zimmerman, B.J. (1990). Self-regulated learning and academic achievement: An overview. *Educational Psychologist, 25*(1), 3–17.

INDEX

advising: education for advisors 249; evaluation 250; future directions 251; goals 246; mentoring and training for advisors 249–250; online 251–252; origins 245; in practice 247–248; research 252; theoretical perspectives 245
advising in language learning (ALL) 244, 245
agency 11, 18, 20, 41, 46, 82, 85–87, 89, 130, 132, 136–137, 150, 159, 161, 174, 224, 263, 383, 385, 396–397, 400, 403, 409–410, 413, 429, 432–433
agentive literacy 85–87, 93
age-related challenges 368
alternative assessment 286–293
anonymization 302
anxiety 101, 147, 172, 234, 240, 247, 315, 332, 355, 358, 363
apps 11, 16–18, 69, 72, 74, 76, 78, 88, 93, 115, 138, 149, 156, 161, 314, 318, 364, 371, 377, 399, 401–403, 432–433
audio technologies 13
augmented reality 10, 20, 37, 39, 40–41, 42, 46, 94, 164, 201
authentic assessment 287
authentic communication 219, 221–223

behaviour mapping 32
behaviour tracking 32
Berlin Declaration 308
big data 399, 426–428, 431
bridging activities 37, 45

CALL in the wild 81
CA-SLA 52, 56, 60–61
child-centred methods 385
classroom research 24, 112
click phenomenon 357, 362
4E cognition 196

cognitive approaches 157, 381, 382, 383, 389, 403
collaborative language learning 143, 146, 148–149
collectivism 265
commercial off-the-shelf games 333
community of practice 156, 158, 183, 190, 252, 259, 261–263, 266
complementarity 347–348
complex systems 25, 67, 79, 138
computer assisted language learning (CALL) 1, 9, 79, 81, 85, 155, 236, 396, 409, 427, 431
computer tracking 313, 321–322
content-and-language-integrated learning (CLIL) 113, 114
conversation analysis 41–42, 57, 183, 186, 191, 195, 201, 203, 416–418
COTS games 333; *see also* commercial off-the-shelf games
counseling 246, 249, 253–254; *see also* advising
cram schools 216–217, 220–221, 223
critical digital literacies 82–84, 89, 92
critical digital pedagogy 89
cultural values 103, 106, 388
cyber-ethnography 329; *see also* digital ethnography

dashboards 147, 149, 430–433
data management plan 306; *see also* DMP
data mining 5, 426, 428–434
decolonising 399
design: conversion 345; explanatory (*see* design, sequential); hybrid 346; mixed method 343; parallel 343; sequential 344
design thinking 62
desire 29, 71, 86, 98–99, 101, 103, 105–107, 220, 238–239, 259–260, 274, 275–276, 316–317, 335, 358–359, 368, 373–374, 400, 423
digital ethnography 318, 328–331, 315

439

digital game-based language learning frameworks 130, 131, 132
digital literacies and identities 158, 159
digital wilds 2, 10, 17, 79, 81–84, 87–88, 91, 93, 312, 327, 408–409, 422
direct method 13
distributed cognition 194
DMP 306

ecological validity 37, 186
ecology 26–27, 63, 209, 223, 224, 359, 383
effectiveness 122–123, 135, 145, 147, 162–163, 217–219, 223, 232–233, 249–250, 275, 291, 319, 397, 426
emic view 186, 377, 378
emotion 68–69, 99, 146, 162, 247–248, 252–253, 293, 320, 354, 358, 381, 383, 430
enactivism 196
equity 28, 137, 286, 290–291, 427
ethics 150, 299–305, 307, 308, 310, 335, 337, 368, 384, 385, 398, 411–412, 427, 433
ethnography 183, 186, 190–191, 318, 328–331, 335, 381–383, 384–385, 408–409, 411–413, 416, 421–422
exam-oriented 216–217, 220–221
exam preparation 218, 221, 223
experiential L2 pedagogy 61
explicit learning 114–116, 121, 168
extra-curricular 14–15, 357
extramural digital game-based language learning 130, 132
extramural English 2–3, 74, 75, 114–115, 117, 119, 121–123, 312, 314, 323
extramural L_n 3–4

fabrication 307–308
fairness 149, 290–293
falsification 307–308
fanfiction 38, 262, 319, 329–330, 334–336
fan translation 330
fan communities 79, 318, 327, 334–335
fandom 11, 18, 36–39, 160, 318, 337, 409
field observations 375, 378
formal education 1, 5, 10, 12, 19, 29, 37–38, 46, 72, 78–79, 114–115, 130, 217, 262, 299, 328, 332–333, 388, 400, 402, 414
formative assessment 76, 287–288, 290–291
formative feedback 288, 290–291

game characteristics 130
gamification 157, 402, 415, 432–433
GDPR 301–302, 334
General Data Protection Regulation *see* GDPR
globalization 15–16, 19, 30, 40
grammar-translation 13–14, 217, 286
group interviews 313, 319–320, 322, 344, 371–372, 376; *see also interviews*
guided tour 332, 376–377

Helsinki declaration 301, 303, 305
heutagogy 397
high-order thinking skills 229
homestay 168–169, 172, 199, 203

identity 4, 11, 17–18, 40, 43, 72, 156, 158–159, 163, 170, 173, 175–177, 182–183, 189–190, 199–221, 265, 328, 336, 357, 359, 362, 397
IDLE 2, 312, 316, 332; *see also* informal digital learning of English
immanent pedagogies 184
immersion 40, 114, 168, 357–360, 363, 386
immersive contexts 356–357, 361–362
implicit learning 113–116, 118, 121–122
incidental acquisition 71, 73
indirect observational methods 384
individual differences 27, 31, 69–70, 168, 169, 173–174, 229–230
individualism 265, 402
inequality 28–29, 222–223, 398, 404
informal digital learning of English 332
informed assent 368
input - output 59
integration (of methods) 341–342
intentional reflective dialogue (IRD) 246
interactional repertoire 60, 197–199, 203
intersubjectivity 44, 60, 196
introspection 354–356
introspective analysis 355, 359

language: accuracy 160–161; assessment 332–333; contact 28–29, 116, 120–123, 168–169, 172–176; diaries 322, 369–371; logs 169, 313, 318–319, 322, 346
language learning: clubs 15; environment 26–30; history 313, 317, 319, 321; strategies 100–103, 143–144, 149, 164, 169
Latin learning 12
learner: beliefs 5, 100, 260, 381, 386, 387–88; community 258–259, 261, 263, 266–267; training 5, 247, 273, 275–278
learning: advisors 245, 247–249, 250, 252; analytics 5, 143, 149–150, 169, 170, 426–430, 432–434; behaviors 52–55; in the wild 10, 37, 42–45, 52, 60–63, 184, 196, 198–199, 204, 209; object, learnable 199, 204, 205; platforms 69, 73, 76, 78, 232, 427; rate 113
learning-in-action 184, 195–197
linguistic development 168–171, 173, 176–177
linguistic landscape 18, 36–40

mapping 5, 24, 30–32, 204, 369, 389, 399
mediation/mediational 19, 183, 190–191, 45, 422
mentoring 174–175, 190–191, 244, 249–250, 432
meta-learning 82, 85, 87
misrepresentation 307–308

Index

mobile-assisted language learning (MALL) 1, 69, 73–74, 78, 88, 165–169, 396–398, 403, 408–414, 418–419, 421–422, 434
mobile-assisted online community 263
mobile phone 25, 32, 44, 90, 147, 410
multiple perspectives 341, 346, 348–349
mutual shaping 10

naturalistic exposure 168, 175
naturalistic learning 3, 11, 74, 112–113, 175, 279–280, 364, 383, 409
neoliberalism 29, 426, 429, 432
non-formal learning 69, 72–74, 76, 78
non-immersive contexts 356, 360, 361, 362
non-introspective analysis 355

observations 186, 313–314, 316, 318, 321–322, 330, 342, 348, 362, 375, 378, 381, 384–385, 422
online ethnography *see* digital ethnography
online fan communities 327
online LBC 30
online tutoring 218, 224, 313
open access 308
outsider research, problems of~ 397–398

paradigm shift 155, 230, 396
participant observation 186, 329–331, 390
participatory extramural digital game-based language learning 136, 137
peer assessment 274, 286, 289–290, 292
personal data 302, 335, 433
personalisation 271, 431–432
personalized learning 162, 230
plagiarism 307–308
portfolio assessment 288, 290
postdigital 396
printing press 10, 12, 19, 68
privacy 149–150, 156, 252, 299, 301–302, 305, 334–336, 427, 433
private tutoring: definition 214, 215–216; modes 216–217
pseudonymize 302

qualitising 342, 345–346; *see also* design conversion
quantitative studies 385–387
quantitising 342, 345; *see also* design, conversion
questionnaires 122, 170, 251, 313–316, 318–322, 328, 330–332, 369–373, 386–387

radio, educational ~ 14, 28, 399
reflective dialogue 244, 245, 246, 254
reflective journals 104, 289, 313, 320
repair 52–55, 57, 60–61, 198–199, 204, 417–418
researching crises 399

retrospection 354–356
rewilding 37, 44–45, 82–83, 92–93, 408–410, 413, 415–416, 421–423

Scaffolding 17, 82, 190–191, 161, 239, 377
Security 93, 149–150, 156, 271, 299, 301, 305, 396, 433
self-access centres 271; definition of~ 272; management of ~ 277; people 275; the future of ~ 279–280; virtual 274, 278
self-access learning: integrating into classes 276–277; learner training 275–276; use of technology 273–274, 278
self-assessment 39, 277, 286, 288–289, 292, 361
self-determination theory 101, 224, 246, 252
self-directed learning 69–70, 82–83, 86, 90, 92, 94, 103–105, 148, 159, 164, 259, 260, 266, 316, 429, 432
self-plagiarism 307–308; *see also* plagiarism
self-regulated language learning 143, 219, 224, 230
self-regulated learning support 143–144, 146–147, 162, 164, 224, 260, 265, 428, 431–432, 434
shadow education 215, 223–225
situated cognition 2, 196
situational factors 102–103
smartphone literacy 88, 93
social constructivism 148, 237
socially desired responses 368, 374
social networking 18, 69, 71, 76–77, 129, 137, 146, 156–157, 159–160, 163, 233, 258, 262, 331–332
socio-cultural approaches 382–384
sociocultural theory 145, 157, 245
spatial theory 24–25
stimulated recall 251, 313, 317, 319, 321–322, 377
structured awareness raising 247
student-centred learning 399, 402
student experience 426

teacher as counselor 61
teacher preparation 156, 164
technology affordance 238, 252
triangulation 348

ultimate attainment 113, 115
usage-based learning 54, 57–60

validity 5, 37, 169, 186, 275, 291, 299–300, 315, 348, 368, 371
Vancouver Protocol 306
visual methods 32, 378, 390

walking interviews 32
washback 221–223, 286, 288
word search 53–54, 57–60, 198–199

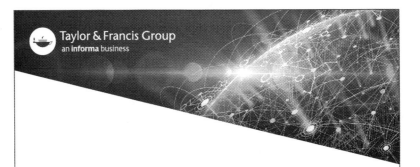